# The Guardian University Guide 2010

# The Guardian University Guide 2010

● what to study ● where to go ● how to get there

Edited by

**Helen Brooks**

**the**guardian

Published by Guardian Books 2009

2 4 6 8 10 9 7 5 3 1

Copyright © Guardian News and Media Ltd 2009

Helen Brooks has asserted her right under the Copyright, Designs and Patents Act 1988 to be identified as the editor of this work.

First published in Great Britain in 2009 by
Guardian Books
Kings Place
90 York Way
London N1 9GU

www.guardianbooks.co.uk

A CIP catalogue record for this book is available from the British Library

ISBN: 978-0-85265-129-2

Text design by Bryony Newhouse
Cover design by Two Associates
Research by Kristen Harrison
Maps by Tony Mills
Map of London boroughs by Ghost

Printed and bound in Great Britain by Clays Ltd, St Ives PLC

# Contents

## Subjects

# University profiles

# Preface

I confess that I don't remember much about my own university application. I certainly don't recall my school giving any advice on the subject whatsoever: perhaps they thought offering information about the place we were going to spend the next three years of our lives would ruin our moral fibre and sense of initiative.

Perhaps it would have done, if I'd had any initiative to start off with. As it was, I was 17 and spent my entire life in a fog of gormless confusion that resolutely failed to lift when the UCCA form (that's what we had in the days before Ucas online applications) arrived: buying a book like this would have helped, but buying a book like this would never have occurred to me. Instead, I nearly died of hypothermia en route to my interview at York. Demonstrating my keen grasp of Britain's provincial geography and accompanying climate, I'd arrived in North Yorkshire in January appropriately dressed for a posting in South America: light suit, no overcoat, flip flops etc. Icy winds gusted down from the Pennines and blew my sombrero off. Meanwhile, on the morning of my interview at Cambridge I rigorously prepared by going to a record shop in King's Street, presumably in the belief that my interlocutor – a professor who'd recently revolutionised the editing of Shakespeare by discrediting the practice of conflating variant editions of plays – was going to quiz me on when the new My Bloody Valentine album was coming out. I didn't have a clue what I was doing.

The only thing I remember really clearly about the whole process was its final denouement: the sound of the door clicking closed as my parents left me at the start of my freshers' week. Too clueless to be apprehensive, it sounded like freedom to me. It probably tells you something about the soul-crushing suburban boredom in which I grew up that Cambridge – a place hardly preceded by its reputation as a 24 hour party city – seemed to be a scarcely-creditable stew of thrills and glamour and nocturnal licentiousness, like Las Vegas with more bicycles and gothic revival architecture. Alternatively, it may just tell you something about being a student, with its excitement and novelty and capacity for outward re-invention. After all, whenever I visited my friends elsewhere in the country, they seemed to feel the same way about their adoptive home. That seemed fair enough when they were living in Manchester or Liverpool or London, but one of them was in Norwich, installed in a windswept hall of residence that had once apparently served as an army barracks and looked at the time like a converted Anderson shelter. This didn't seem to have registered with my friend. You would have thought he was living on Canal Street at the height of Mardi Gras, such was his rabid enthusiasm for his student life. His eyes gleamed with wonder at the world of boundless possibilities that was Norwich: his life seemed to be a constant party, with a computing degree thrown in. It wasn't even where he wanted to go. He got there through clearing.

I'm telling you all this to support my feeling that, in one sense at least, this book is weirdly redundant, because I'm not sure where you go to university is that important. Of course, some places will just appeal to you more than others, some will offer courses better suited to your needs and interests, and it always pays to make an informed decision rather than just getting out the blindfold, the pins and the map, which is where this book comes in. What I mean is that, while you certainly shouldn't follow my example and bumble embarrassingly uninformed through the application process, trusting the whole thing to dumb luck, nor should choosing a university be something that involves agonised fretting over whether or not you've made the perfect choice. You're about to spend three years away from the supervision of your parents, surrounded by people your own age. You'll be gifted vast swathes of time in which to study a topic you'll (hopefully) enjoy: this latter might appear to be the least interesting aspect of university now, but, trust me, it'll seem like an unimaginable luxury with the benefit of hindsight. You will also have more opportunities than ever before to make friends, drink, have sex and pursue extracurricular interests – be they political, artistic, sporting or largely involving sitting around in a ratty dressing gown all day, smoking dope and passing bitingly satirical comment on Cash In The Attic. And if I may be permitted to go a bit hippy on you, you'll be allowed a limitless degree of self-discovery: being a student is the one time in your life you get to endlessly re-invent yourself with impunity. In my case, I displayed a limitless capacity to re-invent myself as yet another variety of idiot, but for my wife – who came from a family where reading books was regarded with the same mystified suspicion as joining a commune and went to a school where the careers advice involved being told to get a job in the local travel agents – the freedom to discover yourself at university was a genuinely life-changing deal.

Taking all that into account, the likelihood is you'll have a good time regardless. Indeed, the likelihood is you'll have such a good time that every time you look back on it in later life you'll first feel a warm glow of affection, then let out a terrible ear-splitting sob of envy at the carefree life you used to lead. You should make the most of it, and this book is a good place to start doing that. But more importantly, you should love it. I hope you do.

**Alexis Petridis**

Alexis Petridis is the *Guardian*'s head rock and pop critic and the music editor of *GQ* magazine.

# Introduction

## Choosing university

Once upon a time, and not even all that long ago, making decisions about university was very much more simple than it is now. There weren't many and not many people went to them. That, obviously, wasn't a good thing: certain types of people, mostly from certain types of school, were expected – or at least encouraged – to go, while for the rest (the vast majority) higher education was something that happened to other people.

These days, fortunately, things have changed. And how. Recent figures show that more than a third of school-leavers choose to study for a degree and that number looks set to carry on rising. While once there were a small handful of universities, now there are well over a hundred. And don't even try to count the courses: you can study anything from aadvarks to zygotes and most things in between.

It is, frankly, an exciting time to be a potential undergraduate. You can decide to attend your local university, or travel to the other end of the country. You can opt to bury yourself in classical literature or theoretical science, or sign up for a vocational degree that will prepare you for a job in a cutting-edge industry. Perhaps you fancy an established, esteemed institution. Or maybe you're leaning towards something younger, leaner, perhaps more flexible. Part-time or full-time, years abroad or in industry, exams or coursework, town or country, campus or not, music, sport, fun, and games: it's all there for the taking.

And that's before we even get on to the great benefits a university education can give you. There is the obvious stuff, of course: the unparalleled opportunity to immerse yourself in study, the skills a degree will cultivate and the talents it will unearth. Your career prospects will improve, your social life will receive a kick up the backside, you'll get a taste of freedom and independence you probably haven't had yet and simply stepping out of your room in the morning will expose you to experiences and opportunities you haven't come across before.

There is a downside, of course. The many thousands of pounds of debt you're likely to tot up just being there, for one thing. If you're currently living on a few quid of parental allowance a week, contemplating owing £20,000 to a combination of banks and loans companies in three or four years' time is enough to make you feel a bit queasy.

But for better or worse it looks like tuition fees are here to stay. And, surprisingly perhaps, most students seem to have taken them in their stride. While numbers of applications to university did drop for courses starting in 2006 – the year fees were introduced – they were back up again for 2007, and again for 2008 and 2009. Perhaps people are figuring their education and future is worth making a financial investment in, even with an uncertain economy. Maybe they think three years of fun is too good a chance to pass up, and they'll worry about the money later. Or perhaps they simply feel that university is something that shouldn't be missed, or left to those who don't have to worry about money. They're right! And it is worth mentioning – though we'll deal with finance more thoroughly elsewhere in the book – that whatever you think about the basic principle of having to pay for your education, the loans and fees system is at least worked out to make it straightforward to pay back what you owe, beginning with the fact that you only start to repay when (the government thinks) you can afford it.

Overall, it seems that the prevailing attitude among Britain's students is one of keep calm and carry on. Yes, the money stuff's a pain, but there's too much that's really great about being a student to let it worry you too much. There are lectures to go to, essays to write (in the middle of the night, more often than not), plays to be in, student newspapers to edit, student elections to campaign in, chemistry prizes to win, books to read, coffee to be drunk, bars to prop up, friends to be made, and a world to be explored.

Feel like joining them? Read on ...

## Why go?

Why not? Really, what else have you got planned for the next three years? Something better than opportunity, freedom, experimentation, and education? If so, please, please write in and let us know what it is so we can do it too.

Because there's a reason so many people want to go to university – and why so many people who did look back on it as the best days of their lives (and why many who didn't regret it bitterly, or go, in the end, as mature students) – because it is, in short, brilliant. It's fun. It's a laugh. It's eye-opening and mind-expanding. If you have even the merest hint of a chance to go you should grab it with both hands and anything else you've got that grabs and thank your lucky stars every minute of the day for the glorious opportunity that's just come your way.

First, let's turn to the first purpose of university: education. It can get lost a bit amongst all the angst over student loans and excitement over freshers' week, but what you're there for is to learn. You'll never have another chance like it, and your brain and your life will never be the same. You can spend years simply soaking up knowledge about something you care about, something that fascinates you, perhaps something that will stand you in good stead in your future career. You will learn from experts and scholars. You will be challenged and pushed and you will love it.

And, of course, a university education is about more than just fastening in your mind chemical equations or dates of important historical events (in actual fact, you're likely to forget 80 per cent of all that information the moment your last exam finishes). What it will also give you is a new way of thinking, an ability to analyse and discuss on a deeper level, a critical approach to information and the skills to deliver your arguments and conclusion in a persuasive and coherent way. Sounds like things that, say, an employer might be interested in? You're right!

Which is why there is even a phrase to describe the material benefits a degree will offer you. It is the "graduate premium", and it means, basically, that if you have a degree you're going to earn more money than someone who doesn't. Now, obviously, it's not a rule without exceptions and we could sit here naming Wayne Rooneys and Victoria Beckhams all day. Nor is there any accounting for the graduate with a double first who elects to live out their life on a remote Scottish island, living off thin air and goodwill. But, yes, on the whole, getting a degree equals more money for you. It's also worth remembering that for some jobs a degree is an absolutely non-negotiable entry requirement and for many more it's pretty much expected that you will have one.

OK, enough of being serious. Let's talk about the fun! Chances are, going to university will see you leaving home for the first time and, my goodness, what place better to go to upon leaving the family nest. You are as free as a bird. You can party all night, eat cake for breakfast, wash less than once a week, cook roast dinner every night for a month, play Mozart at 7 am, and wear what the hell you like out on a Friday night. (You might want to remember that some of these things will really annoy your flatmates. On the other hand, what are they going to do? Ground you?) But at the same time as luxuriating in all this limitless freedom you're safely wrapped up in the cosy security of university life. Whether on campus or in a student flat, you're plugged into a community who are all doing exactly the same thing as you.

And then there are the people who you'll be sharing it all with. You might not believe it when you lay eyes on them for the first time, looking all nervous and sick on the first day, but the people you are at university with are going to be hugely important in your life; in some cases, for the rest of it. You'll never have such a pool of potential mates to chat to, hang out with and share your experiences with again. Among the gawky freshers at your first lecture will be people who will become friends for life. Front row, third seat in? That's the best man at your wedding. The girl chewing her nails by the wall? You'll go travelling for a year with her when you graduate. The guy who's just tripped over a chair and dropped his folder? The funniest person you will ever meet. (Oh, yeah, and he's going to turn out to be a famous comedian, so you really want to keep in touch with him.) And the one sitting in front of you, blocking your view of the stage. Well, remember that wedding we mentioned ... ?

And you'll make these friendships while doing all the stuff that university allows you to do when you're not in the lecture hall or the library (which would be quite a lot of the time, then). Some of that is just sitting about, having a coffee break that lasts for three hours or fashioning a meal for six from three rashers of bacon and a packet of noodles in the communal kitchen. Some of it's even more fun than that. Universities attract things that students like to do – bars, venues, shops, and concerts. And universities themselves, or active student members of them, know that there's more to student life than work, work, work. Hence the proliferation of student media, student politics, student sport, student theatre, student music, student jam-making and student stamp-collecting. At any university you will find people who share your most bizarre and whimsical interests; in fact, you'll probably find a society dedicated to them.

Going back to where we started, university is about learning. But not only the things on your reading list. Without wanting to sound too corny, it will give you a chance to learn about yourself – from learning whether you're the type of person who is ever going to get out of bed at 6 am for an early-morning jog with your keen neighbour, to learning what you are really like, and what you really want. When you get your degree, you'll get a scroll with something fancy written on it. The rest of what you get at university isn't the kind of stuff you can write down anywhere.

## Making a choice

Stick a pin in a map? It sometimes feels as though that's the most logical response to the array of courses and institutions on offer. Or maybe you have known since you were perched on your grandfather's knee that you'd always end up doing Italian at Warwick or physics at Newcastle. In which case, well done you. The other 99.9 per cent of readers might want to consider the following:

There is plenty of information out there for wannabe students. Picking up this book was a smart start, but it is only a start. Like over-eager participants at a speed-dating event, universities are just gagging to talk to you and will virtually trip over themselves in their eagerness to tell you all about what they have to offer. Even the briefest visit to any of their websites will enable you to find out more about their selling points and order a prospectus. Take a trip to your school or college careers service and you'll find a wealth of resources to help you narrow your search.

Don't forget the value of personal experience either. Other people's (do you have friends or family members who could impart some wisdom? Or even just tell you why they chose their university?) and your own. If you can manage it, attend as many open days as you can. There is no substitute for really getting a feel for a university's location and spirit than going for a wander round the campus, meeting some lecturers in your subject and chatting to some of the current students. There's more on open days in the Applying section, starting on page 28.

Equally, remember that this is your life, your education, and a lot of your own (future) earnings. Friends, teachers, and parents might all have strong opinions on the subject and, of course, you should listen to what they have to say. But if everyone wants you to do a nice humanities subject in the south-east, and yet you're drawn to study biology in Scotland, who's to say that you're wrong?

Think big. You might as well. Don't let your choices be narrowed by wanting to follow your current friends to where they're going (you'll make more, and keep the old ones too) or by wanting to choose a sensible option (who can even say what that is?) or stick to something you know you can handle (you never know until you try, and you might amaze yourself). Be realistic too. Have a think about what you like and what you are like. How do you study? What kind of environment do you like to live in? It's time for challenging yourself, but in a way that's going to enable you to flourish and only you know in what kind of atmosphere you're most likely to do that. There's more about the different factors to bear in mind in the Choosing a university section on page 18.

Money might play a part in your choice too. Remember that tuition fees are "variable". Yes, in practice most places charge the same – that is to say, the full amount – but a few plucky institutions are lighter on your pocket. Maybe you'd like to investigate them more thoroughly. Or perhaps you don't want your decision to be influenced by a few hundred pounds a year either way. What does really vary – and quite massively – is the financial support that different universities can offer. All are required to offer some kind of means-tested bursary for students paying fees but that can vary from the bare minimum to really quite lavish awards, depending on a whole host of criteria. At some places, a wealth of scholarships and prizes are on offer; others aim to boost their performance in one particular area by offering financial incentives to people who excel at that subject. If money is an issue for you, it's all worth some really thorough investigation. For more thoughts on money go to our Finance section on page 34.

The last thing to remember? Don't panic! If it seems as though there are a lot of options, well, that's because there are. And whichever one you finally settle on leaves another one – or several other ones – that could get you thinking: "I wonder if I really made the right decision?" It's best not to dwell on that too much or you'll never get round to deciding on anything. And forget, too, any notion that there even is a "right" decision. Furnish yourself with as much information as you possibly can but remember that at the end of the day you will still be taking a leap – albeit a well-informed one – into the dark. It's part of the fun. The nature of university is that you'll almost certainly end up having the best time of your life wherever you go, and swearing blind that University X was the only place you could ever have gone – and you'd have said exactly the same thing if you'd gone to University Y instead. You know, perhaps that map/pin thing isn't such a bad idea after all ...

# Using this guide

Thorough research – and maybe a bit of guesswork and intuition – will form the basis of how you decide where to apply, and what you decide to study. We hope that this book will make a good starting point and a helpful reference.

The institution guides are intended to give a flavour of the universities and higher education institutions they cover. They will give you an idea of what a place is like, what its strengths (and, sometimes, weaknesses) are, anything especially noteworthy about it, and, of course, how expensive it's liable to be. You may already have a shortlist in your head, but browse through them anyway – you could come across some things that surprise you (we did when we were compiling them!). Of course, we can really only scratch the surface here, but the contacts will point you in the right direction to enable you to have a closer look.

Much of this book is given over to the Guardian's unique tables. These are an attempt to help you gauge how good a university is in a particular subject area. Don't make the easy mistake of assuming that a "good" university will teach everything well; every place has its weak spots. And an institution that you perceive to be lacklustre in other ways might turn out to have an internationally renowned department in just the subject you want to study. No matter how good a university's reputation in general, there's no point applying there if the subject you want to study isn't taught well there.

The overall Guardian score is a combination of a number of factors. These are: student:staff ratio; job prospects; the amount of money spent per student; the A-level score (or tariff) of the students who enter the university and a value-added score assess how well those scores are translated into degrees (how many grade Ds at A-level convert into 2:1s at degree level, for example); teaching quality, as rated by graduates of the course in the National Student Survey (NSS); and feedback, which is also taken from the NSS. These tables aren't perfect by any means, as the universities themselves are very quick to tell us, and each year we tweak the methodology, looking to achieve statistical nirvana, but we firmly believe that they are the most rounded league tables there are for prospective undergraduates.

When you examine the tables (divided into subject areas, rather than courses, so also investigate which subject your course comes under) it may be that you rate particular criteria as especially important to you, so examine the data carefully. If you think job prospects are the most important thing, look for universities and colleges that do well in that area; if you think you will benefit most from a lot of personal attention from your tutor, you'll want to consider the figures relating to staff/student ratios.

The overall league table (page 53) is really for interest only. The fact that one university comes top overall is neither here nor there if it doesn't do the course you want to do, or doesn't do it well.

We've also included a short introduction to each subject area, aiming to give an overview of what a course might involve and where it might take you. Space and the virtual impossibility of covering the almost infinite variety of courses on offer mean that these can really be nothing more than a starting point, but hopefully they'll get you thinking and give you some directions for further investigation.

While we've tried to ensure the web addresses in this book are correct, these things can change quickly. There's always Google if we have failed you. We have also tried to recommend useful and reputable sites but editorial policy can change and quality can lapse so we bear no responsibility if you find material there that is useless, wrong or offensive. We will feel quite bad about it, though.

Take your time, consider the choices ahead and make the decision that feels right. Arming yourself with the facts is a good first step. After that it's up to you ...

# Choosing a university

All right, you've decided you're going to apply to university. Well done! Really the only little thing you've got to think about now is ... where? Yes, things get a little bit more tricky from this point on. Narrowing the field from the literally hundreds of options can be a daunting task. But you should relax (at least a little bit): no one expects you to you to be a walking, talking encyclopaedia of facts and figures relating to every university in the land. Even we're not that and we've just spent months putting this guide together.

The best thing you can do is research, research, research. Have a quick look at a large group of institutions, narrow that down to a few strong contenders, really put in the effort to find out about those and that should leave you with some obvious choices.

But before you do that, you might want to consider some of the following criteria that could play a part in making your choice ...

## Stay or go?

The popular image of someone starting university is that of a nervous student loading up the family car with their worldly belongings and being driven hundreds of miles before being dumped at the door of a chilly hall of residence by an emotional mum, stoical dad, and, possibly, gleeful younger siblings.

What is less common is the idea that someone might leave home on the first day of their degree ... and be back again in time for dinner and an early night in their own bed. And yet studying for a degree while living at home is an increasingly popular option. It cuts costs, of course (if you can persuade your parents or whoever you live with that they really do want to support your education by not charging you rent, or at least not at market value), and it's almost certain that your living environment will be more pleasant, quieter, cleaner, and provide better food than if you chose to fend for yourself on campus.

The expansion of the higher education sector means that many more people now have good universities nearby. And many universities are focusing, through recruitment drives or financial incentives, on attracting local students to register with them. In big cities, where you've got the attraction of excellent universities and the problem of high rents, it's always been pretty usual to find students who are happily still living at home.

You also might feel that you just quite like your family, thank you, and enjoy the idea of having a group of people to come home to who are compelled by long-standing affection or genetics to be supportive and interested in what you're doing.

But, then again, a large part of the point of university for many new undergraduates is that it gets them out of the house. For several months at a time. There's no doubt that – unless you happen to inhabit a mansion with extremely liberal (and deaf) family members – staying put in the house you grew up in is going to cramp your style. You might think you can cope with that now ... but are you sure you're still going to be as sanguine when you're leaving the students' union bar early for the third night in a row so you can get the last bus home while everyone else is free to carry on partying because they all live on campus?

And let's not gloss over the fact that leaving home for the first time – no matter when or how you do it or how much you think you're gagging to get out of there – can be a bit of a wrench. Most first-year students admit (through probably not until the second year) to a bit of homesickness. But the nice thing about university is that it lets you experiment with the idea of living alone – yet all the while surrounded by friends, facilities and excellent support networks. And with lovely long holidays that let you go back to the family home for weeks on end and remember exactly why you wanted to move out in the first place.

## Location, location, location

Remember all those times you've gazed out of the window and idly thought, "I wish I lived by the sea/by the mountains/in a big city/in the middle of the country/near a Test cricket ground"? Well, here's the thing: now you can! Nothing beats choosing a university for having a really good think about where you'd like to live and making it a reality. Always lived in the north and fancy seeing if they're really soft down south? Grown up amongst concrete canyons but secretly nurturing a desire to don a pair of walking boots and tramp up and down real grass-covered hills every weekend? Dying to live somewhere that other people pay to go on holiday to? It's all within your grasp!

First, you might want to think about how much you want to super-size your university experience. The lure of big cities is age-old: all those bright lights, the opportunity to lose yourself in infinite choice and variety, the chance to share it all with a diverse group of people and students drawn from all over the world. Cities also have a way of making you feel anonymous, almost invisible, as millions of people busily carry on with their lives all around you and pay you no attention whatsoever. In some ways that can be a liberating – almost exhilarating – experience. You can do anything and be anyone! In others, it can be terribly lonely. Only you know whether you're likely to sink or swim (though bear in mind that the insta-community of a university is likely to make the landing in a big city a little more soft than it might otherwise be).

Other downsides of city life: travelling around it takes a long time, even if the transport links are good; it's expensive, even if part-time work is easy to come by; you might even feel that cities offer a few too many distractions to happily sit with studying for a degree ...

Small towns – or even pretty medium-sized towns in which the university plays a big part – can be lovely places to live for a few years. Everywhere's quick and easy to get to; as you whizz around town on your bike you'll soon get to know it like the back of your hand, you'll see familiar faces wherever you go, and – especially if students make up a significant part of the local economy – there will be plenty of events and facilities laid on just for you. Sure, it gets parochial and claustrophobic from time to time; the fact that the whole place boasts only two cinema screens is a bit annoying; and the last time the local football team got anywhere near the FA Cup is when they took a coach trip to watch the final. Perhaps, if you're going to go small, it would be as well to check that there is a night bus to somewhere that doesn't shut down at 10 pm for when your feet get a bit itchy ...

Another thing to think about is just how far you want to go. It's easy, when that Ucas form needs filling in and your head is swimming with the contents of 14 different prospectuses, to think that that's not exactly a top priority. And you're probably right. But come reading week, when everyone else in your hall of residence is hopping on a train for the quick trip home to get some laundry done and a nice dinner cooked for them and you realise you're stuck in Norwich when your family is in Belfast, or Dundee when your best hope of roast chicken is in Penzance ... well, you might feel it's something you should have paid a bit more attention to. Obviously, it isn't a factor you should let limit you. But at least having an idea of how much it will cost, and how long it will take to get home should you suddenly want or need to, might not be a foolish idea.

## One site fits all?

So, you think you've got it all sorted: you've picked the town or city you want to live in and are busily imaging yourself sauntering along its streets and paths, strolling home at midnight by the gleaming river or going for an early-morning jog through its parks. And then you find that you'll actually be based on a campus eight miles away and the only reason you'd be walking home by the river at midnight is because you missed the last bus.

Don't scrimp on working out *exactly* where you're going to be. A distance of a few miles, or being on the wrong side of the city from your faculty, or just not right in the centre of things, if that's where you want to be, can make a real difference.

Equally, do you want to live on a campus or not? Campuses are remarkable places: self-contained little towns full of just students! Plenty of them have everything you could possibly need right there: shops, banks, bars, cafes, launderettes, doctors, a sports centre, even a cinema or a pool. It can feel as though you're a privileged citizen in some weird student kingdom, and in many ways you are. Some campuses, too, are lovely to look at: rolling parkland and landscaped gardens. All right, you won't spend your *whole* time lolling around on the lawn on sunny afternoons. But you will spend *some* of your time doing that, and what could be nicer?

On the other hand, some campuses are just downright ugly and depressing. If you attend a campus university, you'll end up living off-site for some of the time, but you'll still have to go back most days. A town-based university might be a more appealing choice. These are places where the university buildings are scattered across a town or city, or part thereof. In some – usually the older ones – you're bedded right into the heart of the place where you live, which can really make you feel like part of something. Or sometimes just make you feel as though you're part of a tortuous experiment as you realise you've got five minutes to get from lecture to lab and it's a 20-minute journey across the city centre!

In the end, it just comes down to personal preference. We've said it before, and we'll say it again before the book's over: go for a visit. There really is no substitute for first-hand experience to get a real feel for a place and how much you're going to like it.

## Party time

Oh, yeah, we all know about university, don't we? Three-for-one on alcopops and all the kebabs you can eat, all the while wearing nothing but a vest with ambition and a smile. And the best part is, your parents will never know! Unless they are on Facebook.

And we're not here to tell you that it isn't true – because, frankly, it is, and thank God you can do all that stuff at university because you could certainly never hold down a job and carry on in that fashion.

Nor are we seriously going to suggest that you pick a course on the basis of where has the best social life. You'd be an idiot. A happy idiot, at lots of parties, sure, but an idiot nonetheless. But even we will concede that there's more to university than work, work, work and your studies and your general sense of wellbeing will improve immeasurably if you can let your hair down in the manner that you most enjoy.

So if you're just assuming that a big part of your university social life will revolve around clubbing like a maniac, you might want to just make sure it will be easy for you to make that happen. Those cute little colleges tucked down country lanes? Not so many big-name DJs, as it happens. Similarly, if you're crazy about opera, ballet, classical music, theatre, art or live music, here's an opportunity for you to set up home somewhere where you've got easy access to all of them.

All universities have student bars and the like. But they are not all created equal. Nor do they all boast the same range of student societies and clubs. It stands to reason, most of the time, that the bigger the place the more diverse the offering, the higher the quality and the more opportunities there are to get involved. If you're especially ambitious in one area, you might want to think about the fact that some student organisations are held in national – even international – regard. No aspirant comedian's career was ever hurt by being a member of Cambridge's Footlights comedy troupe, for example, and some of the big student newspapers are recognised by professional journalists as being excellent training grounds for wannabe hacks. Some university sports teams compete internationally too. Picking the right place for you to have fun might be a ticket to more than just a degree.

## Money matters

We've already talked about how tuition fees can vary from place to place (and country to country. Read the Finance section (page 34) carefully!) But there's more to the cost of university than that. Even as a student you don't get special dispensation from the economic forces that govern everyone else … So, broadly speaking, London (and most of the rest of the south) and big cities are more expensive in terms of rent, transport and – oh, just everything, basically – while your quiet northern town is likely to be as cheap as the chips they serve (that will taste better than anything you find south of the Watford Gap).

London students do get extra allowances in their loans/grant package. Will it be enough to tide you over? Only you can decide. And you should remember that it's not all one-way. If you are planning on working part-time you might find that London and other expensive places are also the ones with the most ready supply of money-making opportunities, and, possibly, the highest wages.

Other things need factoring in. OK, you might be living in an "expensive" city – but you're on campus so everything's within walking distance, the bar's amazing and subsidised and because everyone's skint you've learned to be inventive with your money. Whereas your friend in a "cheap" town might not pay as much rent but a big night out means a trip to the nearest city: club prices on drinks and a taxi ride home. And she buys posh sarnies from M&S for her lunch every day because the campus caff is so dire.

It is, frankly, enough to make your head ache. But then so is looking at your overdraft after one year of student life. If you're worried about money it would be worth your while doing a little digging into exactly how pricey various places are likely to be.

# Are you a snob?

It's not an especially palatable truth, but it does exist, so we might as well get it out in the open. In the minds of many – most, probably – people there's a snob's pyramid of UK universities. Right at the top sit Oxford and Cambridge, with the next most venerable institutions arrayed beneath them, the red-bricks beneath them and so on, until you get, at the bottom, to the "new" universities, the higher education institutions and the degree-awarding colleges.

Is it right? Is it fair? Well, and at the risk of causing Guardian-reader outrage, in some cases: yes. It stands to reason that institutions that have been around forever and a day have had the time to accrue the power, the position, the privileges, the experience, and facilities to earn a formidable academic reputation. That reputation attracts the best teachers and students, which in turn boosts their standing, and so it goes on. It's not just a perception; hard statistics (such as our own tables) often demonstrate (though the emphasis is on "often" – not "always") that the places you think are going to be the best are the ones that are.

Should you aim for the top? Again, a resounding yes! Of course you should aim as high as you possibly can. Do not let fears about certain places being "not for the likes of us" put you off. The institutions that are (rightfully) worried about their access figures really do have active programmes in place to encourage applications from everyone who fancies their chances. And while it is sadly true that some places – and, even more sadly, often the best places – are still overpopulated with people from one small section of society, that will only change by more different types of people going. And why not you?

And yet on the other hand ... you might, after sensible deliberation, decide that actually you'd rather be somewhere a bit more free and easy than a place that requires you wear a gown to dinner and listen to someone mumbling in Latin before you get to eat. And you don't need to scrimp on academic quality if you do. Equally, some people literally can't get into certain universities. If you're in a wheelchair, for example, ancient quads and narrow steps might be more of a pain than you can be bothered to cope with. (Not, of course, that it would be an insurmountable problem: Stephen Hawking manages Cambridge just fine and they don't come much more ancient-quadded than Cambridge.)

We've talked in the introduction about how we believe that you should look at the quality of your course, not just the institution. It's the basis of our subject league tables, after all. So if you fall in love with a brilliant course, a passionate tutor (in the platonic sense only, may we just add), a terrific campus or a great city that pulls you to a university "less good" than another one, what is to stop you going there? Nothing, we say.

Though of course we do still live in the real world. While we, and you, might know that course A is lacklustre and limp at University X, and vibrant and thorough at University Y, most lay people – and we mean employers here – only know that, in vague and general terms, X is "better" than Y and so their graduates get an easier ride. We can't pretend that doesn't happen. On the other hand, you might be surprised by how quickly it does filter through to the wider world which courses are better at which places. This is especially true on a course with a vocational bent: you can bet your bottom dollar that employers will have a keen grasp of where the best graduates are going to come from, and it won't just be because of centuries-old reputation.

Similarly, while those little specialist colleges may not have made much impact on the collective consciousness, if they are absolutely the best in the business when it comes to the handful of courses they teach, does it matter that Mr Bloggs in Bolton has never heard of them? In a word: no.

And don't disparage those HE institutions either. They provide significant proportions of graduates in creative arts, teaching, healthcare and land-based subjects, and they could teach some of the "better" places a thing or two about widening participation. If you're interested in non-traditional routes into higher education, or more flexible ways of learning, you could do much, much worse than looking at one of these institutions.

## Oxbridge

But while we're on the subject of snobbery, let's take a look at that most thorny of subjects: Oxbridge. Oh, we could fill a book on this one topic alone. The history! The tradition! The ludicrous public school boys!

There are plenty of reasons for wanting to give Oxbridge a whirl. Both universities are ravishing to look at, for a start. You cannot kid yourself that they are not at the very top of any list of the country's – or the world's – universities. The education you get there will be first-rate, with brilliant – bordering on genius – teachers, excellent facilities and terrific resources. And, sick to the stomach though it might make you feel, the phrase, "Well, I was at Oxford/Cambridge" still carries a lot of currency out in the real world.

But then again, like Monty Python's Camelot, they are ever such silly places. All those traditions and quirks, the Latin and gowns, the language of its own each place has (battells, pidge, bops ... what does any of it mean?), the black tie and balls. It can all border somewhat on the surreal. Of course, all of that may have you salivating to get stuck in – and, if you're up for it, it certainly can be tremendous fun. On the other hand, you may think the whole thing is deranged ...

Applying to either is a bit more of a faff than to other places and you are virtually guaranteed an excruciating interview in which you pit your mock A-level wits against the person who wrote the defining work in your subject. And though of course we are not saying that other degrees aren't challenging or intense, the eight-week terms of Oxbridge, the sheer weight of expectation that seems to leech out of the walls and the one-on-one tutorial style of teaching does seem to lend studying there an extra dose of pressure that can either push you to strive for ever-greater things ... or push you right over the edge.

In the end, you may decide that it's not for you – and that's fine. But whatever you do, don't be put off by the idea that you are not for them. No matter what you think, the streets of these places are not filled with gals in gowns suddenly grabbing you to check that you know which fork you use with fish and whether it's better to say "sofa" or "settee". No one – least of all Oxford or Cambridge – is going to try to tell you that their student body isn't skewed more in one (socially privileged) direction than any other but, even so, they are diverse enough that everyone can find their own comfortable niche. In the end, all students are pretty much the same and reports from Oxbridge students consistently say that the "What school did you go to?" questions ceases to be of interest to anyone after the first five seconds of freshers' week chat.

And Oxford and Cambridge really, really are – no matter what anyone else might tell you – trying to get more people to apply. It's only sensible – the brightest and the best from all areas of the country and all different backgrounds coming to interview gives them the widest choice and the best chance of maintaining their reputations. It's obviously the case that people who've had money flung at their education are going to feel a bit more comfortable with the concept of Oxbridge than someone who'd never heard of it until they saw a rerun of Inspector Morse. But the people who run Oxbridge are – quite famously, actually – not stupid. They understand that people from expensive schools have been primed for it and that other people haven't. They have no vested interest in people from one section of society or another. You think your average bookish tutor, with her head full of advanced physics, cares what her student's mum and dad do for a living? Not at all. They are interested in rooting out potential and the ability to thrive in the system these universities operate. If you think you've got it and you fancy spending some time among the dreaming spires, for heaven's sake go and show them.

## Open season

Turning from one atypical university experience to another ... if, for whatever reason, you decide you don't have the time or the money to commit to a full-time degree right now, don't want to move, don't want to give up your job or don't want to have to rearrange your life around a university timetable there is always the option of studying for a degree with the Open University.

The appeal is obvious: all you need is a computer and a TV, the fees are less, you can fit your study round whatever else you choose, and its academic reputation certainly stands up to scrutiny.

However, the Open is not by any means an easy ride. It still requires a big time commitment and because it's part-time each degree course lasts six years.

Your staying power will certainly be tested – and you won't be immersed in the student experience as you would be on campus.

In any case, although we've included the Open in our institution guides, you won't find it in the league tables. That's not because it's not worthy of being rated, but because its unique set-up means that it can't be fairly compared with other universities.

## Minority rule

Perhaps you think that your race, religion, sexuality or physical ability should play as much of a role in deciding where you're going to continue your education as you think it should in deciding what you're going to have for dinner tonight. If that's you, more power to you. And, indeed, you're probably right if you sense that universities, in general, are far more tolerant to different experiences and points of view among their populations than society in general. University governing bodies will certainly come down hard and fast on discrimination: it goes without saying that if you encounter any you should alert the relevant authorities straight away.

Ethnic minority students may find themselves among only a very few on their course – and the situation gets worse as you approach the top of the pile of UK universities. However, you may not be remotely bothered by that: you'll just take it as a chance to meet plenty of other people from different backgrounds. And it's unlikely that you'll be totally on your own, in any case.

But if being with significant numbers of people from the same race or religion as you is important, head to the big cities. At some of the new London universities, white students are the "minority" section of the student body.

Disabled students may sometimes feel that their way to university is barred – in very literal terms. Old buildings (even "new" universities can occupy ancient structures) with poor facilities for disabled students, coupled with ignorance about what needs to be done, might make for a frustrating mix. But persevere! There are laws in place to ensure that people with disabilities have equal access to education. Most universities will have a dedicated unit to help students with disabilities and ensure the institution meets its responsibilities and will (or should be) keen to make changes that need to be made. It may just require that you point out what needs to be done.

Finally, if you already know you are lesbian, gay or bisexual – or aren't sure but think that university might be a good time to find out – there is probably very little to fear about starting university. Although it would be naive to suggest that homophobia has been totally eradicated, campuses do tend to be fairly tolerant places and most universities will have a community of LGB students and, very likely, an active LGB society too.

If you're nervous about being out at university, however, or want to make sure that you've got ready access to a good LGB scene, you might want to give some thought to where you want to go. Sure, you may relish the thought of being the only out and proud student on some tiny rural campus – and good for you if you do – but if you're more inclined to just want to be one of many, then the larger cities are probably a commonsense option, along with places with an established gay scene.

# Applying

You think you know what you'd like to study, and you've got a fair idea of where you might like to study it. Now all you have to do is make those vague inklings a reality by getting the application process under way. Although it can seem daunting to begin with, it's actually pretty straightforward – as long as you're prepared for what's coming up and when, you will be fine.

## Open days

Not, strictly speaking, a mandatory part of the application process, but we do think that if you can possibly manage it, you should make attendance at a few open days a key stage in your application process.

Of course, it's probably not possible for reasons of time, money or basic inclination to visit every university you have even the vaguest interest in. But if you can, visiting at least the top handful of places on your wish list is a good idea. Scour prospectuses and websites all you like, but they are designed to give a good impression and that nice picture of a handsome building basking in the afternoon sun is handily cropped to leave out the damp 1960s monstrosity that spoils the view for anyone who actually sees it in person. Turning up and having a walk around might be the only way to get a real sense of a place and how you'll fit into it. It's also a great opportunity to meet students and tutors and talk to them about what you might be letting yourself in for. If you don't think you can fund open days independently, check with your school or college to see if they're organising any group trips (or if you could persuade them to).

Open days can be sprinkled throughout the year, though, unfortunately, the traditional season for them has always been mid-May – when many Year 12s are now in the midst of AS-level exams. Universities are (slowly, as is their way) catching on to this development and being more flexible, making them earlier or later in the year. They will be listed on university websites, and the Ucas website also carries details through its institution guide.

You may have to book a place on an official open day, or you may just be able to register your interest and turn up – university websites will have details. Official open days will probably offer you a chance to meet students and lecturers, have a look round facilities, accommodation, and the all-important bar, and give you a taster of academic life.

Have a think beforehand about what you really want to know and use the "Any questions?" slot at the end of the head of department's presentation to find out. Talk to students – and not just the ones officially designated to show you around – they'll probably be able to give you the best impression of the place you're considering spending the next three years.

If you can't make an official open day, you could always call the university and see if you can arrange your own. Ask if you can spend five minutes chatting to a tutor and looking at the facilities. Or you could create a totally ad hoc visit – just dropping by a campus and having a look around. You could probably corner a student or two doing that, but you're unlikely to get much of an idea of the academic side of things in the department you're planning to apply to.

If you *really* can't make any open days then at least cast your net a little further during your research. Student-union-produced alternative prospectuses and student web forums are a good place to start for the uncensored take on what a university is really like – just to balance out the utopian idyll presented in the pages of the official prospectus.

## Applying

Application season begins in early September when Ucas starts accepting applications. Time was, a Ucas form was made of paper and was filled out by anxious students with a Biro clutched in one hand, a bottle of Tippex by their side and frowns of concentration on their faces.

These days you'll almost certainly fill out and submit your form online (and Ucas has a list of centres across the country that will allow you to access their website and fill in the form if you don't have the internet at home, school or college). Unless you are called for interview or asked to submit other examples of your work, this will be the only thing prospective universities have to go on, so it's more than worth making sure you don't make silly mistakes. Take some time to familiarise yourself with the form and think about your responses before you fill it in and click "submit".

Your personal statement is particularly important, and a chance to convince the weary admissions tutor who is on their 30th Ucas form of the day that you really are passionate about your subject and would be a joy to teach. This isn't an excuse to be economical with the truth – these people have made a living out of being clever, remember – but to really talk about why you're interested in the courses you've chosen and the subject; skills and experience you have gained through work, volunteering or placements, especially if it's relevant; and your ambitions and wider interests. Whoever looks at your form will have read the phrase "In my spare time I enjoy socialising with my friends" a hundred thousand times before, so try to be a little bit original.

You can choose up to five courses to apply for (though keep an eye out for entrance criteria; there's no point in applying to do something you don't have the right A-levels for), apart from people who want to study medicine, dentistry or veterinary courses: for those, you can choose up to four courses in one of those subjects, and use your fifth choice for another subject.

The closing date for most applications is January 15 (though see below for some exceptions). After it has received your application, Ucas will forward it on to the places you have applied to. And then all you have to do is sit back and wait for the responses to start coming in. They will be either an unsuccessful decision, an unconditional offer, or a conditional offer (normally based on your exam results). Once you've heard from all of the places you applied to, you can decide which (if any) to firmly accept, accept as your insurance place (if your first choice makes a conditional offer your insurance place should usually be an unconditional offer, or a conditional offer based on lower grades or fewer tariff points) and decline.

If you miss the January 15 deadline for applications, from January 16 to June 30 you can make late applications, which universities may consider if they have places to fill – though obviously the most popular places will probably have filled their courses. You can also apply through Ucas Extra from late February if none of your first round of applications has led to the offer of a place, or none that you want to accept. Using Extra you can apply to courses with spaces left to fill, one course at a time. The details of these courses will be on the Ucas website.

Finally, if you miss the June 30 deadline, suddenly decide you want to go to university when you thought you didn't, or haven't yet managed to find a place on a course, you can apply through Clearing from mid-August. More information about that below.

## Oxbridge

Wouldn't you know it but Oxbridge has a different Ucas applications closing date to the rest of the UK's universities – October 15, a good three months earlier than everywhere else. Which means that if you're giving Oxbridge a go you have to have your Ucas application shipshape and ready to go ages before your friends have even started to think about theirs.

It also means that while they're still dawdling over their personal statements you'll probably be packing your bags and heading to one or other of the universities for interview. These normally take place in December.

Also be aware that you can't apply to both Oxford and Cambridge in the same year. Neither university has their own application form anymore, so you must apply through Ucas.

## Other courses

People applying to do courses in medicine, dentistry, veterinary science or veterinary medicine. The closing date for all these courses is also October 15.

## Art and design

Art and design courses can have a closing date of January 15 or March 24. You will need to use the course search on the Ucas website (www.ucas.com) to check the dates for these courses.

## Clearing

Clearing is often synonymous with a mad scramble for a university place as the summer draws to a close – ending up with slightly baffled students wondering how come they're studying psychology in Scotland when they wanted to be doing chemistry on the south coast. But it needn't be a disordered scuffle: it can actually be a very sensible option, and given a little patience, a little flexibility, and by making sure you don't lose your head, you can end up on a course that is right for you. More than 30,000 people find a university place through Clearing every year: they can't all spend their first year wondering how they ended up where they did.

Clearing opens in mid-August, after exam results, and is a way of matching up students without a place with universities with places to spare. You are eligible for Clearing if any of these apply:

- you have not withdrawn your application
- you hold no offers
- your offers have not been confirmed because you didn't get the required grades
- you have declined your offers or not responded by the due date
- your offers have not been confirmed, and you have declined any alternative offers from the same university
- you sent your Ucas application in after June 30. Ucas won't have sent it to any universities or colleges after this date, so you'll have to use Clearing

When Clearing opens, universities with spaces to fill will list their under-subscribed courses on the Ucas website and in newspapers, including the Guardian. You can then match up your interests and exam results with what's on offer and secure yourself a place on a course starting in a few weeks' time.

It goes without saying that you need an open mind and a degree of flexibility. You may not find the Italian course you are after – but how about film studies with Italian? You may also have to consider universities that weren't on your list before. That's when a cool head — and access to a guide such as this one — will come in handy.

On the other hand, don't get caught up in the momentum of Clearing unless you're sure it's the right thing for you to do. If you aren't sure that you will find something that's going to suit you, it may be better to take an unscheduled gap year and go through the whole application process again rather than make a rash decision and end up somewhere that's wrong for you or doing something you hate.

## Adjustment

Every year some applicants pass their exams with better results than expected. This might mean that they not only meet the conditions of their firm offer, but exceed them. If you find yourself in this position, the Adjustment period gives you an opportunity to reconsider where and what to study — you'll have the option to find an alternative place, while still holding your original confirmed offer.

## Course start dates

Although there are three deadlines for applying to courses through UCAS — October 15, January 15 and March 24 — it's important to check when the course you are interested in will start. If your course starts between January and May, you might need to apply earlier than the set deadlines. You can find details of course start dates on the Course Search area of www.ucas.com but you should also contact the university or college direct for advice on when to apply. While some will be happy to receive applications right up to the start of the course, you should be prepared to send your application early.

Remember that you don't have to apply for all your choices at the same time. You can add further choices as long as you haven't used them all up or accepted a place.

## International applicants

If you are applying from outside the UK or EU, whatever your nationality, you can apply at any time between mid-September and June 30, unless you are applying for Oxford or Cambridge, or for courses in medicine, dentistry, veterinary medicine or veterinary science, in which case you should apply by the dates above. It is advisable to apply as early as possible. Universities and colleges do not guarantee that they will consider applications received after January 15, and some popular courses may not have vacancies after that date. If you're unsure, check with individual universities and colleges.

Remember to allow enough time for entry clearance or immigration, and also travel and accommodation, which take longer during the busy summer period. If you think you may be assessed as a "home" student (UK or EU) for tuition fees, you should apply by January 15.

》 Further information

**University and Colleges Admissions Service (Ucas)** ↗ www.ucas.com

## Applications at a glance

| 2009 | |
|---|---|
| **20 August** | A-level and AS-level results |
| **September 1** | Ucas starts accepting applications |
| **October 15** | Deadline for applications to Oxford and Cambridge, and applications for dentistry, medicine, veterinary medicine, and veterinary science |
| **December** | Interviews for Oxford and Cambridge and some courses at other universities |
| **2010** | |
| **January** | Interviews |
| **January 15** | Deadline for Ucas applications for all courses except those listed above with a October 15 deadline, and art and design courses with a March 24 deadline. |
| **January 16** | Late applications accepted by Ucas. Universities and colleges will consider them if they want to make more offers |
| **Late February** | If you have not received any offers or declined all offers you can apply for other courses, one at a time, through Ucas Extra |
| **March 24** | Deadline for applications for art and design, except those listed with a January 15 deadline. |
| **June** | A-level and AS-level exams |
| **June 30** | Deadline for late applications. Applications after this date are entered in Clearing |
| **August** | A-level and AS-level results. Applicant places are confirmed. Clearing starts on A-level results day. Course vacancies are listed in the Guardian |
| **September/October** | University term starts |

# Finance

Few things in life are certain but, these days, finishing your university studies owing the government a pound or two has got to be one of them. When you first start contemplating higher education you'll very soon realise that it's not going to be a cheap ride – and we're not just talking about overindulgence in the union bar. Over the past few years, debt has become as much a part of the university experience as Pot Noodles and questionable student housing.

The government's decision to allow higher education institutions (HEIs) in England, Wales and Northern Ireland to charge variable fees of around £3,000 a year for their degree courses from 2006 added to already existing concerns that the cost of studying was becoming a barrier to students entering higher education. The National Union of Students estimates that a student beginning their degree in 2006, when the new higher-fee regime was introduced, would graduate with debts of around £27,000.

However, when you look at the detail, things might not appear as gloomy as you first thought. For a start, you don't have to pay your course fees until after you have graduated and are working, rather than finding the money before your first lecture; the government has reintroduced maintenance grants for students from low-income families and universities are offering bursaries and scholarships to tempt you into the fold. There is also extra financial help for part-time students, students with disabilities or those with children. And the threshold for student loans has been raised.

So yes, unless you're wealthy or meticulous in your budgeting you are likely to graduate in some debt, but it may be worth remembering that the investment you make in your education now should benefit you over the course of your working life. The government estimates that graduates earn on average 50 per cent more over their lifetime than someone who stopped studying after their A-levels.

We think it would be a shame for anyone to miss out on the opportunities that a degree offers because of worries about money – especially when there are lots of schemes in place to make the debt manageable. In this chapter we'll guide you through the maze of student finance and hopefully take some of the worry out of higher education's "F" (that's "fees", folks) factor.

## Tuition fees

Let's start with the cost of your course. HEIs in England, Wales and Northern Ireland can charge students around £3,000 a year for full-time degree courses (Scotland has a different arrangement, which is outlined later in the chapter). This goes up a little every year, in line with inflation. So, for entry in 2009, HEIs are allowed to charge up to £3,225 a year. The government has yet to finalise the cost for 2010-11 courses, but if you consider charges for 2008-9 were £3,145 you can get an idea of how much you could pay.

Of course, while universities are allowed to charge this yearly amount it's actually up to the HEI how much it asks students to pay and not all of them are charging the full amount. Prices can vary between universities and courses, so it could pay you to shop around.

The important thing to note is that tuition fees do not have to be paid before you start your course, as they used to be before 2006. You can still pay upfront if you wish, and some universities may even offer a discount if you chose to do so, but most students are expected to pay after graduation.

To defer payment until after your studies, you need to take out a non-means-tested student loan for tuition fees from the Student Loans Company (SLC). The SLC will pay your fees direct to the HEI and you will not have to repay the loan until after you have graduated and are earning at least £15,000 a year. More on repaying your loans later in the chapter.

When the government introduced variable fees in 2006 it said it would review the price of courses in 2009 to assess whether the £3,000 limit needed to be raised. However, reports suggest this review is unlikely to be completed before June 2010 so it should not affect students thinking of applying to study in 2010-11.

## Financial support

Aware that raising the cost of tuition fees would be as popular a concept as an empty beer keg at the students' union bar, the government has beefed up the financial support available to undergraduates so as not to put you off studying. Ministers also told HEIs that if they wanted to charge the full price for fees, they would have to do their bit to help ease the financial burden on students.

This has resulted in the reintroduction of non-repayable maintenance grants, university bursaries and higher borrowing levels to help towards the cost of living. The government estimates that around half of all students applying to university will be eligible for some form of non-repayable financial help.

Details of what is available are outlined below. All figures relate to UK students studying at English universities. The financial support for students studying in Scotland, Wales and Northern Ireland is outlined later in the chapter.

# Student loans for maintenance

In the same way that you can take out a loan to cover the cost of your tuition fees, you can borrow money from the SLC to help cover your living costs while at university – such as accommodation, travel, food, clothes, nights out.

Anyone under the age of 60 can apply for a maintenance loan, although the amount you can borrow is pegged to where you are studying and where you will be living while taking your degree.

There are three borrowing limits.

Students living away from their parents' home and studying in London can borrow the most – for 2009 entry, this will be up to £6,928 in the first year of study.

Those living away from home and studying elsewhere in England can borrow up to £4,950 in their first year, while students who decide to live at their parents' home during their degrees, regardless of where in the country this may be, can borrow up to £3,838.

These amounts are likely to increase for 2010 entry.

If your course includes a placement overseas, the amount you can borrow could change. If you study abroad for a term or more you may be eligible for an overseas rate of loan. In 2009, the maximum loan you can take out while studying overseas is £5,895.

You will be automatically entitled to borrow 75 per cent of the maximum loan amount for which you are eligible, but whether you can take out the remaining 25 per cent will depend on family income and whether you are receiving any other student grants.

Maintenance loans from the SLC will usually be paid directly into your bank account in three instalments during the academic year.


# Maintenance grants

Full-time students from low-income families (earning less than £50,020) studying in England can apply for a non-repayable maintenance grant to help with their living costs.

In 2009, students whose annual household income is £25,000 or less will receive a full grant of £2,906 a year. A partial grant will be paid on a sliding scale to students with household incomes of between £25,001 and £50,020.

Expect these figures to rise slightly if you begin university in 2010.

The money will be paid directly into your bank account three times a year.

If you receive a maintenance grant you will also be entitled to take out student loans, but the amount you can borrow will be slightly less – the government reasons you won't need to borrow quite so much if you receive a grant. For example, if you receive a grant of £1,260 or more, your student loan entitlement will be reduced by £1,260. The smaller the grant you receive the more you will be able to borrow.

---

**Example:** figures based on a student beginning their course in 2009–10, living away from home and studying outside London.

| Household income | Maintenance grant | Student loan for maintenance | Total for 2009–10 |
|---|---|---|---|
| £25,000 | £2,906 | £3,497 | £6,403 |
| £30,000 | £1,906 | £3,997 | £5,903 |
| £40,000 | £711 | £4,595 | £5,306 |
| £50,020 | £50 | £4,925 | £4,975 |
| £60,000 | no grant | £3,564 | £3,564 |

Source: Directgov.gov.uk

## Special support grant

This grant is similar to a regular maintenance grant – it's assessed using household income and is worth the same amount – but it is aimed at helping students pay for those extra costs that come with university, such as books, equipment, travel, and childcare. Eligibility rests on, among other things, whether you're a single parent, have a disability, or have taken time out of a course because of illness or because you've been caring for someone.

The difference between this award and the maintenance grant is that it will not affect the amount you can borrow as a maintenance loan.

## University and college bursaries

As a condition of charging higher fees, HEIs have had to come up with their own bursary schemes to help students manage their finances – and they have come up trumps with the amount of money.

Anyone receiving a full maintenance grant (£2,906) will automatically be entitled to at least £319 a year from their place of study, if it is charging the full price (£3,225) for tuition, in effect allowing eligible students to cover their fee costs each year (maintenance grant + bursary = fee charge). Universities and colleges are also offering bursaries to students who are eligible for partial grants.

However, many HEIs are offering far more than required. It is estimated that last year, students entitled to a full maintenance grant and studying at a university charging the full cost for fees, received, on average, bursaries worth around £800.

But it's not just students in receipt of maintenance grants who may be eligible for financial assistance. Some HEIs are offering money to students who live close to the institution or who apply from a partner school or college.

Some HEIs are also offering scholarships (and of significant sums too) to students studying particular subjects, or if they make the institution their first choice on the Ucas form. There are also sometimes awards available for academic excellence (usually based on your A-level grades). It doesn't take a genius to work out that universities use these tactics to increase the numbers of people applying in certain subject areas, or to attract people with academic prowess. But you could really benefit if you look out for an awards package that matches your course interests and abilities.

To fully benefit from the money that is on offer, you need to check what's available at the university you wish to attend. Most will have this information on their websites or you can use the Bursary Map at direct.gov.uk. It's important to do so as soon as you've decided on a course, as eligibility for some scholarships could be based on written exams, portfolios or interviews. More on applying for financial support later in the chapter.

## Subject-specific bursaries and grants

While universities can offer specific bursaries and scholarships for certain subjects, it's also worth checking with umbrella bodies and societies to see what they are offering, particularly if you want to study a subject with a lower uptake, such as the sciences, technology, engineering, and maths (or STEM) subjects.

There is also extra money available from the NHS for specific nursing, midwifery, and other medical courses, and for social work degrees.

## STEM subjects

Keen to encourage more students on to these very worthy, but perhaps not quite so sexy degree courses, some umbrella organisations are offering financial incentives, so you need to do your research.

The Royal Academy of Engineering (www.raeng.org.uk), for example, offers financial awards to exceptional engineering students, worth up to £5,000 over three years.

Aspiring scientists can also find financial help from the Nuffield Foundation (www.nuffieldfoundation.org), which is offering science bursaries to undergraduates to carry out research during their course.

And the Royal Society of Chemistry lists the institutions that offer scholarships for those studying the subject in the UK, as well as offering funding to attend its conferences (www.rsc.org).

# Healthcare

If you want to study a medical or healthcare course you may also be eligible for financial assistance from the NHS.

Students taking nursing or midwifery degrees and diplomas (which lead to registration with the Nursing and Midwifery Council) could receive an NHS bursary (www.nhsbsa.nhs.uk/students), which could cover the cost of your tuition fees and help towards living expenses.

Students taking a nursing degree can apply for means-tested maintenance grants, while those taking diplomas can apply for a non-income-assessed bursary.

Bursaries may also be available for students studying other medical courses, such as chiropody, podiatry, occupational therapy, physiotherapy, and speech and language therapy.

Be aware that receipt of an NHS bursary will reduce your entitlement to a maintenance loan, but at least that could reduce debts after your studies.

If you are offered a place on a relevant NHS funded course, your HEI will contact the NHS Bursaries Division and they will write to you explaining how to apply for a bursary.

Things are slightly different for medical and dentistry students studying courses lasting five or six years, as you will only be able to apply for an NHS bursary in your final years of training. You are, of course, still able to take out student maintenance loans for the full duration of your course – although this amount will be slightly reduced after your fourth year of study. And you can still apply for a maintenance grant, subject to your family income, which means you could be entitled to receive that precious extra bursary from your place of study for at least the first four years of study.

# Social work

If you are planning to do a degree in social work you may be eligible for a bursary to help cover living costs from the NHS Business Services Authority on behalf of the Department of Health. These bursaries are non-means-tested, but you have to study on an approved course and meet a few other requirements (such as being a UK resident and not receiving support for your studies from an employer), so check with your favoured place of study before you apply.

If you meet the criteria you will be eligible for a basic grant to help with living expenses and the cost of travel during placements. The bursary does not cover tuition fees, but you will be able to take out a loan to cover the cost of those in the same way as other students studying different courses. You will receive a higher grant if you are studying at a HEI in London.

Part-time students will also be eligible for these bursaries.

## Teacher training

Although there have been discussions about tuition fees being waived for undergraduate teacher-training degrees and extra bursaries being made available, particularly to those taking their teacher training in subjects with a shortage of teachers, the extra benefits seem to have gone to students doing postgraduate courses rather than first degrees. So, if you take a regular bachelor of education degree you will be subject to the same financial package as other undergraduate students. If you decide instead to do a three-year degree in another subject and then apply for a postgraduate certificate of education (PGCE) you could get your hands on some extra cash and could qualify for a "golden hello" bursary when you start work, depending on the subject you teach.

## Other financial help

### Access to Learning Fund

As well as their own bursaries, HEIs also offer extra financial support to students through their Access to Learning Funds. These are set up specifically for those moments of financial crisis – an unexpected expense, struggling to keep on top of your bills, or if you think you may be forced to drop out of university for financial reasons.

You can apply for money from this extra pot of cash directly through your HEI, and it is up to it to decide whether you fit the criteria for help and, if so, how much money you will receive. Money from this access fund is usually treated as a non-repayable grant, but sometimes it takes the form of a short-term loan (which is probably still preferable to making extra payments on a credit card).

Priority for money from this fund is given to students from low-income families, those with children, students leaving local authority care, and those in their final year struggling to make ends meet as they approach the end of their course.

### Students with disabilities

If you have a disability – mental or physical – you may be entitled to extra financial help while you study.

Disabled Students' Allowances help to meet any extra costs incurred because of your disability. For example, the money could pay for someone to help you get around campus a little more easily, or to pay for any specialist equipment to help with your studies.

Full-time students can get specialist equipment allowances of up to £5,161, and up to £20,520 a year for non-medical support from a helper. You may also be entitled to extra cash to help meet your travel costs.

Proof of your disability will be needed.

Students with dyslexia may also be able to get extra money, usually to help pay for a computer to aid study. Again, you will need to supply evidence of the condition, usually in the form of an assessment from a psychologist or teacher.

### Students with children and dependents

If you have children and are taking a full-time degree you may be entitled to money to help meet the cost of childcare. It's also worth checking to see if you are eligible for Child Tax Credit.

Those with adult dependents can also apply for an adult dependents grant which, for 2009-10 students, is a maximum of £2,642.

Both these grants are based on household income.

The Parents' Learning Allowance could be another source of welcome cash to help pay for course-related costs, such as books, placements, and extra equipment. Again the amount you get will be based on income, and the allowance does not have to be paid back.

### Distance study

If you decide you would prefer to study by distance learning – perhaps your dream course is at a university in the north of England, but you can't bear to leave your home in the south-east – you may be able to get some funding. This largely depends on which course you are taking and income levels, so contact your local education authority or Student Loans Company for advice.

### Funding for part-time students

For those who want to take a little more time with their studies, perhaps to fit it around work, you will be pleased to know that you can get financial assistance during your course.

Keep in mind that HEIs can set their own tuition fees for part-time courses, so it will be wise to check with the individual institution what it plans to charge for the entire degree before you sign up.

Your household income and the course you wish to study will determine your eligibility for a grant to help cover fees and pay for books, extra materials, and travel. It will usually be assumed your living costs will be met through work or savings if you are studying part-time. However, if your household income is low, you may be able to get some form of help with accommodation. It's always worth inquiring.

## When to apply for money

It's important that you begin researching what you're entitled to as soon as possible. Don't wait until you have an offer of a place at university before applying for financial help, otherwise you could find yourself out of pocket come the first week of term.

You need only fill in one application form to get all the money you might want – although it is a whopper of a form!

The student finance application form covers tuition fees, maintenance loans, and grants, disability and childcare grants and can be downloaded from the government advice website, www.direct.gov.uk. You can also use this website to apply online for funding.

Alternatively, contact your local education authority or the Student Loans Company for a paper application form.


## How to apply

To apply for loans and grants you will need to quote the course for which you have applied and name the university you wish to attend, even if you're not 100 per cent certain what you want to study or where you want to go. These details can be updated later. The important thing is to get your application in as soon as you can. If your details do change, make sure you tell your local authority straight away to avoid any future problems with your application.

If applying for a maintenance grant or loan, your application will need to be supported by evidence of household income, so warn parents, or partners, that they may be asked to show their payslips.

Once your form has been sent off, your local education authority will assess your eligibility and work out how much money you are entitled to receive.

Around six to eight weeks after applying for financial help you should get a letter from Student Finance Direct (SFD), which deals with applications, confirming the amount you will receive and when it will go into your bank account. If you open a new bank account before you start your studies, remember to tell SFD.

When you register for your course, your university will let SFD know you've arrived and signed up and you should start receiving your first student maintenance grant and loan payments. The university will receive the money to cover your fees directly, so you won't have to worry about that.

Getting your hands on a bursary from a university may involve a slightly different process. Some universities administer these bursaries themselves, others leave it to SFD to sort out. Check what the procedure is with your place of study. You may just need to tick the boxes on your student finance application form that allows SFD to pass your details on to the university on your behalf.

# Repaying your tuition and maintenance loans

You will not have to start repaying your tuition fee or maintenance loans until after you graduate and are earning at least £15,000 a year.

The tax office will be notified of your earnings once you start your job and your repayments will be deducted automatically from your pay beginning the April after you graduate. If you decide to work for yourself straight after university, repayments will be collected through the tax self-assessment system.

The good news is you will not pay commercial rates of interest on your student loans. Instead, rates are linked to inflation, so, in real terms, you will be paying back what you borrowed, which means you shouldn't get any nasty surprises about how much you owe.

The rate you pay back will be around 9 per cent of your earnings above £15,000 gross a year. (A £15,000 salary works out to be around £1,250 a month or £288 a week).

So, if you are earning £18,000 a year, you will pay back around £22 a month. Here's how:

An annual salary of £18,000 means you will be paid £1,500 a month gross, which means you are paid £250 over the monthly threshold amount of £1,250. The amount you pay back a month will be 9 per cent of £250, which works out to be around £22, which means a weekly payment of just over £5.

What you'll pay back

| Income each year before tax | Monthly repayment | Repayment as % of income |
|---|---|---|
| up to £15,000 | 0 | 0% |
| £16,000 | £7 | 0.6% |
| £17,000 | £15 | 1.1% |
| £18,000 | £22 | 1.5% |
| £19,000 | £30 | 1.9% |
| £20,000 | £37 | 2.3% |
| £21,000 | £45 | 2.6% |
| £22,000 | £52 | 2.9% |
| £23,000 | £60 | 3.1% |
| £24,000 | £67 | 3.4% |
| £25,000 | £75 | 3.6% |

Source: Student Finance England

You can, of course, choose to pay more each month. If you haven't paid off your loans after 25 years the government will write them off, so you may find it's not worth rushing.

And remember, the figures are recalculated as your income goes up (and down) so if your income drops to below £15,000 for any reason, your repayments will stop.

You may also be entitled to a five-year "repayment holiday", which allows you to take a break from paying back your student loans, perhaps because you want to save money for a house or start a family. Repayment holidays are for those due to start repaying their loan on or after April 2010.

## Studying in different parts of the UK

Where you live could affect how much you pay in tuition fees and how much you receive in grants and loans. Outlined below are the details you need for studying in Scotland, Wales, and Northern Ireland. Remember to contact individual institutions to find out about the bursaries and scholarships they may be offering.

### Scotland

**Students from Scotland studying in Scotland** Scotland did not sign up to the university finance system established in England, Wales, and Northern Ireland, opting instead to introduce a graduate endowment, rather than yearly fees. This endowment was paid by students upon completion of their degrees. However, the Scottish executive recently voted to axe this requirement, which means Scottish students staying in the country to study will pay nothing for their tuition. Means-tested maintenance loans are available and those from low-income households can apply for non-repayable bursaries. You will not have to pay back your loans until the April after graduation when earnings hit £15,000 or more a year. Financial help may be available to cover travel expenses.

**Students from Scotland studying in England, Wales or Northern Ireland** Students will be subject to variable tuition fees, for which you can take out a non-means-tested fees loan, payable the April after you graduate if you are earning at least £15,000 a year. You will be entitled to apply for means-tested student loans, although borrowing limits may be slightly lower. You can also apply for a Students Outside Scotland bursary, which is dependent on family income and will reduce your loan entitlement. You may also be eligible to take out an Additional Loan, which is again dependent on household income. Financial help may be available to cover travel expenses.

**Students from England, Wales, and Northern Ireland studying in Scotland** You will be subject to yearly tuition fees of at least £1,820 (£2,895 for medical students) – bear in mind degrees from Scottish HEIs tend to last four years. You can apply for a non-means-tested loan to cover tuition and for means-tested maintenance loans and grants.

Those in receipt of a full maintenance grant will be eligible for a bursary of around £319 a year.

## Wales

**Students from Wales studying in Wales** You will be subject to variable tuition fees, repayable the April after graduation when you are earning at least £15,000. However, all Welsh students staying in the country to study should be entitled to a yearly non-repayable, non-means-tested tuition fees grant, which should cover more than half the cost of your course. The money will be paid directly to your institution. Means-tested, non-repayable bursaries are also available from HEIs. You can also apply for means-tested maintenance loans. Assembly Learning Grants are also available to help those from low-income families to cover living expenses. Undergraduates training to be secondary school teachers may be eligible for extra funding during their school-based placements.

**Students from Wales studying in England or Northern Ireland** You will be subject to variable tuition fees, repayable the April after graduation if you are earning at least £15,000 a year. You can apply for a non-means-tested loan to cover tuition and for a means-tested maintenance loan. You can also apply for an Assembly Learning Grant to help cover living costs, dependent on household income. You may also be eligible for a bursary from your place of study.

**Students from Wales studying in Scotland** You will be subject to yearly tuition fees of at least £1,820 (£2,895 for medical students). You can apply for a non-means-tested loan to cover tuition, a means-tested maintenance loan and for an Assembly Learning Grant to cover living costs. Those in receipt of a full maintenance grant will be eligible for a bursary of around £319 a year from their place of study.

**Students from England, Scotland, and Northern Ireland studying in Wales** You will be subject to variable tuition fees, repayable the April after graduation if you are earning at least £15,000 a year. You can apply for a non-means-tested loan to cover tuition and for means-tested maintenance loans and grants. You may also be eligible for a bursary from your place of study. Scottish students can apply for a Students Outside Scotland bursary, which is dependent on family income, to help with maintenance.

## Northern Ireland

**Students from Northern Ireland studying in Northern Ireland** You will be subject to variable tuition fees, for which you can take out a non-means-tested fees loan, repayable the April after graduation if you are earning at least £15,000 a year. You will be able to apply for a non-repayable, means-tested maintenance grant (the amount available is slightly higher than the amount offered elsewhere), and could be eligible for a bursary from your chosen place of study. You will be entitled to apply for means-tested student maintenance loans.

**Students from Northern Ireland studying in England and Wales** You will be subject to variable tuition fees, for which you can take out a non-means- tested fees loan, repayable the April after graduation if your salary is at least £15,000 a year. You will be able to apply for a non-repayable, means-tested maintenance grant, and could be eligible for a bursary from your chosen place of study. You will be entitled to apply for means-tested student maintenance loans.

**Students from Northern Ireland studying in Scotland** You will be subject to yearly tuition fees of at least £1,820 (£2,895 for medical students). You can apply for a non-means-tested loan to cover tuition and for means-tested maintenance loans and non-repayable grants. Those in receipt of a full maintenance grant will be eligible for a bursary of around £319 a year from their place of study.

**Students from England, Wales, and Scotland studying in Northern Ireland** You will be subject to variable tuition fees, for which you can take out a non-means-tested fees loan, repayable the April after you graduate if you are earning at least £15,000 a year. You will be able to apply for a non-repayable, means-tested maintenance grant (the Students Outside Scotland bursary for Scottish students) and could be eligible for a bursary from your chosen place of study. You will be entitled to apply for means-tested student maintenance loans.

## » Further information

| | |
|---|---|
| **Directgov** | ↗ direct.gov.uk/studentfinance |
| **Student Awards Agency for Scotland** | ↗ www.saas.gov.uk |
| **Student Finance Wales** | ↗ www.studentfinancewales.co.uk |
| **Student Finance Northern Ireland** | ↗ www.studentfinanceni.co.uk |

# Subjects

# Reading the league tables

Hello, and welcome to the all-singing, all-dancing Guardian league tables. Well, not quite – though if you care to pop by the office, I'm sure we could give you a song – but we are pretty proud of our tables, and hope that they'll be useful in your quest to find the right university.

As with anything that involves statistics, however, university performance is open to quite a lot of interpretation and so here are some notes on how we put ours together.

The tables are compiled, in association with EducationGuardian.co.uk, by Campus Pi, an applied research department at Brunel University. The rankings are compiled from the most recent figures available – official 2007-08 returns from universities and higher education colleges to the Higher Education Statistics Agency (Hesa). They also incorporate data from the National Student Survey (NSS) 2008, published by the Higher Education Funding Council for England.

We have used seven statistical measures to contribute to the ranking of a university or college in each subject, weighted as follows:

- Teaching quality – as rated by final year students on the course (10%)
- Feedback (assessment) – as rated by final year students on the course (5%)
- Spending per student (17%)
- Student:staff ratio (17%)
- Job prospects (17%)
- Value added – comparing students' degree results with their entry qualifications (17%)
- Entry tariff (17%)

Under teaching and assessment the tables show the percentage of students satisfied, or very satisfied, and for entry we give the average Ucas tariff of students accepted on to the course.

We don't publish the actual figures for spending, or for the Guardian's value added calculation. These scores are marked out of 10 in bands, to allow for like with like comparisons – spending on medical students is bound to be higher than on business students, for instance.

For each subject that it teaches, an institution is given a Guardian score, based on these seven measures. The Guardian score for each institution in each subject is derived from a weighted average of the standardised scores for each measure, converted into a scale in which the highest ranked institution gets 100 points and all institutions receive a positive score.

When it comes to the overall score for a university, the subject scores are weighted according to the number of students enrolled on the course taking first degrees. A department with 200 students counts more than one with 50.

The institutional table is determined using average standardised scores in each subject, as opposed to the average teaching score that is displayed for each subject. We believe this is a more robust methodology.

The number of institutions offering a subject affects the influence of that subject in the institutional table. Thus, the institution finishing first in a small subject like agriculture and forestry will not benefit in the overall table as much as the institution that finishes first in a subject like business and management studies, in which 113 institutions are active.

We do not include research ratings or research funding – these are tables aimed at students taking first degrees and so concentrate on teaching and teaching resources.

## Thresholds

It should be stressed that not every one of the thousands of degree courses offered in UK universities appears in the Guardian tables – omission of a subject at an institution should not be taken as criticism. It simply means that student numbers are too low to be used or that data in certain categories is not available.

To be included in a subject table an institution must be teaching at least 35 students (full-time equivalent or FTE) – with at least 25 FTE reported in the relevant cost centre.

This year we have endeavoured to include smaller courses by using data from the previous year as well in cases where student numbers fall below 35. Where there are small student populations involved, spreading the data used over two years promotes stability as well as enabling us to include more courses than last year.

Institutions are excluded from the tables where data for more than two measures are missing. (The NSS scores are counted as one for this purpose.) The process for dealing with the missing data is to subtract the weight of the missing items from 100%, and divide the weighted average of the standardised scores by this figure. In effect, this methodology assumes that the institution would have performed equally well in the missing data items as it did in the measures for which its data was available.

We have also imposed a threshold on the overall universities table: an institution must feature in at least four subject tables. This excludes a number of specialist colleges – in music, for instance – which may be at the top of their subject rankings. These institutions are ranked in a separate table (see page 55).

# The measures

## Teaching quality

We have used results from the NSS 2008, which questions final-year under-graduates about what they think of the quality of the course.

The full NSS survey results are available at www.unistats.com

We used the responses to four questions in the NSS under the heading of the "teaching on my course". These looked at whether staff are good at explaining things, make the subject interesting and are enthusiastic about what they teach, and if the course is intellectually stimulating. This column shows the percentage who "definitely agree" or "mostly agree" with these statements.

## Feedback (assessment)

This column (also taken from the NSS 2008) derives from answers to five questions on feedback relating to whether marking criteria were made clear in advance, assessment arrangements were fair, feedback was prompt, whether they received detailed comments on their work and whether feedback "helped me clarify things I did not understand". Again, we show the percentage who "definitely agree" or "mostly agree".

## Spending per student

The amount of money that an institution spends providing a subject (not including the costs of academic staff, since these are already counted in the staff-student ratio) is compared with the volume of students learning the subject to derive a spend-per-student measure. This figure also includes the money the institution spends on central academic services, and per student FTE.

## Student:staff ratio (SSR)

SSRs compare the number of staff teaching a subject with the number of students studying it, to get a ratio where a low SSR is treated positively in the league tables. At least 25 students and two staff (both FTE) must be present in an SSR calculation. Year-on-year inconsistency and extreme values at either end of the spectrum cause several SSRs to be suppressed.

This is far from being as straightforward as it sounds because the subjects taught do not relate neatly to cost centres in universities and a lot of effort by the Guardian, Campus Pi and the universities has gone into trying to match them up. One size does not fit all, as we have learned (the hard way).

## Job prospects

Based on the 2006-07 Destinations of Leavers from HE Return, we assess the proportion of graduates who find graduate-level employment, or study full-time, within six months of graduation. Graduates who report that they are unable to work are excluded from the study population, which must have at least 24 respondents in order to generate results.

## Value added

Our attempt is to measure how well universities teach a wide range of students, not just the superstars. Scores employ a sophisticated methodology that tracks individual students from enrolment to graduation, comparing qualifications upon entry with the award that a student receives at the end of their studies.

Each student is given a probability of achieving a first or 2:1, based on the qualifications that they enter with. If they manage to earn a good degree then they score points that reflect how difficult it was to do so (in fact, they score the reciprocal of the probability of getting a first or 2:1). Thus an institution that is adept at taking in students with low entry qualifications and converting them into graduates with the best degrees will score highly in the value added measure, since the number of students getting a first or 2:1 will have exceeded statistical expectations. At least 28 students must be in a subject.

## Entry tariff

We take the average Ucas tariff points of first-year first-degree entrants to a subject, subtracting the tariffs for key skills and core skills. There must be at least eight students in this measure.

Five universities – Liverpool Hope, London Metropolitan, Swansea Metropolitan, Wolverhampton and the University of the West of Scotland – declined to let their data be used. We are grateful for the cooperation of everyone who did, though we do try to minimise the hard work by using data they have submitted to Hesa.

There are three joint medical schools: Brighton/Sussex, Hull/York, and the Peninsula medical school established by Exeter and Plymouth. These schools do not have individual institution profiles, but are linked from the tables through to the parent institution.

With regard to data provided by Hesa, it should be noted that Hesa does not accept responsibility for any inferences or conclusions derived from the data by third parties.

# University rankings

This is the overall table, made up of the average Guardian scores across the board.

| Ranking | Institution | Subject appearances | Average Guardian score |
|---|---|---|---|
| 1 | Oxford | 26 | 100.0 |
| 2 | Cambridge | 24 | 97.0 |
| 3 | St Andrews | 19 | 87.0 |
| 4 | Warwick | 22 | 84.0 |
| 5 | London School of Economics | 11 | 82.4 |
| 6 | UCL | 29 | 81.5 |
| 7 | Edinburgh | 34 | 78.3 |
| 8 | Imperial College | 14 | 77.9 |
| 9 | Bath | 19 | 75.6 |
| 10 | Loughborough | 23 | 74.6 |
| 11 | York | 22 | 74.4 |
| 12 | SOAS | 7 | 74.2 |
| 13 | Exeter | 23 | 73.0 |
| 14 | Durham | 25 | 72.7 |
| 15 | Leicester | 20 | 72.0 |
| 16 | Lancaster | 25 | 71.4 |
| 17 | Glasgow | 32 | 70.7 |
| 18 | Sussex | 25 | 70.1 |
| 19 | Aston | 13 | 69.9 |
| 19 | Dundee | 26 | 69.9 |
| 21 | City | 15 | 69.8 |
| 22 | Heriot-Watt | 16 | 69.4 |
| 22 | Southampton | 29 | 69.4 |
| 24 | Birmingham | 38 | 69.1 |
| 24 | King's College London | 24 | 69.1 |
| 26 | Nottingham | 34 | 68.7 |
| 27 | Surrey | 21 | 68.5 |
| 28 | Leeds | 37 | 68.4 |
| 29 | Bristol | 32 | 68.1 |
| 30 | Sheffield | 31 | 67.9 |
| 31 | Royal Holloway | 18 | 67.7 |
| 32 | Bournemouth | 13 | 67.5 |
| 32 | Manchester | 38 | 67.5 |
| 34 | Aberdeen | 21 | 67.2 |
| 35 | UEA | 25 | 66.8 |
| 36 | Robert Gordon | 17 | 66.3 |
| 36 | Stirling | 15 | 66.3 |
| 38 | Strathclyde | 24 | 66.1 |
| 39 | Goldsmiths | 13 | 66.0 |

| Ranking | Institution | Subject appearances | Average Guardian score |
|---|---|---|---|
| 40 | Newcastle | 30 | 65.1 |
| 41 | Reading | 23 | 64.9 |
| 42 | Nottingham Trent | 26 | 64.8 |
| 43 | Edinburgh Napier | 15 | 64.7 |
| 44 | Cardiff | 31 | 64.3 |
| 45 | Kent | 27 | 64.0 |
| 46 | University of the Arts, London | 4 | 63.2 |
| 47 | Liverpool | 32 | 62.3 |
| 48 | Essex | 20 | 62.1 |
| 49 | Queen's, Belfast | 33 | 61.9 |
| 50 | Keele | 22 | 61.6 |
| 51 | Plymouth | 30 | 61.1 |
| 52 | Hull | 28 | 60.1 |
| 53 | Brunel | 24 | 59.7 |
| 53 | Northumbria | 27 | 59.7 |
| 55 | Staffordshire | 17 | 59.2 |
| 56 | Oxford Brookes | 28 | 58.9 |
| 57 | Queen Margaret | 7 | 58.7 |
| 57 | Queen Mary | 19 | 58.7 |
| 59 | UWE Bristol | 25 | 58.3 |
| 60 | Bath Spa | 15 | 56.9 |
| 61 | UC Falmouth | 5 | 56.7 |
| 62 | Sunderland | 17 | 56.6 |
| 63 | Birmingham City | 19 | 56.4 |
| 63 | Gloucestershire | 19 | 56.4 |
| 65 | UWIC | 7 | 56.0 |
| 66 | Glasgow Caledonian | 12 | 55.3 |
| 67 | Sheffield Hallam | 25 | 55.2 |
| 68 | St Mary's UC, Twickenham | 12 | 55.1 |
| 69 | Teesside | 16 | 54.5 |
| 69 | Thames Valley | 10 | 54.5 |
| 71 | Aberystwyth | 19 | 54.3 |
| 72 | Bangor | 20 | 54.2 |
| 73 | Kingston | 27 | 54.0 |
| 74 | Brighton | 23 | 53.9 |
| 75 | Coventry | 24 | 53.5 |
| 75 | Ulster | 29 | 53.5 |
| 77 | De Montfort | 21 | 53.4 |
| 78 | Lampeter | 5 | 53.3 |

| Ranking | Institution | Subject appearances | Average Guardian score |
|---|---|---|---|
| 78 | Portsmouth | 27 | 53.3 |
| 80 | Glamorgan | 24 | 53.1 |
| 81 | Chichester | 10 | 52.9 |
| 82 | Central Lancashire | 22 | 52.7 |
| 83 | Anglia Ruskin | 20 | 52.4 |
| 84 | Bradford | 19 | 51.8 |
| 85 | Cumbria | 15 | 51.4 |
| 85 | Newman University College | 6 | 51.4 |
| 87 | York St John | 13 | 50.7 |
| 88 | Bedfordshire | 16 | 50.0 |
| 89 | Lincoln | 20 | 49.4 |
| 90 | Chester | 20 | 49.3 |
| 91 | Worcester | 14 | 49.2 |
| 92 | Glyndŵr | 9 | 48.9 |
| 93 | Salford | 25 | 48.6 |
| 94 | Winchester | 12 | 48.3 |
| 95 | Swansea | 25 | 48.1 |
| 96 | Huddersfield | 21 | 47.9 |
| 97 | Hertfordshire | 25 | 46.9 |
| 97 | Manchester Met | 30 | 46.9 |

| Ranking | Institution | Subject appearances | Average Guardian score |
|---|---|---|---|
| 99 | Marjon (St Mark and St John) | 6 | 46.2 |
| 100 | Newport | 11 | 45.3 |
| 100 | Northampton | 17 | 45.3 |
| 102 | Leeds Met | 22 | 45.2 |
| 103 | Canterbury Christ Church | 19 | 44.8 |
| 104 | Edge Hill | 14 | 44.3 |
| 105 | Derby | 21 | 43.9 |
| 106 | Middlesex | 17 | 43.6 |
| 107 | Abertay Dundee | 9 | 43.4 |
| 108 | Roehampton | 19 | 43.1 |
| 109 | Greenwich | 29 | 42.5 |
| 110 | Westminster | 16 | 42.4 |
| 111 | Leeds Trinity & All Saints | 8 | 42.0 |
| 112 | Liverpool John Moores | 17 | 40.5 |
| 113 | Bucks New University | 12 | 39.6 |
| 114 | Bolton | 12 | 37.7 |
| 115 | Southampton Solent | 16 | 36.8 |
| 116 | East London | 16 | 34.6 |
| 117 | London South Bank | 19 | 30.1 |

# Specialist institutions

Rankings for colleges that offer one, two or three subjects, but do not compete with universities across a broad range of subjects.

| Ranking | Institution | Subject appearances | Average Guardian score |
|---------|-------------|:-------------------:|:----------------------:|
| 1 | Royal Academy of Music | 1 | 100.0 |
| 2 | Courtauld Institute | 1 | 99.4 |
| 3 | Royal Scottish Academy of Music and Drama | 2 | 90.1 |
| 4 | Central School of Speech and Drama | 1 | 89.2 |
| 5 | Guildhall School of Music and Drama | 2 | 89.0 |
| 6 | Royal College of Music | 1 | 87.0 |
| 7 | Trinity Laban | 2 | 85.7 |
| 8 | Conservatoire for Dance and Drama | 1 | 82.7 |
| 9 | St Mary's UC, Belfast | 1 | 81.3 |
| 10 | The Liverpool Institute for Performing Arts | 2 | 74.9 |
| 11 | Buckingham | 3 | 73.3 |
| 12 | Royal Northern College of Music | 1 | 73.0 |
| 13 | Glasgow School of Art | 2 | 67.6 |
| 14 | Rose Bruford College | 2 | 60.9 |
| 15 | Arts Institute, Bournemouth | 2 | 60.6 |
| 16 | Edinburgh College of Art | 3 | 59.5 |
| 17 | Harper Adams UC | 1 | 59.4 |
| 18 | School of Pharmacy | 1 | 57.7 |
| 19 | Leeds College of Music | 1 | 56.6 |
| 20 | Stranmillis UC | 1 | 54.9 |
| 21 | Writtle College | 2 | 51.0 |
| 22 | Heythrop College | 2 | 49.8 |
| 23 | Bishop Grosseteste UC | 3 | 48.8 |
| 24 | St George's Medical School | 2 | 48.6 |
| 25 | Royal Veterinary College | 1 | 39.8 |
| 26 | Royal Agricultural College | 3 | 37.9 |
| 27 | University for the Creative Arts | 3 | 35.6 |
| 28 | Norwich UC of the Arts | 1 | 35.5 |
| 29 | Trinity UC, Carmarthen | 2 | 34.5 |

# Art and design

## Architecture

Architecture is at the same time a deeply basic feature of social human needs and activity, and a field constantly requiring new ideas and innovation. Big and exciting challenges need to be faced by architects: meeting our dwelling needs in a sustainable way, keeping space meaningful in a society, improving the quality of our public spaces and so on. There is a big difference between producing buildings and spaces that somehow 'work' and making successful and innovative architecture that can become a meaningful and inspiring place for those who use it.

It involves a holistic approach to space, place, and dwelling, which requires students to tackle multi-disciplinary projects and problems. Studying architecture means being exposed to all aspects and facets of what makes a place. Students are expected to look at a problem from the creative and artistic side, as well as from a cultural and historical and a technological and scientific perspective. But above all they face the challenge of integrating all of these into a designed final product — a building or a space. So, studying architecture means learning to be speculative, creative, and research-oriented whilst at the same time translating these skills into the ability to be concrete, practical, and focused on solving very real problems and making better places for people to use and enjoy.

It is both a highly vocational subject leading to a very definite professional profile, as well as something providing a variety of highly transferable skills, given its multi- and inter-disciplinary character. Thanks to skills ranging from creative design, graphic, and spatial awareness to analytical and scientific reasoning, architecture graduates are amongst the most flexible and versatile around.

**Dr Alex Aurigi**, *Director of Architecture, School of Architecture, Planning and Landscape, Newcastle University*

---

In the immortal words of the greatest architect of the 20th century, Le Corbusier, architecture is "the masterly, correct and magnificent play of masses brought together in light".

Sounds wonderful, but if you want to be one, you have to remember it's a very long course of study, comprising a three-year BA or BSc degree at university, a year of practical training in an architect's office, a two-year Dip Arch or BArch at university, and a further year of practical training before the final Professional Practice Examination.

Once you start your course, you will study across a wide range of subjects, from history and theory to IT, technology and management. If a five-year course is a daunting financial prospect, several schools of architecture offer a part-time alternative — taking five years for the BA or BSc degree and three years for the Dip Arch or BArch, during which you'll be able to work while you study.

The breadth of the subject will equip you with plenty of transferable skills, and for those who decide after taking their undergraduate degree, not to pursue a career as an architect there will always be employment opportunities in IT, media, property, design, and planning, to name a few options.

It is a myth that A-level maths and physics are a prerequisite for entry to architecture courses, but it certainly will be an advantage if you have a natural feel for geometry and three-dimensional form and some skill in drawing. Most universities will expect to see evidence of your abilities in a portfolio of work at the time of your application.

You will need a minimum of two A-levels if you enrol on leaving school, but the government's widening access policy encourages candidates from non-traditional academic backgrounds to enrol as mature students if they can demonstrate an aptitude for the subject.

In order to practise as an architect in the UK, it is also necessary to be on the register of architects, which is held by the UK statutory regulator, the Architects Registration Board. ARB is the sole body charged with prescribing the qualifications, so if you want to practise as an architect, it is important you check out whether or not the qualification you are thinking of is prescribed by the ARB. And if you want to be a member of the Royal Institute of British Architects the course needs to be recognised by it too – so check first.

Try to go and see a range of departments in action before making a choice. Course content can vary considerably according to research interests and institutional histories. Some courses are more technical and academic than others, and you will want to ask about their links with architects' practices and investigate what the work placements are like.

Another possibility is architectural technology, which is a relatively new profession and deals with the technical aspects of the specification, design, and construction of a building, often acting as the project manager, connecting client and architect. These courses are shorter than the full requirements for architecture "proper" – three years, or four with a sandwich course, usually followed up with a work placement.

---

66 Architecture is incredibly wide-ranging and well structured: there are several layers of teaching with the studio instruction supplemented by lectures that are further supported by small group teaching known as supervisions. Our projects are really stimulating too, exposing us to all sorts of sources, from Greek philosophy to Alfred Hitchcock, to shape our ideas.

**Elliot Lewis**, *second-year architecture student, University of Cambridge*

---

## 》 Further information

### Architects Registration Board
7 Portland Place
London W1B 1PP

t  020 7436 5269
e  info@arb.org.uk
↗ www.arb.org.uk

### The Royal Institute of British Architects
66 Portland Place
London W1B 1AD

t  020 7580 5533
e  info@inst.riba.org
↗ www.riba.org

**Royal Incorporation of Architects in Scotland**
15 Rutland Square
Edinburgh EG1 2BE

t 0131 229 7545
e info@rias.org.uk
↗ www.rias.org.uk

**Royal Society of Architects in Wales**
4 Cathedral Road
Cardiff CF11 9LJ

t 029 2022 8987
e rsaw@inst.riba.org
↗ www.architecture-wales.com

**Royal Society of Ulster Architects**
2 Mount Charles
Belfast BT7 1NZ

t 0289 032 3760
e info@rsua.org.uk
↗ www.rsua.org.uk

**CABE (Commission for Architecture and the Built Environment)**
1 Kemble Street
London WC2B 4AN

t 020 7070 6700
f 020 7070 6777
e info@cabe.org.uk
↗ www.cabe.org.uk

↗ Online reading

**Architecture** www.architecture.com
**Chartered Institute of Architectural Technologists** www.ciat.org.uk
**Design Council** www.designcouncil.org.uk
**The Architecture Foundation** www.architecturefoundation.org.uk
**Art and Architecture** www.artandarchitecture.org.uk

# Architecture

| | | Guardian score /100 | Satisfied with teaching % | Satisfied with feedback % | Spend per student /10 | Student:staff ratio | Job prospects % | Value added score /10 | Average entry tariff |
|---|---|---|---|---|---|---|---|---|---|
| 1 | UCL | 100.0 | 92 | 71 | 10 | 11.8 | 93 | 8 | 470 |
| 2 | Cambridge | 99.9 | 88 | 69 | 10 | 12.9 | | 6 | 514 |
| 3 | Bath | 97.2 | 95 | 84 | 8 | 17.7 | 98 | 7 | 505 |
| 4 | Cardiff | 84.9 | | | 8 | 13.5 | 90 | 5 | 473 |
| 5 | Edinburgh | 81.0 | 80 | 48 | 10 | 21.5 | 89 | 8 | 444 |
| 6 | Northumbria | 80.1 | 86 | 74 | 4 | 21.5 | 97 | 10 | 318 |
| 7 | Manchester School of Architecture | 77.8 | 81 | 57 | 5 | 14.1 | 97 | 8 | 387 |
| 8 | Newcastle | 76.7 | 85 | 59 | 6 | 20.0 | 97 | 5 | 465 |
| 9 | Sheffield | 74.5 | 91 | 53 | 6 | 17.5 | 96 | 3 | 477 |
| 10 | Glasgow School of Art | 74.3 | | | 3 | 25.3 | 95 | 9 | 433 |
| 11 | Liverpool | 71.0 | 72 | 38 | 9 | 16.1 | 96 | 3 | 405 |
| 11 | Nottingham | 71.0 | 84 | 51 | 8 | 18.0 | 89 | 4 | 443 |
| 13 | Oxford Brookes | 70.6 | 87 | 75 | 4 | 17.7 | 80 | 9 | 369 |
| 14 | Sheffield Hallam | 69.5 | 89 | 70 | 5 | 18.0 | 95 | 5 | 298 |
| 15 | Edinburgh College of Art | 68.7 | | | 4 | 20.5 | 93 | 7 | 393 |
| 16 | Westminster | 67.8 | 77 | 61 | 5 | 17.6 | 83 | 9 | 349 |
| 17 | Strathclyde | 67.4 | 75 | 47 | 5 | 30.8 | 98 | 9 | 403 |
| 18 | Ulster | 66.2 | 88 | 65 | 4 | 23.8 | 100 | 6 | 282 |

| | | Guardian score /100 | Satisfied with teaching % | Satisfied with feedback % | Spend per student /10 | Student:staff ratio | Job prospects % | Value added score /10 | Average entry tariff |
|----|-----|------|----|----|----|------|----|----|-----|
| 19 | Kent | 65.6 | 75 | 68 | 9 | 25.9 | | 4 | 351 |
| 19 | UWE Bristol | 65.6 | 85 | 54 | 4 | 22.0 | 93 | 8 | 321 |
| 21 | Nottingham Trent | 65.2 | 78 | 54 | 7 | 19.9 | | | 329 |
| 22 | Robert Gordon | 63.1 | | | 5 | 21.8 | 94 | 4 | 349 |
| 23 | Birmingham City | 62.9 | 91 | 82 | 3 | 26.2 | | 7 | 290 |
| 24 | University for the Creative Arts | 62.7 | 88 | 51 | 8 | 17.1 | | 4 | 222 |
| 25 | Brighton | 59.6 | 91 | 59 | 4 | 27.2 | 91 | 5 | 329 |
| 26 | Queen's, Belfast | 58.2 | 72 | 50 | 3 | 19.7 | 90 | 7 | 349 |
| 27 | Kingston | 58.0 | 76 | 47 | 4 | 22.1 | 86 | 6 | 348 |
| 28 | Portsmouth | 56.9 | 85 | 65 | 5 | 25.2 | 80 | 6 | 293 |
| 29 | Dundee | 55.9 | 80 | 54 | 5 | 20.1 | 96 | 2 | |
| 30 | Greenwich | 54.9 | 85 | 68 | 6 | 24.5 | 84 | 3 | 239 |
| 31 | Plymouth | 54.8 | 73 | 49 | 4 | 22.2 | 89 | 3 | 356 |
| 32 | Lincoln | 53.8 | 69 | 59 | 3 | 21.7 | 93 | 7 | 283 |
| 33 | East London | 51.1 | 88 | 78 | 4 | 17.4 | 91 | 1 | 235 |
| 34 | Liverpool John Moores | 43.7 | 82 | 65 | 3 | 31.9 | 84 | 4 | 271 |
| 35 | Huddersfield | 41.6 | | | 3 | 27.7 | 90 | 2 | 258 |
| 36 | Southampton Solent | 40.8 | 61 | 43 | 4 | 31.3 | | 6 | 216 |
| 37 | London South Bank | 39.4 | 71 | 54 | 3 | 39.1 | 93 | 7 | 216 |
| 38 | Bolton | 39.1 | 83 | 58 | 1 | 35.2 | | | 208 |
| 39 | De Montfort | 36.1 | 71 | 60 | 4 | 38.6 | 100 | 1 | 274 |
| 40 | Leeds Met | 32.0 | 77 | 56 | 6 | 27.2 | 44 | 3 | 310 |

# Art and design

66 'The world is but a canvas to the imagination,' said the philosopher Henry David Thoreau — and how right he was. An art and design degree offers the opportunity to be creative, innovative, and original, as well as helping to develop skills for life after graduation, whatever direction you choose to go in.

Art and design covers a range of disciplines, from the more traditional fine art courses right through to fashion, product design, and graphics. They are hands-on courses, allowing students to focus on creating and developing, and are often taught by current artists who can help you to develop your ideas and creations. New technology has encouraged the evolution of courses into the 21st century, allowing students to use digital animation and video and moving image, alongside traditional paint and canvas.

Many courses require a foundation year, which provides the opportunity for you to improve your skills and will provide a better indication of which degree subject within art and design is the right one for you.

Studying a creative subject allows you to develop and see your artistic potential through teaching and learning — not just from tutors, but also from other students. We think that's the beauty of studying an art and design course, as it offers a collaborative environment within a vibrant community where people can freely exchange their ideas and experiences.

The creative industries are competitive and so an increasing number of business-facing universities are offering alternative module choices, such as marketing, giving you a wider range of skills for your portfolio.

Art and design is an inspiring and exciting field of study — one that will allow you to truly develop your interests, passions, and ideas.

**Chris McIntyre**, *Dean of the Faculty for the Creative and Cultural Industries, University of Hertfordshire*

---

Choosing a course in art and design could be the first step in achieving a career in fine art, graphics or textiles; or might just help you to a lifetime of art appreciation and personal pleasure. And either is fine. There is no need to feel that your degree is wasted if you don't turn out to be a designer or artist.

Whatever your eventual direction, you'll be entering a very broad church, with subjects ranging from design disciplines (anything from craft-based courses such as furniture design to multimedia work), to fine art (more traditional disciplines such as sculpture or installation art), to the history and theory of art and design, even museum studies.

For your course, you'll probably choose between one of three broad areas: fine art (including disciplines like painting, sculpture, photography, and tapestry), visual communications and design (think things like graphics, animation, illustration) and the applied arts (perhaps fashion, furniture or jewellery design). Once on a course you should have the chance to dabble in other areas, cross-fertilising ideas, and developing your imagination alongside your technical skills.

To do an art degree in art you will most likely need to have a foundation or diploma qualification, which in turn usually means having to do a one-year course after school or college. This foundation year will help you decide whether art and design is really for you before you commit to a further three years.

No one can guarantee that when you complete your studies you'll be able to make a living as a professional artist, but you will learn a wide variety of skills that can be utilised in, for example, design and media companies. You might also decide to go into arts management, work in a museum or gallery, or become an art therapist.

Most art and design courses are in the new universities, but there are some in various "old" universities, higher education colleges, and a few specialist institutions. Check the entry-level qualifications for the course, especially if you haven't done any work to foundation level – some will let you in on A-levels alone.

When making your choice, look closely at the facilities of the department. And investigate also the city's galleries, museums, and cultural life, as these will be invaluable research resources.

Study carefully the elements of the course you are taking and never just take the course name and assume the content is the same for every institution. See also who is teaching you – it could be that you will be studying under a designer or artist of international renown. And while the course content is important, do some research on the reputation of the institution you have in mind. Some are highly prestigious with well-established places on the art scene – it could mean a vital leg-up in your career as a practising artist.

For the more vocational courses – curatorship, for example – it is less important who teaches you than whether the course contains vocational elements that will help you achieve appropriate professional qualifications.

---

  ❝ From a young age I have enjoyed art and my interest in the subject led me to university. Studying art and design at undergraduate level, and currently at a postgraduate level, has increased my awareness of the profound influence it has on daily life, while allowing me to develop a variety of practical skills and transform a hobby into a career.

**Angharad Rees**, *surface pattern design graduate, Swansea Metropolitan University*

---

## ❯❯ Further information

**National Society for Education of Art and Design**
The Gatehouse, Corsham Court
Corsham, Wiltshire SN13 0BZ
**t**  01249 714825
↗ www.nsead.org

**The Arts Councils:**
*England* – www.artscouncil.org.uk
*Scotland* – www.scottisharts.org.uk
*Wales* – www.artswales.org.uk
*Northern Ireland* – www.artscouncil-ni.org

**The Association of Illustrators**
2nd Floor, Back Building
150 Curtain Road, London EC2A 3AR
**t**  020 7613 4328
↗ www.theaoi.com

**EQ (diversity in the creative industries)**
Suite E229, Dean Clough
Halifax HX3 5AX
**t**  01422 381618
↗ www.thinkeq.org.uk

**The Chartered Society of Designers**

1 Cedar Court, Royal Oak Yard
Bermondsey Street
London SE1 3GA

t 020 7357 8088
e info@csd.org.uk
↗ www.csd.org.uk

**The Institute of Engineering Designers**

Courtleigh, Westbury Leigh
Westbury, Wiltshire BA13 3TA

t 01373 822801
e ied@ied.org.uk
↗ www.ied.org.uk

**The Textile Institute**

1st Floor, St James's Buildings
Oxford Street
Manchester M1 6FQ

t 0161 237 1188
e tiihq@textileinst.org.uk
↗ www.textileinstitute.org

**The Association of Photographers**

81 Leonard Street
London EC2A 4QS

t 020 7739 6669
e general@aophoto.co.uk
↗ www.the-aop.org

**The Crafts Council**

44a Pentonville Road
London N1 9BY

t 020 7806 2500
e education@craftscouncil.org.uk
↗ www.craftscouncil.org.uk

**Design Council**

34 Bow Street
London WC2E 7DL

t 020 7420 5200
e info@designcouncil.org.uk
↗ www.designcouncil.org.uk

**The Centre for Sustainable Design**

University College for the Creative Arts
Falkner Road, Farnham
Surrey GU9 7DS

t 01252 892772
f 01252 892747
e cfsd@ucreative.ac.uk
↗ www.cfsd.org.uk

↗ Online reading

**Guardian.co.uk art and design** guardian.co.uk/artanddesign
**Arts Advice** www.netgain.org.uk
**Graphic Arts Online** www.graphicartsonline.com
**Design Week** www.designweek.co.uk
**Design Museum** www.designmuseum.org

# Art and design

| | | Guardian score /100 | Satisfied with teaching % | Satisfied with feedback % | Spend per student /10 | Student:staff ratio | Job prospects % | Value added score /10 | Average entry tariff |
|---|---|---|---|---|---|---|---|---|---|
| 1 | UCL | 100.0 | | | 10 | 11.8 | 64 | 10 | 399 |
| 2 | Oxford | 87.5 | 98 | 84 | 10 | 15.9 | | 7 | 420 |
| 3 | Brunel | 81.9 | | | 9 | 14.6 | 73 | 9 | 371 |
| 4 | Edinburgh | 74.5 | | | 9 | 14.8 | | 7 | 436 |
| 5 | Newcastle | 70.6 | 71 | 59 | 7 | 12.0 | 56 | 8 | 387 |
| 6 | Loughborough | 70.0 | 84 | 71 | 5 | 15.4 | 58 | 9 | 371 |
| 7 | Edinburgh Napier | 68.3 | | | 6 | 14.8 | 74 | 6 | 319 |
| 8 | Glasgow | 67.1 | 83 | 60 | 4 | 15.7 | 57 | | 448 |
| 9 | Goldsmiths | 66.0 | 87 | 60 | 5 | 12.8 | 66 | 7 | 311 |
| 10 | Lancaster | 65.3 | 81 | 69 | 8 | 12.2 | 54 | 3 | 381 |
| 10 | Writtle College | 65.3 | | | 5 | 15.2 | 64 | 8 | |
| 12 | Dundee | 64.5 | 80 | 70 | 8 | 12.5 | 45 | 7 | 344 |
| 13 | Heriot-Watt | 63.0 | 74 | 59 | 6 | 23.3 | 82 | 7 | 331 |
| 14 | Kent | 62.5 | 85 | 62 | 5 | 24.1 | 71 | 10 | 296 |
| 15 | Northumbria | 60.5 | 83 | 69 | 7 | 18.9 | 67 | 5 | 288 |
| 16 | Glamorgan | 60.1 | 83 | 68 | 6 | 10.8 | 53 | 5 | 275 |
| 16 | Glasgow School of Art | 60.1 | | | 7 | 15.1 | 47 | 6 | 360 |
| 18 | Plymouth | 59.4 | 72 | 55 | 10 | 22.9 | 48 | 9 | 257 |
| 19 | Brighton | 59.3 | 81 | 69 | 8 | 15.3 | 50 | 6 | 272 |
| 20 | Robert Gordon | 58.0 | | | 4 | 17.7 | 64 | 7 | 310 |
| 21 | Kingston | 57.2 | 81 | 63 | 4 | 16.8 | 64 | 7 | 247 |
| 22 | Nottingham Trent | 56.9 | 81 | 62 | 5 | 19.9 | 70 | 3 | 324 |
| 23 | Birmingham City | 56.7 | 75 | 66 | 8 | 14.2 | 47 | 7 | 280 |
| 24 | Leeds | 56.6 | 71 | 67 | 5 | 20.2 | 54 | 6 | 379 |
| 24 | Staffordshire | 56.6 | 82 | 73 | 10 | 18.7 | 55 | 2 | 262 |
| 26 | Southampton | 56.5 | 65 | 51 | 7 | 19.4 | 54 | 7 | 374 |
| 27 | Edinburgh College of Art | 56.1 | | | 5 | 15.0 | 44 | 5 | 358 |
| 28 | University of the Arts, London | 55.6 | 70 | 56 | 9 | 22.6 | 61 | 5 | 321 |
| 29 | UWE Bristol | 54.8 | 79 | 73 | 4 | 19.4 | 52 | 8 | 286 |
| 30 | Reading | 54.1 | 70 | 43 | 4 | 14.8 | 55 | 7 | 315 |
| 31 | Arts Institute, Bournemouth | 53.8 | 88 | 77 | 3 | 19.4 | 62 | 3 | 306 |
| 32 | UC Falmouth | 53.7 | 80 | 72 | 5 | 19.3 | 57 | 5 | 274 |
| 33 | Greenwich | 53.2 | 73 | 68 | 5 | 24.5 | 67 | 9 | 206 |
| 34 | De Montfort | 53.1 | 76 | 66 | 4 | 15.1 | 58 | 4 | 272 |
| 35 | Roehampton | 52.6 | 78 | 57 | 5 | 16.0 | 56 | 5 | 279 |
| 36 | Teesside | 52.5 | 92 | 86 | 7 | 19.4 | 42 | 3 | 251 |
| 37 | Bucks New University | 51.8 | 77 | 65 | 7 | 15.6 | 52 | 5 | 236 |
| 38 | Gloucestershire | 51.2 | 72 | 69 | 5 | 17.0 | 47 | 7 | 266 |
| 39 | UWIC | 51.0 | 82 | 75 | 7 | 21.1 | 41 | 5 | 299 |
| 40 | Bath Spa | 50.8 | 78 | 61 | 4 | 20.0 | 52 | 8 | 274 |
| 41 | Canterbury Christ Church | 50.6 | 90 | 76 | 3 | 18.3 | 33 | 9 | 269 |
| 42 | Portsmouth | 50.5 | 80 | 73 | 6 | 21.4 | 50 | 6 | 273 |
| 43 | Aberystwyth | 50.4 | 89 | 68 | 3 | 23.1 | 37 | 8 | 336 |
| 44 | Bournemouth | 49.5 | 68 | 50 | 3 | | 76 | 4 | 281 |
| 45 | Ulster | 49.4 | 75 | 62 | 3 | 16.2 | 49 | 7 | 273 |
| 46 | Huddersfield | 48.8 | 67 | 55 | 4 | 12.1 | 49 | 4 | 270 |

| | | Guardian score /100 | Satisfied with teaching % | Satisfied with feedback % | Spend per student /10 | Student:staff ratio | Job prospects % | Value added score /10 | Average entry tariff |
|---|---|---|---|---|---|---|---|---|---|
| 47 | Cumbria | 47.7 | 79 | 74 | 4 | 17.4 | 41 | 7 | 233 |
| 48 | Sunderland | 47.5 | 82 | 69 | 5 | 13.6 | 43 | 5 | 208 |
| 49 | Manchester Met | 47.1 | 72 | 62 | 4 | 18.9 | 50 | 6 | 276 |
| 50 | Central Lancashire | 46.9 | 73 | 70 | 5 | 24.0 | 60 | 4 | 261 |
| 51 | Oxford Brookes | 46.5 | 84 | 69 | 3 | 27.5 | 47 | 8 | 304 |
| 52 | Thames Valley | 46.3 | 73 | 68 | | 11.2 | 49 | 2 | 216 |
| 53 | Middlesex | 45.1 | 75 | 65 | 10 | 30.0 | 48 | 4 | 211 |
| 54 | Essex | 43.7 | 81 | 63 | 8 | 18.3 | 38 | 3 | 226 |
| 54 | Leeds Met | 43.7 | 74 | 55 | 5 | 18.0 | 44 | 6 | 234 |
| 56 | Hull | 43.4 | 80 | 59 | 5 | 21.0 | 47 | 5 | 233 |
| 57 | Chester | 43.1 | 88 | 66 | 4 | 22.3 | 56 | 1 | 288 |
| 58 | Bolton | 42.6 | 78 | 67 | 2 | 20.2 | 43 | 7 | 237 |
| 58 | Derby | 42.6 | 76 | 63 | 7 | 17.4 | 44 | 2 | 249 |
| 60 | Glyndŵr | 42.1 | 62 | 61 | 5 | 20.8 | 47 | 4 | 282 |
| 61 | Norwich UC of the Arts | 42.0 | 85 | 78 | 4 | 30.7 | 43 | 6 | 268 |
| 62 | University for the Creative Arts | 41.3 | 75 | 63 | 5 | 25.1 | 55 | 3 | 248 |
| 62 | Worcester | 41.3 | 83 | 60 | 2 | | | 4 | 246 |
| 64 | Liverpool John Moores | 41.1 | 76 | 61 | 3 | 17.8 | 47 | 4 | 216 |
| 65 | Newport | 40.9 | 63 | 61 | 3 | 28.1 | 60 | 8 | 257 |
| 66 | Lincoln | 40.8 | 79 | 66 | 3 | 23.8 | 56 | 2 | 275 |
| 67 | Coventry | 40.4 | 68 | 48 | 4 | 23.4 | 62 | 5 | 237 |
| 67 | Southampton Solent | 40.4 | 64 | 52 | 4 | 17.7 | 52 | 4 | 234 |
| 69 | Westminster | 39.5 | 68 | 52 | 4 | 18.4 | 36 | 6 | 265 |
| 70 | Northampton | 39.4 | 77 | 65 | 4 | 21.8 | 40 | 4 | 269 |
| 70 | Ravensbourne College | 39.4 | 74 | 71 | 2 | 29.2 | 68 | 4 | 248 |
| 72 | York St John | 38.7 | 63 | 61 | 8 | 18.0 | 46 | 1 | 241 |
| 73 | Hertfordshire | 38.3 | 60 | 48 | 5 | 14.0 | 52 | 1 | 231 |
| 74 | Salford | 37.3 | 81 | 59 | 3 | 27.4 | 47 | 4 | 252 |
| 75 | Chichester | 36.6 | 76 | 75 | 4 | 18.5 | 36 | 3 | 200 |
| 76 | Anglia Ruskin | 36.4 | 73 | 61 | 6 | 27.9 | 39 | 4 | 261 |
| 77 | Bedfordshire | 32.4 | 66 | 41 | 3 | 16.6 | 56 | 3 | 171 |
| 78 | Sheffield Hallam | 31.4 | 74 | 66 | 4 | 21.7 | 30 | 2 | 258 |
| 79 | East London | 25.8 | 68 | 59 | 3 | 32.5 | 45 | 5 | 214 |

# Building and town and country planning

❝ Planners understand cities — it's what they're trained to do. They develop strategies — for developing London eastward along the Thames; for protecting Europe's historic townscapes; for renewing east European neighbourhoods suffering from decades of underinvestment and social neglect; for upgrading impoverished squatter settlements in Africa; for accommodating projected housing demand in environmentally sensitive regions. They are environmental managers, city shapers, community mobilisers, social entrepreneurs, regulators, inventors, and visionaries.

History and archaeology tell us there have always been planned cities, laid out according to grand designs. Ancient Babylon and Alexandria; the Chinese imperial cities; 18th-century Paris; Britain's 20th-century new towns. Some of these worked according to plan for a while — where their builders and rulers commanded sufficient power and resources. Most cities, even planned cities, however, take on a life of their own. They grow under the influence of millions of individual decisions about where to live, work, invest, play.

Shaping these processes has to be one of the most challenging and important jobs around. This has never been more so than now — the commencement of the urban century. Cities in the rich nations are reinventing themselves in a lively and creative urban renaissance — a dramatic turnaround from the decaying industrial cities of the 20th century. Cities are becoming bigger and more sophisticated.

There are now 30 cities in the world with over 7 million inhabitants, 24 of them larger than London. And as cities grow and city systems evolve, problems emerge — urban water shortages, regional growth disparities, destruction of valuable cultural and environmental assets, rural deprivation, urban poverty, overheated housing markets, congested transportation. Finding mechanisms to address these problems without compromising economic health and vitality is the planner's key skill. Planning is one of the oldest professions — evidence of its abiding importance.

Train as a planner and you're unlikely ever to be out of work. Few other jobs also give you the same kind of chance to shape the future.

**Professor Chris Webster,** *School of City and Regional Planning, Cardiff University*

We don't like to whinge, but creating tables for university subjects can, at times, be a little like tying knots in jelly. The problems come when you find that the figures tend to leave you grouping two (or more) only slightly related subjects. It happens elsewhere and it's not perfect, but here we've grouped together building and town and country planning. They're subjects that can be linked, but these are tables where you should take the rankings with just a small pinch of salt and do more research into the universities which interest you.

To start with building, university courses on building studies (or the built environment) focus on all aspects of buildings — except the design element that belongs to architects. It's a rather practical course, covering construction management, construction techniques, structural and civil engineering, and the planning of infrastructure for major building developments, including airports and railways.

The idea of a building course is to turn out one of the highly skilled professionals who gets to plan and build increasingly complex projects anywhere in the world. Building studies courses have largely developed from university schools of engineering, though many courses also have a grounding in urban policy and history – the best engineers and contractors understand the political ins and outs of projects, and one way of understanding the political sensitivities of particular projects is to understand their history.

The more closely focused courses – those containing engineering or architecture modules, for instance – often require specific A-level subjects, such as maths or physics. These types of degree will also draw more on your numerical skills, whereas more general or management-based building degrees will require a greater emphasis on communication and organisation. But because the learning-through-doing component is so essential in this field, courses are inevitably more "hands-on" than many arts subjects.

An increasing number of women apply to construction engineering and built environment courses; traditionally this has been a male-dominated preserve, but the times they are a-changing.

Most building-related courses are three- or four-year BScs. The range of degrees is so varied that few institutions offer exactly the same degree course so make sure you understand what you're getting into. Certain courses also offer the opportunity to attain chartered engineer status – this requires studying for the Engineering Council examinations – which may help you gain employment further down the line.

Four-year courses nearly always include a sandwich year in industry, which can be a great way to get to know the industry and find your niche in the job market. Ask about the provision an institution has for work placements.

Next up: town and country planning. The subject covers a wide range of activities – advising on the design of new transport systems, tourist sites, conservation areas and, of course, developments in our towns and cities. Issues such as regeneration and environmentally friendly and sustainable development are playing an increasingly important role in the subject.

Town and country planning degrees increasingly reflect the specialisms developing in the planning industry, with courses concentrating variously on things such as urban design, environmental impact, and transport issues. Most courses, though, offer at least one year of training in the general skills of town and country planning. From then on they diverge more – into town and regional planning, city and regional planning or civic design, for example – but they mostly cover a similar curriculum, just with different emphases. There's also the option of joint honours, in planning and geography, for example.

The distinguishing feature for many town and country planning students is the professional accreditation of programmes. The Royal Town Planning Institute (RTPI) accredits courses, meaning that students leaving an accredited course have privileged status and are more likely to get a job if they stay in the field. And as ever, look at the research specialisations of the teaching staff. Try to make sure that those who will be teaching you cover the specific areas you want to study.

With a recruitment crisis in many planning authorities, the employment prospects of graduates are very good, even for those coming from non-accredited courses. As well as being at the local town hall you could also end up in consultancy, environmental management, and rural community councils. After two years in practice, many graduates will sit further exams for professional qualifications, such as membership of the RTPI, the Chartered Institute of Housing or the Chartered Institute of Transport.

> 66 I only started my course this year, but so far it's been great. In one of the modules we had to design student accommodation, which was challenging but really interesting, and of course relevant to us. There's a lot of teamwork involved and we have plenty of access to lecturers through small tutorial groups. The experience I have had so far has been brilliant and I can't wait for more to come.
>
> **Tsui Shan Tracy Au**, *first-year civil engineering student (incorporating building and planning)*, *Loughborough University*

## » Further information

**The Chartered Institute of Building**
Englemere, Kings Ride
Ascot, Berkshire SL5 7TB

t  01344 630700
e  reception@ciob.org.uk
↗  www.ciob.org.uk

**The Association of Building Engineers**
Lutyens House, Billing Brook Road
Weston Favell, Northampton
Northamptonshire NN3 8NW

t  0845 126 1058
e  building.engineers@abe.org.uk
↗  www.abe.org.uk

**CITB-ConstructionSkills**
Bircham Newton, Kings Lynn
Norfolk PE31 6RH

t  01485 577577
e  information.centre@citb.co.uk
↗  www.citb.org.uk

**Town and Country Planning Association**
17 Carlton House Terrace
London SW1 5AS

t  020 7930 8903
↗  www.tcpa.org.uk

**The Royal Town Planning Institute**
41 Botolph Lane
London EC3R 8DL

t  020 7929 9494
↗  www.rtpi.org.uk

**The Chartered Institute of Housing**
9 White Lion Street
London N1 9XJ

t  0247 685 1700
e  customer.services@cih.org
↗  www.cih.org

**BRE (Building Research Establishment)**
Bucknalls Lane, Garston
Watford WD25 9XX

t  01923 664000
e  enquiries@bre.co.uk
↗  www.bre.co.uk

**Centre for Education in the Built Environment**
Bute Building, King Edward VII Avenue
Cardiff CF10 3NB

t  029 2087 4600
↗  www.cebe.heacademy.ac.uk

## ↗ Online reading

**Cyburbia**  www.cyburbia.org
**Construction Education**  www.constructioneducation.com
**Construction Plus**  www.constructionplus.co.uk
**The Chartered Institute of Logistics and Transport**  www.ciltuk.org.uk
**The Landscape Institute**  www.landscapeinstitute.org
**The British Association of Landscape Industries**  www.bali.co.uk
**Internet Town and Country Planner**  www.vts.rdn.ac.uk/tutorial/town
**Sapling** (a portal site for architecture, planning, and environment)  www.sapling.info

# Building and town and country planning

| | | Guardian score /100 | Satisfied with teaching % | Satisfied with feedback % | Spend per student /10 | Student:staff ratio | Job prospects % | Value added score /10 | Average entry tariff |
|---|---|---|---|---|---|---|---|---|---|
| 1 | Cambridge | 100.0 | 78 | 65 | 10 | 12.9 | | 8 | 505 |
| 2 | Loughborough | 98.8 | 87 | 66 | 10 | 10.2 | 95 | 7 | 349 |
| 3 | Manchester | 83.2 | 80 | 52 | 10 | 11.7 | 90 | 7 | 312 |
| 4 | UCL | 80.4 | 86 | 66 | 10 | 11.8 | 73 | 3 | 381 |
| 5 | Sheffield | 77.7 | 90 | 73 | 5 | 17.5 | 97 | 3 | 361 |
| 6 | Reading | 77.6 | 86 | 44 | 4 | 16.7 | 97 | 8 | 327 |
| 6 | Salford | 77.6 | 75 | 55 | 9 | 15.1 | 93 | 7 | 277 |
| 8 | Liverpool | 76.4 | 74 | 39 | 8 | 16.1 | | 9 | 334 |
| 9 | Gloucestershire | 73.9 | 90 | 73 | 8 | 19.9 | 75 | 9 | 259 |
| 10 | Nottingham | 72.6 | 84 | 51 | 7 | 18.0 | | 5 | 376 |
| 11 | Heriot-Watt | 70.2 | 71 | 51 | 6 | 13.3 | 92 | 4 | 332 |
| 12 | Newcastle | 70.0 | 76 | 56 | 6 | 20.0 | 91 | 5 | 344 |
| 13 | Coventry | 69.9 | | | 4 | 21.5 | | 10 | 270 |
| 14 | Cardiff | 69.3 | 69 | 47 | 8 | 13.5 | 84 | 5 | 353 |
| 15 | Sheffield Hallam | 67.5 | 79 | 50 | 5 | 18.0 | 87 | 8 | 268 |
| 16 | Nottingham Trent | 66.7 | 80 | 54 | 6 | 19.9 | 93 | 5 | 270 |
| 17 | Northumbria | 66.4 | 86 | 72 | 4 | 21.5 | 89 | 5 | 285 |
| 18 | Dundee | 66.3 | 82 | 61 | 4 | 20.1 | 79 | 8 | 329 |
| 19 | Anglia Ruskin | 64.1 | 76 | 61 | 8 | | 87 | 4 | 327 |
| 20 | Glyndŵr | 63.2 | 89 | 75 | 4 | 28.1 | | 6 | |
| 21 | Glasgow Caledonian | 62.7 | 76 | 58 | 5 | 24.8 | 79 | 8 | 327 |
| 22 | Edinburgh Napier | 62.6 | | | 3 | 29.0 | 97 | 8 | 284 |
| 23 | Oxford Brookes | 62.1 | 80 | 53 | 4 | 17.7 | 73 | 8 | 295 |
| 24 | Manchester Met | 61.7 | 82 | 53 | 4 | 18.9 | 97 | 2 | 291 |
| 25 | Kingston | 61.0 | 73 | 50 | 4 | 22.1 | 89 | 8 | 258 |
| 26 | Central Lancashire | 60.4 | | | 8 | 23.7 | | 8 | 229 |
| 27 | Glamorgan | 57.7 | 76 | 57 | 5 | 17.4 | | 4 | 241 |
| 28 | Aberdeen | 57.4 | 65 | 49 | 3 | 9.1 | 84 | 1 | 349 |
| 29 | Plymouth | 56.9 | 72 | 51 | 4 | 20.0 | 86 | 4 | 265 |
| 30 | Ulster | 55.2 | 68 | 36 | 4 | 23.8 | 89 | 7 | 281 |
| 31 | UWE Bristol | 54.9 | 73 | 57 | 3 | 22.0 | 80 | 5 | 288 |
| 32 | Leeds Met | 54.3 | 72 | 47 | 5 | 27.2 | 81 | 7 | 260 |
| 33 | Edinburgh College of Art | 54.2 | | | 3 | 20.5 | | 2 | 329 |
| 34 | Robert Gordon | 53.1 | | | 4 | 21.8 | 88 | 2 | 293 |
| 35 | Greenwich | 52.7 | 83 | 59 | 5 | 24.5 | 81 | 4 | 196 |
| 36 | Royal Agricultural College | 50.7 | | | 3 | 20.9 | | 1 | 307 |
| 37 | Westminster | 50.1 | 67 | 61 | 4 | 17.6 | 57 | 7 | 263 |
| 38 | Birmingham City | 49.3 | 82 | 66 | 3 | 26.2 | 77 | 6 | 196 |
| 39 | Portsmouth | 49.0 | 75 | 43 | 5 | 25.2 | 80 | 5 | 237 |
| 40 | Queen's, Belfast | 48.4 | 68 | 54 | 3 | 19.7 | 80 | 2 | 320 |
| 41 | Bolton | 40.1 | 83 | 58 | 1 | 35.2 | | 4 | 221 |
| 42 | Southampton Solent | 34.1 | 65 | 47 | 4 | 31.3 | | 4 | 145 |
| 43 | London South Bank | 31.7 | 71 | 54 | 3 | 39.1 | 76 | 6 | 187 |

# Drama studies

" Drama explores and aids understanding and communication. Performance and social practices shape us as individuals and mould the ways in which we encounter and interact with people, objects, and situations in our everyday lives. Studying performance teaches us about cultures and histories, powers and ideologies, pasts and presents: it offers access to a wider comprehension of human identities and behaviour.

Universities offer students the opportunity to work with leading academics in areas of both theory and practice, in live performance and on screen, across film, theatre, television, and new media. Our degree programme, for example, is not designed to teach vocational skills, but enables students to develop practical capabilities alongside critical and theoretical awareness. Key concepts are explored through a variety of teaching and assessment modes — including performance practice, writing, presentation, filmmaking, and archival research. The breadth of the curriculum and an emphasis on research-led teaching mean that students can study across a range of dramatic forms, or explore one form in greater depth.

As the significance of the creative and cultural industries to Britain's economy increases, studying drama develops and enhances a set of critical, creative, and practical transferable skills. Whilst many graduates do go on to work in areas, such as acting and directing, scenic design, lighting and stage management, as well as producing, editing and sound design for the screen, these skills lend themselves to a variety of careers.

**Dr Catherine Hindson**, *Lecturer in Performance Studies, University of Bristol*

Drama — kind of cool, and very popular. It's a fearsomely difficult course to get on to, but don't go thinking it will be all floodlights and applause.

For while theatre and cinema are extraordinary cultural phenomena, drama at university isn't all about performance, unless you're heading for one of the drama or dance schools to learn acting or dancing and nothing more. If you make that choice, bear in mind that not all the courses at drama schools have degree status, so they don't all appear in the tables in this book.

Many higher education institutions do, however, carry acting modules as part of a broad degree programme — mixing theoretical and practical, studying areas such as film, theatre, and radio, performance techniques, basic technical knowledge, and an academic understanding of historical and critical theory. You'll work with a wide cultural perspective and with a large dollop of critical theory. At the end of it all, you may want to delve into theatre design, production, writing or management. Employment prospects are decent, but there's a lot of competition as you bid for work in the theatre, TV, radio, or in arts management.

If performance is what you want, some drama schools have given their courses degree status, or you can do a joint honours degree, mixing acting with a more academic course. The big advantage is that with a degree qualification you will only have to pay standard university fees. Drama schools can in effect charge privately and it can cost upwards of £10,000 a year, and you may not have the benefit of a student bank account as you won't be technically eligible. However, many drama schools have awards and scholarships you can compete for, which may help you financially.

Courses are rigorous and often very practical – although there has to be an element of written work for courses to qualify for degree status. To begin with, you need to consider your skills, both academically and in terms of performing arts, to make that choice between a performance-based degree and wider theatre or cinematic studies. If you mainly want to act, the other elements of a degree-based drama course may only frustrate you.

It's generally best to think of drama in terms of a vocational degree and investigate accordingly. Does the institution have the expertise and equipment to help you in your specific area of interest? If it's TV, is the technical equipment there? If it's theatre design, does the place put on a number of plays to give you the practice? Are there links with full-time drama courses to provide the cannon fodder (actors) for your experiments?

You might want to specialise in directing, the history of theatre, textual analysis or arts management, so check the structure and choices available on the course.

And what are the contacts like with the real world? Does the institution offer work placements with professional companies to help you gain that vital experience and contacts book that's going to help you find a job on graduation? Some places, on the other hand, bar students from working outside for the duration of the course, reasoning that they're working hard enough already. Financially, this could be an issue, but it could also save you from running yourself into the ground.

And don't forget that in the job hunt later, reputation counts for a lot – much more than for most degrees. It can be a remarkably small world out there and people will know whether somewhere excels in particular areas, so bear that in mind when making your choice.

---

> " Studying drama has been the most challenging, yet rewarding, three years of my life. The structure of the course is based upon the symbiotic relationship of theory and practice, which nurtures and develops each student's ability to move between action and thought fluidly. My knowledge of theatre has broadened immeasurably, and the course has encouraged me to question what I and other people believe, in order to form my own opinions.
>
> **Charlotte Dubrey**, *third-year drama student, University of Exeter*

---

## » Further information

**National Drama**  ↗ www.nationaldrama.co.uk

**The National Council for Drama Training**
1-7 Woburn Walk       t 020 7407 3686
London WC1H 0JJ       e info@ncdt.co.uk
                      ↗ www.ncdt.co.uk

**The Conference of Drama Schools**
PO Box 34252          e info@cds.drama.ac.uk
London NW5 1XJ        ↗ www.drama.ac.uk

**Council for Dance Education and Training**
Old Brewer's Yard     t 020 7240 5703
17-19 Neal Street     e info@cdet.org.uk
London WC2H 9UY       ↗ www.cdet.org.uk          »

**National Operatic and Dramatic Association**
58-60 Lincoln Road
Peterborough PE1 2RZ

t 01733 865790
e info@noda.org.uk
↗ www.noda.org.uk

**Dance and Drama Awards**

e dada@lsc.gov.uk
↗ www.direct.gov.uk/danceanddrama

**Equity**
Guild House
Upper St Martins Lane
London WC2H 8JG

t 020 7379 6000
e info@equity.org.uk
↗ www.equity.org.uk

**British Association of Drama Therapists**

t 01242 235515
e enquiries@badth.org.uk
↗ www.badth.org.uk

↗ Online reading

**The Stage**  www.thestage.co.uk
**Arts Marketing Association**  www.a-m-a.co.uk
**AisleSay**  www.aislesay.com

## Drama and dance

| | | Guardian score /100 | Satisfied with teaching % | Satisfied with feedback % | Spend per student /10 | Student:staff ratio | Job prospects % | Value added score /10 | Average entry tariff |
|---|---|---|---|---|---|---|---|---|---|
| 1 | UEA | 100.0 | 97 | 69 | 10 | 8.6 | 67 | 5 | 401 |
| 2 | Guildhall School of Music and Drama | 93.6 | | | 9 | 7.5 | 73 | 9 | |
| 3 | Royal Scottish Academy of Music and Drama | 93.4 | | | 8 | 7.7 | 75 | 9 | |
| 4 | Trinity Laban | 89.4 | 90 | 70 | 7 | 7.8 | 73 | 10 | |
| 5 | Queen Mary | 85.2 | 96 | 72 | 9 | 11.1 | 51 | 6 | 384 |
| 6 | Warwick | 84.6 | 90 | 67 | 8 | 10.0 | 50 | 6 | 430 |
| 7 | The Liverpool Institute for Performing Arts | 83.5 | | | 4.0 | 12.1 | 77 | 10 | 292 |
| 8 | Conservatoire for Dance and Drama | 83.1 | 90 | 65 | | 11.2 | 64 | 8 | |
| 9 | Central School of Speech and Drama | 82.9 | 89 | 61 | 5.0 | 15.9 | 89 | 8 | 324 |
| 10 | Birmingham | 82.8 | 92 | 60 | 8 | 15.7 | 66 | 6 | 413 |
| 11 | Royal Holloway | 79.6 | 85 | 54 | 5 | 14.0 | 70 | 7 | 395 |
| 12 | Loughborough | 79.5 | 94 | 61 | 6 | 15.4 | 61 | 7 | 386 |
| 13 | Bristol | 78.1 | 62 | 24 | 9 | 14.3 | 60 | 7 | 453 |
| 13 | Goldsmiths | 78.1 | 83 | 41 | 6 | 12.8 | 68 | 7 | 379 |
| 15 | Lancaster | 77.4 | 87 | 42 | 8 | 12.2 | 43 | 7 | 381 |
| 16 | Birmingham City | 77.1 | 88 | 64 | 8 | 14.2 | 57 | 8 | 308 |
| 17 | Glasgow | 76.1 | 87 | 66 | 4 | 15.7 | 56 | 6 | 408 |
| 18 | Glamorgan | 75.0 | 78 | 55 | 7 | 10.8 | 56 | 8 | 274 |
| 19 | Exeter | 74.6 | 94 | 79 | 5 | 22.5 | 48 | 7 | 391 |

| | | Guardian score /100 | Satisfied with teaching % | Satisfied with feedback % | Spend per student /10 | Student:staff ratio | Job prospects % | Value added score /10 | Average entry tariff |
|---|---|---|---|---|---|---|---|---|---|
| 20 | Hull | 73.1 | 92 | 79 | 5 | 21.0 | 57 | 8 | 289 |
| 21 | Middlesex | 72.3 | 79 | 51 | 10 | 30.0 | 69 | 8 | 253 |
| 22 | Plymouth | 71.9 | 85 | 73 | 10 | 22.9 | 52 | 2 | 294 |
| 23 | Essex | 71.7 | 89 | 59 | 8 | 18.3 | 42 | 7 | 318 |
| 24 | University of the Arts, London | 71.5 | 74 | 56 | 9 | 22.6 | 67 | 4 | 357 |
| 25 | Bath Spa | 71.2 | 89 | 54 | 4 | 20.0 | 63 | 8 | 290 |
| 26 | UWE Bristol | 71.0 | 93 | 76 | 4 | 19.4 | 41 | 10 | 282 |
| 27 | Queen Margaret | 70.2 | | | 3 | 18.7 | 71 | 4 | 352 |
| 28 | Reading | 70.1 | 89 | 58 | 5 | 14.8 | 52 | 5 | 324 |
| 28 | Rose Bruford College | 70.1 | 84 | 54 | 5 | 17.4 | 65 | 8 | 255 |
| 30 | Manchester | 69.5 | 81 | 42 | 3 | 17.2 | 60 | 5 | 399 |
| 30 | Thames Valley | 69.5 | 72 | 55 | | 11.2 | | 8 | 234 |
| 32 | UWIC | 68.9 | 88 | 71 | 7 | 21.1 | | 8 | 250 |
| 33 | Leeds | 68.8 | 79 | 55 | 5 | 20.2 | 57 | 6 | 349 |
| 34 | Gloucestershire | 68.6 | 87 | 69 | 6 | 17.0 | 51 | 8 | 237 |
| 35 | Brunel | 68.4 | 84 | 64 | 4 | 9.7 | 47 | 4 | 302 |
| 36 | Northumbria | 68.3 | 84 | 69 | 7 | 18.9 | 55 | 6 | 253 |
| 37 | Dundee | 68.0 | 74 | 67 | 8 | 12.5 | | 2 | |
| 38 | Surrey | 67.9 | 83 | 37 | 4 | 18.8 | | 6 | 371 |
| 39 | Liverpool John Moores | 67.7 | 89 | 68 | 4 | 17.8 | 53 | 6 | 288 |
| 40 | Queen's, Belfast | 66.9 | 82 | 55 | 4 | 19.4 | 52 | 7 | 326 |
| 41 | Bishop Grosseteste UC | 66.8 | 97 | 89 | 1 | 15.0 | 68 | 5 | 212 |
| 42 | Kingston | 66.5 | 88 | 73 | 5 | 16.8 | 36 | 8 | 247 |
| 43 | Kent | 65.9 | 89 | 71 | 5 | 24.1 | 55 | 4 | 332 |
| 44 | Trinity UC, Carmarthen | 65.4 | 84 | 59 | 4 | 13.5 | 62 | 2 | 285 |
| 45 | Brighton | 64.6 | 76 | 59 | 8 | 15.3 | 37 | 4 | 272 |
| 46 | De Montfort | 64.5 | 82 | 71 | 5 | 15.1 | 52 | 3 | 260 |
| 47 | Bolton | 64.4 | 76 | 73 | 3 | 20.2 | | 9 | |
| 47 | Sussex | 64.4 | 81 | 45 | 3 | 19.0 | | 4 | 386 |
| 49 | Nottingham Trent | 64.2 | 72 | 55 | 6 | 19.9 | 75 | 2 | 302 |
| 50 | Manchester Met | 64.0 | 81 | 52 | 4 | 18.9 | 54 | 7 | 248 |
| 51 | Coventry | 63.6 | 89 | 67 | 4 | 23.4 | 47 | 7 | 292 |
| 52 | York St John | 63.3 | 68 | 46 | 8 | 18.0 | 49 | 3 | 313 |
| 53 | Huddersfield | 63.1 | 84 | 58 | 5 | 12.1 | 37 | 3 | 299 |
| 54 | St Mary's UC, Twickenham | 62.1 | 91 | 66 | 2 | 24.6 | 51 | 9 | 253 |
| 55 | Salford | 62.0 | 89 | 61 | 4 | 27.4 | 44 | 9 | 286 |
| 56 | Portsmouth | 60.2 | 87 | 80 | 6 | 21.4 | 35 | 3 | 281 |
| 57 | Edge Hill | 60.1 | 88 | 55 | 3 | 15.7 | 47 | 3 | 268 |
| 58 | Sunderland | 60.0 | 87 | 80 | 5 | 13.6 | 37 | 3 | 218 |
| 59 | Roehampton | 59.9 | 78 | 53 | 5 | 16.0 | 36 | 3 | 296 |
| 60 | UC Falmouth | 59.8 | 79 | 67 | 6 | 19.3 | 40 | 5 | 241 |
| 61 | Ulster | 59.7 | 80 | 46 | 4 | 16.2 | | 5 | 246 |
| 62 | Winchester | 59.4 | 83 | 60 | 2 | 14.9 | 41 | 6 | 246 |
| 63 | Derby | 59.2 | 76 | 58 | 7 | 17.4 | 33 | 7 | 219 |
| 64 | Chichester | 58.6 | 86 | 58 | 4 | 18.5 | 44 | 4 | 251 |
| 65 | Aberystwyth | 58.5 | 86 | 67 | 4 | 23.1 | 38 | 5 | 296 |

| | Guardian score /100 | Satisfied with teaching % | Satisfied with feedback % | Spend per student /10 | Student:staff ratio | Job prospects % | Value added score /10 | Average entry tariff |
|---|---|---|---|---|---|---|---|---|
| 66 London South Bank | 57.0 | 81 | 55 | 4 | | | 7 | 236 |
| 67 Bedfordshire | 56.9 | 81 | 57 | 3 | 16.6 | 39 | 6 | 210 |
| 67 Chester | 56.9 | 70 | 59 | 4 | 22.3 | 51 | 4 | 266 |
| 69 Staffordshire | 56.5 | 84 | 70 | 10 | 18.7 | 40 | 1 | 248 |
| 70 Cumbria | 56.3 | 67 | 51 | 4 | 17.4 | 56 | 4 | 204 |
| 71 Southampton Solent | 55.4 | 71 | 50 | 4 | 17.7 | 46 | 4 | 239 |
| 72 Central Lancashire | 54.8 | 71 | 51 | 5 | 24.0 | 47 | 4 | 244 |
| 73 Anglia Ruskin | 54.7 | 82 | 65 | 7 | 27.9 | 32 | 6 | 261 |
| 74 Canterbury Christ Church | 53.6 | 84 | 60 | 3 | 18.3 | 29 | 3 | 286 |
| 74 Lincoln | 53.6 | 77 | 43 | 3 | 23.8 | 39 | 7 | 263 |
| 76 Bucks New University | 53.0 | 67 | 50 | 7 | 15.6 | 27 | 4 | 206 |
| 77 Oxford Brookes | 52.4 | 77 | 60 | 3 | 27.5 | | 4 | 298 |
| 78 Northampton | 51.5 | 81 | 58 | 4 | 21.8 | 35 | 3 | 247 |
| 79 Newport | 50.3 | 70 | 63 | 4 | 28.1 | 42 | 4 | 261 |
| 80 Hertfordshire | 50.2 | 69 | 57 | 3 | 18.9 | 47 | 2 | 235 |
| 81 Worcester | 48.7 | 93 | 71 | 2 | | 32 | 2 | 246 |
| 82 Leeds Met | 42.3 | 32 | 20 | 5 | 18.0 | 32 | 3 | 248 |
| 83 Ravensbourne College | 40.9 | | | 3 | 29.2 | 45 | 1 | |
| 84 East London | 33.2 | | | 3 | 32.5 | 24 | 2 | 221 |

# Music

❝ Why do people come to university to study music? Music is something you *do*, after all; most students have developed their love of it by playing or singing. Perhaps this has been in some kind of social situation — a choir, an orchestra — and perhaps those social aspects are as important as the music itself. It may seem strange, therefore, that so often reading music at university means studying 'history of' or 'analysis of' a particular repertoire. It almost seems as if that initial impetus has got lost somewhere along the line.

On the other hand, music is too interesting just to play. It has had a massive effect on society over the ages and in different places; more importantly, society has had a massive effect on music. Unless we think about that too, the fascinating web of associations that arise from engaging with different pieces and repertories just gets lost. That, we think, is the point of coming to university — to think, as well as to do. In studying music, we passionately believe in considering musical sources at first hand. As often as possible, we make the study of music begin from direct engagement with the music under consideration. Often this means experiencing music in performance — one's own, and that of others. Scores and writings about music also play their part; developing one's critical responses to music, whether in the form of essays, analyses, performances, or compositions, and finding a space within the material that you can really make your own.

**Dr Nicky Losseff**, *Senior Lecturer in Music, University of York*

There used to be a split between music colleges (or conservatoires), which offered diplomas, and the universities offering degrees. Much of that distinction has now gone and all the institutions offer degrees but, in general, the conservatoires still place more emphasis on the practical aspects of the music rather than the theory and history of the subject, whereas you could do a university degree in music that involves no performance at all.

However, the basics remain the same. After three years (or four at a conservatoire), you should come out with a BMus (although it could be a BA in some places and if you do a music technology degree, you could end up with a BSc). Courses vary hugely — you could choose to study anything from classical performance to how to run a recording studio — but they should all give you a breadth of musical knowledge and appreciation. On many courses you'll find similar core modules, likely to include composition, theory, history of music, performance, and analysis.

Aside from the core subjects, the choice for music degrees is vast, so decide whether the course of modules is of interest to you — whether it's performance, jazz, composition or conducting. In recent times, music degrees have tended to open out to wider influences, and popular music degrees are also experiencing a boom. And if you're heading for the technological end of the spectrum, make sure the facilities are all you would hope for.

Look at the specialisations of those who teach and what links they have. There may be a composer you admire working in the department, or there may be an orchestra or studio to which they have strong links that will help you gain experience via a work placement scheme. Investigate the extra-curricular scene too. As you might expect, music students are often involved in music performance and production beyond the requirements of their degree, sometimes to exceptionally high standards.

When applying, you'll almost certainly need two or three A-levels, including music or a BTec in music technology or studio techniques if that's the direction you're interested in. If you want to be a performer, you'll need to be grade eight in whatever it is you play, as a high degree of technical proficiency is essential. Some (the more old-fashioned) also require a minimum grade on the piano – usually about grade five or six – regardless of your instrument, as they make students do keyboard harmony.

The employment prospects are good, although making it as a performer is notoriously difficult. It's a competitive arena and not well paid, and a large percentage of musicians are self-employed and must teach or find other work to supplement their income. Other music graduates teach full-time or go into arts administration, while music technologists can find a home in the industry as sound engineers or technicians, or work in broadcasting.

Depending on the course you choose, music can in effect be a vocational degree, so it pays to think hard about what you plan to get out of it. And make sure that the way your work is assessed is the best way for you. Assessment methods vary tremendously (from practical tests to written exams and coursework) so don't be caught out.

---

**"** As a performer I am always trying to improve. Practice, practice, practice! The biggest challenge is to be constantly motivated and to always aim high. Studying music is an amazing experience because you get to meet lots of different people from different cultures. I am on the master of opera course at the Academy and the unique thing is that it is an international mix of students. I want to work professionally in the music industry and to be at the top of my game. Studying music is the way to achieve that.

**Marie Claire Breen**, *master of music (opera) student, Royal Scottish Academy of Music and Drama*

---

## » Further information

### Associated Board of the Royal Schools of Music
24 Portland Place
London W1B 1LU

t 020 7636 5400
↗ www.abrsm.ac.uk

### Association of British Orchestras
20 Rupert Street
London W1D 6DF

t 020 7287 0333
e info@abo.org.uk
↗ www.abo.org.uk

### Musicians' Union

t 020 7582 5566
e info@musiciansunion.org.uk
↗ www.musiciansunion.org.uk

### Incorporated Society of Musicians
10 Stratford Place
London W1C 1AA

t 020 7629 4413
e membership@ism.org
↗ www.ism.org

### British Society for Music Therapy
24-27 White Lion Street
London N1 9PD

t 020 7837 6100
e info@bsmt.org
↗ www.bsmt.org

### National Association of Youth Orchestras
Central Hall, West Tollcross
Edinburgh EH3 9BP

t 0131 221 1927
↗ www.nayo.org.uk

↗ Online reading

**Access to Music** www.accesstomusic.co.uk
**Music Everything** www.musiceverything.com
**Awards for Young Musicians** www.a-y-m.org.uk
**Tourdates.co.uk** www.tourdates.co.uk
**Music for Youth** www.mfy.org.uk
**Youth Music** www.youthmusic.org.uk

# Music

| | | Guardian score /100 | Satisfied with teaching % | Satisfied with feedback % | Spend per student /10 | Student:staff ratio | Job prospects % | Value added score /10 | Average entry tariff |
|---|---|---|---|---|---|---|---|---|---|
| 1 | Royal Academy of Music | 100.0 | 92 | 72 | 7 | 9.2 | 89 | 9 | |
| 2 | Oxford | 99.3 | 98 | 83 | 10 | 15.9 | 67 | 4 | 465 |
| 3 | Guildhall School of Music and Drama | 96.2 | | | 8 | 7.5 | 83 | 7 | |
| 4 | Royal Scottish Academy of Music and Drama | 94.0 | | | 7 | 7.7 | 89 | 6 | |
| 5 | UEA | 91.9 | 88 | 60 | 10 | 8.6 | 67 | 6 | 262 |
| 6 | Royal College of Music | 90.5 | 75 | 55 | 8 | 10.1 | 95 | 8 | 311 |
| 7 | Nottingham | 89.8 | 97 | 68 | 7 | 12.6 | 74 | 5 | 446 |
| 8 | Bristol | 88.9 | 91 | 66 | 8 | 14.3 | 77 | 7 | 368 |
| 9 | Cambridge | 87.6 | 90 | 70 | 9 | 19.9 | 80 | 4 | 462 |
| 10 | King's College London | 84.1 | 95 | 58 | 5 | 13.6 | 73 | 5 | 455 |
| 11 | Edinburgh | 83.7 | 92 | 65 | 8 | 14.8 | 60 | 7 | 435 |
| 12 | Royal Northern College of Music | 83.3 | 85 | 72 | 3 | 11.1 | 82 | 7 | |
| 13 | Trinity Laban | 81.2 | 89 | 66 | 6 | 7.8 | 82 | 4 | 292 |
| 14 | York | 80.6 | 92 | 61 | 8 | 13.1 | 51 | 6 | 417 |
| 15 | Newcastle | 78.2 | 89 | 61 | 6 | 12.0 | 69 | 5 | 363 |
| 16 | Manchester | 77.2 | 95 | 71 | 3 | 17.2 | 76 | 4 | 421 |
| 17 | Goldsmiths | 76.7 | 82 | 50 | 4 | 12.8 | 77 | 7 | 333 |
| 18 | City | 76.0 | | | 9 | 10.1 | 62 | 2 | 298 |
| 19 | The Liverpool Institute for Performing Arts | 75.8 | | | 3 | 12.1 | 62 | 10 | 300 |
| 20 | Durham | 74.8 | 88 | 45 | 4 | 14.0 | 78 | 4 | 410 |
| 21 | Southampton | 74.1 | 93 | 70 | 6 | 19.4 | 59 | 7 | 369 |
| 22 | Birmingham City | 73.9 | 81 | 76 | 7 | 14.2 | 85 | 3 | 296 |
| 23 | Sheffield | 73.7 | 95 | 79 | 4 | 13.9 | 68 | 3 | 353 |
| 24 | Strathclyde | 73.4 | 78 | 57 | 7 | 18.1 | 69 | 7 | 396 |
| 25 | Bangor | 73.3 | 83 | 77 | 3 | 16.5 | 69 | 8 | 303 |
| 26 | Queen's, Belfast | 72.9 | 89 | 64 | 3 | 19.4 | 79 | 8 | 337 |
| 27 | Birmingham | 72.8 | 92 | 72 | 6 | 15.7 | 56 | 3 | 436 |
| 27 | Brunel | 72.8 | 81 | 60 | 3 | 9.7 | 69 | 5 | 332 |
| 29 | Edinburgh Napier | 72.7 | | | 5 | 14.8 | 61 | 7 | 351 |
| 30 | Plymouth | 72.3 | 85 | 68 | 10 | 22.9 | 50 | 10 | 156 |
| 31 | Glamorgan | 71.6 | 84 | 49 | 5 | 10.8 | 76 | 4 | 289 |
| 32 | Lancaster | 70.4 | 70 | 62 | 7 | 12.2 | 55 | 7 | 323 |
| 32 | Leeds College of Music | 70.4 | 77 | 46 | 4 | 11.9 | 86 | 5 | 299 |
| 34 | Cardiff | 70.2 | 93 | 64 | 5 | 13.7 | 61 | 4 | 350 |

| | | Guardian score /100 | Satisfied with teaching % | Satisfied with feedback % | Spend per student /10 | Student-staff ratio | Job prospects % | Value added score /10 | Average entry tariff |
|---|---|---|---|---|---|---|---|---|---|
| 35 | Ulster | 69.7 | 80 | 46 | 3 | 16.2 | 85 | 8 | 294 |
| 36 | Coventry | 68.2 | 86 | 61 | 3 | 23.4 | 59 | 10 | 303 |
| 36 | Royal Holloway | 68.2 | 94 | 66 | 4 | 14.0 | 62 | 4 | 342 |
| 38 | Sussex | 67.9 | 85 | 58 | 3 | 16.3 | | 6 | 355 |
| 39 | Bath Spa | 66.8 | 91 | 75 | 3 | 20.0 | 60 | 8 | 309 |
| 40 | Leeds | 64.2 | 91 | 72 | 4 | 20.2 | 61 | 4 | 355 |
| 41 | De Montfort | 64.0 | 96 | 64 | 8 | 11.0 | 60 | 2 | 183 |
| 42 | Hull | 63.6 | 79 | 77 | 4 | 21.0 | 60 | 8 | 261 |
| 43 | Huddersfield | 63.2 | 86 | 68 | 4 | 12.1 | 58 | 3 | 279 |
| 44 | Essex | 63.1 | 92 | 62 | 7 | 18.3 | | 4 | 219 |
| 45 | Gloucestershire | 62.1 | 80 | 71 | 5 | 17.0 | | | 251 |
| 46 | Roehampton | 62.0 | 78 | 53 | 4 | 16.0 | 69 | 7 | 240 |
| 47 | Glasgow | 61.9 | 74 | 45 | 3 | 15.7 | 67 | 3 | 421 |
| 48 | Thames Valley | 61.5 | 80 | 54 | 8 | 20.9 | 55 | 8 | 231 |
| 49 | Liverpool | 61.1 | 84 | 62 | 4 | 16.5 | 54 | 5 | 346 |
| 50 | Middlesex | 60.7 | 79 | 59 | 10 | 30.0 | 67 | 6 | 244 |
| 51 | Rose Bruford College | 60.5 | 83 | 53 | 4 | 17.4 | | 7 | |
| 52 | Westminster | 59.6 | 81 | 38 | 4 | 18.4 | 62 | 8 | 273 |
| 53 | Salford | 57.8 | 88 | 73 | 3 | 27.4 | 56 | 9 | 265 |
| 54 | York St John | 57.6 | 83 | 56 | 7 | 18.0 | 52 | 5 | 236 |
| 55 | Surrey | 55.6 | 87 | 47 | 3 | 18.8 | 56 | 2 | 372 |
| 56 | Kingston | 54.9 | 67 | 66 | 4 | 16.8 | 45 | 9 | 228 |
| 57 | UC Falmouth | 54.2 | 76 | 58 | 4 | 19.3 | | 4 | 270 |
| 58 | Hertfordshire | 53.6 | 86 | 60 | 4 | 14.0 | 39 | 4 | 260 |
| 59 | Central Lancashire | 53.2 | 75 | 48 | 4 | 24.0 | 67 | 7 | 226 |
| 60 | Derby | 52.4 | 78 | 52 | 6 | 17.4 | | 5 | 222 |
| 60 | Keele | 52.4 | 81 | 68 | 2 | 22.8 | | | 296 |
| 62 | Bucks New University | 51.7 | 78 | 56 | 6 | 15.6 | 54 | 2 | 263 |
| 63 | Brighton | 50.7 | 67 | 50 | 7 | 15.3 | 31 | 7 | 224 |
| 64 | Chichester | 47.0 | 87 | 61 | 3 | 18.5 | 51 | 2 | 237 |
| 65 | Canterbury Christ Church | 45.6 | 89 | 57 | 2 | 18.3 | 43 | 3 | 253 |
| 66 | Anglia Ruskin | 40.7 | 89 | 53 | 6 | 27.9 | 52 | 2 | 235 |
| 67 | Southampton Solent | 36.6 | 71 | 49 | 3 | 17.7 | | 1 | 230 |
| 68 | Oxford Brookes | 34.3 | 79 | 63 | 3 | 27.5 | 51 | 2 | 229 |

# Engineering

❝ There is a skills shortage in the UK for qualified engineers who can undertake a broad range of jobs in areas like management, design, development, planning, marketing, and sales. Engineering courses covering a wide range of skills topics could set students above the rest when applying for jobs in industry. Courses cover a range of exciting and innovative topics, including mechanical, electrical, and electronic engineering. In large part they are highly vocational courses suited to individual interests and work needs.

A paid 12-month work placement in a local company is required in some full-time engineering courses, giving students valuable and essential experience in industry and improving their future career prospects. Some courses offer flexibility, with distance learning and work-based learning for people already employed in the industry who are looking to upgrade their skills. Engineering is fast-moving, exciting, and leads to excellent career prospects.

**Professor Phil Picton**, *Head of Division, Applied Sciences, Engineering, University of Northampton*

Asked to name five famous engineers, you might dredge up Isambard Kingdom Brunel, George Stephenson, and maybe James Watt from your memory. Don't know about you, but after that we'd be struggling.

Yet the profession includes an extraordinarily wide spectrum of practitioners, from the designers of great hydroelectric projects to the bloke who fixes your washing machine. The Royal Academy of Engineering has estimated that up to two million people in the UK could be classified as engineers in some way or another, and there are now courses available in anything from film production technology or motor sports engineering, to space technology or medical engineering.

And yet a large number of universities have seen a drop in applicants over recent years, while two-fifths of engineering students say they have no intention of actually becoming engineers when they graduate. That's a real shame because there are huge opportunities right now in UK engineering. Just about every discipline has a shortage of good engineers, and this is particularly acute in the civil and chemical engineering fields. This in turn means employment prospects are good, and salaries, which truthfully have never been spectacular, are now improving as companies chase fewer and fewer graduates.

All courses accredited by the Engineering Council UK are either three-year BEng (four years in Scotland), or four-year MEng qualifications and usually require students to have decent A-levels before applying. In some sectors, especially civil engineering and structural engineering, becoming chartered is a prerequisite to practice, but for all sectors you'll find the financial rewards are higher with it than without.

Once you've graduated, the possibilities are much wider than you might think. You don't have to restrict yourself to engineering – only about a quarter of registered chartered engineers work in manufacturing. You could find your way into financial companies, management consultancies, telecommunications, power and water supply, environmental projects, the armed forces, or the sophisticated IT operations of major banks.

But will you go for a BEng or MEng? Many universities run only the MEng. Look too at the system for gaining chartered engineer status which you can acquire two years after your MEng. Alternatively you could go for incorporated engineer status after taking a BSc, although remember the chartered engineer status is likely to be better rewarded in your pay packet.

It is important to find out how the course is structured, as general engineering degrees can vary hugely. So investigate what modules and options are available to you in the later years of the degree as you begin to specialise. Also, check to see what work placement opportunities there are and what the chances are for study abroad.

We've said this before too – check the research specialisations of the teaching staff and see if they tally with the areas you want to work in. There's no substitute for learning from the leaders in your field.

---

66 Engineering has given me the opportunity for great variety in my studies. I've had the chance to work on individual and group projects, solving real-life problems in anything from renewable energy to investigating heart rate variability in children. I've improved my presentation and team-work skills, as well as gaining management experience. Above all I've enjoyed the course and am in a great position for the future.

**Victoria Cripps**, *fourth-year engineering student, University of Leicester*

---

# General engineering

The general engineering course is, naturally, the best general introduction to the subject and a way of getting into engineering without specialising too early. At the start of the course, you can study across the range and then usually specialise as you go on, graduating in one of the more specific disciplines.

Most MEng courses start with an introduction to engineering for the first two years before moving on to two years of specialisation. It will be based around a core of science, maths, and computing skills, the ability to interpret data, written, and oral communication, presentation skills, teamworking skills and creative approaches, as well as the skills of imagination married to practicality, which are essential to the problem-solving that is at the heart of engineering. It's from such a base that you go on to specialise.

## » Further information

**The Royal Academy of Engineering**
29 Great Peter Street
Westminster, London SW1P 3LW

t   020 7766 0600
↗ www.raengbest.org.uk

**Engineering Council UK**
10 Maltravers Street
London WC2R 3ER

t   020 7240 7891
e   staff@engc.org.uk
↗ www.engc.org.uk

**The Institution of Engineering Design**
Courtleigh, Westbury Leigh
Westbury, Wiltshire BA13 3TA

t   01373 822801
e   ied@ied.org.uk
↗ www.ied.org.uk

**The Institution of Engineering and Technology**
Michael Faraday House
Stevenage
Herts SG1 2AY

t   01438 313311
e   postmaster@theiet.org
↗ www.theiet.org

## ↗ Online reading

**The Engineering Careers Information Service**  www.enginuity.org.uk
**Engineer Girl**  www.engineergirl.org
**Progressive Engineer**  www.progressiveengineer.com
**The Engineer online**  www.e4engineering.com

# Civil engineering

Civil engineering is arguably the most practical of the disciplines and has had the most recruitment problems after the Engineering Council UK's bid to improve academic standards. Strangely, civil engineers seem to be held in rather low regard in the UK, despite the fact that they are essential to our daily life. But at least you'll be pretty much guaranteed a job, possibly with consulting or contracting engineering companies or local authorities, central government or in banking, law, or in the City. You'll be a numerate problem-solver, and those are valuable assets in an employee.

As a civil engineer, you'd be responsible for the design, building, and maintenance of bridges, roads, railway lines, water supply, or sewage systems – facing up to the challenges that make up the creation and use of the infrastructure of a modern country. As well as the practical, it also offers opportunities in design, management, the environment, and buildings and bridges of all shapes and sizes.

You will be involved in studying structural mechanics, geology, surveying, fluid mechanics, and plenty of maths (maths and physics A-levels are essential and a humanities subject is also useful).

## ⟫ Further information

**The Institution of Civil Engineers**
1 Great George Street
Westminster, London SW1P 3AA

t  020 7222 7722
↗ www.ice.org.uk

**The Institution of Structural Engineers**
11 Upper Belgrave Street
London SW1X 8BH

t  020 7235 4535
↗ www.istructe.org.uk

**CITB-Construction Skills**
Bircham Newton, Kings Lynn
Norfolk PE31 6RH

t  01485 577577
e  information.centre@citb.co.uk
↗ www.cskills.org

**The Chartered Institution of Building Services Engineers**
222 Balham High Road
Balham, London SW12 9BS

t  020 8675 5211
↗ www.cibse.org

**European Council of Civil Engineers**
C/o ICE, 1 Great George Street
Westminster , London SW1P 3AA

e  ecce@sksi.sk
↗ www.eccenet.org

## ↗ Online reading

**The Institution of Highway Incorporated Engineers**  www.ihie.org.uk
**Society of Operations Engineers**  www.soe.org.uk
**New Civil Engineer Plus**  www.nceplus.co.uk

# General engineering

| | | Guardian score /100 | Satisfied with teaching % | Satisfied with feedback % | Spend per student /10 | Student:staff ratio | Job prospects % | Value added score /10 | Average entry tariff |
|---|---|---|---|---|---|---|---|---|---|
| 1 | Oxford | 100.0 | 84 | 66 | 10 | 9.9 | 87 | 3 | 544 |
| 2 | Imperial College | 98.2 | | | 10 | 9.9 | | 5 | 473 |
| 3 | Cambridge | 91.6 | 86 | 71 | 9 | 12.1 | 86 | 2 | 561 |
| 4 | Warwick | 81.3 | 75 | 53 | 9 | 10.7 | 89 | 3 | 417 |
| 5 | Brunel | 80.8 | 90 | 77 | 4 | 14.6 | 73 | 9 | 371 |
| 6 | Bournemouth | 80.6 | 80 | 71 | 8 | 10.0 | 52 | 10 | 281 |
| 7 | Leicester | 73.7 | 81 | 69 | 7 | 9.2 | 75 | 4 | 289 |
| 8 | Durham | 67.2 | 81 | 44 | 4 | 14.8 | 86 | 3 | 480 |
| 9 | Exeter | 64.2 | 88 | 64 | 3 | 13.4 | 80 | 3 | 331 |
| 10 | Hull | 62.3 | 77 | 64 | 7 | 13.1 | 72 | 5 | 235 |
| 11 | Swansea | 59.2 | 79 | 57 | 5 | 11.6 | | | 238 |
| 12 | Edinburgh Napier | 58.3 | | | 3 | 15.9 | 73 | 8 | 274 |
| 13 | Sheffield Hallam | 58.1 | 78 | 70 | 3 | 16.2 | 60 | 10 | 200 |
| 14 | De Montfort | 56.4 | 76 | 63 | 4 | 11.0 | 65 | 6 | 198 |
| 15 | Brighton | 52.1 | | | 4 | 11.5 | 66 | 4 | 254 |
| 16 | Central Lancashire | 51.8 | 85 | 67 | 6 | 19.2 | | 3 | |
| 17 | Birmingham | 51.0 | 73 | 53 | 7 | 19.1 | | 4 | |
| 18 | Aberdeen | 47.7 | 72 | 46 | 4 | 19.4 | 81 | 3 | 364 |
| 19 | Birmingham City | 45.4 | 71 | 64 | 5 | 12.3 | 53 | 5 | 180 |
| 20 | Greenwich | 39.5 | 80 | 75 | 3 | 24.1 | 67 | 6 | 173 |
| 21 | London South Bank | 36.1 | 61 | 48 | 2 | 18.6 | | 9 | |
| 22 | Glasgow Caledonian | 31.8 | 77 | 62 | 3 | 22.0 | 52 | 5 | 293 |

# Civil engineering

| | | Guardian score /100 | Satisfied with teaching % | Satisfied with feedback % | Spend per student /10 | Student:staff ratio | Job prospects % | Value added score /10 | Average entry tariff |
|---|---|---|---|---|---|---|---|---|---|
| 1 | Imperial College | 100.0 | 79 | 60 | 10 | 13.6 | 100 | 7 | 475 |
| 2 | Sheffield | 90.8 | 94 | 72 | 7 | 13.5 | 94 | 8 | 427 |
| 3 | Edinburgh | 84.8 | 84 | 35 | 9 | 15.6 | 96 | 8 | 417 |
| 4 | Bristol | 82.7 | 85 | 46 | 7 | 15.0 | 97 | 7 | 458 |
| 5 | Nottingham | 80.3 | 86 | 59 | 9 | 13.1 | 89 | 6 | 373 |
| 6 | Dundee | 79.0 | 84 | 69 | 5 | 13.2 | | | 408 |
| 7 | UCL | 78.6 | 80 | 66 | 10 | 8.5 | 88 | 2 | 432 |
| 8 | East London | 76.8 | 86 | 64 | 10 | | | 10 | 200 |
| 9 | Bolton | 75.6 | 78 | 67 | 3 | 10.9 | | 9 | |
| 10 | Swansea | 74.9 | 74 | 57 | 7 | 11.6 | 95 | 7 | 319 |
| 11 | Newcastle | 74.5 | 89 | 72 | 6 | 13.9 | 94 | 4 | 353 |
| 12 | Southampton | 73.6 | 76 | 49 | 6 | 21.2 | 97 | 8 | 430 |
| 13 | Bath | 73.5 | 91 | 59 | 4 | 21.6 | 95 | 5 | 430 |
| 14 | Nottingham Trent | 71.4 | 89 | 63 | 3 | 16.8 | 100 | 9 | 230 |
| 15 | Abertay Dundee | 71.3 | | | 5 | 11.3 | | 7 | 282 |
| 16 | Birmingham | 66.8 | 77 | 51 | 9 | 19.1 | 89 | 4 | 376 |
| 17 | Cardiff | 66.3 | 87 | 56 | 4 | 23.8 | 94 | 5 | 419 |

| | | Guardian score /100 | Satisfied with teaching % | Satisfied with feedback % | Spend per student /10 | Student:staff ratio | Job prospects % | Value added score /10 | Average entry tariff |
|---|---|---|---|---|---|---|---|---|---|
| 18 | Loughborough | 65.9 | 88 | 70 | 5 | 26.4 | 96 | 4 | 381 |
| 19 | Liverpool | 64.2 | 73 | 57 | 8 | 20.6 | 89 | 6 | 362 |
| 20 | Surrey | 64.1 | 87 | 61 | 5 | 18.3 | 94 | 3 | 342 |
| 21 | Queen's, Belfast | 63.6 | 75 | 47 | 5 | 21.5 | 97 | 6 | 371 |
| 22 | Bradford | 62.3 | 60 | 55 | 5 | 10.4 | | 7 | 261 |
| 22 | Manchester | 62.3 | 79 | 63 | 8 | 27.2 | 92 | 3 | 413 |
| 24 | Heriot-Watt | 61.7 | 74 | 44 | 8 | 13.4 | 83 | 5 | 346 |
| 25 | Strathclyde | 61.3 | 70 | 43 | 7 | 16.7 | 92 | 3 | 388 |
| 26 | Kingston | 59.3 | 89 | 78 | 3 | 24.3 | 88 | 10 | 176 |
| 27 | City | 58.1 | 91 | 58 | 6 | 22.8 | 90 | 4 | 292 |
| 28 | Portsmouth | 55.7 | 91 | 65 | 3 | 18.5 | 95 | 2 | 266 |
| 29 | Teesside | 55.4 | 78 | 68 | 3 | 24.0 | | 8 | 259 |
| 30 | Leeds | 51.8 | 76 | 52 | 5 | 26.2 | 94 | 3 | 353 |
| 31 | Leeds Met | 50.2 | 75 | 57 | 3 | 19.6 | | 7 | 210 |
| 32 | Glasgow | 49.3 | 70 | 30 | 4 | 18.4 | 87 | 3 | 383 |
| 33 | Glamorgan | 48.2 | 71 | 45 | 3 | 19.8 | | 8 | 202 |
| 34 | Ulster | 47.8 | 75 | 43 | 3 | 17.6 | 96 | 3 | 236 |
| 35 | Greenwich | 46.8 | 82 | 71 | 4 | 24.1 | | 4 | 194 |
| 36 | Plymouth | 46.3 | 83 | 64 | 2 | 20.0 | 81 | 7 | 257 |
| 37 | Brighton | 38.9 | | | 3 | 20.9 | | 1 | 294 |
| 38 | Coventry | 36.7 | 70 | 54 | 3 | 24.7 | 71 | 9 | 270 |
| 39 | Salford | 34.2 | 80 | 56 | 4 | 28.6 | | 1 | 259 |
| 40 | Northumbria | 34.0 | 60 | 48 | 3 | 25.1 | | 4 | 256 |
| 41 | Edinburgh Napier | 31.6 | | | 3 | 24.1 | 79 | 4 | 240 |

## Chemical engineering

| | | Guardian score /100 | Satisfied with teaching % | Satisfied with feedback % | Spend per student /10 | Student:staff ratio | Job prospects % | Value added score /10 | Average entry tariff |
|---|---|---|---|---|---|---|---|---|---|
| 1 | Cambridge | 100.0 | 85 | 73 | 8 | 12.3 | 97 | 7 | 532 |
| 2 | Newcastle | 93.2 | 87 | 70 | 9 | 10.4 | 91 | 7 | 399 |
| 3 | Imperial College | 83.1 | 84 | 67 | 9 | 16.8 | 79 | 7 | 479 |
| 4 | Manchester | 79.1 | 81 | 47 | 8 | 13.9 | 82 | 7 | 457 |
| 5 | Edinburgh | 77.1 | 79 | 47 | 6 | 9.9 | | 7 | 420 |
| 6 | Birmingham | 76.9 | 80 | 61 | 8 | 14.6 | | 5 | 409 |
| 7 | Loughborough | 72.6 | 87 | 66 | 5 | 15.7 | 77 | 7 | 392 |
| 8 | Sheffield | 71.7 | 90 | 68 | 6 | 13.0 | | 2 | 399 |
| 9 | Nottingham | 67.9 | 73 | 52 | 7 | 14.3 | 81 | 6 | 358 |
| 10 | UCL | 67.3 | 80 | 56 | 7 | 14.6 | 69 | 8 | 375 |
| 11 | Surrey | 66.9 | 88 | 68 | 3 | 18.3 | | 8 | 315 |
| 12 | Aston | 64.6 | 84 | 81 | 2 | 9.5 | | 3 | 295 |
| 13 | Strathclyde | 63.5 | 75 | 61 | 3 | 23.7 | 90 | 8 | 391 |
| 14 | Swansea | 63.3 | 74 | 57 | 4 | 11.6 | | | 263 |
| 15 | Leeds | 58.4 | 73 | 52 | 5 | 17.6 | 84 | 4 | 326 |
| 16 | Bath | 57.0 | 72 | 44 | 3 | 17.5 | 78 | 4 | 428 |
| 17 | Heriot-Watt | 52.8 | 75 | 47 | 4 | 13.4 | 83 | 1 | 379 |
| 18 | London South Bank | 34.8 | 64 | 49 | 1 | 23.4 | | 7 | 163 |

# Chemical engineering

Almost without exception, university engineering departments report that this discipline comes with great career potential, with some of the best salaries. Chemists and biochemists often need to stay on for a PhD if they're going to get the best jobs, but chemical engineers are straight in there earning the cash.

The jobs – of which there are plenty – could involve working in the chemical, process, food or pharmaceutical industry or in those areas of the City that deal with the large chemical engineering industry.

The subject is – to try to put it simply – about the practical application of chemistry on a large scale, involving the creation and efficient operation of facilities relating to the manufacture of almost anything, from plastic gizmos to cleaning products, from drugs to toothpaste. It's about building a process, one that's economically viable and environmentally responsible. Some students do shy away from working in an industry with a rather poor environmental image, but a big part of the subject is learning how to manage risks properly, and the emphasis on that is getting greater all the time.

## » Further information

**Institution of Chemical Engineers**
Davis Building, Railway Terrace
Rugby CV21 3HQ

t 01788 578214
↗ www.icheme.org

## ↗ Online reading

**ChemWeb** www.chemweb.com
**The Chemical Engineers Resource page** www.cheresources.com
**ChemSoc** www.isc.org/chemsoc
**The Chemical Engineer Today** www.tcetoday.com
**The Association of Institutions concerned with Medical Engineering**
www.aime.org.uk

# Electrical and electronic engineering

Electrical and particularly electronic engineering are among the few disciplines with a clear public perception of what might be involved. There is a very close link with computers, after all, and most people are familiar with this technology. But electrical and electronic engineering can cover a wide range of areas and skills. You could be involved in electricity generation, supply and distribution, software engineering, signal processing, control engineering, computer architecture, communications technology, networking, databases or e-commerce engineering. You'll also end up with a grasp of both the theory and the practical mechanics of electrical and electronic systems, microelectronics, silicon devices and nanotechnology.

Once you graduate, you'll find work in electronics companies, telecommunications of every kind, small systems houses, satellite businesses, and companies in finance – and the City will be keen on your expertise too. In fact, there are very few areas of the economy where your skills will not be useful.

## » Further information

### Institution of Engineering and Technology
Michael Faraday House
Stevenage, Herts SG1 2AY
t 01438 313311
↗ www.theiet.org

### Engineering and Technology Board
Second Floor, Weston House
246 High Holborn
London WC1v 7EX
t 020 7240 7333
↗ www.etechb.co.uk

### The British Computer Society
First Floor, Block D
North Star House, North Star Avenue
Swindon SN2 1FA
t 01793 417424
e bcshq@hq.bcs.org.uk
↗ www.bcs.org

## ↗ Online reading

**Circuit archive** www.ee.washington.edu/circuit_archive
**Engology** www.engology.com
**Helpengine** www.helpengine.org

## Electrical and electronic engineering

| | | Guardian score /100 | Satisfied with teaching % | Satisfied with feedback % | Spend per student /10 | Student:staff ratio | Job prospects % | Value added score /10 | Average entry tariff |
|---|---|---|---|---|---|---|---|---|---|
| 1 | Glasgow | 100.0 | 87 | 64 | 10 | 7.3 | 73 | 7 | 402 |
| 2 | Edinburgh | 97.0 | 91 | 48 | | 8.3 | 91 | 8 | 421 |
| 3 | Southampton | 95.5 | 84 | 63 | 8 | 11.5 | 93 | 7 | 467 |
| 4 | UCL | 94.9 | 72 | 56 | 10 | 7.5 | 79 | 8 | 426 |
| 5 | Imperial College | 93.3 | 87 | 52 | 10 | 14.3 | 82 | 6 | 474 |
| 6 | Surrey | 90.8 | 84 | 66 | 9 | 13.3 | 81 | 8 | 374 |
| 7 | Queen's, Belfast | 88.2 | 78 | 65 | 9 | 8.3 | 82 | 6 | 344 |
| 8 | York | 87.8 | 93 | 81 | 7 | 9.9 | 72 | 4 | 398 |
| 9 | Strathclyde | 87.6 | 67 | 55 | 8 | 7.8 | 85 | 7 | 416 |

| | | Guardian score /100 | Satisfied with teaching % | Satisfied with feedback % | Spend per student /10 | Student:staff ratio | Job prospects % | Value added score /10 | Average entry tariff |
|---|---|---|---|---|---|---|---|---|---|
| 10 | Bristol | 86.2 | 78 | 47 | 7 | 11.1 | 97 | 7 | 406 |
| 11 | Sheffield | 84.5 | 85 | 62 | 7 | 10.5 | 84 | 7 | 353 |
| 12 | Cardiff | 81.0 | 77 | 64 | 7 | 10.6 | 87 | 6 | 342 |
| 13 | Leeds | 77.6 | 72 | 52 | 9 | 10.7 | 76 | 5 | 367 |
| 14 | Nottingham | 77.0 | 76 | 54 | 8 | 12.0 | 85 | 4 | 362 |
| 15 | Loughborough | 76.5 | 88 | 66 | 7 | 16.2 | 95 | 3 | 335 |
| 16 | Birmingham | 75.8 | 77 | 61 | 9 | 13.4 | 86 | 3 | 331 |
| 16 | King's College London | 75.8 | 76 | 68 | 6 | 19.4 | 80 | 10 | 338 |
| 18 | Bath | 74.4 | 76 | 51 | 7 | 10.1 | 82 | 4 | 374 |
| 18 | Manchester | 74.4 | 75 | 47 | 9 | 10.7 | 80 | 3 | 358 |
| 20 | Portsmouth | 72.0 | 94 | 81 | 4 | 15.6 | 76 | 9 | 202 |
| 21 | Lancaster | 71.5 | 73 | 62 | 8 | 10.3 | 75 | 4 | 307 |
| 22 | Essex | 71.2 | 82 | 70 | 3 | 7.1 | | 5 | |
| 23 | Newcastle | 69.7 | 80 | 59 | 7 | 12.2 | 87 | 2 | 347 |
| 24 | Reading | 67.0 | 80 | 54 | 4 | 18.1 | 77 | 7 | 360 |
| 25 | Liverpool | 66.1 | 73 | 57 | 8 | 13.4 | 68 | 3 | 382 |
| 26 | Dundee | 65.8 | 88 | 70 | 5 | 12.4 | | 3 | 309 |
| 26 | UWE Bristol | 65.8 | 87 | 59 | 2 | 20.3 | 79 | 10 | 270 |
| 28 | Sussex | 64.5 | 70 | 63 | 5 | 17.1 | | 8 | |
| 29 | Robert Gordon | 63.9 | | | 6 | 18.2 | 81 | 4 | 334 |
| 30 | Brunel | 62.7 | 85 | 62 | 4 | 15.7 | 75 | 5 | 300 |
| 31 | Bangor | 62.6 | | | 5 | 10.6 | | 5 | 238 |
| 32 | Plymouth | 62.5 | 90 | 72 | 6 | 14.4 | 55 | 5 | 251 |
| 33 | Swansea | 61.5 | 76 | 55 | 5 | 11.6 | 74 | 5 | 253 |
| 34 | Staffordshire | 60.9 | 71 | 49 | 5 | 20.6 | | 10 | |
| 35 | Birmingham City | 60.6 | 66 | 56 | 5 | 12.3 | 66 | 7 | 242 |
| 36 | Heriot-Watt | 60.4 | 84 | 65 | 5 | 15.3 | 81 | 1 | 326 |
| 37 | Southampton Solent | 60.2 | 71 | 53 | 3 | 16.7 | | 9 | |
| 38 | Oxford Brookes | 60.1 | 78 | 45 | 4 | 11.7 | 57 | 9 | 243 |
| 39 | Northumbria | 59.1 | 82 | 61 | 4 | 16.5 | 72 | 6 | 242 |
| 40 | Queen Mary | 58.3 | 78 | 61 | 8 | 12.4 | 70 | 1 | 272 |
| 41 | Aston | 57.5 | 78 | 57 | 5 | | | 2 | 290 |
| 42 | Kent | 56.6 | 85 | 76 | 4 | 13.0 | | 2 | 267 |
| 43 | Coventry | 54.0 | 70 | 54 | 4 | 13.8 | | 6 | 233 |
| 44 | Bolton | 52.7 | 74 | 73 | 3 | 7.4 | | 2 | 227 |
| 45 | De Montfort | 52.3 | 74 | 60 | 5 | 11.0 | 47 | 4 | 232 |
| 46 | Greenwich | 51.1 | 88 | 74 | 3 | 24.1 | 65 | 8 | 189 |
| 47 | Sheffield Hallam | 51.0 | 80 | 65 | 3 | 17.4 | 59 | 8 | 190 |
| 48 | Ulster | 50.7 | 65 | 52 | 3 | 8.2 | | | 206 |
| 49 | Teesside | 50.3 | 80 | 75 | 6 | 19.5 | 54 | 4 | 238 |
| 50 | Salford | 50.1 | 80 | 56 | 3 | 24.6 | | 7 | 276 |
| 51 | Derby | 49.4 | 86 | 65 | 3 | 23.5 | 57 | 8 | 240 |
| 52 | Manchester Met | 47.4 | 67 | 65 | 4 | 15.3 | 58 | 7 | 200 |
| 53 | Glamorgan | 47.2 | 71 | 45 | 3 | 5.8 | 32 | 4 | 266 |
| 54 | Bradford | 46.5 | 68 | 49 | 4 | 19.8 | 69 | 5 | 271 |
| 55 | Ravensbourne College | 42.6 | 80 | 38 | 2 | 24.7 | 55 | 9 | 259 |
| 56 | Huddersfield | 42.1 | 75 | 51 | 3 | 22.3 | 48 | 7 | 262 |
| 57 | City | 41.6 | 68 | 56 | 3 | 17.5 | 60 | 4 | 207 |
| 58 | Glasgow Caledonian | 37.7 | 60 | 50 | 3 | 18.7 | 52 | 4 | 302 |
| 59 | Westminster | 33.7 | 72 | 61 | 2 | 16.2 | 49 | 3 | 183 |
| 60 | London South Bank | 33.3 | 64 | 49 | 2 | 16.0 | 29 | 8 | |
| 61 | Hertfordshire | 32.4 | 74 | 59 | 3 | 17.4 | 49 | 3 | 170 |

# Materials engineering

Materials engineering is increasing in popularity largely due to its non-traditional status and good industrial links. However, there are comparatively few universities offering the course as it remains a specialist interest area and is an expensive course to run. It's really at the junction of chemistry, physics, and engineering and parts of the course can often be hidden away in other degrees as it takes in such a wide, multi-disciplinary approach. It's all about what everything is made of — the properties of materials, how to make them lighter, stronger, more heat-resistant, and cheaper than before — spanning a huge range from metallurgy to textiles and working from the atomic level upwards. It's currently big on recycling.

## » Further information

**Materials Engineering (UK)**
Stephenson House
Railway Technical Centre
London Road, Derby DE24 8UP

t 01332 264452
e reception@meg.co.uk
↗ www.meg.co.uk

**Institute of Materials, Minerals and Mining**
1 Carlton House Terrace
London SW1Y 5DB

t 020 7451 7300
↗ www.iom3.org

## ↗ Online reading

**Engineering Talk** www.engineeringtalk.com
**Internet for materials engineering** www.vts.rdn.ac.uk/tutorial/materials
**The British Institute of Non-Destructive Testing** www.bindt.org

## Material and mineral engineering

| | | Guardian score /100 | Satisfied with teaching % | Satisfied with feedback % | Spend per student /10 | Student:staff ratio | Job prospects % | Value added score /10 | Average entry tariff |
|---|---|---|---|---|---|---|---|---|---|
| 1 | Oxford | 100.0 | 85 | 67 | 10 | 8.2 | | 6 | 509 |
| 2 | Imperial College | 75.7 | 91 | 64 | 6 | 12.2 | 77 | 3 | 431 |
| 3 | Exeter | 71.5 | 86 | 60 | 3 | 16.3 | 84 | 9 | 294 |
| 4 | Sheffield | 69.1 | 85 | 59 | 6 | 8.6 | 83 | 3 | 309 |
| 5 | Loughborough | 68.7 | 92 | 71 | 5 | 12.0 | 77 | 5 | 293 |
| 6 | Birmingham | 62.6 | 87 | 60 | 5 | 13.7 | 79 | 3 | 321 |
| 7 | Leeds | 62.1 | 75 | 47 | 9 | 9.7 | 68 | 3 | 361 |
| 8 | Manchester | 59.9 | 72 | 41 | 6 | 13.7 | 69 | 7 | 353 |
| 9 | Queen Mary | 57.3 | 84 | 73 | 6 | 16.8 | 65 | 5 | 285 |
| 10 | Swansea | 52.2 | 78 | 56 | 3 | 11.6 | | | 242 |
| 11 | Manchester Met | 46.5 | 72 | 57 | 2 | 23.0 | 68 | 10 | 284 |
| 12 | De Montfort | 31.7 | 73 | 57 | 2 | 28.2 | | 5 | 271 |

# Mechanical engineering

There's a range of courses for mechanical engineering, including pure mechanical as well as aeronautical, automotive, and manufacturing engineering. Whatever you choose, you'll be looking at many of the same basics, including solid mechanics, fluid dynamics, thermodynamics, design, materials, propulsion, electrical drives, control systems, computer modelling, and applied engineering, before specialising in a chosen area.

After graduating, you can work in areas such as the car, boat, construction, oil and gas, renewable energy resources, and biomedical industries, or you could move to areas where your expertise and transferable skills will come in handy – IT or the City, perhaps. Either way, the chances are that you won't be on the dole.

## ⟫ Further information

**Institute of Mechanical Engineers**
1 Birdcage Walk
London SW1H 9JJ

t 020 7222 7899
e membership@imeche.org.uk
↗ www.imeche.org

**The Royal Aeronautical Society**
4 Hamilton Place
London W1J 7BQ

t 020 7670 4300
e raes@aerosociety.com
↗ www.raes.org.uk

## ↗ Online reading

**The Society for Experimental Mechanics**  www.sem.org
**Icrank**  www.icrank.com
**The Royal Institution of Naval Architects**  www.rina.org.uk

## Mechanical engineering

| | | Guardian score /100 | Satisfied with teaching % | Satisfied with feedback % | Spend per student /10 | Student:staff ratio | Job prospects % | Value added score /10 | Average entry tariff |
|---|---|---|---|---|---|---|---|---|---|
| 1 | Southampton | 100.0 | 83 | 58 | 7 | 8.0 | 84 | 6 | 444 |
| 2 | Imperial College | 96.2 | 70 | 46 | 10 | 15.8 | 78 | 4 | 492 |
| 3 | Dundee | 94.1 | 88 | 70 | 8 | 9.9 | | | 312 |
| 4 | Sheffield | 93.9 | 82 | 50 | 8 | 16.6 | 94 | 6 | 384 |
| 5 | Bristol | 93.5 | 89 | 52 | 4 | 12.6 | 90 | 5 | 464 |
| 6 | Loughborough | 93.0 | 87 | 72 | 7 | 12.3 | 86 | 3 | 378 |
| 7 | Bath | 91.0 | 91 | 49 | 5 | 16.6 | 84 | 5 | 455 |
| 8 | Newcastle | 90.2 | 84 | 59 | 8 | 17.6 | 90 | 5 | 362 |
| 9 | Cardiff | 88.3 | 81 | 69 | 7 | 17.2 | 84 | 5 | 395 |
| 10 | Nottingham | 87.8 | 84 | 56 | 9 | 14.2 | 70 | 4 | 381 |
| 11 | Strathclyde | 87.5 | 77 | 54 | 5 | 15.6 | 81 | 7 | 420 |
| 12 | Sunderland | 87.4 | | | 8 | 12.0 | | 8 | 211 |
| 13 | Surrey | 86.3 | 86 | 77 | 4 | 18.3 | 87 | 5 | 337 |
| 14 | Lancaster | 85.8 | 77 | 55 | 9 | 10.3 | 85 | 2 | 333 |
| 14 | Leeds | 85.8 | 73 | 46 | 10 | 16.7 | 76 | 6 | 351 |
| 16 | Brunel | 85.6 | 66 | 58 | 5 | 13.9 | 82 | 8 | 359 |

| | | Guardian score /100 | Satisfied with teaching % | Satisfied with feedback % | Spend per student /10 | Student:staff ratio | Job prospects % | Value added score /10 | Average entry tariff |
|---|---|---|---|---|---|---|---|---|---|
| 17 | Edinburgh | 84.7 | 67 | 33 | 8 | 20.0 | 88 | 7 | 414 |
| 18 | UWE Bristol | 83.9 | 75 | 55 | 3 | 13.6 | 75 | 10 | 264 |
| 19 | Plymouth | 81.9 | 88 | 62 | 8 | 12.6 | 60 | 7 | 248 |
| 20 | Kingston | 81.7 | 75 | 59 | 9 | 16.6 | 55 | 9 | 235 |
| 21 | Birmingham | 80.9 | 61 | 47 | 8 | 17.2 | 74 | 7 | 351 |
| 22 | Swansea | 80.2 | 79 | 56 | 6 | 11.6 | 79 | 3 | 306 |
| 23 | Sussex | 79.8 | 72 | 65 | 5 | 17.1 | 70 | 7 | 351 |
| 24 | Queen's, Belfast | 79.7 | 73 | 56 | 5 | 13.8 | 80 | 4 | 360 |
| 25 | Birmingham City | 78.9 | 68 | 57 | 6 | 12.3 | | 8 | 209 |
| 26 | UCL | 78.3 | 68 | 44 | 8 | 13.3 | 68 | 3 | 419 |
| 27 | Glasgow | 77.1 | 78 | 46 | 7 | 15.0 | 67 | 3 | 381 |
| 28 | King's College London | 77.0 | 89 | 61 | 5 | 13.2 | 68 | 2 | 348 |
| 28 | Robert Gordon | 77.0 | | | 8 | 17.2 | 92 | 1 | 322 |
| 30 | Queen Mary | 76.4 | 83 | 68 | 6 | 15.9 | 60 | 4 | 301 |
| 31 | Salford | 76.0 | 68 | 49 | 4 | 14.5 | 64 | 9 | 288 |
| 32 | Heriot-Watt | 75.8 | 74 | 41 | 7 | 11.3 | 76 | 1 | 350 |
| 33 | Portsmouth | 74.0 | 79 | 69 | 5 | 21.0 | 74 | 7 | 224 |
| 34 | Manchester | 73.2 | 66 | 31 | 9 | 21.6 | 70 | 3 | 411 |
| 35 | Manchester Met | 72.4 | 85 | 73 | 3 | 20.1 | 72 | 7 | 258 |
| 36 | Aston | 71.9 | 78 | 47 | 3 | 15.9 | 76 | 4 | 307 |
| 36 | Liverpool | 71.9 | 74 | 51 | 4 | 18.7 | 72 | 4 | 367 |
| 38 | Bradford | 71.7 | 75 | 57 | 4 | 16.0 | 64 | 8 | 227 |
| 39 | Coventry | 70.1 | 72 | 59 | 4 | 22.7 | 65 | 9 | 296 |
| 40 | Northumbria | 68.4 | 87 | 62 | 2 | | 86 | 3 | 277 |
| 41 | Hertfordshire | 67.3 | 81 | 59 | 3 | 19.9 | 65 | 7 | 238 |
| 42 | Huddersfield | 66.9 | 73 | 61 | 2 | 20.5 | 76 | 6 | 247 |
| 43 | Northampton | 66.4 | | | 3 | 18.4 | 53 | 9 | 248 |
| 43 | Oxford Brookes | 66.4 | 86 | 49 | 4 | 29.1 | 70 | 8 | 266 |
| 45 | Staffordshire | 66.3 | 71 | 49 | 4 | 12.9 | 59 | 5 | 249 |
| 46 | City | 64.7 | 78 | 62 | 6 | 19.8 | 57 | 5 | 226 |
| 47 | Sheffield Hallam | 62.5 | 76 | 58 | 3 | 27.4 | 72 | 9 | 200 |
| 48 | Derby | 60.8 | 85 | 66 | 3 | 15.9 | 41 | 4 | |
| 49 | Bolton | 56.9 | 90 | 70 | 2 | 24.4 | | 3 | |
| 50 | Glamorgan | 56.3 | 62 | 50 | 3 | 17.3 | | 3 | 241 |
| 51 | Greenwich | 56.0 | 69 | 64 | 3 | 24.1 | | 6 | 164 |
| 52 | Ulster | 55.6 | 68 | 57 | 3 | 20.2 | 71 | 2 | 212 |
| 53 | Southampton Solent | 41.1 | 63 | 47 | 4 | 31.7 | 57 | 2 | 247 |
| 54 | London South Bank | 38.2 | 60 | 49 | 1 | 23.6 | 49 | 5 | 183 |

# Humanities

## American studies

❝ American studies is the ideal interdisciplinary arts degree that allows students to continue their studies in history and English literature while adding courses in politics and film studies. The focus on America (normally the USA alone, but sometimes also Canada, and in one or two places Latin America and the Caribbean as well) gives an intellectual coherence to the degree. America has been, and remains, the dominant cultural, economic, and military influence in the world, and an American studies degree allows students to learn how this hegemony arose and why it has persisted so long. Many American studies degree programmes in the UK have study abroad opportunities that give students the chance to live in the USA for a year and really immerse themselves in the culture. An American studies degree is one of the few that leaves all career paths open, from the normal 'milk-round' jobs, to those which make specific use of the expertise in American culture that graduates should have.

**Dr Tim Lockley**, *Associate Professor, Department of History and School of Comparative American Studies, University of Warwick*

If you want to understand the nature of the modern world then there is no better way of doing it than to understand the diversity of the country that put a man on the moon, went to war with Britain, Spain, Japan, and Vietnam at various points in its history and still managed to invent jazz, fast food, and bourbon. If you are fascinated by America it makes sense to study it seriously at undergraduate level. While bits of Americana will be included on other courses – you can hardly avoid it if you're studying modern literature, politics or history, for example – you can also get stuck into America's contribution to all those areas and much else besides on an American studies course. What's included under that title varies a good deal, so take a look at the prospectus and find out as much as you can before committing yourself.

American studies is the very definition of a multidisciplinary course, giving you the chance to study literature, history, and politics, film and cultural studies with, possibly, some travel thrown in. It is also interdisciplinary in the way that it asks you to make connections across subjects and to use the knowledge picked up in the study of history, say, to make sense of the literature you will be asked to read. Typically, you might start with an introduction to the literature, politics, and history of the US before specialising in particular periods or areas of interest. Some universities allow greater scope for the study of contemporary culture through areas such as film studies, popular music or visual arts, while others are more akin to a traditional arts course.

Don't go thinking it's a softer option compared to other humanities courses – you're going to have a range of different areas to get to grips with. It is, however, a useful degree course to keep your options open. Employment prospects are good: as with any arts degree, graduates can try their hands at marketing, advertising or the media. You'll be good on analysis and presentation, and will impress employers with your ability to make connections across subjects instead of having tunnel vision in one specialist area.

Entry requirements tend to be pretty flexible, although humanities A-levels are an advantage. Assessment can be exam- or coursework-based.

Choosing a university can be difficult. The multidisciplinary nature of the course means you'll be conducting a virtual health check of the whole of the humanities side of your universities, since you'll be studying with different departments within it. One lame duck of a department in a discipline important to you could really let you down.

Courses last three or four years. It is possible to spend a year, a semester or no time at all on the other side of the Atlantic: consider how much time you would like to and can afford to spend abroad. And if you are going to hop the pond, remember British universities work in collaboration with different American institutions: if you have a burning desire to soak up the LA sunshine or see politics in action at Washington, then remember when filling out your Ucas form that you are in effect choosing two universities rather than one. And try to find out about the level of support offered while you're away. You don't want to feel isolated while you're out there.

American studies tends to mean the United States of, rather than the continents of North and South America, but many universities now offer options to study and live in Canada or Latin America and at least one university has merged its American and Latin American studies department, so it's worth investigating if you don't want to be confined to the US.

---

66 American studies is a very diverse subject, incorporating the study of literature, history, film, and the culture and politics of one of the most fascinating countries in the world. My academic advisors show a real passion for their work. Their enthusiasm has helped me develop my scholarly skills, whilst the opportunity to study abroad proved to be an intriguing life experience.

**Nicola Turek**, *American studies student, University of Manchester*

---

## Online reading

**The British Association of American Studies**  www.baas.ac.uk
**49th Parallel**  www.49thparallel.bham.ac.uk
**American Memory**  www.memory.loc.gov/ammem/amhome.html
**ARNet**  www.americansc.org.uk
**New York Times**  www.nytimes.com
**Washington Post**  www.washingtonpost.com
**The Center for the Study of the Presidency**  www.thepresidency.org
**Smithsonian Institution**  www.si.edu

# American studies

| | | Guardian score /100 | Satisfied with teaching % | Satisfied with feedback % | Spend per student /10 | Student:staff ratio | Job prospects % | Value added score /10 | Average entry tariff |
|---|---|---|---|---|---|---|---|---|---|
| 1 | Warwick | 100.0 | 99 | 87 | 9 | 13.5 | | 8 | 445 |
| 2 | Manchester | 76.2 | 86 | 58 | 9 | 14.0 | 63 | 7 | 359 |
| 3 | Liverpool | 76.0 | 95 | 73 | 8 | 17.4 | 49 | 10 | 344 |
| 4 | UEA | 74.0 | 99 | 81 | 7 | 19.4 | 62 | 7 | 367 |
| 5 | Lancaster | 73.1 | 91 | 66 | 8 | 15.4 | | 8 | 346 |
| 6 | King's College London | 70.5 | 87 | 48 | 9 | 13.5 | 56 | 3 | 383 |
| 7 | Sussex | 70.0 | 93 | 76 | 4 | 19.0 | 71 | 8 | 382 |
| 8 | Birmingham | 64.5 | 82 | 62 | 9 | 17.4 | 44 | 6 | 378 |
| 9 | Nottingham | 61.3 | 90 | 59 | 5 | 19.8 | 66 | 6 | 366 |
| 10 | Essex | 61.1 | 90 | 68 | 5 | 14.8 | 56 | 6 | 277 |
| 11 | Hull | 60.6 | 97 | 90 | 3 | 16.9 | 62 | 4 | 267 |
| 12 | Dundee | 60.3 | 94 | 86 | 6 | 17.2 | 30 | 7 | 322 |
| 13 | Leicester | 58.4 | 92 | 78 | 4 | 19.0 | 69 | 2 | 322 |
| 14 | Keele | 53.6 | 94 | 76 | 3 | 20.6 | 52 | 6 | 318 |
| 15 | Plymouth | 51.8 | 99 | 76 | 3 | 20.8 | | 8 | 228 |
| 16 | Kent | 50.2 | 93 | 77 | 4 | 17.4 | | 3 | 269 |
| 17 | Canterbury Christ Church | 40.4 | 83 | 67 | 4 | 19.5 | 38 | 6 | 224 |
| 18 | Swansea | 37.7 | 91 | 52 | 3 | 21.6 | 38 | 3 | 283 |
| 19 | Portsmouth | 36.6 | 93 | 73 | 4 | 25.8 | 50 | 1 | 285 |
| 20 | Winchester | 34.2 | 94 | 70 | 2 | 19.3 | 26 | 3 | 248 |
| 21 | Lincoln | 29.6 | 84 | 73 | 3 | 24.0 | | | 226 |

# Anthropology

Many people think of anthropology as the study of 'other cultures'. Travelling abroad to a foreign society — to Bali, Sri Lanka, Cameroon, Thailand — is frequently a stimulus for students to decide to study the subject, to make sense of their experiences of the 'differences'. But just as importantly, through a comparative approach, it also helps you to see your own society with fresh eyes. Anthropology is a profoundly liberating subject: things that always seemed natural and inevitable turn out to be just one among many ways of doing things, helping you realise that things can be different.

Because anthropology is 'the study of humankind' [from the Greek *anthropos* ('human')], the world is your oyster. Anthropologists learn about cultures and societies across the world and the ways in which they are increasingly connected through global processes, though they may go on to develop expertise about a specific region (say, South Asia, Europe, or Latin America). It's also a broad church. Anthropologists study pretty much anything that human beings do and create: from making music and art to making a living, from healing to migrating to creating virtual worlds on the internet, from making war to working for peace, environmental sustainability, and human rights. What makes anthropology distinctive is that it considers each of these in context, in relation to other areas of people's lives — that is, holistically.

While anthropology opens you to the diverse range of human experience and challenges your prejudices, it also gives you tools to evaluate cultural and social practices critically. For instance, identifying the power relations that underlie them. More than anything, anthropology is a way of seeing, rather than particular subject matter. It can be used to examine and understand any social setting, but at the same time, can help us all to imagine alternative approaches to the complex problems we now face.

**Jane K Cowan**, *Professor of Social Anthropology, Department of Anthropology, University of Sussex*

---

Do you prefer bones or beliefs? There are few subjects that can offer you specialisms as far apart as the evolution of human beings and the big contemporary issues, such as how universal human rights fit into a multicultural world. But, somehow, anthropology manages it.

There's no aspect of human life that is not touched on by the subject to some degree: you'll cover language, physiology, art, and the way we (or others) organise our societies. You'll start by studying all these different areas before moving on to specialise, usually in one of two areas: social and cultural anthropology or biological anthropology (which is based more in science than in social science). Social and cultural anthropology (related to sociology in many ways) looks at the organisation of societies and their politics, economics and religions, and tries to place those in context.

Biological anthropologists, on the other hand, start from the evolution of mankind and the human race's differing genetics and concern themselves with physical differences between people: skin, blood groups, the shape of the head and so on, and therefore draw on a different range of disciplines — including anatomy, physiology, and biochemistry.

Some courses do lump the two together, but you're more likely to specialise in one side of the subject — so think hard before applying. You'll start by learning the basic theories that cover the mechanics of human societies, before moving on to specialisations, such as moral and ritual systems, kinship, or ethnography. You'll also be expected to do a certain amount of fieldwork, usually as part of your own research project, and often out of term-time. At some places the fieldwork can last a week, at others it can be 20 weeks. Find out what the options are and how much assistance you'll be given.

Those projects can play an important part in the assessment process, otherwise it's a case of large amounts of continuous assessment (often in the newer universities) or the traditional end-of-year exams (the older institutions).

Given its close ties with other social sciences courses, you'd do well to check the relative health of those departments. Where the teaching and facilities cross over, a healthy "partner" department can indicate the health of the one you're entering.

Look at who will be teaching you and what their specialisations are: if you're taught by someone at the leading edge of research, you'll feel right on top of the game. When you make your trip to the open day, try to ask whether that heroic figure you long to learn from will actually have time to be teaching.

Once you've graduated, there are many careers outside academe in which you can use your anthropological knowledge and skills – marketing, international development, consultancy, business, healthcare, law, local government, and the media.

Anthropologists' professional organisations help to keep close contacts between the university world and working anthropologists, and offer training at different stages of your career.

---

66 Anthropology, broadly speaking, is the study of humans, and I've found the course to be a varied and challenging degree programme. From economic and political organisation, nutrition and health, evolution and religion, it provides an exciting view of the world's diverse populations. I have particularly enjoyed studying the new directions anthropology is taking, linking insights into human behaviour with success in the business world. Hence, anthropology provides a fantastic opportunity to explore the world through many eyes.

**Krystyna Lesniak**, *third-year anthropology student, Durham University*

---

## 》 Further information

**The Royal Anthropological Institute**

50 Fitzroy Street
London W1T 5BT

t   020 7387 0455
e   admin@therai.org.uk
↗  www.therai.org.uk

## Online reading

**Anthropology matters** www.anthropologymatters.com

**The American Anthropological Association**  www.aaanet.org

**American Association of Physical Anthropologists**  www.physanth.org

**Intute: Social Science**  www.intute.ac.uk/socialsciences

**Anthrobase**  www.anthrobase.com

**Experience Rich Anthropology**  www.era.anthropology.ac.uk

**Max Planck Institute for Social Anthropology**  www.eth.mpg.de

**Internet Anthropologist**  www.vts.rdn.ac.uk/tutorial/anthroplogist

# Anthropology

| | | Guardian score /100 | Satisfied with teaching % | Satisfied with feedback % | Spend per student /10 | Student-staff ratio | Job prospects % | Value added score /10 | Average entry tariff |
|---|---|---|---|---|---|---|---|---|---|
| 1 | Oxford | 100.0 | 95 | 59 | | 10.8 | | 7 | 509 |
| 2 | Cambridge | 96.3 | 99 | 78 | 10 | 15.5 | 73 | 3 | 504 |
| 3 | SOAS | 87.3 | 98 | 70 | 7 | 14.1 | | 8 | 393 |
| 4 | UCL | 83.6 | 95 | 55 | 9 | 20.1 | 63 | 8 | 435 |
| 5 | London School of Economics | 81.9 | 78 | 49 | 7 | 13.0 | 77 | 4 | 428 |
| 6 | Edinburgh | 78.0 | 82 | 37 | 9 | 14.2 | 50 | 7 | 438 |
| 7 | St Andrews | 77.9 | 95 | 86 | 6 | 17.2 | | 5 | 422 |
| 8 | Goldsmiths | 76.2 | 93 | 68 | 3 | 14.3 | | 10 | 311 |
| 9 | Glasgow | 69.2 | 93 | 68 | 4 | 15.6 | | 5 | 405 |
| 10 | Kent | 68.8 | 98 | 79 | 4 | 16.7 | 52 | 6 | 325 |
| 11 | Durham | 66.5 | 93 | 63 | 5 | 17.9 | 63 | 3 | 383 |
| 12 | Sussex | 66.2 | 94 | 61 | 3 | 19.6 | 58 | 8 | 366 |
| 13 | Manchester | 54.1 | 88 | 30 | 6 | 19.7 | 42 | 4 | 390 |
| 14 | Queen's, Belfast | 52.8 | 87 | 68 | 4 | 18.1 | 42 | 4 | 334 |
| 15 | Aberdeen | 51.4 | 94 | 80 | 3 | 23.3 | | | 314 |
| 16 | Brunel | 46.2 | 83 | 63 | 3 | 20.9 | | | 309 |
| 17 | Oxford Brookes | 45.0 | 85 | 63 | 4 | 19.7 | | 2 | 279 |
| 18 | Roehampton | 34.3 | 82 | 63 | 3 | 23.5 | 51 | 2 | 236 |

# Archaeology

> Archaeology is much more than just fun in the mud! Imagine turning over in your hand a chipped stone axe made 80,000 years ago, or scraping the dirt away from ancient foundations, whether in Egyptian sun or British drizzle. Think about walking across landscapes from the Neolithic to 18th-century gardens, or clambering through the attics of a half-timbered Tudor house.
>
> Archaeology is about understanding human beings over a timespan of many thousands of years, of reconstructing past ways of life from the bones, pots, and metal left behind. It's about the big questions – why humans evolved, why gatherers and hunters settled down to agriculture, the origins of the great civilisations, and of the modern world.
>
> Archaeology can also be political. Entire nations, like Zimbabwe, have named themselves after archaeological sites; the Nazis excavated 'Aryan' sites in eastern Europe. Even simply visiting the Acropolis or Stonehenge tells us about who we think we are. Archaeology students don't just study stones and bones, they think critically about the way the past is used today for political and cultural ends.
>
> On courses like ours, students get to work on projects around the world, from the Caribbean to Hampshire to Egypt. Back on campus, as well as essays and individual and group projects (for example, museum and heritage displays), students handle, draw and classify materials ranging from human and animal bones to Stone Age hand-axes to Roman pottery.
>
> In addition to being highly literate and numerate, archaeologists know all about teamwork – a skill you learn to value when you need to finish digging and recording a trench with three hours to go before the developers' bulldozers move in. But most importantly, students acquire a passion for understanding the material world around them, skills which serve them well regardless of whether they go on to be professional archaeologists. The excitement and relevance of archaeology to the modern world is one of its best-kept secrets.

**Professor Matthew Johnson**, *Professor of Archaeology, University of Southampton*

---

Archaeology is the study of the human past from its physical remains. It's a combination of the heady fresh air and excitement of an excavation and the forensic attention to detail needed to piece together the evidence uncovered. Put broadly, it is the study of human artefacts and remains, in an attempt to see how humans originated, spread across the world, developed tools and technology, and lived and died over the past few million years.

As a subject, it remains highly popular, and it's significant that there are a relatively large number of mature students on archaeology degrees – many opt out of work to study it. But if you're still not sure whether it's for you, try your local museum, which will doubtless be delighted to help you find a short course or dig nearby to give you the chance to see if it's what you want.

After graduation, many find archaeology to be a tough profession – researchers are sometimes desk- and usually budget-bound, while poorly paid field archaeologists are often engaged on high-pressure, short-term developer-funded rescue excavations – the quick dig before the car-park people move in.

Saying that, the employment prospects are pretty good, although students don't by all means end up still working in the profession. Archaeological careers can land you in academia, in a museum, in some form of landscape management, or in work as a consultant.

Consider too the more glamorous (thanks to CSI and the like) world of forensic archaeology – working for the police or for human rights organisations, trying to piece together incidents of murder or genocide. The chances are, though, that you'll end up outside the field (as it were) working in the civil service, banking, the media – anywhere where there is a need for critical and analytical thinking in areas both scientific and human.

Most courses include the opportunity to develop excavation skills, but the approaches vary, from degrees based in the theoretical and documentary to those specialising in particular periods or geographical areas. Most courses offer a range of choices, and students have to take a number of options, including general (that is, theory and methods) and specific (such as human remains or Far Eastern). As ever, check the modules available to see if they cover the areas you are interested in. If you have an interest in languages, you might consider a joint honours degree – someone's got to make sense of all those inscriptions. And check too that the balance between classroom theory and actual digging is how you'd prefer.

While this country's rich historical heritage makes it an excellent place to study the subject, many are keen – for understandable reasons – to travel abroad. Many digs are in remote and fascinating places, so ask about the possibilities of joining an excavation or research programme abroad if you're interested in this.

But for most of your degree, you'll more than likely be in the UK, so check out the city you'll be studying in as well as the institution. See what libraries and museums are around to help broaden your study, and even what local sites of importance there are if you want to go that extra yard.

Investigate whether the institution has a field unit or centre for applied archaeology. Not only is this good for facilitating field trips, it's also handy for consultancy work, from which students might make contacts for a future career.

---

❝ A BSc in archaeology really lets you get to the heart of the subject. You learn how to investigate fundamental questions that can only be answered using science: who, how, why, where and when, I certainly found it a worthwhile degree and now enjoy putting what I learned into practice in my job.

**Lyn Wilson**, *an archaeology graduate from the University of Glasgow, is now a conservation scientist with Historic Scotland*

---

## ≫ Further information

| **The Subject Committee for Archaeology** | |
|---|---|
| | ↗ www.universityarchaeology.org.uk |

| **Council for British Archaeology** | |
|---|---|
| St Mary's House, 66 Bootham | t 01904 671417 |
| York YO30 7BZ | e info@britarch.ac.uk |
| | ↗ www.britarch.ac.uk |

| **Institute of Field Archaeologists** | |
|---|---|
| SHES, University of Reading | t 0118 378 6446 |
| Whiteknights, PO Box 227 | e admin@archaeologists.net |
| Reading RG6 6AB | ↗ www.archaeologists.net |

**English Heritage**
PO Box 569
Swindon SN2 2YP

**t** 0870 333 1182
**e** customers@english-heritage.org.uk
↗ www.english-heritage.org.uk

**The Association of Archaeological Illustrators & Surveyors**
SHES, University of Reading
Whiteknights, PO Box 227
Reading RG6 6AB

**e** admin@aais.org.uk
↗ www.aais.org.uk

↗ Online reading

**The Society of Museum Archaeologists** www.socmusarch.org.uk
**Internet archaeology** www.intarch.ac.uk
**European Association of Archaeologists** www.e-a-a.org
**Archaeology** www.archaeology.org
**Archaeologica** www.archaeologica.org
**The Archaeology Channel** www.archaeologychannel.org
**The Ashmolean Museum** www.ashmolean.org
**Current Archaeology** www.archaeology.co.uk
**Time Team** www.channel4.com/history/timeteam

# Archaeology

| | | Guardian score /100 | Satisfied with teaching % | Satisfied with feedback % | Spend per student /10 | Student:staff ratio | Job prospects % | Value added score /10 | Average entry tariff |
|---|---|---|---|---|---|---|---|---|---|
| 1 | Cambridge | 100.0 | 99 | 78 | 9 | 7.7 | | 5 | 504 |
| 2 | UCL | 96.0 | 94 | 82 | 10 | 7.4 | 47 | 10 | 387 |
| 3 | Oxford | 90.9 | 95 | 61 | 10 | 13.2 | | 8 | 468 |
| 4 | Durham | 84.6 | 97 | 71 | 5 | 9.1 | 84 | 5 | 408 |
| 5 | York | 78.5 | 98 | 85 | 5 | 13.9 | 60 | 9 | 386 |
| 6 | Sheffield | 77.3 | 97 | 82 | 5 | 11.4 | 73 | 6 | 374 |
| 7 | Glasgow | 72.6 | 96 | 79 | 7 | 8.4 | 64 | 4 | 340 |
| 8 | Exeter | 67.1 | 95 | 86 | 4 | 13.3 | 60 | 5 | 355 |
| 9 | Nottingham | 65.2 | 93 | 63 | 6 | 12.5 | 60 | 7 | 337 |
| 10 | Reading | 62.0 | 96 | 77 | 2 | 10.5 | 62 | 7 | 302 |
| 11 | Queen's, Belfast | 61.4 | 90 | 68 | 8 | 12.2 | 62 | 3 | 289 |
| 12 | Leicester | 56.7 | 91 | 73 | 5 | 15.7 | 57 | 5 | 347 |
| 13 | Bournemouth | 55.7 | 87 | 64 | | 9.2 | 52 | 4 | 247 |
| 14 | Kent | 55.0 | 91 | 71 | 3 | 14.1 | | 8 | 296 |
| 15 | Newcastle | 54.4 | 88 | 60 | 3 | 11.6 | 46 | 8 | 334 |
| 16 | Southampton | 53.4 | 90 | 74 | 4 | 10.8 | 48 | 5 | 321 |
| 17 | Bristol | 53.2 | 89 | 46 | 5 | 20.9 | 53 | 9 | 396 |
| 18 | Cardiff | 50.8 | 94 | 68 | 5 | 11.0 | 51 | 2 | 335 |
| 19 | Liverpool | 49.8 | 89 | 64 | 5 | 11.0 | 47 | 4 | 341 |
| 20 | Edinburgh | 49.5 | 88 | 55 | 6 | 19.6 | 45 | 7 | 412 |
| 21 | Birmingham | 48.5 | 85 | 60 | 4 | 11.7 | 47 | 5 | 364 |
| 22 | Bradford | 46.8 | 83 | 52 | 6 | 10.6 | 61 | 3 | 261 |
| 23 | Lampeter | 35.5 | | | 3 | 8.4 | 45 | 2 | 260 |
| 24 | Chester | 34.4 | 84 | 76 | 2 | | 53 | 3 | 237 |
| 25 | Lincoln | 33.7 | 89 | 57 | 4 | 20.8 | 63 | 1 | 284 |
| 26 | Manchester | 32.4 | 95 | 62 | 3 | 25.8 | 49 | 4 | 318 |
| 27 | Winchester | 29.4 | 88 | 58 | 3 | 16.1 | 32 | 9 | 203 |

# Classics

> Classics is the study of ancient Greece and Rome in its broadest sense: language, literature, history, philosophy, art, and archaeology. Athens and Italy are just part of the picture: classics covers the Black Sea, North Africa, Spain, Roman Britain. It is about where we have come from and who we are today. Ever wondered why Washington has a capitol and a senate? Where democracy comes from, or our ideas about law, beauty, justice? The answer is the classical world.
>
> At Cambridge, we think it important for every classics student to learn Latin and Greek. English translations are a wonderful introduction to the classical past but do not provide the same degree of direct engagement. While it is obviously helpful to start these languages early, a large number of our students are studying one or both of them from scratch.
>
> But language is the tip of the iceberg. Few degrees offer the opportunity of acquiring language skills alongside such a wide range of other expertise from essay-writing to critical thinking, from visual analysis to digging. No wonder that classicists are amongst the most employable graduates, and in fields that you might not expect — accountancy, the civil service, law, journalism, banking, media. If you enjoy Plato's Republic, Peterson's Troy, or Shakespeare's Antony and Cleopatra, visiting museums and art galleries or Hadrian's Wall, classics will help you work out why. If you want a truly interdisciplinary experience with plenty of excuses to travel, then classics is the course for you.
>
> **Dr Caroline Vout**, *Senior Lecturer, Faculty of Classics, Fellow of Christ's College, University of Cambridge*

When picking your subject, it's crucial to choose one you'll enjoy studying and will enhance your employment prospects later on. While classics can seem like a determinedly obscure approach — the dry, dusty path that leads on to a career in academia — this is far from the case.

The course — loosely defined as the study of ancient civilisations — combines a variety of disciplines, including language (particularly Latin and ancient Greek), literature, philosophy, art, history, and archaeology. It's about the interlinking of all these aspects in a particular historical context, making the connections between them and thereby developing a variety of analytical skills (which are always appreciated by employers). What's more, your study may not be based exclusively in the ancient world — you can also study how the classical world has been represented in later media.

So a classics degree equips you for far more than simply teaching or academia. Graduates go into law, accountancy, public relations, and many other careers not associated with Cicero and his chums.

There's a huge range of options available to you in a classics department, and as study is often through translation you don't have to have a private school background. There is now less emphasis on the study of languages in university classics departments because Latin and Greek are not generally offered in state schools.

As with any subject, it's worth asking some rigorous questions about what you want from your degree. You could take straight classics, which means a degree with particular focus on the study of Greek and Latin languages. Or you could take classical studies/civilisation or an ancient history course and study through translation, though studying at least some Greek and/or Latin may, however, be a compulsory part of a classical studies/civilisation and ancient history degree in some institutions. If you feel that language study is not your strength, then you need to bear this in mind – it would be beneficial to do some language work if you are aiming to undertake postgraduate work or become a teacher.

There may also be opportunities to travel abroad. The chance to study the classics in Italy or Greece is a valuable one, and if you're combining the course with archaeology, it could offer fascinating possibilities. Pay attention to the wider institution and the city you will be studying in. The older universities tend to have classics as part of their very fabric and so will have the libraries and teaching to match. And investigate the wider city for galleries and museums.

The opportunity to look at genuine artefacts from the period you're studying can make the subject more worthwhile and also offers the possibility of work placements if you fancy curatorial work. Try to get a feel for how the subject is regarded by the institution. Check out the number of teaching staff, their specialisations and the facilities. If you're interviewed in a shed at the back, it could be time to look elsewhere.

---

**❝** Classics is a fabulous degree – it involves a bit of language, history, art, philosophy and even some science. Moreover, you can direct which area you would like to study more. It might be old, but it is never boring. If you study classics, chances are that you'll be in a small, welcoming department. By the end of your degree, going to the library is like going to see your family – and you get the chance to read anything from Homer's mighty epics to Ausonius' "inappropriate" cento poems whilst you are there.

**Joe Taylor**, *fourth-year classics student, University of St Andrews*

---

## 》 Further information

**The Classical Association**
Senate House, Malet Street
London WC1E 7HU

t   020 7862 8706
e   office@classicalassociation.org
↗  www.classicalassociation.org

**The Society for the Promotion of Roman Studies**
Senate House, Malet Street
London WC1E 7HU

t   020 7862 8727
e   office@romansociety.org
↗  www.romansociety.org

**The Society for the Promotion of Hellenic Studies**
Senate House, Malet Street
London WC1E 7HU

t   020 7862 8730
e   office@hellenicsociety.org.uk
↗  www.hellenicsociety.org

## ↗ Online reading

**Classics Web**  www.classics.ac.uk
**The British Epigraphy Society**  www.csad.ox.ac.uk/BES
**The Perseus Digital Library**  www.perseus.tufts.edu
**The Classical Pages**  www.classicspage.com
**Vroma**  www.vroma.org

# Classics

| | | Guardian score /100 | Satisfied with teaching % | Satisfied with feedback % | Spend per student /10 | Student:staff ratio | Job prospects % | Value added score /10 | Average entry tariff |
|---|---|---|---|---|---|---|---|---|---|
| 1 | Oxford | 100.0 | 97 | 76 | 10 | 13.9 | 79 | 6 | 520 |
| 2 | Cambridge | 98.4 | 94 | 78 | 9 | 13.2 | 83 | 7 | 512 |
| 3 | St Andrews | 88.7 | 94 | 81 | 5 | 13.4 | | 9 | 479 |
| 4 | UCL | 84.3 | 84 | 71 | 9 | 9.6 | 67 | 4 | 460 |
| 5 | King's College London | 82.3 | 94 | 82 | 6 | 11.8 | 68 | 6 | 411 |
| 6 | Durham | 77.3 | 94 | 73 | 3 | 15.4 | 76 | 7 | 460 |
| 7 | Warwick | 73.9 | 92 | 69 | 7 | 13.5 | 56 | 5 | 430 |
| 8 | Edinburgh | 71.0 | 90 | 52 | 8 | 15.3 | 56 | 6 | 433 |
| 9 | Glasgow | 69.0 | 96 | 86 | 6 | 15.6 | 51 | 3 | 421 |
| 10 | Exeter | 68.8 | 96 | 73 | 3 | 13.0 | 58 | 4 | 392 |
| 11 | Royal Holloway | 65.8 | 96 | 83 | 4 | 15.3 | 48 | 7 | 350 |
| 12 | Bristol | 65.4 | 83 | 60 | 4 | 18.3 | 79 | 4 | 438 |
| 13 | Manchester | 63.7 | 95 | 68 | 7 | 14.0 | 45 | 3 | 398 |
| 14 | Leeds | 62.1 | 86 | 75 | 4 | 18.1 | 64 | 6 | 352 |
| 15 | Roehampton | 59.9 | 85 | 71 | 3 | 15.7 | | 10 | 239 |
| 16 | Birmingham | 59.3 | 92 | 73 | 7 | 17.4 | 46 | 3 | 358 |
| 17 | Liverpool | 58.2 | 86 | 66 | 6 | 17.4 | | | 338 |
| 18 | Kent | 56.3 | 90 | 66 | 3 | 17.4 | 44 | 8 | 304 |
| 19 | Reading | 55.7 | 89 | 60 | 3 | 18.2 | | 6 | 314 |
| 20 | Nottingham | 54.0 | 85 | 62 | 3 | 19.8 | 55 | 5 | 387 |
| 21 | Newcastle | 52.8 | 84 | 55 | 3 | 24.1 | 53 | 8 | 397 |
| 22 | Swansea | 34.3 | 89 | 74 | 3 | 21.6 | | 1 | 309 |

# English

" For many sixth-formers and college students, undergraduates, and even academics with decades of teaching and research behind them, English literature is the dream subject. It offers intimate access to the experiences, imaginations, and laughter of people who have lived in many parts of the world, over many centuries.

It is always familiar: your favourite poems, novels, short stories, and plays are always at hand to let you into their special worlds. It is always new: the questions you ask can lead you to an unending series of exciting texts and topics, including children's literature, Beowulf, letters, travel books and Gothic in many varieties. Even your old favourites are never quite the same the next time you read them.

Search out programmes that give you some grounding in every period from the Middle Ages to the present day, but also offer you flexibility: it is a principle in the department where I teach that every student who is passionate about a specific topic in English literature should have the opportunity to study it. Small group teaching and essay tutorials are also very helpful. Since no essay is expected to be exactly like any other, all essays require a lot of individual attention.

You will find yourself encouraged to explore beyond the range of the printed page in many fascinating directions: drama studies may take a practical turn, for those with an interest in theatre. Many programmes offer you the chance to enhance your own creative skills, perhaps with a career in the media in mind. What you get out of English literature is very much a reflection of your energy: employers will appreciate your ability to process written data, weigh up evidence, think independently, and put your ideas across, in speech and writing. You will appreciate a lifelong joy.

**Carolyn Lyle**, *Lecturer and Undergraduate Admissions Tutor, Department of English & American Literature, University of Reading*

One of the great attractions of studying English is that most of it was written to give pleasure. The same cannot be said of — say — geography or sociology. The other great attraction is that it cultivates individuality of response. In a maths class, all 30 students can come up with the same answer and get A+. In an English class, 30 students can each get an A+ with wholly different essays.

But while conversing with some of the most imaginative minds in world history (the authors you're reading) is a fine way to pass a few years, you may find the experience quite different from your previous experiences of studying English. For one thing, no book is duller than the one you have to read, and for another, you may well be daunted by the length of the reading list and the fact that you will be much more on your own than ever before — much more so than most students. You'll spend many lonely hours poring over books and criticism as you try to work through your own responses to the material.

Your course should consist of a few lectures per week, plus seminars or tutorials, where you and a number of other students gather with a tutor to discuss a topic. The exchange of views is absolutely central to the degree.

English courses tend to cross-reference politics, the broader arts, philosophy or psychology. There are few barriers to the interests you can develop: you are as likely to find yourself learning about Shakespearean theatre audiences as examining the influence of Trainspotting on contemporary Scottish dialects.

There are few subjects where the possibilities within it vary so much. You might touch on linguistics, cultural studies, the history of ideas and theory, women's writing, as well as the different literary periods, such as Anglo Saxon or Middle English.

An English degree can teach you to respond, think, and articulate thought as one act. You'll be able to present ideas well and formulate your own opinions, and (rightly or wrongly) an English degree is still valued more highly than a BA in media or cultural studies. Graduates with a 2:1 or higher should have no trouble getting on to one of the major graduate training schemes for marketing or business management, or a law conversion course, and plenty go on to do a master's degree or teacher training.

There can be huge differences between the various choices of department on your Ucas form, so look carefully at the prospectus for each of your selections. What you learn, how you learn it, and how you're assessed (most employ a mixture of exams and coursework) can be vastly different things in each institution.

The easy option is often to pick the course with the more contemporary feel – the idea that Hemingway is an easier read than Chaucer. For one thing, that may lead you to apply for vastly oversubscribed courses, as others think the same. And for another, do you really want to be ploughing the same literary furrow for three or four years? This is your chance to expand your mind, so with all that choice out there, you'd be mad to waste it.

Tread carefully through course titles too. Similar-sounding courses can have very different content, but generally you can assume that English language and English literature are quite separate fields of study.

English language looks at syntax, the development of the language from its Old English origins, and how and why it is manipulated by writers. English literature takes literary texts as its main focus, studies their forms and modes, often in relation to literary periods or movements, and studies them in broader contexts, such as social history, philosophy, and politics.

English studies is different again: it adopts a more socio-cultural perspective, and also often uses a broader approach – more theoretical, perhaps involving literature in translation ("literary studies" is also used for this), or an emphasis on modern/contemporary literature.

To confuse matters further, you can take modules in both. So choose carefully, and also check the institution itself. Are the staff well known in their fields? And does it have a good library? If not, does the town have good secondhand bookshops? As always, it pays to do a lot of research before you commit to a course.

---

66 If you like English at A-level then you'll enjoy the degree, but they are very different. The biggest change is the focus on independence – you will be expected to have your own opinions and be original. Seminars take in a huge range of literature, from medieval ballads to 21st-century television, so don't expect three years of Shakespeare. Most of all, the course teaches you to think critically and to form an argument coherently, useful skills for almost any job you choose afterwards.

**Lucy Taylor**, *final-year English and related literature student, University of York*

---

>> Further information

**The English Association**
University of Leicester
University Road, Leicester LE1 7RH

t   0116 252 3982
↗   www.le.ac.uk/engassoc

**Institute of English Studies**
Room NG18, Senate House
Malet Street
London WC1E 7HU

t   020 7862 8675
e   ies@sas.ac.uk
↗   www.ies.sas.ac.uk

↗ Online reading

**Guardian.co.uk books**  guardian.co.uk/books
**The London Review of Books**  www.lrb.co.uk
**New York Review of Books**  www.nybooks.com
**Janus Head**  www.janushead.org
**Eclat (Essential Comparative Literature and Theory)**
    www.ccat.sas.upenn.edu/Complit/Eclat
**Online Literary Criticism**  www.ipl.org/div/litcrit
**The Council for College and University English**  www.ccue.ac.uk

# English

| | | Guardian score /100 | Satisfied with teaching % | Satisfied with feedback % | Spend per student /10 | Student:staff ratio | Job prospects % | Value added score /10 | Average entry tariff |
|---|---|---|---|---|---|---|---|---|---|
| 1 | Oxford | 100.0 | 96 | 71 | 10 | 13.9 | 63 | 7 | 502 |
| 2 | Cambridge | 94.8 | 96 | 81 | 10 | 13.2 | 62 | 6 | 513 |
| 3 | UCL | 89.9 | 95 | 84 | 9 | 10.8 | 67 | 8 | 478 |
| 4 | Warwick | 85.8 | 94 | 71 | 9 | 13.5 | 69 | 7 | 465 |
| 5 | King's College London | 82.9 | 87 | 44 | 9 | 11.8 | 76 | 7 | 445 |
| 6 | St Andrews | 81.2 | 96 | 79 | 8 | 13.4 | 56 | 7 | 455 |
| 7 | Edinburgh | 81.1 | 96 | 55 | 10 | 15.3 | 58 | 7 | 437 |
| 8 | Exeter | 78.7 | 97 | 79 | 5 | 13.0 | 62 | 8 | 423 |
| 9 | Bristol | 78.3 | 94 | 62 | 7 | 18.3 | 77 | 7 | 463 |
| 10 | Durham | 77.1 | 91 | 75 | 4 | 15.4 | 69 | 7 | 488 |
| 10 | York | 77.1 | 91 | 67 | 7 | 17.5 | 65 | 7 | 495 |
| 12 | Glasgow | 75.8 | 91 | 72 | 8 | 15.6 | 60 | 7 | 415 |
| 13 | Sunderland | 74.0 | 94 | 93 | 8 | 15.2 | 50 | 9 | 228 |
| 14 | Liverpool | 73.8 | 94 | 73 | 8 | 17.4 | 53 | 8 | 418 |
| 15 | Buckingham | 73.7 | 93 | 93 | 7 | 6.2 | | 2 | 251 |
| 16 | Leeds | 73.2 | 94 | 73 | 7 | 18.1 | 65 | 7 | 441 |
| 17 | Queen Mary | 72.6 | 95 | 81 | 4 | 20.8 | 67 | 9 | 364 |
| 18 | Dundee | 72.5 | 95 | 86 | 7 | 17.2 | 55 | 9 | 341 |
| 19 | Brunel | 72.0 | 94 | 86 | 8 | 17.9 | 51 | 8 | 306 |
| 20 | Birmingham | 71.9 | 88 | 66 | 9 | 17.4 | 60 | 6 | 415 |
| 21 | Staffordshire | 71.7 | 94 | 65 | 8 | 16.4 | 51 | 10 | 255 |
| 22 | UEA | 70.6 | 94 | 72 | 7 | 19.4 | 59 | 7 | 401 |
| 23 | Manchester | 70.4 | 87 | 52 | 9 | 14.0 | 61 | 4 | 430 |
| 24 | Sheffield | 69.6 | 93 | 69 | 4 | 19.6 | 67 | 7 | 436 |

| | Guardian score /100 | Satisfied with teaching % | Satisfied with feedback % | Spend per student /10 | Student:staff ratio | Job prospects % | Value added score /10 | Average entry tariff |
|---|---|---|---|---|---|---|---|---|
| 25 Stirling | 69.5 | 94 | 66 | 4 | 14.9 | 59 | 8 | |
| 26 Kent | 69.3 | 93 | 77 | 4 | 17.4 | 67 | 8 | 336 |
| 27 Essex | 68.9 | 92 | 71 | 5 | 11.6 | 64 | 6 | 317 |
| 28 Aberdeen | 68.2 | 95 | 81 | 6 | 16.7 | 48 | 9 | 313 |
| 29 Royal Holloway | 67.0 | 90 | 60 | 6 | 15.3 | 60 | 5 | 411 |
| 30 Sussex | 66.2 | 86 | 56 | 5 | 19.0 | 67 | 7 | 416 |
| 31 Hull | 65.4 | 94 | 76 | 3 | 16.9 | 63 | 7 | 309 |
| 32 Loughborough | 65.0 | 95 | 84 | 4 | 21.4 | 62 | 6 | 366 |
| 33 Leicester | 64.8 | 94 | 75 | 5 | 19.0 | 62 | 4 | 378 |
| 34 Nottingham | 64.2 | 90 | 57 | 5 | 19.8 | 60 | 5 | 456 |
| 35 UWE Bristol | 64.0 | 91 | 72 | 4 | 15.4 | 53 | 9 | 285 |
| 36 Southampton | 63.7 | 93 | 73 | 4 | 23.2 | 58 | 7 | 415 |
| 37 Gloucestershire | 63.5 | 88 | 75 | 8 | 13.9 | 40 | 9 | 250 |
| 38 Lancaster | 62.9 | 90 | 67 | 5 | 16.5 | 52 | 5 | 406 |
| 38 Oxford Brookes | 62.9 | 86 | 70 | 6 | 15.0 | 57 | 6 | 331 |
| 40 Nottingham Trent | 62.5 | 91 | 75 | 8 | 14.1 | 57 | 3 | 281 |
| 41 Queen's, Belfast | 61.6 | 93 | 64 | 6 | 15.9 | 56 | 4 | 343 |
| 42 Cardiff | 61.5 | 94 | 62 | 6 | 25.7 | 60 | 6 | 427 |
| 43 Coventry | 61.1 | 83 | 78 | 6 | 14.5 | | | 287 |
| 44 Strathclyde | 60.9 | 91 | 68 | 7 | 21.6 | 44 | 8 | 373 |
| 45 Bolton | 60.6 | | | 3 | 20.0 | 51 | 9 | |
| 45 Kingston | 60.6 | 90 | 75 | 4 | 20.2 | 59 | 9 | 265 |
| 47 Keele | 60.4 | 92 | 71 | 3 | 20.6 | 59 | 7 | 326 |
| 48 Reading | 59.8 | 91 | 68 | 4 | 18.2 | 52 | 7 | 357 |
| 49 Birmingham City | 58.4 | 91 | 75 | 5 | 17.7 | 59 | 5 | 260 |
| 50 Aberystwyth | 58.0 | 90 | 73 | 3 | 15.5 | 48 | 7 | 324 |
| 51 Bath Spa | 57.1 | 89 | 70 | 2 | 22.4 | 61 | 8 | 313 |
| 52 De Montfort | 56.6 | 89 | 79 | 4 | 15.3 | 64 | 3 | 250 |
| 53 Newcastle | 56.5 | 85 | 55 | 5 | 24.1 | 61 | 4 | 443 |
| 54 Hertfordshire | 56.1 | 88 | 61 | 4 | 14.0 | 52 | 6 | 252 |
| 55 Chester | 55.5 | 96 | 84 | 3 | 22.8 | 57 | 4 | 290 |
| 55 Goldsmiths | 55.5 | 88 | 77 | 3 | 15.6 | 59 | 2 | 353 |
| 57 Anglia Ruskin | 55.3 | 83 | 71 | 9 | 26.4 | 56 | 7 | 279 |
| 57 Cumbria | 55.3 | 80 | 64 | | | 74 | 2 | 276 |
| 59 Huddersfield | 55.0 | 88 | 67 | 6 | 16.4 | 38 | 7 | 292 |
| 60 York St John | 54.5 | 91 | 65 | 7 | 19.3 | 46 | 6 | 279 |
| 61 Lampeter | 54.2 | 81 | 65 | 4 | 14.4 | 49 | 6 | 238 |
| 62 Marjon (St Mark and St John) | 54.0 | 88 | 76 | 2 | 17.1 | 49 | 8 | |
| 62 Roehampton | 54.0 | 84 | 64 | 3 | 15.7 | 54 | 5 | 289 |
| 64 Leeds Met | 53.7 | 84 | 57 | 7 | 13.7 | 50 | 2 | 280 |
| 65 Northampton | 52.7 | 86 | 75 | 3 | 15.2 | 39 | 8 | 228 |
| 66 Worcester | 52.5 | 93 | 85 | 4 | 15.8 | 47 | 3 | 235 |
| 67 Sheffield Hallam | 51.8 | 86 | 63 | 6 | 21.3 | 50 | 5 | 287 |
| 68 Bedfordshire | 51.6 | 86 | 78 | 3 | 15.4 | | 5 | 210 |
| 69 Teesside | 51.5 | 87 | 77 | 5 | 16.5 | 42 | 4 | 247 |

| | | Guardian score /100 | Satisfied with teaching % | Satisfied with feedback % | Spend per student /10 | Student:staff ratio | Job prospects % | Value added score /10 | Average entry tariff |
|---|---|---|---|---|---|---|---|---|---|
| 70 | Northumbria | 51.1 | 90 | 79 | 5 | 24.0 | 43 | 5 | 299 |
| 71 | Chichester | 50.9 | 91 | 82 | 4 | 15.1 | 31 | 4 | 261 |
| 72 | Lincoln | 50.4 | 84 | 73 | 3 | 24.0 | 52 | 8 | 280 |
| 72 | Winchester | 50.4 | 93 | 68 | 3 | 19.3 | 55 | 3 | 268 |
| 74 | Swansea | 49.4 | 96 | 64 | 4 | 21.6 | 41 | 6 | 305 |
| 75 | Edge Hill | 49.3 | 92 | 73 | 4 | 17.3 | 43 | 3 | 247 |
| 76 | Westminster | 49.0 | 84 | 69 | 4 | 14.1 | 51 | 2 | 258 |
| 77 | Middlesex | 48.8 | 92 | 75 | 8 | 15.0 | | 1 | 203 |
| 78 | UC Falmouth | 48.2 | 85 | 66 | 6 | 27.3 | 50 | 4 | 281 |
| 79 | Bangor | 46.9 | 89 | 57 | 3 | 20.9 | 40 | 5 | 309 |
| 79 | Central Lancashire | 46.9 | 90 | 76 | 8 | 26.9 | 66 | 1 | 289 |
| 79 | Salford | 46.9 | 95 | 80 | 4 | 19.4 | 31 | 3 | 282 |
| 82 | Leeds Trinity & All Saints | 46.7 | 88 | 76 | 2 | 22.5 | 64 | 3 | 226 |
| 83 | St Mary's UC, Twickenham | 46.6 | 96 | 81 | 3 | 24.6 | 46 | 4 | 264 |
| 84 | Liverpool John Moores | 46.2 | 87 | 72 | 7 | 24.0 | 27 | 8 | 252 |
| 85 | Ulster | 46.1 | 87 | 79 | 5 | 16.5 | 36 | 2 | 251 |
| 86 | Glamorgan | 45.8 | 89 | 71 | 4 | 8.6 | 10 | 5 | 256 |
| 87 | Manchester Met | 45.5 | 88 | 63 | 3 | 21.4 | 44 | 4 | 306 |
| 88 | Newman University College | 44.3 | 84 | 56 | 3 | 24.0 | 79 | 2 | 247 |
| 89 | Portsmouth | 41.7 | 93 | 74 | 5 | 25.8 | 42 | 1 | 299 |
| 90 | Bishop Grosseteste UC | 41.6 | 97 | 90 | 2 | 23.3 | | 2 | 256 |
| 91 | Derby | 40.5 | 83 | 68 | 5 | 21.7 | 39 | 3 | 245 |
| 92 | Newport | 39.6 | | | 4 | 27.7 | 49 | 4 | 251 |
| 93 | Canterbury Christ Church | 39.5 | 83 | 72 | 4 | 19.5 | 38 | 2 | 255 |
| 94 | Plymouth | 39.4 | 84 | 70 | 3 | 20.8 | 49 | 1 | 297 |
| 95 | Brighton | 38.0 | 69 | 67 | 4 | 29.9 | | 7 | 300 |
| 96 | Greenwich | 33.7 | 73 | 58 | 3 | 23.5 | | | 220 |
| 97 | Glyndŵr | 30.0 | 59 | 62 | 3 | 30.5 | 48 | 5 | |

# History and history of art

“ History is as popular a hobby today as it has ever been — the growing number of documentaries on television and books in the shops are ample proof of that. We are clearly fascinated by the lives of people in the past, whether famous rulers, politicians or generals, or the ordinary men, women, and children whose lives were so different from our own. Knowing about the past helps us to develop empathy and a moral compass, to understand different people and societies, and to realise how our own world has come into being, thus defining our own sense of identity.

Yet studying history at university involves far more than passively receiving the fruits of historical research, that is to say the books and television programmes that our modern society consumes so voraciously. Knowing what happened in the past does not make you a historian, any more than being able to use a computer makes you a computer technician. History degrees aim to teach students how to reconstruct the past by interpreting the surviving documents and physical evidence of our ancestors — visual as well as textual — and to sort through diverse and often conflicting interpretations of past events and societies in the history books that we read. This develops in students an advanced capacity to formulate arguments and see the weaknesses (as well as strengths) in those used by others. It is one of the reasons why employers are so keen to recruit history graduates! But ultimately, the real reason for studying history at university must be personal: the joy of exploration and discovery, of peeking behind the curtain and understanding how and why our societies tell stories about the past.

**Dr Simon Ditchfield**, *Reader in History, University of York*

To start with "straight" history: the possibilities of studying the history of the world are so vast that most history degrees begin with general outline courses in the first year and become gradually more specialised from then on. The intention of such broad surveys is to acquaint students with as wide a range of materials and approaches to history as possible in order for you to make informed decisions when it comes to choosing options in subsequent years — during which you might focus on a particular place, period or theme. Those based around the study of foreign countries or earlier periods may encourage you to learn a language; those based around particular methodologies or historical approaches may draw on theories from other branches of the human and social sciences or may encourage a knowledge of statistics.

The standard method of teaching is by a combination of lectures and small group tutorials. The purpose of tutorials is the discussion of assigned reading, and short student presentations may be encouraged. Essays are required at regular intervals and these are included in an element of continuous assessment on some degree courses. Otherwise assessment generally remains weighted towards examinations.

Partly because it has become such a broad discipline, a history degree is widely respected by employers as fostering the ability to read critically and think independently, to gather information and analyse data, and to present ideas both orally and on paper. History graduates go on to pursue a wide variety of careers, including teaching and researching, administration and management, and the media.

When applying, pay attention to the choice of modules and who will be teaching them. Look into related departments as there's often some teaching crossover, and into what scope there is for joint degrees.

# History of art

History of art, meanwhile, is an altogether different degree. It's a valuable inter-disciplinary course that studies how visual art and expression have changed through history, developing a high degree of visual literacy and an awareness of the close relationship between art and its wider historical context. Students use a wide range of historical, theoretical, and critical approaches, developing the skills involved in critical analysis and the critical reading of texts.

There is no doubt that history of art suffers from an image problem as the course of choice for toffs, but things are changing for the better. Institutions are broadening their recruitment strategies and looking to open up the scope of the course to wider influences than the narrow white Eurocentric view of (often painted) art that has traditionally dominated the subject. There is also a growing move away from seeing the subject as connoisseurship towards a more interdisciplinary and academically rigorous approach.

Teaching will be a mixture of classes and lectures, and assessment is nearly always conducted on the basis of analytical essays – either in coursework or exams. A dissertation is also likely to form part of the course.

As with straight history, look closely at the modules on offer and the reputation of the individual staff in the department. There may also be the possibility of spending a year of your degree abroad – this opens up some exciting opportunities and improves employability prospects no end.

Studying in a city that is home to a range of galleries and museums is an obvious advantage, and they can also be valuable for work placements. Look out for these as they are a good chance to get work experience if you want a career in that direction. Also, check if the department has its own slide library. They mostly do, but some are better and easier to use than others.

After graduation you will be ripe for careers in writing, publishing, arts administration, and conservation or teaching.

---

> **""** If there's one thing to say about studying this subject at university, it's that there's no such thing as a 'typical art history student'. The discipline consistently demands new and diverse ways of thinking about art works, historical circumstances and ideological frameworks, giving students the opportunity to engage with philosophy, social and political science and cultural theory as well as the history of art. It is by no means an exaggeration to say that studying art history has transformed the way I see and interact with the world around me.
>
> **Christopher Griffin**, *master's student, Courtauld Institute of Art*

---

## Further information

**The British Academy**
10 Carlton House Terrace
London SW1Y 5AH

**t** 020 7969 5200
↗ www.britac.ac.uk

**The Institute of Historical Research**
Senate House, Malet Street
London WC1E 7HU

**t** 020 7862 8740
**e** ihr.reception@sas.ac.uk
↗ www.history.ac.uk

**Association of Art Historians**
Cowcross Court, 70 Cowcross Street
Clerkenwell
London EC1M 6EJ

**t** 020 7490 3211
**e** admin@aah.org.uk
↗ www.aah.org.uk

**Museums Association**
24 Calvin Street
London E1 6NW

**t** 020 7426 6910
**e** info@museumsassociation.org
↗ www.museumsassociation.org

**The British Association of Paintings Conservator-Restorers**
PO Box 258
Blofield
Norwich NR13 4WY

**t** 01603 516237
**e** office@bapcr.org.uk
↗ www.bapcr.org.uk

↗ Online reading

**Arlis** www.arlis.net
**Economic History Services** eh.net
**Arts Council (of England)** www.artscouncil.org.uk
**History Today** www.historytoday.com
**The Women's Library** www.thewomenslibrary.ac.uk
**The History Channel** www.thehistorychannel.co.uk

## History and history of art

| | | Guardian score /100 | Satisfied with teaching % | Satisfied with feedback % | Spend per student /10 | Student:staff ratio | Job prospects % | Value added score /10 | Average entry tariff |
|---|---|---|---|---|---|---|---|---|---|
| 1 | Oxford | 100.0 | 94 | 67 | 10 | 13.9 | 73 | 7 | 511 |
| 2 | Cambridge | 96.8 | 96 | 83 | 10 | 13.2 | 72 | 7 | 510 |
| 3 | Courtauld Institute | 86.9 | 96 | 86 | | 12.4 | 63 | 8 | 444 |
| 4 | King's College London | 84.6 | 93 | 72 | 8 | 11.8 | 74 | 7 | 467 |
| 5 | St Andrews | 83.1 | 97 | 89 | 8 | 13.4 | 63 | 8 | 451 |
| 6 | UCL | 82.7 | 92 | 69 | 8 | 10.8 | 67 | 8 | 443 |
| 7 | Warwick | 78.8 | 93 | 66 | 9 | 13.5 | 69 | 6 | 456 |
| 8 | Durham | 78.1 | 96 | 86 | 4 | 15.4 | 72 | 7 | 487 |
| 9 | London School of Economics | 77.5 | 80 | 67 | 9 | 13.0 | 87 | 5 | 471 |
| 10 | Edinburgh | 75.3 | 89 | 52 | 10 | 15.3 | 64 | 7 | 448 |
| 11 | Glasgow | 71.6 | 97 | 81 | 8 | 15.6 | 53 | 7 | 405 |
| 12 | SOAS | 70.7 | 96 | 76 | 8 | 11.9 | 54 | 7 | 346 |
| 13 | Exeter | 70.3 | 93 | 77 | 4 | 13.0 | 62 | 7 | 425 |

| | | Guardian score /100 | Satisfied with teaching % | Satisfied with feedback % | Spend per student /10 | Student:staff ratio | Job prospects % | Value added score /10 | Average entry tariff |
|---|---|---|---|---|---|---|---|---|---|
| 14 | York | 70.2 | 93 | 79 | 7 | 17.5 | 62 | 6 | 449 |
| 15 | Bristol | 69.0 | 87 | 61 | 7 | 18.3 | 77 | 7 | 436 |
| 16 | Royal Holloway | 67.9 | 94 | 74 | 6 | 15.3 | 66 | 7 | 378 |
| 17 | UEA | 66.7 | 96 | 87 | 7 | 19.4 | 48 | 8 | 376 |
| 18 | Leeds | 66.4 | 93 | 71 | 6 | 18.1 | 64 | 7 | 416 |
| 19 | Birmingham | 65.7 | 89 | 69 | 9 | 17.4 | 59 | 5 | 395 |
| 19 | Liverpool | 65.7 | 95 | 77 | 8 | 17.4 | 54 | 6 | 386 |
| 21 | Sheffield | 65.1 | 95 | 75 | 4 | 19.6 | 69 | 6 | 443 |
| 22 | Aberdeen | 64.7 | 96 | 79 | 5 | 16.7 | 58 | 9 | 335 |
| 23 | Manchester | 64.6 | 87 | 53 | 9 | 14.0 | 56 | 6 | 405 |
| 24 | Dundee | 61.9 | 90 | 82 | 6 | 17.2 | 38 | 9 | 357 |
| 25 | Lancaster | 60.2 | 94 | 76 | 4 | 16.5 | 53 | 6 | 397 |
| 26 | Kent | 60.0 | 95 | 76 | 4 | 17.4 | 59 | 8 | 333 |
| 27 | Chichester | 59.9 | 97 | 92 | 4 | 15.1 | 42 | 8 | 247 |
| 28 | Oxford Brookes | 59.8 | 89 | 71 | 6 | 15.0 | 62 | 6 | 310 |
| 29 | Leicester | 59.6 | 94 | 74 | 5 | 19.0 | 58 | 7 | 356 |
| 30 | Sussex | 59.0 | 89 | 61 | 4 | 19.0 | 63 | 8 | 376 |
| 31 | Huddersfield | 58.6 | 99 | 88 | 6 | 16.4 | 54 | 4 | 274 |
| 32 | Teesside | 58.5 | 99 | 89 | 4 | 16.5 | 36 | 9 | 258 |
| 33 | Queen Mary | 58.1 | 90 | 77 | 4 | 20.8 | 66 | 7 | 348 |
| 34 | Nottingham | 57.9 | 86 | 60 | 5 | 19.8 | 63 | 7 | 409 |
| 35 | Nottingham Trent | 57.6 | 95 | 75 | 7 | 14.1 | 68 | 2 | 258 |
| 36 | Essex | 57.2 | 94 | 76 | 5 | 11.6 | 46 | 4 | 323 |
| 37 | Gloucestershire | 56.9 | 83 | 74 | 7 | 13.9 | 39 | 9 | 228 |
| 37 | Southampton | 56.9 | 91 | 74 | 4 | 23.2 | 58 | 8 | 404 |
| 39 | Lampeter | 56.5 | 94 | 77 | 4 | 14.4 | 60 | 6 | 258 |
| 40 | Sunderland | 55.8 | 97 | 92 | 8 | 15.2 | 44 | 4 | 230 |
| 41 | Hull | 55.7 | 95 | 84 | 3 | 16.9 | 53 | 6 | 300 |
| 42 | Strathclyde | 55.3 | 91 | 69 | 7 | 21.6 | 56 | 7 | 354 |
| 43 | Bradford | 54.5 | 78 | 57 | 10 | 13.4 | | 2 | 241 |
| 44 | Westminster | 54.4 | | | 4 | 14.1 | 31 | 10 | 251 |
| 45 | Goldsmiths | 54.3 | 90 | 77 | 3 | 15.6 | 52 | 7 | 314 |
| 45 | Kingston | 54.3 | 93 | 73 | 4 | 20.2 | 44 | 10 | 256 |
| 47 | Coventry | 54.1 | | | 5 | 10.1 | | 2 | 281 |
| 48 | De Montfort | 53.3 | 93 | 91 | 4 | 15.3 | 43 | 7 | 247 |
| 49 | Bath Spa | 52.9 | 95 | 78 | 2 | 22.4 | 50 | 10 | 278 |
| 50 | Reading | 52.8 | 94 | 66 | 4 | 18.2 | 49 | 7 | 331 |
| 51 | Newcastle | 52.5 | 88 | 61 | 4 | 24.1 | 63 | 6 | 404 |
| 52 | Newman University College | 52.4 | 99 | 79 | 3 | 24.0 | 52 | 10 | 235 |
| 53 | Stirling | 52.3 | 91 | 84 | 4 | 14.9 | 42 | 4 | |
| 54 | UWE Bristol | 51.5 | 92 | 79 | 4 | 15.4 | 49 | 5 | 275 |
| 55 | Brunel | 51.3 | 79 | 73 | 8 | 17.9 | 55 | 4 | 277 |
| 56 | Cardiff | 49.4 | 92 | 70 | 6 | 25.7 | 50 | 5 | 407 |
| 57 | Glamorgan | 49.0 | 89 | 74 | 3 | 8.6 | 56 | 2 | 220 |
| 58 | Portsmouth | 47.8 | 97 | 88 | 5 | 25.8 | 53 | 5 | 273 |
| 59 | Keele | 46.6 | 93 | 71 | 3 | 20.6 | 55 | 4 | 309 |

| | Guardian score /100 | Satisfied with teaching % | Satisfied with feedback % | Spend per student /10 | Student:staff ratio | Job prospects % | Value added score /10 | Average entry tariff |
|---|---|---|---|---|---|---|---|---|
| 60 Plymouth | 46.5 | 89 | 73 | 3 | 20.8 | 43 | 8 | 270 |
| 61 Queen's, Belfast | 46.4 | 89 | 60 | 6 | 15.9 | 52 | 2 | 334 |
| 62 Aberystwyth | 45.6 | 86 | 79 | 3 | 15.5 | 43 | 4 | 313 |
| 63 Hertfordshire | 44.8 | 92 | 76 | 4 | 14.0 | 38 | 4 | 239 |
| 64 Northumbria | 44.0 | 85 | 74 | 5 | 24.0 | 54 | 6 | 276 |
| 65 Roehampton | 42.8 | 89 | 63 | 3 | 15.7 | 39 | 7 | 246 |
| 66 Leeds Trinity & All Saints | 41.8 | 75 | 61 | 2 | 22.5 | 76 | 2 | |
| 66 St Mary's UC, Twickenham | 41.8 | 98 | 93 | 3 | 24.6 | | 4 | 242 |
| 68 Central Lancashire | 41.3 | 86 | 86 | 7 | 26.9 | 56 | 2 | 275 |
| 69 Derby | 40.9 | | | 5 | 21.7 | | 5 | 238 |
| 69 York St John | 40.9 | 90 | 72 | 6 | 19.3 | 38 | 3 | 253 |
| 71 Chester | 40.4 | 88 | 76 | 3 | 22.8 | 48 | 4 | 270 |
| 72 Sheffield Hallam | 39.7 | 88 | 75 | 6 | 21.3 | 30 | 5 | 272 |
| 73 Leeds Met | 38.6 | 82 | 58 | 7 | 13.7 | 30 | 3 | 238 |
| 74 Northampton | 38.2 | 94 | 86 | 3 | 15.2 | 22 | 6 | 190 |
| 75 Canterbury Christ Church | 37.8 | 93 | 76 | 4 | 19.5 | 32 | 4 | 230 |
| 76 Winchester | 37.7 | 98 | 83 | 3 | 19.3 | 30 | 4 | 255 |
| 77 Ulster | 37.5 | 82 | 71 | 5 | 16.5 | 34 | 3 | 241 |
| 78 Manchester Met | 37.3 | 83 | 67 | 3 | 21.4 | 43 | 5 | 279 |
| 79 Worcester | 36.0 | 88 | 69 | 4 | 15.8 | | 1 | 231 |
| 80 Lincoln | 35.6 | 87 | 76 | 3 | 24.0 | 54 | 3 | 273 |
| 81 Anglia Ruskin | 35.2 | 88 | 79 | 9 | 26.4 | 29 | 3 | 241 |
| 82 Cumbria | 35.0 | 83 | 53 | 8 | 21.5 | 48 | 1 | 292 |
| 83 Edge Hill | 34.2 | 73 | 60 | 4 | 17.3 | 43 | 4 | 219 |
| 84 Salford | 34.0 | 91 | 72 | 4 | 19.4 | 33 | 3 | 236 |
| 85 Swansea | 31.8 | 89 | 68 | 4 | 21.6 | 39 | 2 | 298 |
| 86 Greenwich | 30.5 | 88 | 72 | 3 | 23.5 | 42 | 3 | 220 |
| 87 Liverpool John Moores | 29.1 | 86 | 74 | 6 | 24.0 | 19 | 3 | 225 |
| 88 Bangor | 28.5 | 93 | 71 | 3 | 20.9 | 37 | 1 | 268 |
| 89 Newport | 28.0 | 85 | 70 | 3 | 27.7 | | 4 | |
| 90 Brighton | 27.2 | 83 | 63 | 3 | 29.9 | 36 | 6 | 266 |

# Philosophy

  Studying philosophy gives you a chance to think in depth about the big questions: what is justice? What is morality? What is truth? How are we to understand the mind (perception, experience, belief, desire, imagination, emotion)? When is it reasonable to believe? Is faith opposed to reason? What is an explanation? What is the status of a scientific theory? What is a number? What is a language? What is art?

  But while philosophy is abstract in its content, it is concrete in its benefits. Studying philosophy at university is uniquely able to equip you with the kinds of skills that employers look for: clarity of thought and expression, an ability to reason and analyse arguments, an ability for abstract thought, and an ability to write in a clear and concise way. This combination of abstract content and concrete skills will engender a greater appreciation for the world and your place within it. Philosophy looks at foundations: the foundations of science, of mathematics, of society, of morality, and of humanity. It is quite simply the most fundamental of academic disciplines.

**Dr Sarah Sawyer**, *Senior Lecturer and Head of the Department of Philosophy, University of Sussex*

Philosophy is the perfect subject for those who wonder what on earth it's all about. Don't listen to the sneerers, asking whether you'll find it all worthwhile the moment you have to start repaying your tuition fees, just let them know that philosophy involves a critical examination of our most basic beliefs about truth and reality, right and wrong, interpretation, explanation, and morality. It looks at basic assumptions about what we know and how we should live, and it teaches you how to think and how to argue. Added to that, you might also study the history of philosophy, business or medical ethics, elements of law, and the philosophers themselves, including Plato, Kant, Russell, Descartes, and Locke.

There are four main branches to the study of philosophy: logic and philosophy of language; ontology and metaphysics (abstract stuff about what there is and how it fits together); epistemology and methodology (the theory and nature of knowledge, including the philosophy of science); and ethics. Within these groupings there's even further room for specialisation.

It's not, of course, a directly vocational subject. Instead it gives you the opportunity — perhaps the only chance many people will have in their lives — for extended reflection on and discussion of, as the cliché has it, "life, the universe and everything".

The academic rigour isn't for everyone, but during a philosophy degree you'll learn transferable skills of thought, analysis, and problem-solving and the ability to think logically and to present your thoughts cogently. Employers value such attributes, so your chances of a good job are pretty high, especially in areas such as journalism, publishing, and management consultancy. Some specialisations can help ease the move into the real world; philosophy of law is a good link to a legal career, while business ethics is valued in many areas of commerce.

There are no specific A-level requirements for a course in philosophy, and you shouldn't be at any disadvantage if you have not studied the subject at A-level — nor advantage if you did. If you want to hedge your bets, you could do the course as part of a joint honours degree. Philosophy is often done jointly with English language and linguistics, Greek, German, maths, economics (for those into business ethics), and law.

You might also want to look into the specialisations of the staff, whether you'll get to spend a year abroad, and also investigate how the course is assessed – there's a variety of combinations of exams, coursework, and dissertation, so have an idea which suits you best.

> " The biggest difference between the A-level and the degree is that philosophy at university has so much more discussion. The great thing about this is that you hear others' views and learn new things – taking your thoughts to new places. Philosophy could be described as the search for knowledge, and through the reading of key thinkers coupled with good discussions, it's a deeply liberating subject that frees your mind from normal constraints and teaches you to think for yourself.
>
> **Edward Rushforth**, *first-year philosophy student, University of Greenwich*

## » Further information

**The Royal Institute of Philosophy**
14 Gordon Square
London WC1H 0AG

t  020 7387 4130
↗ www.royalinstitutephilosophy.org

## ↗ Online reading

**The Philosopher's Magazine**  www.philosophersnet.com
**Episteme Links**  www.epistemelinks.com
**Archelogos Projects**  www.archelogos.com
**Philosophy News Service**  www.philosophynews.com
**The Secular Web**  www.infidels.org

## Philosophy

| | | Guardian score /100 | Satisfied with teaching % | Satisfied with feedback % | Spend per student /10 | Student:staff ratio | Job prospects % | Value added score /10 | Average entry tariff |
|---|---|---|---|---|---|---|---|---|---|
| 1 | Oxford | 100.0 | 94 | 69 | 10 | 13.9 | 79 | 7 | 538 |
| 2 | Cambridge | 90.3 | 98 | 80 | 10 | 13.2 | 71 | 4 | 548 |
| 3 | St Andrews | 82.1 | 94 | 71 | 7 | 13.4 | | 9 | 483 |
| 4 | UCL | 80.3 | 86 | 68 | 8 | 10.8 | 63 | 8 | 465 |
| 5 | London School of Economics | 77.8 | | | 8 | 13.0 | 93 | 4 | 474 |
| 6 | King's College London | 74.7 | 94 | 70 | 8 | 11.8 | 56 | 6 | 429 |
| 7 | Warwick | 73.9 | 88 | 64 | 8 | 13.5 | 63 | 5 | 476 |
| 8 | Durham | 72.1 | 91 | 68 | 3 | 15.4 | 74 | 7 | 484 |
| 9 | Stirling | 69.1 | 91 | 82 | 4 | 14.9 | | 8 | |
| 10 | UWE Bristol | 67.1 | 93 | 78 | 3 | 15.4 | | 10 | 262 |
| 11 | Aberdeen | 65.3 | 98 | 86 | 5 | 16.7 | | | 301 |
| 12 | Edinburgh | 64.5 | 82 | 43 | 9 | 15.3 | 54 | 7 | 450 |
| 13 | Dundee | 64.0 | 89 | 76 | 5 | 17.2 | | 8 | 363 |
| 14 | Exeter | 63.6 | 90 | 63 | 4 | 13.0 | | 6 | 400 |
| 14 | Sheffield | 63.6 | 96 | 67 | 4 | 19.6 | 58 | 7 | 435 |
| 16 | Bristol | 63.5 | 93 | 53 | 6 | 18.3 | 65 | 5 | 453 |

| | Guardian score /100 | Satisfied with teaching % | Satisfied with feedback % | Spend per student /10 | Student:staff ratio | Job prospects % | Value added score /10 | Average entry tariff |
|---|---|---|---|---|---|---|---|---|
| 17 Glasgow | 63.2 | 90 | 72 | 7 | 15.6 | 52 | 5 | 383 |
| 18 York | 60.9 | 87 | 53 | 6 | 17.5 | 64 | 4 | 450 |
| 19 Sussex | 60.4 | 91 | 66 | 4 | 19.0 | 54 | 8 | 372 |
| 20 Newcastle | 58.3 | 89 | 64 | 4 | 24.1 | | 10 | 365 |
| 21 Oxford Brookes | 57.6 | 91 | 73 | 8 | 17.8 | | 4 | 289 |
| 22 Essex | 57.0 | 94 | 77 | 4 | 11.6 | 43 | 4 | 303 |
| 23 UEA | 56.7 | 91 | 65 | 6 | 19.4 | 50 | 7 | 345 |
| 24 Manchester | 56.4 | 87 | 51 | 7 | 19.7 | 63 | 4 | 426 |
| 25 Hull | 54.5 | 89 | 75 | 3 | 16.9 | 60 | 6 | 304 |
| 26 Queen's, Belfast | 53.6 | 89 | 52 | 5 | 15.9 | | 5 | 322 |
| 27 Leeds | 53.2 | 93 | 60 | 5 | 18.1 | 54 | 3 | 387 |
| 28 Liverpool | 53.1 | 89 | 48 | 7 | 17.4 | 48 | 3 | 389 |
| 29 Birmingham | 52.9 | 87 | 61 | 8 | 17.4 | 61 | 1 | 393 |
| 30 Nottingham | 52.5 | 90 | 61 | 4 | 19.8 | 68 | 2 | 400 |
| 31 Roehampton | 52.2 | 90 | 53 | 3 | 15.7 | | 9 | 248 |
| 32 Lancaster | 50.9 | 88 | 66 | 7 | 15.4 | 35 | 2 | 375 |
| 33 Heythrop College | 49.8 | | | 4 | 16.1 | | 4 | 303 |
| 34 Cardiff | 49.7 | 97 | 78 | 5 | 25.7 | 44 | 5 | 372 |
| 35 Hertfordshire | 48.7 | 91 | 70 | 4 | 14.0 | 44 | 6 | 227 |
| 36 Anglia Ruskin | 47.5 | 90 | 78 | 8 | 26.4 | | | 253 |
| 37 Lampeter | 47.2 | 87 | 61 | 3 | 14.4 | | | 225 |
| 38 Southampton | 46.4 | 87 | 61 | 4 | 23.2 | 49 | 5 | 381 |
| 39 Kent | 45.9 | 89 | 57 | 4 | 17.4 | 61 | 2 | 315 |
| 40 Central Lancashire | 45.8 | 87 | 87 | 7 | 26.9 | | 6 | 265 |
| 41 Bath Spa | 44.5 | 94 | 73 | 2 | 22.4 | | 4 | |
| 42 Reading | 43.7 | 86 | 61 | 3 | 18.2 | 40 | 4 | 342 |
| 43 Greenwich | 43.4 | 91 | 82 | 3 | 23.5 | | 4 | 272 |
| 44 Manchester Met | 43.2 | 84 | 68 | 3 | 21.4 | 36 | 9 | 262 |
| 45 Keele | 41.7 | 84 | 64 | 3 | 20.6 | | 4 | 320 |
| 46 Brighton | 35.6 | 93 | 84 | 3 | 29.9 | 26 | 6 | 246 |
| 47 Newport | 29.2 | 87 | 66 | 3 | 27.7 | | 2 | 245 |

# Religious studies and theology

> Although some atheists describe God as a 'delusion', religious belief continues to thrive. Why? Reports of the death of religion are much exaggerated, even in so-called 'secular' Europe. Again, why? Institutional Christianity may be in decline, but religion is not. Novelist Philip Pullman may question religion, yet religious themes are evident in many places – from Harry Potter to Doctor Who. What's more, religious traditions continue to make headlines: Buddhist monks resisting Chinese authorities in Tibet, a British archbishop supporting the inclusion of Islamic or Sharia law into UK law, and a man of Christian faith and part-Muslim parentage getting elected as US President.
>
> You'll find the influence of religious traditions everywhere, sometimes in a conservative way and sometimes in a progressive fashion. Because they are attentive to human needs and limitations, religious groups are today at the forefront of debates in medical ethics and genetic manipulation as well as promoting care of the earth in the face of climate change.
>
> 'Why do you do that? What do you hope for? What consoles you?' If you have ever wanted to pose these questions to religious communities, then the study of religion is for you. To appreciate the power of religion – for good and ill – you need to understand religious traditions in all their depth, variety, and complexity. Religious studies and theology enables you to do that. As you study, you also acquire many life skills: from an ability to empathise to the facility to analyse, discuss, and present controversial topics.
>
> Our world is a religious world – to understand how this world is religious prepares you to work in this world. So study religion – you won't regret it!
>
> **Dr Peter M Scott**, *Senior Lecturer in Christian Social Thought and Director of the Lincoln Theological Institute, University of Manchester*

One glance at the newspapers or TV should be enough to convince anyone that religion is an extraordinarily powerful force in the world, used to justify an array of actions, for good and ill. All the more important, then, that we should understand the beliefs and value systems that drive the major faiths.

The teaching of religion at universities has been rapidly transformed in the past few years. Many courses have widened their remit to include a variety of religious traditions, while the profile of students arriving in theology and religious studies departments is very different from even ten years ago. Most noticeably the proportion of female students has risen. Gender studies is now an important part of most theology and religious studies courses.

Students can study for undergraduate degrees in religious studies, world religions, divinity, theology, and biblical studies. Academics are keen to stress that none of these are courses simply for the religiously committed, and that the basic questions about human existence are studied without privileging any single viewpoint. If you are committed to one particular faith, though, you need to be sure you are open to that faith being tested and criticised in an academic setting.

Typically, religious studies courses look at the human phenomenon of religion in all its variety, while theology (or divinity) departments tend to focus on Christianity and the way it understands itself – so be careful to choose the right one. However most departments offer some experience of both types of study. Undertaking theological studies may suggest that you have more than a passing interest in Christianity, but does not require any religious commitment.

Theology students go on to a wide variety of careers and certainly do not all work within religious organisations, although clerical training is part of some theological degree courses, and some departments are linked to colleges that train people for the ministry. Graduates emerge not just with analytical and textual skills, but also skills in language, field research, historical and archaeological methods, philosophy, ethics and sociology, literature, art and music — all hugely valuable assets to any employer.

Be aware of the ever-widening scope of courses available — you could find yourself looking at the philosophy of religion and ethics, the sociology and practice of religion, or even anthropology. There may even be the chance to study abroad or head off on field trips, which is always worthwhile, and the chance to visit holy sites or see religions in their context can add a whole new dimension to your studies.

> The joint degree I'm taking in study of religions and Turkish means that I can learn many languages that fascinate me (such as Persian, Arabic, and Hebrew) and at the same time find out about all sorts of religious belief - even to the point of learning about topics such as "death and the meaning of life". My degree is absolutely perfect for me.
>
> **Sevgi Kaymak,** *second-year study of religions and Turkish student, Soas*

## ≫ Further information

**British Association for the Study of Religions**
Arts Faculty, The Open University          e  basr.open.ac.uk
Walton Hall, Milton Keynes MK7 6AA

## Online reading

**Association for the Sociology of Religion**  www.sociologyofreligion.com
**MultiFaithnet**  www.multifaithcentre.org
**Internet for Religious Studies**  www.vts.rdn.ac.uk/tutorial/religion
**Centre for Reception History of the Bible**  www.crhb.org
**Al-Islam**  www.al-islam.org
**Bible Gateway**  www.biblegateway.com
**Center for the Study of New Religions**  www.cesnur.org
**The Pluralism Project**  www.pluralism.org
**Society for the Study of Theology**  www.exeter.ac.uk/theology/sst

## Faith sites

**Baptist Union of Great Britain**  www.baptist.org.uk
**Buddhism**  www.buddhism.org
**Church of England**  www.cofe.anglican.org
**Church of Scotland**  www.churchofscotland.org.uk
**Hinduism Today**  www.hinduismtoday.org
**Al-Islam**  www.al-islam.org
**Judaism**  www.jewish.co.uk
**Methodist Church**  www.methodist.org.uk
**Roman Catholic Church in England and Wales**  www.catholic-ew.org.uk
**Roman Catholic Church in Scotland**  www.catholic-scotland.org.uk
**Sikhism**  www.sikh.org

# Religious studies and theology

| | | Guardian score /100 | Satisfied with teaching % | Satisfied with feedback % | Spend per student /10 | Student:staff ratio | Job prospects % | Value added score /10 | Average entry tariff |
|---|---|---|---|---|---|---|---|---|---|
| 1 | Oxford | 100.0 | 88 | 65 | 10 | 13.9 | 79 | 7 | 481 |
| 2 | Cambridge | 99.5 | 98 | 84 | 10 | 13.2 | 79 | 4 | 496 |
| 3 | St Andrews | 86.3 | 95 | 77 | 7 | 13.4 | 75 | 8 | 458 |
| 4 | Durham | 76.9 | 97 | 76 | 4 | 15.4 | 78 | 6 | 423 |
| 5 | SOAS | 76.3 | 93 | 57 | 7 | 11.9 | | 9 | 322 |
| 6 | Glasgow | 74.8 | 91 | 72 | 7 | 15.6 | 79 | 8 | 340 |
| 7 | Edinburgh | 72.6 | 93 | 60 | 9 | 15.3 | 64 | 5 | 422 |
| 7 | Exeter | 72.6 | 93 | 71 | 4 | 13.0 | 71 | 5 | 398 |
| 9 | King's College London | 69.2 | 89 | 68 | 8 | 11.8 | 59 | 6 | 411 |
| 10 | Bristol | 67.3 | 92 | 50 | 6 | 18.3 | 73 | 8 | 407 |
| 11 | Aberdeen | 64.1 | 96 | 85 | 5 | 16.7 | 71 | | 320 |
| 12 | Oxford Brookes | 60.3 | 91 | 73 | 5 | 15.0 | | 6 | 319 |
| 13 | Manchester | 60.2 | 89 | 62 | 8 | 14.0 | 65 | 3 | 373 |
| 14 | Heythrop College | 57.7 | | | 4 | 16.1 | | 7 | 331 |
| 15 | Sheffield | 55.3 | 97 | 69 | 4 | 19.6 | 65 | 6 | 361 |
| 16 | Nottingham | 54.7 | 87 | 64 | 5 | 19.8 | 74 | 5 | 389 |
| 17 | Gloucestershire | 54.5 | 87 | 69 | 7 | 13.9 | | 5 | 251 |
| 17 | Queen's, Belfast | 54.5 | 88 | 54 | 5 | 15.9 | 65 | 8 | 316 |
| 19 | Kent | 53.4 | 83 | 66 | 4 | 17.4 | | 8 | 322 |
| 20 | Bangor | 50.1 | 91 | 77 | 3 | 20.9 | 68 | 8 | 288 |
| 21 | Lancaster | 50.0 | 87 | 59 | 7 | 15.4 | 60 | 2 | 370 |
| 22 | Winchester | 49.9 | 92 | 71 | 3 | 19.3 | | 9 | 264 |
| 23 | Hull | 49.0 | 90 | 72 | 3 | 16.9 | | 3 | 333 |
| 24 | Birmingham | 48.3 | 80 | 61 | 8 | 17.4 | 68 | 3 | 349 |
| 25 | Cardiff | 48.1 | 96 | 77 | 5 | 25.7 | 65 | 7 | 357 |
| 26 | Leeds | 47.3 | 90 | 67 | 6 | 18.1 | 49 | 7 | 356 |
| 27 | Lampeter | 43.5 | 87 | 61 | 4 | 14.4 | 76 | 1 | 267 |
| 28 | Newman University College | 41.1 | 98 | 84 | 3 | 24.0 | | 7 | 231 |
| 29 | Leeds Trinity & All Saints | 40.8 | 84 | 68 | 2 | 22.5 | | 5 | |
| 30 | St Mary's UC, Twickenham | 40.6 | 90 | 77 | 3 | 24.6 | | 7 | 244 |
| 31 | Bath Spa | 39.1 | 94 | 73 | 3 | 22.4 | | 4 | 309 |
| 31 | Roehampton | 39.1 | 90 | 53 | 3 | 15.7 | 53 | 9 | 217 |
| 33 | Chester | 38.6 | 93 | 80 | 3 | 22.8 | 73 | 3 | 268 |
| 34 | York St John | 34.8 | 96 | 85 | 6 | 19.3 | 52 | 2 | 262 |
| 35 | Cumbria | 29.6 | 83 | 57 | 4 | 14.5 | 64 | 1 | 278 |
| 36 | Canterbury Christ Church | 28.1 | 88 | 61 | 4 | 19.5 | 49 | 3 | 270 |

# Medical sciences

## Anatomy and physiology

> Human anatomy is concerned with the study of the structure of our bodies, both at the macroscopic and the microscopic levels. It provides an understanding of the relationship between the structure and function of organs and tissues 'beneath the skin'.
>
> Anatomy has a glorious tradition and anatomists can count amongst their number such illustrious historical figures as Galen, Vesalius, Leonardo da Vinci, Michelangelo, William Harvey, Leeuwenhoek, and, more recently, JZ Young and Solly Zuckerman. Of course, the work of these important anatomists continues to be central for the teaching of biomedical sciences — whether for medical and associated healthcare disciplines or for those who are primarily studying anatomy as a scientific subject.
>
> Anatomy is not just of historical importance, as it continues to move with the times and remains a key area for research in contemporary biomedical science. Many advances are being made in our understanding of microscopic structure (using such technologies as electron microscopy and confocal laser-scanning microscopy) and, in the 'post-genomic era', we need to know not just about the human genome but, more significantly, when and where certain genes are being expressed — this is where contemporary anatomists have a crucial role to play.
>
> Furthermore, new imaging technologies, like MRI, rely upon anatomical information. Important discoveries are also being made in neuroanatomy and developmental biology.
>
> So, if you are intrigued by the complexity of the human body, in awe of the wonder and the spectacle of anatomical images, and want a discipline with good vocational and scientific prospects, studying anatomy at university is for you!
>
> **Professor Bernard Moxham**, *School of Biosciences, Cardiff University*

Anatomy and physiology, contrary to popular belief, do not represent easy options for those who can't last the course to become a doctor. While the subjects are, obviously, closely allied with medicine, they are actually of a completely different bent to most other branches of medical study, interesting those who are into the academic side of medicine, but don't wish to become doctors.

Those who do want to stay in the "sector" after graduating are more likely to see themselves as scientists, researchers, paramedical staff or working in the pharmaceutical industry. Of course, they also have the knowledge and skills to enter a whole range of careers, including teaching, scientific journalism, or perhaps less traditional areas of medicine, such as osteopathy or reflexology – although further training would be required.

Anatomy (the structure of the body) and its close cousin physiology (how living organisms and their parts function) are both life sciences, concerned with the study of the body and the relationship between its structure and its functions. Human development, ageing, and response to dysfunction are all likely areas of study, and you'll spend most of that study time in the lab, the lecture hall, and tutorials.

Assessment tends to be largely exam-based, with some emphasis on coursework, practical and research projects or presentations. Most courses also include a significant research project, which is generally in the last year, and occasionally this can lead to those crucial academic publications that will look so fabulous on your CV.

If you want to do anatomy, there is a limited number of institutions to choose from, and these are usually going to be the older universities. It can be combined with developmental biology, biomedical science or cellular science; or included as an option in some biological science or human biology courses.

Physiology is rather more widely offered. Some courses allow for focus on humans, mammals, or areas such as neuroscience, so investigate the possibilities thoroughly. Physiology courses will vary from department to department: there may be focus on how individual organs or tissues work, or on complete systems. Alternatively, you might study how systems interact or how life functions at the cellular level. Where courses do vary is in their number of compulsory study modules, or how much of a free hand you are given to bolt together your own physiology degree.

Also, in many universities the physiology department has come to be closely allied with psychology. Most universities will let you take papers from fields related to physiology, such as biochemistry and psychology, in the course of your degree.

Look carefully at who will be teaching you and what their specialisations are – and those of staff in related departments. There's a great deal of crossover with the teaching staff, so a decent medical school will be of great benefit.

Some universities offer a year abroad or working in industry, so investigate the possibilities – it'll be a challenging experience and look great on your CV.

---

" For some reason, anatomy is a subject that a lot of people are unfamiliar with. I was once accused of learning about space! It is a hands-on approach to learning about the human body. The captivating sessions in the dissection room are, not surprisingly, the favourite aspect for most people as they put lecture theory into practice with real cadavers. Although challenging and accompanied by plenty of work, I have yet to meet anybody who doesn't have a genuine passion for this subject.

**Charlotte Johnston**, *second-year anatomy student, University of Bristol*

---

## » Further information

**The Academy of Medical Sciences**
10 Carlton House Terrace
London SW1Y 5AH

t   020 7969 5288
e   info@acmedsci.ac.uk
↗  www.acmedsci.ac.uk

**British Medical Association**
BMA House, Tavistock Square
London WC1H 9JP

t   020 7387 4499
↗ www.bma.org.uk

**The Royal Society of Medicine**
1 Wimpole Street
London W1G 0AE

t   020 7290 2900
↗ www.rsm.ac.uk

↗ Online reading

**The Center for Human Simulation**  www.uchsc.edu/sm/chs
**MedBioWorld**  www.sciencekomm.at
**The Royal Society**  www.royalsociety.org
**The Virtual Autopsy**  www.le.ac.uk/pathology/teach/va
**Virtual Creatures**  www.k-2.stanford.edu/creatures

# Anatomy and physiology

| | | Guardian score /100 | Satisfied with teaching % | Satisfied with feedback % | Spend per student /10 | Student:staff ratio | Job prospects % | Value added score /10 | Average entry tariff |
|---|---|---|---|---|---|---|---|---|---|
| 1 | Oxford | 100.0 | 88 | 53 | 10 | 13.7 | 72 | 7 | 508 |
| 2 | UCL | 91.1 | 89 | 47 | 9 | 8.0 | 81 | 8 | 395 |
| 3 | Cardiff | 90.2 | 90 | 55 | 9 | 12.7 | 91 | 7 | 409 |
| 4 | Manchester | 89.6 | 89 | 52 | 10 | 7.4 | 75 | 4 | 408 |
| 5 | Aston | 86.6 | 95 | 77 | 7 | 12.7 | 99 | 3 | 359 |
| 6 | Plymouth | 85.6 | 91 | 73 | 8 | 10.3 | | 9 | 378 |
| 7 | Liverpool | 85.0 | 92 | 61 | 8 | 8.9 | 74 | 6 | 382 |
| 8 | Nottingham | 79.2 | 93 | 62 | 6 | 15.0 | 83 | 7 | 415 |
| 9 | Bristol | 76.7 | 87 | 54 | 5 | 6.5 | 72 | 5 | 394 |
| 10 | Birmingham | 74.2 | 95 | 49 | 4 | 13.5 | 74 | 7 | 419 |
| 11 | Queen's, Belfast | 73.0 | 92 | 70 | 7 | 10.2 | 71 | 7 | 338 |
| 12 | Sussex | 72.7 | 84 | 55 | 7 | 9.7 | 65 | 9 | 359 |
| 13 | Anglia Ruskin | 71.5 | 88 | 58 | 7 | 13.8 | 82 | 7 | 312 |
| 14 | Brunel | 65.9 | 96 | 70 | 3 | 15.8 | 60 | 9 | 348 |
| 15 | Bradford | 64.6 | 89 | 57 | 4 | 10.4 | 77 | 4 | 343 |
| 16 | Newcastle | 63.2 | 89 | 65 | 4 | 15.7 | 73 | 5 | 401 |
| 17 | Glasgow Caledonian | 61.9 | 90 | 58 | 4 | 19.9 | 84 | 6 | 389 |
| 18 | Ulster | 61.8 | 77 | 58 | 3 | 9.6 | 80 | 7 | 337 |
| 19 | Leeds | 61.5 | 93 | 71 | 6 | 16.0 | 63 | 5 | 377 |
| 20 | City | 61.4 | 84 | 57 | 4 | 15.8 | 97 | 3 | 342 |
| 21 | UEA | 61.1 | 86 | 46 | 2 | | 82 | 7 | 391 |
| 22 | Hertfordshire | 58.5 | 91 | 62 | 3 | 11.9 | 84 | 4 | 287 |
| 23 | Salford | 57.7 | 92 | 72 | 3 | 15.5 | 75 | 6 | 317 |
| 24 | De Montfort | 57.3 | 91 | 52 | 3 | 15.1 | 85 | 7 | 279 |
| 25 | Robert Gordon | 57.2 | | | 3 | 18.5 | 69 | 6 | 427 |
| 26 | Aberdeen | 54.6 | 93 | 69 | 3 | 17.3 | 60 | 8 | 359 |
| 27 | Cumbria | 54.2 | | | 3 | 19.5 | 98 | 5 | 288 |
| 28 | King's College London | 50.3 | 85 | 45 | 7 | 18.8 | 68 | 4 | 377 |
| 29 | Northumbria | 50.1 | 91 | 74 | 3 | 20.4 | 79 | 4 | |
| 30 | Glamorgan | 44.8 | 76 | 35 | 4 | | | 5 | 337 |
| 31 | Birmingham City | 42.0 | 80 | 61 | 3 | 16.7 | 77 | 3 | 346 |
| 32 | Bedfordshire | 33.0 | 91 | 59 | 3 | 18.0 | 100 | 1 | 273 |
| 32 | Manchester Met | 33.0 | 79 | 57 | 3 | 15.9 | 52 | 3 | 361 |

# Dentistry

The dental undergraduate degree course is action packed. Within the five years students have the opportunity to change peoples' lives, become team leaders, use the latest technology and techniques, and develop skills for business or academia. The course challenges students in many ways: developing skills to carry out very precise procedures including implants and aesthetic restorative dentistry (as seen on makeover shows), teaching an anxious seven-year-old how to clean their teeth or examining a patient with oral cancer.

Students learn the importance of the role they are set to take in the community. Learning does not solely take place within dental schools. Students widen their experience by going on elective studies, often to other parts of the world, and gain work-based learning in local outreach centres. The dental graduate therefore has an understanding of the differing dental needs of patients and has the management skills to provide appropriate treatment.

This degree is the stepping stone to wide-ranging career options — general dental practice, community care, hospital dentistry, specialising in a particular aspect of dentistry (orthodontics, oral surgery, oral medicine, restorative dentistry, to name a few), academic dentistry carrying out research, dentistry in the armed forces or work abroad with charities providing dental care to people in third-world countries.

New techniques and procedures are developing rapidly, expanding the scope and ability of dentists to diagnose and treat disease and gain greater understanding of health education and management. Using scientific knowledge, manual dexterity, interpersonal skills, and a professional attitude dentists can take their skills all over the world and feel fulfilled in their work. Dentistry is a very popular career choice as it offers so many challenges and opportunities.

**Dr Angela Fairclough**, *Director of Learning and Teaching, School of Clinical Dentistry, University of Sheffield*

---

Dentistry is one of the youngest (more than half of all dentists are in their 20s and 30s) and most progressive professions in the UK. Equally, it can be one of the best paid. Even in the NHS, net earnings can be around £80,000 a year, with private practitioners able to set their own fees. So although it's not a licence to print money (most dentistry graduates emerge with a large debt burden, for one thing), it is an extremely popular course to choose — and competition is hot.

You'll be expected to have excellent A-levels — chemistry is a requirement, and while biology is sometimes not specified, it is usually preferred. In any case, a second science A-level is required and usually an AS-level in biology as a minimum. It's almost essential to have had some work experience too — your school or college might run or know of a scheme whereby you can do some observation and work experience at a local practice.

The majority of students are interviewed, and most dental schools also require you to sit the Ukcat (UK Clinical Aptitude Test) before you fill in your Ucas form. For more information on this, including a list of the institutions that currently require it, see the Medical sciences section in this guide.

Once you're in, the form of degree is determined by the General Dental Council, which also sets the minimum standard a dental student must reach upon graduation. After that, what variation there is depends on the individual dental school. The course will involve five years of academic work. In that five years of study you should gain a thorough scientific knowledge and the necessary clinical and practical skills to care for and treat your patients and run a practice. There may also be the option of an intercalated year, in which you will be encouraged to take a science-related course before returning to dentistry.

Teaching includes a wide range of methods from lectures to tutorials, from computer-assisted learning to practical classes as well as the problem-based learning approach favoured by some courses. Exams are generally held at the end of every year, and a percentage of the marks for each exam may be derived from in-course assessment, which may take the form of essays, practical tests or project work. Some schools also assess competency for clinical work and professional attitude.

Remember that the closing date for applications to dentistry courses is earlier than that for most other courses – usually around mid-October. Competition is stiff, and as a safety net for the many who fail to get in, Ucas insists that no more than four of the five choices on your form should be to schools of dentistry. The others can be used to bid for alternative courses, including medicine, without prejudicing your perceived commitment to dentistry.

However, when sizing up the dental options, consider the course carefully. Many courses now introduce you to patients almost at the beginning, while others start with up to two years of pre-clinical work. If you have plans for the intercalated year, consider the wider institution and the courses on offer. Elective periods – which offer the opportunity to extend experience and study elsewhere, either at home or abroad – can also offer invaluable experience, and should be investigated. Look too at the availability and state of the library, IT, laboratory, clinical facilities and also whether they offer outreach placements, which many do.

Specialisations begin after you qualify. Those who wish to concentrate on areas such as orthodontics, restorative dentistry, endodontics, prosthodontics, periodontics, and paediatric dentistry can do so under training and qualifications schemes run by the dental schools. But if you want to go on to postgraduate study, that will be organised by the local postgraduate institute. Investigate the school's links to postgraduate vocational training – the obligatory learning you will have to take on once you start in your practice will, more than likely, start from there. It may seem like a long way away, but it'll soon come around.

---

 The most enjoyable aspect of dentistry is the practical nature of the course. Most teaching is in small groups in the dental clinics with theory followed by treatment of patients. The five-year course is fairly intensive and busy which gives students a good understanding of what the job of being a dentist will be like after graduating.

**Jamie Toole**, *fifth-year dentistry student, Queen's University Belfast*

## Dentistry

| | | Guardian score /100 | Satisfied with teaching % | Satisfied with feedback % | Spend per student /10 | Student:staff ratio | Job prospects % | Value added score /10 | Average entry tariff |
|---|---|---|---|---|---|---|---|---|---|
| 1 | Manchester | 100.0 | 97 | 86 | 7 | 8.4 | 100 | 1 | 449 |
| 2 | Glasgow | 89.1 | 96 | 68 | 2 | 9.0 | 100 | 6 | 499 |
| 3 | Leeds | 79.3 | 98 | 39 | 10 | 10.8 | 100 | 6 | 443 |
| 4 | King's College London | 78.9 | 83 | 35 | 8 | 7.2 | 97 | 6 | 468 |
| 5 | Queen's, Belfast | 71.0 | 95 | 68 | 4 | 7.0 | 100 | 6 | 423 |
| 6 | Dundee | 69.7 | 92 | 30 | 5 | 7.4 | 98 | 7 | 462 |
| 7 | Newcastle | 69.0 | 98 | 59 | 3 | 11.1 | 100 | 6 | 481 |
| 8 | Liverpool | 66.4 | 81 | 61 | 7 | 8.5 | 100 | 7 | 455 |
| 9 | Birmingham | 64.6 | 97 | 80 | 4 | 9.6 | 100 | 6 | 436 |
| 10 | Sheffield | 64.5 | 92 | 69 | 4 | 9.2 | 100 | 6 | 451 |
| 11 | Cardiff | 48.0 | 80 | 33 | 7 | 7.1 | 100 | 4 | 448 |
| 12 | Queen Mary | 45.8 | 74 | 43 | 5 | 7.6 | 96 | 7 | 445 |
| 13 | Bristol | 33.9 | 88 | 43 | 6 | 12.2 | 97 | 7 | 454 |

# Medicine

❝ Ask most doctors about their work and they are quite likely to moan about the NHS or the pressures. Ask them what else they would like to do as a job and most are struggling to find a comparison with medicine. Despite recent problems with job applications and career plans for young doctors, medicine remains an immensely rewarding career. It has huge variety, everything from regular patient contact to research, teaching, and administration. Medicine combines the great privilege of dealing with people's problems, often helping them at their most vulnerable times; at the same time it has the stimulating challenge of keeping up to date with ever-increasing advances in technology and treatments. What could be better than to train for a job that keeps you interested, challenged, and rewarded, while entering a profession that the public still trusts more than any other.

**Professor John Rees**, *Dean of Undergraduate Education, Head of Division, Medical Education, King's College London, School of Medicine*

Each year, thousands of students with lots of As in sciences at A-level sign up for five years of unpaid training. Once qualified, they will work long, long hours for little money. They make life and death decisions without much supervision and there's a high risk of suicide, drug addiction or alcoholism, with potential for high earnings after, oh, 20 years. Yet each year, many of the UK's finest 18-year-old minds decide this is the career for them, leaving Britain's medical schools oversubscribed and able to pick and choose the crème de la crème of the applicants. These applicants know that, despite the pitfalls, medicine can be a uniquely rewarding profession, impacting practically and emotionally on people's lives in a way that only doctors can.

The medical school business is booming, with new schools being launched and established places enrolling both mature and even former arts degree students in response to demand.

The institutions are looking for candidates who are ready for a world of pain (their own as well as their patients'), aware of the daily crises that make up the NHS, and have the inner robustness that means they won't go to pieces at the first sight of blood.

You'll be up against the very best, so in addition to excellent A-levels (which must include chemistry and biology) and GCSEs, achievements in several areas – music, sport, languages, Duke of Edinburgh awards, being head of school, or anything else that shows you have initiative and drive – will all be an important advantage, as will work experience.

Medical courses are changing. Typically they involve five years of academic work, with an optional intercalated year (studying a science course for 12 months before returning to medicine). In the early 1990s, medical schools attracted criticism from the General Medical Council for spending too long on lectures, and so each changed their curriculum to put more emphasis on communication skills, understanding cultural issues, and more patient interaction.

Although the government has promised to pay tuition fees for medical students in their fifth and sixth years (or in years two, three and four of fast-track courses) as one of a number of schemes to attract young people from poor families and ethnic minority communities to train as doctors, the average medical student is still likely to graduate with debts of between £20,000 and £60,000.

Some medical schools run integrated courses, which means that instead of spending a couple of years in university doing your pre-clinical training and being a normal undergraduate in lectures and laboratories you will be seeing patients from the very first term and applying your knowledge to real-life problems. This can be daunting but invaluable, and whether you prefer this is dependent on whether you see yourself as learning a trade or a science.

Location should be a big factor. You'll be attached to the institution for longer than the normal undergraduate's three or four years, so try to establish whether you'll be happy there. A visit, preferably to an open day, is essential. Investigate the social side, and try to find out how supportive the student environment is – things are likely to get very tough over the five years.

Check the options for the intercalated year, where you can study a subject in depth or pursue research, and also for elective periods, which offer the opportunity to extend experience and study elsewhere, either at home or abroad. Look too at the learning resources – what is the availability and state of the library, IT, laboratory, and clinical facilities?

Remember that the closing date for medicine courses is earlier than for most – October 15, and that you can only pick medicine for four of your five allocated Ucas choices. And finally, two words of warning:

As with dentistry, some medical schools may insist that you sit a new aptitude test before you apply. The clinical aptitude test (Ukcat) has been developed by a consortium of universities and has been in place since 2006. The difference between the Ukcat and similar admissions tests that are currently in use to help universities decide between top medical candidates is that it is taken before students fill in their Ucas forms. The consortium hopes to give candidates and admissions officers a better idea of the suitability of the former to a medical career before they apply for courses. The 90-minute Ukcat exam will test candidates' mental abilities and assesses how they might respond to patients. Scientific knowledge is not tested.

The full list of dental and medical schools currently using Ukcat is:

University of Aberdeen
Barts and the London School
  of Medicine and Dentistry
Brighton and Sussex Medical School
Cardiff University
University of Dundee
University of Durham
University of East Anglia
University of Edinburgh
University of Glasgow
Hull York Medical School
Imperial College, London
Keele University
King's College London

University of Leeds
University of Leicester
University of Manchester
Newcastle University
University of Nottingham
University of Oxford (graduate entry)
Peninsula College of Medicine and Dentistry
Queen's University Belfast
University of Sheffield
University of Southampton
University of St Andrews
St George's, University of London
Warwick University (graduate entry)

If your university of choice isn't up there, don't think you've got away with it. A number of universities use the BioMedical Admission Test (Bmat). This is aimed at testing students' thinking skills as opposed to subject knowledge. It is not a pass or fail test but admissions tutors will have the results available alongside candidates' AS-level results and predicted A-level results. You have to register separately for the tests. For dates and more information, check www.bmat.org.uk. The universities who use the Bmat are:

University of Cambridge
Imperial College London
University of Oxford Medical School
Royal Veterinary College
University College London

---

" While medicine is not an easy subject, it is one that I never regret choosing. Although there is a lot of hard work the constant satisfaction you gain from it keeps you highly driven. Imperial was definitely the right choice for me as it fosters both clinical and research science.

**Suha Bachir**, *fourth-year medical student, Imperial College London*

---

## » Further information

**British Medical Association**
BMA House, Tavistock Square
London WC1H 9JP

t   020 7387 4499
↗ www.bma.org.uk

**General Medical Council**
Regent's Place, 350 Euston Road
London NW1 3JN

t   0845 357 8001
e   gmc@gmc-uk.org
↗ www.gmc-uk.org

**The Academy of Medical Sciences**
10 Carlton House Terrace
London SW1Y 5AH

t   020 7969 5288
e   info@acmedsci.ac.uk
↗ www.acmedsci.ac.uk

## » Online reading

**SocietyGuardian.co.uk health section**  SocietyGuardian.co.uk/health
**The British Medical Journal**  www.bmj.com
**Department of Health**  www.dh.gov.uk

# Medicine

| | | Guardian score /100 | Satisfied with teaching % | Satisfied with feedback % | Spend per student /10 | Student-staff ratio | Job prospects % | Value added score /10 | Average entry tariff |
|---|---|---|---|---|---|---|---|---|---|
| 1 | Oxford | 100.0 | 92 | 69 | 10 | 6.7 | 100 | 4 | 536 |
| 2 | Cambridge | 81.5 | | | 9 | 7.0 | 98 | 2 | 554 |
| 3 | Edinburgh | 77.4 | 94 | 42 | 9 | 6.0 | 100 | 4 | 546 |
| 4 | Dundee | 77.2 | 91 | 52 | 8 | 3.0 | 100 | 6 | 503 |
| 5 | UCL | 71.0 | 92 | 46 | 6 | 4.7 | 98 | 9 | 512 |
| 6 | UEA | 62.2 | 97 | 58 | 4 | 5.3 | 98 | 8 | 413 |
| 7 | Imperial College | 61.4 | 87 | 37 | 7 | 6.2 | 100 | 4 | 514 |
| 8 | Leicester | 60.2 | 90 | 60 | | | 100 | 7 | 470 |
| 9 | Aberdeen | 57.4 | 93 | 59 | 4 | 7.4 | 100 | 6 | 482 |
| 9 | Glasgow | 57.4 | 88 | 43 | 4 | 7.3 | 100 | 5 | 517 |
| 11 | St Andrews | 54.3 | 98 | 64 | 3 | 13.3 | 99 | 1 | 503 |
| 12 | Newcastle | 52.4 | 92 | 46 | 4 | 7.8 | 100 | 5 | 481 |
| 13 | Leeds | 50.2 | 92 | 54 | 4 | 8.4 | 99 | 5 | 467 |
| 14 | King's College London | 50.1 | 86 | 35 | 7 | 6.5 | 99 | 6 | 466 |
| 15 | Keele | 49.0 | 91 | 53 | 3 | 10.7 | | 10 | 458 |
| 16 | Hull York Medical School | 47.3 | 91 | 53 | 5 | 10.8 | | 5 | 472 |
| 17 | Southampton | 46.4 | 92 | 50 | 4 | 9.3 | 98 | 7 | 454 |
| 18 | Warwick | 45.8 | 84 | 34 | 7 | 8.9 | 100 | 7 | |
| 19 | Manchester | 44.5 | 82 | 35 | 6 | 9.8 | 100 | 8 | 488 |
| 20 | Peninsula Medical School | 43.8 | 91 | 48 | 7 | 11.1 | 99 | 6 | 422 |
| 21 | Nottingham | 42.3 | 88 | 30 | 4 | 6.3 | 99 | 1 | 478 |
| 22 | St George's Medical School | 41.4 | 89 | 43 | 4 | 11.0 | 100 | 7 | 457 |
| 23 | Queen's, Belfast | 35.5 | 92 | 45 | 3 | 10.2 | 100 | 5 | 446 |
| 24 | Queen Mary | 34.7 | 79 | 45 | 5 | 9.0 | 98 | 6 | 430 |
| 25 | Liverpool | 33.8 | 73 | 31 | 4 | 8.2 | 100 | 5 | 477 |
| 26 | Birmingham | 32.5 | 81 | 27 | 4 | 10.1 | 100 | 4 | 496 |
| 27 | Sheffield | 32.1 | 79 | 27 | 3 | 7.9 | 100 | 5 | 471 |
| 28 | Bristol | 29.0 | 84 | 24 | 5 | 11.9 | 99 | 4 | 472 |
| 29 | Cardiff | 25.9 | 76 | 19 | 4 | 9.2 | 100 | 7 | 469 |
| 30 | Brighton Sussex Medical School | 25.3 | | | 4 | 14.9 | | 6 | 471 |

# Nursing

❝ Nursing is a profession that requires a wide range of skills and aptitudes. Caring and compassion, for instance, are of equal importance as theoretical knowledge, and communication and teamwork skills are as important as technical expertise. Nursing degree and diploma programmes offer the opportunity to develop these abilities, as well as many others, in a variety of practice settings, ranging from NHS Trust hospitals to the patient's own home. They all share a common first year and then you follow your chosen branch of nursing: adult, child health, learning disability or mental health. Both diplomas and degrees in nursing lead to state registration.

In England, most student nurses take a three-year diploma course, which requires five GCSEs or equivalent qualifications, but nursing students with A-levels or equivalent qualifications can take a degree course (on which our tables are based), also lasting three years. All of these courses are run by universities, in partnership with local hospitals. Courses are divided into half theory and half practice.

In theory, this should be a boom time to enter nursing. The government has increased spending in the NHS, employing more nurses and paying them better. Students of all health-related courses can be confident they are heading into an industry that wants them badly.

**Kate Law,** *Assistant Head of School (pre-registration education), University of Brighton*

Nursing is a profession that requires a wide range of skills and aptitudes. Caring and compassion, for instance, share equal importance with theoretical knowledge, and communication and teamwork skills are as important as technical expertise. Nursing degree programmes offer the opportunity to develop these abilities, as well as many others, in a variety of practice settings, ranging from NHS Trust hospitals to the patient's own home.

There are four different nursing degree programmes that you can choose from. They all share a common first year and then you follow your chosen branch of nursing: adult, child health, learning disability or mental health. Both diplomas and degrees in nursing lead to state registration.

In England, most student nurses take a three-year diploma course, which requires five GCSEs or equivalent qualifications, but nursing students with A-levels or equivalent qualifications can take a degree course (on which our tables are based), also lasting three years.

All these courses are run by universities, in partnership with local hospitals. Courses are divided into half theory and half practice. Recent changes mean students now go out to hospitals earlier – usually in the first three months of the course, instead of at six months or later. And the placements are longer – eight weeks instead of three.

In theory, this should be a boom time to enter nursing. The government has increased spending in the NHS, employing more nurses and paying them better. Students of all health-related courses can be reasonably confident they are heading into an industry that wants them badly.

But – and it is a big but to bear in mind – a quarter of student nurses drop out of training before they qualify, according to figures published in early 2006. Financial pressures, the burden of childcare, and bad experiences of ward rounds are thought to be the main reasons why students leave early. The government is attempting to deal with the financial pressures, offering bursaries for living costs, and tuition fees are now paid in full by the NHS. And universities have devoted resources to provide specific support for nursing students to improve retention prospects.

The downside to the increase in places and applications to nursing is the pressure it puts on university departments. Students over the next few years may pay the price in crowded lecture theatres and inadequate supervision. Don't be afraid to ask awkward questions about how well staffed and equipped a department is.

Nurses do most of their training on placements in hospitals, so it is crucial to ask where the placements will be. Does the hospital have a good reputation and is it near enough to make the travel manageable? You may want to have a quick look around the university's hospital "partners" as well as the university itself.

You should also enquire whether the university is good at teaching the type of nursing you want to specialise in (such as children's nursing or mental health). Go to open days and speak to current or past students. Check also the way students are assessed. If you prefer continuous assessment to an exam-based system, choose universities taking that approach, and vice versa.

---

66 A nursing degree is extremely time-consuming — the combination of working shifts, writing assignments, and trying to fit in a social life can be difficult. However, all these aspects are outweighed by the rewarding nature of the work.

The parts of the course I have enjoyed most are the placements, as it is here that you learn the reality of nursing. The course is well structured, as it ensures you spend time in a variety of clinical situations.

**Annie Lowe**, *final-year adult health nursing student, Leeds Metropolitan University*

---

## » Further information

**Royal College of Nursing**
20 Cavendish Square
London W1G 0RN

t   020 7409 3333
↗ www.rcn.org.uk

**Nursing and Midwifery Council**
23 Portland Place
London W1B 1PZ

t   020 7333 9333
e   advice@nmc-uk.org
↗ www.nmc-uk.org

**Health Professions Council**
Park House
184 Kennington Park Road
London SE11 4BU

t   020 7840 9802
e   registration@hpc-uk.org
↗ www.hpc-uk.org

## ↗ Online reading

**SocietyGuardian.co.uk health**  Societyguardian.co.uk/health
**Health Service Journal**  www.hsj.co.uk
**Nursing Standard**  www.nursing-standard.co.uk
**Nursing Times**  www.nursingtimes.net
**Department of Health**  www.dh.gov.uk

# Nursing and paramedical studies

| | | Guardian score /100 | Satisfied with teaching % | Satisfied with feedback % | Spend per student /10 | Student:staff ratio | Job prospects % | Value added score /10 | Average entry tariff |
|---|---|---|---|---|---|---|---|---|---|
| 1 | Edinburgh | 100.0 | 98 | 77 | 10 | 7.1 | 97 | 8 | 395 |
| 2 | Thames Valley | 72.2 | 86 | 72 | 9 | 9.7 | 97 | 6 | |
| 3 | Leeds | 70.6 | 78 | 63 | 10 | 13.4 | 98 | 4 | 322 |
| 4 | Liverpool | 67.2 | 88 | 59 | 8 | 9.7 | 97 | 3 | 325 |
| 5 | Robert Gordon | 65.8 | | | 5 | 15.2 | 93 | 9 | 321 |
| 6 | Nottingham | 65.2 | 88 | 59 | 7 | 15.2 | 93 | 8 | 351 |
| 6 | UEA | 65.2 | 88 | 54 | 9 | 16.7 | 89 | 8 | 339 |
| 8 | Bradford | 63.0 | 84 | 70 | 5 | 11.9 | 88 | 6 | 357 |
| 9 | King's College London | 62.9 | 83 | 47 | 8 | 14.2 | 96 | 6 | 336 |
| 10 | Glasgow | 62.6 | 91 | 61 | 3 | 14.4 | | 8 | 346 |
| 11 | Queen's, Belfast | 62.0 | 89 | 74 | 4 | 17.4 | 98 | 10 | 279 |
| 12 | Essex | 61.1 | | | 5 | 11.7 | | 10 | 242 |
| 13 | Keele | 60.5 | 92 | 59 | 5 | 14.7 | 93 | 7 | 318 |
| 14 | Sheffield Hallam | 59.7 | 93 | 71 | 5 | 12.2 | 89 | 7 | 260 |
| 14 | St George's Medical School | 59.7 | 90 | 49 | | | 91 | 5 | 302 |
| 16 | Kent | 59.1 | 92 | 63 | 9 | 9.3 | 73 | 3 | 293 |
| 17 | Southampton | 58.4 | 90 | 67 | 7 | 14.5 | 89 | 2 | 378 |
| 18 | Stirling | 58.1 | 83 | 56 | 7 | 14.4 | 99 | | |
| 19 | Edinburgh Napier | 58.0 | | | 4 | 16.3 | 95 | 9 | |
| 20 | Birmingham | 57.8 | 91 | 53 | 7 | 13.5 | 78 | 5 | 372 |
| 21 | Northampton | 56.7 | 93 | 54 | 4 | 10.7 | 85 | 8 | 241 |
| 22 | Glasgow Caledonian | 56.0 | 88 | 73 | 4 | 16.5 | 92 | 6 | 332 |
| 23 | Surrey | 55.6 | 88 | 72 | 7 | 20.5 | 98 | 5 | 326 |
| 24 | Cumbria | 55.4 | | | 5 | 14.9 | 88 | 5 | 323 |
| 25 | Ulster | 55.1 | 72 | 56 | 6 | 13.4 | 92 | 7 | 307 |
| 26 | Brighton | 54.8 | 84 | 55 | 4 | 14.1 | 87 | 8 | 299 |
| 26 | York | 54.8 | | | 8 | 11.6 | | 1 | 313 |
| 28 | Glamorgan | 54.1 | 86 | 74 | 5 | 11.3 | 95 | 3 | |
| 29 | Bangor | 53.4 | 86 | 66 | 5 | 12.5 | 98 | 2 | 276 |
| 30 | Chester | 53.3 | 88 | 65 | 2 | 13.5 | 92 | 8 | 274 |
| 31 | Cardiff | 53.2 | 90 | 54 | 6 | 13.2 | 92 | 2 | 297 |
| 32 | UWE Bristol | 52.6 | 84 | 69 | 4 | 14.3 | 91 | 7 | 261 |
| 33 | City | 51.8 | 76 | 58 | 8 | 13.7 | 85 | 6 | 253 |
| 34 | Manchester | 51.7 | 86 | 47 | 7 | 18.7 | 90 | 4 | 325 |
| 35 | Dundee | 51.4 | 90 | 66 | 5 | 18.1 | 96 | | 250 |
| 36 | Queen Margaret | 51.2 | | | 3 | 18.5 | 84 | 9 | 325 |
| 37 | Plymouth | 51.1 | 81 | 58 | 8 | 19.9 | 85 | 9 | 250 |
| 38 | Bedfordshire | 51.0 | 90 | 67 | 3 | 18.0 | 91 | 10 | 194 |
| 39 | Coventry | 50.6 | | | 4 | 15.9 | 83 | 8 | 277 |
| 40 | Staffordshire | 50.2 | 78 | 62 | 7 | 12.9 | 87 | 7 | 218 |
| 41 | Brunel | 49.8 | 72 | 50 | 5 | 15.8 | 77 | 9 | 322 |
| 42 | Oxford Brookes | 48.1 | 76 | 34 | 4 | 15.9 | 88 | 8 | 299 |
| 43 | Hull | 47.9 | 82 | 64 | 4 | 16.0 | 99 | 3 | 269 |
| 43 | Sunderland | 47.9 | 90 | 68 | | 14.3 | | 5 | 209 |
| 43 | Swansea | 47.9 | 77 | 59 | 7 | 14.2 | 91 | 3 | 287 |
| 46 | Bucks New University | 47.4 | | | 4 | 17.8 | 90 | 6 | |

| | | Guardian score /100 | Satisfied with teaching % | Satisfied with feedback % | Spend per student /10 | Student:staff ratio | Job prospects % | Value added score /10 | Average entry tariff |
|---|---|---|---|---|---|---|---|---|---|
| 47 | Anglia Ruskin | 47.2 | 87 | 55 | 8 | 24.1 | 96 | 4 | 259 |
| 48 | Northumbria | 46.7 | 89 | 80 | 4 | 20.4 | 72 | 7 | 327 |
| 49 | Hertfordshire | 46.5 | 80 | 48 | 6 | 11.5 | 84 | 5 | 237 |
| 50 | Birmingham City | 45.3 | 80 | 61 | 5 | 16.7 | 93 | 5 | 251 |
| 50 | Bournemouth | 45.3 | 80 | 59 | 7 | 21.7 | 92 | 8 | 242 |
| 52 | Salford | 45.0 | 87 | 65 | 4 | 15.5 | 84 | 3 | 263 |
| 53 | Central Lancashire | 44.8 | 81 | 68 | 4 | 23.1 | 99 | 4 | 323 |
| 54 | Marjon (St Mark and St John) | 44.7 | 90 | 54 | 2 | 13.3 | 70 | 5 | |
| 55 | Derby | 43.7 | 78 | 51 | 4 | 11.7 | 87 | 4 | 257 |
| 55 | York St John | 43.7 | 89 | 69 | 3 | 15.1 | 72 | 6 | 265 |
| 57 | Edge Hill | 43.3 | 85 | 78 | 3 | 16.0 | 84 | 5 | 209 |
| 58 | Teesside | 42.7 | 84 | 72 | 3 | 20.0 | 88 | 4 | 281 |
| 59 | Huddersfield | 42.6 | 83 | 74 | 4 | 16.2 | 71 | 7 | 248 |
| 60 | Middlesex | 41.9 | 79 | 68 | 8 | 15.6 | 80 | 3 | 215 |
| 61 | Leeds Met | 41.2 | 76 | 69 | 5 | 16.7 | 78 | 4 | 285 |
| 62 | Canterbury Christ Church | 40.3 | 88 | 63 | 3 | 18.2 | 91 | 2 | 260 |
| 63 | Manchester Met | 38.9 | 75 | 56 | 4 | 15.9 | 74 | 4 | 302 |
| 64 | Kingston | 38.6 | 82 | 57 | 6 | 17.8 | 68 | 7 | 241 |
| 65 | Greenwich | 37.3 | 96 | 76 | 3 | 20.0 | 76 | 4 | 229 |
| 66 | Worcester | 37.1 | | | 3 | 18.3 | 99 | 3 | 209 |
| 67 | De Montfort | 36.7 | 78 | 62 | 5 | 17.7 | 76 | 4 | 258 |
| 68 | London South Bank | 35.7 | 87 | 69 | 3 | 24.5 | 93 | 5 | 193 |
| 69 | East London | 35.4 | 72 | 62 | 8 | 12.0 | 81 | 2 | 152 |
| 70 | Glyndŵr | 33.7 | 90 | 79 | 3 | 19.4 | 92 | 1 | 203 |
| 71 | Lincoln | 31.2 | 83 | 63 | 3 | 19.2 | 69 | 6 | 237 |
| 72 | Liverpool John Moores | 25.7 | 75 | 60 | 5 | 17.5 | 65 | 3 | 216 |
| 73 | Abertay Dundee | 25.4 | | | 3 | 20.6 | 73 | 2 | 263 |

# Pharmacology and pharmacy

Lumping these two subjects together is a bit of a problem, as they're very different and, quite frankly, don't belong in the same chapter. But because of the way they are aggregated in university statistics, we can't do anything else. We can't separate them out in the tables (well, we could, and others do, but that wouldn't make any sense statistically speaking), so we've got to consider them together. But you don't have to. They are two different subjects and you should treat them as such.

## Pharmacology

66 Pharmacology is both exciting and challenging. There are few other subjects where you can appreciate the impact that it is making on medical advances, and the enormous benefits to human health and society. Pharmacology is a highly integrative biomedical science, requiring a wide understanding of chemistry, biochemistry, physiology, and genomics. In a nutshell, pharmacology is about understanding how drugs act on biological systems. It is also about using drugs as tools so that we can better understand how cellular systems of the body work.

Pharmacologists are responsible for the discovery of the hundreds of compounds that are used today in the treatment of disease in both humans and animals. Around a quarter of the world's top medicines were discovered in the UK. These include, for example, new drugs for the treatment of asthma; the management of pain; antibacterial and anticancer drugs; and cardiovascular and neuropsychiatric disorders. As well as the discovery of wholly novel drugs, pharmacology has enabled the development of better drugs with far fewer side effects than were used before.

Where is pharmacology going in the next decades, and where are the frontiers of knowledge? In the post-genomic era, the discipline has made extraordinary strides forward.

Career opportunities for pharmacology graduates are vast: many are so enthused by the excitement of the subject, particularly if they have taken a programme with a sandwich year in industry, that they go on to carry out research for a PhD and ultimately join teams in the pharmaceutical industry or academia. Employment prospects for pharmacologists, within the big pharmaceutical companies and biotechnology enterprises, are excellent. The need by industry for pharmacologists goes far beyond laboratory-based research and development, and many may be found involved in clinical trials and drug safety; regulatory affairs; post-marketing drug surveillance; and sales and marketing.

The study of pharmacology provides great opportunities for challenging and rewarding careers, and it is a particularly exciting time to be setting out on this path.

**Peter Roberts**, *Professor of Pharmacology and Chairman of the Committee of Heads of Pharmacology Departments, University of Bristol*

---

Pharmacology is concerned with medicinal drugs: the ways they are administered, how the body distributes and eliminates them and their actual effects — it's where chemistry meets medicine. Pharmacologists study drug action in the whole body, right down to their effects on individual molecules in the cell. Pharmacologists use their knowledge of how cells and organs function to discover drugs to restore the body to health when affected by disease. For such a specialised discipline, it can touch on a remarkably wide variety of topics, including physiology, cell biology, molecular biology, immunology, medicinal chemistry, and biochemistry.

As most drugs are used to treat or prevent disease, pharmacology has a close association with medicine and the pharmaceutical industry, which not only plays an important role in drug discovery and development, but is also a major contributor to the economy, both in the UK and worldwide.

The job prospects for graduates are good, with careers in postgraduate research, teaching, health laboratories, or of course the pharmaceutical industry, where there are also non-lab-based jobs in areas such as drug safety, marketing, quality auditing or product registration.

More than 25 universities run a course in pharmacology, although some run it only in association with other courses. Some provide modules on pharmacology as part of other biomedical science degrees. You'll need three good A-levels, at least two of which will be in the science subjects, plus a good science background at GCSE level. All courses combine practical work and tutorial sessions with a lecture programme. A number of courses in pharmacology also provide the opportunity for "study in industry", involving an industrial placement of up to a year's duration.

---

  I first came across the basic principles that lead to the understanding of pharmacology while studying biology at A-level. The subject is largely based around physiology, rather than chemistry, so a good grasp of how the body works at the molecular and cellular level is needed. When physiological systems go wrong, the really challenging part is discovering how exactly they went wrong and how to put it right. And it's great being kept up to date with the very latest research information.

**Charlotte Mann**, *third-year pharmacology student, King's College London*

---

# Pharmacy

  Pharmacy is an ideal career choice if you wish to combine a broad-based science degree and vocational training leading to flexible and well-remunerated career options. It is an exciting time to study pharmacy and enter a profession whose role as the experts in medicines is expanding as a result of new scientific advances and recent developments like pharmacist prescribing.

Undergraduate curricula integrate key areas of the physical and biological sciences to enable you to critically evaluate and problem-solve both scientific and professional issues, applying these to clinical practice. Subjects taught will include: pharmaceutical and medicinal chemistry, pharmaceutics (the formulation of active molecules into medicines that patients can take), pharmacology (the interaction of chemical substances with biological systems), molecular biology, leading to topics including stem-cell research, pharmacy law and ethics, and health policy. All MPharm courses include a supervised final-year research project. Placements and formal teaching are organised in both hospital and community pharmacies during the course, in preparation for your pre-registration year of 'on the job' training.

Career opportunities in pharmacy are increasing; pharmacists work in community pharmacies, on hospital wards, in GPs' surgeries, in NHS management, in industry, and in teaching and research at universities. If you are good at science and have sound communication skills then consider pharmacy as an excellent career option!

**Dr Philip Rogers**, *Director of Undergraduate Studies in the Department of Pharmacy & Pharmacology, University of Bath*

Pharmacy is seeing a healthy rise in applicants, partly because the unemployment levels for the industry are very low, but also because the perception of the role of the pharmacist is changing.

Whether it be in a community or hospital setting, the government is increasingly acknowledging that pharmacy is one of the primary health professions in the NHS, and that pharmacists are an integral part of most people's experience of NHS care.

Schools of pharmacy teach the study of medicinal substances and the application of their therapeutic uses in the practice of the profession.

The course is a broad-based four-year affair, leading to an MPharm degree, producing graduates for careers in community, hospital, and industry or research pharmacy.

All UK pharmacy degree courses are accredited by the Royal Pharmaceutical Society of Great Britain. In almost all cases, graduates follow their degree with a pre-registration year of professional training in community, hospital or industrial pharmacy before qualifying to join the society's register of professional pharmacists.

Teaching is by a combination of formal lectures and lab-based classes, which may be supplemented by computer-assisted learning, video demonstrations, and tutorials. You will be assessed by a combination of written examinations and coursework.

If you want to study pharmacy, you'll almost certainly need three A-levels, including chemistry, with two subjects from biology/human biology, maths, and physics. Work experience is also a big help, but if you lack the contacts to arrange this, get in touch with the pharmacy school yourself to see if they can help.

Check the learning and teaching facilities – the labs, the state of the medical library, and the IT facilities are all important to your everyday work, so you'll need to be happy with the availability and quality.

Check too the methods of teaching on the course you're considering. Many courses are moving away from the traditional lecture-based approach, and the balance between that and more modern methods (computer simulations, or video-based learning, for example) should also be a consideration. Assessment methods can also vary – it won't just be exams, and it'll pay to consider whether a high number of project-based assignments or dissertations are to your taste.

---

> Pharmacy was an ideal choice of degree course for me after completing science subjects at A-level. I have found the vocational course both challenging and enjoyable, and the blend of science and practice-based course material has prepared me well for my future career as a pharmacist. The excellent academic and research standards here combined with the friendly department atmosphere has provided a fantastic learning environment for me.

**Catherine Golics**, *final-year pharmacy student, Cardiff University*

---

## Further information

**British Pharmacological Society**
16 Angel Gate, City Road
London EC1V 2SG

t 020 7417 0113
www.bps.ac.uk

**Royal Pharmaceutical Society of Great Britain**
1 Lambeth High Street    **t**   020 7735 9141
London SE1 7JN    ↗ www.rpsgb.org.uk

**Association of the British Pharmaceutical Industry**
12 Whitehall    **t**   0870 890 4333
London SW1A 2DY    ↗ www.abpi.org.uk

**The National Pharmacy Association**
Mallinson House    **t**   01727 832161
38-42 St Peter's Street    **e**   npa@npa.co.uk
St Albans, Herts AL1 3NP    ↗ www.npa.co.uk

↗   Online reading

**Pharmweb**   www.pharmweb.net
**Association of Information Officers in the Pharmaceutical Industry**   www.aiopi.org.uk
**Pharmacy Online**   www.priory.com/pharmol.htm
**dotPharmacy**   www.dotpharmacy.com
**Pharmaceutical Journal**   www.pjonline.com
**Pharmaceutical Industry Info**   www.pharmaceutical-industry.info

# Pharmacology and pharmacy

| | | Guardian score /100 | Satisfied with teaching % | Satisfied with feedback % | Spend per student /10 | Student:staff ratio | Job prospects % | Value added score /10 | Average entry tariff |
|---|---|---|---|---|---|---|---|---|---|
| 1 | UCL | 100.0 | 88 | 52 | 9 | 9.9 | 77 | 8 | 411 |
| 2 | Strathclyde | 98.0 | 86 | 56 | 5 | 16.5 | 96 | 10 | 440 |
| 3 | Nottingham | 97.6 | 88 | 47 | 8 | 11.3 | 100 | 6 | 417 |
| 4 | Leeds | 96.2 | 93 | 69 | 9 | 11.3 | 78 | 5 | 445 |
| 5 | UEA | 90.6 | 93 | 71 | 5 | 16.6 | 100 | 6 | 378 |
| 6 | Bath | 90.0 | 90 | 54 | 4 | 14.7 | 96 | 7 | 441 |
| 7 | Liverpool | 89.2 | 88 | 68 | 9 | 6.9 | 70 | 7 | 348 |
| 8 | Bristol | 88.6 | 85 | 66 | 10 | 8.6 | 79 | 3 | 397 |
| 9 | Cardiff | 85.4 | 88 | 56 | 7 | 16.0 | 93 | 6 | 394 |
| 10 | Dundee | 81.8 | 91 | 66 | 3 | 9.0 | | | 400 |
| 11 | School of Pharmacy | 80.0 | 84 | 46 | 5 | 17.6 | 100 | 7 | 395 |
| 12 | Queen's, Belfast | 79.8 | 96 | 63 | 3 | 21.4 | 100 | 7 | 396 |
| 13 | Aston | 77.0 | 88 | 61 | 3 | 17.2 | 100 | 4 | 409 |
| 14 | Manchester | 75.7 | 82 | 42 | 9 | 22.3 | 94 | 5 | 410 |
| 15 | Brighton | 74.5 | 78 | 35 | | 11.1 | 100 | 8 | 358 |
| 16 | Robert Gordon | 69.4 | | | 3 | 21.4 | 100 | | 397 |
| 17 | Sunderland | 69.1 | 90 | 67 | 3 | 17.3 | 94 | 7 | 316 |
| 18 | Greenwich | 68.6 | 91 | 79 | 5 | 24.5 | | 7 | 274 |
| 19 | Hertfordshire | 66.5 | 90 | 68 | 4 | 6.0 | 65 | 5 | 286 |
| 20 | Southampton | 62.9 | 88 | 51 | 4 | 21.8 | | | 391 |
| 21 | De Montfort | 61.3 | 90 | 61 | 3 | 14.2 | 92 | 4 | 296 |
| 22 | King's College London | 59.8 | 84 | 49 | 4 | 15.2 | 85 | 3 | 382 |
| 23 | Bradford | 41.5 | 82 | 63 | 3 | 20.1 | 86 | 2 | 310 |
| 24 | Kingston | 39.6 | 88 | 63 | 4 | 18.1 | 61 | 6 | 256 |
| 25 | Portsmouth | 37.7 | 84 | 53 | 4 | 18.6 | 93 | 1 | 293 |

# Psychology

> There is nothing as fascinating as people. So what could be more enjoyable than spending three years studying them? The differences between people give the world its character, its complexity, as well as its problems. All the problems — and the solutions — to world issues have a psychological foundation because people are at the core of them. That explains the enduring fascination — and usefulness — of studying psychology. Psychologists cut through common sense to take an objective and scientific look at the myriad of human behaviours. From precise brain mechanisms to the broadest patterns of social behaviour, no other subject offers such breadth and diversity.
>
> A psychology graduate will know how to ask the right questions. They'll be skilled at knowing the best way to investigate issues. They'll have the critical thinking skills and methods to quantify and test ideas. Plus, they'll be able to communicate the answers in the most effective manner. With a broad knowledge of animal and human behaviour and thinking, psychologists can understand why things go wrong, what makes people ill, behave in unexpected ways, or contribute to problems in society.
>
> A psychology degree is the first step to becoming a practising psychologist. Graduates can go on to help people make changes for the better in clinical, occupational, sports, forensic, educational, health, environmental, and counselling settings. But because psychology is about understanding human thinking, performance, and behaviour, it's a degree that is valuable in any future career.
>
> **Professor Ben Fletcher**, *Head of School of Psychology, University of Hertfordshire*

Tell someone you do psychology, and people tend to get a bit twitchy, worrying that you're going to psychoanalyse them and reveal the hidden horrors of their twisted minds. Luckily for them, it's not quite like that.

These days, you're less likely to dabble with Freud than with the everyday workings of the human mind, both normal and abnormal, calculating why people think as they do.

Psychology is a relatively young scientific discipline, and is fairly flexible in its approach. Those who study it don't necessarily need science A-levels (but it certainly helps), and you don't necessarily need psychology A-level either. It is possible to find a university to take you if you have an arts background, although a mixture of both art and science is best, and most will require at least a good GCSE maths pass or equivalent.

Once you're in, you'll be studying subject areas such as personality types (introvert/ extrovert, that sort of thing), defining and testing intelligence (and working out whether that's a valid thing to do in the first place), perception, memory, and developmental psychology. Slightly more left-field options could include environmental, consumer, or paranormal psychology. Across all areas, much of the experimental work is computer-controlled so there are plenty of opportunities for computer fiends to develop their skills.

Courses are usually modular with a wide-ranging, scene-setting first year, before settling down to some serious choice in the following years. Most courses are accredited by the British Psychological Society; you'll have the possibility to take further training to become a professional psychologist if you complete an accredited course. You'll be assessed through a mixture of exams and coursework.

The employment rates for graduates are high. You've gained some excellent experience in problem-solving, so if you don't opt to move on to further clinical or forensic psychology, you can head for educational, health or occupational psychology, counselling or neuropsychology – perfect for the physicists amongst you with all that complex technical equipment (MRIs and MEGs). Alternatively you could find work in advertising, marketing or social work, or perhaps the probation and prison services.

When deciding on a course, investigate the modular options that open up in the second and third years. If you know you want to do face perception, visual processing or memory, then make sure they're on offer and try to find out if the tutors specialise in those areas.

Students are often taken by surprise when they realise the scientific nature of the subject. All psychology degrees involve training in statistics, and all require the writing of essays, dissertations, and projects, so ensure that these appeal.

> 66 The beauty of studying psychology is that the more you learn the more you understand its application to daily life. Whether it be the taste of toast or having a word on the tip-of-your-tongue, it covers a diverse range of exciting and challenging topics. One day you could be considering the causes of racism and the next the neurochemistry of drug addiction. The variety will keep even the most curious mind interested.
>
> **Rachel Harlow**, *psychology graduate, University of York*

## » Further information

**British Psychological Society**
St Andrews House
48 Princess Road East
Leicester LE1 7DR

t 0116 254 9568
↗ www.bps.org.uk

## ↗ Online reading

**Association for Humanistic Psychology** www.ahpweb.org
**Experimental Psychological Society** www.eps.ac.uk
**Psychweb** www.psywww.com
**American Psychological Association** www.apa.org
**Encyclopedia of Psychology** www.psychology.org

## Psychology

| | | Guardian score /100 | Satisfied with teaching % | Satisfied with feedback % | Spend per student /10 | Student:staff ratio | Job prospects % | Value added score /10 | Average entry tariff |
|---|---|---|---|---|---|---|---|---|---|
| 1 | Oxford | 100.0 | 92 | 58 | 10 | 12.9 | 79 | 8 | 499 |
| 2 | UCL | 88.5 | 84 | 72 | 10 | 11.7 | 83 | 8 | 469 |
| 3 | St Andrews | 84.4 | 93 | 69 | 10 | 10.2 | 59 | 7 | 466 |
| 4 | Royal Holloway | 75.3 | 92 | 65 | 6 | 13.1 | 71 | 8 | 388 |
| 5 | Bristol | 74.4 | 88 | 52 | 7 | 13.7 | 67 | 8 | 449 |
| 6 | Birmingham | 73.5 | 88 | 57 | 10 | 15.1 | 60 | 7 | 407 |
| 7 | Glasgow | 73.4 | 89 | 62 | 8 | 14.8 | 59 | 9 | 390 |
| 8 | York | 72.3 | 85 | 55 | 9 | 14.5 | 66 | 4 | 457 |

| | | Guardian score /100 | Satisfied with teaching % | Satisfied with feedback % | Spend per student /10 | Student:staff ratio | Job prospects % | Value added score /10 | Average entry tariff |
|---|---|---|---|---|---|---|---|---|---|
| 9 | Aberdeen | 71.8 | 91 | 76 | 7 | 17.1 | 57 | 10 | 338 |
| 10 | Sheffield | 71.6 | 89 | 52 | 8 | 14.2 | 69 | 6 | 407 |
| 11 | Exeter | 70.8 | 89 | 66 | 7 | 16.3 | 62 | 7 | 415 |
| 12 | Stirling | 70.0 | 85 | 66 | 8 | 13.6 | 43 | 10 | |
| 13 | Cardiff | 69.3 | 86 | 53 | 9 | 15.1 | 59 | 6 | 429 |
| 14 | Loughborough | 69.1 | 88 | 66 | 7 | 14.1 | 64 | 6 | 398 |
| 15 | Heriot-Watt | 68.7 | 91 | 62 | 7 | 10.0 | | 7 | 331 |
| 16 | Bath | 67.8 | 84 | 51 | 6 | 15.6 | 57 | 8 | 481 |
| 16 | Nottingham | 67.8 | 84 | 46 | 10 | 14.7 | 53 | 5 | 431 |
| 18 | Leicester | 66.7 | 88 | 59 | 7 | 19.2 | 67 | 9 | 359 |
| 19 | Surrey | 66.4 | 77 | 37 | 8 | 15.1 | 67 | 9 | 392 |
| 20 | Kent | 66.1 | 83 | 56 | 6 | 16.1 | 74 | 7 | 367 |
| 21 | Edinburgh | 65.9 | 83 | 36 | 8 | 15.0 | 57 | 8 | 422 |
| 22 | Southampton | 65.5 | 85 | 58 | 8 | 14.1 | 50 | 8 | 415 |
| 23 | Warwick | 65.2 | 84 | 45 | 7 | 14.9 | 60 | 6 | 414 |
| 24 | Durham | 64.9 | 88 | 67 | 5 | 15.6 | 63 | 4 | 425 |
| 25 | Leeds | 64.0 | 90 | 53 | 6 | 17.8 | 61 | 7 | 428 |
| 26 | Goldsmiths | 63.2 | 89 | 59 | 4 | 9.4 | 51 | 8 | 313 |
| 27 | Sussex | 62.3 | 88 | 58 | 4 | 16.6 | 65 | 7 | 386 |
| 28 | Manchester | 61.9 | 80 | 41 | 8 | 15.1 | 54 | 6 | 416 |
| 29 | Newcastle | 61.0 | 88 | 53 | 7 | 20.6 | 61 | 6 | 419 |
| 30 | Reading | 60.6 | 81 | 51 | 5 | 13.3 | 47 | 8 | 373 |
| 31 | Nottingham Trent | 60.0 | 87 | 58 | 6 | 14.7 | 53 | 8 | 290 |
| 32 | Hull | 59.9 | 87 | 66 | 4 | 19.8 | 70 | 7 | 314 |
| 33 | Oxford Brookes | 59.7 | 86 | 58 | 4 | 15.3 | 56 | 7 | 333 |
| 34 | Brunel | 59.6 | 83 | 78 | 3 | 19.3 | 59 | 8 | 322 |
| 35 | Lancaster | 59.3 | 88 | 53 | 5 | 16.8 | 56 | 4 | 390 |
| 36 | Aston | 58.5 | 90 | 63 | 3 | 16.8 | 64 | 3 | 373 |
| 37 | Queen's, Belfast | 58.3 | 88 | 39 | 9 | 17.5 | 43 | 6 | 348 |
| 38 | Plymouth | 57.8 | 82 | 60 | 7 | 13.4 | 43 | 7 | 297 |
| 39 | UEA | 57.2 | 95 | 77 | 2 | | 55 | 5 | 340 |
| 40 | Edinburgh Napier | 57.0 | | | 5 | 16.2 | 56 | 6 | 308 |
| 41 | Coventry | 56.5 | 84 | 70 | 6 | 15.5 | 47 | 7 | 294 |
| 42 | Staffordshire | 56.1 | 86 | 61 | 7 | 17.0 | 64 | 4 | 253 |
| 43 | Essex | 56.0 | 86 | 66 | 4 | 16.7 | 60 | 4 | 321 |
| 44 | Liverpool | 55.8 | 85 | 60 | 6 | 17.9 | 45 | 7 | 385 |
| 45 | Keele | 55.6 | 83 | 61 | 5 | 16.0 | 53 | 7 | 315 |
| 46 | Northumbria | 55.5 | 90 | 73 | 4 | 21.2 | 60 | 5 | 313 |
| 47 | Dundee | 55.2 | 82 | 61 | 4 | 13.3 | 47 | 5 | 372 |
| 48 | Bangor | 54.5 | 83 | 50 | 8 | 18.0 | 51 | 4 | 307 |
| 49 | Portsmouth | 54.2 | 90 | 56 | 5 | 19.0 | 55 | 6 | 307 |
| 50 | Bournemouth | 54.0 | 80 | 81 | 8 | 17.1 | 52 | 3 | 264 |
| 51 | Worcester | 52.9 | 88 | 59 | 4 | 14.0 | 45 | 7 | 239 |
| 52 | Westminster | 52.8 | 82 | 59 | 4 | 14.1 | 37 | 8 | 295 |
| 53 | Glasgow Caledonian | 52.4 | 87 | 60 | 3 | 20.3 | 40 | 9 | 320 |
| 54 | Canterbury Christ Church | 52.3 | 89 | 76 | 10 | 14.0 | 45 | 1 | 241 |
| 55 | UWE Bristol | 50.1 | 92 | 68 | 4 | 25.2 | 36 | 9 | 291 |

| | | Guardian score /100 | Satisfied with teaching % | Satisfied with feedback % | Spend per student /10 | Student:staff ratio | Job prospects % | Value added score /10 | Average entry tariff |
|---|---|---|---|---|---|---|---|---|---|
| 56 | Strathclyde | 49.7 | 88 | 58 | 5 | 21.1 | 47 | 3 | 377 |
| 57 | Hertfordshire | 49.5 | 80 | 63 | 3 | 12.9 | 47 | 5 | 253 |
| 57 | Northampton | 49.5 | 88 | 72 | 3 | 15.8 | 38 | 7 | 242 |
| 59 | City | 49.1 | 77 | 28 | 4 | 19.1 | 61 | 4 | 367 |
| 59 | Teesside | 49.1 | 85 | 73 | 5 | 17.0 | 49 | 4 | 264 |
| 61 | Lincoln | 47.8 | 90 | 83 | 3 | 23.9 | 53 | 3 | 289 |
| 62 | Bath Spa | 47.7 | 91 | 80 | 2 | 25.3 | 44 | 9 | 285 |
| 63 | Winchester | 47.0 | 92 | 66 | 3 | 15.3 | 50 | 2 | 268 |
| 64 | Huddersfield | 46.8 | 79 | 68 | 5 | 13.6 | 33 | 4 | 265 |
| 65 | Sunderland | 46.7 | 89 | 78 | 6 | 21.3 | 34 | 4 | 248 |
| 66 | East London | 46.1 | 80 | 63 | 5 | 16.9 | 61 | 3 | 189 |
| 67 | Sheffield Hallam | 45.9 | 81 | 62 | 5 | 23.2 | 39 | 8 | 302 |
| 68 | Greenwich | 45.5 | 85 | 45 | 4 | 21.7 | 53 | 7 | 232 |
| 69 | Thames Valley | 45.3 | 76 | 69 | 7 | 20.3 | 52 | 3 | 208 |
| 70 | York St John | 45.2 | 84 | 67 | 3 | 17.9 | 50 | 2 | 281 |
| 71 | Newman University College | 45.1 | 82 | 60 | 3 | 21.5 | | 7 | 241 |
| 72 | Abertay Dundee | 44.9 | | | 3 | 16.2 | 50 | 3 | 260 |
| 73 | Edge Hill | 44.5 | 87 | 69 | 4 | 10.7 | 38 | 1 | 278 |
| 74 | St Mary's UC, Twickenham | 43.9 | 95 | 74 | 3 | 19.0 | 45 | 2 | 239 |
| 75 | Manchester Met | 43.8 | 76 | 60 | 4 | 17.8 | 34 | 6 | 308 |
| 76 | Swansea | 43.7 | 87 | 54 | 4 | 28.6 | 48 | 5 | 349 |
| 77 | Leeds Met | 43.5 | 70 | 55 | 5 | 21.6 | 46 | 6 | 306 |
| 78 | Bedfordshire | 42.4 | 79 | 42 | 3 | 14.8 | 43 | 6 | 182 |
| 79 | Gloucestershire | 42.1 | 72 | 55 | 4 | 18.7 | 40 | 6 | 252 |
| 80 | Ulster | 42.0 | 85 | 66 | 4 | 18.8 | 24 | 6 | 259 |
| 81 | Cumbria | 41.9 | 68 | 40 | 7 | 20.7 | | | 296 |
| 82 | Central Lancashire | 41.8 | 82 | 64 | 6 | 22.5 | 59 | 1 | 274 |
| 83 | Derby | 41.7 | 78 | 52 | 4 | 19.9 | 43 | 5 | 255 |
| 83 | Newport | 41.7 | 76 | 67 | 7 | 23.5 | | | 231 |
| 85 | Glamorgan | 40.8 | 87 | 61 | 3 | 18.6 | 42 | 3 | 244 |
| 86 | Anglia Ruskin | 40.6 | 79 | 45 | 7 | 24.0 | 38 | 5 | 267 |
| 86 | Chester | 40.6 | 86 | 63 | 3 | 24.1 | 50 | 4 | 278 |
| 88 | Bucks New University | 40.0 | 93 | 63 | 4 | 16.1 | 44 | 1 | 207 |
| 89 | Queen Margaret | 39.9 | | | 2 | 26.0 | | 7 | 318 |
| 90 | Southampton Solent | 39.6 | 82 | 52 | 4 | 19.2 | 47 | 2 | 248 |
| 91 | Leeds Trinity & All Saints | 38.6 | 79 | 69 | 2 | 20.5 | 52 | 3 | 244 |
| 92 | Kingston | 38.2 | 81 | 48 | 3 | 19.1 | 34 | 5 | 261 |
| 93 | De Montfort | 38.1 | 84 | 73 | 4 | 17.3 | 38 | 1 | 234 |
| 94 | Liverpool John Moores | 37.0 | 74 | 62 | 4 | 15.9 | 32 | 2 | 271 |
| 95 | Salford | 35.3 | 68 | 52 | 5 | 23.7 | 24 | 7 | 290 |
| 96 | Middlesex | 33.2 | 72 | 50 | 5 | 24.6 | 57 | 2 | 185 |
| 97 | Bradford | 33.1 | 83 | 60 | 3 | 25.5 | 41 | 3 | 223 |
| 98 | Roehampton | 32.4 | 72 | 51 | 3 | 25.2 | 49 | 3 | 230 |
| 99 | London South Bank | 27.6 | 76 | 45 | 4 | 25.7 | 41 | 3 | 207 |
| 100 | Bolton | 27.0 | 82 | 60 | 2 | 28.9 | 27 | 5 | 231 |

# Sports and exercise science

" Throughout history and across cultures, sport and human performance has always held an important position in society. Through studying a sports and exercise science degree you not only learn about the function and limitations of the human body but also about how sport and exercise influence both personal and societal health and wellbeing. You will get to study physiology, psychology, biomechanics, health, and nutrition as well as sociology of sport. Alongside these you will also gain practical experience in not just playing sports but also how to coach, manage, and develop your own, and others', sporting potential.

From a purely pragmatic viewpoint, the degree leads to a greater understanding of the multi-billion pound industries that surround sport, exercise, and health and gives you the background for employment within them. This multi-disciplinary course with both its theoretical and applied aspects, and the fact that employers universally understand what sport and exercise is, also opens up a wealth of job opportunities where employers are looking for well-rounded graduates.

However, sports and exercise science offers more than this as it allows you to investigate what makes us strive to be the best, to push ourselves to the limits, and what those limits are and why. It also allows you to understand why we watch others push themselves, why we have the joy and excitement of shared experiences with thousands of others when our team wins, and why, as a society and as individuals, we invest so much of our recreational time into sport and exercise. The study of sports and exercise science can lead not only to a rewarding career but also gives a window into what it is to be human.

**Dr Matt Pain**, *Senior Lecturer, School of Sport and Exercise Sciences, Loughborough University*

First thing out of the way – you don't have to be good at sports to do this course. However, it helps and if you aren't a natural athlete you do, at least, need to be interested in sport. You should also be careful which sport and exercise course you select as some require participation in a range of sports while others are more theory-based.

Sports science degrees – those concerned with the science of exercise, health, and sport – have blossomed, with the use of increasingly sophisticated techniques to improve performance and training in the sporting world. For further proof of this booming world, just look at the size of the growth of specialists in professional sport – from peripheral vision experts in football to bio-mechanical bowling coaches in cricket.

Sports science courses are, first and foremost, academic programmes of study and are very strongly science-based. The degree courses involve the application of scientific principles through three major areas – biomechanics, physiology, psychology, or an interdisciplinary combination. You will learn how the body responds and adapts to exercise, how and why different energy systems are deployed at different exercise intensities, how the principles of mechanics determine both the flight of a javelin and the gyrations of a gymnast, and how mind and body interact to influence performance.

The other branch of the industry – exercise science – has a central role in physical activity programmes aimed at improving general health, and how sport and exercise fit into the context of the society in which we live. The very fact that the NHS is now keen on physical activity as a form of preventative care means that there is increasing scope in work opportunities for exercise scientists in clinical settings – hospitals, nursing homes, and the like.

The tendency for sports science students is to head for specialisation through module choice or projects. After that, graduates have various career paths. Some head for teaching and research, while others apply their knowledge through related areas such as coaching and sports management. One of the problems with sport scientists is that graduates enter sports-related jobs at quite a low level – jobs such as personal instructor, fitness trainer, and leisure services manager: ones that can be done without a degree. The key to success with a sports-related career is much longer term, so you may need to keep your eye more on the horizon than on the nearest landmark.

There are basically three types of sports and exercise courses. Those with an emphasis on sport, those that focus on science and those that give equal priority to both. Check that the emphasis is in an area that suits you. Similarly, the more broadly based courses that try to cover all options may lack the depth you want in certain areas.

Look, too, at the departments around sports science. Such a multidisciplinary course brings in a lot from other areas, so see how strong the institution is in biochemistry, physiology, and so on, since those departments will feed into the teaching on your course.

The facilities – both sporting and scientific – are obviously essential. A university with good sporting and clinical facilities is a must for sports science. Sporting arenas and facilities get tatty pretty quickly, so see how well it has been maintained: it's an issue of constant investment and that also gives an idea as to how highly they value the course.

---

66 Having come from a biology background at A-level I wanted to discover the other areas involved in the field of sport and exercise science. During my course I have gained in-depth insights into the areas of physiology, biomechanics and psychology. The high scientific content of the course and the fantastic placement opportunities have got me really excited about a career in the field.

**David Green**, *third-year sport and exercise science student, University of Bath*

---

## » Further information

**British Association of Sports and Exercise Sciences**

Leeds Metropolitan University
Carnegie Faculty of Sport and Education
Fairfax Hall, Headingley Campus
Beckett Park, Leeds LS6 3QS

t  0113 812 6162
↗ www.bases.org.uk

**British Association of Sport and Exercise Medicine**

Central Office, 15 Hawthorne Avenue
Norton, Doncaster DN6 9HR

e  basemcentral@basem.co.uk
↗ www.basem.co.uk

**National Sports Medicine Institute**

32 Devonshire Street
London W1G 6PX

t  020 7251 0583
e  enquiry@nsmi.org.uk

**The Centre for Sport and Exercise Science**

Sheffield Hallam University
Collegiate Campus
Sheffield S10 2BP

t  0114 225 2544
e  cses@shu.ac.uk
↗ www.shu.ac.uk/cses

↗ Online reading

**International Federation of Sports Medicine**  www.fims.org
**International Society of Biomechanics**  www.isbweb.org
**Sport England**  www.sportengland.org
**SportEx**  www.sportex.net
**Sports Coach UK**  www.sportscoachuk.org
**Central Council for Physical Recreation**  www.ccpr.org.uk

## Sports science

| | | Guardian score /100 | Satisfied with teaching % | Satisfied with feedback % | Spend per student /10 | Student:staff ratio | Job prospects % | Value added score /10 | Average entry tariff |
|---|---|---|---|---|---|---|---|---|---|
| 1 | Bath | 100.0 | 85 | 62 | | 22.2 | 73 | 9 | 408 |
| 2 | Bournemouth | 99.7 | 83 | 65 | 10 | 10.9 | 77 | 8 | 258 |
| 3 | Exeter | 99.0 | 95 | 86 | 5 | 21.6 | 70 | 9 | 377 |
| 4 | Loughborough | 96.9 | 93 | 68 | 7 | 16.7 | 63 | 8 | 407 |
| 5 | Birmingham | 94.6 | 93 | 67 | 9 | 20.8 | 62 | 8 | 380 |
| 6 | Leeds | 91.1 | 86 | 66 | 10 | 23.2 | 51 | 9 | 358 |
| 7 | Bangor | 90.8 | 92 | 78 | 9 | 21.5 | 75 | 8 | 264 |
| 8 | Edinburgh | 86.0 | 89 | 38 | 10 | 16.7 | 43 | 5 | 390 |
| 9 | Essex | 83.5 | 90 | 52 | 8 | 16.7 | 66 | 7 | 273 |
| 10 | Brunel | 83.3 | 85 | 57 | 6 | 14.7 | 64 | 7 | 320 |
| 11 | Durham | 83.0 | 87 | 68 | 4 | 17.2 | 67 | 5 | 376 |
| 11 | Heriot-Watt | 83.0 | 91 | 62 | 9 | 16.1 | 37 | 8 | 337 |
| 13 | Plymouth | 82.0 | 86 | 51 | 9 | 13.6 | 36 | 10 | 263 |
| 14 | Ulster | 79.2 | 92 | 72 | 5 | 21.3 | 60 | 9 | 281 |
| 15 | Aberystwyth | 79.1 | 98 | 85 | 6 | 20.3 | 50 | 7 | 253 |
| 16 | Nottingham Trent | 77.4 | 92 | 63 | 6 | 18.1 | 67 | 5 | 262 |
| 17 | Glyndŵr | 76.3 | 97 | 88 | 4 | 13.1 | 52 | 7 | 194 |
| 18 | St Mary's UC, Twickenham | 75.0 | 85 | 73 | 3 | 18.8 | 65 | 9 | 228 |
| 19 | Brighton | 73.8 | 89 | 58 | 5 | 30.0 | 75 | 6 | 304 |
| 19 | Manchester Met | 73.8 | 70 | 67 | 6 | 13.8 | 61 | 8 | 226 |
| 21 | Portsmouth | 73.4 | 94 | 76 | 7 | 27.3 | 58 | 7 | 251 |
| 22 | Sheffield Hallam | 73.2 | 84 | 57 | 5 | 21.1 | 56 | 8 | 306 |
| 23 | Swansea | 72.3 | 91 | 76 | 4 | 22.5 | 64 | 5 | 275 |
| 23 | Teesside | 72.3 | 83 | 75 | 4 | 22.4 | 64 | 8 | 246 |
| 25 | Leeds Met | 71.6 | 74 | 52 | 7 | 23.2 | 61 | 8 | 269 |
| 26 | Winchester | 71.3 | 94 | 70 | 2 | 18.7 | 57 | 8 | 240 |
| 27 | Worcester | 70.6 | 86 | 68 | 7 | 23.0 | 63 | 4 | 249 |
| 28 | Northumbria | 70.5 | 86 | 75 | 4 | 21.5 | 59 | 6 | 285 |
| 29 | Chichester | 70.2 | 92 | 82 | 4 | 23.5 | 67 | 5 | 226 |
| 30 | Newman University College | 70.1 | 88 | 81 | 2 | 27.8 | 84 | 7 | 198 |
| 31 | Staffordshire | 69.0 | 85 | 79 | 8 | 23.3 | 62 | 6 | 168 |
| 32 | Chester | 66.7 | 86 | 74 | 5 | 19.2 | 65 | 2 | 239 |
| 33 | UWIC | 66.3 | 84 | 66 | 4 | 20.7 | 55 | 6 | 278 |
| 34 | Hull | 65.6 | 88 | 67 | 4 | 27.0 | 70 | 4 | 240 |
| 35 | Cumbria | 65.5 | 73 | 50 | 10 | 12.1 | 49 | 2 | 248 |
| 36 | Bedfordshire | 65.3 | 81 | 44 | 4 | 13.0 | 63 | 4 | 219 |

| | | Guardian score /100 | Satisfied with teaching % | Satisfied with feedback % | Spend per student /10 | Student:staff ratio | Job prospects % | Value added score /10 | Average entry tariff |
|---|---|---|---|---|---|---|---|---|---|
| 37 | Edinburgh Napier | 63.7 | | | 7 | 25.0 | 52 | 4 | 273 |
| 38 | Hertfordshire | 62.8 | 83 | 44 | 5 | 23.9 | 51 | 5 | 298 |
| 39 | Kingston | 62.6 | 85 | 54 | 8 | 25.6 | 43 | 7 | 206 |
| 40 | Southampton Solent | 61.5 | 75 | 63 | 3 | 4.4 | 55 | 3 | 174 |
| 41 | Southampton | 60.9 | 82 | 69 | 3 | | 58 | 2 | 325 |
| 42 | Kent | 60.8 | 79 | 78 | 4 | 20.3 | 51 | 5 | 226 |
| 43 | Stirling | 60.2 | 87 | 64 | 3 | 21.6 | | 5 | |
| 44 | Greenwich | 59.7 | 80 | 61 | 6 | 29.0 | 68 | 4 | 185 |
| 45 | Glamorgan | 59.3 | 75 | 65 | 6 | 21.4 | 35 | 8 | 229 |
| 46 | Liverpool John Moores | 57.6 | 82 | 67 | 4 | 32.0 | 53 | 7 | 250 |
| 47 | Gloucestershire | 57.5 | 82 | 62 | 7 | 29.1 | 46 | 6 | 221 |
| 48 | Oxford Brookes | 57.0 | 82 | 46 | 4 | 28.3 | | | 281 |
| 49 | Coventry | 55.9 | 85 | 71 | 4 | 21.9 | 43 | 2 | 280 |
| 49 | Leeds Trinity & All Saints | 55.9 | 77 | 59 | 2 | 23.0 | 70 | 4 | 191 |
| 51 | Northampton | 55.7 | 86 | 71 | 3 | 21.3 | 46 | 5 | 190 |
| 52 | Abertay Dundee | 55.4 | | | 4 | | 57 | 2 | 254 |
| 53 | York St John | 55.3 | 84 | 67 | 6 | 28.8 | 50 | 3 | 241 |
| 54 | Middlesex | 52.9 | 82 | 60 | 8 | 42.3 | 63 | 5 | 202 |
| 55 | Bolton | 52.8 | 83 | 65 | 2 | 27.5 | | 8 | 174 |
| 56 | Roehampton | 52.7 | 71 | 53 | 8 | 18.2 | 42 | 3 | 182 |
| 57 | Canterbury Christ Church | 51.3 | 85 | 65 | 3 | 20.5 | 55 | 2 | 201 |
| 58 | Edge Hill | 50.1 | 77 | 62 | 3 | 25.9 | 50 | 3 | 229 |
| 59 | Marjon (St Mark and St John) | 48.8 | 86 | 66 | 2 | 21.9 | 47 | 3 | 202 |
| 60 | Newport | 48.1 | 76 | 67 | 3 | 27.1 | 56 | 3 | 188 |
| 61 | Lincoln | 46.5 | 86 | 66 | 3 | 29.1 | 62 | 1 | 210 |
| 62 | East London | 46.2 | 83 | 60 | 4 | 22.2 | | 1 | 165 |
| 63 | Bucks New University | 37.5 | 67 | 58 | 4 | 31.6 | 47 | 3 | 188 |
| 64 | Derby | 36.6 | 57 | 41 | 6 | 23.0 | 39 | 2 | 194 |
| 65 | London South Bank | 33.8 | 79 | 50 | 3 | 44.3 | | 4 | |

# Veterinary science

❝ Veterinary science is a challenging programme, be in no doubt, but the rewards of a degree in the subject more than repay the effort. Not only does it equip graduates to enter veterinary practice in all its varied forms, it also provides a fantastic applied biology degree. So for those with a passion for all things biological it provides the opportunity to indulge those passions within a secure career framework. Most graduates enter general practice, which can involve work with any species in any country of the world. But there are also opportunities to contribute to human society and animal welfare in other more fundamental ways, such as the control of international disease threats, research into new vaccines and treatments, and in the safeguarding of public health. With a rapidly growing world population demanding more food, with the increasing infectious disease threats posed by climate change and instant travel, and the need for the humane and sustainable production of wholesome food in a volatile world, veterinary graduates are well placed to help address these global challenges to human society.

**Professor Sandy Trees**, *former Dean of Veterinary Science, University of Liverpool*

Veterinary science is the diagnosis and treatment of disease and injury in animals. In addition to veterinary medicine – which we're mostly concerned with here – it also includes dentistry and pre-clinical veterinary medicine. Though getting a place on a veterinary degree course is not easy, competition is not as fierce as you might expect. Naturally, the quality of applicants each year is high, so a strong academic background is essential if you want to apply, but you also need to convince the admissions tutors that you want to be a vet, so make sure you can demonstrate a significant level of commitment to the cause (such as relevant work experience), as well as evidence of a robust, well-rounded personality. While job prospects for graduates from all the veterinary schools are strong, the working life of a vet can be very stressful indeed and you need to able to cope with it.

For most students, a veterinary degree is preparation for an attractive (and sometimes lucrative) career in private practice, but the broad, scientifically based curriculum provides an outstanding background for a wide range of careers in biological and medical fields, in research and in agricultural and food policy roles nationally.

At a time when there is increasing concern about the health and welfare of farm and companion animals, all the schools are giving a higher profile to public health issues, such as BSE, foot-and-mouth disease and avian flu.

A lecture-free final year is common, allowing greater scope for wider study and clinical experience, and more time for teamwork and problem-based learning.

If you plan to study veterinary medicine at Cambridge or the Royal Veterinary College then you face the joys of the BioMedical Admission Test (Bmat), which is aimed at testing students' thinking skills as opposed to subject knowledge and to help universities choose between many high-calibre candidates. The deadline for registering for a Bmat is usually just before the deadline for applying to courses – which, for veterinary sciences is October 15 – but check on www.bmat.org.uk for exact details.

Ucas insists that prospective students include only four veterinary courses among the five choices on their form, in order to give you a safety net if you fail to gain a place.

A few of the universities offering the vet degree are recognised by foreign veterinary associations, such as the American Veterinary Medical Association (AVMA). This means that graduates from those schools can more easily practise abroad. If working overseas is part of your long-term plan, then include this in your criteria for picking a school.

There have been spectacular investments in some veterinary schools recently, so check the facilities, and see if they tally with your own interests, whether it be a new equine centre, new laboratory facilities or a clinical skills centre.

Find out what the student:staff ratios mean at each university. Veterinary faculties often draw staff from other departments to teach on the vet course, particularly in pre-clinical subjects and this can account for apparent variations in staff:student ratios.

---

**66** At the Royal Veterinary College the BSc in bioveterinary sciences was developed to equip graduates with skills for careers within the biotechnology and pharmaceutical industries, veterinary-related professions, and biomedical research. It is an exciting field of study as we play an important part in the promotion of animal — and human — health and welfare.

**Andy Banerjee**, *second-year bioveterinary science student, Royal Veterinary College*

---

## ≫ Further information

**Royal College of Veterinary Surgeons**
Belgravia House
62-4 Horseferry Road
London SW1P 2AF

t  020 7222 2001
e  admin@rcvs.org.uk
↗ www.rcvs.org.uk

**The British Veterinary Association**
7 Mansfield Street
London W1G 9NQ

t  020 7636 6541
e  bvahq@bva.co.uk
↗ www.bva.co.uk

**Society of Practising Veterinary Surgeons**
The Governor's House
Cape Road, Warwick
Warwickshire CV34 5DL

t  01926 410454
e  office@spvs.org.uk
↗ www.spvs.org.uk

**British Equine Veterinary Association**
Mulberry House, 31 Market Street
Fordham, Ely
Cambridgeshire CB7 5LQ

t  01638 723 555
e  info@beva.org.uk
↗ www.beva.org.uk

**British Small Animals Veterinary Association**
Woodrow House, 1 Telford Way
Waterwells Business Park
Quedgeley, Gloucester GL2 2AB

t  01452 726700
e  administration@bsava.com
↗ www.bsava.com

↗ Online reading

**Vetweb**  www.vetweb.co.uk
**European Association of Establishments for Veterinary Education**  www.eaeve.org
**Federation of Veterinarians of Europe**  www.fve.org

## Veterinary science

| | | Guardian score /100 | Satisfied with teaching % | Satisfied with feedback % | Spend per student /10 | Student:staff ratio | Job prospects % | Value added score /10 | Average entry tariff |
|---|---|---|---|---|---|---|---|---|---|
| 1 | Cambridge | 100.0 | | | 8 | 4.6 | 98 | | 527 |
| 2 | Edinburgh | 69.2 | 90 | 34 | 8 | 6.4 | 99 | 8 | 493 |
| 3 | Glasgow | 68.9 | 94 | 50 | 3 | 7.6 | 95 | 9 | 471 |
| 4 | Liverpool | 53.1 | 91 | 46 | 3 | 7.0 | 97 | 4 | 472 |
| 5 | Nottingham | 51.7 | | | 4 | 6.3 | | | 449 |
| 6 | Bristol | 33.3 | 91 | 41 | 3 | 10.0 | 84 | 4 | 431 |
| 7 | Royal Veterinary College | 28.1 | 83 | 24 | 8 | 9.8 | 99 | 3 | 438 |

# Modern languages

> After almost 20 years teaching languages here I think I could summarise my students' views as, 'Yes, it can be tough learning a foreign language, but the rewards are amazing.'
>
> Apart from developing excellent communication and interpersonal skills, students gain maturity and self-reliance during placements spent abroad, as well as the sheer thrill and excitement of actually being able to talk to someone from another culture in their own language. Then there is the pride they feel when they can act as an interpreter, switching from one language to another to order a meal or buy some train tickets. Students have told me that the recognition and respect this gives them more than justifies the hard work they put in to learning the language.
>
> It is often only once students graduate and start a job that they realise that the wide range of academic and personal skills they have acquired gives them far more opportunities for exciting and rewarding careers than people who have not studied a language. Prospective employers not only recognise the value of employing a linguist who can take their business into new markets and deal confidently with overseas clients and suppliers, they also acknowledge the additional maturity and perspective that our language graduates have from their period abroad and the cultural issues they have dealt with.
>
> Most of the rest of the world may want to learn English but this only increases the effect it has on any foreigner when an English person greets them and chats to them in their own language. Lifelong friendships have been forged just as a result of a few words exchanged in an airport lounge between someone returning to Spain or Japan and one of our students, who has ventured to communicate with them in their own language.
>
> I think I agree with my students — yes it can be tough, but the rewards are amazing.
>
> **Graham Webb**, *Principal Lecturer in Languages, Leeds Metropolitan University*

Modern languages is about a whole lot more than learning to order a coffee on holiday — you'll gain an intimate knowledge of another country's literature, culture, history, politics, and people.

As well as the obvious choices — French, German, Italian — you can learn Latin American or Middle Eastern languages, or Serbian and Croatian, or Japanese or Mandarin. The possibilities are as wide as the globe, but whatever you choose, an affection for the country or region linked to your language is rather important.

Most prospective applicants will already be studying a language at A-level, though it is not always necessary to be studying the one you take to degree level, especially for less mainstream languages. Generally speaking, this is a very good time to be aspiring to study languages at university. The number of applicants to language courses has been falling steadily over recent years. Although this is very worrying for universities, it is good news for you if you fail to get the grades they were asking for. You may be able to negotiate your way on to the course, or go elsewhere through Clearing. Bear in mind that due to the ceiling imposed by Government funding allocations it is probable that fewer universities will offer places via clearing.

Once there, you can study a single language or opt for joint honours in two languages; a few places will let you take three. Alternatively, you can combine a language with almost any other subject imaginable: French with music, Spanish with molecular biology, and so on. Most UK universities offer courses in French, German, and Spanish. For less common languages, such as Dutch, Danish, and modern Greek, your choice of institution will be more limited.

Integrated studies, in which the study of a language is one component of, say, a science or technology degree, are also increasingly available. This might well involve you spending a year in France studying, for example, engineering – but in French.

A modern languages degree makes you eminently employable and not just as a teacher or a translator, so don't feel you need to combine a language with a vocational subject merely to improve your job prospects. More than 50 per cent of jobs are open to graduates from any discipline and modern languages graduates have lower rates of unemployment than almost all others. You'll emerge at the end of your degree with highly developed linguistic, analytical, and communication skills – helped greatly by your year abroad.

Before you pick a course, decide what you are hoping to learn. Do you want a literature-based course? If your main interest is in Italian art or Russian politics, does the course cater for this? How much emphasis is given to acquiring language skills? How much of the course is taught in the language? If you are applying for joint honours, can you vary the mix? Are the two timetables really compatible? How is the course taught – is the emphasis on lectures, tutorials or seminars? Will you have to write a dissertation? Read the prospectus and speak to undergraduates to make sure you know exactly what is on offer.

Most places offer a year abroad, so give careful consideration to this. Here are a few questions you'll want to ask: how much help will the university give you with planning your year? Will you be required to produce a dissertation while you are away? Will you be working or studying? Many UK universities have formal exchange links with universities abroad – find out if yours does. Joint language honours applicants should find out if they will be able to split the year between the two countries. Many students spend the year as English language assistants in schools abroad in a scheme organised by the British Council (full details at www.britishcouncil.org/education).

But four years of study might strike you as rather expensive, so bear in mind the (admittedly few) universities, mainly new ones, that have introduced three-year language-related degrees in a bid to address the problem of student debt, and which may involve spending only one term abroad.

---

> The decision to study modern languages was one of the best I have ever made. The structure of the course is completely unique. I love the fact that you don't have to study literature but are encouraged to choose from a range of subjects that interest you including history, politics, film and linguistics among others. Studying languages opens up so many doors in an international graduate environment and I truly don't believe you can quantify the value of doing a year abroad, academically or otherwise.
>
> **Sherin Branquinho**, *fourth-year modern languages student (French and Spanish), University of Southampton*

# Modern languages

| | | Guardian score /100 | Satisfied with teaching % | Satisfied with feedback % | Spend per student /10 | Student:staff ratio | Job prospects % | Value added score /10 | Average entry tariff |
|---|---|---|---|---|---|---|---|---|---|
| 1 | Oxford | 100.0 | 96 | 76 | 10 | 9.5 | 74 | 7 | 515 |
| 2 | Cambridge | 95.4 | 95 | 86 | 9 | 11.5 | 78 | 6 | 527 |
| 3 | UCL | 83.7 | 86 | 60 | 10 | 9.6 | 75 | 6 | 453 |
| 4 | Southampton | 81.5 | 93 | 77 | 10 | 10.5 | 69 | 7 | 431 |
| 5 | Bath | 75.6 | 92 | 74 | 6 | 12.1 | 71 | 7 | 425 |
| 6 | King's College London | 75.4 | 84 | 58 | 9 | 10.2 | 74 | 6 | 397 |
| 7 | St Andrews | 74.7 | 92 | 78 | 4 | 13.4 | 71 | 7 | 456 |
| 8 | Heriot-Watt | 71.7 | 97 | 86 | 6 | 14.9 | 69 | 7 | 384 |
| 9 | Aston | 71.3 | 91 | 73 | 8 | 12.4 | 76 | 4 | 360 |
| 9 | Cardiff | 71.3 | 88 | 63 | | 5.2 | 64 | 4 | 388 |
| 11 | Sussex | 70.8 | 85 | 58 | 3 | 8.5 | 74 | 8 | 398 |
| 12 | Durham | 70.6 | 91 | 58 | 3 | 14.3 | 71 | 7 | 492 |
| 13 | Leeds | 69.1 | 88 | 63 | 9 | 12.4 | 66 | 5 | 394 |
| 14 | Nottingham | 68.5 | 89 | 58 | 7 | 10.3 | 69 | 5 | 394 |
| 15 | Coventry | 67.5 | 83 | 78 | 5 | 14.5 | | 10 | 267 |
| 16 | Edinburgh | 66.4 | 80 | 42 | 9 | 15.3 | 70 | 5 | 459 |
| 16 | Leicester | 66.4 | 93 | 90 | 7 | 15.4 | 55 | 7 | 339 |
| 18 | Lancaster | 66.3 | 92 | 66 | 4 | 13.0 | 80 | 4 | 367 |
| 19 | Bristol | 65.5 | 88 | 64 | 5 | 18.5 | 73 | 7 | 431 |
| 20 | Queen Mary | 65.4 | 91 | 72 | 9 | 12.9 | 55 | 5 | 335 |
| 21 | Kent | 65.1 | 91 | 78 | 4 | 11.9 | 59 | 10 | 297 |
| 22 | SOAS | 64.8 | 87 | 62 | 5 | 10.1 | 64 | 7 | 354 |
| 23 | Warwick | 64.7 | 93 | 76 | 7 | 19.1 | 59 | 5 | 447 |
| 24 | Queen's, Belfast | 64.5 | 83 | 56 | 8 | 11.6 | 71 | 5 | 367 |
| 25 | Manchester | 63.5 | 86 | 54 | 9 | 15.6 | 62 | 5 | 400 |
| 26 | Sheffield | 63.0 | 89 | 67 | 4 | 12.8 | 65 | 6 | 402 |
| 27 | Roehampton | 62.5 | 85 | 71 | 3 | 8.5 | | 10 | 220 |
| 28 | Birmingham | 61.4 | 92 | 64 | 7 | 13.0 | 57 | 4 | 399 |
| 29 | Royal Holloway | 61.3 | 92 | 74 | 4 | 13.3 | 70 | 5 | 346 |
| 30 | Anglia Ruskin | 61.1 | 81 | 66 | 7 | 9.4 | | 5 | |
| 31 | Salford | 60.1 | 84 | 74 | 9 | 11.3 | 52 | 6 | 298 |
| 32 | Newcastle | 56.8 | 83 | 59 | 5 | 18.6 | 67 | 4 | 437 |
| 33 | Exeter | 56.1 | 90 | 66 | 4 | 20.9 | 65 | 5 | 415 |
| 34 | Glasgow | 55.3 | 86 | 56 | 3 | 18.9 | 62 | 8 | 413 |
| 35 | Swansea | 54.7 | 90 | 73 | 3 | 10.5 | 71 | 3 | 306 |
| 36 | Liverpool | 54.5 | 84 | 61 | 7 | 15.2 | 59 | 5 | 351 |
| 37 | Central Lancashire | 54.3 | 91 | 77 | 6 | 6.4 | | 2 | 243 |
| 38 | Portsmouth | 53.3 | 92 | 80 | 6 | 13.1 | 61 | 2 | 258 |

| | Guardian score /100 | Satisfied with teaching % | Satisfied with feedback % | Spend per student /10 | Student:staff ratio | Job prospects % | Value added score /10 | Average entry tariff |
|---|---|---|---|---|---|---|---|---|
| 39 Reading | 52.9 | 88 | 67 | 3 | 13.4 | 53 | 8 | 318 |
| 40 Hull | 52.5 | 93 | 77 | 3 | 25.1 | 76 | 6 | 298 |
| 41 Nottingham Trent | 52.4 | 88 | 71 | 6 | 17.0 | 59 | 7 | 250 |
| 42 Surrey | 52.3 | 77 | 49 | 7 | 7.1 | 53 | 4 | 341 |
| 43 Essex | 52.2 | 86 | 68 | 3 | 12.5 | 52 | 6 | 318 |
| 44 Aberystwyth | 50.9 | 86 | 72 | 4 | 15.9 | 59 | 4 | 307 |
| 45 York | 49.3 | 85 | 52 | 6 | 17.5 | 56 | 2 | 424 |
| 46 Sheffield Hallam | 48.6 | 74 | 60 | 6 | 8.3 | | 4 | 265 |
| 47 York St John | 48.2 | 92 | 81 | 2 | | 48 | 7 | 302 |
| 48 Strathclyde | 48.0 | 89 | 69 | 7 | 27.2 | 58 | 4 | 398 |
| 49 UWE Bristol | 47.0 | 83 | 63 | 3 | 18.3 | 46 | 10 | 278 |
| 50 Westminster | 46.6 | 83 | 65 | 5 | 12.1 | 55 | 4 | 240 |
| 51 UEA | 46.0 | 94 | 76 | 3 | 30.8 | 52 | 8 | 344 |
| 52 Liverpool John Moores | 43.6 | 86 | 62 | 4 | 12.6 | 59 | 2 | 238 |
| 53 Plymouth | 42.9 | 92 | 56 | 2 | 15.9 | | | 256 |
| 54 Oxford Brookes | 41.6 | 81 | 65 | 4 | 16.8 | 47 | 5 | 310 |
| 55 Northumbria | 41.5 | 81 | 63 | 3 | 17.6 | 70 | 2 | 282 |
| 56 Chester | 40.1 | 87 | 63 | 2 | 19.9 | | 6 | 282 |
| 57 Greenwich | 40.0 | 75 | 77 | 2 | 16.1 | 47 | 8 | 235 |
| 58 Bangor | 38.7 | 78 | 68 | 3 | 20.9 | 53 | 3 | 329 |
| 59 Manchester Met | 37.9 | 86 | 63 | 3 | 13.2 | 52 | 2 | 272 |
| 60 Leeds Met | 36.0 | 85 | 59 | 7 | 30.3 | | | 262 |
| 61 Ulster | 31.6 | 71 | 57 | 5 | 7.4 | 47 | 1 | 290 |
| 62 Lincoln | 31.0 | 78 | 65 | 2 | 18.6 | | | 253 |
| 63 Middlesex | 29.2 | 72 | 62 | 4 | 26.1 | | 6 | 201 |

# Physical sciences

## Agriculture and forestry

" Agriculture is the study of how we make the best use of land and other resources to produce crops and animals. It is an exciting time to take a degree in the subject: growing demand for food and biofuels, together with concerns about how agriculture interacts with the environment, have renewed our interest in the problem of how to manage land effectively and sustainably. An agriculture degree gives you knowledge of these exciting areas and equips you for a range of professional careers.

One of the best things about the subject is its breadth. You learn about how crops respond to their environment and how to manage the crop between sowing and harvest to get the best yields. You learn how animals grow, how growth relates to nutrition and about different systems for producing livestock and livestock products. Agriculture is also a great subject to take at a higher level because it is linked to so many other interesting areas of study. It is one of the few degrees that combines science and business management teaching: you learn how to market your produce, draw up business plans and make effective decisions about labour and machinery. You are out in the field, visiting farms, making presentations to business leaders — as well as learning about soils, crop and animal production, business management, and IT.

Agriculture has strong links to the environment. Producing food (and fuel) for a developing world, within environmental limits, is an important and fascinating challenge. An agriculture degree will develop your ability to meet this challenge — and you don't have to come from a farm to apply!

**Dr Stephen Ramsden,** *Associate Professor, Management Division of Agricultural and Environmental sciences, University of Nottingham*

---

The public perception of agricultural courses is that they are finishing schools for ruddy-faced toffs before they drive off in the Range Rover to manage the family estate. Some places may still be like that, but the subject now involves the increasingly complex scientific issues that characterise modern farming and forestry: from genetically modified produce and the use of pesticides to conservation issues and environmental science.

Quality of life, conservation, and "alternatives" such as organic farming are now serious issues for what might be termed rural degrees. Food production may play only a small part, compared with issues of flooding and landscape conservation.

New developments in agriculture increasingly have a strong scientific basis, and biotechnology (such as genetic engineering of crops), embryo transfer in cattle and bio-control of plant diseases are taking their place on the courses, as well as continuing developments of the technology involved in food production. Course content can, therefore, range from cell biochemistry and molecular biology to plant breeding, plant and animal nutrition, and even engineering and computing. The degree has grown up and in many ways leads environmental and political debate – think of GM crops, BSE, and foot-and-mouth.

The course – a three-year BSc – is of use to those who wish to join the agribusiness, run a farm or get involved with research and development or overseas development, or even to environmentalists who want to understand the issues. Employment rates are good, so if those options aren't to your taste, there's always seed or feed companies, or estate and park management.

Those who are looking for land management skills should head for the more vocational courses where you'll learn the skills you'll need, which may also include the now customary fallback for the post-BSE- and foot-and-mouth farmer – rural tourism and marketing. The traditional farming colleges may well be for you.

However if you're more interested in the applied science side of the subject you should head for the more academically biased courses at the universities. Generally, the older institutions teach the more conventional courses and assess work in the same way, with exams and a level of continuous assessment. The newer places go for a more flexible modular approach and a wider range of assessment options – so check if they're offering the areas you're interested in.

The level of debate about the future of farming has not gone unnoticed in the agribusiness world and it is apparent that some departments are linking themselves ever more closely to companies whose agenda may be narrow, to put it kindly. If you have strong opinions on the future roles of agriculture and forestry in this country's ecosystem, then make sure that the department isn't in thrall to a multinational you can't abide. Three years of arguing with your tutors can be exhausting and is unlikely to be rewarded.

And it's worth giving some consideration to the exact location of the course. Some agricultural schools are based in lovely old buildings on acres of land and can be fantastic places to be – or rather isolating.

---

66 I have a particular interest in the role of forest and woodland worldwide as reservoirs of biodiversity, carbon sinks and ecosystems as well as a source of sustainable material. With environmental issues constantly on the political agenda, I'm confident that once I graduate I'll have what it takes to make a difference. What could be more rewarding than that?

**Gareth Waters**, *final-year forestry student, University of Cumbria*

---

## ≫ Further information

**UK Agriculture**
Antrobus House, 18 College Street
Petersfield, Hampshire GU31 4AD

**t** 02392 410000
↗ www.ukagriculture.com

**The Forestry Commission**
Silvan House, 231 Corstorphine Road
Edinburgh EH12 7AT

**t** 0131 334 0303
**e** enquiries@forestry.gsi.gov.uk
↗ www.forestry.gov.uk

**Natural England**
1 East Parade
Sheffield S1 2ET

**t** 0114 241 8920
**e** enquiries@naturalengland.org.uk
↗ www.naturalengland.org.uk

## ↗ Online reading

**Department of Environment, Food and Rural Affairs** www.defra.gov.uk
**Institute for Animal Health** www.iah.bbsrc.ac.uk
**Environmental News Service** www.ens-newswire.com
**National Environment Research Council** www.nerc.ac.uk
**Growing careers** www.growing-careers.com

## Agriculture, forestry and food

| | | Guardian score /100 | Satisfied with teaching % | Satisfied with feedback % | Spend per student /10 | Student:staff ratio | Job prospects % | Value added score /10 | Average entry tariff |
|---|---|---|---|---|---|---|---|---|---|
| 1 | Nottingham | 100.0 | 82 | 62 | 10 | 8.1 | 68 | 5 | 335 |
| 2 | Reading | 83.3 | 83 | 65 | 5 | 12.6 | 79 | 8 | 330 |
| 3 | Bangor | 70.6 | | | 5 | 15.2 | | 9 | 306 |
| 4 | Harper Adams UC | 60.8 | 92 | 74 | 3 | 21.8 | 80 | 5 | 298 |
| 5 | Newcastle | 53.3 | 85 | 61 | 3 | 11.7 | 77 | 2 | 306 |
| 6 | Sheffield Hallam | 52.1 | 89 | 67 | 3 | 19.6 | | 8 | 282 |
| 7 | Aberystwyth | 49.9 | 92 | 75 | 5 | 16.3 | 37 | 3 | 318 |
| 8 | Central Lancashire | 47.9 | 81 | 60 | 9 | 19.2 | 52 | 4 | |
| 8 | Nottingham Trent | 47.9 | 82 | 68 | 3 | 15.8 | 57 | 6 | 297 |
| 10 | Writtle College | 35.7 | 72 | 57 | 9 | 4.9 | 36 | 3 | 250 |
| 11 | Manchester Met | 34.2 | | | 2 | 23.0 | | 6 | 302 |
| 12 | Lincoln | 33.3 | 89 | 65 | 3 | 20.7 | 50 | 6 | 268 |
| 13 | Royal Agricultural College | 31.8 | 86 | 62 | 4 | 17.5 | 54 | 2 | 294 |
| 14 | Greenwich | 29.8 | 84 | 59 | 2 | 19.2 | | 9 | 235 |
| 15 | Salford | 25.5 | 82 | 56 | 4 | 17.0 | | | 247 |

# Biosciences

" To study how living things work is a truly fascinating experience. It's to be able to understand the very nature of life itself — the molecular mechanisms and processes that interact to create a living entity that can grow and divide, to understand how a cell survives in its environment, how it finds energy, how it resists attack from viruses, and how it communicates with its neighbours to build larger, more sophisticated organisms.

Life can seem extremely fragile — but on the other hand living systems have an ability to adapt and repair unlike any human-built device. Cells can carry out the most amazing chemistry with the most basic requirements and at a fraction of the cost of existing technologies. The potential of harnessing living systems is immense and we are only just beginning to realise it.

Living systems have the potential to provide new solutions to a range of challenges that currently face us. For example, living systems will provide alternative forms of energy to avoid the carbon crisis, new treatments to cure human disease and control pests, new materials with self-assembly or repair properties, crops capable of producing more food in poorly fertile or arid regions of the world, and detoxification of harmful waste.

We are now entering a new era of using molecular machines based on living systems to produce greener, non-polluting technologies — an almost limitless potential. It is clear that bioscientists can expect meaningful and rewarding careers for many years to come.

**Dr Richard Williamson**, *Lecturer in Protein Biochemistry, Department of Biosciences, University of Kent*

The science of living things has blossomed in universities over the past 50 or so years as the subject has been transformed by momentous events. From the discovery of DNA to the relatively recent decoding of the human genome, the biosciences truly are at the forefront of human research, with perhaps the greatest excitements lying in the knowledge that we have barely touched the surface. There is so much out there for you to discover.

Put simply, bioscience is the study of the research, development, and manufacture of molecules and biological processes that perform key functions in animals and humans. It is the key to animal life on earth.

There are a number of choices to be made right from the off — more than a hundred universities offer courses, covering an increasingly broad discipline, including biology, botany, zoology, genetics, microbiology, molecular biology and biophysics, biochemistry and biotechnology. And that's just the titles — within those courses there are a whole new set of choices for specialisations you might want to consider.

Once you're there, be prepared for a lot of practical work in the laboratory, as with most science degrees, although before you do any serious work in a white coat there is also a fairly large amount of theoretical work required to understand the processes and latest developments. Most universities encourage some independent study through dissertations and projects, which can be an excellent way to develop your research and presentation skills and give you the confidence in your own original thought.

A BSc in the biosciences is often a good prelude to a more specialised MSc — food biotechnology, virology, and biochemical engineering perhaps, although the options are manifold — or a research degree at MPhil or PhD level. There is increasing demand for biosciences in the job market, and many graduates do move straight into industry —

into the fields of pharmaceuticals, food, hospitals, laboratories or medical research. Science A-levels are virtually a necessity, of course, particularly biology and chemistry.

The majority of universities offer a specialised aspect of bioscience, such as human, marine or applied study – so keep one eye on the employment it might provide when you've graduated.

Within applied bioscience there are even more specialised areas that might be more appealing than a general study, related to agriculture, animals, and the environment. If you want to study a more flexible course, look carefully at the options that are offered, especially in the third and fourth years, when a greater emphasis will be on your individual study and research interests.

The level of laboratory provision and facilities for practical work varies across institutions, so investigate thoroughly and try to get an idea of the amount of time you'll be able to spend doing hands-on work, either in classes or in your own time.

If you're specifically interested in applied bioscience look out for work placement opportunities or links with local industries as these will greatly enhance your career prospects after graduation.

And with this being a particularly fast-moving science, look at who will be teaching you and what their specialisations are – if you're taught by someone at the leading edge of research, you'll feel right on top of the game, although you'll also need to factor in whether all that research means they will be too busy to teach. Don't be afraid to ask questions at the open day.

---

66 The obvious difference between school and university study is the complexity of the work and the increased reading around lectures and lab sessions that a degree requires. Taking lecture notes is a skill you need to acquire rapidly; fortunately, it does come quickly. There weren't too many surprises upon coming to university, although the deadlines are more strictly enforced than at A-level and missing them can have subsequent effects on your grades – but that's a good life lesson.

**Joanne Turner**, *first-year biomedical sciences student, Leeds Metropolitan University*

---

## 》 Further information

**The Institute of Biology**
9 Red Lion Court
London EC4A 3EF

t   020 7936 5900
e   info@iob.org
↗  www.iob.org

**The Biosciences Federation**
PO Box 502
Cambridge CB1 0AL

t   01223 400 189
e   info@bsf.ac.uk
↗  www.bsf.ac.uk

## ↗ Online reading

**Guardian Unlimited Science**  www.guardian.co.uk/science
**The Association of Applied Biologists**  www.aab.org.uk
**The British Society for Cell Biology**  www.bscb.org
**Faculty of 1000 (Biological reports)**  www.facultyof1000.com
**The Biological Inventory Database**  www.ice.ucdavis.edu/bioinventory/bioinventory.html

# Biosciences

| | | Guardian score /100 | Satisfied with teaching % | Satisfied with feedback % | Spend per student /10 | Student:staff ratio | Job prospects % | Value added score /10 | Average entry tariff |
|---|---|---|---|---|---|---|---|---|---|
| 1 | Cambridge | 100.0 | 92 | 76 | 10 | 10.4 | 82 | 5 | 547 |
| 2 | York | 86.5 | 93 | 69 | 10 | 9.0 | 72 | 4 | 444 |
| 3 | Oxford | 85.6 | 91 | 65 | | 10.7 | 71 | 7 | 517 |
| 4 | Leicester | 84.4 | 91 | 67 | 10 | 8.3 | 71 | 5 | 384 |
| 4 | St Andrews | 84.4 | 94 | 63 | 8 | 10.1 | 71 | 8 | 443 |
| 6 | Imperial College | 79.7 | 89 | 49 | 9 | 12.6 | 76 | 4 | 463 |
| 7 | Sussex | 79.6 | 94 | 57 | 7 | 9.7 | 77 | 7 | 365 |
| 8 | Bristol | 79.1 | 92 | 58 | 7 | 8.8 | 72 | 5 | 439 |
| 9 | Edinburgh | 78.4 | 93 | 37 | 10 | 15.2 | 69 | 6 | 426 |
| 10 | Surrey | 77.5 | 85 | 48 | 9 | 11.3 | 79 | 6 | 361 |
| 11 | Sheffield | 77.1 | 94 | 61 | 7 | 14.0 | 70 | 6 | 419 |
| 12 | Aston | 76.9 | 92 | 71 | 6 | 12.2 | 68 | 8 | 314 |
| 13 | Manchester | 76.7 | 91 | 59 | 9 | 11.0 | 66 | 4 | 429 |
| 14 | Nottingham Trent | 75.4 | 94 | 70 | 3 | 11.4 | 79 | 10 | 213 |
| 15 | Warwick | 74.6 | 91 | 57 | | 7.0 | 66 | 3 | 415 |
| 16 | Bath | 74.3 | 86 | 52 | 6 | 13.9 | 74 | 7 | 422 |
| 17 | Newcastle | 72.4 | 88 | 60 | 6 | 13.8 | 69 | 6 | 389 |
| 18 | UEA | 72.3 | 93 | 71 | 6 | 17.7 | 70 | 5 | 377 |
| 19 | Exeter | 71.6 | 91 | 63 | 5 | 15.4 | 72 | 6 | 347 |
| 20 | Loughborough | 71.3 | 95 | 70 | 4 | 19.2 | 69 | 7 | 368 |
| 21 | Ulster | 71.1 | 78 | 58 | 4 | 9.5 | 71 | 9 | 291 |
| 22 | Durham | 71.0 | 89 | 58 | 4 | 14.2 | 74 | 3 | 459 |
| 23 | Reading | 70.9 | 92 | 57 | 9 | 17.2 | 59 | 8 | 332 |
| 24 | Keele | 70.8 | 89 | 70 | 3 | 14.4 | 68 | 9 | 308 |
| 25 | UCL | 70.5 | 87 | 52 | 6 | 18.5 | 69 | 7 | 434 |
| 26 | Portsmouth | 70.3 | 96 | 75 | 10 | 14.7 | 59 | 3 | 243 |
| 27 | Queen Margaret | 69.7 | | | 2 | 11.7 | | 9 | 322 |
| 28 | Aberdeen | 69.0 | 89 | 52 | 8 | 12.1 | 63 | 5 | 303 |
| 29 | Birmingham | 68.9 | 93 | 57 | 9 | 17.5 | 64 | 2 | 398 |
| 30 | King's College London | 68.5 | 81 | 52 | 6 | 17.1 | 73 | 5 | 386 |
| 30 | Liverpool | 68.5 | 84 | 51 | 7 | 12.8 | 64 | 6 | 362 |
| 30 | Robert Gordon | 68.5 | | | 3 | 15.9 | 73 | 8 | 328 |
| 33 | Cardiff | 68.0 | 87 | 36 | 8 | 11.1 | 63 | 3 | 386 |
| 34 | Heriot-Watt | 67.9 | 90 | 58 | 5 | 16.1 | 67 | 7 | 322 |
| 35 | Leeds | 67.6 | 88 | 52 | 9 | 12.7 | 63 | 2 | 357 |
| 36 | Bath Spa | 67.5 | 92 | 80 | 2 | 20.6 | | 10 | 286 |
| 37 | Glasgow | 67.1 | 94 | 74 | 7 | 15.3 | 60 | 2 | 375 |
| 38 | Edinburgh Napier | 66.6 | | | 3 | 16.7 | 70 | 9 | 275 |
| 39 | Nottingham | 66.5 | 86 | 50 | 7 | 15.0 | 73 | 3 | 354 |
| 40 | UWE Bristol | 66.2 | 97 | 85 | 3 | 21.3 | 53 | 10 | 255 |
| 41 | Dundee | 65.8 | 96 | 65 | 5 | 17.8 | 58 | 4 | 385 |
| 42 | Gloucestershire | 65.4 | 80 | 60 | 6 | 5.0 | | | 191 |
| 42 | Lancaster | 65.4 | 87 | 55 | 5 | 13.3 | 74 | 2 | 361 |
| 44 | Queen's, Belfast | 65.3 | 90 | 62 | 4 | 14.0 | 75 | 2 | 334 |
| 45 | Essex | 65.1 | 83 | 63 | 4 | 16.7 | 72 | 5 | 284 |
| 46 | Royal Holloway | 64.2 | 87 | 58 | 5 | 15.3 | 70 | 4 | 306 |

| | Guardian score /100 | Satisfied with teaching % | Satisfied with feedback % | Spend per student /10 | Student:staff ratio | Job prospects % | Value added score /10 | Average entry tariff |
|---|---|---|---|---|---|---|---|---|
| 47 Sheffield Hallam | 64.1 | 93 | 63 | 3 | 19.6 | 69 | 8 | 268 |
| 48 Kent | 63.4 | 91 | 60 | 6 | 13.5 | 63 | 3 | 297 |
| 49 Canterbury Christ Church | 62.7 | 88 | 73 | 3 | 24.4 | | 10 | 206 |
| 50 Anglia Ruskin | 62.1 | 93 | 57 | 6 | 6.7 | 37 | 8 | 209 |
| 51 UWIC | 62.0 | 86 | 66 | 3 | 18.6 | 71 | 8 | 231 |
| 52 Brunel | 61.9 | 81 | 62 | 4 | 17.2 | 75 | 3 | 318 |
| 52 Northumbria | 61.9 | 81 | 42 | 4 | 14.9 | 69 | 7 | 270 |
| 52 Queen Mary | 61.9 | 81 | 51 | 8 | 17.0 | 64 | 3 | 325 |
| 55 Plymouth | 61.6 | 93 | 59 | 5 | 13.6 | 45 | 7 | 300 |
| 56 Stirling | 61.5 | 93 | 59 | 8 | 11.2 | 40 | 5 | |
| 57 Coventry | 61.0 | 85 | 71 | 3 | 21.9 | 81 | 6 | 243 |
| 57 Southampton | 61.0 | 87 | 45 | 4 | 21.8 | 67 | 5 | 380 |
| 59 Swansea | 60.6 | 94 | 47 | 4 | 13.4 | 57 | 4 | 310 |
| 60 Aberystwyth | 59.6 | 89 | 58 | 4 | 17.2 | 40 | 6 | 289 |
| 61 Brighton | 58.6 | 82 | 47 | 4 | | 69 | 6 | 245 |
| 62 Greenwich | 58.2 | 87 | 67 | 8 | 22.3 | 66 | 4 | 192 |
| 63 Glasgow Caledonian | 58.1 | 87 | 61 | 3 | 19.0 | 53 | 7 | 314 |
| 64 Roehampton | 58.0 | 83 | 70 | 7 | 14.7 | 55 | 4 | 191 |
| 65 Hull | 57.4 | 88 | 62 | 5 | 20.9 | 59 | 4 | 276 |
| 66 Worcester | 57.2 | 88 | 63 | 3 | 18.1 | | 7 | 224 |
| 67 Central Lancashire | 57.1 | 73 | 45 | 5 | 23.7 | 80 | 7 | 260 |
| 68 Salford | 56.5 | 80 | 62 | 4 | 18.7 | 59 | 6 | 226 |
| 68 Teesside | 56.5 | 84 | 73 | 4 | 18.2 | | 5 | 231 |
| 70 Manchester Met | 56.3 | 86 | 60 | 3 | 17.3 | 61 | 5 | 252 |
| 71 Bangor | 56.0 | 78 | 47 | 6 | 19.4 | 56 | 6 | 284 |
| 71 Bedfordshire | 56.0 | 91 | 58 | 2 | 22.3 | | 8 | 188 |
| 73 Strathclyde | 55.7 | 84 | 53 | 5 | 21.3 | 71 | 2 | 335 |
| 74 St Mary's UC, Twickenham | 55.5 | 83 | 65 | 2 | 16.5 | | | 242 |
| 75 Chester | 54.1 | 84 | 60 | 6 | 18.9 | 60 | 2 | 304 |
| 76 Staffordshire | 54.0 | 86 | 71 | 4 | 16.9 | 42 | 6 | 198 |
| 77 Oxford Brookes | 53.7 | 73 | 32 | 4 | 18.6 | 60 | 7 | 272 |
| 78 Bradford | 52.3 | 78 | 58 | 6 | 10.3 | 52 | 1 | 249 |
| 79 London South Bank | 50.9 | 81 | 53 | 2 | | 54 | 8 | |
| 80 Hertfordshire | 50.2 | 76 | 53 | 3 | 23.9 | 66 | 4 | 252 |
| 80 Westminster | 50.2 | 84 | 56 | 4 | 17.8 | 52 | 3 | 220 |
| 82 Glamorgan | 49.9 | 83 | 63 | 2 | 30.3 | | 9 | 264 |
| 83 Kingston | 49.3 | 78 | 63 | 3 | 26.1 | 64 | 5 | 205 |
| 84 Sunderland | 49.2 | 87 | 62 | 3 | 27.8 | | | 226 |
| 85 Leeds Met | 47.9 | 75 | 52 | 3 | 21.1 | 59 | 3 | 250 |
| 86 Huddersfield | 44.3 | 87 | 63 | 3 | 31.9 | 51 | 5 | 231 |
| 87 Derby | 38.4 | 84 | 57 | 3 | 24.3 | 36 | 2 | 232 |
| 88 East London | 32.3 | 72 | 50 | 3 | 25.4 | 55 | 1 | 171 |

# Chemistry

❝ A student of chemistry enters a rapidly changing world of new ideas, theories, and proofs. Your subject will lead you towards developing new molecules and materials designed to solve modern-day problems, or towards a better understanding of complex biological systems, or reaching towards the solution to the world's pressing energy problems.

You will come to understand the nanoscale world of atoms and molecules and how to control their synthesis and properties. Ideas that seem abstract at the early stage of learning will become clear and you will have the opportunity to combine your intellectual skills with laboratory research in your pursuit of understanding.

In my early days as a chemist I was energised by the endless opportunities to innovate at all levels. Some people do so through original thinking, some through their skill in converting ideas into reality. All build on the knowledge of past practitioners and benefit from the opinions of the experts around them.

Along with the ability to innovate comes the capacity to contribute. Chemists of the future will work in a multidisciplinary scientific community where their skills will influence the quality of life in tomorrow's world. Not a bad outcome from studies that might well have started with a test-tube and a Bunsen burner. It's certainly a subject that holds as much fascination for me now as it did when I started on my studies a good few years ago!

**Dr Jeremy Hinks**, *School of Chemistry, University of Southampton*

Whether it's why leaves turn red in autumn, why diamonds are hard or even why soap gets us clean, you won't find a better way to explain it than through the study of chemistry. Atoms, molecules, and ions – the fundamental building blocks – are the key actors in the chaotic theatre that is the world in which we live.

Chemistry is the broadest of the traditional physical sciences and covers areas more usually associated with biological, medical or geological studies. It's a challenging degree, requiring a foundation of broad scientific knowledge, as well as an ability to appreciate how different processes interrelate – and an eagerness to conduct investigations and experiments for yourself.

To study it as an undergraduate, chemistry at A-level or equivalent is, as you'd expect, an absolute must, but some universities will also recommend that you have maths, physics or biology – especially if you intend to apply for a more specialised field related to that subject. However, most single subject courses will provide students with support in these areas if it is needed, so entry can still be pretty flexible.

As expected, the early stage of your chemistry degree will revisit (with some additional detail) some of the inorganic, organic and physical chemistry that you studied at A-level or equivalent. You'll find the increased practical work exciting, given that it brings the subject to life. Specialisations in the senior years of your degree will prepare you for the multidisciplinary nature of research. You will then be in a position to choose which of the major global challenges you might want to try and solve: sustainable energy, feeding a growing population or healthcare in an ageing population, to name just a few.

The specialised knowledge required for this degree is such that many graduates decide to stay in scientific fields, either continuing on to higher and research courses or going straight into industry and laboratory work – this could be anything from pharmaceuticals to oceanography. But with the skills you'd develop as a chemistry student you would leave university with many of the numerical, IT, problem-solving, and analytical skills appreciated by employers, and are therefore sought after by employers in a very wide range of professions, including, for example, the City, in government or in commerce.

As well as straight chemistry courses, there are a whole host of chemical science degree courses available that you might like to consider, such as environmental, industrial, medicinal or biological chemistry. In addition you can choose to study chemistry with another related science, such as pharmaceutical sciences or drug design, or as a combined degree if you want to keep your options open.

Most chemistry departments now offer a four-year degree leading to a master's qualification, the MChem – which is fast becoming the desirable qualification for practising chemists.

Alternatively, you could choose to study for a BSc qualification. This three-year programme may be ideal for those unsure whether they wish to spend their career in the discipline. Whichever version takes your fancy, be sure to find out what sort of opportunities for jobs and travel a university offers, as well as the extent of its laboratory and research facilities. Many of the UK's universities are at the cutting edge of chemical research and are, therefore, exciting places to study.

Don't be fooled by appearances when you visit for an open day: an older lab could offer great facilities and a flash new-looking one might not be at all well equipped. Ask the students who are already there.

And as with almost any subject, be aware of the assessment levels used at the institutions you apply for. Chemistry courses will often include more than just the old-style end of year exams – one of the strengths of chemistry programmes is the development of skills during assessment. Increasingly inventive approaches are appearing, such as real-time testing with rapid feedback, verbal examinations and peer and self assessment.

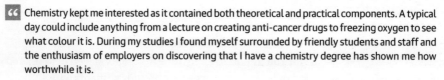

Chemistry kept me interested as it contained both theoretical and practical components. A typical day could include anything from a lecture on creating anti-cancer drugs to freezing oxygen to see what colour it is. During my studies I found myself surrounded by friendly students and staff and the enthusiasm of employers on discovering that I have a chemistry degree has shown me how worthwhile it is.

**Samuel Wright**, *chemistry graduate, University of Leeds*

## Further information

**Royal Society of Chemistry**
Burlington House, Piccadilly
London W1J 0BA

t   020 7440 3344
e   education@rsc.org
↗   www.rsc.org/studentzone

**Chemical Industries Association**
Kings Buildings, Smith Square
London SW1P 3JJ

t   020 7834 3399
e   enquiries@cia.org.uk
↗   www.cia.org.uk

**Society of Chemical Industry**
14-15 Belgrave Square
London SW1X 8PS

t   020 7598 1500
e   secretariat@soci.org
↗   www.soci.org

## Online reading

**ChemSoc**  www.rsc.org/chemsoc
**Chemistry Visualisation**  www.education.ncsa.uiuc.edu
**Royal Society**  www.royalsociety.org
**Chemical Abstracts**  www.cas.org
**Web Elements Periodic Table**  www.webelements.com
**Delights of Chemistry**  www.chem.leeds.ac.uk/delights

## Chemistry

|   |   | Guardian score /100 | Satisfied with teaching % | Satisfied with feedback % | Spend per student /10 | Student:staff ratio | Job prospects % | Value added score /10 | Average entry tariff |
|---|---|---|---|---|---|---|---|---|---|
| 1 | Sussex | 100.0 | 91 | 61 | 7 | 7.4 | | 10 | 403 |
| 2 | Oxford | 94.5 | 86 | 67 | 10 | 17.8 | 89 | 7 | 542 |
| 3 | St Andrews | 87.2 | 94 | 66 | 9 | 9.9 | 82 | 3 | 438 |
| 4 | Warwick | 86.9 | 89 | 67 | 9 | 13.4 | 84 | 6 | 426 |
| 5 | Hull | 85.5 | 92 | 68 | 7 | 13.8 | 91 | 10 | 243 |
| 6 | Imperial College | 85.0 | 78 | 51 | 10 | 12.7 | 86 | 3 | 462 |
| 7 | Durham | 84.9 | 90 | 70 | 5 | 13.1 | 83 | 5 | 507 |
| 8 | York | 82.6 | 95 | 76 | 9 | 11.4 | 82 | 2 | 407 |
| 9 | Southampton | 82.5 | 96 | 70 | 4 | 12.5 | 84 | 6 | 398 |
| 9 | UCL | 82.5 | 87 | 57 | 9 | 10.7 | 76 | 7 | 423 |
| 11 | Liverpool | 81.8 | 80 | 66 | | 10.3 | 89 | 7 | 356 |
| 12 | Leeds | 80.5 | 90 | 63 | 9 | 12.1 | 86 | 3 | 389 |
| 13 | Queen's, Belfast | 78.1 | 91 | 60 | 6 | 12.1 | 87 | 6 | 341 |
| 14 | Heriot-Watt | 77.1 | 93 | 67 | 4 | 12.8 | 85 | 5 | 337 |
| 15 | Sheffield | 77.0 | 92 | 71 | 7 | 14.8 | 79 | 5 | 404 |
| 16 | Robert Gordon | 76.5 | | | 3 | 16.5 | 78 | 10 | 323 |
| 17 | Leicester | 75.9 | 90 | 78 | 6 | 13.7 | 78 | 5 | 345 |
| 18 | Surrey | 74.1 | 83 | 48 | 8 | 14.2 | 92 | 4 | 301 |
| 19 | Bristol | 73.8 | 93 | 51 | 6 | 13.3 | 76 | 4 | 434 |
| 19 | Edinburgh | 73.8 | 81 | 46 | 9 | 16.3 | 78 | 4 | 446 |
| 21 | Nottingham | 73.6 | 90 | 59 | 7 | 12.6 | 75 | 4 | 369 |

| | | Guardian score /100 | Satisfied with teaching % | Satisfied with feedback % | Spend per student /10 | Student:staff ratio | Job prospects % | Value added score /10 | Average entry tariff |
|---|---|---|---|---|---|---|---|---|---|
| 22 | Manchester | 73.5 | 83 | 50 | 8 | 11.8 | 75 | 4 | 409 |
| 23 | Aberdeen | 72.3 | 91 | 66 | 4 | 13.4 | | | 348 |
| 24 | Cardiff | 72.0 | 88 | 42 | 6 | 11.1 | 82 | 5 | 356 |
| 25 | Bath | 71.4 | 91 | 56 | 4 | 12.6 | 83 | 3 | 398 |
| 26 | Glasgow | 69.0 | 86 | 58 | 4 | 17.6 | 86 | 4 | 392 |
| 27 | Loughborough | 68.5 | 90 | 77 | 4 | 14.4 | 80 | 2 | 313 |
| 28 | Strathclyde | 67.7 | 89 | 63 | 4 | 17.7 | 68 | 8 | 396 |
| 29 | Plymouth | 67.3 | 90 | 60 | 5 | 14.2 | | 7 | 235 |
| 30 | UEA | 66.7 | 92 | 64 | 6 | 9.8 | 67 | 1 | 350 |
| 31 | Reading | 66.5 | 77 | 54 | 5 | 13.8 | 74 | 9 | 308 |
| 32 | Birmingham | 65.5 | 82 | 65 | 7 | 14.5 | 62 | 3 | 363 |
| 33 | Northumbria | 61.8 | 89 | 63 | 3 | 14.5 | 68 | 7 | 272 |
| 34 | Queen Mary | 61.1 | 89 | 67 | 3 | 15.9 | 72 | 4 | 281 |
| 35 | Bangor | 60.8 | 83 | 61 | 5 | 13.1 | | 3 | 261 |
| 36 | Huddersfield | 55.9 | 81 | 57 | 4 | 11.7 | 61 | 7 | 204 |
| 36 | Nottingham Trent | 55.9 | 85 | 63 | 3 | 11.6 | | 3 | 216 |
| 38 | Newcastle | 54.6 | 85 | 54 | 3 | 15.3 | 70 | 2 | 324 |
| 39 | Keele | 52.8 | 88 | 65 | 3 | 23.1 | | | 284 |
| 40 | Manchester Met | 50.9 | 85 | 56 | 3 | 15.9 | 65 | 6 | 200 |
| 41 | Greenwich | 50.4 | | | 3 | 18.6 | | 4 | 215 |
| 42 | Kingston | 48.8 | 87 | 57 | 3 | 30.2 | | 9 | 227 |
| 43 | De Montfort | 47.9 | 67 | 40 | 3 | 14.2 | | 6 | 218 |
| 44 | Bradford | 46.7 | 84 | 52 | 2 | 23.1 | | | 244 |
| 45 | Brighton | 41.5 | 74 | 47 | 2 | | 60 | 8 | 215 |
| 46 | Abertay Dundee | 35.0 | | | 2 | 30.3 | 56 | 8 | 247 |

# Computer sciences and IT

" Try to imagine a world without computers. There would be no PCs or laptops, and so no word processing or spreadsheets, no communication using the web, no online shopping or photo enhancement. There would be no mobile phones or digital cameras, because these are computers at heart. There would be no internet or phone system. There would be no modern cars, trains or aircraft: computers control how they work and guide their safety on rails or in the air. There would be empty shops: all their stock is computer-controlled. There would be very few goods: many are made by robots, which themselves are computers. Food would be scarce: supermarkets' distribution systems rely on computers and computers often control food production itself.

Computer science teaches you how to use computers to make the world work as it does. You will learn how to make a computer behave how you want – this might be making a robot move something from one end of a room to another, it might be making a calculation which saves someone's life in a medical ward, or it could be creating a whole new world through building pictures or sound or building a computer system so that other people can do this.

You will learn how computers work together in building networks like the internet, how teams of people build systems worth hundreds of millions of pounds, and how computers can be made to behave like people, among many other topics. You will also learn about how to work together in groups, and what your professional responsibilities are to your colleagues, clients, and society.

Many of you will join universities' industrial partners on sandwich placement schemes, where you work with a company for a year during your degree, putting the theory into practice.

At the end of your degree you will be equipped with lifelong skills that you can use in a whole variety of jobs: from management to consulting, from programming to information systems administration, from IT companies to any company, large or small.

**Professor Simon Thompson**, *Head of Computing Laboratory, University of Kent*

---

Computer science courses cover a broad field, from those that emphasise computer hardware to those that are more mathematical; some have a strong business flavour, while others offer applications such as computer gaming, artificial intelligence or robotics. What is common to nearly all of them is an emphasis on working through tasks in a logical way, particularly when you are writing programs. Many students are attracted because of their own interest in computers, but the courses are more likely to be about building software solutions than the use of information technology and the attractions of gaming and software packages.

The conventional computing science degree (or software engineering degree) typically embraces computer systems, both hardware and software, algorithm development, networked systems, numerical methods, and database design. You'll start by learning the basics – machine architecture, programming languages, algorithms, computer systems, and general theory. Depending on the particular establishment, the mathematical and theoretical foundations of computer science are studied to varying degrees of complexity, hence the need for good mathematical grades for entry to some institutions.

Beyond that, there is a whole range of options under the computing sciences umbrella, including information systems, artificial intelligence, cybernetics, multimedia, and the internet.

Most modules are taught through a series of lectures, tutorials, and practical sessions. Assessment in the majority of cases is through a combination of continuous coursework and a formal examination.

Many universities offer computing science programmes in combination with other subjects. Typically maths, electronic engineering, and business are linked with computing science. Teaching methods generally centre around a lot of practical work, often on a mainframe system and, hopefully, some hi-tech workstations. You'll also work on a number of projects involved with either hardware or software, often as part of a group (as you would in an employment situation).

Computer sciences and IT may not be the most outwardly glamorous of subjects, but graduates will work in a wide field of industrial, governmental, educational or research establishments – often starting with very good salaries. Graduates find employment as programmers, systems analysts, software engineers or IT consultants.

Do plenty of research when choosing your course. To some extent, you are committing yourself to a future career, so ask some serious questions about what, ideally, you want to head towards – although around 50 per cent of IT graduates find employment outside of the sector.

And remember that courses with similar names may not have similar content – there's a wide variation among the different institutions, so look into what compulsory modules you'll be doing and what the discretionary choices are. Also look into lab and computer availability and the ratio of computers to students.

The university may offer sandwich courses, an intercalated year (that will lead you to having experience when you graduate), or perhaps a period studying abroad.

Find out how many employers the department has regular contact with, and the work recent graduates have gone into. Details are available from individual departments or the university careers service.

Also, a number of courses are increasingly incorporating entrepreneurship skills into the curriculum, reflecting the fact that a large number of graduates set up their own business or undertake freelance work and need to understand the issues involved.

> ❝ I wanted to do another degree that gave me practical knowledge of the IT industry. I am very career focused, so City's pathway placement scheme was a major factor in my decision to study at the University. This scheme offered me the opportunity to gain work experience in the IT sector whilst studying for my degree, and as I didn't have any relevant IT experience, I knew this would be invaluable to my future career.
>
> **Scott Dyer**, *first-year computer science student, City University London*

## 》 Further information

**British Computer Society**
First Floor, Block D, North Star House
North Star Avenue, Swindon SN2 1FA

t 01793 417417
↗ www.bcs.org.uk

**The Institute for the Management of Information Systems**
5 Kingfisher House
New Mill Road, Orpington
Kent BR5 3QG

t  0700 0023456
e  central@imis.org.uk
↗ www.imis.org.uk

**The Institute of Engineering and Technology**
Michael Faraday House
Stevenage
Herts SG1 2AY

t  01438 313311
e  postmaster@theiet.org
↗ www.theiet.org

↗ Online reading

**Guardian Unlimited technology**  technology.guardian.co.uk
**IEE Computer Society**  www.computer.org
**Wired magazine**  www.wired.com
**Scientific Computing**  www.scientific-computing.com
**Computer Weekly**  www.computerweekly.com

# Computer sciences and IT

| | | Guardian score /100 | Satisfied with teaching % | Satisfied with feedback % | Spend per student /10 | Student:staff ratio | Job prospects % | Value added score /10 | Average entry tariff |
|---|---|---|---|---|---|---|---|---|---|
| 1 | Oxford | 100.0 | | | 10 | 10.3 | 83 | 3 | 510 |
| 2 | St Andrews | 98.1 | | | 10 | 8.0 | | 6 | 419 |
| 3 | Cambridge | 97.6 | 88 | 75 | 8 | 8.6 | 92 | 2 | 585 |
| 4 | Southampton | 97.5 | 88 | 58 | 9 | 8.7 | 78 | 8 | 405 |
| 5 | Warwick | 94.4 | 83 | 66 | 10 | 9.8 | 83 | 4 | 461 |
| 6 | Edinburgh | 94.3 | 84 | 41 | | 7.5 | 84 | 9 | 437 |
| 7 | Imperial College | 94.1 | 82 | 59 | 10 | 14.3 | 94 | 3 | 462 |
| 8 | York | 93.8 | 88 | 45 | 10 | 9.6 | 80 | 4 | 435 |
| 9 | Surrey | 88.4 | 83 | 66 | 9 | 14.9 | 88 | 7 | 357 |
| 10 | Glasgow | 88.2 | 93 | 57 | 7 | 9.6 | 80 | 7 | 367 |
| 11 | Essex | 88.0 | 88 | 68 | 8 | 6.6 | 69 | 8 | 323 |
| 12 | Sussex | 87.0 | 75 | 48 | 9 | 9.6 | 69 | 9 | 364 |
| 13 | Dundee | 86.7 | 90 | 70 | 6 | 13.2 | 74 | 9 | 359 |
| 14 | Leicester | 86.5 | 82 | 77 | 5 | 9.8 | 72 | 8 | 304 |
| 15 | Reading | 85.8 | 81 | 57 | 10 | 15.3 | 79 | 7 | 330 |
| 16 | Birmingham | 85.5 | 83 | 69 | 9 | 11.2 | 73 | 6 | 374 |
| 17 | Bristol | 84.7 | 76 | 38 | 5 | 12.3 | 86 | 8 | 442 |
| 18 | Bath | 84.5 | 79 | 58 | 7 | 13.5 | 82 | 5 | 431 |
| 19 | Lancaster | 84.4 | 72 | 64 | 9 | 6.4 | 71 | 7 | 318 |
| 20 | Sheffield | 83.9 | 69 | 57 | 8 | 10.5 | 86 | 6 | 362 |
| 21 | Newcastle | 83.8 | 83 | 67 | 6 | 11.1 | 85 | 7 | 323 |
| 22 | King's College London | 83.6 | 74 | 59 | 9 | 14.1 | 89 | 6 | 349 |
| 22 | Manchester | 83.6 | 76 | 52 | 10 | 10.6 | 78 | 4 | 370 |
| 24 | Royal Holloway | 83.4 | 90 | 83 | 5 | 7.4 | 83 | 5 | 295 |
| 25 | Bournemouth | 83.0 | 80 | 62 | 7 | 12.8 | 86 | 9 | 245 |
| 26 | UCL | 82.5 | 70 | 53 | 8 | 9.5 | 80 | 4 | 405 |
| 27 | Stirling | 82.1 | | | 5 | 12.3 | 67 | 10 | |
| 28 | Leeds | 79.6 | 81 | 65 | 8 | 12.4 | 84 | 2 | 362 |

| | | Guardian score /100 | Satisfied with teaching % | Satisfied with feedback % | Spend per student /10 | Student:staff ratio | Job prospects % | Value added score /10 | Average entry tariff |
|---|---|---|---|---|---|---|---|---|---|
| 29 | Loughborough | 79.5 | 90 | 75 | 5 | 17.0 | 87 | 5 | 327 |
| 30 | Aberdeen | 78.6 | 85 | 58 | 5 | 11.9 | 84 | | 339 |
| 31 | Durham | 78.2 | 66 | 41 | 4 | 6.9 | 88 | 3 | 406 |
| 32 | Keele | 76.9 | 86 | 64 | 6 | 10.1 | | | 262 |
| 33 | Plymouth | 76.6 | 79 | 54 | 9 | 13.8 | 66 | 8 | 250 |
| 34 | Heriot-Watt | 75.9 | 82 | 58 | 5 | 12.5 | 73 | 6 | 344 |
| 35 | UWE Bristol | 74.3 | 74 | 62 | 4 | 17.5 | 82 | 9 | 258 |
| 36 | Hull | 74.2 | 84 | 65 | 4 | 18.4 | 82 | 8 | 250 |
| 37 | Liverpool | 74.1 | 78 | 61 | 6 | 9.4 | 62 | 6 | 320 |
| 38 | Kent | 73.6 | 79 | 52 | 5 | 15.3 | 87 | 4 | 306 |
| 39 | Anglia Ruskin | 71.3 | 74 | 58 | 5 | 12.9 | 59 | 9 | 237 |
| 39 | Queen's, Belfast | 71.3 | 73 | 58 | 4 | 15.0 | 76 | 7 | 319 |
| 41 | Swansea | 71.2 | 81 | 43 | 4 | 9.2 | 73 | 3 | 305 |
| 42 | City | 70.5 | 71 | 62 | 5 | 17.3 | 83 | 7 | 248 |
| 43 | Edinburgh Napier | 70.1 | | | 3 | 14.6 | 68 | 9 | 261 |
| 43 | UEA | 70.1 | 86 | 66 | 4 | 17.7 | 77 | 3 | 291 |
| 45 | Queen Mary | 69.6 | 56 | 49 | 8 | 11.8 | 69 | 7 | 275 |
| 45 | Strathclyde | 69.6 | 74 | 54 | 3 | 14.4 | 75 | 4 | 379 |
| 47 | Nottingham | 69.5 | 70 | 54 | 8 | 15.8 | 66 | 3 | 340 |
| 48 | Robert Gordon | 69.0 | | | 4 | 16.6 | 79 | 5 | 297 |
| 49 | Exeter | 68.7 | 77 | 73 | 4 | 19.4 | 72 | 5 | 320 |
| 50 | Cardiff | 67.2 | 69 | 65 | 6 | 15.4 | 82 | 2 | 320 |
| 50 | Chester | 67.2 | 77 | 59 | 3 | 18.0 | 74 | 8 | 235 |
| 52 | De Montfort | 65.7 | 85 | 76 | 5 | 19.7 | 59 | 7 | 196 |
| 52 | Northumbria | 65.7 | 78 | 64 | 4 | 18.3 | 71 | 6 | 238 |
| 54 | Staffordshire | 65.3 | 79 | 52 | 5 | 17.8 | 74 | 5 | 247 |
| 54 | Ulster | 65.3 | 74 | 64 | 4 | 13.2 | 58 | 8 | 230 |
| 56 | Aberystwyth | 65.2 | 81 | 58 | 5 | 17.6 | 62 | 7 | 241 |
| 57 | Oxford Brookes | 65.1 | 73 | 55 | 5 | 17.8 | 68 | 8 | 205 |
| 58 | Glyndŵr | 63.5 | | | 3 | 16.7 | 65 | 7 | |
| 58 | Hertfordshire | 63.5 | 72 | 53 | 7 | 11.5 | 59 | 5 | 192 |
| 58 | Teesside | 63.5 | 77 | 63 | 4 | 16.8 | 50 | 7 | 279 |
| 61 | Kingston | 62.9 | 74 | 55 | 5 | 17.3 | 55 | 9 | 197 |
| 62 | Sheffield Hallam | 62.0 | 68 | 54 | 4 | 18.8 | 65 | 9 | 216 |
| 63 | Glasgow Caledonian | 61.9 | 77 | 66 | 3 | 18.4 | 44 | 9 | 300 |
| 64 | Gloucestershire | 61.7 | 73 | 67 | 4 | 15.7 | 65 | 5 | 201 |
| 64 | Nottingham Trent | 61.7 | 67 | 53 | 4 | 20.7 | 81 | 6 | 223 |
| 66 | Portsmouth | 61.6 | 81 | 66 | 4 | 20.8 | 64 | 4 | 241 |
| 67 | Northampton | 61.3 | 79 | 67 | 2 | 19.5 | 65 | 8 | 200 |
| 68 | Central Lancashire | 61.2 | 84 | 71 | 4 | 22.4 | 72 | 3 | 233 |
| 69 | Brunel | 60.3 | 69 | 60 | 3 | 17.3 | 63 | 4 | 301 |
| 70 | Greenwich | 59.8 | 87 | 82 | 4 | 19.5 | 59 | 3 | 165 |
| 70 | Newport | 59.8 | 69 | 59 | 2 | | 49 | 9 | 236 |
| 72 | Bedfordshire | 59.2 | 67 | 65 | 4 | 8.7 | 57 | 3 | 147 |
| 73 | Bradford | 58.5 | 59 | 45 | 4 | 16.7 | 62 | 8 | 228 |
| 74 | Cumbria | 58.0 | 86 | 61 | | | 64 | 2 | 282 |

| | | Guardian score /100 | Satisfied with teaching % | Satisfied with feedback % | Spend per student /10 | Student:staff ratio | Job prospects % | Value added score /10 | Average entry tariff |
|---|---|---|---|---|---|---|---|---|---|
| 74 | Sunderland | 58.0 | 62 | 60 | 8 | 13.3 | 44 | 6 | 200 |
| 76 | Coventry | 57.7 | | | 4 | 19.4 | 60 | 4 | 275 |
| 77 | Brighton | 57.5 | 69 | 59 | 3 | 18.9 | 64 | 5 | 264 |
| 78 | Middlesex | 57.3 | 80 | 73 | 4 | 15.3 | 65 | 2 | 141 |
| 79 | Edge Hill | 57.2 | 61 | 59 | 3 | 14.1 | 58 | 5 | 228 |
| 80 | Huddersfield | 56.8 | 71 | 61 | 3 | 18.1 | 68 | 3 | 236 |
| 81 | Abertay Dundee | 56.6 | | | 3 | 24.1 | 56 | 7 | 317 |
| 82 | Birmingham City | 56.2 | 68 | 47 | 5 | 14.8 | 51 | 4 | 203 |
| 83 | Lincoln | 56.0 | 78 | 76 | 3 | 26.7 | 57 | 7 | 232 |
| 84 | Roehampton | 55.6 | 75 | 57 | 3 | 15.7 | 54 | 7 | 154 |
| 85 | Aston | 55.1 | 77 | 61 | 3 | 21.2 | 60 | 2 | 322 |
| 86 | Goldsmiths | 55.0 | 69 | 51 | 4 | 11.2 | 57 | 2 | 217 |
| 87 | Leeds Met | 52.6 | 67 | 55 | 6 | 31.1 | 53 | 10 | 210 |
| 87 | Liverpool John Moores | 52.6 | 76 | 56 | 3 | 21.2 | 67 | 3 | 194 |
| 89 | London South Bank | 52.4 | 79 | 66 | 3 | 17.7 | 33 | 9 | 119 |
| 90 | Salford | 51.7 | 64 | 54 | 6 | 26.6 | 58 | 6 | 226 |
| 91 | Worcester | 51.1 | 63 | 64 | 2 | 15.4 | 64 | 3 | 178 |
| 92 | East London | 50.7 | 71 | 59 | 2 | 16.5 | 53 | 4 | 173 |
| 93 | Derby | 49.6 | 71 | 62 | 3 | 14.3 | 67 | 1 | 237 |
| 93 | Manchester Met | 49.6 | 65 | 65 | 3 | 22.6 | 58 | 3 | 242 |
| 95 | Glamorgan | 49.2 | 75 | 67 | 4 | 25.8 | 47 | 4 | 245 |
| 96 | Bucks New University | 48.9 | 76 | 72 | 3 | 20.7 | 50 | 4 | 158 |
| 97 | Westminster | 48.0 | 69 | 59 | 3 | 11.7 | 46 | 2 | 162 |
| 98 | Southampton Solent | 47.6 | 71 | 54 | 3 | 22.7 | 58 | 3 | 198 |
| 99 | Canterbury Christ Church | 47.5 | 83 | 54 | 3 | 19.4 | 55 | 1 | 172 |
| 100 | Bolton | 34.6 | 69 | 53 | 3 | 24.2 | 38 | 1 | |

# Earth and marine science

❝ Why study earth sciences? Well, it's a great way to combine other sciences (chemistry, physics, biology) in the natural laboratory of the earth. Students of earth sciences are equally at home at a computer screen, looking down a microscope, in an analytical laboratory or in the field. I have spent many weeks on remote volcanoes in the Andes, Russia, and Iran. Many of my colleagues are involved in fieldwork examining ancient rocks more than two billion years old from the continents, or young rocks recently deformed in earthquake zones, or participating in research cruises across the world's oceans. It's not bad being paid to study the planet's wonders! Most of our students get jobs with industry, including oil and mineral exploration. There is a lot more appreciation for environmental concerns these days, and students want to be assured that they can make a positive difference before they take up these jobs. A large number also go on to do further research at universities, volcano observatories or geological surveys.

The start of the 21st century is a great time to be an earth scientist. The theory of plate tectonics has been established to the point where it underlies most of our understanding of how the earth works, and the exploration of other worlds has increased our knowledge of how the earth formed and evolved. New technologies enable us to work over a range of scales — to investigate the interior of the planet, or to determine the compositions of tiny parts of minerals. And from a practical perspective, an appreciation of the earth and how it works is critical in making a contribution to mitigating climate change and responsible stewardship of our natural resources.

**Jon Davidson**, *Professor of Earth Sciences, Durham University*

It's a big thing, Planet Earth, and the bits of it that aren't made up purely of rocks tend to be covered with sea, so earth and marine sciences are pretty fundamental to our very existence. The two disciplines — rocks or water — are very different, but either way you'll be interested in the environment and the evolution of the planet and its oceans.

Students tend to be the outdoors type, and as environmental awareness increases, so does interest in the courses — so applications are rising and competition for places is growing.

The major earth science is geology and is concerned primarily with rocks and derivative materials that make up the outer part of the planet earth. As is increasingly the case with most sciences, you'll be taking a multidisciplinary approach, making use of knowledge gleaned from other fields, such as physics, chemistry, and biology, and even looking for clues from other planets as to how the earth has ended up as it has.

You'll study landforms and other surface features of the earth, but also be concerned with the structure and inner parts of the planet, all highly valuable if you're searching for useful minerals or looking for stable environments to build on, or trying to predict earthquakes or the eruptions of volcanoes.

The ocean sciences, meanwhile, are similarly multidisciplinary, as they search for the factors that drive these mind-bogglingly complex masses of water, and can be roughly divided into four disciplines: marine biology (the study of marine plants and animals), marine geology (the study of the composition and formation of the seabed), marine chemistry (the chemical composition of seawater, pollutants, and so on), and marine physics (the study of wave formation, ocean currents, water temperature, density, and tides).

For both courses, you'll spend time skipping between the sciences, before really hitting the specialisations in the final run-in.

Once you've chosen between earth and marine sciences, check how the subject is taught. There will certainly be lectures, but how much practical work? How many field trips? Some courses can be stretched to four years to provide an instant science master's (MSc), while others can be that long in order to incorporate a year of foreign study. Fancy a year of tectonics on the San Andreas fault in California?

Some courses also offer work placement, which may be especially useful if you're planning to move into a particular industry afterwards (oil, for example), so check whether that is possible and, if so, what links the university has with the private sector.

As with all multidisciplinary courses, investigate the related departments – you'll likely be sharing facilities and teaching staff. And if it's cutting-edge research you're into, don't forget to check out the specialisations of whoever's going to be teaching you.

---

66 As a final year earth sciences student you realise how privileged you are to be reading a science that has exciting job prospects. Not only have I been able to study such a cutting edge subject, but thanks to my supportive lecturers and peers I have been able to conduct fieldwork throughout the UK and Europe, building on the knowledge I've gained through lectures and practicals. I can honestly say that geology rocks!

**Laura Phillips**, *third-year geology-geography student, Royal Holloway University of London*

---

## 》 Further information

**Geological Society**
Burlington House, Piccadilly
London W1J 0BG

t  020 7434 9944
e  enquiries@geolsoc.org.uk
↗ www.geolsoc.org.uk

**British Geological Survey**
Kingsley Dunham Centre
Keyworth, Nottingham NG12 5GG

t  0115 936 3143
e  enquiries@bgs.ac.uk
↗ www.bgs.ac.uk

**Natural Environment Research Council**
Polaris House, North Star Avenue
Swindon SN2 1EU

t  01793 411500
↗ www.nerc.ac.uk

## ↗ Online reading

**Geologists' Association**  www.geologists.org.uk
**British Science Association**  www.britishscienceassociation.org
**Jurassic Coast**  www.jurassiccoast.com
**Geology: An Introduction**  www.go4uni.ac.uk/tasters/jigsaw/faq.htm
**Society for Underwater Technology**  www.sut.org.uk
**Proudman Oceanographic Laboratory**  www.pol.ac.uk

# Earth and marine science

| | | Guardian score /100 | Satisfied with teaching % | Satisfied with feedback % | Spend per student /10 | Student:staff ratio | Job prospects % | Value added score /10 | Average entry tariff |
|---|---|---|---|---|---|---|---|---|---|
| 1 | Imperial College | 100.0 | 78 | 54 | 10 | 9.7 | 81 | 6 | 445 |
| 2 | UCL | 97.8 | 84 | 60 | 10 | 7.4 | 78 | 7 | 442 |
| 3 | Oxford | 95.8 | 85 | 67 | | 10.1 | 89 | 4 | 538 |
| 4 | Leicester | 90.6 | 100 | 96 | 6 | 12.1 | 66 | 7 | 374 |
| 5 | Manchester | 85.7 | 91 | 58 | 9 | 10.4 | 67 | 7 | 353 |
| 6 | Royal Holloway | 85.4 | 94 | 75 | 6 | 10.8 | 77 | 7 | 306 |
| 7 | St Andrews | 82.4 | 92 | 68 | 6 | 14.3 | | 7 | 433 |
| 8 | Keele | 81.9 | 93 | 78 | 3 | 18.2 | | 10 | 313 |
| 9 | UEA | 81.7 | 85 | 67 | 7 | 11.3 | 77 | 5 | 392 |
| 10 | Liverpool | 81.6 | 85 | 63 | 8 | 8.3 | 68 | 4 | 380 |
| 11 | Bristol | 81.5 | 90 | 48 | 4 | 11.9 | 93 | 4 | 429 |
| 12 | Durham | 80.5 | 95 | 66 | 3 | 12.8 | 77 | 6 | 408 |
| 13 | UWE Bristol | 78.9 | 93 | 76 | 6 | 8.2 | | | 249 |
| 14 | Lancaster | 77.4 | 80 | 67 | 8 | 10.0 | | 4 | 370 |
| 15 | Southampton | 75.4 | 94 | 65 | 4 | 14.0 | 75 | 4 | 384 |
| 16 | Aberdeen | 74.5 | 94 | 64 | 4 | 13.4 | 85 | 4 | 336 |
| 17 | Leeds | 74.0 | 79 | 49 | 5 | 10.5 | 78 | 7 | 355 |
| 18 | Edinburgh | 73.7 | 90 | 43 | 8 | 16.8 | 74 | 4 | 419 |
| 19 | Bangor | 72.7 | 92 | 61 | 5 | 15.5 | 74 | 7 | 288 |
| 20 | Cardiff | 70.2 | 96 | 52 | 5 | 14.3 | 72 | 5 | 329 |
| 21 | Birmingham | 70.0 | 94 | 75 | 7 | 15.2 | 58 | 4 | 365 |
| 22 | Ulster | 68.6 | | | 3 | 12.0 | | 8 | 235 |
| 23 | Plymouth | 66.3 | 87 | 56 | 6 | 14.2 | 56 | 9 | 260 |
| 24 | Hertfordshire | 65.3 | 87 | 65 | 4 | 4.8 | 59 | 4 | 225 |
| 25 | Aberystwyth | 63.6 | 93 | 72 | 3 | 22.6 | | 4 | 331 |
| 26 | Kingston | 63.4 | 87 | 57 | 4 | 16.0 | | 8 | 217 |
| 27 | Hull | 60.6 | 92 | 71 | 3 | 16.0 | | | 235 |
| 28 | Glamorgan | 50.7 | 82 | 49 | 3 | 5.8 | | 1 | 222 |
| 29 | Derby | 49.1 | 83 | 60 | 3 | 19.3 | | | 222 |
| 30 | Portsmouth | 46.4 | 92 | 63 | 4 | 16.7 | 50 | 2 | 256 |
| 31 | Brighton | 44.8 | 85 | 60 | 3 | | 53 | 5 | 263 |
| 32 | Bournemouth | 36.6 | 83 | 47 | 4 | 29.2 | | | 208 |

# Geography and environmental sciences

> Geography still has quite a public image problem – capital cities, rivers, and chief imports/exports – handy for Trivial Pursuit, but what else? Just as bad is the persistent idea that geographers are all rugged, outdoors types with a secret hankering to be an explorer. We've got those too, but most urban or cultural geographers I know would prefer a cappuccino in Berlin or a chai in Mumbai.
>
> A very positive development for the discipline over the last few years has been the growing public appreciation of the environmental challenges that the world faces, and the growing awareness that geography is ideally suited to examining both the scientific and social dimensions of ecological change and human risk and vulnerability. As the Stern Report stated, dealing with climate change is going to demand political, economic, cultural, and historical knowledge – all of which is covered by contemporary human geography – as well as physical geography subjects like climatology, glaciology, biogeography, and oceanography.
>
> Although most students and academics specialise, the ability to see an integrated picture is a tremendous strength. But geography today isn't just about the environment. It is a discipline that allows extraordinary freedom to explore a huge range of subjects. In my own department, we have people working on volcanoes, ice sheets, and coastal erosion; as well as street culture, the history of the American West, indigenous knowledge, and the economic impact of China and India. Students can follow their interests and enthusiasms across a real spectrum of issues. They emerge with an enviable range of skills, and ready to take up job opportunities in everything from climate science to development NGOs, business, and the media. Geography's public image is gradually changing, and it is about time – it is a fabulous subject that has never been more interesting or important.
>
> **Dr Emma Mawdsley**, *Lecturer in Geography, Fellow of Newnham College, University of Cambridge*

## Geography

Geography has, in the past decade, been given a makeover by cultural and political trends that have seen it shake off the traditional perception of a degree based on precipitation cycles and plate tectonics to become a multidisciplinary subject tackling fundamental questions about the environment, the movement of peoples around the globe, and population patterns.

Geography is unique in bridging the social sciences and the earth sciences. In fact, you can emerge with a BA or a BSc from different institutions with no discernable difference in the course. Like many of the older subjects, it is taking an increasingly multidisciplinary approach, encompassing ecology, geology, economics, and politics to create an applied science with skills of interpretation and analysis, which are invaluable to future employers, and which make geography one of the top courses in terms of graduate recruitment.

The career options available are extremely wide-ranging. You can head off to pursue jobs directly related to geography – such as in town and transport planning or environmental consultancy – or you could use your skills in more general careers, such as IT or marketing. The third option is to continue with full-time study and training to develop a career in teaching or research, or to gain further qualifications for entry into more specialist professions.

The options for modules are pretty vast, so look carefully at what the course offers. There are a number of key common geographical concepts taught across all the institutions, but after that the choice is wider. The options tend to be based around the research interests and specialisations of departmental staff – so see if they tally with your own interests and career plans.

Fieldwork – perhaps including some abroad – is an appealing and integral part of most geography degrees. Check what the options are, and whether they coincide with the course choices you are making.

# Environmental sciences

Everyone tells us the world is going to hell in a deep-fried handbasket, as global warming, the hole in the ozone layer, GM foods, and pollution take an increasingly fevered hold over the public imagination and the end of the world gets more and more nigh. Environmental scientists are generally the ones who think they can do something about it, saving us from ourselves, and taking a degree can be the first step in that process.

The issues facing environmental science have a variety of causes and solutions, so the degree is increasingly multidisciplinary. You'll be studying the principles of (deep breath) ecology, population biology, environmental chemistry, physiology, physical geography, statistics, sociology, law, economics, microbial ecology, energy and biological survey, assessment and conservation (and … breathe out). In addition, you'll need to be able to produce concise accounts of complex problems and communicate them effectively to others.

The degree is generally a three-year BSc. You'll not have come across anything quite like it at school or college, so the first year is often spent building the foundations of the course, before moving on to a more modular format where you venture into deeper waters following particular interests. It's here that the shape of your degree, and perhaps your future career, becomes clearer. That future career may involve working in local government (planning perhaps), environmental agencies, water authorities, industry, consultancy or even the law.

Teaching is a mixture of the traditional lectures and seminars, with a measure of fieldwork thrown in. Assessment is done by varying amounts of coursework and formal exams. The ratio of one to the other can make a difference, so think about what's best for you.

Course content also varies considerably. Some contain mostly science, and no elements of political or social science, while others are at the opposite extreme. Also check the quality of related departments for any area you're particularly interested in studying.

Look too at the detail of the courses and who will be teaching you. Some universities will be better than others at teaching climate change, global warming or environmental chemistry – staff may be at the forefront of research in these fields.

Some courses last four years and include a year studying abroad – a valuable opportunity. Local field trips will also be a possibility, so consider your location carefully – you could end up on the doorstep of the Pennines, for example.

> 66 Geography is an exciting, diverse and increasingly important subject, with geographical issues continually in the media spotlight. Encompassing both human and physical aspects of the world, I especially enjoy computer modelling and mapping technologies to research glacier retreat, past and future climate change, and geomorphological hazards such as landsliding. The fieldwork opportunities across Britain and abroad really illustrate the processes operating in the natural world, making geography one of the most fascinating subjects to study at university.
>
> **Andy Singleton**, *second-year geography student, Durham University*

## )) Further information

**Geographical Association**
160 Solly Street
Sheffield S1 4BF

t  01142 960088
e  info@geography.org.uk
↗  www.geography.org.uk

**The British Ecological Society**
26 Blades Court, Putney
London SW15 2NU

t  020 8871 9797
↗  www.britishecologicalsociety.org

**Royal Geographical Society (with The Institute of British Geographers)**
1 Kensington Gore
London SW7 2AR

t  020 7591 3000
↗  www.rgs.org

**Natural Environment Research Council**
Polaris House, North Star Avenue
Swindon SN2 1EU

t  01793 411500
↗  www.nerc.ac.uk

## ↗ Online reading

**Natural Environment Research Council** www.nerc.ac.uk
**The Center for International Earth Science Information Network (CIESIN)**
   www.ciesin.columbia.edu
**The Global Site** www.theglobalsite.ac.uk

# Geography and environmental studies

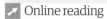

| | | Guardian score /100 | Satisfied with teaching % | Satisfied with feedback % | Spend per student /10 | Student:staff ratio | Job prospects % | Value added score /10 | Average entry tariff |
|---|---|---|---|---|---|---|---|---|---|
| 1 | Cambridge | 100.0 | 96 | 73 | 10 | 10.7 | 81 | 7 | 504 |
| 2 | Oxford | 93.9 | 89 | 58 | 10 | 14.8 | 72 | 8 | 487 |
| 3 | Bristol | 87.9 | 87 | 50 | 8 | 11.9 | 83 | 9 | 452 |
| 4 | St Andrews | 79.1 | 93 | 69 | 3 | 10.2 | 70 | 9 | 457 |
| 5 | UCL | 77.6 | 85 | 52 | 9 | 12.0 | 74 | 7 | 435 |
| 6 | Edinburgh | 76.2 | 86 | 45 | | 6.6 | 68 | 5 | 424 |
| 7 | Durham | 75.9 | 93 | 61 | 6 | 13.1 | 69 | 6 | 462 |
| 8 | Leicester | 74.6 | 93 | 75 | 6 | 12.0 | 69 | 7 | 347 |
| 9 | Southampton | 74.3 | 90 | 57 | 8 | 14.0 | 70 | 7 | 410 |
| 10 | Keele | 70.8 | 94 | 76 | 7 | 8.9 | | | 276 |
| 11 | Leeds | 69.7 | 89 | 66 | 8 | 18.6 | 68 | 8 | 401 |

| | Guardian score /100 | Satisfied with teaching % | Satisfied with feedback % | Spend per student /10 | Student:staff ratio | Job prospects % | Value added score /10 | Average entry tariff |
|---|---|---|---|---|---|---|---|---|
| 12 Nottingham | 69.1 | 88 | 57 | 5 | 15.7 | 63 | 9 | 445 |
| 13 Reading | 67.4 | 85 | 58 | 10 | 21.6 | 69 | 8 | 350 |
| 14 Aberystwyth | 67.3 | 94 | 75 | 6 | 15.5 | 64 | 6 | 334 |
| 15 Dundee | 67.2 | 95 | 62 | 3 | 17.7 | 58 | 10 | 343 |
| 16 Birmingham | 67.1 | 92 | 67 | 7 | 19.1 | 65 | 8 | 377 |
| 17 Royal Holloway | 67.0 | 97 | 71 | 8 | 10.2 | 51 | 4 | 319 |
| 17 York | 67.0 | | | 7 | 12.9 | | 6 | 357 |
| 19 Exeter | 65.6 | 92 | 80 | 4 | 19.3 | 62 | 8 | 369 |
| 20 UEA | 65.5 | 87 | 62 | 8 | 11.2 | 61 | 4 | 361 |
| 21 Loughborough | 65.2 | 95 | 72 | 4 | 17.3 | 65 | 7 | 364 |
| 22 Hull | 65.1 | 89 | 74 | 7 | 12.1 | 61 | 6 | 302 |
| 23 Sussex | 64.9 | 89 | 60 | 5 | 16.6 | 64 | 8 | 379 |
| 24 Lancaster | 63.3 | 95 | 79 | 5 | 19.8 | 63 | 6 | 399 |
| 25 London School of Economics | 63.1 | 73 | 59 | 5 | 14.6 | 81 | 4 | 422 |
| 26 Queen Mary | 62.3 | 86 | 47 | 8 | 9.3 | 55 | 5 | 308 |
| 27 Sheffield | 61.7 | 88 | 60 | 6 | 17.3 | 66 | 4 | 413 |
| 28 King's College London | 61.5 | 88 | 47 | 6 | 15.9 | 72 | 5 | 365 |
| 29 Newcastle | 60.1 | 86 | 56 | 4 | 16.3 | 72 | 4 | 383 |
| 30 UWE Bristol | 60.0 | 92 | 78 | 4 | 13.7 | 46 | 10 | 263 |
| 31 Gloucestershire | 58.2 | 88 | 73 | 5 | 14.4 | 62 | 7 | 257 |
| 32 Glasgow | 57.9 | 94 | 70 | 5 | 19.4 | 58 | 4 | 387 |
| 33 Plymouth | 57.6 | 90 | 62 | 6 | 9.4 | 49 | 6 | 289 |
| 34 Manchester | 57.5 | 88 | 56 | 6 | 22.6 | 60 | 7 | 402 |
| 35 Liverpool | 57.4 | 88 | 50 | 6 | 15.2 | 52 | 8 | 343 |
| 36 Coventry | 56.6 | | | 6 | 16.2 | 58 | 5 | 307 |
| 37 Kingston | 56.0 | 85 | 58 | 4 | 7.2 | 60 | 5 | 228 |
| 38 Bradford | 55.9 | 84 | 52 | 7 | 10.6 | | | 229 |
| 39 Staffordshire | 55.4 | 90 | 70 | 10 | 9.8 | 56 | 1 | 221 |
| 40 Sheffield Hallam | 54.3 | 86 | 82 | 3 | 18.0 | 51 | 9 | 272 |
| 41 Chester | 53.7 | 97 | 78 | 3 | 14.7 | 56 | 3 | 266 |
| 42 Edge Hill | 53.1 | | | 3 | 13.2 | | 3 | 251 |
| 43 Northumbria | 53.0 | 93 | 76 | 5 | 19.5 | 53 | 7 | 275 |
| 43 Queen's, Belfast | 53.0 | 87 | 73 | 5 | 17.2 | 69 | 3 | 312 |
| 45 Nottingham Trent | 52.7 | 87 | 71 | 4 | 20.3 | 70 | 6 | 251 |
| 46 Strathclyde | 51.6 | 88 | 71 | 3 | 24.2 | 62 | 6 | 364 |
| 47 Manchester Met | 51.5 | 88 | 68 | 4 | 14.9 | 55 | 5 | 251 |
| 48 Bangor | 50.3 | 96 | 65 | 3 | 25.7 | | 7 | 328 |
| 49 Aberdeen | 49.0 | 92 | 76 | 6 | 17.4 | 57 | 1 | 309 |
| 50 Bath Spa | 47.9 | 92 | 80 | 2 | 18.5 | 57 | 4 | 277 |
| 51 Canterbury Christ Church | 47.5 | 94 | 85 | 2 | 13.7 | 52 | 2 | 240 |
| 52 Swansea | 45.3 | 90 | 64 | 5 | 16.2 | 46 | 3 | 308 |
| 53 Cumbria | 44.9 | 92 | 79 | 2 | | 58 | 3 | 293 |
| 54 Glamorgan | 44.6 | | | 3 | 7.5 | 39 | 4 | 231 |
| 54 Worcester | 44.6 | 79 | 66 | 4 | 9.2 | | 3 | 201 |
| 56 Derby | 44.0 | | | 8 | 16.6 | 47 | 3 | 205 |
| 57 Northampton | 41.4 | 90 | 74 | 2 | 11.9 | 48 | 2 | 237 |
| 58 Oxford Brookes | 40.7 | 85 | 62 | 3 | 24.5 | 56 | 6 | 285 |
| 59 Portsmouth | 38.9 | 90 | 62 | 4 | 22.4 | 45 | 4 | 273 |
| 60 Ulster | 30.7 | 89 | 62 | 3 | 25.1 | 44 | 4 | 256 |
| 61 Southampton Solent | 29.9 | | | 3 | 16.6 | 44 | 1 | 189 |

# Mathematics

❝ Few people who have not studied a mathematics or science degree will have much idea what modern mathematics involves. Most of the arithmetic and geometry seen in schools today was known to the Ancient Greeks; the ideas of calculus and probability you may have met at A-level were known in the 17th century. And some very neat ideas are to be found there! But mathematicians have not simply been admiring the work of Newton and Fermat for the last three centuries. Since then the patterns of mathematics have been found more profoundly and broadly than those early mathematicians could ever have imagined. There is no denying it: mathematics is in a golden age, and mathematicians are more in demand today than ever before.

The clearest change of emphasis from A-level to university mathematics is in the need to prove things, especially in pure mathematics. Much mathematics is too abstract or technical to simply rely on intuition, and so it is important that you can write clear and irrefutable arguments, which make plain to you, and others, the soundness of your claims. But pure mathematics is more than an insistence on rigour, arguably involving the most beautiful ideas and theorems in all of mathematics, and including whole new areas, such as topology, untouched at school.

Mathematics, though, would not be the subject it is today if it wasn't for the impact of applied mathematics and statistics. There is much beautiful mathematics to be found here, such as in relativity or in number theory behind the RSA encryption widely used in internet security, or just in the way a wide range of techniques from all reaches of mathematics might be applied to solve a difficult problem.

Also with ever-faster computers, mathematicians can now model highly complex systems such as the human heart, can explain why spotted animals have striped tails, can treat non-deterministic systems like the stock market or Brownian motion. The high technical demands of these models and the prevalence of computers in everyday life are making mathematicians ever more employable after university.

**Dr Richard Earl**, *Schools Liaison Officer for the Mathematical Institute and Tutor in Mathematics, Worcester College, University of Oxford*

You might expect a subject that's been around since the days of Pythagoras and the Ancient Greeks to have run its course. But no — maths is pushing the boundaries like never before, with ideas such as chaos theory revolutionising the way we view the world.

More than that, maths is about pattern and structure; it is about logical analysis, deduction, and calculation within these patterns and structures. When patterns are found, often in widely different areas of nature, science, and technology, the mathematics of these patterns can be used to explain phenomena and reveal new truths and insights.

Maths at university is much broader and more varied than maths at A-level — it takes subjects like algebra and geometry into new, abstract dimensions, such as analysis, topology, and group theory. So read the prospectus carefully and make sure you know what you're getting into. Work could be done with the help of a computer, or just an old-fashioned paper, pencil, and furrowed brow.

Recent studies have shown that the average maths graduate consistently earns more than graduates of other subjects — employers are always looking for the strong skills in reasoning and problem-solving you'll acquire. Computing, high finance, management consultancy, risk assessment, information security, and industrial research are all sectors that welcome maths graduates.

The courses students are pitching at can vary dramatically in content, but the first year at least should contain common elements such as algebra, differential equations, probability, and statistics.

After that, the field can be wide open, so investigate thoroughly before applying and check the compulsory elements aren't precisely those areas that scare the living daylights out of you.

You might also consider joint honours — maths and computer science is a popular degree choice, and four-year degrees with a placement in industry are also available. Maths and accountancy is also a good option — many accounting firms prefer it to a straight accountancy degree. Combinations such as these, along with work experience, give graduates plenty of relevant ways to increase their employability. If you get the chance of a work placement, you should always take it, so look into the possibilities.

> By studying mathematics at university you begin to understand how it can be applied in the real world and how you could use your skills in industry to solve problems. One of my favourite modules has been mathematical analysis, where I have learnt about the rigorous foundations of elementary mathematical ideas, such as differentiation and integration. While a mathematics degree is much more challenging than A-level, it is ultimately very rewarding.
>
> **Robert Hicks**, *second-year mathematics student, University of Portsmouth*

## 》 Further information

**The Institute of Mathematics**
Catherine Richards House
16 Nelson Street, Southend-on-Sea
Essex SS1 1EF

t   01702 354020
e   post@ima.org.uk
↗  www.ima.org.uk

**The London Mathematical Society**
De Morgan House, 57-8 Russell Square
London WC1B 4HS

t   020 7637 3686
e   lms@lms.ac.uk
↗  www.lms.ac.uk

**The Mathematical Association**
259 London Road
Leicester LE2 3BE

t   0116 221 0013
e   office@m-a.org.uk
↗  www.m-a.org.uk

## ↗ Online reading

**The Centre for the Popularisation of Maths**  www.popmath.org.uk
**Mega Mathematics**  www.c3.lanl.gov/mega-math
**Maths careers**  www.mathscareers.org.uk
**Plus magazine**  www.plus.maths.org
**The University of Southampton's cipher challenge**  www.cipher.maths.soton.ac.uk

# Mathematics

| | | Guardian score /100 | Satisfied with teaching % | Satisfied with feedback % | Spend per student /10 | Student:staff ratio | Job prospects % | Value added score /10 | Average entry tariff |
|---|---|---|---|---|---|---|---|---|---|
| 1 | Oxford | 100.0 | 85 | 80 | 10 | 12.9 | 78 | 7 | 550 |
| 2 | Cambridge | 92.1 | 86 | 80 | 10 | 13.4 | 91 | 3 | 564 |
| 3 | Warwick | 80.8 | 81 | 60 | 9 | 11.5 | 84 | 5 | 539 |
| 4 | Greenwich | 76.7 | 94 | 83 | 5 | 11.8 | | 10 | 206 |
| 5 | St Andrews | 75.6 | 85 | 67 | 5 | 12.8 | 82 | 7 | 521 |
| 6 | Leicester | 74.4 | 96 | 90 | 8 | 13.9 | 75 | 7 | 365 |
| 6 | Portsmouth | 74.4 | 93 | 74 | | 10.8 | 69 | 10 | 269 |
| 8 | Lancaster | 67.0 | 86 | 71 | 7 | 7.5 | 61 | 6 | 419 |
| 9 | Hertfordshire | 66.6 | 91 | 76 | 3 | 9.2 | 84 | 9 | 218 |
| 10 | UWE Bristol | 64.3 | 89 | 82 | 5 | 15.4 | 74 | 9 | 296 |
| 11 | Imperial College | 63.6 | 72 | 56 | 10 | 14.6 | 71 | 3 | 506 |
| 12 | Heriot-Watt | 63.4 | 78 | 65 | 5 | 15.6 | 84 | 9 | 374 |
| 13 | Bath | 63.0 | 81 | 67 | 4 | 14.6 | 82 | 4 | 488 |
| 14 | Keele | 62.4 | 94 | 77 | 4 | 10.0 | | 6 | 353 |
| 15 | Brighton | 62.3 | | | 7 | 8.9 | | 7 | 259 |
| 16 | Glasgow | 62.2 | 91 | 71 | 6 | 14.0 | 78 | 4 | 410 |
| 17 | Edinburgh | 62.0 | 72 | 57 | 9 | 15.6 | 75 | 5 | 473 |
| 18 | Birmingham | 61.7 | 86 | 74 | 8 | 12.4 | 66 | 3 | 426 |
| 19 | Bristol | 60.9 | 81 | 52 | 6 | 13.4 | 72 | 5 | 495 |
| 20 | Kent | 60.7 | 81 | 73 | 3 | 12.1 | 87 | 7 | 279 |
| 21 | UCL | 60.6 | 84 | 68 | 6 | 17.2 | 77 | 5 | 468 |
| 22 | Kingston | 59.7 | 78 | 75 | 4 | 17.2 | | 10 | 230 |
| 23 | Sheffield | 59.6 | 85 | 75 | 4 | 15.2 | 79 | 5 | 408 |
| 24 | Southampton | 58.4 | 73 | 53 | 6 | 15.1 | 82 | 5 | 448 |
| 25 | Aberystwyth | 57.8 | 78 | 72 | 8 | 12.8 | | 4 | 329 |
| 25 | Durham | 57.8 | 75 | 59 | 3 | 13.6 | 73 | 6 | 530 |
| 27 | Loughborough | 57.5 | 90 | 74 | 5 | 14.5 | 77 | 3 | 383 |
| 28 | Surrey | 56.1 | 78 | 63 | 4 | 10.6 | 77 | 4 | 382 |
| 29 | Leeds | 55.4 | 76 | 60 | 8 | 11.2 | 72 | 3 | 418 |
| 30 | Royal Holloway | 54.4 | 79 | 79 | 6 | 11.6 | 69 | 2 | 364 |
| 31 | Oxford Brookes | 54.2 | | | 6 | 16.1 | | 8 | 281 |
| 32 | King's College London | 53.8 | 81 | 64 | 6 | 15.0 | 70 | 4 | 433 |
| 33 | Nottingham | 53.3 | 77 | 68 | 4 | 14.2 | 68 | 4 | 463 |
| 33 | York | 53.3 | 86 | 64 | 6 | 15.8 | 66 | 4 | 453 |
| 35 | Cardiff | 51.5 | 78 | 66 | 5 | 14.9 | 69 | 4 | 423 |
| 36 | London School of Economics | 51.3 | 72 | 68 | 6 | 19.3 | 79 | 3 | 503 |
| 37 | Nottingham Trent | 49.2 | 63 | 62 | 5 | 15.8 | 81 | 8 | 267 |
| 38 | Sheffield Hallam | 48.9 | 93 | 81 | 6 | 18.8 | 68 | 7 | 259 |
| 39 | Chester | 47.8 | 84 | 71 | 3 | 14.1 | | 7 | 260 |
| 40 | Liverpool | 47.1 | 85 | 74 | 6 | 13.6 | 58 | 3 | 383 |
| 40 | Manchester | 47.1 | 81 | 54 | 7 | 17.0 | 61 | 3 | 442 |
| 42 | Strathclyde | 46.9 | 84 | 71 | 3 | 18.3 | 72 | 5 | 373 |
| 43 | Newcastle | 46.8 | 82 | 58 | 4 | 20.0 | 79 | 3 | 432 |
| 44 | Plymouth | 46.3 | 92 | 85 | 3 | 11.6 | 56 | 6 | 261 |
| 45 | Glamorgan | 46.2 | 84 | 70 | 4 | 18.5 | | 7 | 263 |
| 46 | Sussex | 44.8 | 81 | 71 | 4 | 18.1 | 60 | 5 | 393 |
| 47 | UEA | 43.9 | 94 | 86 | 4 | 24.7 | 66 | 5 | 384 |

| | Guardian score /100 | Satisfied with teaching % | Satisfied with feedback % | Spend per student /10 | Student:staff ratio | Job prospects % | Value added score /10 | Average entry tariff |
|---|---|---|---|---|---|---|---|---|
| 48 Exeter | 42.6 | 82 | 70 | 4 | 21.1 | 72 | 4 | 380 |
| 48 Northumbria | 42.6 | 88 | 74 | 3 | 13.0 | 77 | 1 | 264 |
| 50 Reading | 42.1 | 85 | 69 | 4 | 14.9 | 61 | 3 | 330 |
| 51 Swansea | 41.4 | 73 | 58 | 3 | 14.4 | 65 | 7 | 325 |
| 52 Coventry | 40.0 | | | 5 | 21.5 | | 7 | 284 |
| 53 Aston | 39.0 | | | 3 | 21.2 | | 6 | 347 |
| 54 City | 38.1 | 80 | 74 | 3 | 24.8 | 64 | 9 | 307 |
| 55 Queen's, Belfast | 36.5 | 76 | 69 | 2 | 19.7 | 68 | 4 | 362 |
| 56 Brunel | 33.3 | 71 | 63 | 4 | 16.5 | 56 | 6 | 291 |
| 57 Essex | 32.6 | 74 | 56 | 3 | 14.2 | | 1 | 302 |
| 58 Cumbria | 30.1 | 79 | 62 | 6 | 21.5 | | 3 | 245 |
| 59 Manchester Met | 27.4 | 81 | 70 | 3 | 24.0 | 57 | 5 | 302 |
| 59 Queen Mary | 27.4 | 70 | 56 | 5 | 17.1 | 54 | 3 | 298 |

# Physics

❝ Physics is the study of the nature and properties of energy and matter. As a physics under-graduate you will develop an in-depth understanding of the forces and interactions that take in both the microscopic and macroscopic worlds, from ionisation to isotopes, from quarks to quadrupoles, from superconductors to supernovae. In doing so you will also encounter new and cutting-edge concepts in science such as nanotechnology and supersymmetry.

People who study physics have a hunger for understanding how things work. A physics degree satisfies this hunger by introducing students to new concepts which include exploring the world of quantum physics, discovering how mass and time itself changes in Einstein's special and general relativity, studying the fundamental building blocks of matter in particle physics, and learning how physics concepts underpin a diverse range of technologies, including micro-processors, non-drip paints, quantum computers, and the global positioning system.

As well as developing skills as a scientist it is well recognised that a physics graduate possesses a wide range of other competences and skills including numeracy, problem-solving, teamwork, and communication — all of which are greatly sought after by employers. Taking a physics degree opens up a huge range of stimulating and lucrative careers.

**Dr Lee Thompson**, *Reader in Neutrino Physics, Department of Physics and Astronomy, University of Sheffield*

To study physics is to join a great tradition of scientists, from Newton to Faraday and from Watt to Hawking, to study interactions on the largest scale imaginable (between stars and galaxies) to the smallest scale we know of (between subatomic particles). In short, it's the study of the universe. And it doesn't get any bigger (or smaller) than that.

So it's no surprise that the demand for graduates is growing. Physics courses have a strong emphasis on analytical skills (and often require a fair proportion of maths skills too), and the degree is a highly respected qualification. Graduates end up in a whole range of professions, in areas as diverse as research, teaching, computing, medicine, and engineering.

The usual offering is a BSc of three years' duration, although about a third of physics students do a four-year degree known as an MPhys or MSc. These courses give you the opportunity to specialise in the final year, and get a deeper understanding in the areas of your choice. The courses cover a variety of topics, with many institutions offering modules in medical physics, astronomy, space and science, applied physics, and other related topics, so check if these are available — though the modular course structure at many universities means that you should be able to tailor your course to fit your interests and career aspirations if you look hard enough.

The drop in applicants to "traditional" science courses which has affected some subjects has left physics relatively unscathed. Teaching is based on the usual mixture of lectures, tutorials, lab work and seminars, with the mix dependent on the institution you are at. Most courses also demand a dissertation in the final year, which is an excellent opportunity for engaging in your own experimental or theoretical research.

Once qualified, and if you want to stay a scientist, the Institute of Physics (IoP), the professional body for physicists, can help you to obtain recognised professional status, such as chartered physicist (CPhys) and chartered engineer (CEng). The simplest first step to becoming chartered is to do a degree that has been accredited by the IoP, otherwise you have to prove that the course is equivalent to an accredited degree. It's far easier to check the accreditation before you start.

Most universities still specialise within certain areas of physics. While their under-graduates will study across a broad spectrum, you will find that the researchers work in only four or five regions, so you can select an institution where world-class researchers are working at the frontline of scientific discovery that interests you. But remember to check if they are still actively involved in teaching — it may be that they have "better" things to do.

Some universities offer courses (generally the four-year version) where you can incorporate industrial or laboratory-based placements and other work experience into your studies, or study abroad. Investigate whether this is a possibility, since it's a great opportunity for you to try out your chosen career and see if you like it or not.

A high number of universities have a physics society that organises events in addition to your academic course, such as inviting guest speakers, arranging tours of research facilities and industrial sites, and holding social functions that provide an excellent opportunity to meet the more senior physicists at your department. Events for students are also organised by Nexus, the student wing of the IoP; these include an annual conference (with a hefty social programme). This is the sort of thing that can provide an extra dimension to your course and occasionally restore your faith on those wet Tuesdays when you're wondering what on earth you're doing there.

> Degree-level physics is where you learn to think for yourself and, most importantly, to question. A physicist's most used word is 'why?' (closely followed by 'how?'). Physics is challenging — it's the hard things that are the most memorable and it's the fact that you've overcome them that makes it enjoyable. The 'Oh, wow, that must be difficult!' comments you get from non-scientists when you tell them what you do is also quite good though.

**Rachel Ashley**, *second-year physics student, University of Liverpool*

## » Further information

**Institute of Physics**
76 Portland Place
London W1B 1NT

t  020 7470 4800
e  physics@iop.org
↗ www.iop.org

**Royal Astronomical Society**
Burlington House, Piccadilly
London W1J 0BQ

t  020 7734 4582
↗ www.ras.org.uk

## ↗ Online reading

**Science and Technology Facilities Council**  www.scitech.ac.uk
**Physics World**  www.physicsworld.com
**Royal Society**  www.royalsociety.org
**WiTEC — the European Association for Women in Science and Engineering and Technology**  www.witec-eu.net

# Physics

| | | Guardian score /100 | Satisfied with teaching % | Satisfied with feedback % | Spend per student /10 | Student:staff ratio | Job prospects % | Value added score /10 | Average entry tariff |
|---|---|---|---|---|---|---|---|---|---|
| 1 | Oxford | 100.0 | 86 | 72 | 10 | 9.3 | 77 | 7 | 551 |
| 2 | Birmingham | 85.6 | 97 | 88 | 6 | 10.0 | 78 | 6 | 453 |
| 3 | UCL | 84.5 | 77 | 50 | 9 | 6.9 | 80 | 8 | 435 |
| 4 | Imperial College | 84.0 | 80 | 58 | 8 | 8.4 | 79 | 6 | 518 |
| 5 | Leeds | 76.9 | 91 | 64 | 8 | 9.8 | 84 | 3 | 418 |
| 6 | Warwick | 76.5 | 90 | 70 | 7 | 10.8 | 77 | 5 | 489 |
| 7 | Manchester | 76.2 | 94 | 62 | 8 | 10.2 | 73 | 5 | 478 |
| 8 | Dundee | 75.6 | 95 | 69 | 9 | 5.3 | | | 307 |
| 9 | St Andrews | 74.7 | 86 | 62 | 8 | 8.6 | 75 | 5 | 482 |
| 10 | Sheffield | 72.0 | 97 | 75 | 7 | 10.7 | 75 | 6 | 391 |
| 11 | Heriot-Watt | 71.8 | 87 | 63 | 7 | 10.0 | | 10 | 342 |
| 12 | Royal Holloway | 71.1 | 96 | 74 | 6 | 6.9 | 71 | 5 | 341 |
| 13 | Sussex | 70.6 | 91 | 61 | 6 | 9.7 | 70 | 8 | 405 |
| 14 | Southampton | 69.5 | 96 | 61 | 6 | 9.5 | 75 | 4 | 451 |
| 15 | Queen Mary | 69.4 | 89 | 67 | 7 | 6.0 | | 4 | 312 |
| 16 | Hertfordshire | 66.9 | 92 | 61 | 2 | 3.6 | | 9 | 228 |
| 17 | Glasgow | 66.8 | 91 | 66 | 4 | 8.8 | 84 | 1 | 405 |
| 18 | Durham | 66.7 | 82 | 68 | 3 | 10.6 | 77 | 5 | 526 |
| 19 | Lancaster | 66.3 | 78 | 70 | 7 | 6.7 | 68 | 7 | 375 |
| 20 | Edinburgh | 66.2 | 83 | 48 | | 10.5 | 76 | 3 | 463 |
| 21 | Strathclyde | 64.6 | 89 | 63 | 6 | 8.2 | 61 | 10 | 323 |
| 22 | Leicester | 62.9 | 81 | 44 | 8 | 8.8 | 74 | 4 | 372 |
| 23 | Queen's, Belfast | 62.1 | 92 | 68 | 4 | 7.7 | 67 | 7 | 382 |
| 24 | Liverpool | 61.7 | 85 | 58 | 7 | 8.5 | 69 | 6 | 370 |
| 25 | Glamorgan | 61.2 | 82 | 49 | 2 | 6.2 | | 10 | |
| 26 | Nottingham | 61.0 | 85 | 58 | 7 | 9.7 | 72 | 4 | 418 |
| 27 | Aberystwyth | 60.4 | 93 | 72 | 8 | 9.8 | 71 | 4 | 237 |
| 28 | Loughborough | 59.8 | 90 | 75 | 3 | 9.3 | 69 | 7 | 343 |
| 29 | Cardiff | 59.4 | 90 | 72 | 3 | 11.1 | 80 | 4 | 337 |
| 30 | Swansea | 56.8 | 89 | 66 | 2 | 8.2 | 78 | 3 | 277 |
| 31 | King's College London | 52.9 | | | 6 | 12.5 | | 3 | 415 |
| 32 | Surrey | 52.5 | 84 | 65 | 6 | 12.9 | 70 | 4 | 363 |
| 33 | Exeter | 48.9 | 94 | 70 | 3 | 13.2 | 72 | 2 | 383 |
| 34 | York | 46.8 | 88 | 68 | 4 | 11.8 | 63 | 4 | 397 |
| 35 | Kent | 45.2 | 86 | 55 | 3 | 13.5 | 70 | 8 | 288 |
| 36 | Bath | 40.6 | 77 | 63 | 3 | 11.3 | 71 | 2 | 397 |
| 37 | Bristol | 38.2 | 85 | 46 | 3 | 14.2 | 65 | 3 | 455 |
| 38 | Hull | 37.5 | 92 | 71 | 3 | 19.5 | | 6 | 251 |
| 39 | Nottingham Trent | 33.3 | 81 | 62 | 2 | 12.8 | | 4 | 231 |
| 40 | Salford | 31.7 | | | 2 | 15.2 | 64 | 8 | 221 |

# Social sciences

## Business and management studies

> The growth of business education has been a major success story, with many UK business schools featuring among the most highly rated in the world. This growth has been driven by the demands of industry and commerce for more candidates with relevant, highly transferable skills. Choosing to embark on a business degree is a smart career choice: recent research demonstrates that business graduates can achieve starting salaries well above the average. With business schools offering the opportunity for post-experience courses such as the MBA, specialist masters degrees, executive courses, and doctoral programmes, the possibilities for ongoing career development and increasing earnings potential are all part of the lifelong learning and development package.
>
> Graduates go on work in a wide range of organisations from large multinationals to their own business. Sales and marketing, management consultancy, IT, and human resources are well represented, although increasingly the public sector, such as local government and not-for-profit organisations, are also recruiting business graduates. A business studies course will also introduce you to networking, an important skill for candidates to acquire, who will be going out into a wide range of organisations all over the world. The contacts and relationships built up, both during the course and through alumni associations, will prove a lasting benefit throughout your career. Most business schools will have an excellent career development function that will be able to offer advice and guidance to current students; some also offer their expertise to alumni and this is a valuable service in the current economic climate.

**Vincent Hammersley,** *Director of Communications, Warwick Business School, University of Warwick*

---

More students enrol on business or management courses than any other university degree. So you won't be alone, but you may be bewildered by the choice. Almost all universities will have a programme that falls under the general heading of "business", although the titles of the programmes vary considerably across different institutions – business management, commerce, or business administration. Many degrees also suggest a more specialist focus, such as finance, marketing, retail management, tourism management or international business. And this doesn't take into account joint honours degrees ...

But there are certain common building blocks to all business degrees, such as finance, marketing, and human resource management. Most courses will also touch on business strategy, operations, supply chain and production management. Students are expected to be numerate, so most degrees will have courses in quantitative methods and statistics.

It's a generalisation, but the newer universities tend to be more vocationally orientated, while the older courses are more likely to be based on theory. Whichever you choose, most institutions are pretty flexible about what A-levels you need.

Let's face it, much of the reason for doing a degree like this is to get a job – and finance, management and marketing (for example) certainly do pay well. Remember though, many people who succeed in business do so without a business degree – instead they train afterwards, either on short courses or with an MBA perhaps, so make certain you're interested in the subject for its own sake. No degree is a guarantee of post-graduation success or a licence to print money.

Increasingly in business, technology is key, so make sure a course has more than adequate provision in that area, so you'll be up-to-date with the hardware and software that companies would expect you to use.

Business is a multidisciplinary course – it sits some way between the sciences and the humanities – that can encompass a huge range of extra areas, and the temptation is to take as broad an approach as possible to get to know a little of everything. But this jack-of-all-trades modular approach may not be the best for you in terms of future employment, so consider economics or law or another add-on as a separate degree option entirely.

No matter what you know, it's what you've done that will help impress employers most, so have a look at placement schemes, sandwich courses, and links from the course to employers. If you head off to a job interview with a CV packed with relevant experience, you'll soon be picking out your new suit for work.

For some, reputation is all, so if you're taking the course with a specific goal in mind (working in a City bank, for example), talk to people already employed in that field and find out which institution's graduates are most in demand.

---

> A business and accounting course is perfectly suited to people who are keen on business, but it can also allow flexibility to pursue other interests. Through varied and detailed modules, the course at Exeter has really given me the tools I need to make the most of every opportunity. This level of choice has made me reconsider what I wanted from my studies and I am now taking a range of modules that I believe will help me to develop the skills needed for the top jobs I aim for.
>
> **Lynne Medlock**, *second-year business and accounting student, University of Exeter*

---

## >> Further information

**British Academy of Management**
137 Euston Road
London NW1 2AA

t  020 7383 7770
e  bam@bam.ac.uk
↗ www.bam.ac.uk

**Chartered Institute of Marketing**
Moor Hall, Cookham
Maidenhead, Berkshire SL6 9QH

t  01628 427120
↗ www.cim.co.uk                    »

**Institute of Chartered Accountants in England and Wales**
Chartered Accountants' Hall
PO Box 433, London EC2P 2BJ
t 020 7920 8100
↗ www.icaew.co.uk

**Institute of Chartered Accountants of Scotland**
CA House, 21 Haymarket Yards
Edinburgh EH12 5BH
t 0131 347 0100
e enquiries@icas.org.uk
↗ www.icas.org.uk

↗ Online reading

**Guardian Unlimited business** business.guardian.co.uk
**Bized** www.bized.co.uk
**British Universities Industrial Relations Association** www.buira.org.uk
**Confederation of British Industry** www.cbi.org.uk

# Business and management studies

| | | Guardian score /100 | Satisfied with teaching % | Satisfied with feedback % | Spend per student /10 | Student:staff ratio | Job prospects % | Value added score /10 | Average entry tariff |
|---|---|---|---|---|---|---|---|---|---|
| 1 | Oxford | 100.0 | 84 | 63 | | 8.6 | 88 | 8 | 530 |
| 2 | Leicester | 96.2 | 87 | 81 | 10 | 15.7 | 75 | 7 | 316 |
| 3 | City | 94.5 | 89 | 72 | 10 | 19.2 | 78 | 9 | 390 |
| 4 | St Andrews | 92.6 | 90 | 71 | 5 | 13.3 | 74 | 10 | 430 |
| 5 | Warwick | 91.8 | 78 | 50 | 10 | 16.2 | 83 | 8 | 453 |
| 6 | Imperial College | 85.0 | | | 10 | 20.1 | 67 | 1 | 448 |
| 7 | Exeter | 83.6 | 94 | 82 | 7 | 20.2 | 77 | 6 | 395 |
| 8 | Bath | 82.6 | 83 | 46 | 7 | 19.5 | 87 | 9 | 456 |
| 9 | Glasgow | 82.4 | 85 | 65 | 8 | 17.3 | 73 | 8 | 434 |
| 10 | Strathclyde | 79.2 | 84 | 61 | 9 | 24.1 | 67 | 8 | 421 |
| 11 | London School of Economics | 78.8 | 70 | 63 | 7 | 17.7 | 94 | 4 | 480 |
| 12 | Lancaster | 78.0 | 82 | 60 | 9 | 17.6 | 71 | 6 | 408 |
| 13 | Manchester | 77.2 | 80 | 56 | 9 | 19.1 | 73 | 5 | 414 |
| 14 | Aston | 76.1 | 89 | 70 | 7 | 25.7 | 74 | 7 | 404 |
| 15 | Reading | 75.6 | 84 | 62 | 6 | 18.0 | 78 | 6 | 377 |
| 16 | Loughborough | 75.4 | 94 | 73 | 6 | 27.0 | 78 | 6 | 403 |
| 17 | Nottingham | 75.3 | 81 | 54 | 7 | 20.5 | 77 | 7 | 403 |
| 18 | Birmingham | 74.7 | 80 | 59 | 8 | 19.8 | 72 | 6 | 405 |
| 19 | Heriot-Watt | 73.6 | 80 | 59 | 9 | 26.6 | 72 | 9 | 342 |
| 20 | Buckingham | 72.7 | 95 | 92 | 5 | 7.2 | | 2 | 223 |
| 21 | Leeds | 72.2 | 76 | 50 | 8 | 18.3 | 71 | 5 | 411 |
| 22 | Edinburgh | 71.8 | 82 | 48 | 9 | 29.2 | 67 | 8 | 442 |
| 23 | Queen's, Belfast | 71.5 | 81 | 61 | 3 | 18.1 | 77 | 7 | 372 |
| 24 | Bath Spa | 71.4 | 90 | 81 | 3 | 25.7 | 54 | 10 | 244 |
| 25 | UCL | 71.2 | 77 | 46 | 8 | | 71 | 3 | 408 |
| 26 | Southampton | 71.0 | 76 | 48 | 6 | 22.9 | 78 | 6 | 403 |
| 27 | Robert Gordon | 70.9 | | | 5 | 21.3 | 87 | 6 | 320 |
| 28 | Bristol | 70.1 | 68 | 47 | 3 | 6.8 | 91 | 1 | 421 |
| 28 | Stirling | 70.1 | 79 | 60 | 4 | 13.5 | 64 | 8 | |
| 30 | Keele | 69.6 | 78 | 67 | 6 | 13.2 | 69 | 6 | 288 |

| | | Guardian score /100 | Satisfied with teaching % | Satisfied with feedback % | Spend per student /10 | Student:staff ratio | Job prospects % | Value added score /10 | Average entry tariff |
|---|---|---|---|---|---|---|---|---|---|
| 31 | Aberdeen | 69.5 | 82 | 63 | 4 | 20.6 | 71 | 8 | 340 |
| 31 | King's College London | 69.5 | 75 | 60 | 6 | 20.4 | 70 | 5 | 426 |
| 33 | Edinburgh Napier | 68.9 | | | 4 | 20.7 | 64 | 10 | 279 |
| 34 | Cumbria | 68.7 | 80 | 56 | 8 | 8.4 | 59 | 5 | 232 |
| 35 | Surrey | 68.0 | 72 | 51 | 5 | 23.7 | 74 | 9 | 348 |
| 36 | Sussex | 67.6 | 83 | 69 | 3 | 19.6 | | 6 | 360 |
| 37 | Newcastle | 67.4 | 67 | 53 | 5 | 23.4 | 83 | 7 | 395 |
| 38 | Oxford Brookes | 67.1 | 81 | 62 | 6 | 20.3 | 66 | 7 | 310 |
| 39 | Liverpool | 66.8 | 75 | 57 | 7 | 18.3 | 68 | 6 | 355 |
| 40 | Cardiff | 66.6 | 81 | 55 | 5 | 16.9 | 63 | 4 | 377 |
| 41 | Royal Holloway | 66.4 | 72 | 54 | 5 | 21.7 | 78 | 5 | 371 |
| 42 | UEA | 65.4 | 84 | 63 | 6 | 24.3 | 72 | 4 | 340 |
| 43 | Plymouth | 65.1 | 82 | 61 | 8 | 17.7 | 56 | 5 | 253 |
| 43 | York | 65.1 | 74 | 59 | 6 | 12.1 | 58 | 3 | 336 |
| 45 | Nottingham Trent | 64.9 | 76 | 61 | 6 | 18.3 | 79 | 4 | 267 |
| 46 | Sheffield | 64.3 | 79 | 57 | 4 | 23.9 | 73 | 6 | 357 |
| 47 | Staffordshire | 64.2 | 76 | 62 | 8 | 20.6 | 71 | 6 | 232 |
| 48 | Queen Margaret | 63.8 | | | 2 | 13.1 | 47 | 9 | 279 |
| 49 | Northumbria | 63.2 | 82 | 71 | 5 | 25.6 | 75 | 4 | 303 |
| 50 | Lincoln | 62.6 | 80 | 73 | 2 | 23.8 | 66 | 8 | 253 |
| 51 | Chichester | 62.5 | 92 | 80 | 2 | 16.3 | | 5 | 214 |
| 52 | Bournemouth | 62.3 | 84 | 72 | 5 | 33.8 | 74 | 7 | 304 |
| 53 | Kent | 62.2 | 83 | 73 | 5 | 24.3 | 79 | 2 | 308 |
| 54 | Winchester | 61.5 | 89 | 68 | 2 | 18.6 | 58 | 8 | 225 |
| 55 | Teesside | 60.7 | 77 | 73 | 8 | 18.7 | 47 | 5 | 214 |
| 56 | Queen Mary | 60.4 | 74 | 50 | 5 | 24.7 | 67 | 5 | 329 |
| 57 | De Montfort | 60.3 | 86 | 76 | 3 | 21.8 | 54 | 6 | 232 |
| 58 | St Mary's UC, Twickenham | 60.2 | 84 | 74 | 4 | 18.6 | 51 | 7 | 200 |
| 58 | UWE Bristol | 60.2 | 78 | 62 | 3 | 23.2 | 65 | 7 | 269 |
| 60 | Brunel | 59.5 | 69 | 55 | 4 | 21.7 | 58 | 8 | 305 |
| 60 | Durham | 59.5 | 75 | 64 | 5 | 34.3 | 81 | 4 | 359 |
| 62 | Central Lancashire | 59.2 | 73 | 66 | 6 | 19.1 | 69 | 3 | 258 |
| 63 | Hull | 59.1 | 85 | 71 | 5 | 29.4 | 70 | 5 | 256 |
| 64 | Kingston | 58.5 | 83 | 70 | 6 | 21.8 | 51 | 4 | 217 |
| 65 | Bradford | 58.3 | 72 | 60 | 7 | 19.5 | 52 | 5 | 235 |
| 66 | Dundee | 58.1 | 65 | 55 | 3 | 17.2 | 73 | 3 | 334 |
| 67 | Gloucestershire | 58.0 | 71 | 63 | 4 | 22.4 | 64 | 7 | 238 |
| 68 | Anglia Ruskin | 57.7 | 68 | 55 | 7 | 22.4 | 50 | 8 | 229 |
| 68 | Bangor | 57.7 | 77 | 72 | 5 | 25.0 | 61 | 5 | 271 |
| 70 | Chester | 56.6 | 72 | 55 | 4 | 22.3 | 62 | 8 | 235 |
| 71 | Salford | 56.3 | 77 | 66 | 4 | 17.0 | 49 | 3 | 290 |
| 72 | Ulster | 56.2 | 74 | 58 | 4 | 25.2 | 54 | 8 | 265 |
| 73 | Coventry | 55.8 | 78 | 60 | 5 | 28.3 | 52 | 8 | 275 |
| 74 | Glasgow Caledonian | 55.6 | 77 | 56 | 3 | 26.4 | 55 | 7 | 314 |
| 75 | Glamorgan | 55.5 | 82 | 71 | 4 | 26.3 | 45 | 7 | 261 |
| 76 | Portsmouth | 55.2 | 84 | 64 | 4 | 25.5 | 58 | 4 | 257 |

| | | Guardian score /100 | Satisfied with teaching % | Satisfied with feedback % | Spend per student /10 | Student:staff ratio | Job prospects % | Value added score /10 | Average entry tariff |
|---|---|---|---|---|---|---|---|---|---|
| 77 | Essex | 55.0 | 70 | 54 | 4 | 18.7 | 54 | 4 | 295 |
| 78 | Sheffield Hallam | 54.8 | 80 | 70 | 4 | 30.9 | 59 | 6 | 265 |
| 79 | Huddersfield | 54.5 | 79 | 66 | 3 | 19.5 | 38 | 7 | 245 |
| 80 | Canterbury Christ Church | 54.0 | 81 | 71 | 2 | 29.4 | 48 | 10 | 199 |
| 81 | York St John | 53.9 | 87 | 66 | 4 | 26.0 | 50 | 2 | 337 |
| 82 | Edge Hill | 53.6 | 82 | 67 | 3 | 18.3 | 35 | 7 | 217 |
| 83 | Abertay Dundee | 53.4 | | | 4 | 19.3 | 33 | 7 | 268 |
| 84 | Manchester Met | 52.5 | 69 | 58 | 3 | 25.2 | 59 | 6 | 257 |
| 85 | Birmingham City | 51.9 | 74 | 56 | 5 | 28.6 | 50 | 7 | 227 |
| 86 | Aberystwyth | 51.6 | 75 | 63 | 3 | 21.4 | 42 | 4 | 283 |
| 87 | Royal Agricultural College | 51.1 | 71 | 54 | 5 | 19.0 | 75 | 1 | 248 |
| 88 | Swansea | 50.7 | 72 | 56 | 3 | 25.3 | 66 | 3 | 291 |
| 89 | Worcester | 50.2 | 86 | 64 | 3 | 27.4 | 52 | 4 | 220 |
| 90 | Bedfordshire | 50.1 | 79 | 67 | 3 | 17.7 | 39 | 4 | 179 |
| 91 | Glyndŵr | 50.0 | | | 4 | 26.5 | 49 | 6 | 223 |
| 92 | Brighton | 49.7 | 77 | 57 | 3 | 36.0 | 64 | 7 | 255 |
| 93 | Leeds Trinity & All Saints | 49.1 | 68 | 59 | 3 | 16.3 | 56 | 3 | 201 |
| 94 | Hertfordshire | 48.8 | 73 | 52 | 6 | 24.2 | 53 | 2 | 233 |
| 95 | Sunderland | 48.7 | 76 | 75 | 6 | 26.9 | 47 | 2 | 228 |
| 96 | Thames Valley | 48.0 | 79 | 71 | 5 | 15.3 | 30 | 2 | 173 |
| 97 | UWIC | 47.9 | 73 | 66 | 3 | 19.8 | 45 | 2 | 235 |
| 98 | Northampton | 47.8 | 87 | 73 | 3 | 36.5 | 51 | 7 | 214 |
| 99 | Derby | 47.4 | 77 | 65 | 4 | 21.3 | 39 | 3 | 223 |
| 100 | Leeds Met | 46.9 | 65 | 49 | 4 | 23.9 | 48 | 3 | 266 |
| 100 | Liverpool John Moores | 46.9 | 79 | 58 | 3 | 25.0 | 53 | 3 | 232 |
| 102 | University of the Arts, London | 45.9 | 55 | 51 | 6 | 29.2 | 50 | 5 | 289 |
| 103 | Westminster | 45.2 | 72 | 59 | 4 | 27.3 | 45 | 3 | 235 |
| 104 | Greenwich | 44.8 | 80 | 71 | 4 | 26.7 | 41 | 2 | 190 |
| 105 | Middlesex | 44.6 | 76 | 64 | 5 | 29.8 | 41 | 5 | 158 |
| 106 | University College Birmingham | 44.0 | 74 | 74 | 2 | 38.5 | 46 | 7 | |
| 107 | Newport | 42.7 | 88 | 84 | 3 | 34.1 | 35 | 3 | 228 |
| 108 | Bucks New University | 41.7 | 72 | 60 | 4 | 28.4 | 44 | 3 | 187 |
| 109 | Roehampton | 41.1 | 73 | 41 | 4 | 21.6 | 47 | 1 | 198 |
| 110 | Bolton | 41.0 | 75 | 58 | 4 | 22.1 | 27 | 3 | 185 |
| 111 | Southampton Solent | 39.4 | 70 | 58 | 3 | 34.3 | 54 | 3 | 194 |
| 112 | London South Bank | 34.0 | 77 | 56 | 3 | 38.4 | 35 | 5 | 156 |
| 113 | East London | 30.8 | 77 | 64 | 3 | 34.2 | 30 | 1 | 160 |

# Educational studies

" Pursuing a course in educational studies opens up a complex and exciting investigation into the nature of learning, as well as policies and structures to initiate and develop education. This entails developing an understanding of social, psychological, cultural, historical, political, and ethical factors that affect learning and which structure the pursuit of learning (and teaching) within and beyond institutional contexts.

In more detail, educational studies allows students to consider the dynamics of human development and learning in a variety of disciplines and fields and the politics of education within state education systems as well as alternative approaches to mainstream educational practices. It involves a comparative study of the history of educational practices and policies within the UK and other countries. It deals with philosophical and ethical issues that interrogate the aims and purposes of education and pedagogy. It considers the relations between education and power as well as social and cultural factors that impact upon educational policies and practices.

**Professor Dennis Atkinson**, *Head of Department of Educational Studies and Director of the Research Centre for the Arts and Learning, Goldsmiths College, University of London*

Mention that you're doing educational studies and everyone will think of the classroom, but the subject isn't simply about being a teacher. And if you're just leaving school you might be grateful for that – it seems a bit early to be planning to head right back there. And remember, you'll generally need a PGCE (postgraduate certificate of education) if you want to be a teacher.

As education has come to the forefront of the political spectrum, with tuition fees particularly a recurring area for debate, so there has been a correspondingly dramatic increase in the number of degree programmes in broader educational studies – that is, those that do not lead to qualified teacher status and instead award a BA degree.

These programmes do not view education narrowly. They are concerned not only with schools and children, but with a whole host of other areas, such as the nature of teaching and learning, personal development, the rights of children, law, gender, multiculturalism, and justice, and how these interrelate with education policy and practice. They offer an academic exploration of what governments, organizations, and individuals are doing when they invest – financially, politically, personally – in education.

Students do not simply learn about the history, sociology, philosophy, and psychology of education, but also the portrayal of educational experiences in novels, policy documents, and the findings of important studies.

Teaching methods most commonly involve workshops, seminars, and tutorials. Many programmes take the opportunity to explore matters in practical "real world" contexts and employ collaborative group work activities. There is normally a requirement for students to produce a dissertation, often in the final year of study, which involves the collection and analysis of empirical data associated with, for example, bullying in schools, controversial issues in teaching a school subject or equal opportunities.

Some graduates in educational studies go on to follow education-related careers in the heritage industry, media, management, banking, and administration or of course – following a further year's training – teaching.

How you choose a course depends on what you want to do with it. If you see educational studies as a way of becoming a teacher, check if there is any provision for transfer after graduation to a teacher education programme taught in the same department or institution. It might also be advisable, if you want to teach in a school, to take a joint degree in educational studies and a school subject.

If you want to study education in the broader sense, then look at the topics covered by both your course and the research, specialisations or publications of the teaching staff. The broader the range of choices, the more rounded the degree, but that's no use if there's a particular area you find fascinating that isn't offered. Investigate also whether they have decent computer rooms and can fill you in on the latest developments in e-learning.

---

**“** The course is definitely a challenge, especially if you're working full-time like I am, but it has opened my eyes to better practice and given me a more in-depth knowledge of child care. It helps me to be a better nursery manager and has given me new ideas through talking to other students on the course and a range of modules including children with special needs, child protection and child development. I chose to do the course because I wanted to understand the theory behind what I do every day and to provide better care for the children.

**Lucy Nash**, *second-year student on the early years foundation degree course, Kingston University*

---

## » Further information

**British Educational Research Association**
Association House, South Park Road    **t**   01625 504062
Macclesfield    **e**   admin@bera.ac.uk
Cheshire SK11 6SH    ↗   www.bera.ac.uk

**Institute of Education**
University of London, 20 Bedford Way    **t**   020 7612 6000
London WC1H 0AL    **e**   info@ioe.ac.uk
   ↗   www.ioe.ac.uk

## ↗ Online reading

**EducationGuardian.co.uk**   EducationGuardian.co.uk
**The Training and Development Agency for Schools**   www.tda.gov.uk
**NUT (National Union of Teachers)**   www.teachers.org.uk
**National Union of Students**   www.nus.org.uk
**University and College Union**   www.ucu.org.uk
**Association of University Administrators**   www.aua.ac.uk
**The Commonwealth of Learning**   www.col.org

# Education

| | | Guardian score /100 | Satisfied with teaching % | Satisfied with feedback % | Spend per student /10 | Student:staff ratio | Job prospects % | Value added score /10 | Average entry tariff |
|---|---|---|---|---|---|---|---|---|---|
| 1 | Cambridge | 100.0 | 89 | 73 | 10 | 11.7 | 89 | 7 | 474 |
| 2 | Kingston | 86.5 | 91 | 67 | 10 | 9.9 | 76 | 10 | 259 |
| 3 | Aberdeen | 81.5 | 85 | 50 | 10 | 15.7 | 97 | 8 | 343 |
| 4 | Edinburgh | 79.0 | 80 | 52 | 10 | 16.7 | 94 | 7 | 363 |
| 5 | Stirling | 77.6 | 89 | 73 | 5 | 11.0 | 93 | 7 | |
| 6 | Reading | 77.1 | 93 | 70 | 5 | 19.2 | 92 | 10 | 301 |
| 7 | Huddersfield | 74.8 | 92 | 80 | 10 | 11.8 | | 6 | 225 |
| 8 | St Mary's UC, Belfast | 74.5 | 80 | 60 | 3 | 14.9 | 97 | 9 | 342 |
| 9 | Hertfordshire | 73.9 | 90 | 76 | 8 | 12.2 | 75 | 8 | 274 |
| 10 | Dundee | 71.5 | 91 | 74 | 4 | 18.2 | 93 | 8 | 335 |
| 11 | Leeds | 71.0 | 86 | 75 | 8 | 12.8 | 69 | 6 | 341 |
| 12 | Sunderland | 70.1 | 85 | 82 | 9 | 12.7 | 85 | 4 | 238 |
| 13 | Durham | 68.4 | 85 | 63 | 6 | 17.7 | 89 | 3 | 389 |
| 14 | Central Lancashire | 68.3 | 95 | 74 | | 8.3 | 77 | 3 | 246 |
| 15 | Warwick | 66.3 | 83 | 60 | 10 | 16.1 | 60 | 7 | 311 |
| 16 | Northumbria | 65.4 | 93 | 79 | 7 | 16.5 | 79 | 3 | 313 |
| 17 | Exeter | 64.1 | 92 | 72 | 8 | 21.2 | 55 | 8 | 338 |
| 18 | UWIC | 63.4 | 89 | 79 | 7 | 21.1 | 85 | 6 | 258 |
| 19 | York St John | 62.5 | 89 | 77 | 5 | 18.6 | 80 | 7 | 299 |
| 20 | Plymouth | 62.2 | 88 | 65 | 9 | 18.4 | 68 | 8 | 254 |
| 21 | Goldsmiths | 59.9 | 85 | 52 | 4 | 18.7 | 80 | 9 | 244 |
| 22 | Nottingham Trent | 59.8 | 92 | 68 | 5 | 16.9 | 74 | 6 | 285 |
| 23 | Oxford Brookes | 59.2 | 89 | 64 | 6 | 17.8 | 74 | 5 | 300 |
| 24 | Aberystwyth | 59.1 | 92 | 74 | 6 | 16.6 | | 3 | 264 |
| 24 | Teesside | 59.1 | | | 10 | 31.5 | | 10 | 208 |
| 26 | Birmingham City | 58.9 | 87 | 69 | 4 | 21.2 | 85 | 7 | 256 |
| 26 | Canterbury Christ Church | 58.9 | 82 | 53 | 6 | 17.8 | 94 | 3 | 304 |
| 28 | Brighton | 58.4 | 88 | 73 | 4 | 23.3 | 89 | 5 | 304 |
| 28 | Middlesex | 58.4 | 78 | 65 | 8 | 22.9 | 97 | 8 | 204 |
| 28 | Stranmillis UC | 58.4 | 80 | 55 | 2 | 18.8 | 82 | 9 | 318 |
| 31 | Newport | 58.2 | 82 | 73 | 8 | 18.3 | 81 | 4 | 246 |
| 31 | Sheffield Hallam | 58.2 | 79 | 62 | 4 | 18.4 | 80 | 8 | 277 |
| 33 | Glasgow | 56.2 | 74 | 41 | 4 | 22.1 | 99 | 4 | 341 |
| 34 | De Montfort | 56.1 | 89 | 73 | 2 | 10.4 | 66 | 8 | 231 |
| 35 | Bishop Grosseteste UC | 56.0 | 93 | 80 | 2 | 21.8 | 95 | 3 | 270 |
| 36 | Manchester | 54.2 | 92 | 77 | | 16.8 | 56 | 3 | 299 |
| 37 | Bedfordshire | 53.7 | 77 | 55 | 5 | 14.7 | 87 | 3 | 247 |
| 37 | UWE Bristol | 53.7 | 84 | 65 | 3 | 24.8 | 73 | 10 | 266 |
| 39 | Glyndŵr | 52.8 | 89 | 85 | 4 | 19.3 | 72 | 6 | 230 |
| 40 | Ulster | 52.2 | 75 | 74 | 4 | 17.1 | | | 247 |
| 40 | York | 52.2 | 76 | 68 | 7 | 16.9 | 53 | 5 | 330 |
| 42 | Keele | 51.9 | 81 | 58 | 3 | 20.9 | | | 310 |
| 43 | Brunel | 51.8 | | | 4 | 22.4 | 93 | 1 | 316 |
| 44 | Newman University College | 51.5 | 89 | 70 | 3 | 17.3 | 78 | 4 | 234 |
| 44 | Strathclyde | 51.5 | 78 | 50 | 4 | 21.2 | 84 | 2 | 356 |
| 46 | Winchester | 51.4 | 84 | 70 | 2 | 19.2 | 77 | 4 | 288 |

| | Guardian score /100 | Satisfied with teaching % | Satisfied with feedback % | Spend per student /10 | Student:staff ratio | Job prospects % | Value added score /10 | Average entry tariff |
|---|---|---|---|---|---|---|---|---|
| 47 Chichester | 51.3 | 91 | 71 | 4 | 20.7 | 83 | 2 | 247 |
| 48 Leeds Trinity & All Saints | 50.6 | 92 | 75 | 3 | 26.4 | 88 | 4 | 258 |
| 49 Gloucestershire | 50.2 | 84 | 61 | 8 | 23.5 | 80 | 4 | 249 |
| 49 Hull | 50.2 | 86 | 72 | 5 | 23.3 | 82 | 3 | 250 |
| 51 St Mary's UC, Twickenham | 50.0 | 87 | 66 | 3 | 28.6 | 86 | 7 | 275 |
| 52 Derby | 49.5 | 91 | 76 | 4 | 17.8 | 64 | 6 | 225 |
| 53 Chester | 49.4 | 86 | 62 | 5 | 22.1 | 74 | 5 | 251 |
| 54 Manchester Met | 49.3 | 75 | 54 | 5 | 22.7 | 77 | 5 | 283 |
| 55 Anglia Ruskin | 49.2 | 58 | 44 | 8 | 21.2 | 87 | 6 | 254 |
| 56 Bath Spa | 49.1 | 89 | 77 | 3 | 31.9 | 78 | 8 | 279 |
| 56 Edge Hill | 49.1 | 84 | 66 | 4 | 25.0 | 83 | 4 | 274 |
| 58 Northampton | 47.0 | 89 | 66 | 4 | 21.9 | 75 | 3 | 258 |
| 59 Leeds Met | 46.8 | 74 | 60 | 4 | 26.5 | 78 | 7 | 263 |
| 60 Worcester | 46.4 | 80 | 64 | 4 | 20.6 | 73 | 5 | 247 |
| 61 Roehampton | 46.2 | 85 | 67 | 4 | 21.6 | 67 | 4 | 278 |
| 62 Birmingham | 45.9 | 75 | 59 | 7 | 24.2 | 52 | 4 | 348 |
| 62 Greenwich | 45.9 | 81 | 56 | 6 | 22.8 | 72 | 6 | 231 |
| 64 Cumbria | 44.4 | 80 | 61 | 5 | 21.5 | 79 | 2 | 265 |
| 65 Bangor | 43.6 | 83 | 76 | 4 | 24.8 | 74 | 2 | 274 |
| 66 Trinity UC, Carmarthen | 43.2 | 84 | 63 | 2 | 19.1 | 78 | 2 | 236 |
| 67 Marjon (St Mark and St John) | 39.8 | 83 | 64 | 3 | | 79 | 4 | 216 |
| 68 East London | 29.0 | 69 | 57 | 4 | 18.7 | 61 | 2 | 176 |

# Economics

" Want to understand the world? Want to get to grips with the big issues affecting us all, such as climate change, globalisation, the pensions crisis, meltdown in financial markets, why some countries are rich and others poor? Then economics is for you. Economics provides you with the analytical skills to explore these topics in depth and to dissect issues that are both complex and important. As well as big policy issues, economics can answer more micro-orientated questions including how individuals make choices, how firms compete and even what makes people 'happy'!

Economics touches every facet of our lives and the ability to understand and apply economic concepts provides the tool kit and skills to create insights into the macro and micro issues that affect us all. A combination of theory, quantitative skills, and how they are applied are the key ingredients of the economist's tool kit.

Economics is challenging but, then again, the world is a challenging place. It's a dynamic subject where new issues constantly emerge to which business and governments have to respond. Could we have imagined the liquidity crisis a year ago? Why are oil prices now reaching record highs and what are the implications for the future?

Could we have predicted the liquidity crisis? How do we deal with the consequences? What options do governments have to deal with a crisis as widespread and as deep as the current one, the like of which has not been experienced since the 1930s? Economics provides the tools for understanding and subsequently dealing with these issues.

**Professor Steve McCorriston**, *Head of Economics, University of Exeter*

Next time there's a huge demonstration at a world summit, or the anti-capitalists take to the streets of London, remember what usually motivates the protestors – yep, economics. If single-issue politics is what galvanises young people, the (social) science that informs them is economics – whose money is making the world go round, and why they control it.

Whichever angle you come from, it's economics that runs – or ruins – the world. As John Maynard Keynes, the 20th century's greatest economist, elegantly put it: "Practical men who believe themselves to be quite exempt from any intellectual influences are usually the slaves of some defunct economist."

Post-university employment rates of economists are among the highest for graduates. The subject gives students a good intellectual training – sitting somewhere between science and humanities – which employers like. It also, obviously, has lots of practical applications in the world of business.

Once qualified, you'll have transferable skills in problem-solving, quantitative analysis, and communication. Very few economics graduates work as professional economists, but the majority do find work in related areas – finance, banking, insurance, accountancy, and management and consultancy.

On an economics course, you'll often start with a basic grounding in the social sciences generally, before moving on to economics proper. Then you'll be studying both macro- and micro-economics, and the links between them: the millions of small choices that make up the big ones. To understand economic models, you have to understand both. You'll learn about reasoning and methodology – how economic models fit, or not. In some ways, studying economics becomes a little like philosophy – you'll have to be prepared to defend theories and economic ideologies you may have long held dear. You can also view economics as a science – you'll work to basic assumptions about how people, and therefore economies, will behave and make a set of deductions from that.

If you're not keen on number crunching, you could be in for a nasty shock – you're going to need maths to help formulate theories and extrapolate assumptions and you're going to have to provide statistics to back yourself up. Indeed, your attitude to maths may well influence your choice of course. Some universities require A-level maths, while others ask only for a good grade at GCSE. These requirements are often reflected in the courses, some of which involve more figure-juggling than others. Bear in mind that while you may be able to minimise the maths and stats that you encounter, in doing so you may distort your view of modern economics.

Naturally, you must check what specialisations are open to you. Often the most interesting parts of any degree are the specialist subjects – economic thought from Adam Smith to Milton Friedman, or development economics in sub-Sahara Africa might be just your thing. Alternatively, doing economics as part of a joint degree is very popular: politics, philosophy, and economics, perhaps, or history.

Otherwise, do the obvious things – visit the departments you are considering applying to and ask the students there what they think of the courses. Also look at who is on the academic staff. Learning from those at the cutting edge of thought is always far more likely to keep you on your toes, though if you want to study under a particular economist, make sure they're not too busy to teach and take tutorials.

Some universities offer a sandwich course, enabling you to head off for work placements partway through, while others let you study abroad. And, as with any course, make sure you understand the assessment – exam, coursework or dissertation – and have a good idea as to whether that works for you.

---

66 The main difference between A-levels and my degree has been the increased level of self-discipline needed. Tutors proactively encourage attendance and are more than happy to help when approached, but at the end of the day you're an adult now and it's down to you. This teaches personal responsibility and for you to take ownership of your actions. The most enjoyable aspect of the course has been learning about the UK economy and the business world.

**Murat Haykir**, *first-year business economics with accounting student, University of Plymouth*

---

## » Further information

**Royal Economic Society**
University of St Andrews
St Andrews, Fife KY16 9AL

t 01334 462479
↗ www.res.org.uk

**The Economics Network of the UK's Higher Education Academy**
University of Bristol
8-10 Berkeley Square, Bristol BS8 1HH

↗ www.economicsnetwork.ac.uk

**The Society of Business Economists**
Dean House, Vernham Dean
Andover, Hants SP11 0JZ

t 01264 737552
e support@sbe.co.uk
↗ www.sbe.co.uk

**The Government Economic Service**
HM Treasury, 1 Horse Guards Road
London SW1A 2HQ

t  020 7270 4571 / 5073
e  ges.int@hm-treasury.gov.uk
↗ www.ges.gov.uk

**The Royal Statistical Society**
12 Errol Street
London EC1Y 8LX

t  020 7638 8998
e  rss@rss.org.uk
↗ www.rss.org.uk

↗ Online reading

**Why Study Economics?** www.whystudyeconomics.ac.uk
**Bized** www.bized.co.uk
**The Internet Economist** www.vts.intute.ac.uk/he/tutorial/economist
**Economic History Services** www.eh.net
**National Statistics Online** www.statistics.gov.uk
**The Economist** www.economist.co.uk
**The Financial Times** www.ft.com
**The Adam Smith Institute** www.adamsmith.org
**The Fabian Society** www.fabian-society.org.uk

# Economics

| | | Guardian score /100 | Satisfied with teaching % | Satisfied with feedback % | Spend per student /10 | Student:staff ratio | Job prospects % | Value added score /10 | Average entry tariff |
|---|---|---|---|---|---|---|---|---|---|
| 1 | Oxford | 100.0 | 93 | 67 | | 10.8 | 82 | 9 | 538 |
| 2 | Cambridge | 97.9 | 87 | 67 | 10 | 15.5 | 84 | 7 | 549 |
| 3 | St Andrews | 88.9 | 91 | 70 | 6 | 13.3 | 76 | 9 | 474 |
| 4 | Edinburgh | 87.8 | 80 | 44 | 10 | 14.2 | 85 | 6 | 453 |
| 5 | Warwick | 85.0 | 75 | 51 | 9 | 15.1 | 88 | 7 | 497 |
| 6 | Birmingham | 84.7 | 91 | 74 | 10 | 17.8 | 70 | 7 | 403 |
| 7 | Durham | 84.0 | 81 | 62 | 6 | 17.9 | 92 | 8 | 490 |
| 8 | London School of Economics | 83.6 | 70 | 59 | 8 | 13.0 | 89 | 5 | 519 |
| 9 | UCL | 82.5 | 80 | 61 | 10 | 20.1 | 83 | 5 | 485 |
| 10 | Exeter | 77.8 | 91 | 77 | 3 | 15.9 | 77 | 8 | 386 |
| 11 | Nottingham | 77.4 | 83 | 46 | 6 | 16.7 | 85 | 7 | 467 |
| 12 | Lancaster | 77.1 | 81 | 63 | 10 | 17.6 | 67 | 4 | 406 |
| 13 | SOAS | 75.1 | 85 | 61 | 8 | 14.1 | 73 | 4 | 384 |
| 14 | Heriot-Watt | 74.7 | | | 4 | 16.5 | 76 | 10 | 322 |
| 15 | Bristol | 74.4 | 79 | 48 | 7 | 18.5 | 81 | 7 | 454 |
| 16 | York | 73.0 | 82 | 52 | 8 | 14.0 | 61 | 5 | 454 |
| 17 | Coventry | 72.5 | 90 | 81 | 6 | 22.9 | | 10 | 244 |
| 18 | Bath | 71.0 | 79 | 40 | 6 | 16.9 | 83 | 4 | 452 |
| 19 | Glasgow | 70.0 | 85 | 55 | 5 | 15.6 | 68 | 7 | 408 |
| 20 | Kent | 69.1 | 85 | 78 | 5 | 16.7 | 68 | 7 | 304 |
| 21 | Sussex | 68.4 | 90 | 65 | 3 | 19.6 | 70 | 8 | 343 |
| 22 | Liverpool | 67.7 | 86 | 62 | 5 | 19.9 | 75 | 6 | 384 |
| 23 | Strathclyde | 67.4 | 87 | 50 | 8 | 25.6 | 62 | 8 | 440 |
| 24 | Queen Mary | 67.2 | 72 | 50 | | 16.3 | 67 | 6 | 369 |

| | Guardian score /100 | Satisfied with teaching % | Satisfied with feedback % | Spend per student /10 | Student:staff ratio | Job prospects % | Value added score /10 | Average entry tariff |
|---|---|---|---|---|---|---|---|---|
| 25 Leicester | 66.3 | 88 | 78 | 4 | 24.0 | 73 | 7 | 319 |
| 26 Southampton | 65.1 | 74 | 52 | 5 | 18.6 | 73 | 5 | 421 |
| 27 Leeds | 64.1 | 75 | 51 | 5 | 20.8 | 76 | 6 | 417 |
| 28 Manchester | 63.8 | 74 | 48 | 7 | 19.7 | 70 | 4 | 406 |
| 29 Surrey | 63.4 | 92 | 75 | 5 | 23.0 | 66 | 4 | 327 |
| 30 Essex | 62.9 | 76 | 59 | 4 | 14.8 | 70 | 4 | 322 |
| 31 Newcastle | 62.7 | 79 | 45 | 4 | 22.6 | 82 | 4 | 414 |
| 32 Hull | 62.6 | 91 | 59 | 7 | 29.4 | 78 | 7 | 282 |
| 33 Loughborough | 62.4 | 86 | 64 | 5 | 22.9 | 71 | 4 | 375 |
| 34 Stirling | 62.1 | 87 | 67 | 3 | 18.0 | 52 | 8 | |
| 35 Nottingham Trent | 62.0 | 87 | 62 | 7 | 15.9 | 65 | 3 | 262 |
| 36 UWE Bristol | 61.8 | 84 | 63 | 3 | 20.9 | 77 | 8 | 240 |
| 37 Royal Holloway | 61.0 | 80 | 49 | 3 | 19.1 | 81 | 4 | 364 |
| 38 Queen's, Belfast | 60.4 | 73 | 67 | 4 | 18.1 | 70 | 4 | 351 |
| 39 Ulster | 60.2 | 79 | 56 | 3 | 19.0 | 64 | 10 | 248 |
| 40 Aberdeen | 60.1 | 92 | 72 | 3 | 23.3 | 61 | 7 | 341 |
| 41 Dundee | 59.7 | 70 | 61 | 6 | 17.4 | 57 | 7 | 330 |
| 42 Cardiff | 58.6 | 79 | 54 | 7 | 16.9 | 60 | 2 | 399 |
| 43 City | 58.2 | 66 | 47 | 5 | 17.3 | 59 | 8 | 323 |
| 43 Keele | 58.2 | 68 | 58 | 4 | 16.3 | | | 284 |
| 45 Aberystwyth | 57.6 | 91 | 69 | 3 | 18.5 | | 4 | 235 |
| 46 Sheffield | 57.0 | 86 | 64 | 3 | 23.9 | 68 | 3 | 371 |
| 47 Bradford | 56.4 | 74 | 66 | 5 | 12.8 | | 2 | 253 |
| 48 Leeds Met | 56.2 | 76 | 55 | | 21.8 | 58 | 4 | 277 |
| 49 UEA | 55.4 | 91 | 75 | 3 | 27.9 | 62 | 5 | 330 |
| 50 Staffordshire | 54.9 | 82 | 64 | 5 | 20.0 | | | 199 |
| 51 East London | 54.5 | 83 | 71 | 6 | 18.1 | | 2 | 189 |
| 52 Portsmouth | 54.0 | 83 | 57 | 6 | 16.7 | 69 | 1 | 250 |
| 53 Plymouth | 53.8 | 83 | 60 | 5 | 18.2 | 46 | 7 | 241 |
| 54 Brunel | 53.5 | 75 | 51 | 3 | 20.9 | 57 | 8 | 310 |
| 55 Reading | 50.8 | 75 | 51 | 3 | 20.8 | 56 | 6 | 347 |
| 56 Manchester Met | 49.1 | | | 3 | 19.4 | 47 | 5 | 258 |
| 57 Oxford Brookes | 48.8 | 72 | 61 | 5 | 19.7 | | 2 | 289 |
| 58 Swansea | 47.1 | 88 | 60 | 3 | 22.7 | 71 | 1 | 274 |
| 59 Salford | 46.9 | 82 | 62 | 3 | 23.7 | | 4 | 247 |
| 60 Northumbria | 45.4 | 73 | 61 | 4 | 25.4 | 71 | 2 | 272 |
| 61 Kingston | 43.9 | 79 | 62 | 2 | 27.0 | 48 | 9 | 190 |
| 62 Hertfordshire | 39.8 | 74 | 51 | 7 | 24.2 | 46 | 1 | 231 |
| 63 Middlesex | 37.6 | 92 | 85 | 4 | 37.8 | 61 | 3 | 167 |
| 64 Greenwich | 32.1 | 89 | 75 | 2 | 28.3 | 42 | 1 | 194 |

# Law

❝ Studying law opens doors beyond the traditional route of qualification as a legal practitioner. The skills law graduates are equipped with make them a welcome addition to many varied professions, including journalism, finance, politics, the public sector, and many more. Our course equips undergraduates with a strong set of intellectual, practical, and transferable key skills, such as analytical, communication, and research skills, to give them a head start in the job market. In order to succeed, law students need to be able to study independently, enjoy problem-solving, and be self-motivated.

Options of study include taking a combined degree, for example law and a language. Students are able to take their law degree to many countries, including Europe and the USA, where minimal conversion might be required.

**Lindsay Kelly**, *Widening Participation Officer, School of Law, University of Edinburgh*

Law is one of the most sought-after careers, and it's therefore no surprise that it's also one of the most sought-after degrees in British universities, with more than 17,000 students applying to study it in 2007 alone. If that weren't competition enough, anyone with a good first degree can take a law conversion course after graduation and go on to become a lawyer. It is even possible to bypass university, start work in a law firm and take professional exams, although this is hardly a short cut.

However you do it, it's a slog at times; you need dedication during your course, and even after that, it's at least two years before you're fully qualified. So think long and hard about whether you're ready for it.

And once you've done that, brace yourself again for the LNat. The LNat is the national admissions test for law degrees, which is mandatory for all students applying to study law at 10 universities: Birmingham, Bristol, Cambridge, Durham, Exeter, Glasgow, King's, Nottingham, Oxford, and UCL. It helps admissions tutors to choose the most able students, or to indicate natural ability that may not be shown in A-levels. More information can be found at www.lnat.ac.uk.

Legal education is split, broadly, into two stages: the academic stage and the vocational stage. The academic stage usually comprises a three- to four-year law degree (normally three years in England and Wales, but four in Scotland; four-year degrees in England and Wales are usually combined with another subject). Students should ensure that they study a qualifying law degree if they wish to proceed directly on to courses that allow them to become barristers and solicitors. (Would-be lawyers who take a different undergraduate degree first then take a year-long conversion course, known as the Common Professional Examination (CPE).)

Then the decisions come. To qualify as a barrister requires a year-long bar vocational course (BVC), followed by another year's pupillage in an approved training organisation, usually barristers' chambers. Solicitors take a Legal Practice Course (LPC), followed by a training contract usually lasting two years, before being admitted to the roll of solicitors.

An increasing number of joint degree courses are now on offer at universities, often combining law with sociology, business or politics. You'll generally be graded by a mixture of continuous assessment and exams, although some do expect a dissertation as well.

Once you've graduated, you will at the very least have a good solid professional qualification that your parents will approve of. From that base, you have a degree that can lead to an interesting career within the profession, which, if you get picked up by one of the big City law firms, can be very lucrative indeed. Some of you may even see it as a noble calling and feel the need to take up the shield of justice and fight for what is right. Most will settle for a comfortable career inside the profession either as a barrister or a solicitor, while some will take their training and skills into different arenas, such as the media, marketing or business consultancy.

Whatever course you choose, you'll end up doing the same core subjects you need to earn your professional exemptions, so you'll be studying criminal law, public law, law of the European Union, contracts and tort, land and property law, and equity and the law of trusts. The choice after that is yours to specialise among a range of options, which you need to check are available at your chosen institution, such as tax, international or family law.

In practice, most students have long decided what area they want to specialise in, as applications for sponsorship by law firms have to be made during the second and third years of undergraduate study. Sponsorship for both the LPC and BVC is available.

So how do you choose between being a barrister or a solicitor? The skills of each profession are different, so research and think what you would enjoy most. The barrister is currently the front person in the law courts, while the solicitor is the person who deals with the client and prepares the evidence.

Another factor may be the cost. Few students are sponsored and both the LPC and BVC can cost between £5,000 and £12,770. Once you've done your bar finals you need a pupillage, but you can then practise. It takes longer to be a solicitor, and that extra time means more money.

---

**❝** I have found studying law not only enjoyable but also an excellent way to get my foot in the door at a real law firm. The fast-paced, detailed course can be challenging, but hard work and commitment can lead to outstanding results. The opportunity to choose my modules and gain invaluable hands-on experience from mooting programmes and pro bono schemes provides an experience beyond that at A-level. The well-informed staff, helpful careers service, and superb facilities have also made life easier.

**Matthew Dalley**, *final-year law student, Cardiff University*

---

## » Further information

**The Law Society**
The Society's Hall, 113 Chancery Lane
London WC2A 1PL

t  020 7242 1222
↗ www.lawsociety.org.uk

**Law Society of Scotland**
26 Drumsheugh Gardens
Edinburgh EH3 7YR

t  0131 226 7411
↗ www.lawscot.org.uk

**The Association of Women Barristers**
3 Bedford Row
London WC1R 4DB
www.womenbarristers.co.uk

**The Bar Council**
289-93 High Holborn
London WC1V 7HZ
t  020 7242 0082
www.barcouncil.org.uk

**Faculty of Advocates**
Advocates Library, Parliament House
11 Parliament Square, Edinburgh EH1 1RF
t  0131 226 5071
www.advocates.org.uk

**The Association of Women Solicitors**
114 Chancery Lane
London WC2A 1PL
t  020 7320 5793
www.womensolicitors.org.uk

 Online reading

**The Lawyer**  www.thelawyer.com
**The European Lawyer**  www.europeanlawyer.co.uk
**Consilio**  www.consilio.tv
**Bar Standards Board**  www.barstandardsboard.org.uk
**Institute of Legal Executives**  www.ilex.org.uk
**British and Irish Association of Law Librarians**  www.biall.org.uk
**Clarity**  www.clarity-international.net

# Law

| | | Guardian score /100 | Satisfied with teaching % | Satisfied with feedback % | Spend per student /10 | Student:staff ratio | Job prospects % | Value added score /10 | Average entry tariff |
|---|---|---|---|---|---|---|---|---|---|
| 1 | Cambridge | 100.0 | 95 | 79 | 10 | 15.5 | 88 | 8 | 527 |
| 2 | Oxford | 91.2 | | | | 10.8 | 80 | 9 | 526 |
| 3 | UCL | 89.5 | 88 | 59 | 10 | 20.1 | 92 | 8 | 486 |
| 4 | Edinburgh | 88.1 | 87 | 32 | 10 | 14.2 | 84 | 8 | 477 |
| 5 | King's College London | 87.6 | 93 | 80 | 8 | 13.5 | 81 | 9 | 463 |
| 6 | London School of Economics | 86.6 | 81 | 65 | 9 | 13.0 | 85 | 9 | 513 |
| 7 | Warwick | 84.6 | 91 | 59 | 9 | 15.1 | 79 | 8 | 458 |
| 8 | Birmingham | 81.0 | 92 | 77 | 10 | 17.8 | 80 | 4 | 428 |
| 9 | Queen Mary | 79.4 | 95 | 81 | | 16.3 | 74 | 6 | 404 |
| 10 | Glasgow | 77.7 | 88 | 38 | 6 | 15.6 | 89 | 8 | 481 |
| 11 | Durham | 76.2 | 84 | 53 | 7 | 17.9 | 77 | 8 | 483 |
| 12 | SOAS | 75.8 | 84 | 56 | 9 | 14.1 | 70 | 8 | 400 |
| 13 | Dundee | 74.4 | 87 | 68 | 7 | 17.4 | 83 | 7 | 417 |
| 14 | Nottingham | 74.0 | 92 | 57 | 7 | 16.7 | 83 | 4 | 462 |
| 15 | Bristol | 73.9 | 88 | 48 | 7 | 18.5 | 83 | 7 | 459 |
| 16 | Exeter | 73.5 | 92 | 62 | 4 | 15.9 | 83 | 7 | 414 |
| 17 | Lancaster | 73.2 | 85 | 55 | 8 | 15.4 | 78 | 7 | 403 |
| 17 | Manchester | 73.2 | 85 | 47 | 8 | 19.7 | 78 | 7 | 465 |
| 19 | Aberdeen | 72.8 | 95 | 74 | 4 | 23.3 | 88 | 8 | 417 |
| 20 | Southampton | 72.5 | 91 | 72 | 6 | 18.6 | 77 | 6 | 432 |
| 21 | Cardiff | 72.3 | 86 | 54 | 9 | 17.4 | 76 | 5 | 416 |

| | | Guardian score /100 | Satisfied with teaching % | Satisfied with feedback % | Spend per student /10 | Student:staff ratio | Job prospects % | Value added score /10 | Average entry tariff |
|---|---|---|---|---|---|---|---|---|---|
| 22 | Strathclyde | 72.2 | 87 | 47 | 8 | 25.6 | 84 | 8 | 436 |
| 23 | Buckingham | 71.9 | 94 | 80 | 4 | 11.5 | | 7 | 263 |
| 24 | Robert Gordon | 71.5 | | | 4 | 20.3 | 95 | 8 | 337 |
| 25 | Newcastle | 71.1 | 88 | 78 | 5 | 22.6 | 71 | 8 | 448 |
| 26 | Sussex | 69.6 | 92 | 67 | 4 | 19.6 | 79 | 8 | 374 |
| 27 | Leeds | 67.9 | 82 | 52 | 6 | 20.8 | 75 | 7 | 442 |
| 28 | Edinburgh Napier | 67.3 | | | 4 | 20.7 | 77 | 9 | 323 |
| 29 | Leicester | 67.1 | 90 | 68 | 5 | 24.0 | 77 | 7 | 370 |
| 30 | Liverpool | 66.8 | 84 | 54 | 6 | 19.9 | 78 | 6 | 408 |
| 30 | Queen's, Belfast | 66.8 | 82 | 40 | 5 | 18.1 | 84 | 7 | 405 |
| 32 | Kent | 66.3 | 89 | 65 | 6 | 16.7 | 77 | 4 | 360 |
| 33 | City | 65.4 | 82 | 53 | 6 | 17.3 | 66 | 8 | 360 |
| 34 | Nottingham Trent | 65.1 | 84 | 66 | 7 | 15.9 | 79 | 3 | 314 |
| 34 | Sheffield | 65.1 | 86 | 54 | 4 | 22.5 | 79 | 7 | 412 |
| 36 | Hull | 64.8 | 89 | 65 | 4 | 16.6 | 77 | 5 | 324 |
| 37 | Reading | 64.4 | 86 | 66 | 3 | 20.8 | 74 | 8 | 374 |
| 38 | Portsmouth | 64.3 | 90 | 55 | 7 | 16.7 | 74 | 5 | 294 |
| 39 | Stirling | 63.4 | | | 4 | 18.0 | 69 | 7 | |
| 39 | UEA | 63.4 | 89 | 70 | 4 | 27.9 | 77 | 7 | 382 |
| 41 | Essex | 63.3 | 84 | 54 | 5 | 14.8 | 67 | 7 | 319 |
| 42 | Thames Valley | 63.0 | 80 | 63 | 8 | 9.9 | | 4 | 199 |
| 43 | Keele | 62.2 | 88 | 49 | 5 | 16.3 | 77 | 4 | 328 |
| 44 | Northumbria | 61.6 | 84 | 56 | 5 | 25.4 | 90 | 4 | 362 |
| 45 | Sunderland | 61.2 | 99 | 93 | 8 | 28.5 | 62 | 5 | 223 |
| 46 | Derby | 60.2 | 97 | 87 | 4 | 24.2 | 58 | 8 | 250 |
| 47 | Bedfordshire | 59.6 | 82 | 78 | 3 | 13.5 | 57 | 9 | 206 |
| 47 | Gloucestershire | 59.6 | 94 | 81 | 5 | 26.5 | | 6 | 252 |
| 49 | Sheffield Hallam | 59.5 | 85 | 58 | 6 | 19.9 | 60 | 8 | 275 |
| 50 | Oxford Brookes | 59.0 | 80 | 41 | 6 | 19.7 | 81 | 4 | 327 |
| 51 | Staffordshire | 58.4 | 82 | 63 | 6 | 20.0 | 67 | 7 | 268 |
| 52 | UWE Bristol | 57.9 | 88 | 67 | 4 | 20.9 | 70 | 5 | 306 |
| 53 | Manchester Met | 56.9 | 80 | 55 | 4 | 19.4 | 71 | 6 | 308 |
| 54 | Brunel | 56.5 | 78 | 46 | 4 | 20.9 | 69 | 5 | 359 |
| 55 | Plymouth | 56.0 | 85 | 65 | 6 | 18.2 | 57 | 6 | 264 |
| 56 | Leeds Met | 55.0 | 78 | 57 | | 21.8 | 59 | 3 | 289 |
| 57 | Glasgow Caledonian | 54.9 | 84 | 51 | 3 | 27.7 | 67 | 7 | 371 |
| 58 | Kingston | 54.7 | 87 | 66 | 3 | 27.0 | 65 | 8 | 277 |
| 59 | Aberystwyth | 54.5 | 86 | 59 | 4 | 18.5 | 70 | 3 | 314 |
| 60 | Bangor | 54.2 | 90 | 74 | 3 | 22.4 | 66 | 4 | 306 |
| 60 | Swansea | 54.2 | 92 | 57 | 3 | 22.7 | 60 | 5 | 311 |
| 62 | Bradford | 53.4 | 79 | 71 | 10 | 19.5 | 42 | 3 | 237 |
| 63 | Surrey | 53.3 | 71 | 41 | 6 | 23.0 | 85 | 1 | 364 |
| 64 | Glamorgan | 53.2 | 89 | 75 | 3 | 21.9 | 59 | 5 | 268 |
| 65 | Birmingham City | 53.0 | 72 | 60 | 6 | 18.5 | 63 | 4 | 268 |
| 66 | Coventry | 52.8 | 82 | 66 | 7 | 22.9 | 68 | 2 | 288 |
| 67 | East London | 52.3 | 83 | 64 | 7 | 18.1 | 62 | 3 | 195 |

| | Guardian score /100 | Satisfied with teaching % | Satisfied with feedback % | Spend per student /10 | Student:staff ratio | Job prospects % | Value added score /10 | Average entry tariff |
|---|---|---|---|---|---|---|---|---|
| 68 Bournemouth | 52.1 | 88 | 72 | 6 | | 55 | 5 | 295 |
| 68 De Montfort | 52.1 | 86 | 77 | 2 | 22.5 | 69 | 5 | 229 |
| 70 Teesside | 51.6 | 93 | 85 | 5 | 27.6 | 47 | 4 | 272 |
| 71 Abertay Dundee | 49.9 | | | 3 | 36.3 | | 8 | 346 |
| 71 Ulster | 49.9 | 72 | 62 | 4 | 19.0 | 55 | 5 | 308 |
| 73 Westminster | 47.3 | 68 | 54 | 4 | 19.7 | 64 | 4 | 295 |
| 74 Edge Hill | 46.9 | 95 | 84 | 3 | 20.6 | 41 | 3 | 238 |
| 75 Chester | 45.4 | 80 | 62 | 3 | 24.1 | | 2 | 305 |
| 76 Anglia Ruskin | 44.1 | 74 | 55 | 7 | 30.5 | 57 | 5 | 242 |
| 77 Lincoln | 43.6 | 84 | 71 | 2 | 27.9 | 65 | 4 | 247 |
| 78 Greenwich | 43.3 | 85 | 74 | 3 | 28.3 | 66 | 2 | 242 |
| 79 Central Lancashire | 41.6 | 79 | 67 | 5 | 28.5 | 70 | 1 | 276 |
| 80 Northampton | 41.5 | 88 | 63 | 3 | 27.4 | 37 | 6 | 234 |
| 80 Southampton Solent | 41.5 | 75 | 51 | 4 | 22.5 | 60 | 3 | 202 |
| 82 Brighton | 41.1 | | | 3 | 40.4 | 53 | 9 | 257 |
| 82 Hertfordshire | 41.1 | 89 | 69 | 2 | 26.2 | 58 | 2 | 251 |
| 84 Liverpool John Moores | 39.8 | 85 | 68 | 3 | 27.7 | 47 | 3 | 256 |
| 85 Middlesex | 39.5 | 82 | 67 | 5 | 37.8 | 60 | 4 | 200 |
| 86 Canterbury Christ Church | 39.0 | 79 | 71 | 2 | 25.3 | 40 | 7 | 211 |
| 87 Huddersfield | 38.6 | 85 | 64 | 3 | 28.1 | 67 | 1 | 249 |
| 88 Bucks New University | 34.4 | 88 | 68 | 3 | 27.2 | 70 | 1 | 177 |
| 89 London South Bank | 30.6 | 74 | 53 | 2 | 39.8 | 42 | 8 | 194 |

# Media studies

❝ The average person interacts with the media for the majority of their waking hours. For around 12 hours a day, most of us engage with some form of media whether computer, television, film, radio, internet, mobile phone or iPod. It would therefore be irresponsible, having created a media-drenched society, to deny young people the opportunity to engage in the critical and in-depth study of media products, practices, and principles. How we use media, how media inform our lives, and how their contents can mislead or inspire us are crucial questions.

The shift from 'old' to 'new' media has generated profound changes in the way people communicate with one another, globally and locally. Audiences and news producers seem to converge with the rise of citizen journalism by the amateur capturing of events on mobile phone cameras; professional film and TV programme makers draw inspiration from young YouTubers and vice versa in a postmodern exchange of ideas. Are new media signalling a new democratic era? Or are existing popular cultural fashions and quick fixes being recycled through profit-led multinational media organisations? Is al-Jazeera challenging western notions of 'news', or is 'news' now collapsing into entertainment in an 'info-tainment' culture? These are exciting questions and themes that students of media are exploring and finding the answers to.

The kinds of skills media graduates gain ensure a wide range of career options in the media and cultural industries, PR, advertising, government, and education. Media students are not only eminently employable. They are also among the most savvy: analytical, engaging, and knowledgeable, with a flair for keeping ahead of state-of-the-art ideas, social trends, and cultural developments associated with the media.

**Professor Deborah Chambers**, *Media and Cultural Studies, Newcastle University*

It's been a while coming, but media studies is finally coming out of the shadow of the derision hurled by traditionalists who view the degree as simply three years of watching television. In fact, media and communications courses are concerned with the analysis and understanding of key features of social and cultural life, as well as with creating that cultural life, so remember that if you are interested in drama, or the technical and creative side of the media, a media degree will be an enormous bonus.

Given the power of the mass media in this modern age, the ability to conduct an integrated study of the various tools of the age (newspaper, TV, radio, internet and so on) in social, cultural, and historical context is invaluable. You'll study the way the media represent people and events (and there are rich pickings in these turbulent times), and the way those messages are put over: the use of sound and vision in this information-saturated era.

The courses you can take will vary widely in terms of academic content and vocational intent. In some, you'll be looking more at the sociology, the linguistics, and the cultural hinterland of the media, treating the subject as almost purely academic, with perhaps some practical aspects. Alternatively, you'll be heading for a more job-related course, picking up technical skills that will prepare you for work in journalism, film, photography, production or the interactive media. You could also end up somewhere in between, so look carefully at the modules and make sure you pick the right course.

Whatever the slant of your coursework, you'll be building the skills of research, enquiry, and analysis that older courses have always seen as part of their brief. What's more, media studies graduates still come out as above average in statistics for post-graduate employment.

But be a little wary. This isn't going to sweep you into the director general's seat at the BBC. For most people, success in the media is still about beating the odds: only those willing to make the tea, do the photocopying, or pick up the phone will survive. But if you can do all that, a media studies degree will stand you in as good stead (maybe better) as any other.

If you want a more direct route into the media, then vocational courses might be right for you. If, for example, you want to do journalism, then look for aspects of the course that study news production, elements of bias and propaganda, or the role of the press. Remember too that there are many good postgraduate journalism courses that may be an option if you want to take a different degree later on.

Other courses can be quite technical and almost scientific. Photography, for example, or digital media production teach both the role of those skills in presenting images or rolling news and the technical aspects of running a darkroom or building a website. Digital in particular is the coming element in the media – the dotcom revolution may have stalled but, while it's slower, it's also far more sure-footed.

Since, as many an old hack will tell you, the best way to gain a job in the media is through experience and contacts, check out what links a department has for work placements and make sure that they're in the area you're hoping to work in. Many departments insist that their staff retain links to the real world and you'll need to exploit them if you're going to land that dream job.

---

**&#66;&#66;** University gave me the opportunity to write and direct my first four short films. As well as learning the technical aspects of the equipment, the different roles within production and the theoretical side of TV production, the course gave me the confidence to develop my own ideas and directorial style and crucially build up a network of friends within the industry that I have since worked with professionally.

**Alexandra Kalymnios**, *a TV and video production graduate from Bournemouth University, is now director for Channel 4 TV's Hollyoaks*

---

## 》 Further information

**Skillset**
Focus Point
21 Caledonian Road
London N1 9BG

**t** 020 7713 9800
**⌁** www.skillset.org

**The Institute of Communications Studies**
University of Leeds
Leeds LS2 9JT

**t** 0113 343 8859
**⌁** www.ics.leeds.ac.uk

**National Council for the Training of Journalists**
The New Granary, Station Road
Newport, Saffron Walden
Essex CB11 3PL

**t** 01799 544014
**e** info@nctj.com
**⌁** www.nctj.com 》

**National Union of Journalists**
308 Gray's Inn Road
London WC1X 8DP

t   020 7278 7916
t   training@nuj.org.uk
↗  www.nujtraining.org.uk

**Broadcast Journalism Training Council**
18 Miller's Close
Rippingale, Nr. Bourne
Lincolnshire PE10 0TH

t   01778 440025
e   sec@bjtc.org.uk
↗  www.bjtc.org.uk

↗ Online reading

**MediaGuardian.co.uk** mediaguardian.co.uk
**Media, Communications and Cultural Studies Association** www.meccsa.org.uk
**Periodical Publishers Association** www.ppa.co.uk
**Skillset Careers** www.skillset.org/careers
**New Media Studies** www.newmediastudies.com
**Journalism UK** www.journalismuk.co.uk
**The International Association for Media and History** www.iamhist.org
**The Media and Communications site** www.aber.ac.uk/media
**Media UK** www.mediauk.com

## Media studies, communications and librarianship

| | | Guardian score /100 | Satisfied with teaching % | Satisfied with feedback % | Spend per student /10 | Student:staff ratio | Job prospects % | Value added score /10 | Average entry tariff |
|---|---|---|---|---|---|---|---|---|---|
| 1 | Warwick | 100.0 | 98 | 80 | 9 | 11.1 | 50 | 8 | 428 |
| 2 | Southampton | 93.9 | 73 | 57 | 10 | 10.5 | | 5 | 393 |
| 3 | Sheffield | 91.2 | 94 | 76 | 6 | 19.1 | 83 | 8 | 381 |
| 4 | Cardiff | 89.4 | 92 | 61 | 10 | 17.7 | 72 | 6 | 382 |
| 5 | Birmingham | 85.3 | 87 | 73 | 10 | 17.8 | 48 | 7 | 360 |
| 6 | Newcastle | 84.1 | 81 | 54 | 9 | 16.0 | 70 | 7 | 386 |
| 7 | Loughborough | 84.0 | 89 | 72 | 4 | 17.9 | 66 | 8 | 394 |
| 8 | Leicester | 82.7 | | | 8 | 17.6 | 64 | 9 | 311 |
| 9 | Leeds | 79.5 | 82 | 60 | 8 | 19.4 | 70 | 5 | 374 |
| 10 | King's College London | 79.0 | 81 | 67 | 8 | 21.2 | | | 401 |
| 11 | Birmingham City | 78.9 | 85 | 66 | 10 | 14.0 | 43 | 7 | 310 |
| 12 | Bournemouth | 77.0 | 81 | 61 | 7 | 17.5 | 71 | 6 | 353 |
| 13 | Goldsmiths | 76.8 | 85 | 59 | 5 | 18.2 | 57 | 9 | 349 |
| 14 | University of the Arts, London | 76.6 | 70 | 48 | 9 | 19.8 | 72 | 8 | 294 |
| 15 | Nottingham Trent | 74.8 | 86 | 72 | 7 | 13.6 | 63 | 4 | 305 |
| 16 | Edinburgh Napier | 73.4 | | | 6 | 19.1 | 62 | 8 | 300 |
| 17 | Royal Holloway | 73.0 | 83 | 57 | 8 | 14.4 | 40 | 6 | 368 |
| 18 | Anglia Ruskin | 72.9 | 96 | 78 | 9 | 14.5 | | 3 | 260 |
| 19 | Westminster | 71.8 | 71 | 52 | 7 | 13.7 | 41 | 9 | 333 |
| 20 | Sussex | 70.9 | 88 | 52 | 6 | 22.7 | 58 | 7 | 353 |
| 21 | City | 70.2 | 71 | 56 | 7 | 16.8 | 60 | 7 | 306 |
| 22 | Kingston | 69.5 | 80 | 61 | 6 | 15.4 | 52 | 8 | 257 |
| 22 | Robert Gordon | 69.5 | | | 5 | 20.0 | 70 | 5 | 318 |
| 24 | Aberystwyth | 69.4 | | | 7 | 25.0 | 53 | 10 | 254 |
| 25 | Central Lancashire | 68.8 | 79 | 62 | 6 | 19.5 | 73 | 4 | 322 |
| 26 | Stirling | 68.6 | | | 4 | 16.1 | 54 | 7 | |
| 27 | Keele | 68.0 | 86 | 72 | 4 | | | 8 | 306 |

| | | Guardian score /100 | Satisfied with teaching % | Satisfied with feedback % | Spend per student /10 | Student:staff ratio | Job prospects % | Value added score /10 | Average entry tariff |
|---|---|---|---|---|---|---|---|---|---|
| 28 | Bedfordshire | 67.5 | 80 | 71 | 8 | 11.0 | 31 | 9 | 188 |
| 28 | Surrey | 67.5 | 70 | 53 | 5 | 15.2 | | 8 | 319 |
| 30 | Arts Institute, Bournemouth | 67.2 | 79 | 65 | 5 | 21.7 | | 6 | 357 |
| 31 | University for the Creative Arts | 66.8 | 85 | 70 | 9 | 25.9 | 59 | 3 | |
| 32 | Lancaster | 66.5 | 86 | 77 | 5 | 13.3 | 44 | 3 | 338 |
| 33 | Lincoln | 65.2 | 79 | 66 | 3 | 21.7 | 53 | 10 | 280 |
| 34 | Brunel | 64.7 | 81 | 63 | 4 | 28.5 | 73 | 8 | 303 |
| 35 | Sheffield Hallam | 63.6 | 73 | 61 | 6 | 20.2 | 60 | 8 | 266 |
| 35 | Sunderland | 63.6 | 85 | 71 | 6 | 17.2 | 47 | 7 | 244 |
| 37 | Bangor | 63.4 | 85 | 73 | 5 | 22.2 | | | 280 |
| 38 | Thames Valley | 62.7 | 72 | 60 | | 11.2 | 45 | 8 | 218 |
| 39 | Middlesex | 59.8 | 70 | 57 | 7 | 21.1 | 59 | 7 | 224 |
| 40 | Hull | 59.5 | 92 | 70 | 3 | 16.9 | | 5 | 256 |
| 40 | St Mary's UC, Twickenham | 59.5 | 83 | 72 | 4 | 13.2 | 47 | 4 | 233 |
| 42 | Hertfordshire | 58.9 | 84 | 67 | 3 | 14.0 | | 5 | 235 |
| 43 | Staffordshire | 58.2 | 78 | 64 | 4 | 22.3 | 62 | 6 | 255 |
| 44 | Queen's, Belfast | 58.0 | 76 | 45 | 5 | 19.4 | 38 | 7 | 322 |
| 45 | UWE Bristol | 57.3 | 86 | 67 | 5 | 24.2 | 38 | 8 | 265 |
| 46 | UEA | 56.9 | 86 | 65 | 2 | | | 4 | 340 |
| 47 | Ulster | 56.7 | 76 | 57 | 6 | 18.7 | 46 | 5 | 271 |
| 48 | Portsmouth | 56.5 | 86 | 64 | 5 | | 41 | 3 | 288 |
| 49 | Manchester Met | 56.1 | 76 | 60 | 8 | 20.1 | 44 | 6 | 217 |
| 50 | UC Falmouth | 55.9 | 71 | 55 | 6 | 23.9 | 60 | 6 | 254 |
| 51 | De Montfort | 55.4 | 83 | 69 | 3 | 18.6 | 47 | 6 | 248 |
| 52 | Coventry | 55.2 | 72 | 44 | 6 | 25.1 | 55 | 8 | 268 |
| 53 | Salford | 54.7 | 70 | 53 | 6 | 29.3 | 54 | 8 | 313 |
| 54 | Queen Margaret | 52.8 | | | 2 | | 44 | 7 | 296 |
| 55 | Northumbria | 52.3 | 77 | 70 | 3 | 26.0 | 46 | 7 | 297 |
| 56 | Liverpool John Moores | 51.9 | 80 | 61 | 5 | 17.7 | 49 | 2 | 265 |
| 57 | Gloucestershire | 51.7 | 71 | 57 | 8 | 21.0 | 46 | 3 | 262 |
| 58 | Chichester | 51.3 | 92 | 78 | 3 | 23.8 | 36 | 6 | 239 |
| 59 | Glamorgan | 50.7 | 64 | 49 | 7 | 15.9 | 29 | 6 | 254 |
| 60 | East London | 49.9 | 74 | 61 | 7 | 17.0 | 38 | 4 | 195 |
| 60 | Greenwich | 49.9 | 86 | 77 | 3 | 23.9 | 34 | 7 | 211 |
| 62 | Roehampton | 49.8 | 87 | 72 | 3 | 15.2 | | 1 | 259 |
| 63 | Leeds Met | 47.1 | 69 | 45 | 5 | 22.1 | 47 | 4 | 264 |
| 64 | Southampton Solent | 46.2 | 74 | 60 | 5 | 26.6 | 54 | 3 | 248 |
| 65 | Marjon (St Mark and St John) | 45.5 | 74 | 73 | 2 | 20.0 | 41 | 4 | |
| 66 | Chester | 44.0 | 65 | 57 | 4 | 22.6 | 60 | 2 | 244 |
| 67 | Teesside | 43.5 | 95 | 78 | 8 | 21.3 | 25 | 1 | 227 |
| 68 | Bath Spa | 43.2 | 84 | 59 | 2 | 28.7 | 46 | 5 | 265 |
| 69 | Derby | 43.0 | | | 4 | 25.3 | 52 | 2 | 230 |
| 70 | York St John | 42.1 | 86 | 53 | 3 | 35.0 | | 7 | 267 |
| 71 | London South Bank | 40.4 | 66 | 51 | 3 | 21.6 | 36 | 7 | 187 |
| 72 | Leeds Trinity & All Saints | 38.3 | 71 | 58 | 3 | 21.9 | 43 | 3 | 221 |
| 73 | Winchester | 37.0 | 83 | 67 | 2 | 23.9 | 30 | 3 | 245 |
| 74 | Edge Hill | 36.3 | 77 | 68 | 4 | 19.4 | 24 | 1 | 258 |
| 75 | Canterbury Christ Church | 35.6 | 87 | 63 | 2 | 23.8 | 32 | 3 | 213 |
| 76 | Swansea | 35.3 | 86 | 53 | 3 | 30.7 | 42 | 2 | 266 |
| 77 | Huddersfield | 35.0 | 56 | 50 | 3 | 23.8 | 39 | 3 | 277 |
| 78 | Bucks New University | 34.3 | 68 | 47 | 6 | 26.2 | 42 | 2 | 203 |
| 79 | Northampton | 30.4 | 75 | 72 | 2 | 32.0 | 35 | 4 | 223 |

# Politics

There has never been a better or more important time to study politics at university. Climate change, 9/11 and its aftermath (including the wars in Iraq and Afghanistan) and the rise of China and India have all given a new salience to the need to understand developments in global politics. The transition from Tony Blair to Gordon Brown in the UK and the election of a new president in the United States have provided a significant new context to the formation of domestic and foreign policy agenda.

Studying politics gives students the opportunity to develop a detailed awareness of the relationship between political ideas, institutions, and policy choices at home and abroad. Politics may be studied from a contemporary and national perspective and in a comparative and historical context.

Studying politics opens up a host of exciting career opportunities. Aside from a career in politics itself (numerous politics alumni have gone on to become MPs and even cabinet ministers), typical career destinations for politics graduates include the media, broadcast and written journalism, public relations, the civil service, campaigning non-governmental organisations, think tanks, and international organisations.

**Simon Lee**, *Senior Lecturer in Politics, University of Hull*

Political studies has become somewhat fashionable again, up at the top of the lists when Ucas reveals who applies for what each year. Applications have been rising year on year, which makes it both more competitive to get on a course, and more exciting when you get there. It's a growth in popularity likely to be connected to the increase in single-issue politics amongst the nation's youth. The sight of tens of thousands of people taking to the streets to protest has become a common one again as the war against terror, wars in Afghanistan and Iraq, and the crisis in the Middle East are combined with growing concerns about globalisation and more local worries about tuition fees.

But while you may have been galvanised by single-issue politics, once you get on to a degree course the whole thing of course becomes much, much broader. Most degree courses will first take you on a whirlwind tour of the main philosophers from Plato through to Marx and, more than likely, catch up with the beliefs of the anti-globalisation movement. They will move on to consider the institutions and groupings that make up a political society, including parliamentary and presidential democracies, party politics, electoral behaviour, social and unconventional behaviour, and what happens in every corner of the globe, including military and ethnic dimensions.

From them on, you'll specialise and use your newfound skills to analyse modern-day politics. You could take intelligence studies with international politics, democratic politics, or the environment and Third World development. You'll also come to understand how the public relates to governments, be it via the protest march, revolution, ballot box or focus group.

The chances are, you won't lack for work – the ability to analyse evidence and arguments, oral and written communication, and the knowledge to handle statistics are all in demand by employers not related to the world of party politics. Alternative career choices could include the more apolitical arena of the civil service, or perhaps the ever-growing lobby industry, as well as local authorities, journalism or the public sector.

Look carefully at what options are available to you – there is a wide variance in the ways universities approach the concept and the teaching of politics. But be aware that if your motivation for getting into politics has been single-issue stuff, then the actual nitty-gritty of politics may not be for you – the subject itself (environmental sciences perhaps) may be more pertinent.

How you view politics may help you choose where you study it. If you're a party (political) animal, then you'll want a course with strong elements of parliamentary and democratic studies. If you're more of a theorist, then check the option for political philosophy alternatives, poring over the works of Hobbes or Locke.

Many courses are now taking an increasingly global look at politics and its institutions, so consider those opportunities too – the study of systems entirely different to the western model can add a dimension to your studies which may not have occurred to you at sixth form.

Take note too of the assessment options, and whether it's exams, continuous assessment, dissertations or coursework – different methods work best for different people.

Some universities do four-year courses that include a year working in Westminster, Washington or Ottawa, so try to seize that chance or any other possibilities for vocational work experience. The chances are that it'll be dogsbody stuff for an MP or lobby group, but that experience and the contacts you make could turn out to be invaluable. If you want to stay in politics, it really can be a case of who you know ...

---

66 It's hard not to see politics as just a collection of '-isms': anarchism, conservatism, feminism. But if you take a course involving politics you'll quickly start seeing the 'political' all around you. The world will become this churning sea of institutions, people, and ideas, all open to argument. And you'll use everything from history to philosophy to pick apart the fundamental question of why people interact in the ways they do and whether they can do better.

**Vincenzo Rampulla**, *final-year politics, philosophy and history student at Birkbeck, University of London*

---

## » Further information

### Political Studies Association
Newcastle University
Newcastle-upon-Tyne NE1 7RU

t  0191 222 8021
↗ www.psa.ac.uk

### Civitas (The Institute for the Study of Civil Society)
77 Great Peter Street
Westminster
London SW1P 2EZ

t  020 7799 6677
e  info@civitas.org.uk
↗ www.civitas.org.uk

### Demos
Third Floor, Magdalen House
136 Tooley Street
London SE1 2TU

t  0845 458 5949
e  hello@demos.co.uk
↗ www.demos.co.uk  »

**Unlock Democracy**
6 Cynthia Street
London N1 9JF

t 020 7278 4443
e info@unlockdemocracy.org.uk
↗ www.unlockdemocracy.org.uk

**Policy Network**
Third floor, 11 Tufton Street
London SW1P 3QB

t 020 7340 2200
e info@policy-network.net
↗ www.policy-network.net

↗ Online reading

**Guardian.co.uk politics**  politics.guardian.co.uk
**Politics Direct**  www.politicsdirect.com
**Working for an MP**  www.w4mp.org
**The UK Parliament**  www.parliament.uk
**Global Action Plan**  www.globalactionplan.org.uk

## Politics

| | | Guardian score /100 | Satisfied with teaching % | Satisfied with feedback % | Spend per student /10 | Student:staff ratio | Job prospects % | Value added score /10 | Average entry tariff |
|---|---|---|---|---|---|---|---|---|---|
| 1 | Oxford | 100.0 | 93 | 65 | | 10.8 | 86 | 8 | 532 |
| 2 | St Andrews | 99.6 | 95 | 82 | 8 | 17.2 | 76 | 10 | 497 |
| 3 | Cambridge | 98.4 | 95 | 70 | 10 | 15.5 | 79 | 6 | 498 |
| 4 | King's College London | 93.8 | 96 | 68 | 8 | 13.5 | 80 | 9 | 428 |
| 5 | London School of Economics | 84.5 | 73 | 69 | 8 | 13.0 | 84 | 7 | 449 |
| 6 | Warwick | 82.8 | 88 | 65 | 9 | 15.1 | 65 | 7 | 473 |
| 7 | Birmingham | 80.2 | 90 | 65 | 10 | 17.8 | 61 | 7 | 384 |
| 8 | UCL | 80.0 | 83 | 59 | 10 | 20.1 | | | 474 |
| 9 | York | 78.7 | 88 | 53 | 8 | 14.0 | 65 | 5 | 453 |
| 10 | Durham | 78.5 | 80 | 67 | 7 | 17.9 | 73 | 8 | 461 |
| 11 | Edinburgh | 78.4 | 83 | 40 | 10 | 14.2 | 59 | 6 | 441 |
| 11 | SOAS | 78.4 | 94 | 63 | 8 | 14.1 | 65 | 4 | 427 |
| 13 | Dundee | 76.9 | 98 | 85 | 6 | 17.4 | 41 | 10 | 349 |
| 14 | Queen Mary | 76.6 | 90 | 76 | | 16.3 | 70 | 5 | 359 |
| 15 | Exeter | 75.6 | 92 | 73 | 4 | 15.9 | 69 | 6 | 417 |
| 16 | Nottingham Trent | 74.8 | 90 | 74 | 7 | 15.9 | 67 | 8 | 250 |
| 17 | Bath | 74.1 | 85 | 60 | 7 | 16.9 | 73 | 5 | 433 |
| 18 | Bristol | 72.3 | 81 | 46 | 7 | 18.5 | 68 | 7 | 452 |
| 19 | Bradford | 72.1 | 86 | 68 | 6 | 12.8 | 68 | 6 | 311 |
| 20 | Sheffield | 71.3 | 88 | 66 | 4 | 22.5 | 71 | 8 | 421 |
| 21 | Nottingham | 71.0 | 86 | 47 | 7 | 16.7 | 69 | 6 | 418 |
| 22 | Essex | 70.1 | 89 | 73 | 5 | 14.8 | 65 | 5 | 355 |
| 23 | Glasgow | 69.0 | 88 | 61 | 5 | 15.6 | 55 | 7 | 398 |
| 24 | Sussex | 68.6 | 91 | 71 | 3 | 19.6 | 64 | 7 | 361 |
| 25 | Newcastle | 68.0 | 90 | 65 | 5 | 22.6 | 72 | 5 | 396 |
| 26 | Hull | 67.6 | 93 | 78 | 4 | 16.6 | 70 | 2 | 341 |
| 27 | Manchester | 67.4 | 80 | 48 | 8 | 19.7 | 61 | 6 | 432 |
| 28 | Leicester | 66.2 | 94 | 71 | 5 | 24.0 | 60 | 9 | 326 |

| | | Guardian score /100 | Satisfied with teaching % | Satisfied with feedback % | Spend per student /10 | Student-staff ratio | Job prospects % | Value added score /10 | Average entry tariff |
|---|---|---|---|---|---|---|---|---|---|
| 29 | Kent | 65.3 | 83 | 71 | 5 | 16.7 | 65 | 5 | 293 |
| 30 | Cardiff | 64.4 | 89 | 60 | 5 | 25.7 | 68 | 6 | 412 |
| 31 | Strathclyde | 63.8 | 91 | 68 | 8 | 25.6 | 52 | 6 | 361 |
| 32 | Lancaster | 63.3 | 88 | 57 | 8 | 15.4 | 49 | 2 | 373 |
| 32 | Southampton | 63.3 | 85 | 48 | 5 | 18.6 | 64 | 5 | 373 |
| 34 | Aberdeen | 62.2 | 88 | 75 | 4 | 23.3 | 61 | 7 | 341 |
| 34 | Surrey | 62.2 | 90 | 72 | 6 | 23.0 | | | 300 |
| 36 | Portsmouth | 61.4 | 96 | 84 | 6 | 16.7 | 60 | 1 | 257 |
| 37 | Leeds | 61.2 | 85 | 52 | 5 | 20.8 | 59 | 5 | 392 |
| 38 | Liverpool | 61.1 | 85 | 61 | 6 | 19.9 | 64 | 3 | 358 |
| 39 | Leeds Met | 60.2 | 79 | 56 | | 21.8 | | 7 | 249 |
| 40 | Reading | 59.0 | 88 | 59 | 3 | 20.8 | 66 | 5 | 310 |
| 41 | UEA | 58.9 | 95 | 78 | 4 | 27.9 | 52 | 6 | 344 |
| 42 | Plymouth | 58.7 | 92 | 62 | 5 | 18.2 | 49 | 6 | 261 |
| 43 | Keele | 58.2 | 89 | 67 | 4 | 16.3 | 59 | 3 | 303 |
| 44 | Coventry | 58.1 | 85 | 84 | 6 | 22.9 | | 4 | 296 |
| 45 | City | 57.9 | 73 | 56 | 6 | 17.3 | | | 290 |
| 46 | Aberystwyth | 57.4 | 93 | 69 | 3 | 18.5 | 42 | 5 | 321 |
| 46 | Aston | 57.4 | 90 | 58 | 2 | 20.5 | 52 | 5 | 348 |
| 46 | Goldsmiths | 57.4 | 90 | 58 | 3 | 14.3 | 65 | 1 | 296 |
| 49 | Brunel | 56.7 | 78 | 59 | 3 | 20.9 | 57 | 6 | 293 |
| 50 | Royal Holloway | 56.2 | 81 | 51 | 3 | 19.1 | 55 | 3 | 390 |
| 50 | Stirling | 56.2 | 87 | 67 | 4 | 18.0 | 44 | 5 | |
| 52 | Oxford Brookes | 56.1 | 79 | 58 | 6 | 19.7 | 52 | 5 | 304 |
| 53 | Queen's, Belfast | 55.2 | 82 | 51 | 5 | 18.1 | 57 | 3 | 346 |
| 54 | Huddersfield | 55.0 | 96 | 91 | 3 | 28.1 | | 6 | 230 |
| 55 | Middlesex | 54.9 | 83 | 64 | 5 | 37.8 | | 10 | |
| 56 | Loughborough | 54.4 | 89 | 76 | 5 | 22.9 | 50 | 2 | 316 |
| 57 | Northumbria | 50.4 | 88 | 70 | 5 | 25.4 | 48 | 5 | 268 |
| 58 | UWE Bristol | 49.8 | 87 | 71 | 4 | 20.9 | 48 | 3 | 239 |
| 59 | Westminster | 49.7 | 77 | 52 | 3 | 19.7 | 34 | 10 | 232 |
| 60 | Ulster | 48.7 | 80 | 62 | 3 | 19.0 | 48 | 4 | 242 |
| 61 | De Montfort | 48.3 | 90 | 75 | 2 | 22.5 | 55 | 3 | 218 |
| 62 | Manchester Met | 48.2 | | | 4 | 19.4 | 38 | 6 | 235 |
| 63 | Swansea | 45.8 | 88 | 64 | 3 | 22.7 | 50 | 2 | 279 |
| 64 | Salford | 45.3 | 88 | 71 | 3 | 23.7 | 44 | 3 | 255 |
| 65 | Kingston | 43.8 | 87 | 58 | 2 | 27.0 | | 6 | 206 |
| 66 | Lincoln | 43.6 | 80 | 71 | 2 | 27.9 | 54 | 7 | 252 |
| 67 | Greenwich | 37.1 | 81 | 59 | 2 | 23.5 | | 2 | 215 |
| 68 | Liverpool John Moores | 32.2 | 91 | 61 | 3 | 27.7 | 33 | 2 | 223 |

# Social policy

" Students of social policy explore some of the most pressing issues facing contemporary society. How do societies organise and manage their welfare systems? Who pays, who benefits and who misses out? Governments in the developed world spend huge resources on health and social care, income support and welfare, but how are these resources divided up between different sections of the population? Most importantly, who decides how much to tax and how much to spend to achieve social objectives?

Questions of this kind go to the heart of how societies operate, but they also take students well beyond policy-related concerns to wider issues involving the key moral choices we all face. Different societies approach welfare in different ways, but every society has to make choices about how to treat the poorest communities and marginalised populations. Should we be aiming at achieving as much 'equality' as possible — and what inequalities should we be prepared to put up with?

In one sense, at every stage of the life cycle we each have a stake in one aspect or other of social policy, whether this is through a desire to be educated, a need for childcare or healthcare, or for a decent pension in old age. Studying social policy not only helps us to understand the social and political contexts and processes of policy making, but also who we are, who our neighbours are (locally or globally), and the nature of other people's lives and experiences. Through its attention to social research methods and different forms of social enquiry, a social policy degree will provide significant research skills, which can improve employability in a range of public and private sector occupations.

**Professor Nick Ellison**, *School of Sociology and Social Policy, University of Leeds*

Social policy is a very contemporary degree course, addressing issues that have only arisen in the last 50 years. Its main concern is with how "we" as a society, and "they" as a government, treat the members of our society. At its core, therefore, are issues surrounding the welfare state and the alternatives to it. You'll be asking some fundamental questions about how things are, as well as how they ought to be, merging philosophical and political theories with social science.

As you work through these meaty issues, you'll be acquiring the skills to critically analyse contemporary society. You'll consider topics such as NHS reform, tackling poverty and social exclusion, and changes in the criminal justice system, drawing on a multidisciplinary approach that takes in politics, law, economics, sociology, philosophy, and history.

Very few of you will have come across anything quite like this at school or college, so most degree programmes assume no prior knowledge. Your first year, therefore, is likely to be a general introduction to the topics, followed in the next two years by a mixture of the core and mandatory topics, with optional specialisations, which often focus on particular problems and areas of social policy, such as poverty and social security, housing and planning, crime and penal policy — so check the options tally with your own interests when you apply.

Teaching is usually centred around lectures, seminars, and your own private research and reading. Assessment can be based on exams, coursework, and dissertations, the exact combination depending on where you study.

Once you've graduated, the chances of employment are pretty high. You can view it as a vocational course, so feel equipped to work in the public sector, or perhaps in central or local government or social work. You can also view it as an academic course, in which case you'll have the analytical, research, and technical skills to work in a number of areas – think tanks, policy evaluation and planning, and in academic research.

When choosing a course, it's always handy to check whether the department is engaged with research as well as with teaching. On the one hand, it can mean you have an insight into the very latest thought and initiatives and can be learning from the freshest minds. On the other hand, you may be dealing with a department where the best teachers are too busy elsewhere to deal with you.

As with all multidisciplinary courses, check the health of the related departments. You'll often be taught by, and use the facilities of, the departments which feed into your course.

There are some sandwich courses and some universities run work placement schemes, both of which are handy for taking you out of the theory and planting you in the very real, often with voluntary schemes or charities. This is especially useful if you see the degree as a vocational way of entering social work.

That can of course be an emotionally draining, as well as rewarding, career, so any way of forewarning yourself can help. Check with the course tutors what the possibilities are, including those for a period of foreign study.

And take time to think again about your own motivation. If you fancy social policy as a way of getting into social work, consider doing a social work course instead. Social policy has enormous relevance to such a career, but it usually takes in the in the broader picture, equipping you with the analytical rather than the practical skills for such a choice.

---

66 Social policy provides a wealth of knowledge on the most pressing issues in society. The social policy course is multi-disciplinary in its approach and offers opportunities to consult and discuss the many challenging sources of information on current political affairs among a diverse range of students, which creates interest and understanding. The course offers a range of assessment techniques and a wide and varied choice of interesting essay topics.

**Jennifer McSherry**, *third-year health and social care policy student, University of Ulster*

---

## 》 Further information

**SWAP School of Social Sciences**
University of Southampton
Southampton SO17 1BJ

t  023 8059 9310
↗ www.swap.ac.uk

**The Academy Social Sciences**
30 Tabernacle Street
London EC2A 4UE

t  020 7330 0898
↗ www.acss.org.uk

**Social Research Association**
23-42 Stephenson Way
London NW1 2HX

t  020 7388 2391
e  admin@the-sra.org.uk
↗ www.the-sra.org.uk

↗ Online reading

**SocietyGuardian.co.uk**  SocietyGuardian.co.uk
**The UK Social Policy Association**  www.social-policy.com
**International and Comparative Social Policy Group**  icsp.group.shef.ac.uk
**SocialPolicy.net**  www.socialpolicy.net

## Social policy and administration

| | | Guardian score /100 | Satisfied with teaching % | Satisfied with feedback % | Spend per student /10 | Student:staff ratio | Job prospects % | Value added score /10 | Average entry tariff |
|---|---|---|---|---|---|---|---|---|---|
| 1 | Bristol | 100.0 | 88 | 73 | 10 | 11.7 | 68 | 6 | 347 |
| 2 | London School of Economics | 91.5 | 76 | 55 | 8 | 13.0 | 77 | 6 | 420 |
| 3 | Cardiff | 87.3 | 89 | 53 | 9 | 17.4 | | 8 | 348 |
| 4 | Bath | 83.0 | 87 | 56 | 6 | 16.9 | | 8 | 377 |
| 4 | Leeds | 83.0 | 91 | 60 | 5 | 20.8 | 63 | 10 | 290 |
| 6 | Birmingham | 82.9 | 82 | 63 | 10 | 17.8 | 52 | 8 | 292 |
| 7 | York | 80.8 | 89 | 57 | 8 | 14.0 | 58 | 6 | 321 |
| 8 | Nottingham | 75.8 | 84 | 53 | 6 | 16.7 | | 6 | 329 |
| 9 | Glasgow | 75.1 | 89 | 65 | 5 | 15.6 | 60 | 5 | |
| 10 | Loughborough | 74.6 | 94 | 86 | 5 | 22.9 | 51 | 4 | 356 |
| 11 | Keele | 71.8 | 86 | 60 | 4 | 16.3 | 52 | 6 | 316 |
| 12 | Hull | 71.0 | 87 | 77 | 3 | 16.6 | 61 | 3 | 285 |
| 13 | Nottingham Trent | 70.4 | 76 | 71 | 7 | 15.9 | 52 | 7 | |
| 14 | Birmingham City | 68.5 | 76 | 65 | 5 | 18.5 | | 8 | 240 |
| 15 | Kent | 68.4 | 89 | 68 | 5 | 16.7 | 63 | 3 | 244 |
| 16 | Sheffield Hallam | 64.3 | 78 | 63 | 5 | 19.9 | 40 | 8 | 265 |
| 17 | Manchester | 64.0 | 76 | 27 | 7 | 19.7 | 44 | 5 | 362 |
| 18 | Sheffield | 63.9 | 80 | 56 | 4 | 22.5 | | 6 | 338 |
| 19 | Salford | 59.7 | 88 | 72 | 3 | 23.7 | | 6 | 211 |
| 20 | Central Lancashire | 57.9 | 85 | 65 | 4 | 28.5 | | 5 | 216 |
| 21 | Swansea | 51.1 | 84 | 66 | 3 | 22.7 | 41 | 2 | 268 |
| 22 | Ulster | 49.1 | 76 | 61 | 3 | 19.0 | | 1 | 243 |
| 23 | Anglia Ruskin | 48.9 | 88 | 69 | 6 | 30.5 | 32 | 2 | 251 |
| 24 | Manchester Met | 48.5 | 74 | 60 | 3 | 19.4 | | | 169 |
| 25 | Northampton | 45.1 | 81 | 64 | 3 | 27.4 | | | 186 |
| 26 | London South Bank | 34.5 | 82 | 60 | 2 | 39.8 | | 3 | |

# Social work and community studies

❝ Most people know that social work involves providing practical help for people with problems in their everyday lives, looking after children affected by family breakdown or arranging care for adults who can't manage alone. But studying social work is about much more. It investigates what makes children and adults vulnerable and what can be done to protect them from abuse — and examines what causes people to behave hurtfully to those around them and how intervening in these situations promotes positive outcomes. Sometimes an individual's behaviour prevents them integrating into society; people may experience discrimination and disadvantage because of their race, gender, sexual orientation, disability, or simply because they are different. So social work means exploring social and individual problems from various perspectives and applying theory to better understand and respond to these problems.

An essential part of the course is the 200 days spent in practice learning — working in a real social work agency, supervised and assessed by a practice teacher. Social work students can select from specialist options: bereavement, spirituality, substance misuse, youth justice, and asylum seekers, as well as receiving a solid grounding in child and family practice and adult services. A range of practice placements is available in social work and social care agencies in the area.

**Margaret Holloway**, *Professor of Social Work, University of Hull*

The aim of social work is to provide and manage care, support, and protection in partnership with individuals, families, groups, and communities to enable them to function, participate, and develop in society. Social work is different from, but complementary to, social care, in which personal care is provided to individuals in day, residential or community settings.

The degree in social work, which replaced the two-year diploma, puts social work graduates on a par with the professions they work closely with, such as nurses, teachers, and physiotherapists, and is raising the profession's status and public image. Despite the impression given by the media, applications for the degree have actually risen in recent years.

The generic qualification combines theory with practice — you'll spend around 200 days in practice during the course, with at least two different client groups, and teaching reflects the core skills which social workers require: problem-solving, communication, working with others, personal and professional development, and information technology and numerical skills.

More than 80 universities are accredited by the General Social Care Council to offer the social work degree and, to further encourage people into the profession, the government offers social work students a non-means-tested bursary worth about £4,000 a year. And once you've graduated, the fact that there is still something of a recruitment problem in the profession means employment prospects after graduation are excellent. In addition, and in order to improve recruitment rates in "crisis" areas, social work graduates could be eligible for the reimbursement of their student loans if they sign up to work in boroughs affected by shortages of suitably qualified workers.

Community studies is a markedly different degree, a more academic and less vocational approach to similar issues. It is mainly concerned with concepts of culture and community and cuts across various disciplines, such as sociology, psychology, and anthropology. As such, it can give analytical and problem-solving skills for a range of jobs post-graduation. A community studies course is rather more reliant on traditional methods of teaching – lectures, seminars, and so on – than the more hands-on approach of the social work degree. It's a qualification for those concerned with the issues of society rather than the practicalities. As such, you'll have analytical and problem-solving skills, and that skill of seeing the bigger picture gives you the ability for strategic thought applicable to management jobs in the public and private sectors, and consultancy and journalism, as well as local and central government and the health service.

If you're dithering about which of the two disciplines suits you better, then stop thinking about the degree and think about the job that follows. Are you cut out for social work? If you have an affinity for the subject, but not for the mental and physical bruises of fieldwork, then the broader base of community studies may well be for you. That's not to say that community studies is social work for cowards – it's a new approach to similar issues, and while two graduates from the disciplines will have a lot to say to each other, they will come from totally different standpoints.

In making that choice, talk not just to those who'll be teaching the course, but try those who have graduated and are now working – how do they feel about their job? Remember though that these can be emotionally charged areas to work in. You may get someone on a bad day ...

As ever with the courses in this book, look at the modules of the course and at the research and publications of those who teach and see if they tally with your own interests. Look also at the work experience opportunities and the links the department has for placements. There may even be the opportunity to work abroad.

Consider whether the full-time degree is for you. More so than for most degrees, there are lots of other part-time and short courses that can equip you for work in this field, so look at those and decide if that may be a better option. This might especially be the case for mature students or for those looking for a complete change of career.

All social workers (and social work students) are required to register with the General Social Care Council (GSCC) and abide by their codes of practice, and once you are qualified, you have to give evidence of a minimum level of continuing professional development (90 hours over three years) to maintain registration. Since April 2005 it has been illegal to describe yourself as a social worker if you are not qualified and registered with GSCC.

---

“ The first year of my social work degree has been challenging and thought-provoking. The lecturers are experienced practitioners who encourage creative thinking and further understanding. Social policy, values and ethics, and social theory have been of particular interest to me, and all of the lectures and seminars have been participatory and varied. It's been a fantastic introduction to university study. The first-year preparation for practice placement was inspiring and made me even more determined to qualify and become a social work practitioner.

**Emma Weston**, *first-year social work student, University of Kent*

---

**General Social Care Council**

Goldings House, 2 Hay's Lane
London SE1 2HB

t   020 7397 5100
↗  www.gscc.org.uk

**Scottish Social Services Council**

Compass House
11 Riverside Drive
Dundee DD1 4NY

t   01382 207101
e   enquiries@sssc.uk.com
↗  www.sssc.uk.com

**The Care Council For Wales**

6th Floor, South Gate House
Wood Street
Cardiff CF10 1EW

t   029 2022 6257
e   info@ccwales.org.uk
↗  www.ccwales.org.uk

**The Northern Ireland Social Care Council**

7th Floor, Millennium House
19-25 Great Victoria Street
Belfast BT2 7AQ

t   02890 417600
    textphone: 02890 239340
e   info@niscc.n-i.nhs.uk
↗  www.niscc.info

↗ Online reading

**SocietyGuardian.co.uk**  SocietyGuardian.co.uk
**British Association of Social Workers**  www.basw.co.uk
**Association of Directors of Adult Social Services**  www.adss.org.uk
**Social Care Association**  www.socialcareassociation.co.uk

# Social work

| | | Guardian score /100 | Satisfied with teaching % | Satisfied with feedback % | Spend per student /10 | Student:staff ratio | Job prospects % | Value added score /10 | Average entry tariff |
|---|---|---|---|---|---|---|---|---|---|
| 1 | York | 100.0 | 87 | 54 | 8 | 7.2 | | 8 | 350 |
| 2 | Southampton | 98.1 | 85 | 47 | 10 | 9.9 | | 7 | 347 |
| 3 | Leeds | 97.2 | 93 | 70 | 10 | 5.9 | 59 | 8 | 311 |
| 4 | Sheffield | 91.6 | 85 | 62 | 6 | 8.0 | | | 369 |
| 5 | Kent | 89.2 | 96 | 86 | 9 | 9.3 | 90 | 3 | 268 |
| 6 | Lancaster | 87.4 | 86 | 69 | 5 | 15.4 | | 10 | 268 |
| 7 | Anglia Ruskin | 86.8 | 83 | 62 | 8 | 4.4 | 79 | 7 | 250 |
| 7 | Glamorgan | 86.8 | 87 | 68 | 9 | 10.9 | | | 258 |
| 9 | Portsmouth | 86.2 | 80 | 61 | 6 | 11.6 | 83 | 10 | 235 |
| 10 | UEA | 85.9 | 92 | 72 | 5 | 19.4 | | 10 | 256 |
| 11 | Birmingham | 85.7 | 73 | 50 | 10 | 12.7 | 78 | 4 | 331 |
| 11 | Plymouth | 85.7 | 82 | 66 | 10 | 10.3 | 83 | 5 | 259 |
| 13 | Middlesex | 84.6 | 86 | 70 | 10 | 18.5 | 81 | 4 | |
| 14 | Strathclyde | 83.9 | 80 | 39 | 10 | 15.8 | 75 | | 314 |
| 15 | Goldsmiths | 83.6 | 92 | 73 | 3 | 5.9 | 80 | 6 | |
| 16 | Gloucestershire | 82.8 | 84 | 67 | 8 | 6.8 | 85 | 8 | 187 |
| 16 | Northumbria | 82.8 | 82 | 53 | 6 | 10.3 | 94 | 7 | 250 |
| 18 | Oxford Brookes | 81.1 | 94 | 79 | 3 | 20.7 | 87 | 8 | 279 |
| 19 | Dundee | 80.4 | 83 | 69 | 3 | | 95 | | 315 |
| 20 | Bristol | 80.2 | 54 | 37 | 8 | 11.7 | | 5 | 371 |
| 21 | Bournemouth | 79.3 | 80 | 66 | 9 | 14.0 | 91 | 5 | 236 |
| 22 | Central Lancashire | 79.0 | 83 | 68 | 10 | 13.8 | 84 | 5 | 180 |

| | | Guardian score /100 | Satisfied with teaching % | Satisfied with feedback % | Spend per student /10 | Student:staff ratio | Job prospects % | Value added score /10 | Average entry tariff |
|---|---|---|---|---|---|---|---|---|---|
| 23 | Queen's, Belfast | 77.9 | 88 | 62 | 3 | 18.6 | 92 | 6 | 341 |
| 24 | Sussex | 77.4 | 92 | 64 | 6 | 24.4 | 80 | 6 | |
| 25 | Teesside | 74.3 | 89 | 80 | 7 | 19.6 | 89 | 3 | 241 |
| 26 | Thames Valley | 73.9 | 82 | 73 | 8 | 9.7 | | 2 | 224 |
| 27 | Manchester | 73.0 | 78 | 45 | 5 | 15.5 | | | 317 |
| 28 | Chester | 72.9 | 88 | 71 | 2 | 11.7 | 84 | 5 | |
| 28 | Nottingham Trent | 72.9 | 80 | 57 | 5 | | 86 | 8 | 216 |
| 30 | Reading | 71.8 | 81 | 60 | 3 | 21.9 | 91 | 8 | 264 |
| 31 | Robert Gordon | 71.6 | | | 3 | 15.7 | 92 | 3 | 301 |
| 32 | Bradford | 71.3 | 62 | 57 | 4 | 18.8 | 83 | 9 | 282 |
| 33 | Brighton | 70.2 | 79 | 57 | 7 | 6.6 | 41 | 3 | 299 |
| 34 | Cumbria | 69.9 | 85 | 68 | 8 | 14.8 | 54 | 7 | 209 |
| 35 | Ulster | 68.9 | 78 | 45 | 4 | 20.2 | 84 | 7 | 274 |
| 36 | Sheffield Hallam | 68.5 | 74 | 50 | 4 | 11.3 | 73 | 8 | 210 |
| 37 | UWE Bristol | 68.0 | 84 | 53 | 3 | 23.3 | 98 | 7 | 247 |
| 38 | Marjon (St Mark and St John) | 67.7 | 90 | 78 | 2 | 13.3 | 78 | 5 | |
| 39 | London South Bank | 67.1 | 83 | 50 | 4 | | 78 | 4 | |
| 40 | Salford | 66.9 | 71 | 48 | 5 | 15.7 | 78 | 5 | 271 |
| 41 | Chichester | 66.8 | 88 | 70 | 3 | 16.6 | 65 | 7 | 246 |
| 42 | Manchester Met | 66.7 | 75 | 67 | 4 | 15.4 | 88 | 6 | 207 |
| 43 | De Montfort | 66.6 | 76 | 63 | 3 | 16.8 | 96 | 5 | 209 |
| 44 | Bedfordshire | 66.1 | 91 | 73 | 4 | 17.8 | 83 | 6 | 159 |
| 45 | Kingston | 65.5 | 89 | 71 | 3 | 18.8 | 73 | 9 | 200 |
| 45 | Southampton Solent | 65.5 | 81 | 78 | 4 | 12.6 | 81 | 2 | 255 |
| 47 | Brunel | 64.6 | 63 | 37 | 5 | 12.7 | 69 | 4 | |
| 47 | Leeds Met | 64.6 | 76 | 55 | 6 | 18.4 | 57 | 7 | 241 |
| 49 | Worcester | 64.1 | 86 | 74 | 6 | 16.0 | | 5 | 151 |
| 50 | UWIC | 64.0 | 88 | 75 | 4 | 18.3 | 93 | 2 | 202 |
| 51 | Edinburgh | 63.7 | 80 | 41 | 7 | 26.7 | | 2 | 350 |
| 52 | Lincoln | 63.3 | 80 | 69 | 3 | 19.2 | 82 | 6 | 212 |
| 53 | Northampton | 62.7 | 70 | 57 | 3 | | | 9 | 214 |
| 54 | Huddersfield | 62.5 | 80 | 64 | 4 | 15.8 | 68 | 4 | 231 |
| 55 | Hull | 61.8 | 79 | 51 | 4 | 21.4 | 90 | 3 | 260 |
| 56 | Birmingham City | 60.8 | 46 | 51 | 3 | 24.3 | 82 | 10 | 244 |
| 57 | Sunderland | 60.6 | 85 | 73 | 5 | 24.3 | 67 | 6 | 211 |
| 58 | Staffordshire | 60.5 | 77 | 68 | 5 | 29.2 | 88 | 6 | 206 |
| 59 | Hertfordshire | 60.0 | 67 | 46 | 4 | 15.9 | 94 | 4 | 196 |
| 60 | Royal Holloway | 59.8 | 63 | 42 | 3 | 21.1 | | 6 | |
| 61 | East London | 59.7 | 81 | 61 | 4 | | 66 | 7 | 128 |
| 62 | Winchester | 58.3 | | | 3 | 7.0 | 42 | 3 | 206 |
| 63 | Glyndwr | 57.9 | 79 | 67 | 3 | 19.4 | 73 | 6 | |
| 64 | Liverpool John Moores | 57.1 | 79 | 63 | 7 | 8.4 | 59 | 1 | 208 |
| 65 | Bangor | 54.6 | 72 | 55 | 3 | 22.4 | | | 217 |
| 66 | Newport | 52.7 | 84 | 75 | 3 | | 54 | 4 | 196 |
| 67 | Coventry | 51.2 | 82 | 66 | 3 | 37.2 | 78 | 6 | 241 |
| 68 | Bucks New University | 51.1 | 84 | 61 | 3 | 23.1 | | 3 | |
| 69 | Canterbury Christ Church | 50.0 | 68 | 56 | 3 | 19.3 | 51 | 6 | 210 |
| 70 | Edge Hill | 47.6 | 87 | 76 | 4 | 10.9 | 17 | 2 | 193 |
| 71 | Derby | 47.2 | 72 | 62 | 3 | 22.3 | | 4 | 163 |
| 72 | Greenwich | 47.1 | 62 | 49 | 3 | 20.0 | 73 | 2 | 191 |
| 73 | Roehampton | 35.0 | 82 | 64 | 3 | 24.4 | 33 | 1 | 196 |

# Sociology

❝ Sociology is an exciting and challenging subject that enables students to cultivate a critical approach which takes account of the socio-cultural forces, contexts, and processes that significantly inform individuals' ways of living, group relations, and social institutions in contemporary society. Through studying diverse theories, wide-ranging socio-cultural and geopolitical issues, as well as sophisticated quantitative and qualitative research methods, sociology offers students the knowledge and employable skills to question the familiar, the normative, and the commonsensical. It expands students' horizons in understanding the intricate relationships between individuals and social systems and processes, and the complexity and diversity of social life with its divisions, inequalities, and potential for progressive change. Such engagement equips students with a 'sociological imagination' and important life skills that enable them to live meaningfully as individuals and citizens in an increasingly globalised world.

**Dr Andrew Yip**, *School of Sociology and Social Policy, University of Nottingham*

Sociology's resurgence is due in part to its ability to reinvent itself and broaden its scope of study. The degree is still, essentially, concerned with the way society works, and the way social behaviour and relations and social structures and institutions affect and define people's lives, but more attention is now being paid to what you can study on the fringes of the course.

You'll be introduced to a range of conceptual frameworks, as well as studying issues of social theory, key themes of social change (urbanisation, industrialisation, modernity, postmodernity, globalisation), and social identities and structures. Chances are, you'll also cover the so-called canon of social theory – the birth of sociology and famous historical works of social analysis.

It is important and interesting to look at how people started to formalise social enquiry – to think about what kind of thing "society" is, to ask whether it has coherent rules of organisation, and to consider how we can learn about it.

Some degrees will introduce discussion under the broad area of inequalities – analysing the formation and impact of class, race, and gender. A few places will add consideration of sexuality and sexual identity, religion or youth culture. Related to these debates, there may be consideration of changing local, regional, and national identities – and a larger discussion of how we place ourselves in world. You may also cover social activity – areas such as work, leisure and family, consumption, technology, media, and culture.

Sociology graduates tend to go into social work, teaching, local government, or the civil service, but their analytical skills also come in useful for careers in personnel, marketing, and journalism.

Sociology courses are now much more varied than they once were. One big question is how much quantitative sociology you are prepared to do. This can involve a fair amount of statistics and number crunching, so it doesn't suit all students to have this as a compulsory element.

Furthermore, decide whether you want a more traditional course that centres on theory, or a more applied course, which teaches primarily contemporary issues. You can also find courses that concentrate on a specific area — taking a whole degree on crime and society is now possible and such courses are popular. Alternatively, you could choose one with a modular structure that allows you to change focus.

A bolder option would be to pick a joint honours degree; combinations with media studies, sociology or psychology are popular examples. Be aware, though, that this can be a greater commitment — joint honours schools often require higher grades and demand more of students attempting to integrate different disciplinary traditions. Finally, take a careful look at how the course is assessed and choose one that will suit your strengths. Formal exams, coursework, and dissertation can all play a part, just make sure the balance is in line with the way you prefer to work.

And, as with many courses, check the research specialisations of the university teaching staff. If you're being taught by those who are at the leading edge of research in your subject, it can be rewarding and you'll learn a heck of a lot more. The downside could be that some of them might have less time to teach you, so do investigate.

---

> ❝ I am one of those people who didn't set out to major in sociology, but due to great tutors and the very friendly atmosphere of the department, I discovered my true passion. The department gives students the chance to learn about what they are interested in by offering advanced seminars and the feeling of community through contact with PhD students and members of staff.
>
> **Diana Stypinska**, *second-year sociology student, Lancaster University*

---

## ⟩⟩ Further information

### The British Sociological Association
Bailey Suite, Palatine House
Belmont Business Park
Durham DH1 1TW

t  0191 383 0839
e  enquiries@britsoc.co.uk
↗ www.britsoc.co.uk

### The Socio-Legal Studies Association
SLSA Chair, School of Law
Queen's University Belfast
Belfast BT7 1NN

t  0289 097 3468
↗ www.slsa.ac.uk

## ↗ Online reading

**SocietyGuardian.co.uk** SocietyGuardian.co.uk
**Sociology Central** www.sociology.org.uk
**Intute: Social Sciences** www.intute.ac.uk/socialsciences
**The British Sociology Journal** www.lse.ac.uk/serials/bjs
**Internet Sociologist** www.vts.rdn.ac.uk/tutorial/sociologist

# Sociology

| | | Guardian score /100 | Satisfied with teaching % | Satisfied with feedback % | Spend per student /10 | Student:staff ratio | Job prospects % | Value added score /10 | Average entry tariff |
|---|---|---|---|---|---|---|---|---|---|
| 1 | Cambridge | 100.0 | 95 | 70 | 10 | 15.5 | 80 | 8 | 498 |
| 2 | Warwick | 81.7 | 88 | 76 | 10 | 15.1 | 70 | 7 | 409 |
| 3 | Edinburgh | 77.0 | 81 | 42 | 10 | 14.2 | 48 | 9 | 432 |
| 4 | Birmingham | 76.3 | 89 | 65 | 10 | 17.8 | 53 | 8 | 355 |
| 5 | Sussex | 71.7 | 90 | 65 | 4 | 19.6 | 62 | 10 | 370 |
| 6 | Bristol | 70.4 | 90 | 51 | 8 | 18.5 | 69 | 6 | 391 |
| 7 | Bath | 69.4 | 86 | 58 | 7 | 16.9 | 71 | 7 | 342 |
| 8 | Glasgow | 69.2 | 85 | 61 | 6 | 15.6 | 56 | 9 | 409 |
| 9 | Durham | 67.3 | 87 | 63 | 7 | 17.9 | 55 | 7 | 406 |
| 10 | Loughborough | 65.8 | 94 | 80 | 6 | 22.9 | 54 | 6 | 358 |
| 11 | London School of Economics | 65.5 | 73 | 58 | 9 | 13.0 | | 7 | 398 |
| 12 | Cardiff | 65.1 | 89 | 51 | 9 | 17.4 | 48 | 8 | 349 |
| 13 | Lancaster | 64.5 | 87 | 66 | 8 | 15.4 | 44 | 7 | 357 |
| 14 | Surrey | 63.9 | 88 | 67 | 7 | 23.0 | 64 | 8 | 324 |
| 15 | Exeter | 63.3 | 87 | 60 | 4 | 15.9 | 54 | 9 | 356 |
| 16 | Leeds | 62.3 | 92 | 61 | 6 | 20.8 | 52 | 8 | 356 |
| 17 | Nottingham Trent | 62.2 | 84 | 64 | 8 | 15.9 | 63 | 7 | 250 |
| 18 | Essex | 61.6 | 85 | 76 | 6 | 14.8 | 65 | 3 | 311 |
| 19 | York | 61.5 | 91 | 54 | 9 | 14.0 | 41 | 5 | 333 |
| 20 | Nottingham | 60.8 | 84 | 54 | 7 | 16.7 | 61 | 5 | 322 |
| 21 | Brunel | 60.1 | 86 | 66 | 4 | 20.9 | | 10 | 285 |
| 22 | Aston | 59.3 | 90 | 56 | 3 | 20.5 | 55 | 9 | 328 |
| 23 | Manchester | 58.2 | 84 | 56 | 8 | 19.7 | 39 | 8 | 369 |
| 24 | Northumbria | 58.0 | 88 | 67 | 6 | 25.4 | 56 | 9 | 261 |
| 25 | Edinburgh Napier | 57.2 | | | 5 | 20.7 | 51 | 8 | 296 |
| 25 | Strathclyde | 57.2 | 82 | 58 | 9 | 25.6 | | | 365 |
| 27 | Liverpool | 56.4 | 87 | 63 | 7 | 19.9 | 47 | 5 | 334 |
| 28 | Glasgow Caledonian | 56.3 | 94 | 79 | 4 | 27.7 | 42 | 9 | 297 |
| 29 | Portsmouth | 56.2 | 96 | 65 | 7 | 16.7 | 52 | 3 | 283 |
| 30 | Sheffield | 56.1 | 77 | 54 | 5 | 22.5 | 60 | 8 | 361 |
| 31 | City | 56.0 | 79 | 64 | 7 | 17.3 | 54 | 6 | 271 |
| 31 | Robert Gordon | 56.0 | | | 5 | 20.3 | 58 | 5 | 302 |
| 33 | Oxford Brookes | 55.9 | 84 | 71 | 7 | 19.7 | 45 | 7 | 309 |
| 34 | Keele | 55.7 | 85 | 69 | 5 | 16.3 | 52 | 4 | 317 |
| 35 | Southampton | 55.6 | 81 | 65 | 6 | 18.6 | 48 | 6 | 341 |
| 36 | Hull | 55.5 | 86 | 71 | 4 | 16.6 | 52 | 6 | 261 |
| 37 | Staffordshire | 54.8 | 86 | 64 | 6 | 20.0 | 49 | 8 | 234 |
| 38 | Stirling | 54.1 | 89 | 66 | 5 | 18.0 | 61 | 2 | |
| 39 | Sheffield Hallam | 53.0 | 83 | 61 | 6 | 19.9 | 44 | 9 | 239 |
| 40 | Kent | 52.4 | 87 | 66 | 6 | 16.7 | 52 | 2 | 282 |
| 41 | Worcester | 52.3 | 92 | 77 | 3 | 18.4 | | 5 | 264 |
| 42 | Gloucestershire | 52.2 | 82 | 77 | 5 | 26.5 | | 8 | 231 |
| 43 | Bath Spa | 51.5 | 84 | 77 | 1 | 16.8 | 45 | 7 | 275 |
| 44 | Edge Hill | 51.4 | 86 | 76 | 3 | 20.6 | | | 265 |
| 45 | Aberdeen | 51.2 | 94 | 80 | 4 | 23.3 | 39 | 3 | 323 |
| 46 | Goldsmiths | 50.6 | 82 | 55 | 4 | 14.3 | 60 | 2 | 274 |
| 47 | Chester | 50.5 | 84 | 63 | 3 | 24.1 | 55 | 7 | 253 |

| | Guardian score /100 | Satisfied with teaching % | Satisfied with feedback % | Spend per student /10 | Student-staff ratio | Job prospects % | Value added score /10 | Average entry tariff |
|---|---|---|---|---|---|---|---|---|
| 48 St Mary's UC, Twickenham | 49.8 | 91 | 79 | 1 | 18.4 | | 9 | 214 |
| 49 Bradford | 49.5 | 77 | 63 | 7 | 12.8 | | 5 | 185 |
| 50 Glamorgan | 49.1 | 87 | 71 | 4 | 21.9 | | 8 | 212 |
| 51 Newcastle | 48.1 | 80 | 61 | 6 | 22.6 | 54 | 2 | 349 |
| 52 East London | 47.5 | 84 | 75 | 7 | 18.1 | 36 | 4 | |
| 52 UEA | 47.5 | 88 | 79 | 4 | 27.9 | 41 | 4 | 307 |
| 54 Bedfordshire | 46.8 | 87 | 74 | 4 | 13.5 | 54 | 2 | 219 |
| 55 Queen's, Belfast | 45.9 | 85 | 63 | 6 | 18.1 | 48 | 1 | 325 |
| 56 Lincoln | 45.7 | 91 | 76 | 2 | 27.9 | 51 | 7 | 257 |
| 57 Anglia Ruskin | 45.5 | 89 | 64 | 7 | 30.5 | | 4 | 237 |
| 58 Coventry | 45.4 | 85 | 68 | 7 | 22.9 | 38 | 4 | 251 |
| 59 Salford | 44.6 | 89 | 78 | 4 | 23.7 | 52 | 2 | 246 |
| 60 Teesside | 44.3 | 83 | 71 | 5 | 27.6 | 43 | 7 | 230 |
| 61 Bangor | 44.2 | 84 | 66 | 4 | 22.4 | 42 | 5 | 259 |
| 61 Central Lancashire | 44.2 | 86 | 65 | 6 | 28.5 | 54 | 2 | 242 |
| 63 Plymouth | 44.0 | 80 | 53 | 6 | 18.2 | 32 | 6 | 257 |
| 64 Birmingham City | 43.6 | 85 | 67 | 6 | 18.5 | 31 | 3 | 243 |
| 65 Sunderland | 43.0 | 85 | 67 | 8 | 28.5 | 38 | 5 | 222 |
| 66 Derby | 42.2 | 91 | 78 | 4 | 24.2 | | 1 | 234 |
| 67 Westminster | 42.1 | 81 | 64 | 4 | 19.7 | 36 | 5 | 224 |
| 68 Ulster | 41.7 | 79 | 73 | 4 | 19.0 | 32 | 3 | 259 |
| 69 Leeds Met | 40.6 | 79 | 61 | | 21.8 | 33 | 2 | 237 |
| 70 Southampton Solent | 40.2 | 89 | 62 | 4 | 22.5 | 33 | 4 | 232 |
| 71 Canterbury Christ Church | 39.6 | 90 | 75 | 2 | 25.3 | 44 | 3 | 233 |
| 72 Manchester Met | 39.4 | 73 | 58 | 3 | 21.4 | 40 | 7 | 246 |
| 73 Northampton | 39.2 | 77 | 65 | 4 | 27.4 | | 7 | 238 |
| 74 Roehampton | 38.9 | 76 | 50 | 4 | 23.5 | 36 | 6 | 233 |
| 74 UWE Bristol | 38.9 | 87 | 67 | 4 | 20.9 | 22 | 4 | 244 |
| 76 Kingston | 38.4 | 80 | 57 | 3 | 27.0 | 45 | 6 | 220 |
| 77 Huddersfield | 37.6 | 82 | 67 | 3 | 28.1 | | | 218 |
| 78 Abertay Dundee | 33.5 | | | 4 | 36.3 | 35 | 5 | 273 |
| 79 Greenwich | 33.0 | 83 | 69 | 3 | 28.3 | 38 | 3 | 203 |
| 80 London South Bank | 31.8 | 84 | 65 | 2 | 39.8 | 53 | 6 | 172 |
| 81 Bucks New University | 30.1 | 84 | 60 | 3 | 27.2 | 43 | 1 | 210 |
| 82 Brighton | 29.3 | 79 | 57 | 3 | 40.4 | 42 | 4 | 286 |
| 83 Middlesex | 28.1 | 81 | 51 | 5 | 37.8 | 42 | 4 | 161 |
| 84 Liverpool John Moores | 26.1 | 78 | 62 | 3 | 27.7 | 35 | 1 | 218 |

# Tourism and leisure management

> Tourism is a people industry. It's the world's largest industry, and its range is vast both on the supply side and the demand. It is global in reach and if properly managed offers destinations — both in developed and developing countries — a route to economic growth. It offers graduates career opportunities in all parts of the world in many different arenas, both in the private and public sectors.
>
> How many disciplines offer such a wide range of careers, with employers such as tour operators and travel agents, tourist attractions and transport providers, the accommodation sector, national and regional tourist boards, local authorities, the education sector, and the not-for-profit sector? How many disciplines allow the graduate to work with such a diverse range of consumers as leisure visitors, business tourists, conference and incentive travel consumers, and those visiting friends and relatives, to name just a few?
>
> Tourism is the world's fastest growing industry, it is diverse, vibrant, and exciting, and, above all, it needs new young professionals, well trained and skilled, with good business acumen and management capabilities.
>
> However, tourism needs professionals for another reason — its ability to harm our planet. No other industry has such an impact on our environment, the economic balance of our world, and the social and cultural lives of communities touched by tourism. Tomorrow's world needs people with the skills to manage tourism responsibly, to guarantee sustainability for the industry, and to make sure the benefits from tourism are shared.
>
> Tourism students graduate having had an exciting, enjoyable, and educational experience and are vocationally desirable, with good transferable management skills to enter the global tourism industry.
>
> **Greig Headley,** *Tourism Undergraduate Programme Leader, Leeds Metropolitan University*

Tourism and leisure management is a relatively new course to British universities. It is more likely to be found in former polytechnics and further education colleges than in the more traditional universities, but as the industry grows, so it demands increased professionalism, and with that comes a need for graduates.

The tourism industry is now widely recognised as the world's largest and its growth is creating rapid social, economic, and environmental changes across the globe, which require detailed understanding and measures to manage them.

As a subject, tourism isn't just concerned with how the masses flood towards the Costa del Sol. It has much wider concerns, beyond the developed world, and often looks instead at its global impact.

You'll study how people journey to their destination, how people choose where to go, and what they do when they are there. You'll gain an understanding of how people travel and how that interaction gives rise to changes in society, the economy, and the environment on a global scale.

Leisure management courses cover more practical areas, as befits a vocational degree. In a typical degree, you'll be able to study human resource management, accountancy, computing, and marketing. From there, you can specialise in the specific study of operational issues alongside courses related to strategic development. You might, for example, study topics in tourism and the environment, heritage, public and private sector leisure management or leisure and special needs.

As with many vocational courses, there is always the sandwich option, whereby you can spend a year working in a part of the tourism industry, or else the possibility of a shorter period of work experience. Either is invaluable – experience is key to finding the right kind of future employment: it both impresses your future bosses and gives you a far better idea of the areas you might want to work in. Some courses, international hotel management, for example, have foreign travel as an integral part of the course.

Graduates can look forward to careers with transport providers (airlines, ferry operators), tour operators, hotels, government tourism organisations, travel agents, leisure developments and not-for-profit organisations such as the National Trust. There are also possibilities in sports centre management, both private and public, and a relatively large number head off for teacher training courses each year.

In the tourism and leisure industries, there are a number of professional bodies that validate courses. Graduates of those courses are then entitled to membership of the body and thus professional status. If you're treating this as a vocational degree, then check that the appropriate bodies (the Tourism Society or the Institute of Travel, for example) validate the course. It could save a lot of bother later.

And check the nature of the study. Some courses demand a dissertation, and it can come as a shock to those who think they have opted for a work-based qualification to find that they have to undergo such an academic test. Such things are not for everyone. Similarly, the methods of assessment vary widely – from end-of-term exams to projects to continuous assessment. These all tend to prompt different stress patterns, so work out which is right for you.

Make sure a degree course is best suited to your needs. Many higher education and further education colleges offer excellent higher national diplomas (HNDs) which are usually two-year courses when taken full-time or can be done part-time when you're already working. Think hard – and talk to your careers advisers – before you take on a full degree course.

---

66 My favourite part of the course so far has been the fieldtrip to Majorca. Not only did I have an amazing time, but I learnt so much by putting the theory learnt in lectures into practice. My placement year has already proved invaluable, teaching me lots about the working world. I have learnt skills that you could never learn doing a straight degree, particularly with computer programs and also about professional behaviour, how to act with colleagues and outside organisations.

**Amanda Colbran**, *final-year tourism management student, University of Surrey*

---

» Further information

**Institute of Travel and Tourism**
PO Box 217, Ware
Herts SG12 8WY
t 0844 499 5653
e enquiries@itt.co.uk
↗ www.itt.co.uk

**Visit Britain**
Thames Tower, Blacks Road
Hammersmith, London W6 9EL
t 020 8846 9000
↗ www.visitbritain.com

**Tourism Management Institute**
41 Charlton Street
London NW1 1JD
t 01926 641 506
↗ www.tmi.org.uk

**Tourism Concern**
Stapleton House
277-81 Holloway Road
London N7 8HN
t 020 7133 3800
e info@tourismconcern.org.uk
↗ www.tourismconcern.org.uk

## Tourism, transport and travel

| | | Guardian score /100 | Satisfied with teaching % | Satisfied with feedback % | Spend per student /10 | Student:staff ratio | Job prospects % | Value added score /10 | Average entry tariff |
|---|---|---|---|---|---|---|---|---|---|
| 1 | Surrey | 100.0 | 85 | 79 | 8 | 22.3 | 58 | 8 | 333 |
| 2 | Bournemouth | 87.2 | 82 | 66 | | 12.2 | 65 | 6 | 266 |
| 3 | Sunderland | 86.3 | 76 | 76 | 10 | 11.8 | | 7 | 228 |
| 4 | Robert Gordon | 79.3 | | | 5 | 17.4 | 59 | 7 | 275 |
| 5 | Edinburgh Napier | 78.6 | | | 3 | 28.9 | 47 | 10 | 274 |
| 6 | Brighton | 77.4 | 81 | 71 | 9 | 11.1 | 49 | 4 | 231 |
| 7 | Plymouth | 70.9 | 88 | 69 | 10 | 17.7 | 35 | 4 | 231 |
| 8 | Oxford Brookes | 69.3 | 82 | 62 | 7 | 24.4 | | 8 | 271 |
| 9 | Gloucestershire | 66.2 | 79 | 60 | 8 | 16.9 | 52 | 6 | 222 |
| 10 | Central Lancashire | 65.2 | 90 | 78 | 8 | 27.7 | 60 | 3 | 229 |
| 11 | Ulster | 63.7 | 78 | 65 | 7 | 11.9 | 21 | 8 | 243 |
| 12 | Glasgow Caledonian | 60.7 | 78 | 56 | 5 | 26.3 | 43 | 7 | 301 |
| 13 | Manchester Met | 57.4 | 68 | 58 | 5 | 21.2 | | 8 | 250 |
| 14 | St Mary's UC, Twickenham | 56.0 | 86 | 75 | 3 | 18.6 | | | 204 |
| 15 | Hertfordshire | 55.2 | 82 | 60 | 7 | 24.2 | 47 | 4 | 227 |
| 16 | Sheffield Hallam | 54.4 | 84 | 73 | 4 | 30.9 | 43 | 8 | 236 |
| 17 | Bath Spa | 54.0 | 90 | 81 | 3 | 25.7 | | | 228 |
| 18 | Lincoln | 52.5 | 82 | 74 | 2 | 23.8 | | 7 | 220 |
| 19 | London South Bank | 51.8 | 77 | 55 | | 4.3 | | 3 | 166 |

| | | Guardian score /100 | Satisfied with teaching % | Satisfied with feedback % | Spend per student /10 | Student:staff ratio | Job prospects % | Value added score /10 | Average entry tariff |
|---|---|---|---|---|---|---|---|---|---|
| 20 | Portsmouth | 50.8 | 85 | 66 | 5 | 25.5 | | 4 | 240 |
| 21 | Derby | 50.4 | 77 | 63 | 7 | 18.9 | 30 | 4 | 228 |
| 22 | Queen Margaret | 50.1 | | | 2 | | 35 | 3 | 304 |
| 23 | Huddersfield | 48.2 | 72 | 78 | 7 | 18.8 | | 1 | 235 |
| 24 | Leeds Met | 41.7 | 69 | 39 | 5 | 35.4 | 54 | 5 | 252 |
| 25 | Thames Valley | 38.9 | 77 | 72 | 5 | 15.3 | 32 | 4 | 160 |
| 26 | Bedfordshire | 37.7 | 61 | 58 | 3 | 17.7 | | 6 | |
| 27 | Salford | 34.1 | 81 | 71 | 4 | 24.6 | 18 | 4 | 207 |
| 28 | Greenwich | 33.2 | 69 | 51 | 4 | 26.7 | 42 | 4 | 205 |
| 29 | Liverpool John Moores | 31.5 | 73 | 64 | 4 | 27.5 | 47 | 3 | 175 |
| 30 | University College Birmingham | 28.9 | 77 | 69 | 2 | 25.7 | 30 | 3 | 219 |

# University
# profiles

# Reading the profiles

What follows are short introductions to more than 150 universities and higher education institutions to help you as you take your first steps towards that all-important selection. This book would be too heavy to lift – and far too long to read – if we tried to include exhaustive information on every place. What we provide here is merely a taster, so if something appeals do follow the links to that university's website or drop them an email (contact details are included in our profiles): they'll be happy to do all they can to convince you to give them a whirl.

But in the meantime, with universities from the north of Scotland to the southern tip of England just waiting to welcome you as a potential student, you should get cracking with the job of sifting through them. Enjoy it! And here are a few notes on the profiles to keep things clear …

## Accommodation

Usually when we say that accommodation is guaranteed, we mean for young, full-time undergraduates who apply during the normal admissions cycle (rather than through Clearing, say) accept an offer and get their forms in by the deadline. Though often the criteria are much less stringent than that: check with the accommodation offices for exact details.

## Prices

Prices (for accommodation, for example) are generally provided by the university and refer to 2009-10, unless otherwise stated. Bear in mind that a slight rise should be expected for your year of entry. And the cost of university accommodation usually refers to a room in halls, including utility bills. Where private accommodation prices are mentioned, they usually refer to sharing a house or flat and don't include bills.

## Statistics

Stats included in the profiles have typically been supplied by the university in question and are the most recent available.

## Fees

Unless otherwise stated, the fees quoted here are for full-time home or EU students and refer to courses beginning in 2009-10 – for the very good reason that at the time of researching and writing this book the fees for entry in 2010-11 hadn't been set. Check with the university for the most up-to-date figure and expect a rise on this year. (To give you an idea of how much, the increase from 2008-09 to 2009-10 was from £3,145 to £3,225 – £80.)

## Bursaries

Bursaries are non-repayable awards, typically aimed at full-time UK undergraduates. Universities charging the maximum fee must offer some level of bursary support to any student who qualifies for the full maintenance grant or special support grant. But many institutions offer awards well beyond the statutory requirement and to students on less than full grants, too.

As with fees, most bursary packages have yet to be finalised: details here generally refer to 2009-10.

And in the case of bursaries and financial support, it really is worth doing plenty of your own research. We can only give a summary here, not a comprehensive run-down of what's available, so make sure you take a look at the relevant sections of the website or prospectus of any university you are interested in.

### » Useful websites

**Ucas** www.ucas.com

**Aim Higher** www.direct.gov.uk/uni

**Department for Business, Innovation and Skills** www.dcsf.gov.uk/studentsupport

**Student Awards Agency for Scotland** www.student-support-saas.gov.uk

**Department for Employment and Learning Northern Ireland** www.delni.gov.uk

**Student Finance Northern Ireland** www.studentfinanceni.co.uk

**Student Finance Wales** www.studentfinancewales.co.uk

**Training and Development Agency for Schools** www.tda.gov.uk

**National Union of Students** www.nusonline.co.uk

**Union of Students in Ireland** www.nistudents.org

**Office for Fair Access** www.offa.org.uk

### Note on the University of London

The colleges and institutes of this federal university are bound together by the prestigious London degree. As far as central facilities go, students have access to the University of London Union (ULU), some student accommodation in intercollegiate halls and some central sporting facilities. Teaching and social events are collegiate.

The following colleges and schools have individual profiles: Birkbeck, Central School of Speech and Drama, Courtauld Institute of Art, Goldsmiths, King's College London, London School of Economics and Political Science, Queen Mary, Royal Academy of Music, Royal Holloway, Royal Veterinary College, St George's, School of Pharmacy, Soas, University College London. Other specialist colleges, institutes and schools that also belong to the University of London: Heythrop College, Institute of Education, London Business School, London School of Hygiene and Tropical Medicine.

## Note on the University of Wales/Prifysgol Cymru

The University of Wales/Prifysgol Cymru is a large federal university. It was founded by Royal Charter in 1893, bringing together the aims and aspirations of three existing colleges in Aberystwyth, South Wales and Monmouthshire, and Bangor.

The following institutions award University of Wales degrees: Aberystwyth; Bangor; Glyndŵr, University of Wales; Lampeter; University of Wales, Newport; Swansea; Swansea Metropolitan University; Trinity University College; and University of Wales Institute, Cardiff (UWIC). These institutions all have separate profiles in the guide.

Degrees of the University of Wales are also offered in certain subjects at Cardiff University and the Royal Welsh College of Music and Drama (also profiled separately), as well as other HE institutions in the rest of the UK and overseas.

---

### Key to symbols

The following statistics (in each profile) are drawn from the 2006–07 Higher Education Statistics Agency (Hesa) performance indicators, the most recent publicly available (www.hesa.ac.uk):

 Total number of full-time, first-time degree entrants

 The percentage of entrants from state schools or colleges

 The percentage of young full-time first degree entrants from NS-SEC classes 4, 5, 6 and 7 (the lowest four socio-economic classes in the data)

 Non-continuation rates, as a percentage: the projected outcomes for full-time students starting first degree courses in 2005–06

 Graduate employment rates: these refer to leavers obtaining degrees from full-time courses in 2006–07. The employment indicator is based on the new Destinations of Leavers in Higher Education (DLHE) survey. It expresses the number of graduates who say they are working and/or studying as a percentage of all those who are working, or studying or seeking work, six months after graduation

---

The profiles also include an (anonymous!) quote from a current student or recent graduate, to give you a tiny flavour of a "real" experience. So they'll be subjective, biased and unreliable. They may just be right, though! And there's only one way for you to find out …

# London institutions

1. University of the Arts London
2. Birkbeck, University of London
3. Brunel University
4. Central School of Speech and Drama
5. City University London
6. Conservatoire for Dance and Drama
7. Courtauld Institute of Art
8. University of East London
9. Goldsmiths, University of London
10. University of Greenwich
11. Heythrop College
12. Imperial College London
13. King's College London
14. Kingston University
15. London Metropolitan University
16. London School of Economics
17. London South Bank University
18. Middlesex University
19. Queen Mary, University of London
20. Roehampton University
21. Rose Bruford College
22. Royal Academy of Music
23. Royal College of Music, London
24. Royal Holloway, University of London
25. Royal Veterinary College, University of London
26. St George's, University of London
27. St Mary's University College, Twickenham
28. School of Oriental and African Studies (Soas)
29. School of Pharmacy, University of London
30. Thames Valley University
31. Trinity Laban
32. University College London
33. University of Westminster

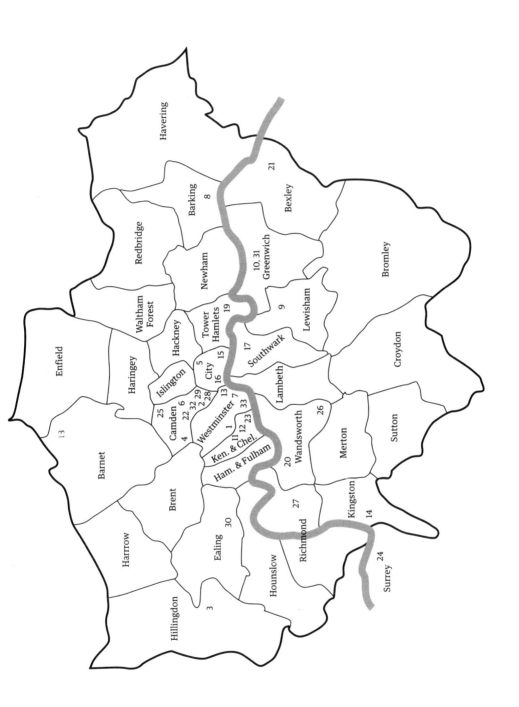

Havering

Barking 8

Bexley 21

Redbridge

Greenwich 10, 31

Newham

Waltham Forest

Bromley

Tower Hamlets 19

Hackney

Haringey

Lewisham 9

Enfield

Islington

City 5

Southwark 17

Croydon

16

13

2, 28

29

Lambeth

25

22 6

Camden

32

Westminster

Wandsworth 26

Barnet

4

1

Ken. & Chel. 11 12 23 33

7

Merton

Sutton

Brent

20

Ham. & Fulham

Harrow

Ealing 30

Kingston

14

Hounslow

Richmond 27

Hillingdon 3

Surrey 24

# University of Aberdeen

University Office
King's College
Aberdeen  AB24 3FX

**t**  01224 272090/91
**e**  sras@abdn.ac.uk
↗  www.abdn.ac.uk/sras

**》 further links**

ACCOMMODATION  www.abdn.ac.uk/accommodation
STUDENTS' UNION  www.ausa.org.uk

Aberdeen

| 2105 | 81.8 | 25.3 | 14.9 | 96.5 |

Aberdeen is an ancient university with a strong academic reputation. Its picturesque 15th-century King's College campus lies just 20 minutes' walk out of the city centre. The university is investing £230m in new facilities – a library, student centre and sports village, for starters. Aberdeen (or the Granite City, after the rock it is built of) is a charming, student-friendly city with plenty of good pubs.

**Fees**  Scottish and EU students pay no tuition fees. For other UK students, annual tuition fees are £1,820 in 2008–09 (£2,895 for medicine).

**Bursaries**  There is a wide range of scholarships available.
See abdn.ac.uk/sras/undergraduate/bursaries

**Accommodation**  Guaranteed for all new first-year students. Weekly prices range from £72 to £103 for self-catering accommodation, and from £116 to £137 for catered halls. The university has invested £20m in new accommodation.

**Facilities**  There's a big focus on keeping the library (one of the largest and best-equipped in Scotland) and computing facilities state-of-the-art, and Aberdeen is especially proud of its museum collections. A £28m sports centre is due to open in 2009 and a new library in 2011.

**Transport**  There's an airport, a station that connects directly to Edinburgh and London, and plenty of good road links. It's an easy stroll or quick bus ride from the university into town. See abdn.ac.uk/central/vcampus/

**❝ STUDENT VIEW ❞**
*"My time at Aberdeen has been fantastic. The campus is beautiful, facilities first-rate and my lecturers are both approachable and leaders in their field."*

# University of Abertay Dundee

40 Bell Street
Dundee DD1 1HG

**t** 01382 308080
**e** sro@abertay.ac.uk
**↗** www.abertay.ac.uk

**»» further links**

ACCOMMODATION accommo@abertay.ac.uk
STUDENTS' UNION www.abertaystudents.com

960    96.8    36.9    15.4    93.3

Dundee

---

You could never accuse Abertay of being stuck in the past. It offers world-leading courses in computer arts and computer games technology, has some of the best IT facilities in the UK and, in 2009, was accredited as the first UK centre of excellence for computer games education. In recent years, Abertay has built a new library and a student centre with cinema, coffee shop, nightclub and exhibition space. Dundee itself is a bustling, hard-working city, the fourth largest in Scotland and also, apparently, the warmest, thanks to its south-facing aspect. There are good local arts scenes, with a particularly good track record in music.

**Fees** Fees for all undergraduate courses are £1,820 for new students in 2009-10. Scottish students have their fees paid for them.

**Bursaries** Means-tested hardship fund, with an average payout of £1,000. Another similar fund for mature students. Other scholarships and bursaries available.

**Accommodation** Priority is given to first-year students and the accommodation office can help to find private rooms. A new development of 500 rooms is currently under way, due for completion August 2010. Average rent is about £65 a week.

**Facilities** A higher rate of PCs to students than almost any other university. There are new teaching facilities and the brand new student centre, too.

**Transport** The campus is right in the city centre, so short walks will take you most places you want to be. Dundee is 90 minutes by train from Glasgow and an hour from Edinburgh. There's an airport with direct links to London.

**‹‹ STUDENT VIEW ››**

*"The lecturers at Abertay are extremely enthusiastic, which really helps bring out the best in the students and the real-world working environments are a great advantage when you go on to apply for jobs."*

# Aberystwyth, University of Wales

Old College, King Street
Aberystwyth
Ceredigion  SY23 2AX

**t**  01970 622021
**e**  ug-admissions@aber.ac.uk
**↗**  www.aber.ac.uk

Aberystwyth

**》》 further links**

ACCOMMODATION  accommodation@aber.ac.uk
STUDENTS' UNION  www.aberguild.co.uk

| 1770 | 94.9 | 28.4 | 10.8 | 90.4 |

The university is central to life in "Aber": in a town of 12,000 people, the addition of 8,000 students is going to make an impact. It's frequently rated highly in student satisfaction surveys. Encouragingly, more than 90% of the undergraduate population comes from the state sector. The town itself, while small, has a lovely, breezy position on the west coast of Wales, and is known for a thriving local music scene. Good transport links, too, should you need to get away.

**Fees**  £3,225 a year for all full-time undergraduate courses in 2009-10. Welsh students will qualify for a fee subsidy paid directly to the institution and will in effect be liable for a fee of approximately £1,285.

**Bursaries**  Comprehensive range of means-tested bursaries from £1,000 for students on a maximum grant to £200 for students who receive the minimum grant. There are also subject-specific excellence bursaries available of £2,000 over three years, dependent on Ucas points. See www.aber.ac.uk/en/scholarships

**Accommodation**  Guaranteed for first-years. Weekly rates for 2008-09 from £64.75 a week self-catered to £95 catered.

**Facilities**  Aberystwyth arts centre, recognised as a national centre for arts development, is a department of the university, so expect lots of arty goings-on. The university library is very well equipped, but should it fall short you can always pay a visit to the National Library of Wales, which is based in Aberystwyth. It's a copyright library, which means it is entitled to a copy of every book published in Britain.

**Transport**  Although it's out on the west coast, trains will whisk you to Birmingham and beyond. Road links will take you to north or south-west Wales with ease.

**❝ STUDENT VIEW ❞**

*"The quality of life is amazing — the town is dominated by students and that gives it a real community feel. I can't imagine not living by the sea once I leave Aber!"*

# Anglia Ruskin University

Bishop Hall Lane
Chelmsford  CM1 1SQ

**t**  0845 271 3333
**e**  answers@anglia.ac.uk
↗ www.anglia.ac.uk

**Cambridge Campus**  East Road, Cambridge  CB1 1PT

**》 further links**

ACCOMMODATION  www.anglia.ac.uk/accommodation
STUDENTS' UNION  www.angliastudent.com

2225      97.8      36.6      21.7      91.4

Chelmsford

Based at two main campuses in Cambridge and Chelmsford, Anglia Ruskin is fiercely committed to widening access to higher education. It is one of the largest universities in the east of England, and has 25,500 students, more than 95% of whom are from state schools. Much of its research is rated as world-leading and, at 92%, it has one of the highest employability rates in the higher education sector. Cambridge-based students will have access to a lovely and deeply student-centric historic city. Chelmsford, while not so much of a tourist trap, still has enough going on to keep you occupied.

**Fees**  £3,225 a year for all full-time undergraduate courses in 2009-10, with a mandatory bursary of £319. See www.anglia.ac.uk/studentfinance

**Bursaries**  See www.anglia.ac.uk/scholarships09

**Accommodation**  There is no official guarantee of accommodation for first-year students, but in reality the university can accommodate all first-year Chelmsford applicants and more than 95% of Cambridge applicants. Rents from £68 to £120 a week.

**Facilities**  Good sports facilities, particularly at Chelmsford. Both sites have bars, computing facilities and libraries. The university has invested £85m in state-of-the-art learning environments, including the health and social care building. Award-winning student radio station shared with the University of Cambridge.

**Transport**  Both Cambridge and Chelmsford have easy access to motorways, main roads, rails links and Stansted airport. See www.anglia.ac.uk/findus

**❝ STUDENT VIEW ❞**

*"I enjoyed every aspect of the course. Self progression was amazing — this was possible with the support and understanding given by the lecturers and social policy staff."*

# University of the Arts London

**Camberwell College of Arts**  Peckham Road, London  SE5 8UF
**Central Saint Martins College of Art and Design**  Southampton Row, London  WC1B 4AP
**Chelsea College of Art and Design**  Millbank, London  SW1P 4JU
**London College of Communication**  Elephant & Castle, London  SE1 6SB
**London College of Fashion**  20 John Princes' Street, London  W1G 0BJ
**Wimbledon College of Art**  Merton Hall Road, London  SW19 3QA

**t**  020 7 514 6000
**e**  info@arts.ac.uk
**↗**  www.arts.ac.uk

**》》 further links**

ACCOMMODATION  www.arts.ac.uk/housing
STUDENTS' UNION  www.suarts.org

2135     95.1     26.6     14.1     86.5

London

University of the Arts London is Europe's largest university for art, design, fashion, communication and the performing arts. It is a federation of six internationally renowned colleges: Camberwell College of Arts, Central Saint Martins College of Art and Design, Chelsea College of Art and Design, London College of Communication, London College of Fashion and Wimbledon College of Art. In 2006, the student hub opened in the West End as a point of contact for students from across the university. Saint Martins is due to move to its new multimillion-pound, state-of-the-art premises in the heart of King's Cross in 2011.

**Fees**  For 2009-10, undergraduate home students will pay £3,225.

**Bursaries**  Students in receipt of the full government grant will receive a bursary of £319 a year. Students who receive a proportion of the grant will be eligible to apply for an access bursary of £1,000. There is a wide range of other bursaries available, including privately funded scholarships.

**Accommodation**  University accommodation costs for 2008-09 range from £76 to £166 a week. The university provides 2,243 places in 12 residences in north, south, south-east and east London. Disabled students and students under 18 at the start of their course are guaranteed accommodation. Priority is also given to students from outside London.

**Facilities**  The university's nine libraries provide students with access to over 400,000 books. Electronic databases and online periodicals and books are also available. The university is home to the Stanley Kubrick archive, made up of film, costumes, scripts, photography, set designs and sound recordings.

**Transport**  All sites are easily accessible and well served by underground, bus and mainline train services. Students receive 30% off travelcards and season tickets.

**❝ STUDENT VIEW ❞**
*"University of the Arts London doesn't streamline its students into one way of thinking or approaching things, or force them to adopt any style; rather, it encourages them to be individuals."*

# Arts University College at Bournemouth

Wallisdown, Poole
Dorset  BH 12 5HH

**t**  01202 533 011
**e**  general@aib.ac.uk
↗ www.aib.ac.uk

**》 further links**

ACCOMMODATION  studentadvice@aib.ac.uk
STUDENTS' UNION  www.aib.ac.uk/studentinformation
/studentunion.aspx

495      95.3      33.2      10.1      95.3

Bournemouth

The Arts University College at Bournemouth (or Arts Institute at Bournemouth as it was known until July 1 2009) offers high-quality specialist education in arts, design and media. The institute offers courses ranging from film production, illustration and graphic design, architecture and events management through to fashion, photography and acting. The campus is situated two miles from the centre of Bournemouth, and consists of a series of purpose-built studios accommodating 2,000 or so students on full-time courses. As you'd imagine, there's plenty of lovely scenery and seaside fun in the vicinity.

**Fees**  £3,225 for full-time undergraduate programmes in 2009-10.

**Bursaries**  All students who receive the full grant of £2,906 will receive £350. These students will also receive a bonus of £150 on successful completion of their first year, £250 after their second year and £500 upon completion of their final year. All students who receive a grant of between £1,075 and £2,905 will receive £200.

**Accommodation**  Halls of residence on campus or in town cost £89 to £120 a week, including all bills. Places are allocated according to need and are not guaranteed. The majority of students live in privately rented accommodation during their first year. Average cost is £72 to £85 a week.

**Facilities**  A purpose-built library supplies material to support the courses taught. The Enterprise Pavilion provides business incubation units for graduates from the institute and other higher education providers. The institute also boasts a contemporary arts gallery.

**Transport**  London is less than two hours away, with regular train and coach services, and good road networks. A sponsored bus service runs in term time, which links students to the places they are likely to want to go. There are good cycle routes from the institute into Bournemouth.

**❝ STUDENT VIEW ❞**

*"The lecturers really know their material as many still work in their industry in addition to teaching, so not only do we get some great lectures, but we also make fantastic contacts with people who could be our future employers."*

# Aston University, Birmingham

Aston Triangle
Birmingham B4 7ED

**t** 0121 204 3000
**e** ugenquiries@aston.ac.uk
⌁ www.aston.ac.uk

**》》 further links**

ACCOMMODATION www.aston.ac.uk/accommodation
STUDENTS' UNION www.astonguild.org.uk

1775    91.5    36.2    7.9    95.9

Birmingham

Aston offers a broad range of courses. Some 70% of the 9,000 or so undergraduates take sandwich placement years or years abroad. The university is proud both of its student diversity, and of its excellent graduate employment rate (83% of 2007 graduates entered graduate-level jobs, against a UK average of less than 70%). Aston is located on a green, self-contained campus right in the centre of Birmingham. The university is building 1,350 fully networked, en suite rooms on campus, ready for 2010 entry. Other recent developments include a £22m extension to the business school and a £4m IT network upgrade.

**Fees** £3,225 for all full-time undergraduates in 2009-10. Sandwich placement year fees are £1,610.

**Bursaries** Means-tested bursaries of up to £800 a year. Students whose family income is below £18,000 receive £800, then on a sliding scale for incomes of between £18,000 and £39,000. All UK/EU students on a placement year (and paying the fee) will receive a placement bursary of £1,000 for that year. Students on a year abroad get £500. The vast majority of Aston students take paid placement years in year three; the average salary is around £15,000, which can also help with finances in the final year.

**Accommodation** Guaranteed for eligible first-years. Self-catering accommodation ranges from £68 to £106 a week for 39-week letting periods. Meal plans available: about £270 a term will buy you two square meals a day.

**Facilities** The campus boasts two sports centres, a 25m pool and a 75-station fitness suite. All student accommodation has internet access. The library is open 24 hours a day for most of the academic year. Off-campus, the university sports grounds include grass and all-weather pitches, floodlighting and a pavilion.

**Transport** Excellent road and train links.

**◀◀ STUDENT VIEW ▶▶**

*"Aston is a small university with a big reputation. It was only when I started looking for a graduate job that I realised how true this is. The campus has a community spirit that I'm proud to be part of."*

# Bangor University

Bangor
Gwynedd  LL57 2DG

**t**  01248 351151
**e**  admissions@bangor.ac.uk
↗  www.bangor.ac.uk

**>> further links**
ACCOMMODATION  halls@bangor.ac.uk
STUDENTS' UNION  www.undeb.bangor.ac.uk

| 2020 | 95.5 | 32.8 | 15.4 | 93.5 |

If you're the outdoor type, Bangor could be the place for you. It's close to the sea and the mountains. The cost of living is low and part-time work is fairly easy to come by. The town — actually one of the UK's smallest cities — has a significant proportion of Welsh speakers. As for the university itself, major investment is taking place to provide more student accommodation and it is expanding academically, too: funding for 50 new academic posts has been announced and new courses are being introduced every year. The university counts Danny Boyle, the Oscar-winning director of Slumdog Millionaire, among its alumni.

**Fees**  £3,225 for all undergraduate degrees in 2009-10.

**Bursaries**  Bursaries totalling more than £2.5m and new £5,000 excellence scholarships are available for 2009 entry. Bursaries of up to £1,000 a year for those from lower-income families. Specific awards for certain subjects, merit scholarships and other awards available.

**Accommodation**  A range of accommodation is available, including catered and en suite options priced from just over £66 to just under £104 a week.

**Facilities**  Three main library sites, one each for arts and sciences, as well as extensive access to online databases and journals. Nine computer rooms are open 24 hours a day and there is broad wireless coverage, and laptop loan and purchase schemes. A new arts and innovation centre project is planned as part of an ongoing 10-year estates development strategy.

**Transport**  Although not a campus university, most parts of the university are within walking distance of each other. Bangor is on the main rail line between London and Holyhead, and has good road links to the motorway network along the A55.

**⟨⟨ STUDENT VIEW ⟩⟩**

*"Everything about Bangor is appealing to students — the friendly sociable atmosphere, the location and environment that surrounds the city, the ease of everything being within walking distance and how affordable it is."*

# University of Bath

Bath  BA2 7AY

**t**  01225 388388
**e**  admissions@bath.ac.uk
**↗**  www.bath.ac.uk

**University of Bath in Swindon**
Oakfield Campus, Marlowe Avenue, Walcot, Swindon  SN3 3JR

**》 further links**

ACCOMMODATION  www.bath.ac.uk/accommodation
STUDENTS' UNION  www.bathstudent.com

1720     76.2     18.0     4.4     94.7

Lovely, honey-coloured, stately Bath could hardly be more visually charming, and the location of the campus on a hill overlooking the city means you're perfectly placed to soak up the view. The droves of tourists ensure there are plenty of shopping and leisure activities to join in with, and you can always dash off to neighbouring Bristol for some urban grit. Sport is a big deal at the university, with excellent facilities and teams that will vanquish all comers. But sporty or not, everyone seems to have a good time: the university boasts impressive student satisfaction results.

**Fees**  £3,225 for all undergraduate courses in 2009–10.

**Bursaries**  Up to £1,200 for students with a family income of £25,000 or less, on a sliding scale after that. Other merit- and subject-based awards available.

**Accommodation**  Accommodation is guaranteed for first-years, usually on campus. Prices from £75 to £115 a week. A complex of 355 en suite rooms was completed in October 2008 and several campus residences are undergoing refurbishment.

**Facilities**  The library is one of the few in the country to stay open 24 hours a day, seven days a week. Sports facilities were already some of the best in the country, even before the addition of a £30m training village.

**Transport**  A frequent bus runs into town and takes about 10 minutes. The train to Bristol takes 15 minutes, and it's an hour-and-a-half to London.

**❝ STUDENT VIEW ❞**
*"A unique place to study, set in a world heritage city, with a friendly and diverse campus. The sports facilities are fantastic and we have an incredibly active students' union. I have loved every minute."*

# Bath Spa University

Newton Park, Newton St Loe
Bath  BA2 9BN

**t**  01225 875875
**e**  enquiries@bathspa.ac.uk
**⌕**  www.bathspa.ac.uk

**Sion Hill Campus**  Sion Hill, Bath  BA1 5SF
**Somerset Place**  Landsdown, Bath  BA1 5HA
**Culverhay**  Rush Hill, Bath  BA2 2QL

**》 further links**

ACCOMMODATION  accommodation@bathspa.ac.uk
STUDENTS' UNION  www.bathspasu.co.uk

1310     94.9     29.5     10.0     96.8

Bath

Bath Spa is a relatively new university and prides itself on its teaching focus and emphasis on employability. Applications are on the increase and the university is expanding its range of courses. The university is split over three sites. Newton Park may be a few miles from town, but it's so lovely-looking you couldn't possibly mind. Bath city itself is equally dreamy, and nearby Bristol is the place to party.

**Fees**  £3,225 for all full-time undergraduate courses in 2009-10.

**Bursaries**  Means-tested bursary of up to £1,200. An extra £1,000 non-means-tested scholarship is also available for certain science subjects. Emergency and other financial support available.

**Accommodation**  A range of accommodation is available, priced from about £64 to £112 a week. The university houses all first-year students who want accommodation either on campus, in university-managed accommodation or in reserved private housing off-campus.

**Facilities**  Each campus has a library whose content reflects the courses taught there, as well as study areas and access to computing resources. The student union is a well-established music venue.

**Transport**  About 90 minutes to London by train; Bristol is virtually on the doorstep.

**❝ STUDENT VIEW ❞**

*"This is an exciting place to live — from the new Bath Spa complex to the redevelopment of the city centre, Bath is a world heritage site moving into the 21st century. And sports fans can get a kick out of the successful rugby and high-flying football teams."*

# University of Bedfordshire

| | |
|---|---|
| **University of Bedfordshire** | **t** 01234 400 400 |
| | **e** admission@beds.ac.uk |
| | ⌐ www.beds.ac.uk |

**Luton Campus** Park Square, Luton, Bedfordshire LU1 3JU
**Bedford Campus** Polhill Avenue, Bedford MK41 9EA
**Putteridge Bury Campus** Hitchin Road, Luton, Bedfordshire LU2 8LE

**》 further links**

ACCOMMODATION accommodation@beds.ac.uk
STUDENTS' UNION www.ubsu.co.uk

| 1955 | 98.8 | 41.6 | 20.6 | 90.3 |
|---|---|---|---|---|

Bedfordshire was born from the merging of the University of Luton with the Bedford campus of De Montfort University. Both towns are within striking distance of London. Luton has a busy social scene and Bedford boasts a nice riverside position. It is a forward-thinking university with an excellent graduate employment record, and a diverse student population of more than 18,000 students from more than 100 countries. A sizeable proportion of students hail from the local area.

**Fees** £3,225 a year for undergraduate courses in 2009-10.

**Bursaries** The most generous bursary package in the south of England, the university says. Most first-years will receive up to £4,262, and, at the very least, can expect to receive £319, regardless of personal circumstances. There is also a wide range of scholarships. See www.beds.ac.uk/money

**Accommodation** All first-years are offered accommodation on the Bedford or Luton campus. A new £20m block has opened in Bedford; a similar £40m development is planned for Luton. Rents are reasonable.

**Facilities** A massive £134m redevelopment plan is due for completion in September 2010. Includes a £20m en suite halls of residence, a £6m campus centre, which houses a 280-seat theatre, and an £8m physical education and sport science centre where athletes will train for the 2012 Olympics.

**Transport** The airport is close by, the bus station is a short walk from Park Square and there are regular trains to London.

**❛❛ STUDENT VIEW ❜❜**
*"I chose to study at the University of Bedfordshire because of its location and also because of its reputation. The facilities are very good and of a high standard, and are also very accessible."*

# Birkbeck, University of London

Malet Street
Bloomsbury
London  WC1E 7HX

t  0845 601 0174 (Bloomsbury); 0845 602 4169 (Stratford)
e  info@bbk.ac.uk  or  info@birkbeckstratford.ac.uk
↗  www.bbk.ac.uk  or  www.birkbeckstratford.ac.uk

 **further links**

ACCOMMODATION  housing.london.ac.uk/cms
STUDENTS' UNION  www.bbk.ac.uk/su

London

Formerly Birkbeck College, London, the institution was founded in 1823 by George Birkbeck to extend educational opportunities to working Londoners who might otherwise miss out. Almost 200 years on, it's still fulfilling the same role. As well as being a respected teaching and research institution, Birkbeck is unique among the colleges of the University of London for its emphasis on part-time, non-residential teaching for non-traditional students. Undergraduate teaching takes place in the evening and a degree takes four years to complete. Fees are competitive and the ability to work while studying makes Birkbeck a good choice for those concerned about debt. Birkbeck has a central London location, and since 2007, a range of courses has also been available in Stratford, east London. Applications are direct to the college and not through Ucas.

**Fees**  Fees vary. See the website for details.

**Bursaries**  Contact the college directly. There is an excellent package of financial support for students, including government grants and college bursaries.

**Accommodation**  No on-campus accommodation, as most students live and work in London. Students from elsewhere can use the University of London housing services.

**Facilities**  There is a modern library on four floors, which is open at evenings and weekends, and there is good access to computing facilities. The bar, dining hall and cafe are open in the early evening. You have access to the University of London student union, with great facilities for sport and socialising.

**Transport**  Both the Bloomsbury and Stratford campuses are easily accessible by public transport.

**❝ STUDENT VIEW ❞**

*"I knew I wanted to go to a quality institution, and Birkbeck's got a great reputation. It's really paid off for me; I've seen how highly my University of London qualification is thought of."*

# University of Birmingham

Edgbaston
Birmingham  B15 2TT

**t**  0121 414 3344
**e**  admissions@bham.ac.uk
↗  www.bham.ac.uk

**》 further links**

ACCOMMODATION  www.housing.bham.ac.uk
STUDENTS' UNION  www.guildofstudents.com

4360      78.1      22.1      4.9      94.0

Large, prestigious and rather grand – you wouldn't expect anything less from Birmingham's university. Established in 1900, it was the first redbrick university to receive its royal charter. Striking examples of Victorian architecture remain on the large, leafy campus in Edgbaston, which comes equipped with all mod cons: bars, cafes, shops, a hair salon, a concert hall, banks, an art gallery, a medical practice, a nursery ... even its own train station (only two stops to the city centre). It has one of the largest student unions in the country, as well as excellent employment figures. There's a strong emphasis on sport: there was even a Birmingham student at the last Olympics.

**Fees**   £3,225 for all full-time undergraduate programmes in 2009-10.

**Bursaries**   In 2009, there will be a bursary of £860 available to all students with a household income of less than £35,460. Students who qualify will also be eligible for a scholarship of £1,290 based on academic achievement (for example, AAB at A-level). Other scholarships in selected subjects and for excellence in music and sport.

**Accommodation**   Guaranteed for first-years meeting the criteria. Approximate rents are from £78 for a standard single rising to £125 for an en suite room.

**Facilities**   Great facilities and even an art gallery housing Monets, Turners and Picassos on campus.

**Transport**   Good for rail, road and air.

 **STUDENT VIEW 》**

*"The campus is the perfect blend between traditional and modern. It is uplifting to walk around historic buildings, while learning the most recent ideas and concepts with the most up-to-date technology."*

# Birmingham City University

Perry Bar
Birmingham  B42 2SU

**t**  0121 331 5000
**e**  choices@bcu.ac.uk
↗  www.bcu.ac.uk

**》 further links**

ACCOMMODATION  accommodation@bcu.ac.uk
STUDENTS' UNION  www.birminghamcitysu.com

Birmingham

| 3175 | 97.5 | 45.1 | 19.8 | 91.8 |

Birmingham City University is a forward-looking university of approximately 23,000 students, spread across eight campuses around the city. The largest campus is situated at the modern Perry Barr site, three miles north of the city centre. Courses have a strong focus on relevance for the job market and there's an excellent careers service. In the recent research assessment exercise, much of the university's research was rated as excellent. The university prides itself on its reputation for widening participation and you'll find a broad spectrum of cultures, nationalities and ages here. The city itself is similarly diverse, with plenty to see and do around town, and excellent transport links, should you feel the need to escape for any reason.

**Fees**  £3,225 a year for all full-time undergraduate courses in 2009-10.

**Bursaries**  There is currently a bursary of up to £525 available for students receiving a full or partial maintenance grant.

**Accommodation**  Applicants are guaranteed a room in halls of residence for their first year provided they have accepted an offer on a full-time course. For other applicants, accommodation is subject to availability. Most halls are self-catering and prices range from £64 to £96 a week.

**Facilities**  New state-of-the-art faculty of health learning equipment at the Edgbaston campus, including virtual hospital wards, simulation dummies and a mock operating theatre. A £7m sports facility is due to open in September 2009 comprising a sports hall and 80-station fitness suite. A further £150m is to be invested to create a big city centre campus in the central eastside district of Birmingham.

**Transport**  Birmingham is easy to get to by road or rail.

**《 STUDENT VIEW 》**

*"Birmingham City University offers much more than just an academic qualification.  It is not just a place to study but a university in which to really get involved and meet a whole variety of people, from different backgrounds and with different ideas."*

# University College Birmingham

Summer Row
Birmingham B3 1JB

**t** 0121 604 1000
**e** marketing@ucb.ac.uk
**↗** www.ucb.ac.uk

**》 further links**

ACCOMMODATION accommodation@ucb.ac.uk
STUDENTS' UNION www.bcftcs.ac.uk/asp/STU-studentGuild.asp

540    98.9    48.8    12.9    89.1

Birmingham

University College Birmingham (formerly the Birmingham School of Food, Tourism and Creative Studies) offers a range of undergraduate courses, mainly centred around the hospitality industries. There are 3,900 HE students on a range of short courses, and engaged in full- and part-time degree and postgraduate degree studies. The specialist nature of the university college means that students have access to tailored facilities. There are also close links with employers. Birmingham is a fun place to study with all the attractions of a big city on your doorstep.

**Fees** £3,225 for full-time undergraduate students in 2009-10.

**Bursaries** If your household income is £25,000 or less, you will receive a bursary of £1,080 a year. Between £25,001 and £42,516, you will receive a bursary of £648 a year. Between £42,517 and £60,032, you will receive a bursary of £324 a year. Students in receipt of a disabled students' living allowance will receive a bursary of £1,624 a year regardless of household income.

**Accommodation** More than 1,000 students can be accommodated in halls. Rent is between £69 and £88 a week.

**Facilities** There are restaurants and a spa, which are used both as learning resources and as commercial centres: the public is actively encouraged to make use of them and, of course, so can students.

**Transport** A convenient location within easy reach of the city centre. Birmingham itself is well served by road, rail and air.

**❝ STUDENT VIEW ❞**

*"The student body is really international, which is great. I have made friends with people I never would have met if I hadn't come here. It quickly feels like home."*

# Bishop Grosseteste University College Lincoln

Lincoln  LN1 3DY

**t**  01522 527347
**e**  info@bishopg.ac.uk
↗  www.bishopg.ac.uk

>> **further links**

ACCOMMODATION  rachel.crane@bishopg.ac.uk
STUDENTS' UNION  www.bishopgsu.co.uk

| 380 | 100.0 | 43.0 | 6.6 | 97.0 |

Lincoln

Robert Grosseteste was a 13th-century bishop of Lincoln. The college bearing his name was established in 1862 and has a long-standing reputation as an independent Anglican higher education institution; its mission statement recognises faith as part of human experience, and provides for its practice and nurture. As well as that, it offers courses in arts and education (it was until recently a teacher training college) and is firmly committed to diversity and opening access to higher education. Lincoln itself is a charming historical city — perhaps a touch on the quiet side, but who's complaining about that?

**Fees**  £3,225 for full-time undergraduate students in 2009–10.

**Bursaries**  £1,075 will be paid to students with a household income of £39,333 or less. Further means-tested and discretionary support is available.

**Accommodation**  Accommodation is guaranteed for first-years who have Bishop Grosseteste as their firm choice. Costs are reasonable.

**Facilities**  A sports and fitness centre opened in 2006, and there are good library and IT facilities, too. The student union has enjoyed some recent revamping.

**Transport**  One to two hours to London by train. It's a 25–30 minute (uphill!) walk from the station to campus.

❝ **STUDENT VIEW** ❞

*"The best aspect of my time at BG was the quality of teaching on my course and the support provided by my tutors."*

# University of Bolton

Deane Road
Bolton  BL3 5AB

**t** 01204 900600
**e** enquiries@bolton.ac.uk
↗ www.bolton.ac.uk



>> **further links**
ACCOMMODATION  accomm@bolton.ac.uk
STUDENTS' UNION  www.bisu.co.uk

1070      98.9      45.8      38.0      87.9

Still a relatively new university, Bolton is enjoying large rises in applications and a multimillion-pound development programme to match. £8m has been spent in the past two years to move all subjects to the main Deane campus in the centre of town, where a new student union and social learning zone have been built. Of the 9,000 or so students, about three-quarters are north-west natives. Perhaps it's not surprising they haven't strayed too far. Bolton itself may not be massive, but there's a rich cultural heritage and plenty to do – not to mention the fact that Manchester is just a short hop away for some real big-city life.

**Fees**  £3,225 for all full-time undergraduate courses in 2009-10.

**Bursaries**  £320 annual bursaries to those receiving a full grant, then support on a sliding scale for those receiving partial grants, down to £70 a year. £730 annual scholarships for those who have completed a preparatory course or period of study at the university or a partner institution, irrespective of financial means.

**Accommodation**  The university is usually able to accommodate all first-years who have requested a place in halls. Self-catering accommodation costs £60 a week.

**Facilities**  There's a range of sports teams to join or classes to take part in at the sports centre, and the university is currently finalising a joint venture with Bolton council and NHS Bolton to build a £30m health and fitness centre. The library is open late and there is 24-hour access to computing facilities.

**Transport**  Bolton station is half a mile away with frequent connections to Manchester. The motorway network is on the doorstep.

**◄◄ STUDENT VIEW ►►**
*"I chose to study at Bolton because I liked the atmosphere, the people and the environment. The lecturers are very knowledgeable and supportive, and are always willing to spend extra time with students."*

# Bournemouth University

Fern Barrow
Talbot Campus, Poole
Dorset  BH12 5BB

**t**  08456 501501
**e**  askBUenquiries@bournemouth.ac.uk
**↗**  www.bournemouth.ac.uk

**》 further links**

ACCOMMODATION  www.bournemouth.ac.uk/accommodation
STUDENTS' UNION  www.subu.org.uk

2755    94.5    28.6    13.1    94.7

Bournemouth

There's nothing head-in-the-clouds about Bournemouth – and that's not only because the lovely weather on the south coast means there rarely are any clouds. The university is firmly rooted in the professional application of education. It works closely with key employers and courses are designed with future professional success in mind. The 17,000 or so students enjoy all the benefits of living in a tourist town, touted by some as the new Brighton, no less. It's sunny and boasts some of the best beaches in the UK – great if you're a fan of watersports, or even just of lying on the sand eating an ice cream.

**Fees**  £3,225 for full-time undergraduate courses in 2009–10.

**Bursaries**  Every full-time undergraduate UK/EU student (except those on NHS courses) who meets the income criteria will receive a cash bursary. Other bursaries and a range of scholarships also available.

**Accommodation**  The university expects to offer all new students somewhere to live. All university-managed accommodation is within five miles of the two campuses. In September 2009, a new student block opens in the town centre, right opposite the student union's nightclub – handy, that. Costs average £75 to £98 a week.

**Facilities**  Award-winning learning facilities. There's a Sony HD TV studio (the only one at a UK university) and the National Centre for Computer Animation. There's a great county-standard cricket ground, and unrivalled sailing and watersports facilities.

**Transport**  There are inter-campus buses, extensive cycle routes in town, ferry cross-channel services, and rail and road links. And Bournemouth International airport, of course.

**❝ STUDENT VIEW ❞**

*"My time at Bournemouth University has not only developed my subject knowledge, but also improved my communication, interpersonal and presentation skills so I'm equipped for a job in a competitive market."*

# University of Bradford

Richmond Rd
Bradford West
West Yorkshire  BD7 1DP

**t**  0800 073 1225
**e**  course-enquiries@bradford.ac.uk
✎  www.bradford.ac.uk

**》》 further links**
ACCOMMODATION  halls-of-residence@bradford.ac.uk
STUDENTS' UNION  www.ubuonline.co.uk

Bradford

| 1930 | 93.9 | 49.0 | 16.9 | 91.1 |

Bradford is a bustling, diverse, friendly and energetic city – and the university follows suit. It continues to attract large numbers of applicants, drawn by the promise of good employment prospects, a low cost of living and arguably the best curry in the country. The city-centre campus fosters a close-knit student community and is undergoing a huge refurbishment. The university is committed to sustainable development: campus cafes sell Fairtrade products and new student accommodation will aim for low environmental impact.

**Fees**  £3,225 for full-time undergraduate courses in 2009-10.

**Bursaries**  Two levels of bursary for 2009-10, means-tested up to £40,000 and £60,032 household income respectively: £400 or £500 in a foundation year; £400 or £500 in the first year, rising to £500 or £700 in the second year, and £600 or £900 in the final and subsequent years. Most students receive a bursary of up to £2,100 in total for a three-year degree programme.

**Accommodation**  Prices range from £60.53 to £91.50 a week.

**Facilities**  The student union boasts no fewer than three nightclubs and the university has one of the highest PC-to-student ratios in the country. There is an art gallery, theatre and music centre on the campus. The university plans to spend £68m on building projects over the next few years, to include a major refurbishment of the laboratories in the school of life science, creation of a new MBA suite and library at the school of management, and improvement of the student union building and the sports centre.

**Transport**  Walking to the town centre takes about 15 minutes. Leeds is approximately 20 minutes away by train and Bradford is within reach of Leeds Bradford international airport and the M62 motorway.

**❝ STUDENT VIEW ❞**

*"One of the things I enjoy most about the University of Bradford is the interaction between students and lecturers. It is an excellent university with high-quality teaching. The cutting-edge research will help you develop your career."*

# University of Brighton

Mithras House
Lewes Road
Brighton  BN2 4AT

**t**  01273 600900
**e**  admissions@brighton.ac.uk
**↗**  www.brighton.ac.uk

**Moulsecoomb Place**  Lewes Road, Brighton  BN2 4GA
**Falmer Campus**  Village Way, Brighton  BN1 9SF
**Eastbourne Campus**  Trevin Towers, Gaudick Road, Eastbourne  BN20 73P

>> **further links**

ACCOMMODATION  accommodation@brighton.ac.uk
STUDENTS' UNION  www.ubsu.net

3085       93.0       28.6       13.0       92.2

Brighton

---

Despite its size (20,000 or so students), Brighton is a laidback university. Its varied degrees have a strong professional focus — 94% of undergraduate courses have opportunities for work-based learning — with good graduate employment rates. The university actively nurtures students' entrepreneurialism through its Beepurple network, holding monthly workshops to develop business ideas and provide startup advice. The student body is diverse, with many part-time and mature students. The university is split over campuses in Brighton and Eastbourne. The appeal of the former is legendary, and the steady spread of smart bars and boutiques by Brighton's pebble beach shows no sign of slowing. Eastbourne is a more sedate seaside resort, but it's not too hard to get to Brighton for some ritzy fun.

**Fees**  £3,225 for full-time undergraduate students in 2009-10.

**Bursaries**  All full-time undergraduate students from the UK with household incomes of up to £40,330 a year are eligible for a bursary worth between £540 and £1,080 a year. Additional bursaries are available for local students and there are scholarships for exceptional achievement.

**Accommodation**  Over 80% of first-years who meet the criteria get a place in halls. Various types available in halls of residence and student houses. Weekly rents range from £70 to £128.

**Facilities**  Extensive sporting facilities. The student union hosts its own club nights and there are good computing resources. Two major building projects are under way: a new academic building at Falmer and a new building to house the university's work in biosciences at the Moulsecoomb site.

**Transport**  London is less than an hour by train. Gatwick airport and Newhaven port are both nearby. Eastbourne is about 40 minutes away from Brighton by car and 30 minutes by train.

---

**66 STUDENT VIEW 99**

*"All of the staff are really approachable and enthusiastic about their subjects. Due to the cosmopolitan nature of Brighton there is always something fun and interesting happening at the university."*

# University of Bristol

Senate House
Tyndall Avenue
Bristol  BS8 1TH

**t**  0117 928 9000
**e**  ug-admissions@bristol.ac.uk
↗  www.bristol.ac.uk

**》 further links**

ACCOMMODATION  accom-office@bris.ac.uk
STUDENTS' UNION  www.ubu.org.uk

3050      63.1      14.3      4.2      95.2

From humble beginnings as a university college in 1876 with just 99 students, Bristol has become an internationally respected academic powerhouse with around 12,500 undergraduates and 3,500 postgraduates. The university is one of the most popular in the UK, partly because of its excellent research and teaching, and partly because Bristol is an attractive city with a great social scene. Most of the university's main buildings are located within a few minutes' walk of each other in a lively part of the city centre, which is itself only a 30-minute walk from the student residences in leafy Stoke Bishop. You can see why so many people are clamouring to get into Bristol.

**Fees**  £3,225 for full-time undergraduate students in 2009-10.

**Bursaries**  All new undergraduate students with a household income of £50,000 or less, and in receipt of a grant receive a bursary of up to £1,200. Other support and awards available. See bristol.ac.uk/studentfunding

**Accommodation**  Guaranteed for non-local first-years. Various types available in halls of residence and student houses. Weekly rents range from £52 to £152.

**Facilities**  The library has the largest academic collection in south-west England: 1.4m volumes. The university has invested more than £8m in facilities for sport and exercise in recent years    these include a £5m indoor sports centre, a tennis centre, a 33m swimming pool and a rowing facility. Drama and music are also well catered for.

**Transport**  Good road and rail links including the M4 and M5. Convenient for Bristol airport.

**❝ STUDENT VIEW ❞**

*"My tutors are friendly and always happy to discuss my ideas and interests. The university has some great facilities and I love the diversity of the city. Bristol offers everything I wanted from a university."*

# Brunel University

Uxbridge   UB8 3PH

**t**  01895 274000
**e**  admissions@brunel.ac.uk
**↗**  www.brunel.ac.uk

**»» further links**

ACCOMMODATION  accom-uxb@brunel.ac.uk
STUDENTS' UNION  www.brunel.ac.uk/life/ubs

2940      92.5      37.7      11.6      92.7

London

Since becoming a university in 1966, Brunel's mission has been to combine academic rigour with the practical, entrepreneurial and imaginative approach pioneered by its namesake, Isambard Kingdom Brunel. It's proving successful. The university has invested £250m in social, teaching, accommodation and sporting facilities in recent years. Its 14,000 students are now all on a single campus at Uxbridge – a rarity in London – and enjoy a strong sense of community. And more than 2,500 international students from more than 110 different countries at Brunel help to create a diverse and cosmopolitan atmosphere. Uxbridge town centre, 20 minutes' walk away, may not be all big city lights, but it's compact and less frenetic than central London – which is, after all, very easy to get to.

**Fees**  £3,225 for full-time undergraduate students in 2009–10.

**Bursaries**  £1,000 each year of study to all undergraduates entitled to receive a full grant; £500 a year to undergraduates eligible for a partial grant whose annual household income is between £25,001 and £33,000.

**Accommodation**  Guaranteed for all first-years; from £81.41 to £99.66 a week.
See brunel.ac.uk/life/accommodation

**Facilities**  The library has enjoyed recent investment, and there is good access to computing facilities.

**Transport**  Brunel is within easy walking distance of Uxbridge underground, which is at the end of the Metropolitan line, so it's easy to get to London. A short bus ride gets you to West Drayton railway station, where trains run to/from London Paddington and Bristol. The university is a short drive from the M4, M40 and M25, and close to Heathrow. See brunel.ac.uk/about/where

**«« STUDENT VIEW »»**
*"The brilliant facilities almost invite students to say, 'What can't I achieve?' and the courses inspire you to take your work to the next level."*

# University of Buckingham

Hunter Street
Buckingham MK18 1EG

t 01280 814080
e info@buckingham.ac.uk
↗ www.buckingham.ac.uk

>> **further links**

ACCOMMODATION accommodation@buckingham.ac.uk
STUDENTS' UNION www.buckingham.ac.uk/life/social/su

80    79.5    0.0    90.0

Buckingham is a unique institution: Britain's only private university. Just under 900 students study here and the university offers intensive two-year degree programmes, with four 10-week terms a year. Even taking that into account, a Buckingham degree is still more expensive than your regular kind, though you do get an impressive staff-student ratio and Buckingham students are among the most satisfied with their university experience. The pretty campus is compact, but big enough to boast its own cinema. It has a rural feel, but is between Milton Keynes and Oxford should you need a shot of urban adrenaline. More than 61% of the student population is from overseas.

**Fees**  £8,000 a year for most undergraduate courses.

**Bursaries**  A range of scholarships is available.

**Accommodation**  Campus accommodation is guaranteed for all first-years who apply for it. Self-catering accommodation costs between £67 and £111 a week.

**Facilities**  The student union is based at the hub of student entertainment in Tanlaw Mill at the Hunter Street campus. Facilities include a bar, refectory, gym, studio and common room. The local cinema is housed in one of the university lecture halls.

**Transport**  The town boasts a good public transport service with regular buses to Oxford, Milton Keynes and Cambridge. Milton Keynes railway station is 20 minutes away from the university and there are regular trains to London, which is a 30-minute journey. The university has a minibus that runs five times a day between the two campuses.

**❝ STUDENT VIEW ❞**

*"The University truly is 'a gem in the rough' with its staff that are experts in their fields, and a most diverse community of students — all round a unique experience, especially with its two-year degree programme."*

# Buckinghamshire New University

**High Wycombe Campus**  Queen Alexandra Road, High Wycombe  HP11 2JZ
**Wellesbourne Campus**  Kingshill Road, High Wycombe  HP13 5BB
**Chalfont Campus**  Gorelands Lane, Chalfont St Giles  HP8 4AD

t  0800 0565 660
e  advice@bucks.ac.uk
↗ www.bucks.ac.uk

**》 further links**

ACCOMMODATION  www.bcuc.ac.uk/accommodation
STUDENTS' UNION  www.bucksstudent.com/student_marketing

     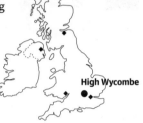

| 1285 | 96.8 | 36.0 | 14.2 | 91.2 |

High Wycombe

Buckinghamshire New University nestles in the beautiful countryside of the Chiltern Hills. Formerly Buckinghamshire Chilterns University College, Bucks was awarded full university status in 2007. From September 2009, all of its courses, with the exception of nursing, will be based at its campus in High Wycombe. The university offers a varied range of vocationally targeted degrees and studying options not widely available, from commercial pilot training to music management, textiles and furniture. Its faculties are aligned to employment markets: the creative and cultural industries, the management and information management sectors, and the public sector. Ucas figures show that the university had a 33.7% increase in applications last year. There is a large proportion of mature students, and many students come from the Buckinghamshire region. The town centre is within easy walking distance, and London is a short train ride away.

**Fees**  £3,225 for full-time undergraduate courses in 2009-10.

**Bursaries**  The Big Deal package includes a £500 cash bursary paid to all full-time UK and EU students, plus additional faculty-based support and free access to all gigs and club nights.

**Accommodation**  Costs range between £65 and £85 a week. New student accommodation is currently being built in High Wycombe. All students living outside a 25-mile radius of the High Wycombe campus are guaranteed an offer of a room in halls.

**Facilities**  The campus boasts a brand new learning resources centre, including music, drama and sports facilities, and newly refurbished workshops and seminar rooms.

**Transport**  The local mainline station connects to the London underground in 40 minutes.

**❝ STUDENT VIEW 》**

*"Not only is my course preparing me in the best possible way to get a job at the end of it, I am having a brilliant time at Bucks, and have made loads of new friends."*

# University of Cambridge

The Old Schools
Trinity Lane
Cambridge CB2 1TN

**t** 01223 333308
**e** admissions@cam.ac.uk
**↗** www.cam.ac.uk

**》》 further links**

ACCOMMODATION   See individual college websites for details
STUDENTS' UNION   www.cusu.cam.ac.uk

2820      57.6      11.5      0.9      94.3

With a history stretching back 800 years (making it the second oldest university in Britain), a solid-gold academic reputation, a wealth of lore and tradition, and some truly glorious architecture, Cambridge has plenty of justification for its boast of being one of the best universities in the world. It's also slightly tainted by the accusation that only posh types need apply, but the university is vigorous in its attempts to encourage people from all backgrounds. It's made up of 29 undergraduate colleges and the college you belong to will be the focus of your university life. They all have their own character, so choose with care. Cambridge itself is a dreamy place to be, with plenty going on if college life gets too insular.

**Fees**   £3,225 for full-time undergraduate students in 2009-10.

**Bursaries**   Means-tested and calculated on a sliding scale. Up to £3,250 for eligible students. Further awards and bursaries also available.

**Accommodation**   Almost all students are housed by their college for the full length of their course. Standard rents are between £70 and £100 a week.

**Facilities**   Extensive resources are offered to students at Cambridge and include access to 149 libraries, eight specialist museums and collections, and the university botanic garden. Most student rooms are connected to the university network and wireless hotspots are available throughout the university. The colleges offer a variety of other resources and amenities, and each has its own common room and bar.

**Transport**   Cambridge is a small city and most students walk or cycle everywhere. The Uni4 bus service connects many departments and colleges, and a discounted fare is available to students. London is about an hour away by train. Stansted airport is nearby.

**66 STUDENT VIEW 99**

*"I'm the first in my family to go to university and I'm really happy at Cambridge. It's incredibly friendly, with a good social scene and while the work's challenging, the environment and teaching is inspirational."*

## Cambridge colleges

**Christ's College**
St Andrew's Street, Cambridge CB2 3BU
t 01223 334 900
www.christs.cam.ac.uk

**Churchill College**
Storey's Way, Cambridge CB3 0DS
t 01223 336 000
www.chu.cam.ac.uk

**Clare College**
Trinity Lane, Cambridge CB2 1TL
t 01223 333 200
www.clare.cam.ac.uk

**Clare Hall** (postgraduates)
Herschel Road, Cambridge CB3 9AL
t 01223 332360
www.clarehall.cam.ac.uk

**Corpus Christi College**
Trumpington Street, Cambridge CB2 1RH
t 01223 338 000
www.corpus.cam.ac.uk

**Darwin College** (postgraduates)
Silver Street, Cambridge CB3 9EU
t 01223 335 660
www.dar.cam.ac.uk

**Downing College**
Regent Street, Cambridge CB2 1DQ
t 01223 334 800
www.dow.cam.ac.uk

**Emmanuel College**
St Andrew's Street, Cambridge CB2 3AP
t 01223 334200
www.emma.cam.ac.uk

**Fitzwilliam College**
Storey's Way, Cambridge CB3 0DG
t 01223 332000
www.fitz.cam.ac.uk/index.jsp

**Girton College**
Huntingdon Road, Cambridge CB3 0JG
t 01223 338999
www.girton.cam.ac.uk

**Gonville & Caius College**
Trinity Street, Cambridge CB2 1TA
t 01223 332400
www.cai.cam.ac.uk

**Homerton College**
Hills Road, Cambridge CB2 2PH
t 01223 507111
www.homerton.cam.ac.uk

**Hughes Hall**
Mortimer Road, Cambridge CB1 2EW
t 01223 334898
www.hughes.cam.ac.uk

**Jesus College**
Jesus Lane, Cambridge CB5 8BL
t 01223 339339
www.jesus.cam.ac.uk

**King's College**
King's Parade, Cambridge CB2 1ST
t 01223 331100
www.kings.cam.ac.uk

**Lucy Cavendish College** (female)
Lady Margaret Road, Cambridge CB3 0BU
t 01223 332190
www.lucy-cav.cam.ac.uk

**Magdalene College**
Magdalene Street, Cambridge CB3 0AG
t 01223 332100
www.magd.cam.ac.uk

**New Hall** (female)
Huntingdon Road, Cambridge CB3 0DF
t 01223 762100
www.newhall.cam.ac.uk

**Newnham College**  (female)
Sidgwick Avenue, Cambridge  CB3 9DF
  t  01223 335700
  ↗ www.newn.cam.ac.uk

**Pembroke College**
Trumpington Street, Cambridge  CB2 1RF
  t  01223 338100
  ↗ www.pem.cam.ac.uk

**Peterhouse**
Trumpington Street, Cambridge  CB2 1RD
  t  01223 338200
  ↗ www.pet.cam.ac.uk

**Queens' College**
Silver Street, Cambridge  CB3 9ET
  t  01223 335511
  ↗ www.queens.cam.ac.uk/splash.asp

**Robinson College**
Grange Road, Cambridge  CB3 9AN
  t  01223 339100
  ↗ www.robinson.cam.ac.uk

**St Catharine's College**
Trumpington Street, Cambridge  CB2 1RL
  t  01223 338300
  ↗ www.caths.cam.ac.uk

**St Edmund's College**
Mount Pleasant, Cambridge  CB3 0BN
  t  01223 336250
  ↗ www.st-edmunds.cam.ac.uk

**St John's College**
St John's Street, Cambridge  CB2 1TP
  t  01223 338600
  ↗ www.joh.cam.ac.uk

**Selwyn College**
Grange Road, Cambridge  CB3 9DQ
  t  01223 335846
  ↗ www.sel.cam.ac.uk

**Sidney Sussex College**
Sidney Street, Cambridge  CB2 3HU
  t  01223 338800
  ↗ www.sid.cam.ac.uk

**Trinity College**
Trinity Street, Cambridge  CB2 1TQ
  t  01223 338400
  ↗ www.trin.cam.ac.uk

**Trinity Hall**
Trinity Lane, Cambridge  CB2 1TJ
  t  01223 332500
  ↗ www.trinhall.cam.ac.uk

**Wolfson College**
Barton Road, Cambridge  CB3 9BB
  t  01223 335900
  ↗ www.wolfson.cam.ac.uk

# Canterbury Christ Church University

University Centre Folkestone
Mill Bay
Folkestone  CT20 1JG

**t**  01227 782900
**e**  admissions@canterbury.ac.uk
**↗**  www.canterbury.ac.uk

**Canterbury Campus**  North Holmes Road, Canterbury, Kent  CT1 1QU
**Broadstairs Campus**  Northwood Road, Broadstairs, Kent  CT10 2WA
**Medway Campus**  Rowan Williams Court, 30 Pembroke Court, Chatham Maritime,
Kent  ME4 4UF
**Salomons Campus**  David Salomons Estate, Broomhill Road, Southborough,
Tunbridge Wells, Kent  TN3 0TG

**》 further links**

ACCOMMODATION  accommodation@canterbury.ac.uk
STUDENTS' UNION  www.ccsu.co.uk

1855    96.9    34.5    15.6    92.0

Canterbury

Canterbury is the largest centre in the region for training people for careers in public service, such as education, policing, health and social care. It has undergone a major expansion in recent years and now has campuses all over Kent, in Canterbury, Broadstairs, Folkestone, Chatham and Tunbridge Wells. More than 15,000 students study a broad range of courses with often innovative approaches to learning. Whichever campus you end up on, you'll always be handily placed for London, but also perfectly poised to enjoy life in the "garden of England". The university fosters a friendly, co-operative atmosphere and getting involved in all aspects of student life is actively encouraged.

**Fees**  £3,225 for full-time undergraduate students in 2009-10.

**Bursaries**  £860 for students with a household income of less than £25,000. £510 for students with a household income of between £25,001 and £49,305. Sports scholarships are also available.

**Accommodation**  Guaranteed for first-years who meet the university's criteria. A range of accommodation is available, most within walking distance of the campuses. Prices start at £70 a week.

**Facilities**  A multimillion-pound sports centre within walking distance of the Canterbury campus has just opened, and Augustine House, a state-of-the-art library and learning facility, opens in the autumn. The student union boasts CTV, its own TV production facility, the Unified student newspaper and CSR Radio – a full FM community radio licence shared with the University of Kent. It even has its own record label, C3U Records. The library at the Medway campus is reputed to be the longest library in Europe.

**Transport**  London by train or car is one-and-a-half hours away.

**❝ STUDENT VIEW ❞**

*"My time at Canterbury Christ Church has helped me to become a reflective and creative primary school teacher. The teaching staff are very helpful and friendly and I have learnt a great deal from lectures and seminars, as well as having lots of fun."*

# Cardiff University

McKenzie House
30-36 Newport Rd
Cardiff CF24 0DE

**t** 029 2087 4455
**e** enquiry@cardiff.ac.uk
**↗** www.cardiff.ac.uk

**》 further links**

ACCOMMODATION  residences@cardiff.ac.uk
STUDENTS' UNION  www.cardiffstudents.com

4325    85.8    21.5    6.5    96.1

Cardiff

Cardiff has grand civic architecture in a breezy waterside location, super-smart city bars and lovely countryside. The university has an excellent reputation for the quality of its teaching and research. Almost 60% of its research is ranked as world-leading and it is a member of the Russell group of leading research universities. There are approximately 26,000 students, including more than 3,000 from more than 100 countries outside the UK, helping to create a vibrant, cosmopolitan community.

**Fees** £3,225 for all full-time undergraduate courses. Eligible Welsh students can apply for a Welsh assembly fee grant of £1,940, meaning that students only pay an annual fee of £1,285. The arrangements for Welsh students beginning their studies in 2010 are currently under review by the Welsh Assembly government.

**Bursaries** The university bursary scheme is available to full-time undergraduate students from lower-income households, valued at up to £1,050 a year. Also available are subject-specific scholarships awarded for academic achievement.

**Accommodation** A place in one of the university's 5,300 single study bedrooms is guaranteed to all first-year undergraduates applying through the normal Ucas admissions cycle. Prices range from £56 to £84 a week.

**Facilities** The university's 18 libraries contain over 1m books and journals. Computer rooms with 24/7 access and wireless connections across the campus. The student union boasts a 1,500-capacity concert hall. Facilities include a sports centre, a fitness centre with a gym and six squash courts, 13 hectares of grass pitches and four county-standard cricket wickets.

**Transport** There are regular bus services between both campuses throughout the day. Good for road and rail; London is two hours by train, Manchester three. Closer in, Swansea takes 40 minutes and Bristol 45 minutes.

**⁶⁶ STUDENT VIEW ᵓᵓ**

*"Although it's not a typical campus university, the schools on the main site near the city centre are so close together it feels like one. There are great pubs, great parks, and nice old university buildings to have lectures in."*

# University of Central Lancashire

Preston PR1 2HE

**t** 01772 892400
**e** cenquiries@uclan.ac.uk
↗ www.uclan.ac.uk

**》 further links**

ACCOMMODATION  saccommodation@uclan.ac.uk
STUDENTS' UNION  www.uclansu.co.uk

3845      96.9      37.7      22.5      95.4

Uclan is one of the country's largest universities, with 32,000 students, and it aims to provide an excellent experience for every single one of them. It's certainly working for the sports science students – in the latest national student survey they gave the university a 100% satisfaction rating, ranking it number one in the UK. Some £60m is currently being invested in new facilities and the recently opened £15m media factory will support work in art, design and performing arts, as well as providing business facilities for entrepreneurial graduates. All courses have an employability strand, and there are some interesting ones to choose from: how about the UK's first foundation degree in nuclear decommissioning, taught on the doorstep of Sellafield power station?

**Fees**  £3,225 for full-time UK/EU undergraduate students in 2009-10.

**Bursaries**  £500 in the first year of study and £310 in subsequent years where the principal earner in the student's household is on less than £60,000 a year. Other excellence scholarships and bursaries also available.

**Accommodation**  Weekly costs range from around £71.96 (flats) to £82.95 (en suite flats); £82.95 to £84.98 in university-leased halls of residence. The university can offer advice on private-sector accommodation.

**Facilities**  New facilities include a £5.5m school of dentistry, a £6.5m student union, a £10m Brook building for health and business, and a £10m investment in science through the new Darwin building. Its new £10m campus in Burnley will open in September 2009.

**Transport**  The campus is located on the edge of the city centre – it's a 10-minute walk/ two-minute bus ride into the main shopping area. Under three hours on the train to London or Glasgow, and an hour from Manchester.

**❝ STUDENT VIEW ❞**

*"The lecture theatres and classrooms are spacious, and the teaching staff friendly and approachable, which makes all the difference. The tutors are always available for advice and guidance while the balance between theory and practice is just right."*

# Central School of Speech and Drama

Embassy Theatre
Eton Avenue
London  NW3 3HY

**t**  020 7722 8183
**e**  enquiries@cssd.ac.uk
↗ www.cssd.ac.uk

**》 further links**

ACCOMMODATION  accommodation@cssd.ac.uk
STUDENTS' UNION  www.ulu.co.uk

155        82.9       17.9       3.9        96.2

Founded in 1906, Central is a highly regarded drama and theatre school near Swiss Cottage in north London. Undergraduate courses range from acting to costume, design, lighting, sound, prop-making, puppetry and stage management – plus a course in drama, applied theatre and education. Famous alumni include Peggy Ashcroft, Harold Pinter and Vanessa Redgrave, so to say you've got the chance to follow some big footsteps at Central would be something of an understatement ...

**Fees**  £3,237 for full-time undergraduate courses in 2009-10.

**Bursaries**  There is a range of scholarships and bursaries that students can apply for.

**Accommodation**  There is very limited provision for Central students at the University of London's intercollegiate halls. Renting in the private sector will cost from £90 a week.

**Facilities**  Facilities include the £5m, 224-seat Embassy Theatre, plus the Embassy Studio and New Studio, each of which can accommodate 100 people.

**Transport**  Located in London with access to good tube, bus and rail services.

 **STUDENT VIEW** 》

*"One of the best things about studying at Central is how much of a family we are. The class sizes are small so you build up a great relationship with your lecturers and begin to know them as friends."*

# University of Chester

Chester Campus
Parkgate Road
Chester  CH1 4BJ

**t**  01244 511000
**e**  enquiries@chester.ac.uk
↗ www.chester.ac.uk

**Warrington Campus**  University of Chester, Crab Lane, Warrington  WA2 0DB

**»** **further links**

ACCOMMODATION  accommodation@chester.ac.uk
STUDENTS' UNION  www.chestersu.com

| 2295 | 96.6 | 36.4 | 15.2 | 95.8 |

Chester is a handsome, historical city in the north-west of England – and thankfully, the majority of its residents don't disport themselves in the manner of the local soap, Hollyoaks. The appeal of the place may be revealed in the fact that about a third of the students at the university come from the local area. They may also be attracted by the wide array of subjects: how about Muslim youth work or zoo management? There are two campuses, one in Chester and one in Warrington. A new £2m student union building was opened in 2007 on the Chester campus and a business/lifelong learning centre at Warrington. Both campuses are student-friendly, manageable and close to Liverpool and Manchester for some big nights out.

**Fees**  £3,225 for students on full-time undergraduate courses in 2009-10.

**Bursaries**  A non-repayable maintenance grant of £2,906 a year is available to new full-time students whose family income is less than £25,000 a year, while those whose family income is higher may qualify for a partial grant. Those who qualify for the full maintenance grant will also be entitled to receive a bursary of £1,000 a year.

**Accommodation**  Approximately 65% of first-year students are housed in halls of residence. In 2008-09, weekly prices range from £48.40 to £125.65.

**Facilities**  A new library and learning resources centre has recently opened in Warrington, to complement the rather larger one at Chester. Specialist degrees in sports science are run at both campuses, so facilities are good.

**Transport**  There is a shuttle bus service between the campuses and sites, and the city centre is walkable from the Chester campus. Good connections to Manchester and Liverpool.

**❝ STUDENT VIEW ❞**

*"I thoroughly enjoyed my time here and my student experience. In the end, I not only graduated with a good degree, but got enough experience and knowledge to equip myself for the real world."*

# University of Chichester

Bishop Otter Campus
College Lane, Chichester
West Sussex PO19 6PE

**t** 01243 816000
**e** admissions@chi.ac.uk
✓ www.chiuni.ac.uk

**Bognor Regis Campus**
University of Chichester, Upper Bognor Road, West Sussex PO21 1HR

>> **further links**

ACCOMMODATION accommodation@chi.ac.uk
STUDENTS' UNION www.chisu.org

915    96.4    35.3    7.8    95.5

Chichester

Chichester gained full university status in 2005 and prides itself on its friendly, close-knit feel. It is one of the smallest universities in the UK, with just over 5,000 students. The university feels accessible and integrated, being based on two historic campuses in Chichester and Bognor Regis, both relatively small places. West Sussex boasts some genuinely gorgeous scenery and the coast is within easy reach. You don't have to go anywhere to enjoy the benign climate. They must be doing something right – as well as good graduate employment rates, Chichester has an excellent student satisfaction rating and some of the best retention rates in the country.

**Fees** £3,225 a year for all full-time undergraduate courses in 2009-10.

**Bursaries** All students receiving full grant will receive bursaries of £1,077 a year, then on a sliding scale for those receiving partial grant, down to £256 a year.

**Accommodation** Halls of residence are available on both campuses in Chichester and Bognor Regis, both catered and self-catered. Prices for 2009-10 range from £83.75 to £142 a week.

**Facilities** Chichester will be an Olympic training camp leading up to the 2012 London Olympic games, so there are some pretty nifty sports facilities. The modern learning resource centre at Bishop Otter campus is award-winning.

**Transport** Free bus service between Chichester and Bognor Regis campuses. Both campuses are within 15 minutes' walk of the town centre. The Bognor Regis campus is a five-minute walk from the beach, and London is an hour-and-a-half away.

**❝ STUDENT VIEW ❞**

*"I would certainly recommend the University of Chichester as the standard of education is very good and the staff are very kind and always want to help. The location is beautiful and I am really happy here."*

# City University London

City University
Northampton Square
London   EC1V 0HB

**t**   020 7040 5060
**e**   ugadmissions@city.ac.uk
↗   www.city.ac.uk

**》 further links**

ACCOMMODATION   www.city.ac.uk/accommodation
STUDENTS' UNION   www.city.ac.uk/disability/students_union.html

1490     88.5     39.7     14.7     94.2

London

---

As the name suggests, City is located in the heart of London but its outlook is truly international. Students are drawn from 156 countries around the world, while staff come from over 40 different countries. There are commendable graduate employment rates, state-of-the-art facilities and an extensive public lecture and events programme. You're unlikely to find it a cheap place to study, but where better to spend your student loan? Both the West End and the City of London are virtually on your doorstep.

**Fees**   £3,225 a year for full-time undergraduate courses in 2009-10.

**Bursaries**   £770 for students in receipt of full maintenance grants, and £360 for students with household incomes of between £25,001 and £30,000. Merit-based scholarships in certain subjects.

**Accommodation**   The university can generally house all first-years from outside London.

**Facilities**   In 2008, the student union was refurbished to the tune of £1.5m — a new venue called Ten Squared can seat 160 diners during the day, while at night it hosts a wide range of events, making use of its state-of-the-art sound and lighting system. Many of the university's classrooms have recently been upgraded with audiovisual equipment, and a student centre opened in 2007.

**Transport**   City's central London location ensures that it benefits from excellent transport links. There are several bus routes, and the tube and mainline stations of Angel, Farringdon and Barbican.

**⟪ STUDENT VIEW ⟫**

*"I have always found the tutors at City very friendly, willing to help and feel that they genuinely care about the students here."*

# Conservatoire for Dance and Drama

1-7 Woburn Walk
London WC1H 0JJ

**t** 020 7387 5101
**e** info@cdd.ac.uk
↗ www.cdd.ac.uk

**»» further links**

ACCOMMODATION  Contact each affiliate school direct
STUDENTS' UNION  www.cdd.ac.uk/student-info/student-support

165      86.9      5.8      84.4

London

CDD was founded in 2001 and is a higher education institution that provides practice-based and vocational education and training in dance, acting, circus arts, technical theatre and theatre directing. It is made up of eight schools around the country: Bristol Old Vic Theatre School, the Central School of Ballet, Circus Space, London Academy of Music and Dramatic Arts, London Contemporary Dance School, the Northern School of Contemporary Dance, the Rambert School of Ballet and Contemporary Dance, and the Royal Academy of Dramatic Art. CDD doesn't have its own degree-awarding powers, so degrees are validated by different universities.

**Fees**  £3,225 for full-time undergraduate courses in 2009-10.

**Bursaries**  Up to £1,650 a year for students with a household income of £25,000 or less, then on a sliding scale.

**Accommodation**  Depends, naturally, on where you're living and studying. Each affiliate school should have someone on hand to help you find housing.

**Facilities**  The constituent institutions of CDD are specialist and well-respected: expect their facilities to be of a high standard and tailored to the demands of your course.

**Transport**  Depends on which school you're at: see their individual websites for details.

 **STUDENT VIEW »»**

*"I think this is the busiest I have ever been in my life. What with long hours, hard projects and challenging plays, there is barely time to catch my breath … and I love it!"*

# Courtauld Institute of Art

Somerset House
Strand
London  WC2R 0RN

**t**  020 7848 2645
**e**  ugadmissions@courtauld.ac.uk
⬈  www.courtauld.ac.uk

**》》 further links**

ACCOMMODATION  www.lon.ac.uk
STUDENTS' UNION  www.ulu.co.uk

50          42.9          22.5          6.8          100.0

As far as undergraduates go, the Courtauld is a one-trick pony: the only BA course it offers is history of art. But what a trick! The Courtauld is one of Britain's most famous galleries and art institutes, and the 400 or so students (of whom undergraduates make up about a third) have unrivalled access to it. As well as that, the spectacular location at Somerset House means that all of London's resources are on your doorstep. The emphasis is on small-group teaching, and the institute prides itself on its friendly feel and academic excellence. Degrees are awarded by the University of London, so you have access to the main university library at Senate House.

**Fees**  £3,225 for undergraduates in 2009-10.

**Bursaries**  There is a range of scholarships on offer, some very generous.

**Accommodation**  The institute aims to house as many first-year students as possible in intercollegiate halls in Bloomsbury or its own residence near Somerset House. About half of first-years (and all subsequent years) find private accommodation.

**Facilities**  Outstanding libraries and the gallery's collection of paintings, drawings and prints, and sculpture and decorative arts.

**Transport**  Located in central London and, therefore, connected to most underground, rail and bus networks.

**❝ STUDENT VIEW ❞**

*"It's a privilege to be part of such a diverse, intergenerational research community and to be taught by a world-class faculty defining the discipline of art history today."*

# Coventry University

Priory Street
Coventry CV1 5FB

**t** 02476 887688
**e** studentenquiries@coventry.ac.uk
**↗** www.coventry.ac.uk

›› **further links**

ACCOMMODATION accom.ss@coventry.ac.uk
STUDENTS' UNION www.cusu.org

| 2930 | 96.6 | 39.4 | 20.0 | 94.4 |

Perhaps you won't mind being sent to Coventry when you realise it means life on an impressive 13-hectare campus in the heart of one of the largest cities in England. A pleasant cathedral quarter and city centre showcase 1,000 years of history, and the city has all the facilities you'd expect. The university thinks of itself as modern and forward-looking. Courses have close vocational links with major global corporations and employability is a key concern.

**Fees** £3,225 a year for undergraduates in 2009–10.

**Bursaries** A bursary of £320 is available to all eligible undergraduates who qualify for a full or partial grant. A range of generous excellence scholarships is also available.

**Accommodation** Guaranteed for eligible first-years. Catered accommodation costs approximately £99 a week; self-catering accommodation £84 (standard) to £105 (en suite) a week.

**Facilities** Students benefit from an award-winning library, a new sports centre and a £5m student centre. A £160m investment in the campus will see the development of several new buildings, including a student building and a faculty of engineering and computing.

**Transport** Close to the M1/M6 intersection and half an hour from Birmingham by train; an hour-and-a-quarter to London.

**❝ STUDENT VIEW ❞**

*"Coventry's a place that can bring out the best in you, and the city's just the right size to feel at home and part of the local community."*

# University for the Creative Arts

New Dover Road
Canterbury  CT1 3AN

**t**  01227 817302
**e**  info@ucreative.ac.uk
**↗**  www.ucreative.ac.uk

**University College for the Creative Arts at Epsom**
Ashley Road, Surrey  KT18 5BE       **t**  01372 728811

**University College for the Creative Arts at Farnham**
Falkner Road, Surrey  GU9 7DS       **t**  01252 722441

**University College for the Creative Arts at Maidstone**
Oakwood Park, Kent  ME16 8AG       **t**  01622 620000

**University College for the Creative Arts at Rochester**
Fort Pitt, Kent  ME1 1DZ       **t**  01634 888702

**》 further links**

ACCOMMODATION  accommodation@ucreative.ac.uk
STUDENTS' UNION  www.uccasu.com

| 1440 | 98.2 | 34.3 | 10.9 | 88.8 |

**Canterbury**

Granted full university title last May, the University for the Creative Arts is one of the leading providers of specialist art and design education in Europe. A diverse community of about 6,500 students from 76 countries is spread across the south-east in the five constituent colleges (Canterbury, Epsom, Farnham, Maidstone and Rochester). Students come from all over the world to study at the university, win industry awards, and showcase their work at national and international festivals. Many members of staff here are creative practitioners as well as academics, so students are well prepared for the world of work. There is an impressive list of famous alumni, including the late TV animator Tony Hart.

**Fees**  £3,225 for full-time undergraduates in 2009-10.

**Bursaries**  A minimum of £310 for students in receipt of the full grant. Generous excellence scholarships also available.

**Accommodation**  Demand is high, but priority is given to new full-time students who don't live locally. There is a wide range of accommodation available and the university college maintains a list of private accommodation. Prices vary.

**Facilities**  Fully equipped specialist workshops for honing creative arts skills across alll subjects (ie pattern-cutting centre for fashion, glass and ceramics workshops). Good specialist libraries and active student support networks in place.

**Transport**  All campuses are close to motorways, rail networks and international airports.

**❝ STUDENT VIEW ❞**

*"When I joined UCA I never imagined I would be prepared so well for the future. My course leader's industry contacts alone have led to amazing and invaluable experiences that are preparing me really well for finding a job when I graduate."*

# University of Cumbria

Fusehill Street, Carlisle
Cumbria  CA1 2HH

**t**  01228 616234
**e**  admissions@cumbria.ac.uk
↗  www.cumbria.ac.uk

**Carlisle Campuses**  Brampton Road, Carlisle, Cumbria  CA3 9AY
Paternoster Row, Carlisle, Cumbria  CA3 8TB
**Lancaster Campus**  Bowerham Road, Lancaster  LA1 3JD
**London Campus**  English Street, Bow, London  E3 4TA
**Penrith Campus**  Newton Rigg, Penrith, Cumbria  CA11 0AH
**Ambleside Campus**  Rydal Road, Ambleside, Cumbria  LA22 9BB

**》 further links**

ACCOMMODATION  www.cumbria.ac.uk/accommodation
STUDENTS' UNION  www.thestudentsunion.org.uk

1555    98.5    37.2    14.5    92.7

Carlisle

The University of Cumbria was formed on 1 August 2007, from an amalgamation of St Martin's College, Cumbria Institute of the Arts, and the Cumbrian campuses of the University of Central Lancaster. The university has campuses in Carlisle, Newton Rigg, Penrith, Ambleside and Lancaster, and a specialist teacher education centre in London. It is committed to learning that is innovative, flexible and student-centred, and that utilises the latest technology. It prides itself on preparing its students for employment, and on its links with local schools, colleges, businesses and the community it serves.

**Fees**  £3,225 for full-time undergraduates in 2009–10.

**Bursaries**  Means-tested grants of between £1,290 and £215 are available to most students. Those on a four-year undergraduate teaching course receive £1,935 (non-means-tested) in their first year. Other scholarships also available.

**Accommodation**  First-year students are likely to find a place in university accommodation. There's a wide variety on offer and prices vary, though rents in the area are fairly reasonable.

**Facilities**  Sport plays a significant part in the life of the university, and facilities are extensive and of a high standard. Integrated services for library, media and IT support.

**Transport**  Good links by motorway and rail. International airports and big cities, including Manchester and Glasgow, are accessible.

**❝ STUDENT VIEW ❞**

*"The tutors here have a real passion for their subject and all the courses are delivered with real enthusiasm … you can't help but enjoy yourself!"*

# De Montfort University

The Gateway
Leicester  LE1 9BH

**t**  08459 454647
**e**  enquiry@dmu.ac.uk
**↗** www.dmu.ac.uk

**Charles Frears Campus**  266 London Road, Leicester  LE2 1RQ

**»  further links**

ACCOMMODATION  housing@dmu.ac.uk
STUDENTS' UNION  www.demontfortstudents.com

3825       97.0       41.9       14.4       93.3

The De Montfort of today has emerged from the unification of a wide range of specialist institutions and has an impressive way of re-inventing itself. Most recently this has meant allowing the Bedford campus to merge with the University of Luton to create the new University of Bedfordshire, and there is a constant programme of investment and development. Which leaves De Montfort a dynamic, forward-thinking and sizeable university. The main campus is in Leicester's city centre, with a second – the Charles Frears campus, offering courses in nursing and midwifery – on the outskirts. Leicester is England's 10th largest city, with good transport links and all the facilities you'd expect. It's also brilliantly multicultural: the Diwali celebrations in Leicester are something to be seen.

**Fees**  £3,225 for full-time undergraduates in 2009-10.

**Bursaries**  £500 for students in receipt of a full grant. Further regional bursaries and generous excellence scholarships are available.

**Accommodation**  Guaranteed for all first-years. University accommodation ranges from £74 to £90 a week. Rental cost in the city/town ranges from £35 to £161.50 a week.

**Facilities**  September 2009 will see the opening of a £35m building for the faculty of business and law, to include several major lecture theatres, an integrated law library and a mock courtroom. State-of-the-art facilities at the university's centre for excellence in performing arts and one of the most advanced recording and broadcast studios in a UK university. £1.7m has been spent on revamping the library. Good sports and social facilities.

**Transport**  Both campuses are within walking distance of the city centre. Road and rail links to the rest of the UK are excellent.

**❝ STUDENT VIEW ❞**

*"I chose DMU because of its growing reputation for academic excellence. The skills I'm learning are so relevant and practical and I know it will help me to play my part in building a better community."*

# University of Derby

Kedleston Road
Derby DE22 1GB

**t** 01332 591167
**e** askadmissions@derby.ac.uk
↗ www.derby.ac.uk

**University of Derby Buxton** 1 Devonshire Road, Buxton, Derbyshire SK17 6RY

## >> further links

ACCOMMODATION www.derby.ac.uk/accommodation
STUDENTS' UNION www.udsu.co.uk

| 2560 | 98.4 | 38.0 | 23.5 | 92.7 |

Flexibility is something of a watchword at Derby. It invites you to create your own degree, study part-time or choose a fast-track degree. It also emphasises its vocational slant — links with employers and other partners are carefully maintained — and 2008 saw the launch of an initiative called University of Derby Corporate, dedicated to engaging with employers and businesses, as well as developing enterprise and entrepreneurship. Derby is a pleasant, historical city, and Buxton, location of the university's grade II-listed Devonshire campus, is an equally charming spa town. Both are handy for some lovely countryside and easygoing enough to make you feel right at home.

**Fees** £3,225 for all full-time degrees in 2009-10.

**Bursaries** £830 for students eligible for the full government grant; then on a sliding scale for those eligible for a partial grant, down to £210. Further awards for local students are also available.

**Accommodation** Guaranteed for first-years, in one of seven halls of residence: six in Derby and one in Buxton. The halls are close to the campuses and you can opt to live in them for a second year. The costs range from £73 to £91.25 a week.

**Facilities** Sir Richard Branson opened the university's £21m arts, design and technology site in November 2007. Tennis courts and an all-weather sports pitch were opened in spring 2009, and £13.5m is currently being spent on refurbishing the three main towers.

**Transport** The university has an excellent sustainable transport plan throughout Derby, also servicing the Buxton campus during term-time. Frequent shuttle bus services run between Derby sites and into the city centre. Derby is 10 minutes from the M1 and on the main railway line from London St Pancras.

## ❰❰ STUDENT VIEW ❱❱
*"A quality place to live, work, and study. You get more than just a degree at Derby and it really shows. A brilliant experience for your entire time here."*

# University of Dundee

Nethergate
Dundee  DD1 4HN

**t**  01382 384000
**e**  university@dundee.ac.uk
↗  www.dundee.ac.uk

>> **further links**
ACCOMMODATION  residences@dundee.ac.uk
STUDENTS' UNION  dusa.co.uk

2000    88.3    25.7    15.1    95.5

Thanks to its south-facing position, Dundee has claims to be the sunniest city in Scotland. It's large enough to be interesting (and the most densely populated bit of Scotland after Glasgow), but compact enough to be friendly and manageable. It's close to Edinburgh, and there's nice countryside and coast if you have a surplus of physical energy to expend. The university has recently invested £200m in campus improvements, including £39m in new student accommodation. Expect your digs to be pretty fancy, then. Snow Patrol was formed by Dundee students.

**Fees**  Currently, Scottish students pay no fees. Other students are liable for £1,775 fees (£2,825 for degrees in medicine) in 2009.

**Bursaries**  Young students' bursaries available for Scottish students under 25 from low-income families. Students applying for and going on to study one of the three-year honours degree programmes can apply for the chancellor's scholarship of £1,000 a year for three years. Additional academic, musical and sporting bursaries available.

**Accommodation**  Guaranteed for applications received by July of the year of entry. New accommodation has recently been opened and there are four residence sites in total. Prices range from £56 to £105.

**Facilities**  The main library has been extended at a cost of £5.5m and has excellent modern facilities for silent and group study. Indoor sports facilities have been extended at a cost of £4m. The union has bars and clubs over five floors.

**Transport**  The main campus is in the city centre. Transport links to the rest of the country are excellent. Edinburgh and Glasgow are both within 90 minutes' travel by car or rail. The airport has a direct link to London City that takes 90 minutes.

**◀◀ STUDENT VIEW ▶▶**

*"Though occasionally cold and windy, Dundee is a great place to live as a student. As the city is fairly small, it has a great student-community atmosphere. It also has a good multicultural feel, with many students from all over the world."*

# Durham University

University Office
Old Elvet
Durham  DH1 3HP

**t**  0191 334 6128
**e**  admissions@durham.ac.uk
**↗**  www.durham.ac.uk

**Queen's Campus**  Stockton University Boulevard, Thornaby, Stockton-on-Tees  TS17 6BH

**»** **further links**

ACCOMMODATION  www.dur.ac.uk/colleges
STUDENTS' UNION  www.dsu.org.uk

| 3160 | 61.8 | 14.8 | 2.5 | 93.8 |

Durham

Durham is home to one of the country's top universities. The city is picturesque, wooded, hilly and aching with heritage. The Norman cathedral dominates the skyline — and it tells you something about the prestige of the university that one of its colleges is housed in the castle right next door. Durham is a collegiate university, meaning that student life has a real sense of focus and community to it. There's also more than a whiff of Oxbridge to proceedings – fun, if you like that sort of thing. If you don't, you'll probably be relieved to know that Durham has put its money where its mouth is when it comes to widening participation. Its Queen's campus in nearby Stockton-on-Tees boasts plenty of local and mature students.

**Fees**  £3,225 a year for full-time undergraduates in 2009-10.

**Bursaries**  Full-time undergraduates with a household income of less than £25,000 are eligible for a grant of up to £1,300 a year.

**Accommodation**  Approximately 99% of first-years live in college accommodation, and many second- and third-years are housed, too. Accommodation is provided by colleges and varies accordingly. Room-only accommodation is about £65 to £85 a week in Durham city and about £45 at Queen's campus.

**Facilities**  Excellent, well-stocked library in an award-winning building. It is one of only six libraries in the UK with national archive status. Good IT facilities and 26 hectares of sports fields. Each college provides its own range of services. They vary, but you'll find a good standard wherever you go.

**Transport**  Both Durham city and Stockton have road and rail links to the rest of the east coast and country, with two regional airports providing links to major UK and European cities. A free shuttle bus operates between campuses in term-time.

**❝ STUDENT VIEW ❞**

*"Durham University students, staff and alumni collectively contribute to a supportive and ambitious community; diverse in its achievements, dynamic in its goals and constantly striving to improve."*

# University of East Anglia

Norwich NR4 7TJ

t 01603 591515
e admissions@uea.ac.uk
www.uea.ac.uk

**»» further links**

ACCOMMODATION www.ueaaccommodation.com
STUDENTS' UNION www.ueastudent.com

| 2440 | 87.3 | 23.8 | 13.5 | 94.1 |

The campus is just a couple of miles from the centre of Norwich, though you may wonder why anyone would ever venture off campus: the 130 landscaped hectares boast excellent sports facilities, bars and cafes, and the excellent Sainsbury centre for visual arts. In the 2008 national student satisfaction survey, the overall satisfaction rating was 92%. An excellent reputation and a wide mix of courses probably helps to impress. The university prides itself on being at the forefront of green awareness, and aims to have its energy needs met by an on-campus biomass generating plant due for completion in 2009.

**Fees** £3,225 for the majority of full-time undergraduate courses in 2009–10. Fees for students studying physiotherapy, occupational therapy, speech and language therapy, nursing and midwifery will continue to be covered by the NHS students grant unit. First years of the science with a foundation year programme and the medical foundation year programme will cost £1,255.

**Bursaries** £600 for students in receipt of the full grant and £300 for students in receipt of a partial grant. Scholarships (some based on academic excellence) of up to £4,000 available.

**Accommodation** Guaranteed for eligible first-years. All accommodation is self-catering and most is based on campus. There is a range to choose from and it costs from £60 to £96 a week.

**Facilities** The library is open seven days a week and holds more than 800,000 volumes. Current facilities include a 50m Olympic pool, an athletics track, an indoor arena, squash and tennis courts, a climbing wall, a fitness centre, dance studios, and 16 hectares of playing fields and pitches.

**Transport** There's a 24-hour bus service. It's a two-hour trip by road or rail to London. Norwich airport is nearby and Stansted 90 minutes away.

**⁶⁶ STUDENT VIEW »**

*"I have found the lecturers on my course both helpful and knowledgeable. Campus life is one of the best things about the university and the atmosphere is lively. There's no other university quite like it."*

# University of East London

Docklands Campus
4–6 University Way
London  E16 2RD

**t**  020 8223 3000
**e**  admiss@uel.ac.uk
↗  www.uel.ac.uk

**Stratford Campus**  University House, Romford Road, London  E15 4LZ
**Duncan House**  Stratford High Street, London  E15 2JB

》 **further links**
ACCOMMODATION  www.uel.ac.uk/residential
STUDENTS' UNION  www.uelsu.net

3090    98.8    45.6    19.9    93.0

The University of East London is centred on the ultra-modern Docklands campus by the Thames, with another base at Stratford in east London, the hub of one of Europe's largest urban regeneration programmes, thanks to the 2012 Olympics. The university prides itself on developing new ways of teaching and learning that make the university as accessible and flexible as possible. Almost all its 21,000 students come from state schools and a large proportion are from ethnic minorities. Courses are innovative and responsive to the needs of students and industry.

**Fees**  £3,225 for all full-time undergraduate courses in 2009-10.

**Bursaries**  £300 for students in receipt of the full grant, plus a £500 progress bursary to all students who complete the first semester and progress to the second. The progress bursary is also available to students in receipt of a partial grant. Further scholarships for excellence also available.

**Accommodation**  Available for first-years who live outside the Greater London and Essex area. All rooms are en suite and range from £92 to £124 a week.

**Facilities**  Modern and inspiring buildings at the Docklands campus, with purpose-built teaching and learning facilities. Good libraries and some unexpected additional attractions, such as an on-site manufacturing facility and two industry-standard television studios.

**Transport**  It's London, so you've got the overground rail, tube, buses and Docklands Light Railway. And the rest of the UK links to the capital quite nicely.

 **STUDENT VIEW** 》
*"The courses are good. They are well thought out and teach skills that will be helpful after you graduate. It's so multicultural and a very modern place to study."*

# Edge Hill University

St Helens Road
Ormskirk
Lancashire  L39 4QP

**t**  01695 575171
**e**  enquiries@edgehill.ac.uk
**↗**  www.edgehill.ac.uk

**Aintree Campus**  University Hospital Aintree, Longmoor Lane, Liverpool  L9 7AL
**Woodlands Campus**  Woodlands Centre, Southport Road, Chorley, Lancashire  PR7 1QR
**Gateway House**  Faculty of Health, Piccadilly South, Manchester  M60 7LP
**Woodford Lodge Professional Centre**  Woodford Lane, West Winsford, Cheshire  CW7 4EH
**Wirral Education Centre**  Acre Lane, Bromborough, Wirral, Merseyside  CH62 7BZ

**》 further links**
ACCOMMODATION  accommodationteam@edgehill.ac.uk
STUDENTS' UNION  www.edgehillsu.com

1855     98.3     39.9     18.4     95.3

Edge Hill is growing rapidly and now has almost 23,000 students. An investment of £200m over the next 10 years means the main campus — a 65-hectare site located in west Lancashire — is set to expand significantly. An £8m state-of-the-art business and law school opened in 2009, and a £14m faculty of health opened in 2008. A lead institution for widening participation to higher education, the university ranks in the top four nationally for attracting young students from working-class families.

**Fees**  £3,225 for full-time undergraduate courses in 2009–10. Fees for siblings of those studying at Edge Hill are reduced by £1,000.

**Bursaries**  £500 if your household income is less than £25,000 a year. £200 learning support bursary for all students. Other bursaries and scholarships also available.

**Accommodation**  Most first-years live on campus, though it isn't guaranteed. Self-catering costs from £51 to £66 a week, and catered halls are £82.

**Facilities**  The campus boasts a lake, piazza area and plenty of green space. Well-resourced learning resource centre, good IT facilities across the campus and a 24-hour IT suite at the learning innovation centre. Resident DJs and live gigs are regularly hosted by the Venue at the student union, and a range of theatre, music and comedy is performed at the Rose theatre. Sporting Edge, the on-campus sports centre, provides high-quality facilities that were recently included in the Olympic pre-games training guide for London 2012. The centre includes a fully equipped gym, a swimming pool, a running track and sports fields.

**Transport**  The motorway connections to the rest of the UK are easy enough, but the train journey means a change at Liverpool or Preston.

**❝ STUDENT VIEW ❞**
*"Edge Hill University is like a mini-community. The course is teaching me so much and the staff are so friendly and supportive. They have really helped me believe in myself and my academic ability."*

# University of Edinburgh

Old College
South Bridge
Edinburgh  EH8 9YL

**t**  0131 650 1000
**e**  sra.enquiries@ed.ac.uk
**↗**  www.ed.ac.uk

**》 further links**

ACCOMMODATION  accommodation@ed.ac.uk
STUDENTS' UNION  www.eusa.ed.ac.uk

3490       68.0       15.7       5.8       95.4

Edinburgh

Edinburgh has an excellent national and international reputation, and a large, diverse and multinational student body. Edinburgh itself is vibrant and cosmopolitan, with stately architecture and green spaces. University buildings are spread throughout the city. Many of them are historic, but the university continues to develop: a state-of-the-art informatics forum opened in 2008.

**Fees**  Scottish and EU students from outside the UK pay no fees up front. For other UK students, there is an annual non-means-tested fee of £1,820 (£2,895 for medicine) in 2009-10.

**Bursaries**  Scottish students under 25 receive up to £2,640 a year in 2009-10, depending on parental income. Students from England, Wales and Northern Ireland who are in receipt of a maximum grant are eligible for an additional bursary. There is a large range of other scholarships and bursaries. See www.scholarships.ed.ac.uk

**Accommodation**  First-year undergraduates from outside Edinburgh are offered a range of catered options in single study bedrooms from £148 a week (sharing bathrooms) to £198 (en suite). Self-catering options in single rooms in flats with shared facilities cost from £81 to £102 a week. Options to share twin rooms, at cheaper rates, are available in both catered and self-catered accommodation.

**Facilities**  There are 17 libraries covering different subject areas, and you can use any of these. The centre for sport and exercise has several state-of-the-art gyms, a swimming pool, sports halls and a climbing wall. A complete range of exercise classes is available in addition to the 63 sports clubs on offer.

**Transport**  The university is spread throughout the city, with the majority of buildings within walking distance. Edinburgh has the excellent transport links you'd expect of a capital city. Edinburgh airport is eight miles away.

**❝ STUDENT VIEW ❞**

*"Edinburgh is a beautiful city and I trust the quality of teaching here. There are so many new things happening, it is impossible to keep up, it's the perfect setting for a fabulous student lifestyle!"*

# Edinburgh College of Art

Lauriston Place
Edinburgh  EH3 9DF

**t**  0131 221 6027
**e**  registry@eca.ac.uk
↗  www.eca.ac.uk

**》 further links**

ACCOMMODATION  ss@eca.ac.uk
STUDENTS' UNION  www.eca.ac.uk/index.php?id=335

 430
 82.8
 20.6
 3.7
 96.3

Edinburgh

Based near the famous Grassmarket, Edinburgh College of Art offers specialist programmes in art, design, architecture, landscape architecture, and visual and cultural studies. The college traces its origins back to 1760. Today there are approximately 1,700 students from all over the world. Art and design students take a shared first-year course, which provides a broad preparation for subsequent specialisation in any of 15 art or design subjects. The newly aligned Edinburgh school of architecture, a joint venture between the college and the University of Edinburgh, scored highly in the latest research assessment exercise and is already proving popular.

**Fees**  Full-time fees for 2009–10 are £1,820.

**Bursaries**  Bursaries and scholarships may be available to students who meet certain criteria.

**Accommodation**  Students who enrol for programmes run jointly with the University of Edinburgh are eligible for university accommodation. The college has no dedicated student accommodation, but it works closely with a privately run hall of residence across the road from the college. Student services offers an inquiry and flatmate-matching service.

**Facilities**  There is a wealth of studios, workshops and other facilities for design and architecture students. The college library lies at the heart of the newly developed learning zone, which provides an innovative environment for learning, teaching and research resources. The campus is Wi-Fi enabled and laptops may be borrowed. The Wee Red Club on campus is famed for its music nights.

**Transport**  Edinburgh is about four hours by regular train services from London and one hour by plane. The airport, with direct links to 98 UK and international destinations, is about 30 minutes from the college.

**《 STUDENT VIEW 》**

*"The teaching staff at Edinburgh College of Art were fantastic and have continued to give me support and advice even after my graduation."*

# Edinburgh Napier University

Craiglockhart Campus
Edinburgh  EH14 1DJ

**t**  08452 606040
**e**  info@napier.ac.uk
↗ www.napier.ac.uk

**Merchiston**  Edinburgh  EH10 5DT
**Craighouse Campus**  Craighouse road, Edinburgh  EH10 5LB
**Canaan Lane**  Edinburgh  EH9 2TB
**Comely Bank**  Edinburgh  EH4 2LD
**Marchmont Campus**  Edinburgh  EH9 1HU
**Morningside Campus**  Edinburgh  EH10 4BY

≫ **further links**

ACCOMMODATION  accommodation@-napier.ac.uk
STUDENTS' UNION  www.napierstudents.com

Edinburgh

1880   96.0   33.3   16.7   97.5

Edinburgh Napier is Scotland's top modern university and one of the largest higher education institutions in the country, with almost 15,000 students, including 3,000 international students from more than 100 countries. It has a number of campuses within easy reach of the buzzy city centre. The university has an excellent employability record, with 97.5% of graduates in employment or further study within six months of graduating.

**Fees**  Scottish and EU students can get their tuition fees paid. Students from England, Wales and Northern Ireland should apply to their local authority or awarding body to determine the level of fees they must pay.

**Bursaries**  A range of scholarships and trust funds for new students, particularly those in need, also for mature students, overseas students, or those with dependants. Students from the UK (not Scotland) paying fees and claiming a full grant are entitled to a bursary of about £300.

**Accommodation**  Available to most new undergraduate students for the full academic year. Rent works out at about £80 a week.

**Facilities**  The 500-seat Jack Kilby computing centre is open 24/7 and students have access to online lecture notes and study aids. There are fully networked libraries at each campus, and a state-of-the-art mulitmedia language lab and adaptive technology centre for students with special needs. The Craiglockhart campus even has a fitness suite with qualified staff to provide inductions, health advice and personalised fitness programmes.

**Transport**  Good train links from Edinburgh to London via Newcastle and York. Access to motorways and a nearby airport.

**❝ STUDENT VIEW ❞**

*"Edinburgh Napier's graduate employability record was one of the biggest reasons for me coming here."*

# University of Essex

Wivenhoe Park
Colchester  CO4 3SQ

**t**  01206 873666
**e**  admit@essex.ac.uk
↗  www.essex.ac.uk

**East 15, Loughton Campus**  Hatfields, Rectory Lane, Loughton  IG10 3RY
**Southend Campus**  Elmer Approach, Southend-on-Sea  SS1 1LW

》 **further links**

ACCOMMODATION  accom@essex.ac.uk
STUDENTS' UNION  www.essexstudent.com

1740      95.2      31.8      12.1      90.3

Essex has just over 9,000 students on three campuses – Colchester, Loughton and Southend – with 80 hectares of landscaped grounds at the oldest and largest campus on the outskirts of Colchester. The student union has invested more than £3m at the campus over the past five years and recently opened a nightclub, following a £1.25m redevelopment. The £25m Southend campus was opened in spring 2008. Essex boasts a consistently strong academic performance and was ranked ninth in the UK for the quality of its research in the 2008 research assessment exercise.

**Fees**  £3,225 for all full-time undergraduate courses in 2009–10.

**Bursaries**  If your household income is less than £25,000, you will receive £319 a year. Between £25,001 and £34,000, you will receive bursaries to top up your partial grant, to bring your overall support to £3,225. Then on a sliding scale for students with household incomes of between £34,001 and £50,020.

**Accommodation**  From £63 a week for standard accommodation and £93 a week for en suite. All first-year students not living within the respective campus borough are guaranteed accommodation.

**Facilities**  The union nightclub has been named the best student venue in the UK and there are three further bars to tempt you. 16 hectares of the Colchester campus are devoted to sport.

**Transport**  Colchester campus is two miles from the town centre on major bus routes. There are two railway stations in the town. London is an hour away. The Southend campus is near the town's two railway stations with direct routes into London, while central London is accessible from the Loughton campus by the underground (Central line). All three campuses are within driving distance of Stansted airport.

❝ **STUDENT VIEW** ❞

*"My decision to go to the university, I feel is the best of my life. The excellent teaching, research facilities and friendly campus have provided me with new skills and experiences that will benefit me in every aspect of my future."*

# University of Exeter

Streatham Campus
Northcote House
Exeter EX4 4QJ

**t** 01392 263855
**e** ug-ad@exeter.ac.uk
**↗** www.exeter.ac.uk

**St Luke's Campus** Heavitree Road, Exeter EX1 2LU
**Tremough Campus** Penryn, Cornwall TR10 9EZ

**》 further links**

ACCOMMODATION www.exeter.ac.uk/accommodation
STUDENTS' UNION www.exeterguild.org

2600    72.8    16.7    8.3    94.7

Exeter

Students at Exeter are likely to have permanent smiles on their faces: it has campuses in the cathedral city and also near Falmouth, in Cornwall, as well as plenty of coastline, countryside and glorious weather. Add to that the fact that the Streatham campus is widely regarded as one of the most beautiful in the country, and that Exeter is rated one of the best universities in the UK for "ents", and it's no wonder that increases in applications far exceed the national average. Of course, you'll have to do some work, too — Exeter has an excellent academic reputation.

**Fees** £3,225 for full-time undergraduate courses in 2009-10.

**Bursaries** Means-tested bursaries of up to £1,500 a year are available for students from low-income backgrounds and the south-west bursary scheme allows students resident in the region to apply for additional top-up awards. Other scholarships are available.

**Accommodation** Guaranteed for first-year students. Costs range from £69 to £171 a week.

**Facilities** Library facilities are currently undergoing a £9m investment and users benefit from 24/7 access, self-service machines, state-of-the-art multimedia facilities, enhanced group and silent study areas, and an extended Wi-Fi network. Excellent sports facilities, too. The university has invested £140m in new buildings and facilities over the last five years, and is now planning to substantially improve campus facilities.

**Transport** Short walks into town from either campus in Exeter. The Cornwall campus is a 15-minute bus ride into Falmouth. The M5 is handy for Exeter and London is two hours by train. Two hours or more in the other direction to Falmouth from Exeter.

---

**❝ STUDENT VIEW ❞**

*"My time in Exeter has been an experience I will never forget. It has really formed the person I am today from what I have learned both through academic teaching and the societies and activities I have been involved in."*

# University College Falmouth
## Incorporating Dartington College of Arts

Woodlane
Falmouth
Cornwall  TR11 4RH

**t**  01326 211077
**e**  admissions@falmouth.ac.uk
↗  www.falmouth.ac.uk

**Tremough Campus**  Tremough, Penryn, Cornwall  TR10 9EZ

**》 further links**

ACCOMMODATION  www.tremoughservices/accommodation
STUDENTS' UNION  www.fxu.org.uk

675      97.6      31.7      11.9      94.3

Falmouth

Courses at University College Falmouth focus on art and design, and they are taught in Falmouth and on the Tremough campus of the Combined Universities in Cornwall. Falmouth is famous for its beautiful harbour, and the rest of Cornwall is no less enticing. Such inspiring settings should get your creative juices flowing nicely.

**Fees**  £3,225 for full-time undergraduates in 2009-10.

**Bursaries**  Means-tested bursaries of up to £850 a year. Additional grants for living expenses and for students with dependants and with special educational needs.

**Accommodation**  The weekly rental cost for halls of residence is £70 to £105 a week; all are self-catering. Private-sector housing costs between £65 and £100 a week.

**Facilities**  The college is proud of its high-spec design, photography and media centres. A performance centre is due to open in October 2010.

**Transport**  Falmouth and Penryn are situated on the A39, which links to the A30 trunk road that runs the length of Cornwall. Regular trains link the town to London and elsewhere. Truro to London Paddington takes just over four hours. Newquay airport is approximately 20 miles away and flights operate daily to Gatwick and Stansted — the journey takes about an hour.

**❝ STUDENT VIEW ❞**

*"With so many different disciplines studying here, the diversity of ideas is really inspiring. Not only are our facilities some of the best in the country, but you can just step out of the door, and take in the beautiful scenery and subtropical gardens."*

# Glamorgan University

Pontypridd  CF37 1DL

t  0800 716925
e  enquiries@glam.ac.uk
↗ www.glam.ac.uk

>> **further links**

ACCOMMODATION  accom@glam.ac.uk
STUDENTS' UNION  www.glamsu.com

3295      98.4      42.0      29.0      94.2

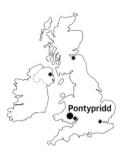

Pontypridd

The University of Glamorgan boasts three modern campuses, two in Treforest near the town of Pontypridd and a brand new, state-of-the-art facility in the heart of Cardiff city centre. Glamorgan is committed to innovation in teaching and learning, and to equipping students with the skills they will need for their chosen careers. The university attracts more than 21,000 students across its campuses and is known for its friendly, community atmosphere. There has been an impressive 18.4% increase in applications this year. Glamorgan's status as one of Wales's research-active universities was confirmed by its excellent results for the quality of its research in the 2008 research assessment exercise.

**Fees**  £3,225 a year for all full-time undergraduate courses. Wales and EU (non-UK) students are eligible for a non-means-tested grant of £1,940 a year from the Welsh Assembly government.

**Bursaries**  For 2009 entry, a scholarship for full-time undergraduates worth £3,000; £1,000 each year to students who have achieved 300 or more Ucas points. A residential allowance worth £1,500; £500 to be paid each year to students whose home address is more than 45 miles away. Other funding also available.

**Accommodation**  Weekly rent for self-catering accommodation is about £82. Private halls of residence available at the Cardiff campus.

**Facilities**  The campus boasts good IT facilities and sports facilities that are some of the best in the country (used by international rugby and football teams for training). A brand new student union building will be completed in 2010, as well as new halls of residence on the Treforest campus.

**Transport**  Pontypridd campuses: on the M4 corridor, and 20 minutes by train or car to Cardiff. The Atrium campus is in Cardiff city centre.

**❝ STUDENT VIEW ❞**

*"The University of Glamorgan has so much to offer students in terms of courses and the great facilities on its campuses. The lecturers on my course couldn't be more supportive and the quality of teaching is superb. Definitely the best decision I've ever made!"*

# University of Glasgow

University Avenue
Glasgow  G12 8QQ

**t**  0141 330 6062
**e**  ugenquiries@gla.ac.uk
↗  www.gla.ac.uk

**»** **further links**

ACCOMMODATION  accom@gla.ac.uk
STUDENTS' UNION  www.theguu.com

3620    86.6    21.9    13.1    94.9

Glasgow is Scotland's second oldest university, the UK's fourth oldest, and an important pillar of Scotland's biggest city. As well as excellent teaching and a worldwide reputation, students enjoy a compact campus at the heart of the city's stylish West End. A flexible system of study means that those who aren't studying for a professional degree can make the final decision about their honours subject/s at the end of the second year. Glasgow is a confident and dynamic city that has reinvented itself in recent years. Facilities for shopping, entertainment and cultural pursuits are excellent, and there is dramatic countryside nearby.

**Fees**  Eligible Scottish and EU-domiciled students studying full-time are entitled to free tuition. Tuition fees are charged for English, Welsh and Northern Irish students, currently £1,820 (£2,895 for medicine) a year in 2009-10.

**Bursaries**  Young students' bursaries for Scots under 25 from low-income families. Students from England, Wales and Northern Ireland who are in receipt of a maximum maintenance award are eligible for a bursary of £315. A further range of scholarships and bursaries available.

**Accommodation**  Most first-years live in university accommodation; a wide range, at varying costs, is available.

**Facilities**  Travel within Glasgow is made easy by an underground system that connects the university to the city centre in about 10 minutes. There are bus and overground train services, too. And two train stations, good road links and two airports nearby.

**Transport**  Travel within Glasgow is made easy by an underground system that connects the university to the city centre in 10 minutes. There are bus and overground train services, plus two train stations, good road links and an airport nearby, too.

**❝ STUDENT VIEW ❞**

*"I chose Glasgow because of its stellar international reputation as a research university. Right from first year I got the opportunity to delve into the subjects I was most interested in, taught by professors actively engaged in research in the field."*

# Glasgow Caledonian University

Cowcaddens Road
Glasgow  G4 0BA

t  0141 331 3000
e  admissions@gcal.ac.uk
↗ www.gcal.ac.uk

» **further links**
ACCOMMODATION  accommodation@gcal.ac.uk
STUDENTS' UNION  www.caledonianstudent.com

3210     96.2     35.0     20.6     94.8

With approximately 17,000 students, Glasgow Caledonian University is one of Scotland's largest universities in terms of recruitment. Its campus is in the Cowcaddens area, right in the middle of the city. Key academic strengths are health, the environment, creative culture, business and social justice. Widening access is central to Glasgow Caledonian's philosophy, as is being known for social entrepreneurship, and actively engaging in social and economic regeneration in Glasgow. Like the city it is in, its confidence is high.

**Fees**  Scottish students receive free tuition. Students from England, Wales and Northern Ireland are liable for tuition fees of £1,820 in 2009-10.

**Bursaries**  Young students' bursaries for Scottish students under 25 from low-income families. Other grants, scholarships and bursaries available.

**Accommodation**  Awarded according to criteria that include age, special needs, distance from campus and international status. Self-catering accommodation costs from £73.30 to £84.50 a week.

**Facilities**  The Saltire centre, the hub of the campus, is the first university building of its kind to integrate all learning and student services: library, study spaces, a student services mall and a learning cafe. Innovative teaching facilities, such as the virtual hospital, too.

**Transport**  As you would expect in a big city: extensive public transport and good links. The airport is seven miles away.

 **STUDENT VIEW** »
*"Glasgow Caledonian University presents a vibrant and modern environment, not only for learning and teaching but also for individual development and group work. It's the place to learn!"*

# Glasgow School of Art

167 Renfrew Street
Glasgow  G3 6RQ

**t**  0141 353 4500
**e**  registry@gsa.ac.uk
↗  www.gsa.ac.uk

**》 further links**

ACCOMMODATION  welfare@gsa.ac.uk
STUDENTS' UNION  www.gsa.ac.uk/gsa.cfm?pid=23

Glasgow

270    87.0    18.0    5.0    81.7

The Glasgow School of Art (GSA) was founded in 1845 as a government school of design. One of the few remaining independent schools in the UK, GSA is one of the UK's pre-eminent institutions for the study of fine art, design and architecture. In fact, a quarter of the artists shortlisted for the Turner Prize since 2005 have been GSA graduates. At the heart of the campus lies the Mackintosh building designed by the famous Scottish architect Charles Rennie Mackintosh, an alumnus of the college. Courses are offered within the schools of architecture, design or fine art, and about 15% of the 1,900-strong student body is international.

**Fees**  £1,820 a year for undergraduates in 2009–10. Scottish students do not pay the fee.

**Bursaries**  The GSA offers a range of scholarships with different eligibility criteria. There is also a hardship fund.

**Accommodation**  There is one purpose-built hall of residence, located within a couple of minutes' walking distance from the campus. It also subleases residential accommodation from the University of Glasgow, located in the West End of the city: half of all GSA bed spaces are located on this site.

**Facilities**  A digital design studio, a centre for advanced textiles, and several galleries and exhibition spaces. The school also boasts a nightclub and a venue, the Arts School.

**Transport**  Five hours by train to London. Short walk to the city centre from campus.

**❝ STUDENT VIEW ❞**

*"The GSA is an amazing creative environment, there is always so much going on and every show and exhibition I have seen here has inspired me to work harder and get better at what I do."*

# University of Gloucestershire

The Park
Cheltenham  GL50 2RH

**t**  08707 210210
**e**  admissions@glos.ac.uk
**↗**  www.glos.ac.uk

**Pittville Studios**  Albert Road, Cheltenham  GL52 3JG
**Francis Close Hall Campus**  Swindon Road, Cheltenham  GL50 4AZ
**Oxstalls Campus**  Oxstalls Lane, Longlevens, Gloucester  GL2 9HW

**》 further links**

ACCOMMODATION  accommodation@glos.ac.uk
STUDENTS' UNION  www.yourstudentsunion.com

1680      95.2      32.1      10.1      96.8

Students are spread over five campuses: three in Cheltenham, one in Gloucester and one in London. Cheltenham, in particular, is attractive, but it and Gloucester can both support a decent social life and have good links to bigger cities, as well as some appealing rural surroundings. The university is proud of its green credentials and sustainable policies: it was ranked number one in the People & Planet's green league of universities (2008). Learning is flexible – there are large groups of mature and part-time students – and courses are innovative. There is emphasis on industry links and work placements, with an eye to preparing you for a future career.

**Fees**  £3,225 for full-time undergraduate courses in 2009-10.

**Bursaries**  Students qualifying for a full grant are eligible for a bursary of £319. A one-off payment of £500 is available to students with 360 or more Ucas points. Students from partner colleges are eligible for a payment of £1,000. Further scholarships and support available.

**Accommodation**  There are halls on or near all campuses with space for 1,000 students. Most students (and some first-years) live in private accommodation. Rooms cost from £69 a week.

**Facilities**  All learning centres offer free internet and email access, and are open seven days a week during term-time. Wireless network facilities are available on all campuses. The university boasts an aerobic and resistance fitness suite with accompanying dance studio, competition-standard cricket facilities, laboratory facilities and an all-weather pitch.

**Transport**  Good (free) bus links are provided between campuses. Road and rail links are generally pretty good, depending on which campus you are on.

**❝ STUDENT VIEW ❞**

*"The university has a great working and living environment. But for me the main attraction was the lecturers – they are the people who can help you get the best degree possible."*

# Glyndŵr University

Plas Coch Campus
Mold Road
Wrexham  LL11 2AW

**t**  01978 293439
**e**  sid@glyndwr.ac.uk
↗  glyndwr.ac.uk

**》 further links**

ACCOMMODATION  accommodation@glyndwr.ac.uk
STUDENTS' UNION  www.newisu.com

720       99.7      46.2      22.8      91.7

Glyndŵr was born in July 2008 when the North East Wales Institute of Higher Education was granted university status and changed its name to that of Welsh hero Owain Glyndŵr. The university has two main sites: Plas Coch and the North Wales school of art and design. The university has approximately 8,000 full-time students and prides itself on its enterprising spirit. Students benefit from the university's links with companies such as Kellogg's, JCB, Tetrapak, Cadbury and Sharp. Based near the centre of Wrexham, north Wales's largest town, means pubs, clubs and restaurants are covered. As is shopping, thanks to Eagles Meadow, a new shopping and entertainment complex. But if you're one for the great outdoors, a short drive takes you into the spectacular Welsh hills and countryside.

**Fees**  For 2009 entry, £3,225 for all full-time undergraduate students from the UK. Eligible Welsh full-time students can apply to receive a Welsh Assembly government fee grant of up to £1,940.

**Bursaries**  Bursaries from £500 to £1,000, dependent on household income. Sports awards are available, as well as an excellence scholarship.

**Accommodation**  Rooms in university accommodation cost as little as £50 to £77 a week. Rooms with shared facilities also available off campus in Wrexham town centre.

**Facilities**  A well-resourced library and plenty of computer suites across campus. There is an on-campus sports centre, a second-language learning centre and a new £3m performing arts centre.

**Transport**  Wrexham has direct train links to London, Birmingham and Cardiff.

**❝ STUDENT VIEW ❞**

*"The facilities and the accommodation are close together and give us the opportunity to meet different people and build up relationships. Glyndŵr is a nice place for student life."*

# Goldsmiths, University of London

New Cross
London SE14 6NW

**t** 020 7078 5300
**e** admissions@gold.ac.uk
**↗** www.goldsmiths.ac.uk

**》》 further links**

ACCOMMODATION accommodation@gold.ac.uk
STUDENTS' UNION www.goldsmithsstudents.com

| 1265 | 91.6 | 30.2 | 14.4 | 95.5 |

London

Subjects offered cover the arts, social sciences, humanities and computing. The college is almost entirely based on one site in New Cross, south-east London, an area regularly described as "up and coming". It is certainly vibrant, with excellent links to the centre of London and a burgeoning artistic scene. The cost of living is also more reasonable than in many areas. There is plenty of creative energy flowing among the 8,000 or so students; a high proportion are mature and a quarter come from outside the UK, which makes for a diverse student body. Add to that the potential of one of the world's greatest cities and you can pretty much do whatever you set your mind to at Goldsmiths.

**Fees** £3,225 a year for all full-time undergraduate courses in 2009-10.

**Bursaries** Details for 2010 entry were not finalised at time of printing.
See goldsmiths.ac.uk/ug/costs for updates. A range of scholarships is available.

**Accommodation** Priority is given to full-time first-years from outside London. Accommodation is self-catering and the average weekly cost for a single room was £85 to £114 in 2008-09. Catered accommodation in University of London intercollegiate halls was £109 to £250.

**Facilities** An award-winning student union, including a new fitness centre, a well-equipped library (including excellent IT facilities), wireless hotspots and a virtual learning environment. There are nine specialist research labs, workshop facilites, a 160-seat theatre and three performance studios, and a radio and TV studio.

**Transport** Just 15 minutes by train to central London. The campus is also well placed in terms of bus (including night bus) routes and Deptford Bridge DLR station (which links to the tube network) is a 10-minute walk away.

**❝❝ STUDENT VIEW ❞❞**

*"No student here is treated like a number, but as an individual with worthwhile things to say. I've always felt encouraged to explore new ways of thinking and writing, without being bound to any one 'right' way of doing things. "*

# University of Greenwich

Old Royal Naval College
Park Row
Greenwich SE10 9LS

**t** 0800 005006
**e** courseinfo@gre.ac.uk
**↗** www.gre.ac.uk

**Avery Hill** Mansion Site, Bexley Road, Eltham, London SE9 2PQ
**Medway** Central Avenue, Chatham Maritime, Kent ME4 4TB

**》 further links**

ACCOMMODATION gre.ac.uk/about/accommodation
STUDENTS' UNION www.suug.co.uk

3125    97.8    46.4    20.8    87.5

The university boasts a world heritage site. The main campus is on the banks of the Thames in three baroque buildings designed by Sir Christopher Wren. Other sites are Avery Hill, in an 35-hectare park in Eltham, south-east London, and Medway, another charming campus full of Edwardian redbrick and ivy, near Chatham's historic dockyard. As a result, the 28,000 students are spread between city and more rural locations, though all are part of an institution that is proud of its diversity and committed to widening participation.

**Fees** £2,900 for full-time undergraduates in 2009-10. Fees for some programmes, including programmes taken at partner colleges, vary. See gre.ac.uk/students/finance

**Bursaries** Greenwich offers mature student bursaries and scholarships for students with high Ucas points. More specialised scholarships available. See gre.ac.uk/students/finance/uni_support/bursaries

**Accommodation** Guaranteed for first-years. Prices range from about £74 to £163 a week.

**Facilities** Major libraries, computing facilities, student union facilities, catering facilities and bars at all campuses. Avery Hill has a new gym and sports fields. Medway has a sports centre. Greenwich is close to a council-run sports centre, as well as plenty of bars, restaurants and takeaways. It is also just down the river from the O2 arena. New developments include a student hall of residence at Medway and a refurbished cafe at the Medway campus.

**Transport** The Greenwich campus can be reached by Docklands Light Railway, rail and boat. You can be at London Bridge in 20 minutes. Avery Hill to London Bridge involves a 10-15 minute walk to the station and a 25-minute rail journey. The Medway campus takes just under an hour-and-a-half from London by train, then bus in Medway. Greenwich provides an inter-campus bus service linking Avery Hill to Greenwich and Medway.

**❝ STUDENT VIEW ❞**

*"The Greenwich campus has beautiful surroundings, it is often used as a film location and is just upriver from the O2. The tutors are very helpful and provide great support for students adapting to university life."*

# Guildhall School of Music & Drama

Silk Street
Barbican EC2Y 8DT

**t** 020 7628 2571
**e** registry@gsmd.ac.uk
**↗** www.gsmd.ac.uk

**》》 further links**

ACCOMMODATION  accommodation@gsmd.ac.uk
STUDENTS' UNION  gsmd.ac.uk/school/student_facilities
/students_union.htm

95      61.5      93.8

London

The Guildhall School of Music & Drama is one of Europe's leading conservatoires, offering musicians, actors, stage managers and theatre technicians an inspiring environment in which to develop as artists and professionals. The school first opened its doors in 1880 to 62 part-time students in a disused warehouse in the City of London. Today it is situated in the heart of one of Britain's most important arts venues at the Barbican and has more than 800 full-time music and drama students, with a growing international reputation for its teaching and research. More than a third of the school's students are from outside the UK and represent more than 40 nationalities. Its degrees are validated by City University London.

**Fees**  £3,225 for full-time undergraduate programmes in 2009-10.

**Bursaries**  The school offers a wide range of bursaries and scholarships to all students. It provides additional support for UK undergraduate students from disadvantaged backgrounds via the Guildhall bursary scheme, which pays bursaries equivalent to 50% of the value of the grant to those already in receipt of the grant.

**Accommodation**  Sundial Court, the school's hall of residence, is located around the corner from the main building and has 177 bedrooms in 39 flats. Anticipated cost in 2009-10 is £112 a week.

**Facilities**  The Silk Street building includes a 186-seat music hall, an 80-seat lecture recital room and a 308-seat theatre, all of which are open to the public. There is a studio theatre, 41 teaching/practice rooms, electronic music studios, recording and sound studios, the students' common room and IT facilities. A new building, due to open in 2012, will house additional world-class performance facilities: a 609-seat concert hall, a 225-seat training theatre, a studio theatre, and a space for teaching, office and support services.

**Transport**  The Guildhall School is right in the heart of London. Barbican, Moorgate, Liverpool Street, St Paul's and Bank tube stations are all nearby.

**❝ STUDENT VIEW ❞**
*"When you walk into Guildhall, the whole foyer feels alive and bustling. It's this atmosphere, along with the motivated lecturers and inspired students, that got me to accept the offer of a place here."*

# Harper Adams University College

Newport
Shropshire  TF10 8NB

**t** 01952 820280
**e** admissions@harper-adams.ac.uk
↗ www.harper-adams.ac.uk

**》 further links**

ACCOMMODATION  01952 815286
STUDENTS' UNION  www.harper-adams.ac.uk/su

335        80.8        61.0        13.3        99.0

This specialist agricultural and rural institution has just 2,000 students, giving them the chance to experience living in a close-knit community. Set in the lovely Shropshire countryside, there's little around but peace and quiet, and the small town of Newport. Despite this, or perhaps because of it, the on-campus entertainments will easily satisfy the part of you that thirsts for noise, raucous fun and beer. It will come as little surprise that most of the courses focus on rural and land-based subjects. And its course list is ever-expanding as it aims to educate the future leaders and guardians of a sustainable, rural economy.

**Fees**  £3,225 for full-time undergraduate courses in 2009-10.

**Bursaries**  If you have a household income of up to £25,000, you will receive £1,500. Between £25,001 and £28,500, you will receive £750. Between £28,501 and £38,330, you will receive £500. Students who do not qualify for a means-tested scholarship can apply for a merit scholarship, which can be from £250 to £750.

**Accommodation**  All first-year students are guaranteed a place in university-managed accommodation. The university offers a choice of en suite and standard rooms in catered or self-catered halls of residence. Charges range from £89 to £131 a week in 2009-10.

**Facilities**  The modern library and IT suite are at the heart of the campus, which also contains a working farm. There are specialist facilities for students studying engineering, animal health and veterinary nursing programmes, as well as sports pitches, a sports hall, a gym and a swimming pool.

**Transport**  There is a bus service to Newport, about two miles away. The larger towns of Shrewsbury and Telford (for the nearest station) are also conveniently located.

**◀◀ STUDENT VIEW ▶▶**

*"The quality of teaching at Harper is excellent. All the lecturers have recently worked in practice or excel in a particular area, and the placement year puts everything into context, making you want to learn more!"*

# Heriot-Watt University

Edinburgh EH14 4AS

t 0131 449 5111
e enquiries@hw.ac.uk
↗ www.hw.ac.uk

**Dubai Campus** Dubai International Academic City, UAE
**Scottish Borders Campus** Netherdale, Galashiels, Selkirkshire TD1 3HF

**》 further links**
ACCOMMODATION www.hw.ac.uk/welfare/accommodation
STUDENTS' UNION www.hwusa.org

1175 91.8 27.6 11.8 94.9

Edinburgh

Uniquely among Scottish universities, Heriot-Watt can boast near-constant sunshine, a glamorous beachside position and sky-scrapers as far as the eye can see. Admittedly, this is only if you are studying at the Dubai campus, but other students don't do too badly, nonetheless. The Edinburgh campus occupies 154 hectares of meadow and woodland, and the Scottish borders campus in Galashiels, south of Edinburgh, is right in the very heart of the borders. Heriot-Watt emphasises career progression and flexible learning. Strengths include subjects related to the petroleum industry, brewing and distilling. Well, it is Scottish, even if it does have a Middle Eastern outpost.

**Fees** If you are from Scotland, you won't have to pay fees. Students from England, Wales and Northern Ireland will pay fees, yet to be set, but with a loan to cover the cost.

**Bursaries** The young students' bursary is available for Scottish students from low-income families. A wide range of further bursaries and scholarships also available. See scholarships.hw.ac.uk.

**Accommodation** Guaranteed for first-years, with rents ranging from £57 to £94.50 a week.

**Facilities** The Heriot-Watt university archive and museum contains many unique records relating to the history of science, engineering, technology and business, going back to 1821. The textile collection at the Scottish borders campus houses one of the finest collections of textile records and artefacts in the world.

**Transport** Edinburgh's the capital, so all the links by road, rail and air are what you would expect.

**❝ STUDENT VIEW ❞**
*"Heriot-Watt University has given me much, both socially and academically, as I am developing every day. By studying here I have obtained great expectations for the future and hopefully a solid base for job prospects."*

# University of Hertfordshire

College Lane
Hatfield
Hertfordshire  AL10 9AB

**t**  01707 284000
**e**  ask@herts.ac.uk
**↗**  www.herts.ac.uk

**Law Studies**  7 Hatfield, St Albans, Hertfordshire  AL1 3RS

**》 further links**

ACCOMMODATION  accommodation@herts.ac.uk
STUDENTS' UNION  uhsu.herts.ac.uk

| 4235 | 97.9 | 39.5 | 15.7 | 93.0 |

The university is located on two sites in Hatfield, within easy reach of each other, and a third in St Albans. The purpose-built De Havilland campus offers excellent facilities for sport, 24/7 learning and stylish undergraduate accommodation. Hertfordshire takes a flexible approach to learning, with possibilities for e-learning and part-time study. A new focus on creative and cultural industries has given rise to a host of new courses. A £10m media centre in Hatfield houses the latest technology for the teaching of music, animation, film, television and multimedia.

**Fees**  £3,225 for undergraduate courses in 2009-10.

**Bursaries**  The university will pay £1,000 of the value of your grant from 2009-10. Students may receive one of two main scholarships: those with at least 360 Ucas points will receive the chancellor's scholarship of £2,500 in their first year; science and engineering scholarships worth up to £3,000 over four years are available for students on specific courses who receive at least 280 Ucas points.

**Accommodation**  Accommodation is guaranteed for first-years. Prices range from about £66 to £102 a week.

**Facilities**  A pool and climbing wall are among the sports facilities. There's also the Weston auditorium, for arts events. Two art galleries and one of the best teaching observatories in the UK. September 2009 sees the opening of the Forum; an auditorium for live gigs, bars, a club and a restaurant.

**Transport**  Good transport links to the rest of the UK. Only 25 minutes by train to London King's Cross tube and railway station. A frequent university shuttle bus travels between university campuses. The university's own bus company, Uno, runs a service around Hertfordshire and north London for staff, students and members of the public.

**◀◀ STUDENT VIEW ▶▶**

*"I'm impressed with the constant free events happening within the University, from career fairs to guest entrepreneur lectures. With the focus on developing the practical experience of students, I'm confident I'll graduate with the skills employers want."*

# University of Huddersfield

Queensgate
Huddersfield  HD1 3DH

**t** 01484 422288
**e** admissions@hud.ac.uk
↗ www.hud.ac.uk

>> **further links**

ACCOMMODATION  accommodation@hud.ac.uk
STUDENTS' UNION  www.huddersfieldstudent.com

3265      97.5      41.9      15.5      90.7

The University of Huddersfield's roots go back some 160 years but its sights are firmly set on the future of its students and it has close links with industry, business and the cultural community. Courses are modular, with a strong vocational emphasis, and many offer the option of a year abroad or working in industry. The university is among the top 10 providers of sandwich courses, where students undertake a paid work placement in industry. Huddersfield is a pleasant town with an expanding social scene, thanks, in large part, to the 23,000 or so students who make up the university. The campus straddles the old canal and there's a continuing programme of investment in facilities for students. The latest is a £15m creative arts building, completed last year, which has become a landmark building in the town.

**Fees**  £3,225 for full-time undergraduate courses in 2009-10.

**Bursaries**  The university offers £500 a year to eligible students with a household income of less than £25,000.

**Accommodation**  The university does not have its own accommodation, but recommends a couple of private providers.

**Facilities**  The student union is active, with great facilities including a stylish bar and a restaurant providing "home-style" cooking. The newly renovated library and computing centre is at the heart of the campus, alongside the new creative arts building.

**Transport**  Transport links to Manchester and Leeds are good, with the M62 and the M1 within striking distance. Good rail links, too.

**❝ STUDENT VIEW ❞**

*"It's got everything. Living in halls in your first year will mean you'll make hundreds of friends and have the absolute time of your life. Huddersfield itself is bursting with life and the university is relaxed yet focused."*

# University of Hull

Hull  HU6 7RX

**t** 0870 126 2000
**e** admissions@hull.ac.uk
**↗** www.hull.ac.uk

**Scarborough Campus** Filey Road, Scarborough  YO11 3AZ

**»** **further links**

ACCOMMODATION  www.hull.ac.uk/accom
STUDENTS' UNION  www.hullstudent.com

3005    92.6    30.8    10.2    96.1

Anyone who goes to Hull will tell you it's friendly and down to earth, with a diverse population and a very low cost of living. No wonder it rates highly for student satisfaction. And it's no slouch when it comes to the smarts, either. It has a strong research reputation and its teaching is very well regarded: two-thirds of students emerge with a first or 2.1. The Hull campus is 15 minutes' walk from the city centre and there are plenty of student-friendly bars and venues to investigate. The smaller campus in Scarborough is close to the faded seaside glamour of the resort. The coastline here is marvellous and a lunchtime surf is a real possibility.

**Fees**  £3,225 a year for all full-time undergraduate courses in 2009–10.

**Bursaries**  If your family's annual income is £25,000 or less, you will receive a bursary of £1,000 a year. Between £25,001 and £40,000, you will receive a bursary of £500 a year. Excellence scholarships of £1,500 are also available, as well as other awards.

**Accommodation**  Guaranteed for all first-years. Costs are currently under review.

**Facilities**  Hull is nearing the end of a three-year, £16m programme of investment in student residential accommodation. The £2.4m Enterprise Centre opened in December 2008, providing resources and expertise for entrepreneurs. There's an award-winning student union nightclub and good sports provision, too.

**Transport**  Road links are good, but rail links can be slightly cumbersome.

**❝ STUDENT VIEW ❞**

*"Hull offers more than just a degree; excellent teaching staff, good employment prospects, a great union with hundreds of societies, a beautiful campus and affordable accommodation. Its reputation and friendly atmosphere are the icing on the cake."*

# Imperial College London

Exhibition Road
South Kensington
London SW7 2AZ

**t** 020 7589 5111
**e** info@imperial.ac.uk
**⬈** www.imperial.ac.uk

**Charing Cross** Reynolds Building, St Dunstan's Road, London W6 8RP
**Chelsea & Westminster** 369 Fulham Road SW10 9NH
**Hammersmith** The Commonwealth Building, The Hammersmith Hospital, Du Cane Road, London W12 0NN
**Northwick Park** Watford Road, Harrow, Middlesex HA1 3UJ
**Royal Brompton** Dovehouse Street, London SW3 6LY
**Silwood Park** Buckhurst Road, Ascot, Berks SL5 7PY
**St Mary's Campus** Norfolk Place, London W2 1PG
**Wye Campus** Ashford, Kent TN25 5AH

**》 further links**

ACCOMMODATION accommodation@imperial.ac.uk
STUDENTS' UNION www.imperialcollegeunion.org

1370    62.0    18.3    2.9    93.5

London

Imperial's reputation places it as one of the best academic institutions in the world. Not surprisingly, competition for places is stiff, and there is a certain grandeur about the institution that is only reinforced by its main location among the pomp and circumstance of one of London's swankiest boroughs. Hyde Park, the V&A and the Albert Hall are all on your doorstep.

**Fees** £3,225 for all full-time undergraduate courses in 2009-10.

**Bursaries** Home students who are in receipt of a grant will be entitled to a study support bursary of £3,300. Further bursary and scholarship schemes available.

**Accommodation** Undergraduates are guaranteed a place in their first year. Prices vary from £55 a week for a triple room to £156.60 for a single room en suite.

**Facilities** Newly refurbished central library, free sports facilities for students; for a one-off fitness orientation fee of £15, Imperial students have use of the pool, sauna, steam room and gym.

**Transport** It's extremely central London. The closest tube is South Kensington.

**❝ STUDENT VIEW ❞**

*"Imperial is a really special place where one can come from absolutely any background and feel proud of the outstanding academics and the supportive and embracing scene of clubs and societies here."*

# Keele University

Keele
Staffordshire  ST5 5BG

**t**  01782 734005 / 733994
**e**  undergraduate@acad.keele.ac.uk
     bursaries@keele.ac.uk
**↗**  www.keele.ac.uk

**»  further links**

ACCOMMODATION   01782 733086
STUDENTS' UNION  www.kusu.net

1570      90.8      26.5      8.6      95.0

The UK's largest campus university was founded in 1949, the first new university after the second world war. It occupies a 250-hectare estate of wood and parkland in Newcastle-under-Lyme, near Stoke-on-Trent (midway between Manchester and Birmingham). Keele offers a distinctive dual-honours degree for most students. New undergraduate courses from 2009 include an interdisciplinary BSc in environment and sustainability. Many students and staff live on campus, making for a good atmosphere. The sense of community helps new students feel at home very quickly and there are many societies and part-time job opportunities available. Sport and leisure facilities are excellent.

**Fees**  £3,225 a year for undergraduates in 2009-10.

**Bursaries**  £319 for students who receive a full grant but also receive other public funding; £800 for students who receive a full grant and no other public funding. £1,000 for students who make Keele their first or insurance choice, receive a full or partial grant, have an annual household income below £40,000 and attain three A grades at A-level (or equivalent) in one sitting.

**Accommodation**  On-campus accommodation guaranteed for first-years holding Keele as their firm choice. Self-catering from £64 to £105 a week.

**Facilities**  There is a lively student union that has no fewer than five bar areas; the "ents" department is a dab hand at booking top bands such as Scouting for Girls. Good IT facilities, with 3,200 network connections for student study rooms. Excellent sports facilities include a well-equipped fitness centre, basketball courts and an indoor climbing wall.

**Transport**  Frequent bus service between the university and Stoke-on-Trent, Newcastle and Crewe.

**◄◄ STUDENT VIEW ►►**

*"Keele is a university quite apart from anything else; away from stressful pace of life in the cities, you can really spend time on getting the most out of your university life. You will not find anywhere else with such a communal, village feel, where you can have the experience of a lifetime."*

# University of Kent

Canterbury
Kent  CT2 7NZ

**t**  01227 764000
**e**  recruitment@kent.ac.uk
**↗**  www.kent.ac.uk

**The Medway Building**  Chatham Maritime, Kent  ME4 4AG
**Bridge Wardens' College**  Clocktower Building, Chatham Historic Dockyard, Kent  ME4 4TE
**University of Kent at Brussels**  Boulevard de la Plaine 5, 1050 Bruxelles, Belgium
**Tonbridge Centre**  Avebury Avenue, Tonbridge, Kent  TN9 1TG

**》 further links**

ACCOMMODATION  01227 766660
STUDENTS' UNION  www.kentunion.co.uk

| 3090 | 91.9 | 24.6 | 11.1 | 95.2 |

Canterbury

Kent describes itself as the UK's top European university, and many courses offer a foreign language option or a year abroad. It's part of the Franco-British University of the Transmanche and there's even a campus in Brussels. But no matter how much it gazes towards the continent, it takes its regional role seriously. The leafy main campus is about two miles from Canterbury centre, and is friendly and vibrant. The newer Medway campus has some stunning buildings and a great sense of community. The university rates highly for student satisfaction in the national student survey, and was voted number one in the south-east in 2007 and 2008. Canterbury is a historic city with plenty of visitor attractions, and good shopping, bars and leisure facilities.

**Fees**  £3,225 for full-time undergraduate courses in 2009-10.

**Bursaries**  Up to £1,000 for students from households with an income of less than £25,000, then on a sliding scale down to £250 a year for students with a household income of up to £40,000. Academic excellence scholarships of £1,000 also available.

**Accommodation**  All first-years can live in halls providing Kent is their first choice. Prices vary.

**Facilities**  The self-contained Canterbury campus includes student accommodation, a library, a theatre, a nightclub, eating places, bars, a medical centre and a chapel. The sports centre is one of the best and cheapest on-campus university sports facilities. There are well-stocked libraries and a good range of social facilities. The careers service, in particular, is active on behalf of students.

**Transport**  The Canterbury campus is a half-hour walk from the city centre. The Medway campus is 30 minutes from London.

**❝ STUDENT VIEW ❞**

*"The academic and leisure facilities are fantastic, with a huge library and affordable pubs and restaurants. Kent is a friendly and welcoming place and it has a brilliant reputation amongst alumni and employers."*

# King's College London

| | |
|---|---|
| Strand<br>London WC2R 2LS | **t** 020 7848 7070<br>**e** studentenq@kcl.ac.uk<br>↗ www.kcl.ac.uk |

**Waterloo Campus** The Franklin-Wilkins Building, Stamford Street, London SE1 9NN
**Guy's Campus** New Hunts House, London SE1 1UL
**Hampstead Campus** Kidderpore Avenue, London NW3 7ST
**King's College Hospital** Denmark Hill, London SE5 9RS

》 **further links**

ACCOMMODATION accomm@kcl.ac.uk
STUDENTS' UNION www.kclsu.org

2560     71.3     21.5     7.6     97.0

Based in the heart of London, King's is ranked in the top 25 universities worldwide. It offers world-class teaching and research at its nine schools and five Medical Research Council centres. Four of the five campuses are clustered together on a landmark-packed stretch of the Thames. Waterloo Bridge? London Eye? Houses of Parliament? People fly across the world to see these things; you'll pass them on the way to your lectures. The fifth campus is the college's own hospital in Denmark Hill, in south-east London, a quick trip on the overland train. Graduates have an employment record much higher than the national average – and among the highest starting salaries, too.

**Fees** £3,225 for all full-time undergraduate courses in 2009-10.

**Bursaries** For all new full-time undergraduate students in receipt of a grant, King's will award a bursary linked to this amount. The amount can vary year to year; see kcl.ac.uk/funding for current levels. Various scholarships also available.

**Accommodation** Full-time undergraduates are guaranteed one year, though not necessarily their first, in either a college, Liberty Living or intercollegiate residence. Prices for 2009-10 at kcl.ac.uk/accomm

**Facilities** The main Maughan library used to be the Public Record Office and is now the largest new university library in Britain since the second world war. It's got the original Victorian zinc ceilings, lots of computers, and wireless, too. The college is investing in its IT in order to achieve a state-of-the-art virtual campus. Good sports facilities include the redevelopment of the sports ground at Brockley Rise, where two new all-weather pitches will be soon be in place.

**Transport** Its central location means that King's is close to many forms of transport: tubes, bus, trains and even the river.

**❝ STUDENT VIEW ❞**

*"Studying at King's has been both a challenging and enjoyable experience.*
*I have made friends and memories that will span a lifetime."*

# Kingston University

River House
53-57 High Street
Kingston upon Thames  KT1 1LQ

**t**  08700 841 347
**e**  admissions-info@kingston.ac.uk
**↗**  www.kingston.ac.uk

**Kingston Hill Campus**  Kingston Hill, Kingston upon Thames, Surrey  KT2 7LB
**Penrhyn Road Campus**  Penrhyn Road, Kingston upon Thames, Surrey  KT1 2EE
**Knights Park Campus**  Grange Road, Kingston upon Thames, Surrey  KT1 2QJ
**Roehampton Vale Campus**  104 Friars Avenue, Roehampton Vale, London  SW15 3DW

**》 further links**

ACCOMMODATION  accommodation@kingston.ac.uk
STUDENTS' UNION  www.kusu.co.uk

4440      95.6      36.7      16.4      91.8

Kingston is based on four campuses scattered around Kingston upon Thames. Approximately 21,000 students study in seven faculties and at partner colleges, with a couple of thousand more abroad. Its portfolio of foundation degree programmes has recently been extended and includes plenty of interesting vocational options. The university has invested in cutting-edge e-learning systems with students now able to access at least 80% of course modules online. Over the past 18 months, it has embarked on an ambitious investment programme that will cost £123m. Three new buildings are up and running, including an impressive £20m six-storey building for teaching and studying.

**Fees**  £3,225 for full-time undergraduate courses starting in 2009-10.

**Bursaries**  All students eligible for a full or partial grant will be entitled to some level of bursary, ranging from £1,000 a year down to £310. Every UK/EU student who starts the first year of a full fee-paying degree course through the local compact scheme will receive an extra £300 a year.

**Accommodation**  The university is able to offer self-catering accommodation to most first-years who make Kingston their firm or insurance choice. All other applicants will be offered accommodation subject to availability. Weekly prices are £105 to £113.50 for en suite rooms, £99.50 for standard rooms and £90.50 for budget en suite rooms.

**Facilities**  There are specialist learning resources centres at each campus, with 24-hour opening at the two larger campuses during key teaching weeks in term-time. The recently refurbished fitness centre includes a 65-station gym sporting the latest cardiovascular equipment.

**Transport**  Two campuses are based within the town centre, with the other two a 10-minute bus ride away. Central London is less than half an hour away by train. Frequent and free bus service for students during term-time.

**❝ STUDENT VIEW 》**

*"Consistent and first-class support from tutors — many of whom are also still working in the industry themselves — plus of course the proximity to London has made Kingston University a fantastic all-round choice."*

# University of Wales Lampeter

Ceredigion  SA48 7ED

**t**  01570 422351
**e**  recruit@lamp.ac.uk
**↗**  www.lamp.ac.uk

**》 further links**

ACCOMMODATION  p.thomas@lamp.ac.uk
STUDENTS' UNION  www.lamp.ac.uk/su

295      92.8      38.7      16.0      91.1

Lampeter is the oldest degree-awarding institution in Wales, founded in 1822. It's also the smallest, with just 1,000 or so students on campus. As a result, the university has a close-knit atmosphere and staff pride themselves on being approachable. Lampeter is a small town, and the campus has a beautiful setting in the Ceredigion hills, on the banks of the River Teifi. The campus also boasts some handsome old buildings. Town/gown relations are excellent, and if you're in search of some peace and quiet and lots of lovely green you could do a lot worse, though both Swansea and Cardiff are reachable and the student union's entertainment officers ensure campus life has its fair share of fun. Academically, the university rates highly in theology and religious studies, and English language and literature. About a third of students are over 21 when they start their course. Lampeter and Trinity University College are due to merge in 2010 to create a new university.

**Fees**  £3,225 a year for all full-time undergraduate courses in 2009-10.

**Bursaries**  Bursaries of approximately £300 available to eligible students. There are departmental scholarships of up to £2,000, and numerous other smaller scholarships and prizes.

**Accommodation**  Guaranteed for first-years. Weekly prices from about £55 to £65 a week.

**Facilities**  Significant investment in online library resources in the past year means Lampeter now holds one of the largest collections of e-books in Wales. A new research centre opened in January 2008 to house the priceless special collections in a climate-controlled environment.

**Transport**  Everything is within walking distance. Bus to Carmarthen or Aberystwth to connect to the trains.

**❝ STUDENT VIEW ❞**

*"Lampeter is a fantastic environment in which to study, develop, meet new people and try different activities. Set in beautiful Welsh countryside, it's a place where you can throw yourself into life. Lampeter is unique!"*

# Lancaster University

Bailrigg
Lancaster  LA1 4YW

t  01524 65201
e  ugadmissions@lancaster.ac.uk
↗ www.lancaster.ac.uk

 **further links**

ACCOMMODATION  cro@lancaster.ac.uk
STUDENTS' UNION  www.lusu.co.uk

| 2250 | 90.3 | 21.9 | 6.7 | 95.0 |

Lancaster is a collegiate university with eight undergraduate colleges on campus (and a ninth for graduates). All students are members of one or other of the colleges which, as well as providing accommodation, also have their own bars and common rooms, and an instant sense of community and belonging. Academic staff are also affiliated with a college and often have an active role. The campus is located outside Lancaster and students make up about a fifth of the town's population, so they are well catered for. Here, you're within easy reach of the north-west coast, the Lake District, Manchester and Liverpool. Academic standards at the university are high.

**Fees**  £3,225 for full-time undergraduate courses in 2009-10.

**Bursaries**  If your household income is below £18,360, you are eligible for £1,315. Between £18,360 and £27,800, you are eligible for £500. Excellence scholarships of £1,000 based on A-level grades also available.

**Accommodation**  Accommodation is guaranteed to all students who put Lancaster as their first choice, firmly accept an offer from the university and apply before the deadline. Self-catering accommodation is from £70 for a basic room up to £131.70 for a twin studio apartment. Most rooms on campus are en suite and cost £95 a week.

**Facilities**  £300m has been invested in transforming the campus. There is a theatre, a gallery and a concert series. A new student learning hub will open in 2009, with 24-hour computer access. And a new sports centre is planned.

**Transport**  There are direct trains to the major cities, and good bus and coach networks, with the M6 within spitting distance. It's only three hours to London.

**◀◀ STUDENT VIEW ▶▶**

*"At Lancaster I realised there was much more to the degree than just a well-structured curriculum taught by a world-class faculty. The staff were friendly and made me feel very welcome. An added bonus was the international atmosphere with students from all parts of the world."*

# University of Leeds

Woodhouse Lane
Leeds  LS2 9JT

**t**  0113 343 2336
**e**  ask@.leeds.ac.uk
**↗**  www.leeds.ac.uk

**》 further links**

ACCOMMODATION  www.leeds.ac.uk/accommodation
STUDENTS' UNION  www.luuonline.com

5955    73.3    19.7    7.9    96.1

Leeds is a top redbrick university – in fact, a top university of any colour brick – and one of the giants of the higher education system. With a student population of 31,000, Leeds remains popular with applicants. They are drawn by the excellent standards for teaching and research, and the chance to live in Leeds itself. A large, student-friendly, dynamic city, Leeds is a great place to study, and opportunities for going out and having fun abound. There's also some impressive civic architecture and it's the regional centre for enjoying the arts. Leeds students have the benefit of a large single campus between the city centre and Headingley, where many students also live. There's an active student union, with an award-winning student newspaper and radio station.

**Fees**  £3,225 a year for all full-time undergraduate courses in 2009-10.

**Bursaries**  £2,786 to £2,906 for all students receiving a full grant. Bursaries on a sliding scale from £335 to £1,540 for students receiving partial grants. Many additional scholarships, including various subject awards, and awards of £3,000 a year for entrants from under-represented groups or low-participation areas.

**Accommodation**  Guaranteed to eligible single first-years. Single rooms in catered accommodation range from £95 to £153 a week; single rooms in self-catering accommodation between £75 and £130 a week.

**Facilities**  Some of the best computing resources in the country and a renowned library with more than 2.9m items in stock. The student union is one of the biggest and best in the country.

**Transport**  London is two-and-a-half hours away by train, with good links (by road and rail) to the rest of the country. Leeds Bradford international airport takes you further afield.

**❝ STUDENT VIEW ❞**

*"Leeds can offer you an amazing and unique experience. With a great academic environment and amazing social networks, it provides an exciting opportunity to enjoy the next three years or more at a top university."*

# Leeds College of Music

3 Quarry Hill
Leeds  LS2 7PD

**t**  0113 222 3400
**e**  enquiries@lcm.ac.uk
↗ www.lcm.ac.uk

**》 further links**

ACCOMMODATION  0113 222 3514
STUDENTS' UNION  www.lcm.ac.uk/about-lcm
/student-life/student-union.htm

155    88.2    20.0    98.2

Leeds College of Music is the UK's largest music college, with more than 1,000 full-time and 1,500 part-time students. Undergraduate courses include music (classical music), jazz, music production, sound design and pop music studies. By offering both further and higher education courses, the college also aims to allow students to progress from BTec courses through to degree-level study. The college is situated on Quarry Hill, at the very heart of the city's emerging arts and cultural quarter, where its neighbours include the West Yorkshire Playhouse, the live music venue The Wardrobe, South Asian Arts UK, Yorkshire Dance and BBC Yorkshire.

**Fees**  £3,225 for full-time undergraduate courses in 2009-10.

**Bursaries**  The college will provide an annual bursary to students whose household income is below £39,333, ranging from just over £500 to just over £1,000, depending on income. Other scholarships — including scholarships for the endangered species instruments of which there is a national shortage — are available.

**Accommodation**  Many first-years live in Joseph Stones house, which has 190 study bedrooms. Prices start at £79 a week. The average private-sector rent in Leeds is about £63 a week.

**Facilities**  The Venue, a 350-seat performance space hosts an annual concert season. The Centre for Jazz Studies was established in 2005. The 13 studios are designed to meet a variety of needs ranging from the live recording of bands and ensembles, and multi-track recording, through to sound design, sampling, production of sound for moving image, digital editing and mastering. There is a specialist library.

**Transport**  The central bus and coach station is opposite the college. Leeds train station is a 10-minute walk from the college. A bus to the main student areas of Hyde Park and Headingley takes about 15 minutes.

**❝ STUDENT VIEW ❞**

*"With such a wide selection of courses, Leeds College of Music has equipped me with a vast and diverse network of brilliant musicians. A great place to meet like-minded people who you are likely to work with even after graduating."*

# Leeds Metropolitan University

Civic Quarter
Leeds LS1 3HE

**t** 0113 812 3113
**e** course-enquiries@leedsmet.ac.uk
**↗** www.leedsmet.ac.uk

**Headingley Campus** Beckett Park, Leeds LS6 3QS
**Harrogate Campus** Hornbeam Park, Harrogate, North Yorkshire HG2 8QT

>> **further links**

ACCOMMODATION accommodation@leedsmet.ac.uk
STUDENTS' UNION www.lmusu.org.uk

5525    92.5    31.9    15.8    90.9

Leeds Metropolitan is a university with a lot of clout. It has more than 29,000 students and is lauded for its contribution to the local area. The majority of its students are from the region, and the university puts its money where its mouth is on widening participation by electing to charge well under the maximum possible fees. The university has a charming parkland campus in the pleasant Leeds suburb of Headingley and a cluster of buildings (including many recently acquired) in the city centre.

**Fees** Fees for all full-time undergraduates are currently £2,000 a year.

**Bursaries** Leeds Met says it prefers the approach of overall lower fees to charging a higher fee and redistributing some of that money through a system of bursaries. Some sports and other scholarships are available.

**Accommodation** Guaranteed for eligible first-year undergraduates. Prices range from £58 to £112.56 a week.

**Facilities** Excellent sports facilities, good access to IT resources (including some specialist software) and libraries with 24-hour access during term-time weekdays.

**Transport** Handy for just about anywhere, Leeds is well served by road and rail links.

**❝ STUDENT VIEW ❞**

*"Leeds Met has helped me to grow in confidence and I love everything about being here. I had the opportunity to work abroad during my placement year, which was an amazing experience."*

# Leeds Trinity and All Saints

Brownberrie Lane
Horsforth
Leeds  LS18 5HD

**t**  0113 283 7150
**e**  enquiries@leedstrinity.ac.uk
⬈  www.leedstrinity.ac.uk

**》 further links**

ACCOMMODATION  accommodation@leedstrinity.ac.uk
STUDENTS' UNION  www.leedstrinity.ac.uk/services/su

690      95.7      32.5      16.9      94.1

Leeds Trinity and All Saints is an independent higher education institution, accredited by the University of Leeds. Approximately 2,500 students attend the college, making for an pleasant, intimate atmosphere. There is a focus on employment, reflected in the mainly vocational or humanities courses run by the college, with business, media, health and education featuring prominently. All courses include a professional work placement, and graduate employment rates are good. The campus is in Horsforth, six miles from Leeds city centre, on the edge of the Yorkshire Dales. Leeds Trinity is investing heavily in new accommodation and facilities on campus.

**Fees**  £3,225 for full-time undergraduates in 2009-10.

**Bursaries**  Leeds Trinity offers a means-tested bursary of £500 to £1,000. £1,000 excellence scholarships also awarded. See www.leedstrinity.ac.uk/studentfinance

**Accommodation**  Leeds Trinity can normally accommodate all first-year students who wish to live on campus. Students can apply for self-catering or part-catered accommodation, with en suite rooms or shared facilities, and many rooms now have internet access. Prices for 2008-09 ranged from £2,724 to £4,278 for the academic year.

**Facilities**  A state-of-the-art sports and fitness centre opened in 2007. The modern, purpose-built learning centre has the study resources you'll need, plus you can use the University of Leeds' libraries.

**Transport**  Leeds is about two hours from London by train and there is a local station at Horsforth. There's ready access to the A1, M1 and M62.

**❝ STUDENT VIEW ❞**

*"I chose Leeds Trinity for its supportive environment.  People notice you here and are interested in what you are doing - there's a personal touch that I think makes studying here unique."*

# University of Leicester

University Road
Leicester LE1 7RH

**t** 0116 252 2522
**e** admissions@le.ac.uk
**↗** www.le.ac.uk

**》 further links**

ACCOMMODATION  accommodation@le.ac.uk
STUDENTS' UNION  www.leicesterstudent.org

1945      89.5      26.0      7.0      94.9

Leicester students – all 21,000 of them – certainly appear to be happy bunnies: it has recorded some of the highest scores for overall satisfaction in the national student survey for four years in a row and the drop-out rate is notably low. The appeal might lie in the friendly and compact campus, a 10-minute walk from one end to the other, providing you don't get sidetracked by any of the on-campus facilities. Victoria Park next door is a convenient and popular place to relax when the weather is good. Leicester puts up a consistently strong academic performance across all its subject areas. It's understandably proud of its most famous research achievement: the development of DNA genetic fingerprinting. Add on Leicester itself, a lively, multicultural city with great facilities and transport links, and it's no wonder everyone is so pleased to be there.

**Fees**  £3,225 a year for all full-time undergraduate courses in 2009-10.

**Bursaries**  If you have a household income of up to £20,000, you will receive £1,319. Up to £40,000, you will receive between £100 and £1,019, on a sliding scale. Non-repayable entrance scholarships of £1,000 for students achieving ABB or above at A-level or equivalent in some subjects.

**Accommodation**  Guaranteed for first-years. Costs vary significantly depending on the package chosen by students. Basic but good-quality rooms start at about £72 a week. A top-of-the-range en suite room in the new £25m hall of residence can cost up to £150 a week including meals.

**Facilities**  A new library has just opened, with access to computer facilities, a bookshop and cafe.

**Transport**  There are direct rail services to all parts of the country, and the city is well served by the M1 and M69 motorways.

**❝ STUDENT VIEW ❞**

*"My experience at Leicester has been fantastic. It's exciting and inspiring to be taught by people who have a genuine love for their subject; it has helped me to achieve so much more than I thought possible."*

# University of Lincoln

Brayford Pool
Lincoln LN6 7TS

**t** 01522 882000
**e** enquiries@lincoln.ac.uk
↗ www.lincoln.ac.uk

**》 further links**

ACCOMMODATION 01522 886195
STUDENTS' UNION www.lincolnsu.com

2840    97.5    36.1    14.1    89.7

Lincoln is a sweet cathedral city that attracts a million tourists a year. The main campus of the university offers great views up to the cathedral, though you might be too busy looking around you: the waterfront developments at Brayford Pool include a multiscreen cinema, restaurants, nightclubs, accommodation and the new student union building with great concert space and bars. The university's city-centre buildings are known as the Cathedral Quarter and there's a lovely rural campus, Riseholme Park. It must be doing something right: in the 2008 national student survey, Lincoln recorded one of the most significant improvements for student satisfaction of any university in the country.

**Fees**  £3,225 for full-time undergradate courses in 2009–10.

**Bursaries**  Students receiving a grant of up to £2,835 will be eligible for up to £600, then on a sliding scale. Other scholarships and support available.

**Accommodation**  Good availability for first-years in university or private accommodation on or near campus. Costs range between approximately £85 and £95 a week. En suite rooms and a variety of catered and self-catered options are available.

**Facilities**  The library is located in the impressive Great Central Warehouse building, and the Engine Shed is the region's largest live music venue, home to the student union. Work on Enterprise@Lincoln — a hub for the university's enterprise and employer engagement activity — began in November 2008, and the £3.5m performing arts centre opened in January 2008. The media building is fully equipped with the latest broadcast television, radio and sound equipment.

**Transport**  Lincoln railway station is five minutes' walk away and has train services to London (approximately two hours) and other major cities. The A1 is about 20 minutes away.

**❝ STUDENT VIEW ❞**

*"The tutors are very supportive and make you feel part of a team. They are passionate about the subjects they teach and take the time to ensure that every student understands each aspect."*

# University of Liverpool

Liverpool  L69 3BX

**t** 0151 794 2000
**e** ugrecruitment@liv.ac.uk
↗ www.liv.ac.uk

**》 further links**

ACCOMMODATION  accommodation@liv.ac.uk
STUDENTS' UNION  www.lgos.org

3650    84.8    24.7    8.1    96.4

Liverpool has everything you'd expect from a classic redbrick university: excellent ratings in teaching and research, a large and diverse student body, a strong sense of self and a location in a top city. Now would be a great time to apply to Liverpool – in 2008 it became the European Capital of Culture, and the investment is paying off. In 2006, the university opened the first independent Anglo-Asian university in China in partnership with Xi'an Jiaotong University in Suzhou. Students can opt to take work placements in Suzhou. £200m of investment is also taking place on the university's campus near the centre of Liverpool. Facilities for fun are great (the student union building is the largest in the country), the cost of living is low, and there is a real commitment to opening access and to the local community.

**Fees**  £3,225 for full-time undergraduate courses in 2009-10.

**Bursaries**  If your household has an income less than £25,000 a year, you will receive £1,400. Less than £20,817 a year (and you achieve AAB at A-level or equivalent), you will receive £4,000. Further attainment scholarships in certain subjects and awards for academic excellence also available.

**Accommodation**  Guaranteed for eligible first-years. A range of accommodation is available. Costs range from £80.15 a week for self-catered halls to £106.05 a week for catered halls.

**Facilities**  Two main libraries, one of which enjoyed a spruce-up in summer 2008. Extensive sports grounds and the student union offers a choice of three bars. The university has invested £200m in an extensive capital programme.

**Transport**  The campus is situated about 10 minutes' walk from the city centre. Good for trains and coaches, and there are motorways almost on the doorstep.

**❝ STUDENT VIEW ❞**

*"The university is a vibrant and active community, with a real breadth of opportunity to build on your student experience and make the most of your time studying in the heart of a great city."*

# Liverpool Hope University

Hope Park
Liverpool  L16 9JD

**t**  0151 291 3000
**e**  course-enquiry@hope.ac.uk
**↗**  www.hope.ac.uk

**Everton Campus**  Hope at Everton, Haigh Street, Liverpool  L3 8QB

>> **further links**

ACCOMMODATION  accommodation@hope.ac.uk
STUDENTS' UNION  www.hopesu.co.uk

1565    98.1    41.4    25.6    97.3

Liverpool

True to the history of its founding institutions – religious colleges training women to be teachers – Hope is the only ecumenical university in Europe, with a significant female population, and is strong in teacher training. The number of applications to Hope continues to rise. It has two campuses in the thriving and confident city of Liverpool, where 7,500 students are taught. Hope has a high-quality careers service and opportunities for part-time work and work experience are plentiful, including the chance to gain Hope's service and leadership award through community work, in the UK or overseas. Campus developments of some £13m are planned, including a new centre for music, performance and innovation and a new building for the education deanery.

**Fees**  £3,225 a year for all full-time undergraduate courses.

**Bursaries**  Every undergraduate will receive a bursary of no less than £400 a year irrespective of family income. Those receiving a full grant will be given an annual bursary, averaging £1,000. Those on partial grant will get £700 a year. Other scholarships available.

**Accommodation**  All first-years are guaranteed accommodation. There is a variety on offer and prices vary accordingly.

**Facilities**  Hope uses Moodle, the fastest growing and most used virtual learning environment in the UK. Hope's library has extended opening hours designed to fit around student needs and claims to be the most flexible of any university. The university aims to provide the most up-to-date computer facilities.

**Transport**  Excellent transport links to and from the city centre. Intercity trains from Liverpool Lime Street station and international flights from Liverpool John Lennon airport.

**◀◀ STUDENT VIEW ▶▶**

*"The tutors at Hope make you feel valued as an individual and are always approachable and willing to hear your ideas whilst continually motivating and encouraging academic development. I am so glad I chose to undertake my undergraduate degree at Liverpool Hope University."*

# Liverpool Institute for Performing Arts

Mount Street
Liverpool  L1 9HF

**t**  0151 330 3000
**e**  admissions@lipa.ac.uk
↗ www.lipa.ac.uk

**》 further links**

ACCOMMODATION   0151 330 3084

170      88.0      21.5      10.4      91.2

LIPA was the brainchild of Sir Paul McCartney, who wanted to save the site of his former school, and Mark Featherstone-Witty, who wanted to provide training for people intent on entering showbusiness. Together, they poured £20m into the institute, which opened in 1996. LIPA is a small, specialist institution with approximately 650 students. It provides education and training for performers and those who make performance possible, and currently offers nine undergraduate degrees in performing arts subjects. Its curriculum is designed to give graduates a sense of the business side of the industry as much as the creative aspects.

**Fees**  Expected to be £3,225 for undergraduates in 2009–10.

**Bursaries**  Students qualifying for a full maintenance grant may be eligible for a bursary of just over £500. Students who qualify for certain levels of the partial maintenance grants may be eligible for a bursary of just over £250.

**Accommodation**  The institute doesn't have any of its own accommodation, but has partnerships with local providers. Availability is excellent for all first-years, with a choice of halls of residence-style accommodation within five to 10 minutes' walk of LIPA. Prices range from £64 to £105 a week.

**Facilities**  The grand grade-II listed building houses world-class facilities, including two performance spaces. There are recording studios and music practice rooms, dance and acting studios, and classrooms. The learning resources centre provides books, e-books, CDs, DVDs, journals and e-journals, as well as ICT and study support facilities.

**Transport**  Liverpool is a transport hub with good access by road via the M62, by intercity rail to Lime Street station, and by air from Liverpool John Lennon and Manchester airports.

**◄◄ STUDENT VIEW ►►**

*"The business and networking opportunities at LIPA are unrivalled. Without LIPA I would never have dreamt that I could do some of the things I've done during my time here and I now feel equipped to go into the industry."*

# Liverpool John Moores University

Roscoe Court
4 Rodney Street
Liverpool  L1 2TZ

**t**  0151 231 5090
**e**  recruitment@ljmu.ac.uk
↗ www.ljmu.ac.uk

**》 further links**

ACCOMMODATION  accommodation@ljmu.ac.uk
STUDENTS' UNION  www.l-s-u.com

4295    96.1    40.4    21.1    92.3

Liverpool

At Liverpool John Moores University, graduate skills development and work-related learning are integral to all undergraduate degrees. Backed by an advisory panel of senior business leaders in national and international companies, students are encouraged to develop "world of work" skills that give them a competitive edge. Plus the university's graduate development centre offers an extensive range of "ready for work" training courses. Liverpool is a fun place to be a student and it's fairly cheap for a big urban centre. And with three large campuses in the city, you're never far from a university base.

**Fees**  £3,225 for full-time undergraduates in 2009-10.

**Bursaries**  If you have a household income below £25,000, you will receive a bursary of £1,075. Between £25,001 and £50,000, you will receive £430. Up to six awards of £10,000 a year are available for academically gifted students who can also demonstrate achievement, excellence and commitment in areas such as volunteering, citizenship or the arts. Other awards available.

**Accommodation**  Guaranteed for all first-years, including those who apply through Clearing. Self-catering halls range from £64 to £105 a week.

**Facilities**  A new £27m art and design academy, a new life and sciences building and social learning zones within the three learning resource centres. Sporting facilities include a 25m pool, an Astro pitch, an indoor sports hall, gymnasiums and dance studios, and outdoor netball and tennis courts.

**Transport**  Two campuses are in the middle of town; a third is a 15-minute bus ride away.

**❝ STUDENT VIEW ❞**

*"The teaching is excellent and I have felt supported throughout my course, with very well-qualified tutors more than willing to help at any time. The library services are fantastic, especially with their extended opening hours."*

# London Metropolitan University

31 Jewry Street
London EC3N 2EY

**t** 020 7133 4200
**e** admissions@londonmet.ac.uk
↗ www.londonmet.ac.uk

**London City Campus** Calcutta House, Old Castle Street, London E1 7NT
**London North Campus** Student Services, London Metropolitan University,
Tower Building, 166-220 Holloway Road, London N7 8DB

**»» further links**

ACCOMMODATION accommodation@londonmet.ac.uk
STUDENTS' UNION www.londonmetsu.org.uk

| 3495 | 97.3 | 42.9 | 21.6 | 82.0 |

London

London Met is London's largest single university and Europe's largest business school, with two impeccably placed campuses. One is in the heart of the City, close to Liverpool Street. Another is in trendy north London, near the smart shops and bars of Highbury and Islington. Of the 34,000 students, almost a third are from overseas. Courses have a firm professional and vocational bent. New buildings include a striking graduate centre and a £30m state-of-the-art science centre, featuring a "super lab", and excellent sports and fitness facilities. London offers everything a student could want. The great student union facilities at both campuses are good places to start.

**Fees** £3,145 a year for all full-time undergraduate courses in 2008-09.

**Bursaries** University bursaries are available to all eligible home students and can be worth up to £1,000, calculated on a sliding scale. London Met offers a wide range of full scholarships, including sports and excellence scholarships.

**Accommodation** London Met has access to a range of halls of residence in buildings managed both by the university and by approved organisations, all within easy reach of the North and City campuses.

**Facilities** Extensive libraries with integrated facilities, as well as the specialist women's library and TUC collections. There's an ultra-modern science centre, sound and recording studios, a mock courtroom and seven floors of IT facilities at the Technology Tower.

**Transport** Both campuses are within easy striking distance of central London via tube, bus or train.

**❝ STUDENT VIEW ❞**

*"London Met offers more than just an education, it helps you to grow and develop as a person."*

# London School of Economics and Political Science

Houghton Street
London  WC2A 2AE

**t**  020 7405 7686
**e**  ug-admissions@lse.ac.uk
↗  www.lse.ac.uk

**》 further links**

ACCOMMODATION  accommodation@lse.ac.uk
STUDENTS' UNION  www.lsesu.com

London

615        65.9        18.2        3.4        94.4

LSE is the only university in the UK specialising in the study of social sciences and has a worldwide reputation in the field. The world's largest social sciences library is housed here. Of the 8,000 or so students, half are postgraduates and only about a third are from the UK, making for the largest proportion of overseas students at any university in the world. LSE students have a reputation for being academic and determined; the fact that the university library has a borrowing rate four times the national average speaks volumes. Graduates enjoy top employment rates and starting salaries. The school is located in the heart of London, just over the road from King's College London, with which it enjoys a traditional rivalry. It's close to the amenities of the West End, the river and Bloomsbury.

**Fees**  £3,225 a year for all UK/EU full-time undergraduate courses in 2009-10.

**Bursaries**  A maximum bursary of £2,500 a year for those students with the lowest household income, and then on a downwards sliding scale for those receiving a partial grant. Other forms of financial support available, including scholarships.

**Accommodation**  Guaranteed for all first-year undergraduate students. Prices for university halls vary. With new halls opened in 2006, LSE can now offer rooms in residences to 41% of its students.

**Facilities**  Excellent. Great libraries and other learning resources. The student union attracts plenty of non-students, which is a nice compliment if you don't mind them taking up bar space. The New Academic Building (opened November 2008) has added eight floors of state-of-the-art teaching and lecture rooms.

**Transport**  All roads lead to London, and so do quite a lot of train tracks and flight paths. Tube, bus and rail once you've breached the city limits. LSE is central: walk or cycle most places you need to be.

**❝ STUDENT VIEW ❞**

*"LSE is different, to say the least. You meet so many different people from every corner and background in the world. LSE teaches you a hell of a lot of life skills while you gain a sought-after degree that employers will value highly. You will come out of LSE a different person, but usually for the better."*

# London South Bank University

90 London Road
London  SE1 6LN

**t** 020 7815 7815
**e** enquiry@lsbu.ac.uk
↗ www.lsbu.ac.uk

**》 further links**

ACCOMMODATION  accommodation@lsbu.ac.uk
STUDENTS' UNION  www.lsbsu.org

1995       98.3       44.2       27.3       83.4

London

LSBU is based at the Elephant & Castle in south London. It's an area that is always described as up and coming, and it may actually fulfil its promise soon, as major investment in the area is planned. LSBU is doing its bit, with £47m being put into its campus. In any case, the area has its own rough'n'tumble charm and buckets of history, and it's hard to beat the location, within easy reach of London Bridge, Southwark, the South Bank, Waterloo and Westminster. The 23,000-strong student body is diverse and culturally rich. Half are from ethnic minorities, 3,000 come from outside the UK. Of the home students, a third are from Southwark and another third from elsewhere in London. A large proportion are mature students. Courses are built with future careers in mind – a tactic that's paying off, as graduate salaries are very good.

**Fees**  £3,145 for full-time undergraduates in 2008-09.

**Bursaries**  Bursaries currently worth £2,250 over three years. The bursary is available to all students. Other financial assistance and scholarships available.

**Accommodation**  LSBU offers a range of self-catering halls and flats within close proximity to the Southwark campus, which houses 1,400 students. The cost per week is between £86.50 and £106. Low-cost private accommodation is also available nearby.

**Facilities**  Good on-site sports facilities, and access to libraries and computing resources.

**Transport**  Easy access to the tube, plentiful bus routes and overland rail services.

 **STUDENT VIEW 》**

*"Many of my lecturers have been inspirational, very supportive and encouraging.
They're excellent role models for future nurses."*

# Loughborough University

Loughborough
Leicestershire  LE11 3TU

**t**  01509 263171
**e**  admissions@lboro.ac.uk
↗  www.lboro.ac.uk

**»» further links**

ACCOMMODATION  sac@lboro.ac.uk
STUDENTS' UNION  www.lufbra.net

2925      81.7      21.7      5.5      93.8

Loughborough

Academically strong across the board it may be – and it is – but Loughborough is still famous for its strength in sport. It's proud of its reputation in teaching, studying and participating in all sorts of sweaty activities, though it probably is possible to be a student here without once being compelled to don a sweatband and take to a pitch of some variety. Indeed, art and culture are taken seriously here, too. The Midlands market town is about a mile away from campus. The university is the town's biggest employer and students are a major part of the population here. The student union is unique as it's the only one in the country that is physically owned by the students. The rest of the 177-hectare campus is a safe and pleasant place to spend time, with good facilities for all aspects of student life, including – what else? – sport.

**Fees**  £3,225 for full-time undergraduate courses in 2009-10.

**Bursaries**  £1,390 for students with a household income up to £18,360, then calculated on a descending sliding scale. Merit-based scholarships are also available in some subjects.

**Accommodation**  Loughborough encourages first-years to live in halls. A range of housing is available. Self-catering options cost from about £62 to £130 a week. Catered options from about £118 to £145 a week.

**Facilities**  The university has the country's largest concentration of world-class training facilities across a wide range of sports. The recently refurbished Sir Robert Martin theatre and the Cope auditorium regularly host concerts, dance and drama productions, both by visiting artists and the university's own highly successful students.

**Transport**  A 20-minute walk from the town centre, or take the shuttle bus. Train to Nottingham, Derby or Leicester in 30 minutes.

**❝ STUDENT VIEW »**

*"Choosing Loughborough was an easy decision for me and it has certainly paid off. Everything I need – friends, social life and a great education – is all located on one great campus."*

# University of Manchester

Oxford Road
Manchester  M13 9PL

**t**  0161 275 2077
**e**  ug.admissions@manchester.ac.uk
↗  www.manchester.ac.uk

**»  further links**

ACCOMMODATION  accommodation@ manchester.ac.uk
STUDENTS' UNION  www.umsu.manchester.ac.uk

5335    77.2    21.3    8.4    93.6

Manchester

---

Manchester is massive: almost 30,000 students and 10,000 staff make it the biggest university in the UK (bar the Open University). It's the most popular in the country, too, according to Ucas applications, and the most targeted by the UK's graduate employers. Given all that, it's easy to find like-minded friends to spend your time with; Manchester's continuing success is due in part to the positive experience that graduates report. The city is also a big draw – down-to-earth and friendly, but increasingly hip and happening. Shopping and bar-hopping are practically compulsory here and there are plenty of venues for both. Even just for an amble around, you can enjoy the epic architecture of the city's industrial past and vibrant present; it's all a short walk from the university.

**Fees**  £3,225 for full-time undergraduate courses in 2009-10.

**Bursaries**  Details can be found at manchester.ac.uk/undergraduate/funding

**Accommodation**  Guaranteed for first-years. Prices range from about £78 a week for a single, self-catered room to about £130 for a catered, single en suite room near the city centre.

**Facilities**  You've got access to one of the UK's largest academic libraries, more than 10,000 PCs across campus, e-learning facilities, and excellent teaching resources for both arts and sciences.

**Transport**  There are two mainline stations, an international airport and good motorway connections.

**❝ STUDENT VIEW ❞**

*"Manchester is the next best thing to London, with an array of shops, restaurants, bars, and nightclubs. You are always guaranteed a good night out. It offers a great selection of courses and the teaching staff are friendly, helpful, and approachable."*

# Manchester Metropolitan University

| | |
|---|---|
| All Saints Building | **t** 0161 247 6969 |
| All Saints | **e** enquiries@mmu.ac.uk |
| Manchester  M15 6BH | ✗ www.mmu.ac.uk |

**Alsager Campus**  Hassall Road, Alsager ST7 2HL
**Aytoun Campus**  Aytoun Street, Manchester M1 3GH
**Crewe Campus**  Crewe Green Road, Crewe CW1 5DU
**Didsbury Campus**  Wilmslow Road, Didsbury, Manchester  M20 2RR
**Elizabeth Gaskell Campus**  Hathersage Road, Manchester M13 0JA
**Hollings Campus**  Old Hall Lane, Manchester M14 6HR

》 **further links**

ACCOMMODATION  accommodation@mmu.ac.uk
STUDENTS' UNION  www.mmunion.co.uk

| 7060 | 94.7 | 35.7 | 20.1 | 91.7 |
|---|---|---|---|---|

MMU is one of the largest universities in Britain, offering approximately 700 courses and giving students the opportunity to undertake a range of industry placements and exchange programmes with international universities. It's investing £300m in brand new facilities at Manchester, Didsbury and Crewe, and has a great social scene, having been voted best place to be a gay student by Diva magazine, ahead of London and Brighton. The student union has recently undergone a massive transformation and its bars are always heaving. Manchester boasts a rich cultural life, with a huge range of museums and live music venues.

**Fees**  £3,145 a year for all full-time undergraduate courses in 2008-09.

**Bursaries**  £1,000 a year for students receiving full grant, then on a sliding scale, to those with a family income of £39,290, who get £100.

**Accommodation**  The university will do its best to find accommodation for all first-year students, either in halls or private accommodation. Costs range from £63 to £130 a week.

**Facilities**  Great for sport: the Manchester Aquatics Centre is a £30m purpose-built swimming pool complex located on the Manchester campus, boasting two Olympic-standard main pools. The Sugden sports centre features a new 100-station fitness suite with state-of-the-art resistance and cadiovascular training machines. High-spec engineering and science labs, and good arts facilities, too.

**Transport**  Transport around either Manchester or Cheshire is easy and there are great links to the rest of the country and (via the international airport) the world. The university operates a free bus between Cheshire campuses.

◀◀ STUDENT VIEW ▶▶

*"There is so much to get involved in and you can take advantage of so much, whether it's politics, sports, a society, job opportunities, or just the shopping! You really will love this city!"*

# Middlesex University

The Burroughs
Hendon
London NW4 4BT

**t** 020 8411 5555
**e** enquiries@mdx.ac.uk
**↗** www.mdx.ac.uk

**Cat Hill Campus** Chase Side, Barnet, Herts EN4 8HT
**Enfield Campus** Queensway, Enfield, Middlesex EN3 4SA
**Trent Park Campus** Bramley Road, London N14 4YZ
**Middlesex University Dubai** Knowledge Village, P O Box 500697, Block 16, Dubai, United Arab Emirates

**》 further links**

ACCOMMODATION accomm@mdx.ac.uk
STUDENTS' UNION www.musu.mdx.ac.uk

| 3065 | 97.7 | 47.7 | 33.9 | 90.1 |

Middlesex University is located in north London and spread over four campuses. Hendon, undergoing a continuing process of redevelopment, is the flagship campus. Cat Hill is the specialist centre for art and design. Trent Park, surrounded by lakes and woods, is home to performing arts, languages, media communications, philosophy, and teaching and education. And Archway specialises in healthcare. Oh, and there's also a campus in Dubai should you fancy studying in the sun. All campuses — except for Dubai — are less than an hour from central London, meaning the perks of the big city are there on your doorstep, but so is some peace and quiet, should you need it. Middlesex is one of the most multinational universities in the country, with a fifth of its students coming from outside the UK and well over 100 different countries represented.

**Fees** £3,225 for all full-time undergraduate courses in 2009-10.

**Bursaries** £319 for all students who qualify for a grant. Middlesex offers some unique scholarships, including internships with organisations such as Apple and Channel 4. See mdx.ac.uk/scholarships

**Bursaries** Middlesex prioritises first-year students who have made the university their first choice and those from furthest away. Rents are about £80 to £97 a week.

**Facilities** State-of-the-art teaching facilities and laboratories at the brand new Hatchcroft science building, and £4.5m has been spent on a student venue, the Forum. The university's Museum of Domestic Design and Architecture houses an important collection of decorative art and design. Each campus has its own learning resources.

**Transport** It's virtually in London, with all the transport benefits that that implies. Each campus is within short walking distance of a tube station.

**❝ STUDENT VIEW ❞**

*"Middlesex gave me the opportunity to meet people from all over the world — such a unique experience as it is so diverse and you get to study in London — it's great. The new facilities are fantastic, there is so much to do."*

# Newcastle University

Newcastle upon Tyne   NE1 7RU

**t**   0191 222 5594
**e**   enquiries@ncl.ac.uk
**↗**   www.ncl.ac.uk

**》 further links**

ACCOMMODATION   accommodation-enquiries@ncl.ac.uk
STUDENTS' UNION   www.unionsociety.co.uk

3890      70.0      20.1      7.5      96.1

Newcastle
upon Tyne

---

Newcastle has an impressive academic track record and is located in a city that inspires immense affection in locals and visitors alike. Newcastle is famous for its nightlife, and with a relatively low cost of living and a compact city centre, going for a trawl around its varied pubs and clubs couldn't be easier. But it's also a regional centre for the arts, theatre and live music. It's close to great countryside and the dramatic coastline. And there's a little local football team that seems to be quite popular ... The university has a modern outlook – it has Fair Trade status, is a smoke-free campus and was the only university to formally back the Jubilee Debt Campaign for the cancellation of debt in developing countries.

**Fees**   £3,225 for all full-time undergraduate courses in 2009-10.

**Bursaries**   If your family income is up to £25,000, you will receive £1,340. Between £25,001 and £32,284, you will receive £700. See ncl.ac.uk/undergraduate/finance/scholarships

**Accommodation**   Guaranteed for eligible first-years. Prices from £68.74 to £96.11 a week for self-catered and £97.79 to £113.19 for catered (two meals a day).

**Facilities**   The library has more than 1m books, 15,000 electronic journals, 2,000 study places and many specialist collections. There is excellent computer provision and access. Around 95% of student bedrooms are wired for internet access. 2009 sees the opening of the Hancock Museum, part of the Great North Museum, which will showcase internationally important collections. A new 24-hour music building is due to open in 2009, comprising studios, band rehearsal facilities and studio spaces.

**Transport**   The campus is in the middle of the city and close to the Metro. There are easy links to London and Edinburgh, a ferry port and an airport.

---

**❝ STUDENT VIEW ❞**

*"I fell in love with the city as soon as I got here, and Newcastle University's academic and teaching reputation meant the choice to come here was a no-brainer."*

# Newman University College, Birmingham

Genners Lane
Bartley Green
Birmingham  B32 3NT

**t**  0121 476 1181
**e**  registry@newman.ac.uk
↗ www.newman.ac.uk

**》 further links**

ACCOMMODATION   0121 483 2219
STUDENTS' UNION   www.newmansu.org

555      100.0      45.2      19.9      95.3

---

Newman University College is located in a purpose-built campus eight miles from Birmingham city centre. Once a teacher training college, it has expanded its portfolio, and now offers single and combined honours degrees in a variety of subject areas. Research and work-based foundation degrees remain important. All students take a work placement module and there are European placement opportunities. Newman has one of the best graduate employment records in the country.

**Fees**   £3,225 for full-time undergraduates in 2009-10.

**Bursaries**   Bursaries of up to £1,025 are awarded based on academic achievement and household income in the second year, and £525 in years 1 and 3. Students who pass the first year at their first attempt receive an achievement bursary of £500 payable in year 2.

**Accommodation**   First-years get priority; costs about £73 a week.

**Facilities**   A big sports centre with an all-weather pitch, a library with computing resources, and a lively student union.

**Transport**   Birmingham is well served by transport.

**❝ STUDENT VIEW ❞**

*"I have been very impressed not only with the people at Newman, but also with the energy and intellectualism. They are exceptionally accommodating even when you approach them for help in a module that is not run by them."*

# University of Wales, Newport

Caerleon Campus
Lodge Road
Newport  NP20 5DA

t  01633 432432
e  uic@newport.ac.uk
↗  www.newport.ac.uk

**》 further links**

ACCOMMODATION  accommodation@newport.ac.uk
STUDENTS' UNION  www.newportunion.com

| 1170 | 99.0 | 38.1 | 26.0 | 87.7 |

The university is on two campuses, one near the city centre, another in Caerleon. Accommodation and the student union are on the latter. In 2010, a new campus will open in central Newport. The university has been highly rated in the national student survey and applications are leaping.

**Fees**  £3,225 for full-time undergraduate courses in 2009-10.

**Bursaries**  £1,000 for students with a household income of up to £20,000, then calculated in a downward sliding scale. The university also offers a further range of bursaries and scholarships.

**Accommodation**  Guaranteed for eligible first-years. Self-catered accommodation costs between £65.50 for a standard room and £79 for an en suite per week.

**Facilities**  A good sports centre and an elite school of golf. Also a useful online learning scheme.

**Transport**  It's two hours' drive to London on the M4 and has direct train links, too.

**❝ STUDENT VIEW ❞**

*"Newport has a very 'homely' feeling. Everyone is very friendly and willing to help one another. Tutors encourage us to work with professionals, which has helped me to find my true potential, be confident and show what I'm good at."*

# University of Northampton

Avenue Campus
St Georges Avenue
Northampton  NN2 6JD

**t** 0800 358 2232
**e** study@northampton.ac.uk
↗ www.northampton.ac.uk

**Park Campus**  Boughton Green Road, Northampton  NN2 7AL

## ›› further links

ACCOMMODATION  accommodation@northampton.ac.uk
STUDENTS' UNION  www.northamptonunion.com

1775    96.7    35.5    17.1    93.8

Northampton

More than 11,000 students attend courses in the arts, applied sciences, business, education, health and social sciences on two campuses close to Northampton town centre. The university has seen a substantial investment in campus facilities in the past few years, with a further £80m planned. The student union regularly has live entertainment at its two locations. Northampton is a big market town with some attractive green spaces and architecture.

**Fees**  £3,225 for full-time undergraduate courses in 2009-10.

**Bursaries**  Undergraduate students from the UK with household incomes of up to £40,000 may be eligible to receive a bursary of £500 to £1,000 a year.

**Accommodation**  Prices for 2009-10 are expected to range from £39 a week for a small twin to £86.95 for a single en suite room. All halls are self-catering.

**Facilities**  Park campus has a nightclub and Avenue campus has a student union bar, as well as dance and drama studios, and computer-aided design suites. There is 24-hour access to IT resources.

**Transport**  Northampton town centre is close by and easily accessible. Bus transport is provided for students between campuses and across the city. Northampton is one hour by train to Birmingham and London, and is accessible via three junctions on the M1.

## ‹‹ STUDENT VIEW ››

*"I have always been impressed with the facilities and resources. The academic librarians are fantastic and the technicians will help you in any way they can. If I've needed any help, it's always been available."*

# Northumbria University

Newcastle City Campus
Ellison Place
Newcastle upon Tyne NE1 8ST

**t** 0191 232 6002
0191 227 4064 (prospectus requests)
**e** er.admissions@northumbria.ac.uk
↗ www.northumbria.ac.uk

**Coach Lane Campus** Coach Lane, Benton, Newcastle upon Tyne NE7 7XA

**》 further links**

ACCOMMODATION rc.accommodation@northumbria.ac.uk
STUDENTS' UNION www.mynsu.co.uk

4525 91.3 31.9 17.8 95.7

Newcastle upon Tyne

Northumbria has invested £136m in its city-centre campus and is attracting more students every year (they currently number a whopping 40,000) – no surprise when you consider it is based in a city renowned for its culture, friendliness and nightlife. Northumbria's teaching has a good reputation and courses allow for flexibility. The university has two campuses in Newcastle upon Tyne: City campus is located in the heart of the city – ideal for sampling that legendary Newcastle nightlife – and Coach Lane campus is three miles from the city centre in the leafy suburbs of Newcastle. The university eagerly awaits its new, three-storey, state-of-the-art sports facility, which will boast some of the most impressive fitness and training amenities in the country, due to open in June 2010.

**Fees** £3,225 a year for full-time undergraduate courses for 2009 entry.

**Bursaries** About £300 a year to those receiving full grant. Awards of between £250 and £1,000 in the first year, depending on subject studied. The amount received in subsequent years will depend on academic performance.

**Accommodation** Self-catering is from £64 to £96 a week (the more expensive rooms are en suite), catered from £96 to £106 a week.

**Facilities** The City campus east has won numerous awards. Sports facilities keep the university in the top 10 UK sporting institutions.

**Transport** The train station is a short walk from the university; it is under three hours to London and one-and-a-half to Edinburgh. There is a Metro and an international airport.

**❝ STUDENT VIEW ❞**

*"I chose Northumbria mainly because of the course. It was recommended to me by my tutors at college. It has a very good national reputation. I also came to Newcastle because of the city itself, which has a great buzz about it."*

# Norwich University College of the Arts

Francis House
3-7 Redwell Street
Norwich  NR2 4SN UK

t  01603 610561
e  info@nuca.ac.uk
↗  www.nuca.ac.uk

## ›› further links

ACCOMMODATION  accommodation@nuca.ac.uk
STUDENTS' UNION  nuca.ac.uk/student-life

315    97.8    34.3    5.9    88.5

Norwich

Norwich University College of the Arts (Nuca), formerly Norwich School of Art and Design, is in central Norwich and has almost 1,500 full-time students. Established in 1845, it offers a wide range of the sort of courses you would expect from an arts institution, including graphic design, fine art, film and video, and animation. Norwich Gallery, which runs the Aurora festival, is based at Nuca. Norwich itself is a very pleasant city, with excellent shopping, an impressive Norman castle and cathedral, and lovely river walks. And the Norfolk Broads are on your doorstep.

**Fees**   £3,225 for full-time undergraduate courses in 2009–10.

**Bursaries**   Tied to the amount of maintenance support you receive, and between £300 and £800 a year.

**Accommodation**   There are a couple of residences charging between £74 to £98 a week. Allocation is based on how far away your home is.

**Facilities**   The recently renovated library houses over 30,000 volumes, a collection of more than 80,000 images, and 2,500 DVDs. The university college also has a contemporary gallery.

**Transport**   The train station is a short walk away and it's less than two hours to London. Norwich international airport has regular flights to Amsterdam and Manchester, and through connections to over 400 cities worldwide.

## ❝ STUDENT VIEW ❞

*"Norwich University College of the Arts is a very inspiring and innovative place to work. With exhibitions going on all the time all over college you are always inspired, as well as being pushed to keep up with the high standard of work around you."*

# University of Nottingham

University Park
Nottingham  NG7 2RD

**t**  0115 951 5151
**e**  undergraduate-enquiries@nottingham.ac.uk
**↗**  www.nottingham.ac.uk

**Sutton Bonington Campus**
Sutton Bonington, Near Loughborough, Leicestershire  LE12 5RD
**Jubilee Campus**  Wollaton Road, Nottingham  NG8 1BB
**Kings Meadow Campus**  Lenton Lane, Nottingham  NG7 2NA
**The University of Nottingham China Campus**
199 Taikang East Road, Ningbo, 315100, China
**The University of Nottingham Malaysia Campus**
Jalan Broga, 43500 Semenyih, Selangor Darul Ehsan, Malaysia

**》 further links**

ACCOMMODATION  ugaccommodation@nottingham.ac.uk
STUDENTS' UNION  www.su.nottingham.ac.uk

4585      67.4      17.4      3.3      96.1

Nottingham is traditionally one of the most popular universities for undergraduates. And not only with students from the UK. People from 150 different nations come here and there are also campuses in Malaysia and China; UK students can spend part of their degree studying at either of those. Nottingham is great for shopping, restaurants and nightlife. There's a lively and mixed social scene, and it's very student-friendly. The attractive campus is a short distance away, with landscaped grounds and lots of trees. It has great facilities for sports and the arts, and the student union is one of the largest and most active in the UK, with over 200 societies, sports clubs, student-run services, associations and a variety of events on offer. There's also an award-winning student radio station. Academic standards are very high and there is an excellent graduate employment record, helped by a good careers service.

**Fees**  £3,225 for full-time undergraduate courses in 2009–10.

**Bursaries**  Between £270 and £1,080 for each year of an undergraduate degree, dependent on residual household income. Students may also be eligible for additional bursaries.

**Accommodation**  Guaranteed for full-time first-years. Weekly prices range from £106.31 (shared study bedroom) to £172.99 (single en suite study bedroom) in catered halls, and start at about £78.75 for a room in a self-catered flat.

**Facilities**  Library facilities include the new Hallward library learning hubs. There is a new £2.4m sports centre on the Sutton Bonington campus and a new floodlit artificial pitch on University Park.

**Transport**  A free bus between campuses, good rail and road links, and an international airport nearby.

**❝ STUDENT VIEW ❞**

*"Whilst independent study is strongly encouraged, the support and guidance offered by faculty staff is outstanding. This, combined with the great times had along the way, guarantees a fantastic university experience"*

# Nottingham Trent University

Burton Street
Nottingham  NG1 4BU

**t** 0115 941 8418
**e** admissions@ntu.ac.uk
**↗** www.ntu.ac.uk

**Clifton Campus**  Clifton Lane, Nottingham  NG11 8NS
**Brackenhurst**  Nottingham Roadm Southwell  NG25 0QF

**》 further links**

ACCOMMODATION  accommodation@ntu.ac.uk
STUDENTS' UNION  www.trentstudents.org

4275   92.6   35.5   11.5   96.7

---

NTU is one of the largest new universities in the country, with about 25,000 students. They are spread over three campuses: one in the city centre, another about five miles away, and a third in the country, about 12 miles out of town. Guess which one has its own dairy farm ... The university is one of the top places in the country for graduate employment. NTU has close links with more than 6,000 employers across the world; most courses are vocational, with many students spending up to a year on work placements. The student community is diverse. Newton and Arkwright, two of the university's iconic buildings, are being redeveloped as part of a £130m estates regeneration programme to build a creative learning environment. Nottingham is a vibrant city with a proud history. The city centre has the full range of leisure options, from sleek cocktail bars to grungy clubs.

**Fees**  £3,225 for full-time undergraduates in 2009-10.

**Bursaries**  £1,075 a year for those on full grants, then on a sliding scale between £665 and £360 for those on partial grant. Those whose family lives in Nottinghamshire get an extra £115 to £265. Scholarship bursaries of £2,000 a year go to at least 25 students on full grant.

**Accommodation**  All new students who have NTU as their first choice are guaranteed an offer of university-allocated accommodation. Self-catering accommodation ranges from £67 to £111 a week.

**Facilities**  24-hour computing facilities.

**Transport**  The city centre is easily accessible. Nottingham has great transport links. Award-winning Unilink bus service between City and Clifton campuses.

**❝ STUDENT VIEW ❞**

*"Everybody involved with the uni seem to be great people and the education provided is superb, helped by the great facilities on offer to the students. I can't fault NTU so far."*

# Open University

PO Box 197
Milton Keynes  MK7 6BJ

**t**  0845 300 6090
**e**  general-enquiries@open.ac.uk
↗  www.open.ac.uk

The UK's largest university and a world leader in distance education. Consistently rated top for student satisfaction, quality of teaching and research performance in independent surveys. There are 180,000 students enrolled: 150,000 undergraduate and 30,000 postgraduate. Undergraduate degrees have no prerequisite entry requirements. The university uses YouTube, OU View and award-winning mobile learning technologies to support learning. Students work in their own time, but are supported by staff at regional centres. The average cost of an OU undergraduate degree is under £3,860 – so you can see the appeal for students wanting to avoid heavy debt.

**Fees**  Vary. See the website for more details.

❰❰ STUDENT VIEW ❱❱

*"I studied alongside work, so I'm already earning more money than a lot of my friends who went to traditional 'brick' universities as they're still working their way up. Plus, I have no debt!"*

# University of Oxford

University Offices
Wellington Square
Oxford  OX1 2JD

**t**  01865 288000
**e**  undergraduate.admissions@admin.ox.ac.uk
↗  www.ox.ac.uk

**》 further links**

ACCOMMODATION  Contact individual colleges for details
STUDENTS' UNION  www.ousu.org

2825    53.0    9.8    2.4    95.2

There's no doubt that Oxford's history is very present. You'll probably live in at least one beautiful, centuries-old building, sit at the same desk as your favourite prime minister or Nobel prize-winner. But Oxford is also a modern university: at, or near, the top of national and global rankings, year after year, at the forefront of research and teaching, and with tip-top facilities. As a collegiate university, whichever of the 38 colleges or six permanent private halls you call home will be the focus of your university life: where you'll live, eat, party and usually receive the one-to-one tutorials that are the keystone of Oxford teaching.

**Fees**  £3,225 for full-time undergraduate courses in 2009–10.

**Bursaries**  Oxford has one of the most generous bursary schemes in the UK. If your household income is less than £25,000, you will receive £3,225 a year, and, if less than £18,000, you qualify for an extra £875 in year 1. If you have a household income of between £25,001 and £49,999, you will be entitled to a partial award, based on a sliding scale. Other scholarships and bursaries also available.

**Accommodation**  All students live in accommodation provided by their college. All colleges house first-years; many house students for subsequent years, often for the entirety of their course. Standard accommodation in most colleges is approximately £121 a week over 26 (term-time) weeks.

**Facilities**  Oxford has the largest university library system in the UK, with more than 100 separate libraries. There are four major museums, as well as botanic gardens. Great for sport. University provision is supplemented by colleges' own libraries, sports grounds and IT facilities.

**Transport**  Within Oxford, everything is walk- or bike-able. Good links to London; frequent trains and coaches.

**❝ STUDENT VIEW ❞**

*"Oxford offers the perfect balance between academic and extracurricular opportunities, allowing me to learn directly from expert mathematicians and play lots of sport and music too. Whatever your interests, there is always something fun to do."*

# Oxford colleges

**All Souls College**
High Street, Oxford   OX1 4AL
t   01865 279379

**Balliol College**
Broad Street, Oxford   OX1 3BJ
t   01865 277777

**Blackfriars**
St Giles, Oxford   OX1 3LY
t   01865 278400

**Brasenose College**
Radcliffe Square, Oxford   OX1 4AJ
t   01865 277830

**Campion Hall**
Brewer Street, Oxford   OX1 1QS
t   01865 286100
↗   www.campion.ox.ac.uk

**Christ Church**
St Aldate's, Oxford   OX1 1DP
t   01865 276150
↗   www.chch.ox.ac.uk

**Corpus Christi College**
Merton, Oxford   OX1 4JF
t   01865 276700
↗   www.ccc.ox.ac.uk

**Exeter College**
Turl Street, Oxford   OX1 3DP
t   01865 279600
↗   www.exeter.ox.ac.uk

**Green Templeton College**
At the Radcliffe Observatory
Woodstock Road, Oxford   OX2 6HG
↗   www.gtc.ox.ac.uk

**Harris Manchester College**
Mansfield Road, Oxford   OX1 3TD
t   01865 271006
↗   www.hmc.ox.ac.uk

**Hertford College**
Catte Street, Oxford   OX1 3BW
t   01865 279400
↗   www.hertford.ox.ac.uk

**Jesus College**
Turl Street, Oxford   OX1 3DW
t   01865 279700
↗   www.jesus.ox.ac.uk

**Keble College**
Parks Road, Oxford   OX1 3PG
t   01865 272727
↗   www.keble.ox.ac.uk

**Kellogg College**
62 Banbury Road, Oxford   OX2 6PN
t   01865 612000
↗   www.kellogg.ox.ac.uk

**Lady Margaret Hall**
Norham Gardens, Oxford   OX2 6QA
t   01865 274300
↗   www.lmh.ox.ac.uk

**Linacre College**
St Cross Road, Oxford   OX1 3JA
t   01865 271650
↗   www.linacre.ox.ac.uk

**Lincoln College**
Turl Street, Oxford   OX1 3DR
t   01865 279800
↗   www.lincoln.ox.ac.uk

**Magdalen College**
High Street, Oxford   OX1 4AU
t   01865 276000
↗   www.magd.ox.ac.uk

**Mansfield College**
Mansfield Road, Oxford   OX1 3TF
t   01865 270999
↗   www.mansfield.ox.ac.uk

**Merton College**
Merton Street, Oxford   OX1 4JD
t   01865 276310
↗   www.merton.ox.ac.uk

**New College**
Holywell Street, Oxford   OX1 3BN
t   01865 279555
↗   www.new.ox.ac.uk

**Nuffield College**
New Road, Oxford   OX1 1NF
t   01865 278500
↗   www.nuffield.ox.ac.uk

**Oriel College**
Oriel Square, Oxford   OX1 4EW
t   01865 276555
↗   www.oriel.ox.ac.uk

**Pembroke College**
St Aldate's, Oxford   OX1 1DW
t   01865 276444
↗ www.pmb.ox.ac.uk

**The Queen's College**
High Street, Oxford   OX1 4AW
t   01865 279120
↗ www.queens.ox.ac.uk

**Regent's Park College**
Pusey Street, Oxford   OX1 2LB
t   01865 288120
↗ www.rpc.ox.ac.u

**St Anne's College**
Woodstock Road, Oxford   OX2 6HS
t   01865 274800
↗ www.st-annes.ox.ac.uk

**St Antony's College**
Woodstock Road, Oxford   OX2 6FJ
t   01865 284 700
↗ www.sant.ox.ac.uk

**St Benet's Hall**
38 St Giles, Oxford OX1 3LN
t   01865 280 556
↗ www.st-benets.ox.ac.uk

**St Catherine's College**
Manor Road, Oxford   OX1 3UJ
t   01865 271700
↗ www.stcatz.ox.ac.uk

**St Cross College**
St Giles, Oxford   OX1 3LZ
t   01865 278490
↗ www.stx.ox.ac.uk

**St Edmund Hall**
Queen's Lane, Oxford   OX1 4AR
t   01865 279000
↗ www.seh.ox.ac.uk

**St Hilda's College**
Cowley Place, Oxford   OX4 1DY
t   01865 276884
↗ www.sthildas.ox.ac.uk

**St Hugh's College**
St Margaret's Road, Oxford   OX2 6LE
t   01865 274910
↗ www.st-hughs.ox.ac.uk

**St John's College**
St Giles, Oxford   OX1 3JP
t   01865 277300
↗ www.sjc.ox.ac.uk

**St Peter's College**
New Inn Hall Street, Oxford   OX1 2DL
t   01865 278900
↗ www.spc.ox.ac.uk

**St Stephen's House**
16 Marston Street, Oxford OX4 1JX
t   01865 613500
↗ www.ssho.ox.ac.uk

**Somerville College**
Woodstock Road
Oxford   OX2 6HD
t   01865 270600

**Trinity College**
Broad Street, Oxford   OX1 3BH
t   01865 279900
↗ www.trinity.ox.ac.uk

**University College**
High Street, Oxford   OX1 4BH
t   01865 276601
↗ www.univ.ox.ac.uk

**Wadham College**
Parks Road, Oxford   OX1 3PN
t   01865 277545
↗ www.wadham.ox.ac.uk

**Wolfson College**
Linton Road, Oxford   OX2 6UD
t   01865 274100
↗ www.wolfson.ox.ac.uk

**Worcester College**
Walton Street, Oxford   OX1 2HB
t   01865 278300
↗ www.worcester.ox.ac.uk

**Wycliffe Hall**
54 Banbury Road, Oxford OX2 6PW
t   01865 274200
↗ www.wycliffehall.org.uk

# Oxford Brookes University

Headington Campus
Gipsy Lane, Headington
Oxford OX3 0BP

**t** 01865 484848
**e** query@brookes.ac.uk
**↗** www.brookes.ac.uk

**Westminster Institute of Education** Harcourt Hill Campus, Oxford OX2 9AT
**School of Health & Social Care** Jack Straw Lane, Oxford OX3 0FL
**Wheatley Campus** Wheatley, Oxford OX33 1HX

**》 further links**
ACCOMMODATION accomm@brookes.ac.uk
STUDENTS' UNION www.thesu.com

2620　　72.9　　41.3　　13.1　　95.0

Brookes is consistently rated as one of the best of the newer universities, and it is ambitious to be one of the best of any type of university in the country. Its students are spread over three campuses: Headington and Harcourt Hill are each a little distance from the city centre; Wheatley is about seven miles away, in the Oxfordshire countryside. Headington and Wheatley are at the start of a 15-year redevelopment plan. Oxford is a student-friendly city and there are all the facilities you could want in town. However, as Brookes's own Venue is the largest, erm, venue in Oxford, with regular club nights and concerts, you won't have far to go for some great entertainment. Brookes's modular degree system aims to provide opportunities to tailor-make your own course. Introductory modules in subjects such as video production, statistics and business can be added to many of the undergraduate degree programmes.

**Fees** £3,225 for full-time undergraduate courses in 2009-10.

**Bursaries** Awarded on a sliding scale according to family income, from a minimum of £150 to a maximum of £1,800. Scholarships also available.

**Accommodation** Not guaranteed for first-years, but last year the university was able to meet all requests for accommodation. There's a range to choose from and prices vary accordingly; some accommodation is undergoing refurbishment and should be brand spanking new in 2009.

**Facilities** The centre for sport caters extensively for the active, while the libraries provide a well-stocked alternative. And then there's the Venue.

**Transport** A bus connects campuses. Well connected to London and the rest of the south. You're not bang in the city centre at Brookes, so a bike or a bus pass will come in handy.

**❝ STUDENT VIEW ❯❯**
*"Oxford is a fresh and interesting place to be with a high proportion of foreign students — which I absolutely love. At Brookes you're treated like an adult but the back-up is always there and the tutors are always on hand."*

# University of Plymouth

Drake Circus
Plymouth  PL4 8AA

**t**  01752 585858
**e**  prospectus@plymouth.ac.uk
**↗**  www.plymouth.ac.uk

**»** **further links**

ACCOMMODATION  accommodation@plymouth.ac.uk
STUDENTS' UNION  www.upsu.com

3820      93.8      31.1      14.4      92.4

Plymouth

Plymouth is one of the largest universities in the country, and certainly the largest in the south-west, with approximately 30,000 students. The university's aim is to be known as the enterprise university and it is investing heavily in its future: a £35m arts and community complex opened in 2008, with further developments in 2009. The main campus is within easy walking distance of the city centre, and is a great, sunny seaside spot. Given its proximity to some of the country's loveliest beaches, watersports are popular with students – but then, so is sitting by the sea eating ice-cream. The location also plays a part in studies here: courses relating to marine life and the oceans are particularly well regarded. And where else could you find a degree in surf science?

**Fees**  £3,225 for full-time undergraduate courses in 2009-10.

**Bursaries**  A wide range of bursaries and scholarships is available. See plymouth.ac.uk/money

**Accommodation**  About half of all new students will be offered a place in university-managed or allocated accommodation. Weekly cost for university-managed accommodation: £80 to £125. Weekly cost for private accommodation: £65 to £130.

**Facilities**  A £35m award-winning building for arts and community; new £40m development, including student accommodation and a cafe; new £10.75m building for health and social work students. Plymouth is the only UK university to have its own diving and marine centre where students can gain an internationally recognised diving qualification as part of their marine-based degree.

**Transport**  The campus is in the city centre, with everything you need – whether it be the coast or buzzing nightlife – a short walk away. About three hours on the train to London; slightly longer by road.

**《 STUDENT VIEW 》**

*"I've gained so much from studying here. Tutors are inspirational and facilities are fantastic.*
*There's a friendly feel and the location couldn't be better: in the city centre but just a short walk from the sea."*

# University College Plymouth
# St Mark and St John

Derriford Road
Plymouth
Devon  PL6 8BH

**t**  01752 636700
**e**  admissions@marjon.ac.uk
↗ www.marjon.com

**》》 further links**

ACCOMMODATION   01752 636711
STUDENTS' UNION   www.marjonsu.co.uk

670      97.5      44.0      19.2      94.8

Plymouth

The University College Plymouth St Mark and St John (and breathe) unsurprisingly shortens its name to UCP Marjon, and is a small (about 5,000 students), single-campus higher education institution, based in the south-west. It prides itself on its warm, welcoming and inclusive atmosphere. Courses are mostly sport, health, coaching and PE, and education and teacher training. Other degrees include speech and language therapy, media, and music and performance arts. The campus is on the outskirts of Plymouth, but that just means you're closer to the moors.

**Fees**  £3,225 for undergraduate courses in 2009-10.

**Bursaries**  A hardship fund is available. All new students are supplied with a free laptop.

**Accommodation**  There are places on campus for around 500 students, with priority given to first-years. Accommodation is affordable, at about £67 a week.

**Facilities**  £12.3m is being invested in a new sports centre due for completion in 2010. It will include a 25-metre pool, full-size Astroturf, a 90-station fitness suite, a 12-court sports hall, grass pitches, a sports science lab and a video analysis suite. The library is at the heart of the campus and there is 24-hour access to computing facilities.

**Transport**  Rail and road links to most big cities, plus ferry services. Plymouth airport is very close by.

**⟨⟨ STUDENT VIEW ⟩⟩**

*"The variation of teaching styles is brilliant, always keeping you actively involved in your professional development.  Being a small campus means there is a great friendly and warm social circle. I've made some fantastic friends for life."*

# University of Portsmouth

University House
Winston Churchill Avenue
Portsmouth  PO1 2UP

**t**  02392 848484
**e**  info-centre@port.ac.uk
⌖  www.port.ac.uk

**》 further links**

ACCOMMODATION  student.housing@port.ac.uk
STUDENTS' UNION  www.upsu.net

3805      94.8      31.1      13.0      93.7

Portsmouth

Portsmouth is based on two sites: the Langstone campus and the University Quarter, which include impressive modern buildings and green park space. Portsmouth is compact and easy to navigate, and the seaside location is a real plus. There are good opportunities for part-time and holiday work, not to mention an active careers service. The university is currently riding high: 88% of students said they were satisfied with their course in the 2008 national student survey and, in the 2008 research assessment exercise, Portsmouth came joint first for applied mathematics, along with Cambridge, Durham and Oxford; and was in the top ten for European studies and applied health professions and studies.

**Fees**  £3,225 for full-time undergraduate courses in 2009–10.

**Bursaries**  £900 awarded to home students in receipt of a full grant. £600 for those in receipt of a partial grant. A further £300 is available to students from eligible local schools and colleges. Other bursaries are available.

**Accommodation**  75% of first-years are offered university accommodation, allocated on a first-come, first-served basis. The weekly cost of self-catered accommodation is £72.52 to £110.60.

**Facilities**  A state-of-the-art newsroom for the journalism course and the Expert centre, equipped with computerised mannequins that breathe, bleed and react to drugs (for people on health courses, not just for fun). The student union is award-winning, as is the new library extension. Recent builds include the £9.4m Dennis Sciama building, the home of the Institute of Cosmology and Gravitation. A dental academy opens in 2010 to train dentists, dental technicians and dental nurses.

**Transport**  London is just over an hour away. The station is near the university, so there's easy access to much of the rest of the south too.

**❝ STUDENT VIEW ❞**

*"Portsmouth is large enough to supply the variety students want but small enough to feel like you know the place. The huge seafront is popular with students who want to hang out on the beach or have long, lazy Saturdays on one of the many green seaside areas."*

# Queen Margaret University, Edinburgh

Queen Margaret University Drive
Musselburgh  EH21 6UU

**t**  0131 474 0000
**e**  admissions@qmu.ac.uk
↗  www.qmu.ac.uk

**»» further links**

ACCOMMODATION  accommodation@qmu.ac.uk
STUDENTS' UNION  www.qmusu.org.uk

| 850 | 94.7 | 30.1 | 19.2 | 92.5 |

Edinburgh's fourth university, granted full status in 2007, is on a new, purpose-built campus in Musselburgh, just to the east of the city. There are about 5,000 students, almost 80% of them women. There's an emphasis on vocational education, and the university boasts good graduate employment rates. Queen Margaret values its supportive atmosphere and engagement with the community.

**Fees**  Scottish and EU students from outside the UK pay no tuition fees. For other UK students, annual tuition fees will be £1,820 in 2009–10.

**Bursaries**  Young students' bursaries available for Scottish students under 25 from low-income families. Other funds available.

**Accommodation**  The new campus offers 800 en suite rooms in modern shared flats. Prices range from £90 to £95 a week.

**Facilities**  At the heart of this modern purpose-built campus is an innovative learning resource centre with a multitude of flexible learning spaces for students. There are bustling learning spaces, individual study booths, group study rooms, as well as IT, quiet and silent-study rooms.

**Transport**  The new campus is well served by buses (every 10 minutes) and trains. Musselburgh train station is located next to the campus and transports students into Edinburgh city centre in six minutes, exactly. Edinburgh International airport is approximately 16 miles away.

**❝ STUDENT VIEW ❞**

*"The unique selling point about Queen Margaret is its size. It's small and friendly so it feels like everyone knows each other. It is also a new campus so the facilities are ultra-modern and eco-friendly!"*

# Queen Mary, University of London

327 Mile End Road
Poplar
London  E1 4NS

**t**  020 7882 5555
**e**  admissions@qmul.ac.uk
↗  www.qmul.ac.uk

**»  further links**

ACCOMMODATION  residences@qmul.ac.uk
STUDENTS' UNION  www.qmsu.org

2775      85.8      32.6      11.5      95.0

Queen Mary is one of the UK's top universities, ranked 11th nationally out of 132 universities in the 2008 research assessment exercise. Besides good teaching and research, it is one of the best universities for student employability and graduate starting salaries. Degree programmes cover an impressively broad range of disciplines: arts and humanities, science and engineering, and medicine and dentistry at Barts and the London. Queen Mary offers life on a contained campus, but in the middle of a huge city; the main campus is in Mile End, east London. It's a multicultural area and, fittingly, a fifth of students are from overseas — from more than 125 countries.

**Fees**  £3,225 for full-time undergraduate courses in 2009–10.

**Bursaries**  1,078 for students with a full grant and £861 for those on a partial grant. Further scholarships available.

**Accommodation**  2,280 places in university-owned accommodation, and more in University of London halls. £66 to £116 a week.

**Facilities**  Excellent. A state-of-the-art gym and fitness centre opened in September 2008, alongside the newly refurbished Drapers's bar and student union facilities. Students also have access to the world-famous Senate House library and can get involved with the University of London Union, one of the UK's largest student unions.

**Transport**  Easy access to the London transport system for travel between campuses, around the city and beyond.

**❝ STUDENT VIEW ❞**

*"Queen Mary's academics are leaders in their field — many of them are world authorities in their areas of research. Being taught by them is truly inspirational; I'm proud to study at Queen Mary, one of the top research-led universities in the country."*

# Queen's University Belfast

University Road
Belfast BT7 1NN

**t** 028 9024 5133
**e** comms.office@qub.ac.uk
**↗** www.qub.ac.uk

**》 further links**

ACCOMMODATION accommodation@qub.ac.uk
STUDENTS' UNION www.qubsu.org

3815    99.1    35.2    14.5    96.6

Queen's has a good academic reputation. It is home to three centres of excellence: inter-professional education, active and interactive learning, and creative and performing arts. The university launched an employability and skills initiative in 2008, which includes a unique programme that officially recognises extracurricular activities such as sport or voluntary work. Students receive the degree plus award alongside their degree when they graduate. The campus is a 15-minute walk from the city centre, by the lovely botanical gardens and the Ulster Museum. Queen's takes its role in the community seriously: there's the annual Belfast festival, a film festival, art gallery and Northern Ireland's only arthouse cinema.

**Fees**   £3,225 for full-time undergraduate courses in 2009–10 for students on sandwich-year placements; students entering at stage 0 will pay £1,290 in their first year.

**Bursaries**   If you have a household income of up to £18,820, you will receive £1,185. Between £18,821 and £23,820, you will receive £655. Between £23,821 and £33,820, you will receive £110. Other support too.

**Accommodation**   Guaranteed for about 80% of freshers, from £65 to £90 a week. Prices for renting in the city are £50 to £55 a week.

**Facilities**   New student guidance centre and a £7m extension to the university's physical education centre, which has led to Queen's being selected as an official training camp for the 2012 Olympics. £9m has been spent on the student union, which is currently ranked fourth in the Russell group.

**Transport**   Most major British cities are within an hour's flying time from Belfast's two airports, which offer flights to many locations in Ireland and mainland Europe, as well as direct services to North America. Regular ferry services to Scotland and England.

**❝ STUDENT VIEW ❞**
*"The university has a great deal to offer both academically and socially. My first year has been a real adventure and university staff have been enormously helpful in helping me to settle in and make the most of student life!"*

# Ravensbourne College of Design and Communication

Walden Road
Chislehurst
Kent BR7 5SN

**t** 020 8289 4900
**e** info@rave.ac.uk
**↗** www.rave.ac.uk

**》 further links**

ACCOMMODATION   info@rave.ac.uk
STUDENTS' UNION   www.rave.ac.uk/life/student_union.htm

205       94.1       37.2       8.4       85.0

London

Apart from being the higher education institution with the most memorable web address (www.rave.ac.uk), Ravensbourne is a single-campus college of design and communication, based in seven hectares of parkland south-east of London, near Chislehurst in Kent. Courses are offered within two faculties: design, where courses include fashion, interior design and product design; and communications media, where courses include broadcasting, graphic and sound design, and animation. Undergraduate degree programmes are validated by the University of Sussex. Ravensbourne is moving to a new building in Greenwich Peninsula next to the 02 arena in 2010.

**Fees**   £3,225 for full-time undergraduate courses in 2009-10.

**Bursaries**   £310 for students receiving a full grant. Other awards and support available.

**Accommodation**   100 students can be accommodated on campus. One house is fully equipped for students with disabilities. Rent is approximately £80 a week, depending on room size.

**Facilities**   Students enjoy a world-class broadcasting studio, a virtual reality suite, 3D proto-typing facilities and a high standard of individual workspaces.

**Transport**   Central London is just 20 minutes away by train.

 **STUDENT VIEW 》**

*"Ravensbourne has excellent links in the media industry and has a brilliant reputation with big companies that I would like to work for. The tutors are knowledgeable and very approachable."*

# University of Reading

Whiteknights
PO Box 217, Reading
Berkshire  RG6 6AH

t  0118 987 5123
e  student.recruitment@reading.ac.uk
↗ www.reading.ac.uk

**》 further links**

ACCOMMODATION  accommodation@reading.ac.uk
STUDENTS' UNION  www.rusu.co.uk

2795    82.4    23.9    6.7    95.8

The University of Reading is a traditional, academic university that celebrated its 80th birthday in 2006. It is ranked as one of the UK's top research-intensive universities. Reading is academically sound with an innovative slant to its course portfolio. As well as all the old favourites, there are courses in subjects such as cybernetics. The main Whiteknights campus is one of the most charming in the UK, with a lake, woodland and even meadows to admire on your way to lectures. Reading has excellent facilities for shopping and leisure.

**Fees**  £3,225 for full-time undergraduate courses in 2009-10.

**Bursaries**  £1,385 bursary if household income is less that £25,000; £923 if less than £35,000; £462 if less than £45,000. A wide range of other support and awards is available, including entrance scholarships of £2,000.

**Accommodation**  Accommodation comprises both self-catered and catered halls, and more than 95% of first-years who request a hall place will get one. Costs range from about £68 to £143 a week.

**Facilities**  The library contains more than a million volumes; there's advanced electronic media available and online study resources. Recent developments include a £2.2m refurbishment of the sports centre, and a new student services centre and library.

**Transport**  Located just outside the M25, there's easy access to central London by train.

**❝ STUDENT VIEW ❞**

*"Reading has the best of both worlds: a campus-based community that is minutes away from a buzzing town centre!"*

# Robert Gordon University

Schoolhill
Aberdeen AB10 1FR

t 01224 262000
e admissions@rgu.ac.uk
↗ www.rgu.ac.uk

》》 **further links**

ACCOMMODATION accommodation@rgu.ac.uk
STUDENTS' UNION www.rguunion.co.uk

Aberdeen

| 1525 | 94.9 | 33.1 | 14.0 | 97.4 |
|------|------|------|------|------|

RGU is a modern university in Aberdeen of more than 30,000 students. The city-centre campus at Schoolhill is the hub of student social life; a second campus lies just under three miles away at Garthdee. The emphasis at RGU is firmly on vocational and professional courses – indeed, it calls itself "the professional university" – and a wide range of placement options is on offer. As a result, RGU has one of the best graduate recruitment records in the UK. In the past decade, the university has invested more than £100m to improve its facilities, and intends to make the Garthdee site "the best riverside campus in Europe".

**Fees** Scottish and EU students from outside the UK pay no tuition fees. For other UK students, annual tuition fees will be £1,820 in 2009-10.

**Bursaries** Young students' bursaries for Scottish students under 25 from low-income families. Supplementary grants are also available for eligible students. A range of scholarships is available.

**Accommodation** Accommodation is well equipped and usually shared with between four and seven other students. Some flats are en suite. Rents range from £76.50 to £97.50 a week.

**Facilities** Include a technologically advanced hospital environment and a purpose-built television studio. £10m has been invested in a modern sports facility, which features a 25-metre swimming pool, three gyms, a climbing wall and bouldering room, a cafe bar, three exercise studios and a large sports hall.

**Transport** Aberdeen's compact size makes it easy to get around the city and between the two campuses. Aberdeen is two and half hours' drive from Edinburgh or Glasgow, and there are regular rail and bus services to most major towns and cities in the UK.

**◀◀ STUDENT VIEW ▶▶**

*"The university provides me with opportunities and prepares me well for the working environment, particularly through the work placements. The facilities are first class and the staff are very approachable and helpful."*

# Roehampton University

Erasmus House
Roehampton Lane
London  SW15 5PU

**t**  020 8392 3232
**e**  enquiries@roehampton.ac.uk
↗  www.roehampton.ac.uk

**》 further links**

ACCOMMODATION  accommodation@roehampton.ac.uk
STUDENTS' UNION  www.roehamptonstudent.com

2215      96.5      35.7      21.2      93.4

Roehampton is a campus university based in a scenic parkland location, complete with lakes and woodland walks, overlooking Richmond Park. The campus contains a mixture of architectural styles ranging from 18th-Century, grade-I listed buildings to brand new modern structures. It's close to the chichi London districts of Richmond and Putney, and central London is only a few minutes away by train. A significant number of Roehampton's 8,000 students are mature or from an ethnic minority, and women outnumber men by three to one. The university was rated first in the UK in the latest research and assessment exercise for its research in dance and anthropology.

**Fees**   £3,225 a year for all full-time undergraduate courses in 2009–10.

**Bursaries**   £500 for full-time UK students in receipt of a full grant. A range of scholarships is also available.

**Accommodation**   Most first-years can live in university accommodation on or near campus. Costs range from £80 to £116 a week.

**Facilities**   The library contains a cybercafe, there are innovative teaching facilities, and sports resources are enjoying multimillion-pound development work.

**Transport**   Only 20 minutes to London by train. From there, the world's your oyster.

**❝ STUDENT VIEW ❞**

*"Our campus is beautiful and serene, our teachers are leaders in their fields and our colleges provide a community feel inside and outside the classroom. As soon as I arrived I felt like I belonged."*

# Rose Bruford College

Burnt Oak Lane
Sidcup
Kent   DA15 9DF

**t**  020 8308 2600
**e**  enquiries@bruford.ac.uk
**↗**  www.bruford.ac.uk

## »  further links

ACCOMMODATION   020 8308 2638
STUDENTS' UNION   www.bruford.ac.uk/students/union.aspx

205        94.2        26.2        14.8        87.7

London

Rose Bruford College is a drama school based in attractive grounds near Sidcup, Kent, on the outskirts of south-east London. Founded in 1950, the college pioneered the first acting degree in 1976. It offers a range of honours degree courses in theatre and performance, validated by the University of Manchester. Facilities include two theatres – the 330-seat Rose, a theatre in the round, and the end-stage Barn Theatre – plus studios for rehearsals, design, lectures, teachings and recording; lighting design labs; and a workshop complex.

**Fees**  £3,225 for full-time undergraduate courses in 2009–10.

**Bursaries**  Eligible students can apply for a bursary of around £300 from the college. Other awards also available.

**Accommodation**  There are limited places available for first-years in university-owned accommodation at about £85 a week.

**Facilities**  There's an extensive library, including impressive specialist collections. Unsurprisingly, facilities for performance are good.

**Transport**  25-minute journey into London.

**❝ STUDENT VIEW »**

*"I think what sets Rose Bruford apart is the diversity of theatre disciplines.  When I left I already had a wealth of experience working with every department of theatre."*

# Royal Academy of Music

Marylebone Road
London  NW1 5HT

**t**  020 7873 7373
**e**  registry@ram.ac.uk
**⌁**  www.ram.ac.uk

**》 further links**

ACCOMMODATION  www.lon.ac.uk/halls
STUDENTS' UNION  www.ram.ac.uk/whoswho/students%20union
/pages/students%20union.aspx

| 55 | 42.3 | 22.4 | 8.9 | 100.0 |

London

Founded in 1822, the Royal Academy of Music is one of the oldest and most prestigious conservatoires in the UK. It is based in upmarket Marylebone, central London, and musicians study for University of London degrees in varying programmes of study, including instrumental performance, composition, jazz, musical theatre and opera. There is a huge range of orchestras and ensembles that give public performances in spaces such as the 400-seat Dukes Hall. The student community is international, with more than 50 countries represented; there is even an English for musicians course. Musicians who have studied at the academy include Lesley Garrett, Sir Elton John and Myleene Klass.

**Fees**  £3,225 for full-time undergraduate programmes in 2009-10.

**Bursaries**  Means-tested bursaries are available, as well as a range of other awards and scholarships.

**Accommodation**  The academy cannot provide accommodation, but students can apply for a place in one of the University of London's intercollegiate halls.

**Facilities**  Truly impressive facilities for performance and rehearsal.

**Transport**  The academy is in the heart of London, providing easy access to and from all parts of the city and beyond.

**❝ STUDENT VIEW ❞**

*"Being surrounded by such a high standard of students and teachers in a supportive environment has made it an inspiring and enjoyable time for me here."*

# Royal Agricultural College

Stroud Road
Cirencester  GL7 6JS

t  01285 652531
e  admissions@rac.ac.uk
↗ www.rac.ac.uk

**》 further links**

ACCOMMODATION  lettings@rac.ac.uk

185      37.5      39.2      10.9      91.2

Cirencester

The Royal Agricultural College is a single-campus university college in Cirencester, Gloucestershire, which offers BSc honours degrees in the schools of agriculture, business, equine management, and rural economy/land management. Situated in an Oxbridge-style quadrangle in attractive parkland, the college is a charming place to live and study — though it has a reputation for being a refuge of the Land Rover-driving classes.

**Fees**   £3,225 for full-time undergraduate courses in 2009–10.

**Bursaries**   Students are entitled to a means-tested bursary of up to £1,615.

**Accommodation**   The college has study bedrooms for up to 350 students, 76 in twin rooms and the rest in single-study bedrooms, many en suite. Most are catered, with students getting three meals a day, seven days a week. Costs vary. There is a lettings service to help students find private sector accommodation in Cirencester.

**Facilities**   Facilities include three working commercial farms, with a 250-cow dairy herd, a 1,650-ewe breeding flock, and 250 hectares of crops including organic produce.

**Transport**   A shuttle bus operates between the college and Cirencester, from where there's easy public transport.

**ᏦᏦ STUDENT VIEW ᎒᎒**

*"I've met some great friends here and there's an excellent feeling on campus. The course is varied enough to keep anyone interested and the resources are good too."*

# Royal College of Music

Prince Consort Road
London  SW7 2BS

**t**  020 7589 3643
**e**  info@rcm.ac.uk
↗  www.rcm.ac.uk

 **further links**

ACCOMMODATION  collegehall@rcm.ac.uk

60        3.4        97.6

Students at London's Royal College of Music have no excuse not to feel inspired:
not only are they at one of the top conservatoires in the country, attracting more than
600 students from 49 countries, they also practise directly opposite the Royal Albert Hall.
The undergraduate BMus lasts for four years; tuition covers up to 90 minutes a week of
principal study, plus extra options and ensemble activities. There is also a BSc in physics
with studies in musical performance, taught at both RCM and Imperial. Facilities are
top-notch and the RCM is aware that it has a duty to prepare its students for viable careers
in a difficult industry, not just teach them how to make beautiful music.

**Fees**  £3,225 for full-time undergraduate courses in 2009–10.

**Bursaries**  £1,000 a year for students receiving a grant of at least £2,350.

**Accommodation**  The college has a hall of residence, College Hall, near Ravenscourt Park in west
London. It sleeps about 170 students, and includes practice rooms. Fees are about £65 to £115 a week
including bills. In the private sector, rents are about £75 to £110 a week excluding bills.

**Facilities**  Facilities include the 400-seat Britten theatre, the RCM's digital studios and the
newly refurbished 400-seat Amaryllis Fleming concert hall.

**Transport**  Very easy: you're in the middle of London.

 STUDENT VIEW

*"It's full of like-minded people who want to have a great time as well as making great music."*

# Royal Holloway, University of London

Egham
Surrey  TW20 0EX

**t**  01784 434455
**e**  admissions@rhul.ac.uk
**↗**  www.rhul.ac.uk

**»** **further links**

ACCOMMODATION  accommodation@rhul.ac.uk
STUDENTS' UNION  www.surhul.co.uk

1490        78.5        24.0        7.1        95.8

London

---

Though part of the University of London, and certainly within easy reach of the capital, Royal Holloway is actually based in Egham, Surrey, giving a sense of space and calm that students at other London institutions might sometimes kill for. The campus is 55 hectares of parkland, within walking distance of Windsor Great Park. It is dominated by the simply incredible Founder's building, a Victorian copy of the Chateau de Chambord in the Loire Valley, which really has to be seen to be believed. Teaching and research are both of the highest order, and graduates enjoy a noticeably good graduate employment rate. It was announced in 2008 that Royal Holloway is to merge with St George's, University of London, to create a single college in 2010.

**Fees**  £3,225 a year for all full-time undergraduate courses in 2009–10.

**Bursaries**  £750 a year bursaries for all students who qualify for partial or full grants. Other awards for excellence also available.

**Accommodation**  Prioritised for eligible first-years. Prices range from about £65 to £125 a week, with a choice of self-catering or catered pay-as-you-go subsidised meals. Halls range from the Victorian splendour of the Founder's building to new state-of-the-art halls with en suite study bedrooms in flats.

**Facilities**  Victorian Boilerhouse theatre and the state-of-the-art lecture hall add to the architectural merit of the campus. A comfortable, hi-tech library, thanks to a recent investment of £1.3m.

**Transport**  Pretty well serviced by road and rail, not least because London is less than 20 miles away.

**❝ STUDENT VIEW ❞**

*"Royal Holloway is a dynamic and exciting place to study. Coming here has enabled me to achieve my goals and meet people from different countries and cultures and I will leave here having achieved much more than a degree."*

# Royal Northern College of Music

124 Oxford Road
Manchester  M13 9RD

**t**  0161 907 5200
**e**  info@rncm.ac.uk
↗ www.rncm.ac.uk

 **further links**

ACCOMMODATION  0161 907 5219
STUDENTS' UNION  www.rncmsu.co.uk

135      12.0      95.0

The Royal Northern College of Music is based in a single building in the south of central Manchester. Students take the four-year BMus in order to develop their performance or composition skills to professional standards, but the course also includes supporting professional studies, such as the music business or the art of teaching, plus academic studies, which relate theoretical studies to practice. There is a huge range of ensembles, plus programmes in opera, chamber music and early music; and performance opportunities range from informal late-night jazz in the cafe bar to large-scale symphony orchestra concerts at venues such as the Bridgewater Hall.

**Fees**  £3,225 for full-time undergraduate courses in 2009-10.

**Bursaries**  Up to £1,050, means-tested. Scholarships also available.

**Accommodation**  The college has a hall of residence two minutes' walk away with places for 316 RNCM students. Costs for 2008-09 were £90.50 a week.

**Facilities**  The 616-capacity Bruntwood theatre is one of the largest performance spaces in Manchester. The college boasts more than 120 pianos, half of which are grand. Well-stocked library with over 87,000 books and items of printed music, more than 20,000 sound recordings, 20 listening stations and 24 IT workstations.

**Transport**  Pretty well serviced by road, rail and bus in the Greater Manchester area. Oxford Road station is an eight-minute walk from campus and London is two and a half hours by train. Manchester airport is 15 minutes away.

**❝ STUDENT VIEW ❞**

*"At the RNCM there are so many opportunities to perform with different kinds of people. The college is a really supportive place — you feel supported by your tutors and fellow students. I think if you feel supported and comfortable you can do your best work."*

# Royal Scottish Academy of Music and Drama

100 Renfrew Street
Glasgow  G2 3DB

**t**  0141 332 4101
**e**  musicadmissions@rsamd.ac.uk
      dramaadmissions@rsamd.ac.uk
↗  www.rsamd.ac.uk

**》》 further links**

ACCOMMODATION  www.libertyliving.co.uk
STUDENTS' UNION  www.rsamd-su.co.uk

175         87.1        10.8        96.4

Glasgow

---

In September 2009, Glasgow's Royal Scottish Academy of Music and Drama will add dance to its portfolio to become the UK's first conservatoire of dance, drama and music. Its history can be traced back to 1847, and today it attracts students from approximately 40 countries. Music courses include the four-year BMus, plus a BEd for prospective music teachers and a BA in Scottish music (with or without piping). Drama courses include acting, digital film and television; there is also a four-year BA in contemporary performance practice. And from 2009-10, the academy will offer BAs in modern ballet and musical theatre.The alumni list is impressive: Alan Cumming, James McAvoy and David Tennant, for starters. Glasgow is a fun place to be a student, and opportunities for performance are ample.

**Fees**  Undergraduate full-time fees will be £1,820 for new entrants in 2009-10, though Scottish students have this paid for them.

**Bursaries**  Bursaries and scholarships available.

**Accommodation**  The academy aims to offer all first-year students a place in its contracted hall of residence, Liberty House, in the centre of Glasgow. It offers advice to students seeking accommodation in the private sector.

**Facilities**  The academy boasts facilities that are among the best in the world. They include the Alexander Gibson opera school, the 344-seat New Athenaeum theatre, the Academy concert hall and the Academy dance studios.

**Transport**  Easily accessible from major approach roads. The airport is handy, as are the stations.

**◄◄ STUDENT VIEW ►►**

*"Every day is different. First you'll be in a camera class, then screenwriting. Other times you'll be on set. I've been on a shoot with Lord Attenborough and James McAvoy. Where else would you get that?"*

# Royal Veterinary College

Royal College Street
London  NW1 0TU

**t**  020 7468 5149
**e**  enquiries@rvc.ac.uk
**↗**  www.rvc.ac.uk

**Hawkshead Campus**  Hawkshead Lane, North Mymms, Hatfield, Hertfordshire  AL9 7TA

**》 further links**
ACCOMMODATION  www.lon.ac.uk/halls

270   76.7   24.5   6.1   98.7

London

Founded in 1791, the Royal Veterinary College (RVC) was the UK's first veterinary school, and remains its largest. A college of the University of London, RVC is based at two campuses: Camden, in the north of central London, and Hawkshead in Hertfordshire. Undergraduates can choose from the BVetMed, a five-year programme leading to qualification as a vet; a BSc in bioveterinary sciences for students looking for a career in the biotechnological, agricultural and pharmaceutical industries, as well as in organisations such as the Institute of Animal Health; and a foundation degree or BSc in veterinary nursing. Students may also take a gateway course, which leads on to the first year of the veterinary medicine degree.

**Fees**  3,225 for full-time undergraduates in 2009-10.

**Bursaries**  Bursaries of up to £1,750 are available for undergraduates who qualify for a grant. The college is introducing merit scholarships to the value of £3,000 for every year of the course.

**Accommodation**  RVC can provide places in halls for 95% of first-year undergraduates, either in self-catering facilities or catered intercollegiate halls. Charges in self-catering halls for 2008-09 ranged from £108 to £127 a week, though self-catering halls have a 50-week minimum let.

**Facilities**  Research and treatment facilities are used by the profession, meaning students have access to top-class resources.

**Transport**  Located in and around London, providing easy access to and from all campuses and other parts of the city — and beyond.

**❝ STUDENT VIEW ❞**

*"What attracted me to the RVC over other vet schools was the marriage of studying in the metropolitan setting of London while being able to work in the countryside. In addition, the RVC has a terrific reputation for research and the standard of teaching."*

# Royal Welsh College of Music & Drama

Castle Grounds
Cathays Park
Cardiff CF10 3ER

**t** Music admissions 029 2039 1363
Drama admissions 029 2039 1327
**e** music.admissions@rwcmd.ac.uk
drama.admissions@rwcmd.ac.uk
↗ www.rwcmd.ac.uk

**》 further links**

ACCOMMODATION studentservices@rwcmd.ac.uk
STUDENTS' UNION www.rwcmd.ac.uk/student_life
/students_union.aspx

Cardiff

---

The Royal Welsh College of Music and Drama is the national conservatoire of Wales, and a leading UK provider of specialist practical and performance-based training. The college is proud of its student success rate, with many rising to the top of their professions. The campus is in the centre of Cardiff, the vibrant capital city of Wales and a thriving centre for the creative industries. Work has recently begun on redeveloping the college's performance and rehearsal facilities. £22.5m will be spent on a 450-capacity recital hall, a 160-seat theatre, purpose-built rehearsal spaces and an impressive entrance arcade/exhibition space. For those budding pianists among you, take note: in early 2009, the college took delivery of 62 Steinway pianos, making it the first all-Steinway conservatoire, thanks to a groundbreaking deal with the piano-makers.

**Fees** 3,225 for undergraduate courses in 2009-10.

**Bursaries** Competitive entry scholarships are available of up to the full amount of the tuition fee. The national bursary scheme in Wales means students in receipt of a full grant get another £310.

**Accommodation** New students are guaranteed a room in halls. The cost is £79.95 a week for a 42-week contract including bills (Sky Digital and broadband are included). Private sector rents are about £220 a month plus bills and you can use a Find-A-Friend service to find fellow students to share with.

**Facilities** Facilities include the Anthony Hopkins centre, two recital galleries, studio theatres, a recording studio, courtyard performance space, Bute theatre, workshops and 50 music practice rooms.

**Transport** Cardiff International airport is close at hand. There is a frequent coach service to London as well as frequent trains.

**❝ STUDENT VIEW ❞**

*"The college makes you feel welcome immediately. The staff are what make it — there is so much importance placed on you as an individual, and what you want to get out of the course."*

# University of St Andrews

St Andrews
Fife KY16 9AJ
Scotland

**t** 01334 476161
**e** student.recruitment@st-andrews.ac.uk
↗ www.st-andrews.ac.uk

**》 further links**

ACCOMMODATION  studacc@st-and.ac.uk
STUDENTS' UNION  www.yourunion.net

1020  58.7  15.7  5.5  95.0

St Andrews is the oldest university in Scotland, and the third oldest in the English-speaking world, after Oxford and Cambridge. It is a prestigious academic centre renowned for the quality of its teaching and research, and a reputation for being a bit posh – Prince William did study here, after all. There's a high independent-school intake and a raft of arcane traditions. But St Andrews does have an active commitment to widening access. The location is special, too – a small, historic town tucked up on the coast of north-east Scotland. Despite the lack of cavernous nightclubs, there's plenty to do, and lots of student societies. And lest we forget, St Andrews is the home of golf.

**Fees**  Scottish and EU students from outside the UK pay no tuition fees. For other UK students, tuition fee of £1,820 (£2,895 for medicine).

**Bursaries**  Subject-based scholarships are available. Other bursaries and awards available.

**Accommodation**  Guaranteed for eligible first-years. Price range of accommodation supplied by the university is from about £55 to £168.

**Facilities**  The university spends about £1.4m on books and journals each year; an extensive refurbishment of the library is due to begin this year. Work began in June 2008 on a £45m school of medicine and the sciences. Revamped £35m eco-friendly student residences and 500 new beds in a new halls of residence are planned. Sports facilities extend over 60 acres near the university halls.

**Transport**  The nearest train station is Leuchars (five miles away and served by a bus from St Andrews every 15 minutes). The nearest city is Dundee, approximately 30 minutes by bus or car. There is a small airport at Dundee and an international airport at Edinburgh.

**《 STUDENT VIEW 》**

*"The ancient university, seaside town and creativity and vision of both students and staff means that life here is completely unique. We're part of 600 years of history here, and that's pretty inspiring."*

# St George's, University of London

Cranmer Terrace
London  SW17 0RE

**t**  020 8725 2333
**e**  See individual courses on the website
for contact details
↗  www.sgul.ac.uk

**》 further links**

ACCOMMODATION  www.sgul.ac.uk/halls
STUDENTS' UNION  www.student.sgul.ac.uk

| 530 | 81.8 | 23.3 | 6.4 | 99.2 |

St George's is one of the UK's best-known specialist providers of medical and healthcare education. Located in Tooting, a lively, cosmopolitan part of south-west London, it shares a site and clinical resources with St George's hospital, one of the busiest in Europe. Student satisfaction here is extremely high and is likely to remain so once they've left – the university has a 99% graduate employment rate with an average starting salary of £26,655, the third highest of full-time first-degree qualifiers in the country. As well as the five-year MBBS in medicine, St George's offers undergraduate degrees in healthcare sciences (diagnostic or therapeutic radiography, and physiotherapy), biomedical informatics, biomedical science and pharmacy, nursing, midwifery, social work, and a four- or five-year master's in pharmacy. The university is also active in clinical research.

**Fees**  £3,225 for full-time undergraduate courses in 2009–10.

**Bursaries**  Between £165 and £1,295 for students entitled to a full or partial grant, on a sliding scale.

**Accommodation**  The new halls of residence are modern and competitively priced. There are 332 en suite bedrooms and specially designed accommodation for wheelchair users on the ground floor.

**Facilities**  Specialist library resources and overnight computer access with a huge range of clinical study material to work with.

**Transport**  It's in London, near Tooting Broadway underground station, so good for transport.

**❝ STUDENT VIEW ❞**

*"The environment of St George's instils a work hard-play hard attitude from day one. The support networks, friendly atmosphere and amazing modern facilities make George's the very best place to study the healthcare sciences."*

# St Mary's University College, Belfast

191 Falls Road
Belfast  BT12 6FE

**t**  02890 327678
↗ www.stmarys-belfast.ac.uk

**》 further links**

ACCOMMODATION  02890 327678
STUDENTS' UNION  www.smsu.co.uk

300    100.0    52.4    12.1    98.9

Belfast

St Mary's is academically integrated with Queen's University Belfast, based in the Falls Road in the west of the city, which mostly provides teacher training in the Catholic tradition. It currently offers two undergraduate degrees: a four-year BEd in either primary or secondary education (including specific subject studies), and a three-year BA in liberal arts, which includes modules in human development studies, Ireland in Europe, and options from a range of humanities subjects including Gaeilge (Gaelic) and religious studies.

**Fees**   £3,225 for full-time undergraduate courses in 2009-10.

**Bursaries**   Students in receipt of a full grant will receive a bursary of £1,230, while those getting a partial grant will receive a bursary of £530.

**Accommodation**   Available either in the private sector, or in halls at Stranmillis University College or Queen's University Belfast.

**Facilities**   There's a modern library and high-quality computing facilites. Students are also entitled to use the library, recreational and computing resources at Queen's University Belfast.

**Transport**   Frequent buses to Great Victoria Street bus and rail centre two miles away. Central station is 15 minutes by bus. Belfast's airports are easily accessible.

**◀◀ STUDENT VIEW ▶▶**

*"Unlike other colleges where I have studied, I found that the uniqueness of St Mary's is the family atmosphere it creates. St Mary's ethos of support is clearly seen between lecturer and student and also between student and student."*

# St Mary's University College, Twickenham

Waldegrave Road
Strawberry Hill
Twickenham TW1 4SX

**t** 020 8240 2314
**e** recruit@smuc.ac.uk
↗ www.smuc.ac.uk

**》 further links**

ACCOMMODATION accommodation@smuc.ac.uk
STUDENTS' UNION www.smuc.ac.uk/student-life/su.htm

845      95.4      33.3      14.4      96.9

London

St Mary's was founded in 1850 as a Catholic teacher-training college, and about a third of its students still take teaching courses, including PGCEs. Other courses include drama, health and exercise, humanities, media, social sciences, sports, theology and management. The university college is obviously popular with its 3,500 undergraduates, who gave it good ratings in recent national student surveys. St Mary's was granted its own taught degree-awarding powers in 2006 (it had previously been awarding Surrey University degrees) and is making plans to slightly increase its size to gain university status.

**Fees** £3,225 for full-time undergraduate courses in 2009–10.

**Bursaries** All students are eligible for £310, and up to £700, means-tested.

**Accommodation** First-years are generally guaranteed accommodation. There's a wide range available and prices vary.

**Facilities** Good sports facilities — it is the Institute of Sports' leading centre in London. The college has also been identified as a training base for the 2012 Olympics.

**Transport** Trains to Waterloo station from Strawberry Hill every 30 minutes. Or take the train to Richmond underground station from where you can travel on the District line. The M3 and M4 are close by.

**❝ STUDENT VIEW ❞**

*"The best thing about St Mary's is its size — you soon get to know loads of people on campus, there's a friendly atmosphere here and it feels much more personal than larger universities I visited."*

# University of Salford

Salford
Greater Manchester  M5 4WT

**t**  0161 295 5000
**e**  course-enquiries@salford.ac.uk
↗  www.salford.ac.uk

**» further links**
ACCOMMODATION  www.accommodation.salford.ac.uk
STUDENTS' UNION  www.salfordstudents.com

| 3195 | 96.5 | 40.2 | 22.0 | 91.6 |

The university has an attractive waterside location in regenerated Salford. It's about a mile and a half from Manchester city centre, with its great Victorian architecture, endless bars, clubs and shops, and fabulous galleries and museums. Just under 20,000 students study here, with a hefty proportion of international students among them. The university is renowned for its friendly atmosphere. Courses are created with future careers in mind and there are some interesting options to choose from. This university has plans. The BBC is relocating five major departments to Salford Quays in 2011 and the university will have a building next door full of hi-tech facilities. By autumn 2012, the school of media, music and performance will be the proud owners of a £47m state-of-the-art building. Oh, and Smiths fans, take note: guitarist Johnny Marr has been appointed as a visiting professor and will be teaching on the popular music course.

**Fees**  £3,225 for full-time undergraduate students in 2009-10.

**Bursaries**  £320 for students in receipt of a full grant.
See salford.ac.uk/study/undergraduate/money_matters/bursaries

**Accommodation**  Weekly cost is between £56 and £78.54, among the lowest in the country. University accommodation is guaranteed for all students.

**Facilities**  The leisure centre is open seven days a week and boasts a gym, a swimming pool, a sauna and spa, squash courts, a climbing wall, a snooker room and a multi-use sports hall. There are five libraries and good access to computers.

**Transport**  The campus is less than a mile and a half from Manchester city centre. It has excellent transport links with Salford Crescent railway station on campus and a regular bus service. Manchester international airport is less than 20 minutes' drive away. The university provides a free bus service.

**« STUDENT VIEW »**

*"I love the buzzing atmosphere here. The students and teaching staff are always coming up with new and interesting ideas. It really keeps you on your toes!"*

# School of Oriental and African Studies

Thornhaugh Street
Russell Square
London WC1H 0XG

**t** 020 7898 4034
**e** study@soas.ac.uk
↗ www.soas.ac.uk

》 **further links**

ACCOMMODATION  www.soas.ac.uk/admissions/ug/accommodation
STUDENTS' UNION  www.soasunion.org

525    74.9    20.3    17.5    95.4

The School of Oriental and African Studies (Soas) is part of the University of London and enjoys a central location in student-centric Bloomsbury, with a second campus a short distance away near King's Cross. It was initially founded in 1916 as a place to train British administrators for postings across the empire. These days, it's the UK's only higher education institution to focus on the languages, cultures and societies of Africa, Asia and the Middle East, with a worldwide reputation for its teaching and research. There are approximately 4,600 students (about half of them are postgraduates) representing over 130 countries, making for a close-knit, cosmopolitan and fascinating student population.

**Fees**  £3,225 for full-time undergraduate courses in 2009–10 for UK/EU students.
£12,000 for non-EU students.

**Bursaries**  £860 for students who receive the maximum grant. £420 for students who receive a partial grant.

**Accommodation**  First-years are accommodated wherever possible and Soas has access to a range of halls of residence, both its own and intercollegiate University of London halls. Costs vary, but anticipate about £120 a week.

**Facilities**  The library is recognised as a collection of national importance and IT provision is very good.

**Transport**  It's very central London, near Euston, St Pancras and King's Cross.

**❝ STUDENT VIEW ❞**

*"Soas is a place that accepts everyone for who they are, and where your individual talents are encouraged to shine. I have developed a greater understanding and appreciation for the world around me."*

# School of Pharmacy, University of London

29-39 Brunswick Square
London  WC1N 1AX

t  020 7753 5800
e  registry@pharmacy.ac.uk
↗  www.pharmacy.ac.uk

**》 further links**

ACCOMMODATION  www.lon.ac.uk/halls
STUDENTS' UNION  sop-su.co.uk/www.sop-su.co.uk/Welcome.html

145        84.8        39.8        3.4        100.0        London

The School of Pharmacy is a specialist college of the University of London. Its only undergraduate degree programme is the master of pharmacy, or MPharm, which entitles graduates, after a further year of pre-registration training, to sit Royal Pharmaceutical Society exams and register as a pharmacist. The programme aims to "integrate the teaching, learning and understanding of pharmaceutical science in the context of pharmacy practice". Near the end of the course, students can choose specialist options or undertake a research project, and there is also a chance to study abroad in the spring of the third year. The college is based in the university district of Bloomsbury, in the heart of London.

**Fees**  £3,225 for the MPharm in 2009-10.

**Bursaries**  Students receiving the full grant will be eligible for just over £500, and then on a sliding scale. Students will be eligible for the same amount again if they achieve certain high grades at A-level.

**Accommodation**  Students from outside London can apply to live in the University of London's intercollegiate halls. Most first-years are allocated a place.

**Facilities**  You can join two student unions: the school's own and the University of London Union (ULU), a 10-minute walk away. ULU has great sports and recreational facilities. Teaching facilities are state of the art.

**Transport**  Located in the heart of London, it provides ready access to ... anywhere, really.

**❝ STUDENT VIEW ❞**

*"All the lecturers bring their enthusiasm and charisma to the classroom. It's just a shame that it all ends after four years because the last year is best!"*

# Scottish Agricultural College

Edinburgh Campus
King's Buildings, West Mains Road
Edinburgh EH9 3JG

**t** 0800 269453
**e** recruitment@sac.ac.uk
**↗** www.sac.ac.uk

**Aberdeen Campus** Craibstone Estate, Aberdeen AB21 9YA
**Ayr Campus** Auchincruive, Ayr KA6 5HW

**》 further links**

ACCOMMODATION Edinburgh 0131 535 4041/49, 0131 535 4391
Aberdeen 01224 711012
Ayr 01292 525203

The Scottish Agricultural College (SAC) offers undergraduate and postgraduate courses designed to support the land-based industries and rural economy. Courses range from agriculture to business studies, environment, conservation, garden design, sport, outdoor pursuits and tourism. SAC has three campuses across Scotland (Edinburgh, Ayr and Aberdeen), all of which are pleasant places to live and study.

**Fees** Scottish and non-UK/EU will normally have their fees paid for them. £1,820 for students from elsewhere in the UK in 2009-10.

**Bursaries** Scottish students benefit from a range of support from the Scottish executive, but SAC also has a limited number of centenary bursaries up to £2,000. It also has up to three honours-year bursaries available to successful participants in the SAC trust placement/traineeship scheme.

**Accommodation** Edinburgh, students can apply for privately managed halls of residences. In Aberdeen and Ayr, there are self-catering halls, and most first-years wanting to live on campus can be accommodated. Costs are about £85 a week in Aberdeen (en suite) and £68 a week in Ayr.

**Facilities** SAC has farms distributed around Scotland with a comprehensive range of farming activities represented, including organic, livestock, arable and dairy. Science courses at SAC are supported by modern, well-equipped teaching laboratories and each campus has its own library.

**Transport** Good train and road links with major airports close to each campus.

**《 STUDENT VIEW 》**

*"There is an excellent mix of guest speakers, practicals and field trips, which makes the courses interesting and relevant to what is currently happening in the rural and land-based business world."*

# University of Sheffield

Western Bank
Sheffield  S10 2TN

**t**  0114 222 1255
**e**  ug.admissions@sheffield.ac.uk
**↗**  www.sheffield.ac.uk

**》 further links**

ACCOMMODATION  studentoffice@sheffield.ac.uk
STUDENTS' UNION  www.shef.ac.uk/union

3990    85.3    21.3    7.0    96.0

Sheffield is always a popular choice with students. There are almost 24,000 of them enjoying life in the lively and friendly northern city, and many of them get involved in the union, or in the wealth of societies and activities the university boasts. The student media is especially well thought of. University buildings are clustered close together about a mile to the west of the city centre, where you can find all the shops, bars and pubs you could desire. The clubbing here is particularly good. Sheffield has a strong academic reputation and provides good career prospects.

**Fees**  £3,225 a year for undergraduate courses in 2009-10.

**Bursaries**  Income-based: £700 a year for those from a household with income below £17,219; £430 if your income is between £17,220 and £35,515. Prior achievement: up to £1,665 dependent on A grades at A-level, subject of study and household income. Other bursaries available.

**Accommodation**  Guaranteed for eligible non-local first-years. Catered accommodation from £98 to £130 a week, self-catering from £70 to £110 a week. Brand-new accommodation opened in September 2007, with further development due to be completed in 2009.

**Facilities**  The Jessop West building opened in January 2009 and is home to the history and English departments, and the school of modern languages and linguistics. The Soundhouse provides practice studios, rehearsal spaces and recording rooms for the department of music. The student union was voted the best at the NUS 2008 awards, so expect great facilities and events.

**Transport**  The central position makes it good for getting around the country and there's a decent local public transport system.

**ʺ STUDENT VIEW 》**

*"I just love Sheffield — a beautiful city mixed with an amazing university with a fantastic union, great facilities and great departments — what more could anyone wish for?"*

# Sheffield Hallam University

City Campus
Howard Street
Sheffield S1 1WB

**t** 0114 225 5555
**e** enquiries@shu.ac.uk
↗ www.shu.ac.uk

**》 further links**

ACCOMMODATION  accommodation@shu.ac.uk
STUDENTS' UNION  www.shu.ac.uk/university/union

5335 95.5 33.2 14.5 92.3

Sheffield

With approximately 30,000 students, Sheffield Hallam is one of the largest universities in the country, and the biggest provider of health and social care and teacher training in the UK. It's based on two campuses, one in the bustling city centre and the other out in the leafy suburbs. Investment of £115m over the past 10 years has provided the university with modern, well-equipped teaching facilities. Sheffield Hallam takes its links with business seriously and has the highest number of placement courses of any UK university. Sheffield has great facilities and good transport links. It claims to be the greenest city in England, and is within easy reach of Leeds, Manchester and the Peak District.

**Fees**  £3,225 for undergraduates in 2009-10.

**Bursaries**  £700 for eligible students in receipt of the full grant. An access bursary of £300 is also available for students from partner schools and colleges.

**Accommodation**  Guaranteed for first-years in either university-owned, partnership or privately owned accommodation. Prices vary, but are reasonable.

**Facilities**  Good learning and teaching facilities, a lively student union, plentiful sports provision and one of the UK's leading universities in e-learning.

**Transport**  Easy to hop on a train to London, Leeds or Manchester. Good public transport in town.

**❬❬ STUDENT VIEW ❭❭**

*"Studying at Sheffield Hallam has been a fantastic experience for me. The tutors are really accessible, they've been a massive help and given me loads of feedback and encouragement, so I can feel my confidence growing."*

# University of Southampton

Highfield Campus
University Road
Southampton  SO17 1BJ

**t**  023 8059 5000
**e**  prospenq@soton.ac.uk
↗  www.soton.ac.uk

**Bodrewood Campus**  Biomedical Sciences Building, Bassett Crescent East, Southampton  SO16 7PX
**Southampton General Hospital**  Tremona Road, Southampton  SO16 6YD
**National Oceanography Centre**  Waterfront Campus, European Way, Southampton  SO14 3ZH
**Winchester School of Art**  Park Avenue, Winchester  SO23 8DL

**》 further links**

ACCOMMODATION  accommodation@soton.ac.uk
STUDENTS' UNION  www.susu.org

3540     83.2     19.9     5.3     94.1

**Southampton**

Founded in 1952, Southampton is an innovative university with a diverse student population. Its main Highfield campus is located two miles from the centre of Southampton, with other sites spread across Southampton and Winchester. The active student union recently launched a TV station to accompany its award-winning radio station. The campus has benefited from considerable recent investment, including an £8.4m indoor sports complex and swimming pool, major refurbishment of the student union and Hartley library, contemporary halls of residence, and the newly built, distinctive EEE (education, engineering and entrance) building. The National Oceanography Centre is here, and the university performs well academically on all fronts.

**Fees**  £3,225 for undergraduate courses in 2009–10.

**Bursaries**  If your household income is less than £25,000, you will receive £1,000. Between £25,001 and £32,000, it's £500. A wide range of other bursaries is also available. Many subject-specific scholarships.

**Accommodation**  Guaranteed for eligible first-years. Part-catered halls or flats: £101.85 to £145.60 a week.

**Facilities**  Highfield campus hosts three internationally celebrated arts venues. There are seven libraries based around the university and more than 2,000 computer workstations in dedicated rooms on all campuses and halls of residence.

**Transport**  Excellent road and rail links, and Southampton International airport is on the outskirts of the city. There is also Uni-link, the award-winning bus service.

**‹‹ STUDENT VIEW ››**

*"The course has been an ideal mix of theory and practice and there is a real sense of community here, with the halls and the other campuses close by. It feels like a big family, where everything is in one place."*

# Southampton Solent University

East Park Terrace
Southampton  SO14 OYN

**t**  0845 6767000
**e**  enquiries@solent.ac.uk
↗ www.solent.ac.uk

**» further links**

ACCOMMODATION  accommodation@solent.ac.uk
STUDENTS' UNION  www.solentsu.co.uk

2275       96.7       36.0       21.2       93.8

**Southampton**

Southampton Solent is one of the UK's newest universities, with more than 18,000 students based at city-centre and waterfront campuses. The university has particularly good graduate employment rates, focusing on courses that offer real-life job opportunities. Work experience is key here, and students benefit from some fantastic placements. For example, the media students are part of the official Glastonbury festival filming team. As if that weren't enough, top radio, TV and music presenters, performers, promoters and managers give lectures on courses ranging from popular music to comedy. Unsurprisingly, maritime studies is a particular strength, with courses in yacht design producing some of the most influential designers in the industry. The alumni list includes gold-medal Olympians and record-breaking solo sailors.

**Fees**  £3,225 for undergraduate courses in 2009-10.

**Bursaries**  £1,050 for students with a household income of less than £18,360, then on a descending sliding scale. Other awards also available.

**Accommodation**  Fees range between £77 to £101.85 a week, inclusive of bills (the more expensive rate is for en suite).

**Facilities**  The university has its own watersports centre at its Warsash campus, at the mouth of the river Hamble. It has just been named a Skillset media academy and has professional standard HD television studios and an outside broadcast truck with multi-channel audio recording equipment. It has also opened new £1m music recording studios, a performance space with HD filming facilities, and a £1.3m hi-tech sports laboratory.

**Transport**  The city has excellent transport links by road, rail and air, thanks to the nearby Southampton international airport, which links with a number of cities in the north of England, Scotland, Ireland and the Channel Islands.

**« STUDENT VIEW »**

*"Southampton Solent has a really modern atmosphere and a great vibe. The people make you feel really welcome and there are some unique courses."*

# Staffordshire University

College Road
Stoke-on-Trent
Staffordshire  ST4 2DE

**t**  01782 294000
**e**  admissions@staffs.ac.uk
**↗**  www.staffs.ac.uk

**Leek Road Campus**  Stoke-on-Trent  ST4 2DF
**Stafford Campus**  Beaconside, Stafford  ST18 0AD
**Lichfield Campus**  The Friary, Lichfield, Staffordshire  WS13 6QG

**》 further links**

ACCOMMODATION  www.staffs.ac.uk/study_here/student_services
/accommodation/index.jsp
STUDENTS' UNION  www.staffsunion.com

2545    97.7    39.2    21.2    91.9

Stoke-on-Trent

---

Staffordshire University is located on two main campuses, in Stoke and Stafford, with a satellite campus in Lichfield. The Stoke campus lies close to the centre of Stoke-on-Trent, with easy access to the railway station and the amenities of the city. A £285m project to create a state-of-the-art learning quarter in the city is set to transform the campus and surrounding area (see www.uniq-stoke.com). The Stafford campus is a mile and a half from the town centre. The university boasts a lively student union and the cost of living is relatively low, making it one of the most affordable universities. In total, there are about 15,000 students at the main campus, plus another 10,000 studying on university awards overseas or at partner colleges in Staffordshire and Shropshire. And if three or four years spent doing a degree seems like too much of a commitment, the university offers a fast-track option in a number of subjects.

**Fees**  £3,225 for undergraduates in 2009–10.

**Bursaries**  Guaranteed cash bursaries of up to £1,000 a year throughout the course to home students.

**Accommodation**  University-managed accommodation costs £95 a week for rooms with en suite facilities and £55 a week for standard rooms.

**Facilities**  Facilities include a professionally equipped media centre, a crime scene house, a nature reserve, a drama studio and mock courtrooms. The new technologies centre at the Stafford campus includes an industry-standard television centre.

**Transport**  Both campuses are five minutes' drive from the M6. Stoke station is a minute's walk away from the Stoke campus and has pretty good links in all directions.

**❝ STUDENT VIEW ❞**

*"My tutors can be summed up in one word — brilliant. In fact they are more like friends. For me, university is worth every minute. Not only am I learning so much about myself every day but I'm learning such a great deal about the subject that I love."*

# University of Stirling

Stirling  FK9 4LA

**t** 01786 467044
**e** recruitment@stir.ac.uk
↗ www.stir.ac.uk

Stirling

**》》 further links**

ACCOMMODATION  www.studaccom.stir.ac.uk
STUDENTS' UNION  www.susaonline.org.uk

| 1350 | 93.5 | 27.1 | 8.7 | 96.4 |

Stirling's campus is regularly described as one of the most beautiful in the world, set in 122 hectares at the foot of the Ochil Hills. It boasts its own loch and Airthrey Castle. Stirling, two miles away, is also pretty, with a castle and historical old town. There are excellent facilities for sport and a recently refurbished arts centre on campus. A significant proportion of the 11,511 students are from the local area, but there's a good representation of international students too. Stirling was the first university in the UK to introduce the semester system and is proud of the flexibility of its degrees. With no faculty boundaries, students can choose from one of the widest variety of subject combinations.

**Fees**  Scottish and EU students from outside the UK pay no tuition fees. For other UK students, annual tuition fee of £1,820.

**Bursaries**  Young students' bursaries for Scottish students under 25 from lower-income groups (level is dependent on family income). Other grants also available, plus a range of scholarships.

**Accommodation**  All first-years are guaranteed accommodation. Weekly prices start at £60 for a self-catering room with shared shower and kitchen, and go to £88 for an en suite room sharing a kitchen.

**Facilities**  There are 24-hour computer labs, the MacRobert arts centre with theatre and cinema; extensive indoor and outdoor sports facilities, including a newly extended tennis centre and gym; a 50m swimming pool; a nine-hole golf course, driving range and golf academy; and a publicly accessible art collection. Not to mention the lively students' association with cafes and bars.

**Transport**  Stirling is well connected to the UK road and rail networks, and is only 45 minutes from both Edinburgh and Glasgow.

**⁶⁶ STUDENT VIEW ⁹⁹**

*"What I love about Stirling is its community feel and I'm confident that the skills I've developed and experiences I've had here will set me in good stead for whatever it is I settle on in my future."*

# Stranmillis University College

Stranmillis Road
Belfast  BT9 5DY

**t**  028 9038 1271
**↗**  www.stran.ac.uk

**»** **further links**

ACCOMMODATION  www.stran.ac.uk/informationfor/undergraduatestudents
/studentservices/accommodationcatering

STUDENTS' UNION  www.stran.ac.uk/informationfor/undergraduatestudents
/studentservices/studentsunion

260   100.0   33.5   3.9   93.2

Belfast

Founded in 1922 as a teacher training institute, Stranmillis is now a college of Queen's University Belfast, offering three undergraduate degrees: a BEd in either primary or post-primary education, a BA in early childhood studies, and a BSc in health and leisure studies. Its campus is based in a conservation area, part of 18 hectares of wooded parkland, one mile south of the city centre. The college is proud of being an inter-faith institution "with staff and students of all religions and none".

**Fees**  £3,225 for undergraduates in 2009–10.

**Bursaries**  Up to £1,050, means-tested.

**Accommodation**  The college can provide rooms for 400 students. Rents are £85 a week.

**Facilities**  There's a well-stocked library that will loan laptops to students.

**Transport**  An hour by air from London. Good links with Northern Ireland and the rest of Ireland.

**❝ STUDENT VIEW ❞**

*"I was amazed at how easy it was to settle in. I am really enjoying my time at Stranmillis and would encourage anyone wanting a challenge whilst having a good time to consider this course."*

# University of Strathclyde

John Anderson Campus
16 Richmond Street
Glasgow G1 1XQ

**t** 0141 548 2814
**e** scls@mis.strath.ac.uk
↗ www.strath.ac.uk

**Jordanhill Campus** 76 Southbrae Drive, Glasgow G1 1XQ

**»** **further links**

ACCOMMODATION student.accommodation@strath.ac.uk
STUDENTS' UNION www.strathstudents.com

3140    92.3    26.7    14.0    95.1

Strathclyde emphasises "useful learning" by tailoring degrees and teaching towards the requirements of future employers and the wider society. It also takes a holistic approach to university life, acknowledging students come to university to do more than just attend classes, and encouraging them to get involved in student activities or check out what Glasgow has to offer. There are more than 15,000 students, split between the central John Anderson campus (where many students also live) and another in the west of the city. The student union building is one of the largest in the country, though Glasgow also has plenty to offer, from top music venues and swanky bars to hushed art galleries and plenty of green spaces. Indeed, the city was in the top 10 must-see locations in the 2009 Rough Guide.

**Fees**  Scottish and EU students from outside the UK pay no tuition fees. For other UK students, annual tuition fee of £1,775. See strath.ac.uk/feenews

**Bursaries**  There is a range of scholarships on offer. The university has a searchable database of bursaries and scholarships.

**Accommodation**  Guaranteed for first-years. A range of residences is available in the city-centre campus village from approximately £60 to £90 a week.

**Facilities**  Some of the best student libraries in Scotland, with specialist collections for the subjects taught here. There are 2,000 reader spaces and more than 1m resources, including 7,000 print and e-journals. 24-hour online IT resource centre, online learning systems and other multimedia support. More than 400 hotspots for Wi-Fi access across the campus. Student laptop initiative provides discounted laptops and support packages.

**Transport**  Close to Glasgow's main railway stations, bus station, subway and central airport.

**❝ STUDENT VIEW ❞**

*"I'm glad I chose Strathclyde. The classes are always interesting and instil a desire to learn more about the subjects, and when classes are done the union ALWAYS makes for a fantastic night out! I've made friends here that I know I'll have for the rest of my life."*

# University of Sunderland

City Campus, Edinburgh Building
Chester Road
Sunderland SR1 3SD

**t** 0191 515 2000
**e** student-helpline@sunderland.ac.uk
**↗** www.sunderland.ac.uk

**Sir Tom Cowie Campus at St Peter's** St Peter's Way, Sunderland SR6 0DD

**»** **further links**
ACCOMMODATION residentialservices@sunderland.ac.uk
STUDENTS' UNION www.sunderlandsu.co.uk

| 2285 | 98.2 | 48.0 | 19.9 | 92.5 |

The University of Sunderland has a student population of more than 14,000, based on two main sites, and they're a pretty happy bunch according to the latest national student survey, which ranked them as the most satisfied in the north-east. The Sir Tom Cowie campus at St Peter's is a riverside development that has seen an investment of over £50m in recent years. At the City campus, an ambitious redevelopment programme is well underway with a range of new sport and leisure facilities opening in September 2009. Sunderland is a modern coastal city, right at the heart of the vibrant north-east. The city has been the focus of regeneration and investment, and is continuing to grow and develop.

**Fees** £3,225 a year for undergraduates in 2009-10.

**Bursaries** £325 a year for those with a household income of less than £39,305. Scholarships in subject-specific areas also available.

**Accommodation** The university tries to accommodate all first-year undergraduates in halls of residence. There is a wide range of accommodation available and prices vary accordingly, but expect them to compare very favourably with costs in other parts of the country.

**Facilities** The Sir Tom Cowie campus was recently voted one of the top 10 student campuses in the UK. CitySpace, a new sport and social centre, will open in September 2009, and new state-of-the-art library and social learning facilities will be available.

**Transport** The metro is a light railway network with a station at the heart of City campus. Bus and road links are excellent, and rail transport to the rest of the UK is good too. London is under three hours away by train.

**❝ STUDENT VIEW ❯❯**

*"It's a different world over here for me compared to Northern Ireland but the people in this city have made it easy for me to fit in. The quality of the university courses offered is better than anywhere else and the nightlife is amazing."*

# University of Surrey

Guildford
Surrey  U2 7XH

t  01483 683948
e  ug-enquiries@surrey.ac.uk
↗  www.surrey.ac.uk

**》 further links**

ACCOMMODATION  www.surrey.ac.uk/accommodation
STUDENTS' UNION  www.ussu.co.uk

1530     90.9     22.3     9.5     97.0

Guildford

---

The University of Surrey's main campus is on Stag Hill, in Guildford, adjacent to the cathedral. It has charming parkland with its own lake. A major expansion of the campus is underway at Manor Park, which will include academic buildings, sports facilities, and accommodation for students and staff. Guildford is a rather smart town, with easy links to London. As befits a university that pioneered sandwich degrees, 80% of the 12,000-strong student population study on courses that include a work-based professional training year. The university is famous for its consistently outstanding employment record.

**Fees**  £3,225 for undergraduate courses in 2009–10.

**Bursaries**  Up to £2,050. A further range of scholarships is available. See surrey.ac.uk/undergraduate/fees/bursaries

**Accommodation**  All first-years are guaranteed university accommodation if they apply by the deadline. There's a wide range available and prices vary accordingly.

**Facilities**  Great resources for sport and physical activity, including a programme of 25 dance classes a week. There's a dedicated art gallery on campus and a good library and study facilities. The student union has some of the best facilities in the country, and a packed calendar of events and activities.

**Transport**  London is half an hour away by train. Guildford is on the main lines between London Waterloo and Portsmouth with regular services.

---

**‹‹ STUDENT VIEW ››**

*"I have gained real life experiences and opportunities that I would never have been privilege to, had I not been at Surrey"*

# University of Sussex

Sussex House
Brighton  BN1 9RH

**t**  01273 606755
**e**  ug.enquiries@sussex.ac.uk
↗  www.sussex.ac.uk

## 》 further links

ACCOMMODATION  housing@sussex.ac.uk
STUDENTS' UNION  www.ussu.info

2075    86.1    22.3    9.9    92.8

Brighton

---

The University of Sussex is the only university surrounded by a (newly designated) national park, the South Downs. Yet, it's just 50 minutes from London by train and four miles from lovely Brighton, with its vibrant nightlife, great shops, Royal Pavillion and seaside attractions. As well as good amenities on campus, there is a large and active student union. Sussex has a good academic reputation (the English department is particularly strong) and a history of innovative approaches to teaching and learning. The alumni list includes Hilary Benn, author Ian McEwan and Vogue editor Alexandra Shulman.

**Fees**  £3,225 for full-time undergraduate courses in 2009-10.

**Bursaries**  £1,000 a year for all students receiving the full grant. If your family income is less than £30,000 you can also apply for one of 200 scholarships worth £1,000 a year, which are awarded on the basis of criteria such as overcoming disadvantage or contribution to the community. Other departmental scholarships also available.

**Accommodation**  Guaranteed for eligible first-years. Accommodation costs from £70 to £108 a week.

**Facilities**  2011 is the university's 50th anniversary and plenty of developments are planned, including a revamped Gardner arts centre to reopen as the Attenborough centre (in honour of its former chancellor Lord Atttenborough) and a new £10m teaching building for arts and science, to open in 2010.

**Transport**  London is under an hour by train. Gatwick is half that. Train services direct from central Brighton to campus at Falmer — journey takes just eight minutes. Good bus services too. Many people cycle.

---

**❝ STUDENT VIEW ❞**

*"Sussex is the perfect choice — a world-leading university, with inspiring people, in a great location."*

# Swansea University

Singleton Park
Swansea  SA2 8PP

**t**  01792 205678
**e**  admissions@swansea.ac.uk
**↗**  www.swansea.ac.uk

**》 further links**

ACCOMMODATION  accommodation@swansea.ac.uk
STUDENTS' UNION  www.swansea-union.co.uk

2810      93.1      29.0      12.0      95.5

Swansea

A hot contender for any "best campus" award going, Swansea is virtually unparalleled for its location. It sits in parkland overlooking the Swansea Bay, on the edge of the stunning Gower peninsula. Surfers, walkers and climbers adore it here. When you tire of gazing at the natural splendour, it's a short trip into the centre of Swansea – not so lovely to look at, but, as Wales's second city, a good place to shop, party or get some culture. The university is a consistently popular choice with applicants. The student population numbers 10,463 undergraduates and 1,849 postgraduates. Swansea has a solid academic reputation and an excellent 95% graduate employment rate.

**Fees**  £3,225 for home and EU students for full-time undergraduate courses in 2009-10. Students who live within the EU are eligible for a fee grant of £1,940 and will pay a fee of £1,285.

**Bursaries and scholarships**  The university offers a number of scholarships, bursaries and prizes. See swan.ac.uk/scholarships

**Accommodation**  Approximately 99% of first-years are guaranteed accommodation and prices range from £69 to £85 a week. Rent in the city/town is about £55 to £67 a week.

**Facilities**  With 1,800-plus computers available for student use, Swansea has one of the best rates of computing provision in the country, and the library has the longest opening hours of any academic library in Wales (8am to 2am). As for the sports village, it houses the Wales national pool, the only 50m pool in Wales.

**Transport**  An efficient bus service runs from the student village to the main university campus, and the city centre is only a 10-minute journey from campus. Cardiff is an hour away by car and is well served by road and rail links. London Paddington is under three hours away by train and Cardiff International airport is just over one hour away.

**《 STUDENT VIEW 》**

*"I will never forget my time at Swansea University, or the friends I made along the way. I would recommend the Swansea experience to anyone."*

# Swansea Metropolitan University

Mount Pleasant
Swansea  SA1 6ED

**t**  01792 481010
**e**  enquiry@smu.ac.uk
↗  www.smu.ac.uk

**》 further links**

ACCOMMODATION  01792 482082  or accommodation@smu.ac.uk
STUDENTS' UNION  www.metsu.org

| 785 | 97.9 | 42.7 | 23.1 | 94.1 |

Swansea Metropolitan University has been a major centre for vocational higher education for more than 150 years. It is based on several campuses in and around the city of Swansea, with easy access to Mumbles and the breathtaking Gower peninsula. Swansea Met offers courses under three main faculties: arts and design; applied design and engineering; and a third faculty broadly called humanities, but also encompassing accounting, business and tourism. It remains true to its historical focus of vocational education, and maintains close links with industry, commerce and public services. Its approach pays off, as graduate employment rates are above the UK average.

**Fees**  £3,225 for full-time undergraduate courses in 2009–10.

**Bursaries**  The university offers a means-tested bursary of up to £310. A non-means-tested bursary of £500 is available to students who live more than 45 miles away from campus.

**Accommodation**  There's a range to choose from and prices range from £56 to £66 a week.

**Facilities**  There are three libraries, each with their own computing facilities attached. Each faculty is equipped with the relevant industry-standard facilities.

**Transport**  Swansea enjoys excellent road and rail links with all parts of Britain. A regular bus service runs from all campuses to the city centre and Swansea is easily navigable on foot, on bicycle or by road.

**❝ STUDENT VIEW ❞**

*"Swansea Metropolitan University has provided me with some experiences that I might not have had elsewhere. There is a wealth of support from the lecturers and a wide range of activities to get involved with."*

# University of Teesside

Middlesbrough
Tees Valley   TS1 3BA

**t**  01642 218121
**e**  registry@tees.ac.uk
**↗**  www.tees.ac.uk

**》 further links**

ACCOMMODATION  accommodation@tees.ac.uk
STUDENTS' UNION  www.tees.ac.uk/sections/studentlife
/students_union.cfm

2275    99.1    47.1    15.7    91.3

Middlesbrough

---

Teesside's campus is close to the centre of Middlesbrough, a town undergoing a transformation — alongside a wide range of bars, cafes and clubs is a stunning new art gallery, Middlesbrough Institute of Modern Art. And if you want to get away from the hustle and bustle, the charming old town of Whitby and the stunning North York Moors are just on your doorstep. Almost £100m has been invested in the university over the past decade. Student numbers have reached 24,000, with widening participation a priority: 98.5% of young, full-time degree entrants attended state schools or colleges. The university enjoys an international reputation for computing teaching and research, and is ranked in the top three for learning resources in the 2008 national student survey.

**Fees**  £3,225 a year for all full-time undergraduate courses in 2009–10.

**Bursaries**  £1,025 a year for those from families earning £25,000 or less. Elite athlete bursary scheme of up to £2,000. Scholarships are currently under review. See tees.ac.uk/scholarships

**Accommodation**  Priority for halls is given to first-year students, although the university is normally able to offer accommodation to all students who apply. Rents in the range of £40 to £78 a week.

**Facilities**  An award-winning student union and a learning resource centre branded excellent by 91% of students. Some first-rate resources, including a hi-tech mock courtroom, an environmental chamber for sports science students, and broadcast-quality video production facilities. A new dental technology training and sports therapy centre opens in 2010.

**Transport**  City-centre campus, with good coach and rail links to York and Newcastle (both an hour away), Leeds and Manchester. London is two and a half hours by train from Darlington. The airport is 20 minutes away.

**❝ STUDENT VIEW ❞**

*"Teesside is a great place to study. New buildings are going up all around, the facilities we use are worth thousands of pounds, and the staff are very good at putting time aside for you if you show an active interest in your studies. What more could you want!"*

# Thames Valley University

**Thames Valley University**

t 0800 036 8888
e learning.advice@tvu.ac.uk
↗ www.tvu.ac.uk

**Ealing Campus** St Mary's Road, Ealing, W5 5RF
**Slough Campus** Wellington Street, Slough, Berkshire SL1 1YG
**Brentford Campus** Paragon House, Boston Manor Road, Brentford, Middlesex TW8 9GA
**Reading Campus** Kings Road, Reading, Berkshire RG1 4HJ

>> **further links**

ACCOMMODATION uas@tvu.ac.uk
STUDENTS' UNION www.tvusu.co.uk

1630    98.0    38.9    28.9    94.8

London

Thames Valley University (TVU) is based across three campuses in west London: Ealing and Brentford, Reading and Slough. It's not too far to go to get to the wild and crazy heart of London, but life around here is a bit more sedate and manageable. There is a large, mixed student body, with lots of mature, part-time and ethnic minority students. Courses are designed with students' career prospects in mind and 2008 figures from the Higher Education Statistics Agency showed that at 95% TVU had the best graduate employment record against its benchmark in the country. Programmes of study cover just about everything – from psychology to international culinary arts, business studies to nursing.

**Fees** £3,225 for full-time undergraduate courses in 2009-10.

**Bursaries** If your household income is below £25,000, you may be eligible for a bursary of £1,060. Between £25,000 and £40,000, you may be eligible for £530. Other support – including a £5,000 excellence award – is available.

**Accommodation** The university has student accommodation in Brentford. Expect to pay about £100 a week.

**Facilities** Learning resource centres at each campus are well stocked and updated regularly, with an ever-expanding selection of electronic resources. The centres have long opening hours; some with 24-hour access.

**Transport** There are shuttle buses between campuses, and excellent public transport links provide easy access into London.

**❝ STUDENT VIEW ❞**

*"Because of the diversity and where TVU is based, I am able to benefit from excellent teaching staff and great industry links. I'm at ease knowing lecturers understand their industry and are guiding me on the best path to success."*

# Trinity Laban

King Charles Court
Old Royal Naval College
Greenwich, London  SE10 9JF

**t**  020 8305 4300
**e**  info@trinitylaban.ac.uk
↗ www.trinitylaban.ac.uk

**》 further links**

ACCOMMODATION  www.opalstudents.com

130       81.2       15.3       19.7       94.6

London

Trinity Laban is a conservatoire for music and dance, formed in 2005 from the merger of Trinity College of Music with Laban. It is based in Greenwich — a very pleasant corner of south-east London. Trinity is housed at the glorious King Charles Court at the Old Royal Naval College, while Laban is based to the west of Greenwich, nearer Deptford, in a landmark building designed by Herzog & de Meuron (of Tate Modern fame). There's a range of specialised programmes available, including degrees in dance theatre, performance and Indian music.

**Fees**  £3,225 a year for undergraduates courses in 2009-10.

**Bursaries**  There are several scholarships and bursaries available — more information can be found on the website.

**Accommodation**  The nearby privately owned McMillan student village can house most new students. Prices start at about £115 a week.

**Facilities**  As you may expect, there are superb resources for both practice and performance.

**Transport**  It's in London, so ready access to the DLR, national rail and bus services.

**《 STUDENT VIEW 》**

*"The wonderful thing about studying at Trinity Laban is that you're always being inspired, whether by the teaching staff or by your fellow students. There are so many opportunities, and the courses are incredibly rewarding."*

# Trinity University College

Carmarthen  SA31 3EP

**t**  01267 676767
**e**  registry@trinity-cm.ac.uk
↗  www.trinity-cm.ac.uk

**》 further links**

ACCOMMODATION  d.doyle@trinity-cm.ac.uk
STUDENTS' UNION  www.trinitysu.co.uk

400      99.6     40.8     17.0     97.9

Trinity University College (Coleg Prifysgol y Drindod) – formerly Trinity College Carmarthen (Coleg y Drindod Caerfyrddin) – is a church college that is due to merge with Lampeter to become University of Wales: Trinity Saint David by July 2010. It offers arts and humanities degrees in a range of subjects from acting and film studies, to Christianity and community studies; as well as a range of education-based degrees. Students are based on a picturesque single campus in south Wales, with easy access to lovely countryside and the busy market town of Carmarthen.

**Fees**  £3,225 a year for undergraduate courses in 2009-10.

**Bursaries**  Means-tested bursary of about £400 for students from low-income homes. Also, a range of support for specific purposes, such as accommodation or childcare.

**Accommodation**  The vast majority of first-years can live on campus, in single study bedrooms. Rent is about £90 a week.

**Facilities**  There's a sports hall (featuring a climbing wall) and a fitness suite. The student union is active and arts facilities in particular are very good, including a fully equipped theatre.

**Transport**  Close to the town centre and to the station for major rail links. Good access to the main road network.

 **STUDENT VIEW 》**

*"My time at Trinity has been brilliant. Everyone is really friendly and it doesn't take long to feel at home. Living on campus is an excellent way of getting settled into a new place."*

# UHI Millennium Institute

Executive Office
Ness Walk  IV3 5SQ

**t**  0845 272 3600
**e**  info@uhi.ac.uk
↗  www.uhi.ac.uk

**》 further links**

ACCOMMODATION  uhi.ac.uk/accommodation
STUDENTS' UNION  www.uhisa.org.uk

365    100.0    52.5    29.9    90.2

UHI is the only higher education institution based in the Highlands and Islands of Scotland, covering 15 sites as far away from each other as Shetland, Lewis, Argyll and Perth. As well as more general vocational courses, such as computing or business studies, UHI offers degrees that reflect the industries and culture of the region, such as aircraft engineering, engineering with renewable energy studies, culture studies of the Highlands and Islands, Gaelic music and culture, marine science, sustainable forestry … and, for outdoors types, adventure tourism management and golf management.

**Fees**  £1,820 for new students in 2009-10. Scottish students have their fees paid for them.

**Bursaries**  There is a young person's bursary for eligible Scottish students, and further financial support available.

**Accommodation**  There is a wide variety of accommodation available at the 15 sites. Some have halls and others will assist you in finding private accommodation. Prices vary.

**Facilities**  Vary according to where you study. UHI is good at off-campus delivery.

**Transport**  Depends on where you are, of course, but plan seven hours for the train to London; fewer by air. All campuses are easily accessible by bus.

**❝ STUDENT VIEW ❞**

*"I have been very fortunate in that all my lecturers loved their jobs — their passion for the subject was, at times, infectious."*

# UHI colleges

**Aygrll College UHI**
West Bay, Dunoon, Argyll  PA23 7HP    t 0845 230 9969

**Highland Theological College UHI**
High Street, Dingwall, Ross-shire  IV15 9HA    t 01349 780000

**Inverness College UHI**
3 Longman Road, Longman South, Inverness  IV1 1SA    t 01463 273000

**Lews Castle College UHI**
Stornoway, Isle of Lewis  HS2 0XR    t 01851 770000

**Lochaber College UHI**
Colaisde Lochaber OGE, An Aird, Fort William, Inverness-shire  PH33 6AN    t 01397 874000

**Moray College UHI**
Moray Street, Elgin, Morayshire  IV30 1JJ    t 01343 576000

**NAFC Marine Centre UHI**
Port Arthur, Scalloway, Shetland  ZE1 0UN    t 01595 772000

**Ness Foundation**
Ness House, Dochfour Business Centre, Inverness  IV3 8GY    t 01463 220 407

**North Highland College**
Ormlie Road, Thurso, Caithness  KW14 7EE    t 01847 889000

**Orkney College UHI**
Kirkwall, Orkney  KW15 1LX    t 01856 569000

**Perth College UHI**
Crieff Road, Perth  PH1 2NX    t 0845 270 1177

**Sabhal Mòr Ostaig UHI**
An Teanga, Slèite, Isle of Skye  IV44 8RQ    t 01471 888000

**Scottish Association for Marine Science UHI**
Dunstaffnage Marine Laboratory, Oban, Argyll  PA37 1QA    t 01631 559000

**Sustainable Development Research Centre**
The Enterprise Park, Forres, Moray  IV36 2AB    t 01309 678111

**Shetland College UHI**
Gremista, Lerwick, Shetland  ZE1 0PX    t 01595 771000

# University of Ulster

York Street
Belfast
Co. Antrim  BT15 1ED

**t**  08700 400 700
**e**  registryjn@ulster.ac.uk
**↗**  www.ulster.ac.uk

**Jordanstown Campus**  Shore Road, Newtownabbey, Co. Antrim  BT37 0QB
**Coleraine Campus**  Cromore Road, Co. Londonderry  BT52 1SA
**Magee Campus**  Northland Road, Londonderry  BT48 7JL

**》 further links**

ACCOMMODATION  ulster.ac.uk/-accommodation
STUDENTS' UNION  www.uusu.org

4125    100.0    47.6    21.3    94.0

The University of Ulster is home to 25,000 local, national and international students, spread over four campuses in Belfast, Coleraine, Jordanstown and Magee (Derry). A fifth, Campus One, is a fully online e-learning service. Sport is big at Ulster — its vision is to establish itself as the leading university for sport in Ireland. The Sports Institute Northern Ireland resides at the Jordanstown campus, which is also home to the Ulster Sports Academy, a major indoor sport and recreation facility that opened in 2008.

**Fees**  £3,225 for full-time undergraduate courses in 2009–10. For more information see ulster.ac.uk/finance/fees

**Bursaries**  If your household income is below £18,360, you will receive £1,070 a year. Between £18,821 and £21,525, you will receive £640. Between £21,526 and £40,238, you will receive £320. See prospectus.ulster.ac.uk/geninfo/uu-bursaries.html

**Accommodation**  Guaranteed for eligible first-years. Weekly prices range from about £50 to £100.

**Facilities**  State-of-the-art libraries at all four campuses. Expect lovely aromas floating around the Belfast campus as it is home to the Academy training restaurant. It also hosts the Ulster festival of art and design, which was launched in 2008. The Coleraine campus boasts the Riverside theatre, the third largest professional theatre in Northern Ireland. And the Magee campus is home to the centre for the creative and performing arts.

**Transport**  Excellent road and rail connections between the campuses. There are three airports in Northern Ireland, all under an hour away from most British and Irish cities. Plenty of international flights too. If you're in the car, daily ferry services run between Scotland and England to Larne and Belfast.

**❝ STUDENT VIEW ❯❯**

*"The University of Ulster is a friendly place to study with helpful staff, top-class lecturers and modern facilities. The students here make the experience what it is — a great one!"*

# University College London

Gower Street
London  WC1E 6BT

**t**  020 7679 2000
**e**  Enquiries via the website
**↗**  www.ucl.ac.uk

**》 further links**

ACCOMMODATION  www.ucl.ac.uk/accommodation
STUDENTS' UNION  www.uclu.org

2350      66.6      18.9      8.0      95.9

UCL is big and is consistently ranked among the best universities in the world, with an emphasis on innovative teaching and research excellence (it got its 20th Nobel prize in 2007). Its alumni include Gandhi, Alexander Graham Bell and, of course, Coldplay. Its Bloomsbury base is convenient for all of central London, and is famous for its literary and educational heritage. At least 50% of staff were ranked as of world-leading quality or internationally excellent in the 2008 research assessment exercise.

**Fees**  £3,225 a year for full-time undergraduate courses in 2009-10.

**Bursaries**  Up to £2,775 a year, depending on household income.

**Accommodation**  Guaranteed for eligible first-years. Weekly prices range from £101 to £144 for catered accommodation and from £68 to £145 for self-catering.

**Facilities**  Excellent library facilities, on-campus theatre, a fitness centre and a great student union.

**Transport**  Easy access to the London underground network and a couple of mainline stations; and the Eurostar terminal is only up the road. A number of bus routes stop just outside the main entrance, and there are cycle racks at UCL residencies and on campus.

**❝ STUDENT VIEW ❞**

*"This prestigious institution instantly attracted me. The RAE scores were high, it's located in the coolest city in the world, not to mention it has been ranked seventh best university in the world."*

# University of Wales Institute, Cardiff

Western Avenue
Cardiff  CF5 2YB

**t** 029 2041 6070
**e** uwicinfo@uwic.ac.uk
↗ www.uwic.ac.uk

**》 further links**

ACCOMMODATION  accomm@uwic.ac.uk
STUDENTS' UNION  www.uwicsu.co.uk

| 2100 | 94.9 | 29.8 | 16.1 | 93.4 |

UWIC is one of the leading new universities in Wales, mainly because of its career-orientated courses that make graduates popular with employers. It's also a top sporting university with first-class facilities and a proud tradition of competition — and success. Cardiff is a lively, cosmopolitan and fun-loving capital city, but still manageable and easy to get around. There's some lovely countryside within easy reach and good transport links to the rest of the UK.

**Fees**  £3,225 a year for all full-time undergraduate courses for 2009–10. Welsh students are eligible for a non-means-tested fee grant from the Welsh assembly of £1,890.

**Bursaries**  Means-tested bursaries based on a family income of £300 to £500 are available, as well as other bursaries. Also, entry scholarships of up to £1,000. See uwic.ac.uk/bursaries

**Accommodation**  Not guaranteed, but UWIC will help with finding suitable private accommodation if necessary. Rooms cost between £72.50 and £106 a week.

**Facilities**  Resources for sport are especially good. A recent investment of £50m will pay for a new Cardiff school of management building, a new food industry centre and a multi-purpose student centre.

**Transport**  Free student transport between the four campuses, the city centre and popular student housing areas. Cardiff is good for road and rail: London is two hours by train.

 **STUDENT VIEW 》**

*"The quality of teaching was great with the perfect balance of lectures and tutorials; the programme prepared me for work and was designed to give me skills that I wasn't aware I had."*

# University of Warwick

Coventry CV4 7AL

**t** 02476 523523
**e** student.recruitment@warwick.ac.uk
↗ www.warwick.ac.uk

>> **further links**

ACCOMMODATION accommodation@warwick.ac.uk
STUDENTS' UNION www.warwicksu.com

2565    76.4    17.6    4.0    94.8

● Coventry

The first fact you should know about Warwick is that it's not in Warwick. It actually lies about three miles outside the centre of Coventry and on the border of Warwickshire. Warwick itself does have its own castle, though, so you may like to go there for a day trip. Coventry has all the other mod cons you require, though the modern (well, modern in the 1960s) main campus is charming and very well equipped. Consistently rated among the best universities in the country, Warwick is something of a leader in the academic field, with innovative approaches to community involvement and widening participation.

**Fees** £3,225 for full-time undergraduate courses in 2009-10.

**Bursaries** £1,800 to all students with a family income of £36,000 or less.
Further support also available.

**Accommodation** Guaranteed for all first-years. There are about 6,000 on-campus rooms, and a stock of off-campus rooms too. Self-catering halls range from about £70 to £115 a week.

**Facilities** There's an impressive art collection on show at the arts centre, good sports facilities and a large library.

**Transport** Close to the M1/M6 intersection and half an hour to Birmingham by train; an hour and a quarter to London.

**❝ STUDENT VIEW ❞**

*"Warwick as a whole is a great environment in which to study and to live. Campus is lively and vibrant, offering all the facilities you could possibly need, together with a very active students' union providing a range of extra-curricular activities."*

# University of the West of England, Bristol

Frenchay Campus
Coldharbour Lane
Bristol BS16 1QY

**t** 0117 32 83333
**e** admissions@uwe.ac.uk
**↗** www.uwe.ac.uk

**Bower Ashton Campus** Kennel Lodge Road, Bower Ashton, Bristol BS3 2JT
**St Matthias Campus** Oldbury Court Road, Fishponds, Bristol BS16 2JP
**Glenside Campus** Blackberry Hill, Stapleton, Bristol BS16 1DD
**Hartpury College** Hartpury House, Hartpury, Gloucester GL19 3BE
**Bath Education Centre** First floor, Education Centre, Royal United Hospital,
Combe Park, Bath BA1 3NG
**Gloucester Education Centre** Hartpury House, Hartpury, Gloucester GL19 3BE
**Swindon Education Centre** Great Western Hospital, Marlborough Road,
Swindon SN3 6BB

**》 further links**

ACCOMMODATION accommodation@uwe.ac.uk
STUDENTS' UNION www.uwesu.org/ez/

4970  89.0  28.9  19.5  94.0

Bristol

UWE Bristol has grown considerably since it gained university status in 1992, and now has a student population of almost 30,000. Students are drawn from a wide range of backgrounds, and the university is keen to take on students with a broad range of qualifications and experience. The graduate employment record is consistently impressive and the university has started running its own unique graduate development programme. The four campuses are spread across the lovely city of Bristol, which is the largest city in the south-west with an impressive music scene and cultural life, and gorgeous historic buildings. It's very student-friendly and many first-time visitors instantly fall in love with it.

**Fees** £3,225 for all full-time undergraduate courses in 2009-10.
**Bursaries** £1,000 annually for those with a household income below £25,000. £1,000 for UK undergraduates who have completed a recognised access course.
**Accommodation** Guaranteed for first-years. Self-catering accommodation costs from £60 to £121 a week (2008-09 rents). There's a new student village on the Frenchay campus.
**Facilities** 24/7 access to library and computing facilities. Continuing investment, including new student village and sports centre.
**Transport** A bus service run by the university links the campuses and the city centre. Close to the M4 and M5, not far from Bristol airport and on all major rail routes. Hubs for 24/7 pay-as-you-go cycle stations at UWE's Frenchay, St Matthias and Glenside campuses.

**❝ STUDENT VIEW ❞**

*"The university provides you with every possible opportunity you could want. It has such a friendly atmosphere you would be hard pushed to find somewhere better."*

# University of the West of Scotland

Paisley PA1 2BE

**t** 0800 027 1000
**e** uni-direct@uws.ac.uk
↗ www.uws.ac.uk

**Ayr Campus** Beech Grove, Ayr KA8 0SR
**Dumfries Campus** Maxwell House, Dumfries DG1 4UQ
**Hamilton Campus** Almada Street, Hamilton ML3 0JB

**》 further links**

ACCOMMODATION accommodation@uws.ac.uk
STUDENTS' UNION www.sauws.org.uk

2250 99.1 38.4 21.4 91.5

Paisley

The University of the West of Scotland (UWS) was formed in 2007 following the merger of the University of Paisley with Bell College. UWS is Scotland's biggest modern university, with just under 20,000 students. The university has campuses in Ayr, Dumfries, Hamilton and Paisley. It also has Scotland's largest school of Health, Nursing and Midwifery. The university is one of Scotland's most career-focused higher education institutions, boasting strong links with industrial and commercial partners. Students can take the option of a year's paid work placement as part of many degrees.

**Fees** Students resident in Scotland or in non-UK EU countries may be eligible for free tuition, but may have to pay the graduate endowment upon completing their course. For other UK students, annual tuition fee of not less than £1,820.

**Bursaries** The university is supported by organisations who offer scholarships/bursaries to students each year. See uws.ac.uk/finance

**Accommodation** Students from outside a 40-mile radius are given priority. University self-catering accommodation costs about £64 a week. The university offers advice on private accommodation.

**Facilities** Well-equipped libraries at all four campuses. Wi-Fi access spots in residences and on campus. Computing students have access to a PlayStation games development lab sponsored by Sony. The £5m student union smack bang in the middle of Paisley has a cyber-cafe, bars, a 450-capacity venue and games areas.

**Transport** Paisley campus is two miles from Glasgow airport and 10 minutes from the centre of Glasgow by train. Hamilton campus is 15 minutes by train from Glasgow, Ayr campus is 40 minutes from Glasgow by car or train. Dumfries campus is reached by bus from Dumfries centre.

**◀◀ STUDENT VIEW ▶▶**

*"It is refreshing to work in an environment that creates a balance between the theoretical and practical and gives you access to industry-standard equipment and facilities."*

# University of Westminster

309 Regent Street
London  W1B 2UW

**t**  020 7911 5000
**e**  course-enquiries@westminster.ac.uk
↗  www.westminster.ac.uk

**》 further links**

ACCOMMODATION  unilethousing@westminster.ac.uk
STUDENTS' UNION  www.uwsu.com

| 3670 | 95.6 | 44.4 | 19.6 | 88.1 |

London

If you want to be right at the heart of London, you couldn't do better than Westminster. Three of its campuses are bang in the middle of town; Harrow is slightly further-flung, though still on the tube. In London, everything you could want is within easy reach. As the country's first polytechnic (in 1838), Westminster has a longstanding commitment to equal opportunities; lots of courses can be studied part-time and the student body is exceptionally diverse. It puts careers at the centre of its mission and is diligent about preparing students for their chosen profession.

**Fees**  £3,225 a year for all full-time undergraduate courses in 2009–10.

**Bursaries**  £319 a year for those receiving a grant. The university's scholarship programme is the largest of its kind in the UK, with £4.3m being awarded annually to over 500 students.

**Accommodation**  There are 1,427 beds available to students across six halls in Harrow, Hoxton, Highgate, Victoria, Marylebone (refurbished in 2008) and Lambeth. Priority is given to those living more than 25 miles from campus. All halls are self-catered, and cost between £73.08 and £153.02 a week for the 37-week academic year.

**Facilities**  There are 4,000 computers across the university's four sites and all of the student rooms have internet access. Libraries on all sites, with 24-hour access in Harrow and Marylebone. The university's 18-hectare sports grounds are located at Chiswick and include a boathouse, a pavilion, six recently refurbished tennis courts and an all-weather pitch. The student union boasts a £1m venue and an underground exhibition space; the student radio station is award-winning.

**Transport**  Three of the four campuses are in central London with excellent links. The fourth, in Harrow, is a 20-minute tube ride away, or there's a 24-hour bus service.

**‹‹ STUDENT VIEW ››**

*"The University of Westminster is a cosmopolitan community and I have got to know so many different people and cultures. My studies are really challenging and I have received all the help I need from staff and tutors."*

# University of Winchester

West Hill
Winchester  SO22 4NR

**t**  01962 841515
**e**  course.enquiries@winchester.ac.uk
↗  www.winchester.ac.uk

**Chute House Campus**  Church Street, Basingstoke  RG21 7 QT

**》 further links**

ACCOMMODATION  housing@winchester.ac.uk
STUDENTS' UNION  www.winchesterstudents.co.uk

1195       96.8       31.8       11.9       95.3

Winchester

Winchester is a fairly small university, with approximately 3,000 full-time students and a similar number on part-time courses, which makes for a friendly, informal environment where students are free to develop as individuals. Its long history as a teacher training college means that education is still a focus, but there's a wide range of other degrees on offer, too. Winchester is a lovely cathedral city with a refined atmosphere, excellent shopping, and great pubs, cafes and restaurants to suit all tastes. There's another campus, in Basingstoke, which has a major shopping centre but lacks a cathedral.

**Fees**  £3,225 for full-time undergraduate courses in 2009–10.

**Bursaries**  All students who are entitled to a full grant will receive £820 a year. Students whose household income is between £25,000 and £39,333 will receive £410. Other scholarships and awards available.

**Accommodation**  On-campus or university-managed accommodation guaranteed to all first-year full-time undergraduates who hold Winchester as their firm choice. The university tries to house all students with insurance offers and those who apply through Clearing. Costs range from £79 to £102 a week.

**Facilities**  The £10m student union includes a 1,200-capacity venue space. Excellent sports facilities with an Olympic-standard athletics track and an all-weather hockey and general sports pitch.

**Transport**  A 10-minute walk to the city centre and the train station. Winchester is one hour away from London and 20 minutes from Southampton. Bus services are good.

**❝ STUDENT VIEW ❞**

*"There is something about being a student here that you can't quite put your finger on. Whether it's due to the sense of family or the feel of the city itself, it's both a great place to live and study."*

# University of Wolverhampton

Wulfruna Street
Wolverhampton  WV1 1SB

**t**  0800 953 3222
**e**  enquiries@wlv.ac.uk
**↗**  www.wlv.ac.uk

**Compton Park Campus**  Compton Road West, Compton, Wolverhampton  WV3 9DX
**Telford Campus**  Shifnal Road, Priorslee, Telford  TF2 9NT
**Walsall Campus**  Gorway Road, Walsall  WS1 3BD

**》 further links**

ACCOMMODATION  residences@wlv.ac.uk
STUDENTS' UNION  www.wlv.ac.uk

3245        99.0        51.3        20.9        91.2

Wolverhampton has approximately 23,000 students, including a growing number from Europe and overseas. It's coming to the end of a seven-year programme of investment and expansion costing £60m, so expect to see some swanky new buildings on its four campuses. Like many of the newer universities, Wolverhampton focuses on employability. Each of the 10 schools has a dedicated placement officer to help students gain relevant work experience. Unsurprisingly, graduate employment rates are good. Wolverhampton is a bustling place in its own right and is also just down the road from Birmingham if you feel there are gaps that need filling in your shopping/clubbing/cultural life. Plus some lovely scenery nearby for a bit of rest and relaxation.

**Fees**  £3,225 for undergraduates in 2009–10.

**Bursaries**  If you have a family income of less than £25,000, you will receive £500 a year. Between £25,001 and £35,000, you will receive £300 a year.

**Accommodation**  The university has more than 2,000 accommodation places available in its halls of residence with rooms allocated on a first-come, first-served basis. Prices range from £58 to £85 a week — not bad considering that includes internet access, utilities, laundry facilities, basic content insurance and 24-hour caretaking.

**Facilities**  The new technology centre holds about 500 PCs, rapid prototyping facilities for construction and engineering, and professional-standard TV and radio stations. Walsall campus's sports centre is an official training base for the 2012 Olympics. And the Arena theatre, based at the City campus, is one of the most successful small theatres in the Midlands.

**Transport**  All campuses and campus towns are linked by a free shuttle bus. Wolverhampton has excellent transport links and Birmingham is just a short train or tram ride away.

**⟨⟨ STUDENT VIEW ⟩⟩**

*"I found that staff were always on hand to help with any problems. Emails were answered very quickly by all lecturers and one-to-one contact with teaching staff was routine. The quality of teaching was excellent."*

# University of Worcester

Henwick Grove
Worcester  WR2 6AJ

**t**  01905 855000
**e**  study@worc.ac.uk
↗  www.worcester.ac.uk

**》 further links**
ACCOMMODATION  accommodation@worc.ac.uk
STUDENTS' UNION  www.worcsu.com

1095      98.1      33.6      15.5      93.7

● Worcester

---

Worcester seems to be on the move. It enjoyed an applications increase of 10.6% this year and has seen applications increase by more than 100% in the past five years. It is currently investing more than £100m in the development of a new city-centre campus, the first phase of which will be completed in September 2009, and a further £60m on a unique library and history centre, which will be the first joint university and public library in the UK. There are currently 8,000 students at Worcester and the majority come from the West Midlands, but applications from further afield are increasing. Worcester itself is a charming city with plenty to see and do. There's some lovely countryside nearby too.

**Fees**  £3,225 a year for undergraduate courses in 2009-10.

**Bursaries**  £500 for every new student, rising to £640 for students in receipt of a partial grant, and £770 for those on full grant. Forty scholarships of £1,000 available after the first year of study to reward outstanding achievement. Other awards and support also available.

**Accommodation**  All first-year undergraduates who accept a conditional or unconditional offer by the Ucas deadline are guaranteed a place. Prices begin at £69 a week.

**Facilities**  The Peirson library has over 150,000 books and 600 journal print titles, and 150 computers are available. Computers are also available in 24-hour open access rooms across the campus. Excellent sports facilities, too.

**Transport**  The campus is a 15-minute walk from the city centre. A frequent bus service also links the two. Worcester has good rail and motorway links (M5), which put Birmingham within 45 minutes and London just over two hours from the city centre.

**⁶⁶ STUDENT VIEW ⁹⁹**

*"Worcester is a great place — it offers loads to do, with a great city backdrop. There is an overriding sense of community, making it a really friendly place to live and study."*

# Writtle College

Chelmsford
Essex CM1 3RR

**t** 01245 424200
**e** info@writtle.ac.uk
↗ www.writtle.ac.uk

**》 further links**

ACCOMMODATION  student.services@writtle.ac.uk
STUDENTS' UNION  www.writtlesu.com

170    94.8    35.1    17.9    88.9

Chelmsford

---

Set in a 220-hectare estate, Writtle College is a land-based college, two miles from Chelmsford in Essex. Established in 1893, it is now a partner college of the University of Essex and offers a range of courses within the four schools of higher education: design, equine and animal science, horticulture, and sustainable environments. The main campus is surrounded by its own estate, farm and gardens – the college says this serves as a "green laboratory" for students.

**Fees**  £2,906 a year, less than the maximum level.

**Bursaries**  Eligible students are entitled to a means-tested bursary, starting at about £300; you get more in your second and third years.

**Accommodation**  There's a range available costing between £92 and £114 a week. Contracts are for the full year, including the Christmas and Easter holidays. Rents include a meal allowance of 10 meals a week (term-time).

**Facilities**  There are conservation areas; landscaped gardens; design studios; animal, equine and stud units; and a working farm. Students have access to 15 high-spec computer suites and the library provides one of the leading specialist book and information collections in England.

**Transport**  Situated two miles from the town centre of Chelmsford and just a few minutes' walk from the main bus route through Writtle village. There are buses from Chelmsford station to the campus.

---

**ᴳ STUDENT VIEW 》**

*"After visiting Writtle I knew it was where I would be happiest; the course was just what I wanted to do without compromise and has allowed me to explore all aspects of the industry."*

# University of York

Heslington
York  YO10 5DD

**t**  01904 430000
**e**  admissions@york.ac.uk
↗  www.york.ac.uk

**King's Manor**  University of York, Exhibition Square, York  YO1 7EP

》 **further links**

ACCOMMODATION  accommodation@york.ac.uk
STUDENTS' UNION  www.yusu.org

2030      79.9      16.9      4.1      94.5

York opened in 1963, part of the new wave of British universities, and since then has gone on to secure its place as one of the best places in the country to study. It enjoys a collegiate system similar to Oxbridge, though the divisions don't seem to be as rigid. Most students are based on the landscaped campus on the outskirts of the city. The modernist concrete buildings may be an acquired taste, but you'll probably end up quite fond of them; in any case, the wide grassy spaces and leafy interludes, not to mention the large lake, take the edge off. York is a superlative historic city, with a history stretching back to Roman times and the evidence of it all around you. The present day makes its presence felt, too, with a lively social scene and plenty of facilities for having fun in whatever form you like it.

**Fees**  £3,225 for full-time undergraduate degrees in 2009-10.

**Bursaries**  For students with a household income of up to £25,000, there is a bursary of £1,436. Between £25,001 and £35,910, the bursary is £718. Between £35,911 and £41,040, the bursary is £360. Other support is available.

**Accommodation**  Guaranteed for first-years. University-owned or managed residences cost between £78 and £93 a week.

**Facilities**  Libraries, computer rooms, restaurants, bars, shops, a fully equipped sports centre, tennis and squash courts, health centre, theatres and concert halls are all within easy walking distance on campus.

**Transport**  York city centre is 20 minutes' stroll away, or under 10 minutes by bus; a fast, direct service runs every 10 minutes. Much of the city is pedestrianised and there are plentiful cycle routes. A fast all-night train places Leeds and Manchester within easy reach.

**❝ STUDENT VIEW ❞**

*"The university, the surrounding area, and the city are fantastic places to live. The pleasant aura that surrounds the university enables students to study as they wish to. York attracts some of the best and most exciting staff around. And literally every student is involved in campus life in some way."*

# York St John University

Lord Mayor's Walk
York  YO31 7EX

**t**  01904 624624
**e**  admissions@yorksj.ac.uk
**↗**  www.yorksj.ac.uk

**》》 further links**

ACCOMMODATION  accommodation@yorksj.ac.uk
STUDENTS' UNION  www.ysjsu.com

1395      93.2      29.0      10.7      93.5

York St John University descends from two Victorian Anglican teacher training colleges. Over the past 168 years, it has gone through various incarnations and gained full university status in 2006. Its courses have diversified a bit, too, though you can, of course, still train to teach here. There are approximately 6,000 students and almost half of them are over 21. There's also a male to female ratio of 28:72. The campus is located literally a stone's throw from York Minster, the stunning medieval cathedral where the graduation ceremonies take place. All other amenities of this charming and compact city centre are on your doorstep.

**Fees**   £3,225 for all full-time undergraduate degrees in 2009–10.

**Bursaries**   If your household income is less than £18,360 you will receive a bursary of £1,610. Between £18,361 and £20,970, you will receive £1,075. Between £20,971 and £25,000, you will receive £540.

**Accommodation**   Nearly all first-years who want to can live in student accommodation. A range of catered and self-catered accommodation is on offer, ranging from £69 to £125 a week.

**Facilities**   There is good sports provision, an internet cafe, impressive lecture theatres and approximately 400 PCs in the learning centre. In December 2008, the university opened its new £15.5m development, De Grey Court, which includes a 150-seat state-of-the-art lecture theatre, a boardroom, seminar and teaching spaces, and specialist teaching environments such as a kitchen space for occupational therapy students.

**Transport**   The university is just a few minutes' walk from the city centre, which is easily navigable on foot or bike. The train station is approximately 15 minutes' walk and is on the main east coast rail line — handy for London and Edinburgh, both approximately two hours away. Leeds and Manchester are also easy to get to.

**❝❝ STUDENT VIEW ❞❞**

*"York St John is a small but very friendly university. I'm really enjoying the course — it's everything I hoped it would be (and more). The tutors are great and are extremely helpful in supporting us to succeed."*

# Help finding your institution

If you're struggling to find an institution either because it is referred to by an acronym, or has recently changed name, the following list will help you.

- Arts Institute at Bournemouth  *see* **Arts University College at Bournemouth**  236

- Dartington College of Arts  *see* **University College Falmouth (incorporating Dartington College of Arts)**  282

- Marjon  *see* **University College Plymouth St Mark and St John**  335

- Napier University  *see* **Edinburgh Napier University**  279

- North East Wales Institute of Higher Education  *see* **Glyndŵr University**  288

- Norwich School of Art and Design  *see* **Norwich University College of the Arts**  326

- SOAS  *see* **School of Oriental and African Studies**  358

- Trinty College Carmarthen  *see* **Trinty University College**  377

- UCL  see **University College London**  381

- UEA  *see* **University of East Anglia**  274

- UWE Bristol  *see* **University of the West of England, Bristol**  384

- UWIC  *see* **University of Wales Institute, Cardiff**  382

# Acknowledgments

Thanks to

The universities who responded to requests for information and also to
Matt Hiely-Rayner, Julie Whittaker and Lorna Lines of Campus Pi at Brunel
University, Jon Bentham, Lisa Darnell, Liz Ford, Kristen Harrison, Amelia Hodsdon,
Donald Macleod, Bryony Newhouse, Alexis Petridis, Katie Shimmon, Laura Wheadon,
Alice Wignall and Faye-Anne Wilkinson.

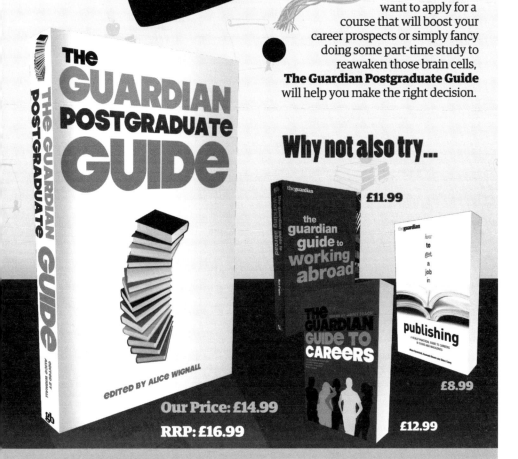